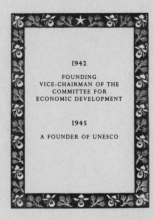

1942

FOUNDING
VICE-CHAIRMAN OF THE
COMMITTEE FOR
ECONOMIC DEVELOPMENT

1945

A FOUNDER OF UNESCO

1943

CHAIRMAN OF THE
BOARD OF

1768

ENCYCLOPAEDIA BRITANNICA
INC. AND

ENCYCLOPAEDIA BRITANNICA
FILMS INC.

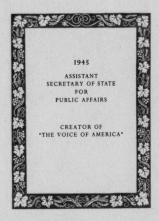

1945

ASSISTANT
SECRETARY OF STATE
FOR
PUBLIC AFFAIRS

CREATOR OF
"THE VOICE OF AMERICA"

1949

SENATOR FOR CONNECTICUT

SENATOR REIPUBLICÆ
CONNECTICUTENSIS

1951

PROPOSER OF
MOTION FOR EXPULSION OF
JOSEPH McCARTHY FROM
THE U.S. SENATE WHICH
CONDEMNED HIM IN 1954

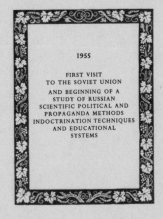

1955

FIRST VISIT
TO THE SOVIET UNION

AND BEGINNING OF A
STUDY OF RUSSIAN
SCIENTIFIC POLITICAL AND
PROPAGANDA METHODS
INDOCTRINATION TECHNIQUES
AND EDUCATIONAL
SYSTEMS

1958

AUTHOR OF
"THIS IS THE CHALLENGE"
WRITTEN TO AWAKEN
AMERICA TO A RESPONSE TO
RUSSIAN INTENTIONS

1961

AUTHOR OF
"THE VOICE OF LATIN AMERICA"
WRITTEN WHILE ON
A JOURNEY WITH
GOVERNOR ADLAI STEVENSON

1963

UNESCO

UNITED STATES AMBASSADOR
TO
UNESCO

1964

AS PUBLISHER OF
ENCYCLOPAEDIA BRITANNICA

ACQUIRES
MERRIAM-WEBSTER

SUCCESSOR
LEXICOGRAPHERS TO
NOAH WEBSTER

D1212671

The decorative panels reproduced on the endpapers are from designs by the late British scholar and typographer Stanley Morison. The wood engravings are by the noted British designer and engraver Reynolds Stone. They were executed for a surprise keepsake presented to William Benton on his sixty-fifth birthday.

THE
LIVES
OF
WILLIAM
BENTON

THE
LIVES
OF
WILLIAM
BENTON

SIDNEY
HYMAN

THE UNIVERSITY OF CHICAGO PRESS
CHICAGO AND LONDON

Standard Book Number: 226-36548-4
Library of Congress Catalog Card Number: 72-88231

The University of Chicago Press, Chicago 60637
The University of Chicago Press, Ltd., London

TO
ANN,
MY SISTER

Contents

5 *Synthesis*

Illustrations

Preface

I was in my last year as a student at the University of Chicago when the thirty-seven-year-old William Burnett Benton, Yale '21, and a recently resigned partner in the New York advertising firm of Benton and Bowles, arrived on the university campus as a newly appointed vice-president. The time was October 1937, and from then until 1960, a detail about the man in motion would suddenly flash into my view and just as suddenly fade out. It was like a newsreel, a thing of snippets without context.

At first, the snippets were confined to comic anecdotes about Benton. The net impression they gave was that at some point in his past he had started on a cross-country race against the absolute of time itself and that, in running it, he always looked for short cuts so that a minute saved on one task could be used on another. It was never said that Benton looked for short cuts to and through Heaven. But I did hear that he once bustled into the office of John Howe, his University of Chicago assistant, and said earnestly: "John, I've talked to three different people today at three different times, and all brought up the name of Saint Thomas Aquinas. Will you please give me a one-page memorandum stating what Saint Thomas is all about, and why he is so much discussed on the campus?" It was a little hard to explain that Saint Thomas was about thirteen volumes in a Sheed and Ward edition, plus a vast commentary accumulated over seven centuries of Western thought.

Though I was a student collector of "Bentonisms," I never met the man, never heard him speak, never read anything he wrote, and I saw him only twice. Once was at a distance. Once was closer, when our paths crossed on campus while he was talking with the university's president, Robert Maynard Hutchins, also Yale '21. In that fleeting moment, I saw only that Benton was a man of medium height and of compact athletic build. His hair was brown and wavy. His eyes were neither "soft" nor "hard" nor "piercing." "Alert" would be the more apt word. His nose had a broken ridge and a sharp

point, and his face had a squarish cut and a freshly scrubbed pinkish
tone. The clothes he wore looked expensive and neat. But above all,
he had the jaunty bounce of a man who took seriously Emerson's
injunction: "First, be a good animal."

In later years I read or heard about the different turns Benton's
career had taken—in education, publishing, the State Department,
the United States Senate, and many private associations. It was not
until 1959 that I had my first direct contact with Benton, and then
only by letter. At the request of former Secretary of State Dean
Acheson, the chairman of a panel under the Democratic Advisory
Council to the Democratic National Committee, I had prepared a
draft paper called "The Reconstruction of the Presidency." When
the draft was sent to the panel members for comments, most of the
members failed to respond at all. The few who did confined themselves to correcting the misdemeanor of a comma in the wrong place.
The saving exception was Benton's response. It came back to me
within a day in the form of a long letter packed with precise suggestions for changes. Nothing of what he said quite matched the
memories I had of the man about whom so many comic anecdotes
were told at the University of Chicago.

There was a postscript to his response, revealing certain personal
experiences he had in connection with the emergence of General
Dwight D. Eisenhower as the 1952 Republican presidential candidate. In my own reply, thanking Benton for his work on the draft
pamphlet, I mentioned the postscript and said that it had shed new
light on a story I thought I knew by heart. I added that he doubtless
had other personal experiences which, if told, could light up many
corners of contemporary American history. Had he, I asked, ever
thought of writing his autobiography?

I did not know at the time that Benton responded to questions in
a split-level way. Those put to him on paper, however embarrassing,
are answered promptly and fully. But at his invitation and expense,
you can go half way around the world to question him face to face,
only to find on arrival that because he is absorbed in other things,
the chance of asking the question and getting an answer can be as
slow in materializing as is the promise in the road signs reading
"Christ is coming."

Since my question about the autobiography was in writing, there
was a swift reply to it. Benton said that the idea had been urged
on him by others, but that he had rejected it. Autobiographies, said

he, were a form of necrophilia. They forced a person to look back on his life. He preferred to look ahead and, in fact, was busy at that very moment with a number of new projects which would give him no time to write an autobiography. Further, while he doubted that he could tell the *full* truth about himself, he was positive that he would not and could not tell the full truth about his friends. He valued their good opinion and saw no point in dwelling publicly on their shortcomings. These considerations, said he, operating in other cases, explained why so few good autobiographies were ever written. Casanova's, to be sure, was a good one, but Casanova had no wife, no children, no family. His autobiography, written when he was in his seventies, was designed primarily to entertain the German princeling for whom he worked as a librarian. To this Benton added another tidbit of contemporary American history to which he had been a party, and which was wholly new to me.

Our subsequent exchanges about an autobiography came to nothing. The man, nonetheless, remained on my mind.

In February 1960, in New York with several hours to spare, I called at Benton's office to visit John Howe, his assistant and my friend since University of Chicago days. The office at 342 Madison Avenue had none of the features associated with a Hollywood version of a high-styled "Madison Avenue suite." When you opened the door, you found yourself in a place of work whose furnishings were in the style of Grand Rapids Utilitarian. There was no waiting room, and no one waiting. The secretaries in sight seemed friendly in an unaffected way. Several worked at desks in an open room to the right. Several worked at desks in an open room to the left. Leading off from the open rooms were three small enclosed offices. John Howe, the chief of staff, and the only man on it, used one of these. A larger one was equipped for use by Benton's friends or business associates passing through New York. Benton himself occupied an office of about the same size. It had a "homey" atmosphere, and what made it so were the walls covered with news photographs, cartoons, plaques, scrolls, framed ribbons, and medallions. Each had a meaning at a particular stage of Benton's life, and all together they formed a graphic biography of it.

In the course of my talk with John Howe, I mentioned my correspondence with Benton concerning a proposed autobiography. John, who had followed the correspondence, turned the case around. Would I, he asked, consider writing a *biography* of the man? He went on to explain that Benton, whose career as a Democratic United States senator from Connecticut had been aborted by the Eisenhower landslide in 1952, had a reasonable chance to get the 1962 Connecticut Democratic nomination to the Senate seat. If so, a biography focused on his public career since leaving the advertising agency of Benton and Bowles in 1936 might help lay to rest the old charges that he was just a "slick Madison Avenue huckster." There would be no constraints on what I wrote. "Beardsley Ruml," said John, quoting a man I knew and admired, "will tell you that Bill Benton is an open book who hides nothing about himself. That's the kind of biography you will be free to write if the proposal interests you."

After much yes and no talk back and forth, it was agreed that I would spend several weeks studying Benton's files and would then decide whether or not to undertake the biography.

In the weeks that followed, I encamped in a room lined with Benton's files. All were superbly organized. All were open to inspection regardless of the intimate nature of the material they contained. Nothing was under lock and key. Nothing was withheld. I cannot say that the sampling process brought a coherent view of the whole of Benton's life. I saw but a fraction of that life—as may still be the case. But what I saw was enough to provide some connecting links between seemingly unrelated details I had previously known, and they added up to the fact that here was an outsized man in American life.

At the end of the sampling process, I told John Howe that I was ready to undertake the biography on a schedule that called for six months of work in 1960 and another six in 1961. The book would be ready for publication by June 1962.

Subsequently, when Benton returned from a Latin-American tour with Governor Adlai Stevenson, I finally met him for the first time. The place was in his New York office at noon on his sixtieth birthday, 1 April 1960.

Against the retained image of the man I once saw walking with Hutchins on the University of Chicago campus, Benton's hair was graying; he had put on a little weight—but not too much; he still had the same freshly scrubbed pinkish look; there were a few lines around his eyes, and some which bracketed his mouth. But the rest of his face was free of the grooves formed by the afflictions of life. He seemed a singularly happy man, a little high-pitched in voice, and

charged with a vitality that made a younger man like myself feel
old by comparison.

He was courtly in the manner of his greeting, and he made complimentary references to things I had written. But now, too, I
learned first hand that in Benton's Decalogue, the first command-
ment was "Thou shalt not kill time." He was in a great hurry. He
had another appointment, and he could talk to me only while walking out of his office, down the corridor, then in the crowded elevator,
out of the office building, and during the taxi ride to the place of his
appointment. He talked as if no one else were nearby, or had ears,
or he didn't care what other people overheard since he had nothing
to conceal.

He said he had as many objections to the idea of a biography as
to an autobiography. However, I could go ahead with the book on
the terms proposed, but I must understand at the outset that he was
too busy to give me very much time.

I managed to say that lengthy conversations would not be necessary; his files were exceptionally orderly and comprehensive—and
became the source for many of the quoted passages in this book.
(For many years he had made it a habit to jot down the key words
and the essence of virtually every significant conversation he had,
committing the whole exchange to a voluminous memorandum the
minute he got back to a dictating machine.) I went on to explain
that this did not mean that I could write a biography from written
records alone. Written records can produce their own distortions
of line simply because they *exist* and are at hand for ready use—
while the truth of what actually happened could be retrieved only
from faded or tangled memories of things spoken, said, seen, or
sensed. I would naturally interview Benton's family, friends, and
associates, and his critics as well. But I had an instinctive feeling
that despite the limitations of written records, I would be relying
more heavily than usual on his files because of their unique nature.
I would follow lines of action in them until they led to dead-end
streets or to crossroads with confused directional signs. I would
then have to appeal to him for help.

Benton responded with a quick, "Yes, yes." And that was about
all that was said on April Fools' Day, 1960. No contract was ever
signed between us. My project was not to be an "authorized" biography.

Except for a week in August 1960 spent as Benton's guest aboard the *Flying Clipper,* a yacht he had chartered for a cruise around the North Sea, I did not see him again for more than a year. All our exchanges were by letter. Thus, when he was at his winter home in Phoenix in March 1961, he wrote to say that he was sending to his New York office a trunk full of material which he had not examined in any detail. Perhaps it might contain something of interest to me.

What he had sent on was the kind of treasure trove biographers dream of finding, yet few do. The trunk was crammed with the letters he had written his mother from the time he had entered Shattuck School in 1913 until 1942—the cutoff point being his mother's death. The trunk also contained many letters she had written him in that same stretch of years, along with her own unpublished autobiography, diaries, letters to and from grandparents, aunts, uncles, and cousins, and family records going back to the earliest days of America.

In the case of the mother-son letters alone, the mass of confessional detail, running into millions of words and extending over three decades, gave me an inside view of Benton's life as he was passing through various stages of growth on the way to maturity. Indeed, in the writing of this biography, I was strongly tempted at one point to confine the story to the mother-son relationship and then add an abrupt QED—since everything else seemed to follow from it. The temptation was resisted, but strong traces of it appear in the extensive use of these letters in the first portions of this biography.

In the spring of 1962 the original reason for writing this biography was nullified. Abraham Ribicoff resigned as President Kennedy's secretary of health, education, and welfare, in order to seek Connecticut's Democratic nomination for a United States Senate seat. The decision put an end to Benton's chances for the nomination. The decision also removed the shadow of a "campaign biography" from my writing project, besides removing the pressure of the deadline previously set for finishing it.

With no deadline to work against, the biography moved forward in spurts, between which it seemed to stop altogether. There were dead-end streets, and open roads—as in the great mass of father-son correspondence made available to me by Benton's oldest son, Charles. One year followed another. One draft followed another. Old friends died. New ones were made. Hopes deferred were fulfilled. Hopes about to be realized were frustrated. Old ventures were reorganized. New ones were launched. And as the passing years revealed what the days hid, chapters of the biography which seemed beyond need of further change had to be revised.

But there had to be a cutoff point somewhere. The point decided on was the year 1968—the two hundredth anniversary of the *Encyclopaedia Britannica,* and the twenty-fifth anniversary of Benton's work as its publisher and chairman of the board. There the matter stands, though Benton's own life continues to branch and flare in new directions.

There are many Bill Bentons and the different angles of vision brought to bear on him can lead to different reactions ranging from awe to outrage. Speaking for myself as a biographer, from an initial interest in the man, my own reactions evolved into a deepening respect and then to a deepening affection for him. I know many of his crotchets, and much about the way he can bruise the nerves of other people without consciously intending to do so. I know that like other strong personalities, he pays a price in weakness at some points for the many elements of strength he possesses. But I also am convinced of something else. Here is a man in ferment whose name may be unknown to most Americans yet who, in the act of educating himself, has had a profound effect on the education of an ever widening circle of people in the United States and the world over. That central fact forms the focal point for all the pages that follow.

In the writing of the book, I accumulated debts of gratitude. I owe them to the many people whose lives touched Benton's, and who either provided me with material for the manuscript, corrected my errors of fact, or clarified my perceptions. This includes many of the men and women whose names appear in connection with episodes treated in the main text. Here, however, I must acknowledge the special debt I owe to John Howe, and to Anne Cronin, Marie Oginski, Harriet Kirby, Mildred Gorelik, and Kay Hart for the infinitely patient way they answered my many questions bearing on the difference between the real and seemingly real in the story to be told, and helped otherwise. I am grateful also to Fairfax Cone, chairman of the board of trustees of the University of Chicago, who suggested the title for the book, and to Professor Frank Freidel of Harvard, who read the text from the standpoint of its worth as a work of scholarship. Above all, I am in debt to Bruce L. Felknor, who undertook an editorial task that was beyond my own capacity.

He brought a fresh pair of eyes to an oversized manuscript and, in a word-by-word reading of the text, showed me where to cut some 50,000 words—and to reorganize many of the rest—so that the essential elements of the narrative could emerge with greater clarity. There would have been no book at all without his help, and without the judgment he showed in outflanking difficulties which had seemed insuperable to me.

THE
LIVES
OF
WILLIAM
BENTON

1

The Turning Point

Before there could be a Moses, said Machiavelli, there must first have been Children of Israel who wanted to get out of Egypt. William ("Bill") Benton got at least halfway out of Egypt all by himself. On 1 April 1936, his thirty-sixth birthday, his resignation as head of the New York advertising agency of Benton and Bowles became official. Twelve days later, the news was released to the press. But there was a question to be asked. What was he to do with himself? He was not born for leisure and never had any experience with it.

Some persons on Madison Avenue who read the press report thought they knew what Benton would do next, and they could support their views by citing the history of the Benton and Bowles agency. When it was founded by Benton and Chester Bowles in July 1929, on the eve of the great crash, the books showed that each of the two partners put only $9,000 into starting their venture—and Benton had borrowed $4,000 of his share from Bowles. Yet in less than seven years and despite the Great Depression, the agency had become one of the most prosperous in the advertising world. So much so, that Benton's personal income at the age of thirty-six was said to be a half-million dollars annually, while the stock he turned in when he resigned was reportedly valued at around a million dollars. It made no sense to think that he was quitting forever a business in which he excelled. What he would surely do next—and soon—would be to start a new advertising agency. It was this conviction that accounted for the many calls he received from Madison Avenue figures asking that they be remembered in case there was a place for them on the ground floor of any new agency he might start.

Others who knew Benton a little better had specific suggestions

3

about what he should do next, and many of them had the power to make good on the offers that went along with the suggestions. He could move to Hollywood and become the president of the RKO film company, which was then in trouble. He could become president of the Better Business Bureau. He could be, on a part-time basis, the chairman of the board of David Stern's *New York Evening Post*. He could perhaps be the president of the New York Stock Exchange. He could have the Coca-Cola franchise for the continent of Australia. He could be the publicity director for the Republican National Committee.

None of the offers was to his liking. When he resigned from Benton and Bowles he was naive about everything except how to run an advertising agency. He didn't think he wanted much money, and it had not seriously occurred to him that he might lose the money he had made. All he knew—and strongly felt—was that he was determined to turn his back on business of any kind. True, he was still enmeshed in the complications of resignation from the firm, and he had promised his former partners that he would give them "half-time" throughout 1936 in order to help tidy up business matters he had previously handled. Then toward the first of 1937 he would take a planned trip around the world with his wife, Helen. But after that, what? After the complications were overcome, the business matters settled, the trip taken, what was he to do with himself?

The question was still unresolved on a Monday morning in late April when he walked into his office. There, waiting for him, were a telegram from Chicago, a special delivery letter from Chicago, and a stack of messages about telephone calls from Chicago. All originated with one man—who at noon on that same Monday walked into Benton's office. He was Robert Maynard Hutchins, president of the University of Chicago, and a classmate of Benton's at Yale, where the two had been on the debating team in 1921. Hutchins, however, had not come just to talk over old times. He had a serious problem to discuss with Benton—one that had been featured in the national press—and he had a serious proposal to make in connection with it.

The problem arose out of the "Walgreen case."

Charles Walgreen of Chicago, the owner of a large chain of drugstores, had a niece who had lately been a student at the University of Chicago. From what she told him about her studies he gained the impression that she was being "indoctrinated" by "Communist professors." Mr. Walgreen, as a patriot and protective uncle, publicly withdrew the young girl from the university. The great play the Chicago newspapers gave the story led the Illinois state senate to appoint what was known as the Broyles Commission on Higher Education in Illinois. The commission never got around to investigating other universities but concentrated on "communism at the University of Chicago." The Walgreen case was the center of the affair, and while the hearings ran their course in the ballroom of Chicago's Stevens Hotel, all the city's newspapers joined in pummeling the university, except the *Chicago Times*. This young tabloid defended the university, and suffered for doing so. Financially weak, it was further weakened when Walgreen withdrew his advertising from its pages.

Hutchins, for his part, resisted all demands that he sacrifice the faculty members who had been singled out for attack. Instead he led the counterattack on the investigating committee's demagoguery.

The committee could prove none of the Walgreen charges, for the charges were a fantasy from the beginning. Yet the University of Chicago itself as an institution was hurt by the pounding it took from the press during the investigation. The Illinois state legislature threatened to suspend the university's tax-exempt status. There was a threatened drop in applications for admission to the undergraduate college. There was also a threatened decrease in gifts from prospective benefactors and from conservative alumni.

Hutchins drew the picture for Benton in a few broad strokes, followed by a proposal. Now that Benton was "unemployed," would he consider accepting an appointment as Secretary of the University of Chicago? The work would resemble Hutchins's own work years earlier when he began his university administrative career as Secretary of Yale. Benton would direct the University of Chicago's public relations, alumni relations, and fund-raising activities—all of which were in disarray because of the Walgreen case. All these could benefit from the touch of a man experienced in the advertising business. What did Benton think of the proposal?

The answer was laughter. If he was going to "advertise" a university, Benton said, why resign his partnership in the thriving firm of Benton and Bowles, where the work was far more exciting and infinitely more profitable than anything he could do on the campus?

"There would be," said he, "a greater intellectual challenge in advertising a bar of Palmolive soap or a can of Maxwell House coffee." Besides, he really didn't know what he wanted to do next. He meant to take a year in which to look around before reaching a decision. That was that.

But not quite. Hutchins, with his personal gift for imagining the other person, was brighter, quicker, and more resourceful than was Benton in personal confrontations. He knew that the shortest distance between two human points can sometimes be a circle; so he dropped his original proposal in favor of a new one. Would Benton at least come to Chicago in order to study the Walgreen case and to prepare a report for the trustees on how best to deal with its consequences? If so, he would not only be of great help to Hutchins personally but would be rendering an important service to a great university.

The answer this time was not laughter. "I'll think it over," said Benton.

Not much more passed between the two men on the Monday noon in April 1936. Little as it was, it is almost certain that no other university president in America would then have thought, or had the nerve, to put the case as Hutchins did to an advertising man—least of all to one like Benton who seemed to epitomize Madison Avenue mores. But then, Hutchins was no ordinary university president, nor was Benton wholly a product of Madison Avenue. His family background was much like Hutchins's, and this Hutchins knew from their acquaintance at Yale. What Hutchins said during the Monday noon call would eventually change the direction of Benton's life—by taking him back to the world of his forebears.

1

MOTHER
AND
SON

2

Puritans and Cavaliers

William Benton was the child of a marriage between westward moving carriers of the Puritan culture from New England and the Cavalier culture from the South. On both sides, his ancestors had come to America in early colonial times. Both engaged in a ceaseless fight for life. They fought the denying hand of nature as they farmed the rocks of Connecticut, the clay soil of Loudon County, Virginia, and scratched for a living in the forests of the Carolinas and Georgia. They fought the denying hand of the Indians who barred their passage to the promised land of milk and honey. They fought the army of George III in order to have an independent right to be the authors of their own political, economic, and religious life. They fought another English army, this time in the War of 1812, in order to clear the way for a westward march.

Among Benton's forebears, his two grandfathers stand out like placard figures from a morality play, one marked Puritan, the other marked Cavalier. It was Benton's fate to combine the traits of both in his own makeup—sometimes in an unreconciled state; sometimes, too, with outcroppings that baffled associates unaware of the mixed inheritance in his bones.

The Puritan was Grandfather William Benton, Phi Beta Kappa, Yale, class of 1843. Ordained as a Congregationalist minister after his graduation, Grandfather William had served for a while as the principal of the Fairfield Academy at Fairfield, Connecticut. Since his college days, however, he had been drawn to missionary work, and in 1847 he informed the American Board of Commissioners for Foreign Missions of his desire to be sent abroad. When his application was rejected because he was a bachelor, he asked the board to suggest a possible wife-designate. The board obligingly directed his attention to a Miss Loanza Goulding who was working for a doctor in Ware, Massachusetts. Her application for admission to medical schools had been rejected because of her sex; it was a time when women got into medical schools only as cadavers to be dissected. Yet in her determination to get the training she needed in order to be a medical missionary—perhaps the first woman in American history to be one—she worked for the doctor in Ware in order to absorb whatever he could teach. Loanza's sister Harriet had been killed by Choctaw Indians in Oklahoma while working among them as a missionary, and this, instead of cooling Loanza's missionary zeal, only made it more ardent. She would take the place of the life that had been lost.

When Reverend William Benton learned something of this, he got on a horse and rode to Ware. He liked what he saw when he met Loanza. He liked what he heard when she talked. A few days later, back in Connecticut, he wrote her a letter proposing marriage on the straightforward ground that since they both meant to labor for the Lord in a foreign vineyard, their labors would be more fruitful if they made a team of it. Loanza, though surprised by the proposal, agreed with the logic behind it. The Board of Commissioners for Foreign Missions, duly apprised of their marriage, blessed the couple with apt quotations from Scriptures and satisfied their highest desires by sending them as the first Congregational missionaries to Syria, a three months' sail from Boston.

Syria, which also included what is now Lebanon, Israel, and Jordan, was then a province of the Turkish sultanate. It was a brutal and bloody province soon to explode in revolution, anarchy, and civil war, all growing out of old conflicts between the wild Druse tribes and the Maronite Christians. Yet the Bentons, to judge from Loanza's diary, were indifferent to the dangers around them when they reached Aleppo near the end of 1847. There was the Lord's work to do, and they were soon happily busy doing it, William by establishing missions and schools, and Loanza by completing her medical training in the office of a Scottish doctor in Aleppo—who was busy translating the Bible into Arabic and who encouraged her to take over his practice.

Their firstborn child, a son, died of a pestilential fever in Aleppo; the Bentons themselves were forced to return to Tolland, Connecticut, to regain their health; but in October 1852, following the birth of their son Charles—who was to be William Benton's father—the

Bentons went back to Syria. This time they established their base in the mountain village of B'hamdoun on Mount Lebanon, not far from Beirut. Here two more sons and two daughters were born. Here is where William created the background for what would come to be known as the Benton School, which his descendants were to maintain until the school was closed forever by World War II. Here too is where Loanza developed her cost-free medical practice of some four thousand patients, and here is where a turn of events in 1860, recorded in Benton family papers and sung about in B'hamdoun folklore, could have meant the destruction of the Benton family and of most other inhabitants in the village.

Though the inhabitants were mainly Christians, the village was ruled by a Druse sheik, who was favorably disposed toward Loanza because all the women in his household were her patients. As it happened, in 1860 a Christian from B'hamdoun killed a son of the Druse sheik who ruled the nearby village of Zehlah. The father, bent on vengeance, assembled four hundred warriors and rode with them toward B'hamdoun, vowing to kill every Christian in it. When news of this reached the Sheik of B'hamdoun, he went to William and Loanza Benton to apprise them of their peril. He added that he meant to intercept the oncoming sheik and to try to avert the planned massacre. William insisted on going along, and so he did, arming himself only with a large Bible. Somewhere on the outskirts of B'hamdoun, the hosts of the sheik of Zehlah came into view, and William approached them alone with the Bible opened wide and held aloft for all the warriors to see. Then he called out to them again and again: "In this book it is written, 'Thou shalt not kill.'" Drawing still nearer, he took the hostile sheik by the hand and spoke long to him until the sheik finally said: "Because of you, Reverend Benton, I will not let even a chicken of B'hamdoun be killed. But my men are hungry and tired and thirsty and they want to eat." William agreed to feed them for three days; the invading Druse left peacefully and B'hamdoun was saved. Ever after that, until this day, it was sung in the village:

> The rivers in the field
> The mountains, the valleys,
> And all living things cry:
> Long life to Reverend and Signora Mrs. Benton.
> Long life to all who are born of them!

After a quarter of a century in Syria, the Bentons returned to Connecticut. William's pension made for genteel poverty, and even before his death in 1880, Loanza became the family breadwinner, touring the United States and thrilling Sunday night audiences in Congregational churches with tales of her missionary experiences. Her daughters, Mary and Harriet, were part of the supporting cast. Dressed in the clothes of Arab children, they passed the collection plate; the proceeds were Loanza's fees, and by such means she helped send her three sons through Yale, beginning with the oldest, Charles.

William Benton's Cavalier grandfather, on the maternal side, was Daniel Webster Hixson, born near Burlington, Iowa, with forebears from Virginia, the Carolinas, and Georgia who, around 1800, had begun to migrate north by northwest into and beyond the Ohio Valley. Daniel, the seventh son in a family of fourteen boys, united on northern free soil all the traits associated with southern Cavaliers—zest, impulsiveness, stubbornness, a good disposition and a bad temper, financial improvidence, a refusal to admit the reality of pain, animal courage, imagination, impatience, and a wit that made any room in which he sat rock with laughter. He talked freely to people he liked—and to people he didn't like in order to prevent *them* from talking. His formal education ended in his early teens, and his life nearly ended before he began to live it.

When the Civil War broke out, Daniel, aged sixteen, lied about his age and followed two older brothers into the Thirtieth Iowa Infantry. On the second day of the battle of Vicksburg, when the regiment made a frontal assault on the Rebel defenses, Daniel was hit in the left arm by a bullet, pitched backward, and tumbled down a hill out of the range of guns. He made his way to an aid station and was evacuated to a Vicksburg hospital, the first wounded man to be received in it. The doctors wanted to amputate the arm, lest he die of gangrene. He flatly refused, and kept himself awake the first night in the hospital, fearing the loss of his arm if he fell asleep. His arm did become gangrenous; an operation was imperative; Daniel agreed but refused ether, still fearing amputation if he became unconscious. What had to be done was done without sedatives, and the youth seemed impervious to pain.

The first wounded soldier from Burlington to be furloughed home, Daniel Hixson, the young war hero, began to court sixteen-year-old

Helen Orr, one of the most eligible young girls in the area. "Accomplished in all the graces," as the saying went, Helen was the only child of "the rich John Orr," a Presbyterian Scot who stemmed from a New Hampshire family. The farm he owned embraced two thousand acres of very fertile bottom land along the west bank of the Mississippi River near Burlington. Malarial mosquitoes came with the place; yet the bountiful yield of the land supported in local terms an almost baronial style of life. Here Daniel and Helen settled after their marriage.

There could be no complaints about Daniel's willingness to do his share of physical labor. Despite his war wound, he had more than enough animal energy in reserve to set the pace for the hired hands on the Orr farm. But when the place eventually passed to Helen as her inheritance, it became clear that her husband had never learned the multiplication part of arithmetic, only the subtraction part. He used Helen's money freely to help out the needy, especially Civil War widows and orphans. He also used her money to invest in glittering "get rich quick" schemes, only to fill an attic trunk with worthless certificates, stocks, and bonds. When Helen tried to curb her husband's financial vagaries, he would fly into a rage; that silenced her except for remarks about how he was "wasting the inheritance of their three children." The oldest of these was Edwin; the youngest, Capitola; the middle child, Elma, was to be William Benton's mother.

In 1883, the Hixsons leased their Iowa bottom land and moved to a 640-acre farm in Grant County, Minnesota. Six years later the care of this farm was entrusted to the son Edwin, while the rest of the family moved on to Fergus Falls, Minnesota. Here they bought a house in town and a new farm on the outskirts—which received only as much attention as Daniel could spare from his flowering passion for politics. Politics was his métier; he excelled in it, and he had a cause—the Grange movement with its program of political and economic reform.

In Minnesota, the Grange largely took over the Democratic party, and though the Democrats had been called "the party of treason" during the Civil War, the party attracted enough Union army veterans to contend vigorously for all state offices. Daniel Hixson, with his extensive private philanthropic work among veterans, stood for election as a Democratic state senator in 1886 and won the seat. When he was reelected two years later, his Democratic colleagues in the state senate made him their leader in the fight to end a cruel, conspiratorial practice common in that day. Briefly, the owners of grain elevators and flour mills gave their freight business to a particular railroad on condition that the railroad managers not rent freight cars to individual farmers. Thus, when a farmer arrived in a place like Fergus Falls with a wagon full of wheat, he had no way to ship the produce to Minneapolis but was forced to sell his wheat to the owner of a local grain elevator at a price which could run from 5 to 15 percent below the Minneapolis market price, plus shipping charges.

A bitter war was fought at the state level against this conspiracy, and even before the practice was made illegal on a national plane by federal antitrust laws, Daniel Hixson and his senate associates prevailed in the fight to make it illegal in Minnesota. Their investigation of rail and flour magnates earned the hostility of men like James J. Hill of the Great Northern, who once seized Hixson's lapels on the capitol steps and demanded, "Hixson, why do you persecute me?" Governor John Pillsbury of flour and lumber fame— who played a decisive role in building the University of Minnesota— was largely responsible for Hixson's ultimate loss of his senate seat. But laws were enacted regulating freight rates and compelling railroads to rent cars to individual farmers at a fair price.

The legislative victory did not by itself put an end to all things plaguing Minnesota farmers and those elsewhere in the decades after the Civil War. But the collective efforts of men like Daniel Webster Hixson—they were to be called "Sons of the Wild Jackass" —generated at least a ray of hopeful light in an otherwise dark western sky.

Before coming to the next generation, William Benton's parents, I digress briefly to a moment in 1960 when Benton was introduced to the young fiancée of one of his older associates. Benton knew his associate's age, asked the age of the young woman, and swiftly computed the difference. "I want to congratulate you again," he suddenly said to her in a burst of enthusiasm, "because you are a very brave woman." "Brave?" she asked. "Yes," said he, "because you are going into a marriage knowing in advance that you will probably be a widow for a long time." Actuarial statistics were all on his side. Yet to congratulate a young woman for her bravery in facing widowhood, just a few weeks before her marriage? It seemed outlandish—except for one unspoken detail. The congratulations were not really addressed to the young woman but to the memory of Benton's mother, who had married a much older man and then had shown great gallantry in *her* long widowhood.

Elma Hixson, the daughter of the Cavalier who fought in the Union army and later fought the trusts, was twenty-five years old when she married the forty-eight-year-old Charles William Benton, the son of the Puritan who fought a missionary's battle for the Lord in far-off Syria. The bond which united them was a mutual interest in teaching.

In an autobiographical sketch, Elma stated that since early childhood she had wanted to teach school, and she was barely out of childhood when she began to do just that. The place was a one-room school in Grant County, Minnesota, in a district where her father paid most of the taxes. She was fourteen years old at the time, and of her thirteen pupils a number were her senior by several years. The school term, for which she was paid $100, was limited to three months of winter weather when child labor could be spared from the farms. In her late teens she managed to get a year of university training, and then returned to teaching. By the time she was twenty-five she was superintendent of schools in Otter Tail County, Minnesota, the first woman in the state ever to be a county superintendent.

Like her mother before her, she was also a leader in the Minnesota Department of the Daughters of the American Revolution; she attached great importance to the DAR as did other ladies in Minnesota's small towns—principally to set themselves apart from the newly arrived German and Scandinavian immigrants by emphasizing their own pioneer American heritage. Also like her mother before her, she was a leader in the Women's Christian Temperance Union, and in her teens was a well-known speaker on the subject of the evils of drink. Yet these formidable biases detracted nothing from her beauty; she had many admirers, one of them being a "rich cousin"— Will Burnett, a member of the Ohio state legislature. "Cousin Will," so Elma wrote in her biographical sketch as though she were correcting a paper in English composition, "lacked unity, coherence and emphasis in his overtures toward a marriage proposal. In the end he sighed and said that the age difference between us was too great. He was shocked into a permanent state of bachelorhood when he later heard of the even greater age difference between me and the man I married—Professor Charles William Benton, Chairman of the Romance Language Department at the University of Minnesota."

Charles Benton had come to the University of Minnesota after several shifts in his career. As a youth in Syria, he had mastered Arabic and Turkish and, through a tutor, French as well. His scholastic attainments in other subjects when he was a Yale undergraduate were not high enough to win him a Phi Beta Kappa key, but he was awarded a prize as the best language student in his class. After commencement, in preparation for an intended career as a Congregational minister, he spent an additional two years at Yale studying theology and another year at the Union Theological Seminary studying Hebrew. Then, upon being ordained, he held a pulpit in Darien, Connecticut.

So far, he belonged (as did his father before him) to the natural aristocracy of Connecticut. These were not the monied families whose heads rarely went so far as to graduate from high school. The true aristocracy were the Congregational clergymen and their children, who might be the only persons with a university education in the towns where they settled. Their homes, generally on the town green, often contained the only books in town and were the intellectual centers of their communities. But, especially in the light of the controversy over Charles Darwin's *Origin of Species*, Reverend Charles William Benton decided against the ministry. His fundamentalist faith was shaken. He remained within the church but gave up the Darien pulpit in 1879 and entered Harvard with the intention of securing a Ph.D. degree in Semitic philology.

Charles Benton was by no means the only Congregational clergyman trained at Yale who migrated out of the ministry in the 1870s and 1880s after an encounter with Charles Darwin. It happened to many others, and so, ironically, Yale could boast of being the mother of university presidents and professors. For these disillusioned Congregational clergymen constituted a large part of the small number of Americans who held any kind of university degree. The new colleges and universities founded throughout the West after the Civil War had few sources of supply for presidents and faculty members other than the former Congregational ministers, who thus brought the Yale influence to the expanding sphere of American higher education.

Charles Benton might have resisted the new call of "Go West ex-

Congregational clergymen" until he at least secured his Ph.D. degree from Harvard. But the death of his father in the spring of 1880 led to a financial crisis in the family. Loanza could not support everybody by her lectures. She needed help. None could be expected from her two younger sons, Edwin and Henry. Though they were Yale graduates, they had not as yet become self-supporting. The two daughters, Mary and Harriet, had yet to start college. There were no rich kinsmen who could be turned to in time of distress. If help was to be forthcoming, it could only come from the twenty-eight-year-old Charles. This Charles knew, and he began to inquire about employment opportunities in the teaching profession. One such opportunity came in the spring of 1880 when academic talent scouts from the young University of Minnesota appeared on the Harvard campus and engaged Charles as assistant professor in Semitic languages starting in the 1880 fall term.

Dr. Cyrus Northrop, president of the University of Minnesota at the time, was, like Charles, a former Yale man. The university itself was little more than a name and a hope for the future—an enlarged version of the Benton School in B'hamdoun. It had no elms, no commons, no ivied halls, no celebrated graduates, or any traditions of excellence. The whole of its undergraduate faculty consisted of some 25 persons, and their students numbered barely 500. Salaries were low; Charles Benton, even at the peak of his career, made an annual salary of only $2,600. Yet he provided for three powerful women who outshone the male members of the family and who also dominated Charles until he married. First, there was his mother Loanza, who lived with him and whom he continued to support until her death. Then there was his younger sister Harriet, who also lived with him while she attended the University of Minnesota and whom he supported until her marriage to Professor William Clark, chairman of the university's Latin Department. Then, most awesomely of all, there was his sister Mary. With Charles's support, Mary attended and was graduated from the University of Minnesota in 1885 with Phi Beta Kappa honors. It is enough to add that in 1897 she became professor of Latin and French at Smith College, with a sideline in Greek and mathematics. After seventeen years the college honored her with the award of an LL.D. degree; she left Smith in 1914 to become dean of women at Carleton College, where she remained until her retirement in 1922.

Charles Benton's first year in Minneapolis proved academically embarrassing. Though he had come to the university to teach Old Testament tongues, the students were majestically indifferent to his courses. Not one enrolled in any of them. So the next year, he offered courses in Romance languages, and became a full professor in the process.

Later, in 1889, his department and others in the field of the humanities almost starved to death for want of funds from the state legislature, the chief legislator responsible being none other than Professor Benton's future father-in-law, State Senator Daniel Webster Hixson. Hixson was in no way hostile to learning; though he had been in modern terms a youthful "drop-out," he had educated himself by extensive reading. Where the University of Minnesota was concerned, however, he felt that a hard but necessary choice had to be made in the matter of priorities when it came to allocating funds. In his view, the first thing to be done was to increase the efficiency and profitability of the state's agriculture, since agriculture was then the source of practically all the taxable wealth that could go to pay for all other public programs, including the further development of higher education. With this line of reasoning, Hixson persuaded the Minnesota state legislature in 1889 to reduce its appropriations for university studies in fields like the humanities and to use the net savings in improving the quality of the School of Agriculture.

Many present-day students of "stages of educational development" would agree with Daniel Hixson's order of priorities. But, at the time, students at the University of Minnesota made known their hostile feelings by sending him a leather medal bearing a sarcastic tribute: "AWARDED TO SENATOR D. W. HIXSON of the 42nd district for his wise, persistent and self-sacrificing efforts on behalf of the UNIVERSITY OF MINNESOTA in this hour of trial and need. BY admiring students of the University. APRIL 22ND, 1889." On the reverse side of the medal, the students underlined their biting intent, but expressed themselves in French: A BAS HIXSON! VIVE L'UNIVERSITÉ! Some of the students, perhaps, learned these few French words in one of Professor Benton's classes. If so, there is no family record indicating what State Senator Hixson thought of Professor Benton—or vice versa. Nor are there any records revealing how the senator, who could endure great physical pain, viewed the marriage between his education-minded daughter and Charles Benton, who, besides being dominated by women, suffered from hay fever.

3

Mother Superior

William Benton was born to Elma and Charles on April Fools' Day, 1900, at the start of a century full of optical illusions. Though he was promptly called "Billie," the full name given him at birth was William Burnett Benton. This was meant to be a salute to Will Burnett, the "rich cousin" who had been interested in marrying Elma. It also said something about Elma's capacity for long-range planning. She hoped that by naming her firstborn son after her rich cousin, the latter would remember the child in his will, and thus leave him enough money to pay for his college education. It was one of the few times in her life when Elma's foresight did not result in the hoped-for event.

Eighteen months after William's birth, Elma bore another son, named Daniel Hixson after his grandfather. Dan was at home in the outdoors, loved to hunt, cared little for reading, and was indifferent to being almost always the low man on the scholastic totem pole. Bill viewed the outdoors solely from a utilitarian standpoint— it was good for his health. His life was centered indoors. He was a top scholar in any class and read everything he could lay his hands on. In their early life the two brothers had little in common but valor. They fought constantly, even after Grandfather Hixson tried to cool their taste for battle by knocking their heads together with a crack that left both boys nearly senseless.

The household where they grew up was itself a calm place. Arguments between the parents were generally on an intellectual level, or on a point of "principle." A long remembered case of this kind occurred when Dr. George Edgar Vincent, soon after he succeeded Dr. Northrop as president of the University of Minnesota, caused a great crisis in the Benton home by reducing

19

the father's salary by $100 from its peak of $2,600 annually. "My mother," Benton later recalled, "lashed at my father for not being aggressive enough in defense of his rights, and to make matters worse for him, his sister, Dr. Mary Benton of Smith College, happened to be in Minneapolis at the time. She took it upon herself to descend on Dr. Vincent and to upbraid him for his cruel conduct toward her defenseless brother."

Professor Charles Benton never made a name for himself in the academic world, not even completing work on his Ph.D. degree. Nor did he ever publish anything, partly because his undergraduate students took up so much time, but perhaps mainly because of a tragedy that would shatter any scholar. At great expense over a period of years, he had collected a personal library of rare books which he meant to use in writing a book of his own. The entire collection was consumed by a fire that destroyed the main building at the University of Minnesota in 1904. The flames seemed to devour Professor Benton's aging spirit as well as the books and the notes.

Still, there is as much strength in self-abnegation as there is in a naked will to power, and this subtle kind of strength Charles Benton had. If he failed to win a scholar's renown in the world beyond Minneapolis, he enjoyed a full measure of respect from the people whose lives he touched. He was an intellectual leader of Minneapolis, first deacon of the First Congregational Church, and he opened his home to hundreds of townspeople, students, faculty members, and visitors. In particular was this true for visiting Frenchmen— Charles Benton was the president of the Alliance française of the Northwest—and for all European scholars in residence at the university.

Conversations in the Benton home when foreigners were present were normally conducted in French, to the vast annoyance of young "Billie." His ear was not good. He had no gift for mimicry. He could not even catch the nuances of words in English, much less those in a foreign language. As a child, therefore, he cut his losses by simply snapping his ears shut when animated grown-up talk swirled around him in a language he did not understand. The mental block he apparently developed in the process was the source of his frequent complaint in later years that he was unable to do well in foreign languages.

With his mother, Elma, the case was different. She doggedly learned French to hold her own with her guests. Just as doggedly she completed some unfinished business in her general education. When her two sons were five and three and a half years old, Elma entered the University of Minnesota. She attended classes in the morning, managed household affairs upon her return home, studied at night. After five years of this, she was graduated from the university, Phi Beta Kappa. The experience also made for impatience with any signs of backsliding in her older son. She often scolded him, punished him often, and often severely.

The son's relationship with the father was different. He tended to ignore his father, though he was conscious of his love. Nothing delighted the boy more than rides on the handlebars of his father's bicycle. Professor Benton would stop off to chat in Arabic with Syrian fruit and candy store proprietors, who would shower him with sweet Near Eastern candies, causing his son to conclude that knowledge of Arabic was the most valuable asset in the world. But on the whole, the boy's consciousness of his father's love served only to spur the youth into taking shameless advantage of his father's tolerance. When he played hookey from school in order to go to the nickelodeon, it was always when Elma was out of the house; the youth counted on his father not to be aware of the truancy, or to forgive it if he were. But woe unto the son if he ever strayed from the path his mother expected him to walk! Perhaps as a result, he grew into a man who seemed unafraid of anything, including God's final judgment—unafraid of anything, that is, but his mother's frown, while longing for her approving smile, which he never got.

Part of the reason for the lack of direct contact with his father was an annual ritual in which the father took no part. The ritual entailed a move by Elma and the two boys to Fergus Falls to spend the summer months with her parents. When the University of Minnesota shut down for the summer season, Professor Benton, as a sufferer from hay fever, got away from pollen by removing himself to Grand Marais, Minnesota, on the shores of Lake Superior. Sometimes he camped alone, sometimes with a university colleague who was a nature lover or also suffered from hay fever. Yet his absence from Fergus Falls, at a time when his son Bill could have profited the most from shared vacation experiences, meant that the youth was all the more dominated by his mother—and all the more fascinated by his free-wheeling grandfather, Senator Daniel Webster Hixson.

Fergus Falls had another meaning for the boy. A year-round

avid collector of marbles and stamps and engaged in an extensive
trade in these items, he needed capital to finance some of his trans-
actions. He earned the capital in Fergus Falls by picking berries at
ten cents a quart, working long hours even when his small arms
were a mass of scratches from brambly gooseberry bushes. The bulk
of his earnings he turned over to his father for safekeeping, but
when Charles Benton died, he owed his son thirty dollars. The son
wondered for a long time whether to tell his mother about this, and
to insist that *she* owed him the money. In the end he decided to keep
quiet, though this was the largest sum of money with which he had
ever been directly connected.

Young Benton's religious education posed a different kind of
problem. He had no trouble summoning up enthusiasm for tangen-
tial things in his religious environment. He basked in the deference
shown his Grandmother Hixson by the members of the Fergus Falls
Congregational Church. He was enchanted by the stories his father
and aunts told about their youth in Syria and the Lebanon, and
about the bravery of their missionary parents. His competitive instincts spurred him to excel in making fudge or selling tickets for
church bazaars. He starred at reciting poetry in school and at
church socials. He was warmed by an inner light when he was in
Fergus Falls or in Minneapolis, and all his family and near relatives
gathered round while Grandfather Hixson or his mother read aloud
from the Bible.

But he was restless when forced to attend church every Sunday.
A child who could never stay still, stay down, or stay put in one
place for very long—except when concentrating on a book—he
had a low opinion of long sermons. Elma, wishing to ease his distress, let him bring his own books from home to read during the
hour-long Sunday sermon. When this method of relief proved short-
lived, she hit upon an alternative plan, growing out of her own
special talent for vocal music.

In fact, the rich timbre of her voice sometimes embarrassed her
son. When he was about nine, Elma, in a moment of bargaining with
him, offered to agree to any reasonable request he made. "Mamma,"
said he quickly, "I wish you wouldn't sing so loudly in church!"
More than three decades later, when Elma was near death and her
successful and busy son was at her bedside, Benton received a long-
distance call from one of his associates. Not wishing to tax his
mother in any way, he tiptoed out of her bedroom and took the

call in an adjacent room, where he promptly assaulted the telephone with one of his high, piercing, and protracted declamations. But then he suddenly thought of his ailing mother. He broke off the telephone connection, tiptoed back to Elma's bedside, and asked with great solicitude: "Mother, am I talking too loud?" "No," she answered tartly, "but the suit you are wearing is."

In Minneapolis in 1909 it occurred to Elma that if she introduced her son to choral music, this might solve his problem with long sermons. He could spend the second part of his Sunday devotions by attending Sunday school in the First Congregational Church. The first part, and the evening service, would be spent five blocks away in the choir of Holy Trinity Episcopal Church. The plan meant split-second timing and a dash down the five blocks, if the boy was to profit from split-level religion. But it was worth a trial. If it worked out, her son would be spared the boring service in the First Congregational Church while he was expressing himself in his high soprano voice in Holy Trinity Church.

Elma's strategic approach to her son's religious life was a distinguished success. Young Benton, for the next four years, was faithful and well behaved in his attendance at Holy Trinity. He liked being part of the choir. He liked going to the church choir camp two weeks during the summer, and he swelled with pride when he was assigned a minor role as a boy soprano soloist. The child who used various ruses to skip off to the nickelodeon without getting caught was still there but well hidden on Sundays beneath the vestments sedately worn by a model choirboy who sang an excellent soprano which could hit high C without effort even when he was an advanced thirteen-year-old. His singing ability led to a new turn in his life less than two weeks after the life he had known suddenly ended with the death of his father in November 1913 at the age of sixty-two.

Upon Professor Charles Benton's death, the rector of Holy Trinity Episcopal Church, Reverend Stanley Kilbourne, paid a condolence call on the family. He had come to know Elma because her son sang in the choir, and his good impressions of the boy were confirmed by William Ripley Dorr, a young man who worked his way through the University of Minnesota as Holy Trinity's organist and choirmaster. Mr. Kilbourne now asked Elma if she had any plans in mind for the youth and suggested that, since his father had been an ordained clergyman, young Benton might qualify for a scholarship at Shattuck School.

Shattuck, an Episcopal school for boys at Faribault, the Episcopal "cathedral city" of Minnesota, was founded on the eve of the Civil War by Bishop Henry Benjamin Whipple, the same Bostonian who founded Saint Paul's at Concord, New Hampshire. Shattuck was the first military school for boys in the United States, and the first in which a regular army officer directed the specifically military aspects of the training program. There had been a good reason for military emphasis when Shattuck first opened its doors. Settlers in what was then the West lived in danger of Indian insurrections, and the school fitted into the regional defense plan as a source of trained soldiers and officers for the home guard. But the last Indian uprising was in the 1880s and no longer did Sitting Bulls, Crazy Horses, and Geronimos wait in ambush over the next hill. Still, by the prevailing standard of academic excellence—how much miscellaneous information could be crammed into a boy's head and retained there until he took his college entrance examinations—Shattuck was the best boarding school for boys in the broad region from Chicago to the Pacific Coast.

Its fees were also among the highest. Excluding uniforms, supplies and allowances, but including laundry, the tuition in 1913 was $650 a year, a large sum compared to the per capita income of the average American in those days. In practice, however, the full amount was paid mainly by despairing well-to-do parents who hoped that a stiff dose of military discipline was worth any price if only it enabled them to survive being parents to the kind of boys they brought into the world. At the same time, subject to available facilities for a cadet corps of two hundred boys in 1913, qualified sons of clergymen and army officers were accepted at half the standard fees.

With Elma's approval, and taking young Benton with him, Mr. Kilbourne journeyed to Faribault to bargain with Reverend Dr. James Dobbins, Shattuck's white-bearded, octogenarian headmaster, for a reduction in fees. Dr. Dobbins slowly gave ground before arguments stressing the boy's ancestry, the virtues of his mother and late father, and especially the fine addition his soprano voice would make to the school choir. He reduced the fee to $200, and the deal was sealed. In mid-November 1913 William Benton was entered as a cadet at Shattuck. All he was expected to do for his scholarship was to sing, and he was unquestionably the leading "ringer" in the choir.

Elma's financial plight as a widow at the age of thirty-nine was not desperate, but it allowed for no grand gestures. There was a small sum of money from her husband's insurance policy and she could realize another small sum if she sold her Minneapolis home. There was also a "Carnegie pension" of $63 a month, granted retired professors or their widows.[1] But that was all. Her father, by now living principally on his pension as a Civil War veteran, could offer her but little help. Her brother and sister had problems of their own. It was clear that she would have to go to work to educate her two sons. More immediately, it was also clear that even though "Billie" had a partial scholarship to Shattuck, she would be hard pressed to meet his other expenses, which would be around $400 a year.

Young William Benton was ordinarily a cheerful boy, full of frisky bounce; and even when things were black for him, he was like a brave boxer in the ring who, the more he is hurt, smiles the more for the benefit of spectators. So it was with the face he showed the other cadets at Shattuck. One thing, however, is clear enough. He had very little to sing about when he was suddenly propelled into the military academy. Straightaway, he lost his nickname "Billie." He was now called "Benton." Straightaway, too, he discovered that he was the fourth smallest and second youngest boy in the school. The smallest and youngest was his roommate, Thomas S. Matthews, the son of an Episcopal clergyman who was dean of the cathedral in Faribault and would soon become the Episcopal bishop of New Jersey. In later life, the younger Matthews was to be a celebrated managing editor of *Time* magazine.

There was another thing Benton discovered straightaway. Nothing ever happened at Shattuck except drill and compulsory athletics and chapel and classes and studying—all in lock step, company by company—with severe penalties for any cadet who strayed from the prescribed daily regimen that began at 6:45 in the morning and

---

[1]Available funds for these pensions were eventually exhausted, largely because of the longevity of the women who qualified for and received them. Benton's two aunts, Dr. Mary Benton and Mrs. John Clark, also received Carnegie pensions. The three ladies averaged thirty years or more apiece. The Carnegie pension fund once wrote Benton that this was a family record.

extended to taps and "lights out" at 9:30 in the evening. The only time of the day which a boy could claim as his own was a twenty-minute period right after dinner. Some who couldn't endure the ordeal ran away, only to be caught and brought back in disgrace. One distraught boy climbed a telephone pole and announced that he would jump and break his neck unless he was allowed to leave Shattuck. But when an officer threatened him with something worse than a broken neck if he jumped, the youth slid meekly down the pole.

Benton's feelings about all this were chronicled in the semiweekly letters he faithfully wrote his mother, and the many letters he regularly wrote to his brother, to his Grandfather and Grandmother Hixson, to his aunts, his uncles, and his many cousins.[2] Besides, his mother gave him a diary in which he was expected to record his most private thoughts. This he faithfully did. She also gave him an account book as if to teach him the mathematical detail her father never mastered—namely, the difference between addition and subtraction. He was expected to note each penny he spent and to mail her regular reports justifying how he used his weekly allowance of fifty cents. This, too, he faithfully did.

His letters to his mother read like a serialized tale of woe. But in his diary there is an entry describing one instance of how he outwitted the authorities who were the source of his woe. He had caught scarlet fever, and upon his recovery was in no hurry to get back to his classes and to military drills. The Shattuck infirmary was a haven for his bruised soul, and he meant to stay there as long as his teeming mind could invent the means. One of these was to get a cup of hot tea from an orderly minutes before he knew a nurse was scheduled to appear with a thermometer to take his temperature. He kept a hot last mouthful in the cavity of his cheek, shoved the teacup out of sight and, just as the nurse drew near his bed, swallowed the hot mouthful. The thermometer put in his mouth seconds later naturally showed a gratifying fever, followed by instructions from a puzzled doctor to the effect that though the stricken youth seemed well in all respects except the fever, he should be kept in bed a few days longer.

---

[2]When Benton had children of his own, he managed on the run to bombard them with letters and memos of every kind in order to keep them abreast of what he was doing, and what he thought about what *they* were doing. He expected a certain reciprocity in this matter, and few things in his life annoyed him more than their failure to write him with any regularity.

Despite such tricks, Benton more than overcame the handicap of having entered Shattuck three months late. He soon forged to the front of his class in all subjects except Latin, standing second only to Tommy Matthews. In promptness, cleanliness, respectfulness, and all other minor virtues valued at the school, he also led his class, with a near perfect score in "conduct." This record set the stage for an encounter between Benton and a Mr. Matthison, Shattuck's assistant headmaster—after which the youth breathlessly reported to Elma that his educational future was happily "settled."

As a Yale graduate, Matthison was a member of a Saint Paul–based club comprised of Yale graduates who lived in the Northwest. It was the practice of the club to award a scholarship every year to a worthy boy from the region who wanted to go to Yale and passed the necessary entrance examinations. Matthison had noticed that, in filling out a school form, young Benton had indicated that he meant to follow in the footsteps of his father, grandfather, and two uncles by going to Yale. The youth was summoned to appear before the assistant headmaster and was told that he had made a very wise decision in his choice of a college. More than that, Matthison himself had already spoken about Benton to the president of the Yale Club in Saint Paul, who agreed that the youth should get the club's scholarship when he passed the entrance examinations to Yale.

Elma, meanwhile, had her hands full with a project of her own, so full that she was unable to visit her son at Shattuck for five months after he had entered the academy. She had been persuaded by her father and her brother to rent her Minneapolis home and join them in a Montana homestead venture which could be the start of a "cattle empire." Elsewhere in the nation, homesteading had gone out of fashion. But the Great Northern Railroad, being anxious to create sources of freight along its route in Montana, kept the fashion alive in that state by a clever advertising pitch. It publicized the government's offer of 320 acres to a settler, subject to the terms of the homestead law. The size of the offering, twice the normal 160-acre homestead of earlier years in states to the east where the land was fertile, should have made a prospective settler wary; two times zero is still zero.

Elma could do sums, but this time, under the coaxing of her father and brother, she, like them, was beguiled by the Great Northern slogans: "Three hundred and twenty acres sure look good to me," and "Montana or bust." The three entrepreneurs staked out claims to adjacent homesteads about twenty miles north of Zurich, Montana. The time was the dead of winter when snowdrifts concealed the true nature of the land. To make matters worse, Elma spent $3,250 of her meager capital in building a clapboard house on the site of her homestead—as if to make clear that she had no mental reservations about complying with every syllable of the homestead law. The law provided that a settler gained title to the land upon completing three years of residence on it for a minimum of seven months a year ;[3] the settler must also clear for cultivation at least 40 acres, besides other "improvements." The clapboard house certainly qualified as an "improvement." But what would support it? And who would clear the rocks from the prescribed 40 acres out of 320? Her father and brother could help if they had any strength left over from "proving up" on their own claims. But it was understood that the main job of removing the rocks would fall to Elma's two boys during their vacations from school. It was understood more specifically that the job would fall to the dutiful son "Billie" who never shirked the chores, while the son Daniel, in contrast, had a charming way of evading them.

A felon sentenced to hard labor in punishment for his crime could hardly find a more forbidding place to pay his debt to society. The general area in Montana where Elma, her father, and brother had staked out claims to homesteads was called the Bench, a vast plateau running east from the Rockies about 3,500 feet above sea level. Without snow, the plateau was covered with coarse grass and low cactus and sage brush. Nothing grew to a height of over three feet, and not a tree could be seen in any direction in the 20 miles between the homestead and Zurich, or between it and the foothills of the Rocky Mountains 150 miles to the west. There wasn't enough grass to attract cattle ranchers, but sheepmen did drive their herds across the area toward better grass to the north. The winter temperature could drop to forty degrees below zero ; summers were mild, but it seldom rained except in a sudden torrential downpour, which accounted for the great ravines that crisscrossed the Bench ; only at the bottom of the ravines did the soil retain enough water for an occasional crop.

While Elma battled the emerging hard facts about the Montana

---

[3]Throughout his life in the East, the only person Benton met who had ever "filed and proved up" on a homestead was "Big Ed" Johnson of Colorado. Johnson and Benton were colleagues in the United States Senate.

homestead, almost the only prospect with a ray of hope was the report that her older son might secure a scholarship to Yale. When she came to Shattuck in March 1914, Dr. Dobbins held out another ray of hope for her. After praising the performance of her son and describing him as "precisely the kind of youth Shattuck wants to help," he volunteered to try to offer "something special" in the way of a scholarship for her younger son, if Elma wanted to send him to Shattuck also.

On that note she returned to Montana, where her sons were to spend three summers with her. As her money ran out, with no hope of crops in sight from the "dry land farming," she made plans to resume her teaching career. The place, a comedown for a woman who had been in the center of the intellectual community at the University of Minnesota, was a one-room pineboard school in Blaine County, Montana, a couple of miles from the homestead, at a salary of $40 a month for eight months a year. The homestead would be retained in the hope that her money would last long enough to meet residence requirements and prove the claim. But after a year Elma was compelled to take a more lucrative teaching post at Fergus Falls, Minnesota, and the following year she moved on to North High School at Minneapolis. In the long run she won title to the homestead only by means of a "private bill" put through Congress by Minnesota's Senator Frank B. Kellogg, who had once been her father's office boy in the state senate. The bill was signed by President Wilson on his last day in office. Thus owning her 320 acres, she was able later to sell the clapboard house for $250 to a neighbor, who hauled it off behind a team of horses.

Young Benton, who was to start work on the homestead in the summer of 1914, was reprieved at the last minute. Elma had heard that William Ripley Dorr, the twenty-two-year-old organist and choirmaster of Holy Trinity Church in Minneapolis, was planning a bicycle trip with a friend through Scotland and England, visiting the great cathedrals, listening to the great choirs, and inspecting the organs. The friend had dropped out, Elma learned, and feeling that her older son could profit from such a venture, she asked Dorr if he would take the boy along instead. The answer was yes. Elma by some sort of alchemy, then turned rocks into the necessary $500, and on 16 June 1914 her son and Dorr left for Europe.

There was no hint of war in the air when they reached Glasgow and toured the Lake Country. The highlight of their trip for the remainder of June and July was a visit to Durham castle, where the pair were shown around by the noted Dr. Henley Hensen, the bishop of Durham. The latter afterwards invited the two young Americans to dinner, and as Benton reported in a letter to Elma: "I sat between two bishops and felt pretty shaky. It ended up with Dr. Hensen giving us each a nice copy of one of his books, and he put his name in the front." What the youth did not report was that Dr. Hensen also gave him a gold sovereign.

Six days later, 2 August, the two tourists were in Lincoln, and young Benton crackled with excitement at being the first with the news as he wrote his mother:

> We've just learned of England's mobilization (it is not yet known to the public). A rich American from Boston found it out and told us. We also just learned of Germany's declaration. Everybody is very excited. We would be stranded except that we happen to have tickets on the American line, the only line running to N.Y. Our tickets will be worth an awful lot. We are very, very lucky. It's funny seeing cathedrals when everybody is talking of war. I suppose you get the papers. Imagine what it is in England. We are very lucky with our tickets. England has taken no stand yet.

The next day, when England declared war, found him in Cambridge. But it was not until 6 August that he summarized for his mother the whole of the event he had lived through:

> There were three days when the banks were closed and we couldn't get money. For a while I didn't have a cent. Money scarce. Everybody frightened. Parliament wanted 100,000,000 pounds. Banks to dig up. Crash, rushes on banks, banks close. Country in a state of excitement. I will remember this all of my life.

Elma cabled to say that if he could not come back by ship, he should enter school in England. There was, however, no trouble in coming home, except for an incident in Liverpool where Benton had his first taste of "security regulations." He and Dorr were arrested for taking pictures on the docks, but the suspect choirmaster and choirboy were finally released and their cameras returned. Their homebound ship carried double its normal quota of passengers but it was smooth sailing in all other respects.

Benton was back in Shattuck in time for the start of the 1914 fall term, without first seeing his mother, who was in Montana. Though still a private in the cadet corps, he had been an eyewitness to the outbreak of the European war—and hence, at fourteen, a "seasoned veteran" of that conflict. But other boys were in the feeder lines leading to the battlefield itself. Some forty Canadian youths failed to return that fall, many of them having volunteered for service in the Canadian army.

4

Would-Be Soldier

As the fall of 1914 turned into winter there were reminders that the war overseas was no Indian uprising of the kind the Shattuck cadets were originally trained to put down. There was an occasional announcement that a former student who had volunteered in the Canadian army had lost his life on the western front. At intervals, too, an antique Englishman who had fought in some forgotten colonial war would show up at Shattuck and regale the boys with tales of derring-do against the Fuzzy-Wuzzies. Whether or not this was the British propaganda machine in subtle motion, young Benton had aesthetic reservations about the performance. "The stories this retired English officer told," he said in a letter to his Grandfather Daniel, "were not half as good or as interesting as those you tell of the Civil War." To which he added a sudden postscript: "My voice is changing."

At Shattuck, Benton's mood had been swinging wildly from the depths of pessimism to the heights of optimism and back again, although in the month before Christmas there was no sign that he was suffering more than his usual range of agonies. He and Tommy Matthews were the only two boys in the school studying first-year Greek, and as Bill wrote Elma, "I don't stand up very well in comparison with Matthews who is a shark at Greek. He is always on top of the day's lesson, and I always get bawled out because I am not." He hoped, however, "to beat him all hollow in algebra."

When Benton arrived in Fergus Falls for Christmas with his mother and his grandparents, his rebellion toward Shattuck was at once apparent. He had brought with him all his worldly goods and announced that he would not go back. Why? Two girl cousins had written him that students in the Fergus Falls High School were having a wonderful time, and this piece of intelligence made military life seem all the more grim. Further, Tommy Matthews, "the shark at Greek," would not be back at Shattuck. He was transferring to Saint Paul's in New Hampshire to be a bit nearer New Jersey, where his father had just been made the Episcopal bishop. It was hard enough to be one of two boys studying Greek. With Matthews gone, he dreaded the prospect of being the *only* Greek scholar.

It is not clear whether his mother had ever intimated that there was a connection between Bill's record at Shattuck and the prospect Dr. Dobbins had held out that Dan might also get some sort of scholarship. But it is clear that when the older son said flatly that he wouldn't return to Shattuck, Elma—though she had not seen him for almost a year—just as flatly said he would. In a protracted test of wills, the mother did not flinch. The son fell on his knees and cried. His sobs did not move her, except for one concession. He could have the option of not taking *second*-year Greek. Otherwise, she crushed his rebellion, and personally took him back to Shattuck like a prisoner of war being led into a stockade. He appeared subdued; if there was any wrath left in him, he could take it out on the reconditioned typewriter Elma gave him as a Christmas present.

At first, there was plenty of wrath left in him, and he voiced it in his typewritten letters to his mother whenever he saw an opening to be brusque. Thus to her in early January 1915. "I want you to tell me whether I should be confirmed as an Episcopalian or not. Do you want me to be confirmed in some other church than the Congregational? Do you want me to be confirmed at all? Do not leave that to my own judgment, or say you do not care; because if you do, I will wait until you tell me definitely. Please answer this *immediately*, if only by card." This was followed in the next few weeks by a series of medical reports, based on self-diagnosis and reading like the ten plagues. In all these he seemed to imply that his mother was responsible for every ache and pain he was suffering, from eyestrain to insomnia, from "rheumatism" to earaches and hives. The only good thing he had to report was that he had a new roommate, Phil Works, and got along well with him.

Still, since Benton knew that he would have to stay the course at Shattuck, he began to make the most of all things that came his way. He was "pledged" to a fraternity—and eventually became its president. He made one of the scrub football teams comprised of leftovers from the first and second varsity teams, and he eventually became its captain, suffered a broken nose, but had a "successful" season. He was, in his own words, "a damn good captain but a lousy right end."

There was also his recovery from a shattering surprise. In an ad sent out by a firm specializing in old coins, he thought he read that buffalo nickels of a certain date brought many times their worth. And so he wrote to his mother: "I wish you would send me all your buffalo nickels because I can sell them for twenty-five cents each. I will make my fortune. I have got sixteen nickels already but I have not sold them yet. I am paying ten cents for them and am doing a thriving business." At last he was ready to cash in and make his fortune. "I sent away twenty 1914 buffalo nickels," he wrote his mother, "and a couple of days later I got a postal card saying that they were worth five cents each and are waiting for return postage." He eventually found a more reliable source of pocket money. He became the school's sole agent for memory books, stationery, class pins, and other emblems. Best of all, he invented a binder, on which he secured a monopoly from the memory book company, to hold the newly founded weekly school paper, of which he was sports editor. He sold this at $1.50—twice his purchase price—to virtually every cadet in school. This was his introduction to the specialty selling of books in which he later became the world leader.

One aspect of life at Shattuck seemed to depress Benton more than any other. Until his senior year, he was denied his ardent ambition to be made at least an NCO in the corps of cadets. But he eventually made in local terms something better than an officer. After many palpitations of the heart, all recorded like electrocardiograms in letters to his mother, he made the "crack squad." This was a special drill team of twelve boys, the pride of Shattuck, supreme and unique in the entire United States, with special black and white uniforms setting them off from the herd at the proms at which they were featured. No triumph of later life meant so much to him.

Benton's last two years at Shattuck revolved in general around an ironclad promise he got in the early summer of 1915 from Mr. Edward T. Gale of Minneapolis. Gale was a key figure in the Yale Club, which annually awarded a scholarship to a young man from the Northwest who wanted to go to Yale, and Benton wanted to know if the sixteen-month-old commitment he had from Shattuck's assistant headmaster, Mr. Matthison, concerning that scholarship still stood. It did. The scholarship would be held for him even if he flunked the entrance examinations on a first try. Harvard, as "the mother of movements," might stress academic excellence in its students. Yale, as "the mother of men," stressed the old Puritan virtue of "character." Bill Benton had "character," besides other virtues. His father and grandfather had graduated from Yale. Further, he had been brought up a close playmate of Gale's only son, who lived a block away from the Bentons in their Minneapolis days. The son was Richard Pillsbury Gale, the only grandson of Governor Pillsbury who had founded the flour mills—and helped unseat State Senator Hixson.

Young Benton did not know how small the scholarship would prove to be—$250 a year. Its promise became a golden vision he clung to for the remainder of that summer as he worked a grinding routine on the desolate Montana homestead. He cleared rocks with a pick and horse-drawn stoneboat. On the same stoneboat he hauled drinking water from a spring three and a half miles away, where he would fill the hogshead by pail. Each week he rode more than forty miles on horseback for any mail waiting in Zurich.

It is hard for a contemporary reader to imagine what that frontier was like in 1915—perhaps like Ohio a hundred years before, but devoid of fertile soil. There were no doctors, no schools save a single room for eight elementary grades. Running water and electricity were unknown. Bathing meant a Saturday scrubbing with water heated by wood fire, in a rubber tub dragged onto the living room floor. Reading was by kerosene lamp. A single horse provided power for chores, a pony took care of transportation, and one cow gave fresh milk. Rarely, there would be enough rain to raise a meager crop of some vegetable. Drinking water came from the hogshead— and Benton remembers that the trick was to get the dipper in, filled with water, and out again without collecting slime. Meat—except canned salmon and chipped beef, cooked in various ways—was unknown unless Bill shot a jackrabbit; he did get one sage hen in four summers. He used to hope that sheepherders heading north might give the Bentons one of their flock, but they never did—even when he rode out to the moving herd and asked for a sheep in exchange for passage across his mother's homestead. Compared to Montana, Shattuck in the fall of 1915 seemed like the life of Utopia. He was even glad to hear that his younger brother would be joining him at school after Christmas. "I will help Dan all I can with his work," Bill wrote Elma. He tried to do just that when Dan came to Shattuck, but with little effect.

Girls were now beginning to put their mark on Benton's young life, and he often appealed to his mother for advice on how to meet certain problems they posed. Elma, in a comprehensive reply to all his questions, took a position that was sharply beside the point of her son's inquiries. She voiced her deep concern over the repetitive new note he had been striking about "girls." It could only mean that he was "squandering" his money. He was neglecting his studies. By having "joined the pleasure-seeking throng" so early in life, he was "forming bad habits that would prove disastrous in college."

He was quick to assure her that she was "dead wrong" on every count of this indictment. "Believe me!" said he emphatically, "I'm going to study when I go to college, and I am going to get Phi Beta Kappa. It is one of my ambitions." As for her other charges: "I don't think I'm extravagant, Mother. I don't spend money on frivolity, that's a cinch. I want to help myself through college. I've always intended to. I don't know what I can do, but that will develop." In this, he spoke with the assurance of a successful entrepreneur (he was then earning around $16 a month on his stationery business).

Toward the end of the school year, before returning to the Montana homestead for another round of loneliness and back-breaking toil, his announced hope to make Phi Beta Kappa was subordinated to another ambition. The Wilson administration in Washington had taken a few faltering steps in the direction of a defense preparedness program, and this prompted Benton to inform his mother that he wanted to enlist in the army "as soon as war breaks out in earnest." Further, "the whole school was taken down to see the moving picture, 'The Battle Cry of Peace.' It is an instructive movie on the preparedness question, advocating it. It is wonderful. Everybody liked it. When it comes your way, be *sure* to see it, because I know that you will like it very much, even though it is a little horrible." His mother forwarded the letter to his aunt, Dr. Mary Benton. Aunt Mary tried to cool the blood of the young warrior by sending him some pacifist pamphlets. Their receipt prompted him again to write Elma: "Perhaps the 'Battle Cry of Peace' is exaggerated. But there must be something in it. I want to enlist as soon as I can get out of Shattuck."

Benton's letters to his mother during his last year at Shattuck reflected a youth torn by eagerness to enlist in the army and by concern about possible disaster in the coming entrance examinations for Yale. "Don't tell me I can't fail," he wrote her, "because I very well may." In June 1917, as his graduation from Shattuck drew near, one would have supposed that his expressed fear of failure was just a flaming arrow shot into the air for the sake of the awesome beauty of its trajectory. The examinations for Yale coincided with his final examinations at school, but even that seemed no ground for concern. On a four-year average, Benton stood second in his Shattuck class every year, and first when all the years were averaged.

But then came the fiasco. William Burnett Benton, son, grandson, and nephew of Phi Beta Kappa preachers, teachers, or university department heads, failed his entrance examinations to Yale.

The news reached Elma Benton in a form letter, saying that her son had failed each of his four examinations. Benton, in agony, wrote to the Yale authorities to say that surely a mistake had been made. The answer was that he had indeed passed the examinations in English and mathematics, but had failed in French and Latin— which made their original notice correct for all practical purposes. Under the "new plan" it was necessary for a boy to pass all four of the so-called comprehensive examinations.

Under the "old plan," had he taken his examinations at the end of each year, subject by subject, he would have doubtlessly piled up the credits required to be admitted to Yale. But as he had been the No. 1 man in academic standing in his class on a four-year average, his teachers did not think of keeping him after each year's commencement exercise for the few days required to take examinations subject by subject. Since they would have had to supervise the examinations—and hence delay their own departure from the school— they were happy to send the boy home so that they could go home themselves.

Benton later learned that he had scored 100 in his mathematics examination and was the only Yale applicant that year who did so. But that did not make him feel any better. The massive fact remained that Yale, following its rules, had slammed the door in his face.

The summer of 1917, again spent working on the Montana homestead, did nothing to alleviate Benton's depression. First, there was his doleful experience at a Fourth of July dance held at Cherry Ridge, a tiny place consisting of a general store which included a post office and a school. Benton, fresh from school and not yet broken to the saddle, wanted to go. Wearing his best, and only, store suit, a fancy one by Montana standards (where Sears, Roebuck styles prevailed), he set off on horseback to ride the thirty-five miles straight over the prairie with no roads or trails of any kind.

The dance started at five o'clock in the evening and was to last until five the next morning, since almost everyone present had come across the prairie and could not find his way home in the dark. At least three or four men were on hand for every woman, but young Benton was choosy. From the time of his arrival until nine in the evening, he was on the lookout for a girl of his own age to dance with. Finally his watchful waiting seemed about to pay off. He saw an attractive girl of about sixteen sitting on the bench along the wall across the room. Benton approached the girl, introduced himself in the approved Shattuck style for correct manners, and asked if he could have the pleasure of a dance with her. The girl hesitated and said: "I don't know whether my husband would like it." And she added: "Besides, I don't know what to do with my baby." It was only then that young Benton noticed the baby bundled next to her. But he was desperate. So was she. They danced, danced again, and then again—while young Benton fought to suppress his bitter disappointment and unhappiness over his partner.

He started home on horseback at five in the morning and did not reach his mother's homestead until noon. He tumbled off the horse so tired and saddle sore that he thought he would never be able to get on a horse again. With no sleep since nine o'clock the previous morning, he had ridden seventy miles. It was a big price to pay for a few dances with a sixteen-year-old married girl who had a baby. Still, there were no other young girls at the dance and he didn't see another one all summer long. That was part of life on the frontier. Years later, he supposed that his mother was right when she said to him: "Billie, Montana was *good* for you." But when he looked back on the time he spent there it seemed like the suburbs of hell, especially in the summer of 1917.

There was another thing his mother later said to him: "Don't forget that you owe Shattuck a great deal." He didn't forget, came to serve on its board of trustees, and made impressive financial contributions to it. But the more he thought about the prisonlike military aspect of the place, the more he hated it retroactively. Resolving to do something to spare other youths his own torment, he offered the school a large extra gift on condition that all its military features be cast aside. The offer was not accepted.

The plans Elma made for her older son's further education took their cast from a change in her own life. Throughout the summers of 1916 and 1917, on the Montana homestead, Elma reflected at length on her own long-range prospects. If she was to return to teaching on a permanent basis, she should have academic credentials qualifying her for higher positions, perhaps in a university. This meant at least a master's degree in education. Accordingly, she applied for and was admitted as a graduate student in Columbia University's Teachers College, starting in the fall of 1917. Her friends could not see the logic behind her decision. Elma was forty-two years old; she had a fine job with North High School in Minneapolis; and with her salary she could educate her two boys. Why, then, make the kind of break that would take her to New York? Her mind, however, was made up, and no arguments advanced by her friends could change her decision.

Since she could not afford to take her sons with her, she arranged to have Bill enroll in Carleton College, where his aunt, Dr. Mary Benton, was dean of women. Carleton, at Northfield, Minnesota, would put Bill only twenty miles north of his brother Dan in Faribault. The two boys would be about forty-five miles south of Minneapolis, where other relatives and many friends lived, and close enough to Fergus Falls to spend the Christmas holidays with their grandparents.

Another factor in Elma's decision was that her older son, by attending Carleton (or any other accredited college), would have two options. He could enter Yale as a sophomore provided he passed the entrance examinations, or he could drop back a year and enter the freshman class without taking the examinations he had come to dread. Elma was so determined to see her son get into Yale that she was willing to write off the year at Carleton and have him go to New Haven as a freshman.

When Benton entered Carleton, his being the nephew of the dean of women caused "a sensation." He was the "best known freshman in the class." True, he didn't have any money "to take the girls to the movies like the other fellows" did. True, his clothes were so worn and threadbare that once when he bent over, he split his pants "wide open." But there were compensations. He was promptly made a corporal in the Carleton Company, "with good chances of promotion." He was elected to the Philomathean Literary Society, "the oldest and the best in school, and the one every freshman wants to make." And not only did he make the freshman debating team but he also won a place on the "Philo" debating team, and it was "very unusual for a freshman to make it."

Then, on the eve of a Carleton varsity basketball game, Benton was asked to substitute for the regular cheer leader at a basketball game played by Carleton's second-string team. This activity prompted his mother to dash off several warning notes about the adverse effect cheer leading would have on his throat. "I do not see why you are always talking about my throat not being strong," he said in a sharp rejoinder. "It is even stronger than the average." Then, without meaning to venture into prophecy, he added: "My throat will stand plenty of yelling. I may get hoarse but that does not mean that my throat is sore."

Nor did his academic standing suffer from his debating and yelling. He again held the No. 2 academic rank among the men in his class and was enjoying himself so much and was doing so well on every front—social, military, and academic—that he argued the advantage of continuing at Carleton for four years, after which he would go to Yale for *graduate* work. "I am telling you these things," Benton concluded, "so that if you think it would be better for me to do something else, I should do it, because I know that whatever you think is best is sure to be best."

Before Elma could state what she thought was best, she had a *non sequitur* from her son to weigh along with everything else. "Biology," he suddenly informed her, "is getting to be *very* instructive. We have been studying all about the venereal diseases, birth control and its evil effects in France, etc., and about reproduction in all animals and man in particular. I think it is something that everyone ought to know." Elma tabled that one for a while, but fired away at the other thoughts he was juggling. She insisted that he keep a steady course pointing to Yale—even if it meant taking the entrance examinations or entering as a freshman.

Her son provisionally agreed to the general plan, but he warned that he didn't think he would be able to "stick it out at Yale," since he "wanted to get in the Army pretty badly." He would not be an exception to a family tradition. He was the great-great-great grandson of soldiers in General George Washington's army during the Revolutionary War. He was the great-grandson of soldiers in General Andrew Jackson's army during the war of 1812. He was the grandson of a soldier in General Ulysses S. Grant's army during the Civil War. He was the grandson of missionaries who were soldiers of the Lord in the Middle East. Now it was his turn to be a soldier in General John Pershing's army during the world war. Evidence of his earnestness appears in a letter which his Aunt Mary Benton sent to Elma on 11 May 1918:

> I must talk to you about Billy. His desire to enlist seems to be very strong. I have tried to say what I could to dissuade him. I cannot feel that it is best. All the word from Washington seems to be that it is wiser for boys of his age to wait at least until they are twenty-one and to pursue their studies. He says that he is just as strong as any of those boys that are going. I cannot help wishing that Billy could content himself with going on with his studies. There is no question about the strength of his desire to enlist.

Elma knew what to say. "When the United States government wants boys of 18," she wrote her son, "it will draft them. You are the eldest son of a widow and have an extra reason for waiting until the government tells you it wants you." She won her point for the time being, but the debate was not over.

Benton, however, won a point of his own in a different debate. Instead of returning in the summer of 1918 for work on the Montana homestead, he joined Phil Works, his former Shattuck roommate, in taking a job on a roadbed construction crew of the Duluth, Mesabi, and Northern Railway serving the Mesabi iron range in northern Minnesota. What he saved out of his pay (the offered rate was $70 a month, plus room and board in the labor barracks or small hotels) would help meet the initial costs of the fall move to New Haven. Elma, after much discussion, agreed to the summer job, though she took a pessimistic view of where it might lead.

The early reports Elma had from her son as his work took him over the iron range were reassuring. But then came a series of notes telling of many new friends in Duluth, where he met college men with "millionaires for fathers." By the end of July 1918, thanks to the sons of the "millionaires," he and Phil Works had been accepted by the circle of well-to-do girls in Duluth, and there were regular get-togethers whenever a weekend brought the boys near that city.

A letter referring to these activities reached Elma in Montana coincident with the news from Fergus Falls that her mother, then in her mid-seventies, had died. The funeral would be in Fergus Falls and the interment in Burlington, Iowa. Elma called Bill by a rail-road telephone line. Before the bad connection was broken off, she told him about the death in the family and then abruptly turned to the living present. She accused her son of "squandering" his money by trying to keep up with a "dissipated pack of rich boys," and by slipping off with them for "a frolic in Duluth with a dissipated group of rich young girls." She was appalled to see his "principles breaking."

Benton promptly wrote a letter that would be waiting for his mother upon her return to Zurich from Burlington. First he com-mented on the "numbing" news of his grandmother's death. Then he turned abruptly to his mother's "unjust, warped conclusions." He was not walking any primrose path over the iron ranges, and he enclosed an itemized account to show how he had spent his earnings to date. His mother should remember that, with her previously given consent, he had bought a new suit he had needed but had no money to get when he was at Carleton. Otherwise, in seven weeks of work under the blazing sun, he had spent a total of only $34 on himself. This came to roughly $5 a week for clothes, laundry, pressing, and everything else, including stamps for his extensive correspondence with assorted people. "Is that very extravagant?" he asked rhetori-cally. Nor could he see why his mother thought his "principles were breaking." This was the unkindest cut of all. "I never," said he, "met so clean a bunch of young fellows in my life, or such a splendid, pure-minded group of girls."

Several days later, as if to clinch the argument, he sent his mother a picture of a girl named Cordelia Collins, a student at Smith, whom he was taking to a dance in Duluth. "Cordelia," he noted, "reminds me a great deal of you, for she is so very practical and sensible. I get very, very, sick of these little butterfly girls who don't know what it is to think a serious thought."

Meanwhile, a draft law was passed in August 1918 covering men between the ages of eighteen and forty-five. Benton, age eighteen, registered in Duluth, giving as his home address the place in New York where his mother would be staying on her return to Columbia in the fall, where she had a new appointment to the Teachers College faculty, at $900 a year, as supervisor of secondary school teachers in the training school connected with the college. By the terms of the draft law, it was understood that when Benton entered Yale he would automatically be inducted into the army as a member of the Student Army Training Corps, receive the regular private's pay of $30 a month, live in a barracks, and eat in a mess hall—all paid for by the government. He would go into training as a field artillery officer, a program unique at Yale and begun there even before the war. He was not clear about what the new turn of things meant to his academic status, or how much academic work he would be taking along with the military. The Yale authorities didn't know what the army had in mind for their institution.

In any case, within a week after the draft law was passed, Benton was the only "college man" left on the construction crew. He needed every cent he could earn, and he worked right up to the day in mid-September when his mother came from Minneapolis to Duluth, where the pair boarded a Great Lakes passenger boat for a trip to Buffalo, New York, and then by train to New York City.

Benton was so eager for military service that in Buffalo he briefly slipped away from his mother and walked into a Marine recruiting station seeking to enlist. An old-line Marine recruiting sergeant took young Benton into a nearby bar and offered him some beer to make sure that he would capture his boy. The boy refused the beer, and for good measure added primly that he had never tasted liquor of any kind. Whatever the sergeant made of this, he advised the youth not to enlist but to stick to his studies and become an officer. When Benton later confided the episode to his mother, she promptly threatened to enroll him in Columbia in order to keep him under surveillance, but she relented, and he proceeded to Yale.

Under the new draft law, a boy qualified for college could enter the army and enroll for officer training right at his college. The ablest ones would then be shipped on to the regular officer training camps of the United States Army. Yale, however, was an exception to the rule. Instead of its being a processing center for boys destined for regular army camps, various draft centers shipped some twenty-five hundred men to Yale to train for field artillery commissions— simply because Yale had the horses and what passed for dormitories and mess halls. Most of the tramees were not really Yale students. They did only a minimum of academic work. But from reveille until taps their day was a round of standing formation, routine drills, and mass descents on the mess hall.

Benton was inducted into this life on 28 September 1918, got his typhoid shots, and promptly began to run a high fever—though not from the shots alone. He was aflame with frustration because none of his "training for the infantry" at Shattuck or at Carleton could be converted into a ground for distinction in Yale's artillery setup. Even when he had a chance to show his power of command by once putting a platoon through a snappy bit of drill, the lieutenant in charge was looking elsewhere and didn't notice the performance at all. Nor was there any sign of action on his application for a transfer to infantry training at a regular army camp. He was ready to settle for anything—even a "good sergeancy," if this meant getting out of Yale, into the regular army, and from there to France.

On 10 November 1918 he wrote to his mother that along with two thousand trainees, he had recently taken a "final test" involving trigonometry, and that almost everyone's mark was raised 20 points because the instructors giving the test had allowed only one hour instead of the two that were prescribed. It had also been announced that only one man completed the examination with a perfect 100 without the 20-point bonus. He was Private Benton of Battery C.

It was the high point of Benton's military career. The day after his success, the armistice was signed on the western front. "I didn't go anywhere," Private Benton informed Elma in describing the noise that greeted news of the armistice. "I was so intensely disappointed in having missed the war that it made me sick. The war was the greatest experience of my generation, and I was not part of it." He had lost twenty pounds from the bad food at Yale, but because of his "contribution to the war effort" he had a $10,000 government insurance policy which he would convert when he was twenty-five years old into an "endowment" policy paying off when he was sixty-two.

Three days after the armistice, his depression had deepened to a point where he wanted to drop out of school entirely just as soon as he was mustered out of the Student Army Training Corps. He thought of going to New York if he could get a job. He thought of transferring anywhere that would have him as a sophomore if only to get his schooling over as quickly as possible. "It is very peculiar how my ambition and everything has gone," he wrote his mother. "I don't seem to be able to awaken it or to care about anything." He hadn't the slightest idea "what to do next."

His mother, as usual, had a very strong idea of what he should do next. She ordered him to stick to his academic work at Yale until he completed his work on the B.A. degree. Benton, obedient to her will, remained at Yale after the Student Training Corps was demobilized on 15 December, in order to take the entrance examinations. If he passed them, he would get credit for the year spent at Carleton. If he failed, he would have to enter as a freshman.

After the examinations, he joined his mother in New York for the Christmas holidays, then doubled back to New Haven, where he had left his trunk at the railroad station in line with a plan he kept to himself. If he again failed his entrance examinations, in his determination not to forfeit the year he had spent at Carleton, he meant to pick up his trunk and head for Williams College, which his grandfather, William Benton, had attended in his own time before transferring to Yale. However, he was spared the need to put the plan into effect. Yale's dean of admissions was "Toots" Farr, and the dean of the college was Dean Jones, a man who had once been a faculty colleague of Professor Charles Benton at the University of Minnesota. The case of young Benton may have already been discussed between the two deans when Benton appeared in Farr's office and put a trembling question to him: "Did I pass the entrance examinations and will I be admitted as a sophomore?" Farr replied cryptically: "You are admitted as a sophomore." Benton pursued the matter no further. He assumed that he had failed Latin again but was being admitted as a sophomore in honor of his deceased father. Later, he discovered that the university needed sophomores badly; the class which entered in 1917 was so depleted by the war that it was the smallest in decades.

Along with other demobilized students who stayed at Yale or who returned in large numbers from the war, Benton shifted to an academic track in early January. He was not reconciled to the fact of his aborted military career. Nor would he be reconciled for more than a decade afterward. The matter would periodically come to the forefront of his consciousness, to disrupt his relationship with his mother—and with himself.

5

Outsider at Yale

The Yale Benton faced was not the college of his father's or grandfather's day, when Puritan clergymen held all the strategic places as administrators and professors. Their educational mission, as they saw it, was to train prospective Congregational clergymen or teachers, and undergraduate instruction at Yale College was based largely on the principle of austere exposure to and triumph over pain.

The last clergyman president of Yale, Timothy Dwight, was succeeded in 1899 by Arthur Twining Hadley, Yale's authority on railroads. Hadley, until he retired in 1921, often exhorted students to prepare themselves for a career of public service, and he also wrote a great deal about the relationship among ethics, political economy, and business. But this seemed only a ceremonial bow to Yale's long history as a training ground for ministers, and college presidents.

The main body of students in Benton's day did not follow Hadley even in a ceremonial bow to the past. Undergraduate life still drew its intellectual tone from the scions of New England's Puritan aristocracy—and its branches which settled the West—scions who were largely trained at eastern "prep" schools. A handful of students did lend themselves to the traditional molding process and traditional careers. But to an increasing degree, young men aiming at a business career converged on Yale from around the nation believing that its high academic reputation and high social prestige would help them in business later on. The days of the week and the hours of the day at which courses were offered were often the most important factor in determining their courses of study. Benton had a comment to make about the matter later in life. In November 1937, as the new vice-president of the University of Chicago, when he spoke over a CBS national hookup on "The Education of a Business Man," he said:

> The professor's job was to conduct classes, to keep us awake in them, and at the end of the semester to engage us in a battle for grades.... Few of my classmates even considered the merits of further education once we were entitled to call ourselves "Bachelor of Arts," unless we wanted to become high-priced lawyers or doctors and had to stay on. It seldom occurred to us that a life of scholarship or university research might be a career for a man. To us, the graduate student, to quote Dr. George E. Vincent, was a fellow who didn't know enough to go home when the party was over.

In January 1918, Benton was not so critical. He was eager to get into "the party," but found many obstacles.

First, there was Yale's arbitrary class system. Students were accepted by classes, made their friends by classes, were assigned rooms by classes, were promoted by classes, engaged in athletics by classes, loafed on the Yale fence by classes, took up the various customs and privileges of college life by classes, and were accepted into the secret societies by classes. Benton's status, as a sophomore who had not spent his first year at Yale, automatically made him an outsider on the social track the main body of his class was following. Moreover, he had chosen Richard Gale of Minneapolis as a roommate, and Gale, as a freshman, had to live in freshman quarters. So did Benton—which again removed him from the main body of the sophomore class.

Something else made him an outsider. Gale's father had come through for Benton with the promised scholarship awarded by the Minneapolis–Saint Paul Yale Club. But it amounted to only $250 for the sophomore year, and this gave Benton no margin of funds with which to preen himself. Social lines could be blurred when everyone wore the same uniform and lived in barracks. But the lines suddenly re-formed when the students changed to civilian clothes, lived in the dormitories, chose their own eating places, and squired girls around to "the dances." Everything about Benton now stamped him at Yale as a westerner who was poor, who had no taste in clothes, and who had no high and mighty connections in the world of Yale. Finally, though he overflowed with physical energy, he lacked the athletic skills that could boost the depressed state of his stock on the Yale social exchange and mark him a candidate-designate for the most prestigious of the fraternities and, prospectively, of the senior societies.

Yet the road blocks aroused his competitive instincts. He began to contribute to the *Yale Record,* the undergraduate humor magazine, and had a number of items published. He tried out for the Yale dramatic club. He also tried out for the collegiate debating team, but without initial enthusiasm. "Debating amounts to practically nothing in the college," he informed his mother, "and very few take an interest in it. Only rubes are supposed even to go out for it. I may make it, but even if I do, there is not the honor connected with it as at Carleton. Here in college, it would mean much more to make the wrestling team or do anything else."

But while he got at least a toehold in spheres where free competition prevailed, a month before the junior prom to be held in April, he was hurled back on his own loneliness and poverty. If he took a girl to the three-day festivities grouped around the prom, he would have to lay out $75, and he had no such money to spend on just having a good time. He consoled himself, and his mother, with the wild hope that he might be able to go to the junior prom in his senior year. But for the moment, he doubted that it would be worthwhile to invest $6 in a stag ticket. "I could not," he said, "make out a program as I do not know anyone in my class. I am sorry to say, Mother, that I don't think I'm going to amount to anything in the social line around here."

But he kept trying. During a dance called the "Sophomore German" held before the junior prom, he waited in his dormitory until midnight, when the ticket takers at the door wandered off. Benton then walked over to the place where the dance was being held and got into it for nothing—only to be mortified by his own conspicuousness. He was one of the few youths in the place who was not dressed in a tuxedo. Worse, his best suit never appeared more forbidding. It was the heavy brown suit he had bought with money earned in summer work in and around the Mesabi iron range. In Duluth, it had seemed the height of fashion. Against the background of the "Sophomore German" dance, he felt as though he were a garishly illuminated mud pie. "I didn't have a very good time," he reported to his mother. "I did not know any of the girls—or perhaps they didn't want to know me."

Still, said he in a subsequent note to his mother, he was never really "bewitched by girls" the way so many of his contemporaries were. His main interest for the moment was centered on getting material published in the *Yale Record*. Here he was increasingly successful. He was also getting along well in his studies. He had "received Honors" in economics, logic, geology, and English, and did "particularly well in logic." Spanish alone was giving him trouble in his tests. "I have absolutely no ability for languages," he confessed, "and never have had, and I only wish I did not feel I have to take them. I know that Spanish next year will be my lowest mark. I doubt if I will get over 65 in it—and if anything keeps me from a high average, that will be it." Even so, if it were not for all his outside student activities, he had "a strong chance to make Phi Beta Kappa by his senior year." He discovered that he was in "an awfully dumb class."

In May 1919, a new source of academic distinction opened up for him when he applied for and was awarded a Rhodes scholarship from Connecticut. Many had accumulated during the war. His mother, being informed, did not thrill with delight. She could not see what bearing the scholarship would have on the business career her son seemed bent on pursuing, to her own voluble disappointment. "If," said she, "you will accept my advice and guidance and go into a career of scholarship or research, or theology or even law, then you should take the Rhodes scholarship. If, however, you persist in your mistaken ideas of going into business, you'd better get at it." The obedient son turned the scholarship down.

In the spring of 1919, Benton made a decision of his own which changed the course of his university education.

New international trading and financial patterns had come to the surface of the post-armistice world, and many investment markets, as in Latin America where English and German interests had been dominant, now lay open to penetration by American banks. But the latter were short of trained personnel who could be sent abroad to help exploit the new opportunities. The largest American bank—the National City Bank of New York—hit upon a solution other banks were to imitate. At the instigation of its president, Frank Vanderlip, it had organized what was euphemistically called a "college training class" to provide itself with a manpower pipeline from the colleges and universities.

The program embraced twenty-five universities. Students recom-

mended by their economics professors could apply at the end of the
sophomore year for summer work with the bank. Two applicants
would be chosen from each institution and would be rotated among
the departments of the bank during two succeeding summers. They
would be paid $80 a month the first summer and $100 the second. If
their performance was satisfactory, upon graduation they would be
employed by the bank at a starting salary of $125 a month. Then
they would be sent to a branch office in Latin America or elsewhere
overseas with the assurance that if they did well they could count on
earning as much as $2,500 a year in three years' time.

Benton's economics professor at Yale was a volunteer missionary
working to convert students to the revealed truth of the bank's plan.
He emphasized that the National City Bank was the "biggest bank
in the Western Hemisphere with many overseas branches," and its
"scholarship training program" was a passkey to prestige, position, and, presumably, a fortune. It was a new gospel, a Third Testament, which differed from the Old and New Testaments that had
resounded from Yale's lecterns in the days of Benton's father and
grandfather. It found an eager convert in young Benton.

A passkey to prestige, position, and a fortune seemed all the more
welcome to him as the academic year at Yale neared its end, and he
appraised where he stood on New Haven's social stock exchange. He
was clearly among the low men on it. True, he had won the freshman-
sophomore debating contest—and the only silver cup he would ever
win in his life. But as he had suspected, debating at Yale, unlike
Carleton, was the road to social ostracism rather than prestige.
Further, he had not yet accumulated enough "points" to be elected
to the board of editors of the *Yale Record*, though he had amassed
a formidable number in a few brief months. He was on the eligibility
list of the Yale drama club, but had never been cast in any of its
plays. He had submitted some pieces to Yale's literary magazine,
but all were rejected. Nor would he have Dick Gale as his roommate
in the year ahead. He had urged Gale, in his own interest, to find a
roommate from among the members of his own class of 1922, while
he himself moved in with his own class of 1921.

It was a bleak summary, and, as usual, Bill poured out his heart
to his mother:

Sometimes I hate this college, and wish I had never seen it.
It seems very aristocratic and it certainly is very hard to get

acquainted. It is not like the West at all, where it makes no difference which year you enter. Here the boys have all got their friends, and they do not care to try to make any new ones. It is very, very discouraging at times. I hope next year to do a great deal, and to devote all my time to studying and trying to make Phi Beta Kappa, to the oratorical contests, to the Record, to debating, to dramatics, and perhaps to the Lit. Even if I can't get to know the fellows, I am going to do a lot here and satisfy myself, and I am going to do more in three years than the rest of the class has in four, and enough to make a senior society two or three times over if I were a junior fraternity man. I am going to do all I can in college, earn all the money I can, and let everyone else go to the devil.

In this half-dispirited, half-belligerent mood, he secured the necessary recommendations from his professors for the college training class at the National City Bank and then was interviewed by E. R. Naar, the assistant cashier of the bank who came to Yale to pick the actual trainees. Some one hundred Yale students were among Benton's competitors for the two open places. Naar, who had originally come from the West, questioned Benton closely about his life in Minnesota and Montana and may have seen something of himself in the youth before him. In any case, the exchange between two transplanted westerners of different generations went well. On 19 June, Benton was informed by letter that he was one of the two students at Yale who had been chosen for the college training class at the bank and was "congratulated" for "the excellent showing" he had made in his interview.

Benton was pleased by his triumph over ninety-eight competitors from Yale but had a moment of doubt before he accepted the National City Bank's job offer. If he deducted from the projected monthly salary of $80 the monthly cost of transportation, laundry, pressing, shoe repair, razor blades, stamps, stationery, magazines, newspapers, and "entertainment," he did not see how he could manage to survive unless his mother helped out. He put the case to her in a letter, and apologized for doing so.

Elma by now was about to receive her master's degree, and the work she had done meant two years toward her Ph.D. degree. But economic troubles, never far removed, had lately been intensified by worries about her father. Daniel Webster Hixson still kept his home in Fergus Falls, but, on the Montana homestead where he was living with his son, matters had gone from bad to dreadful. Severe winters in 1917–18 and 1918–19 had been followed by a drought that began in early spring of 1919, with rainless days becoming rainless weeks and months. By early June, dust storms were already blowing across the face of Montana, and many families in their despair over crop prospects were abandoning their homesteads. How long could or should Edwin Hixson hold out? Yet if he left the land, where would their father live and who would look after him?

An offer to Elma to join the faculty of the University of California in Los Angeles suggested a possible answer. Her widowed sister, Capitola, by now was remarried and living in that city, and if Elma also established herself there, they could bring their father to Los Angeles and jointly look after him. She put the plan to her father, who rejected it. His people for two centuries in America had fought the elements as farmers, and his son was the only man in his own direct line of descent who was left to carry on the old fight. If Edwin walked off the homestead, it would mean a final uprooting of the family from the soil that had always nurtured it. Nor was the father ready for a Los Angeles refuge where he would have nothing to do "except breathe until death collapsed his lungs." As long as Edwin still had the will to fight the droughts and dust storms, his father would back him up with his own labor and money. He would even sell his home in Fergus Falls and use part of the proceeds to tide them over the 1919 crisis. Next year, surely, there would be plenty of rain and good crops.[1]

The stand her father took ended Elma's flirtation with the University of California. In casting about for other academic posts, she learned that the trustees of Hosmer Hall, a private school for girls in Saint Louis, were looking for a new head. There were several other private schools in Saint Louis at the time, but they all had men as headmasters. Moreover, Hosmer Hall had had a very distinguished tradition, southern style. The wives of many of the leading citizens of Saint Louis, then very much of a southern town, were either graduates of the institution or were on its board of trustees. "Hosmer Hall," Elma herself would later say laughingly, "also had the highest tuition west of Pittsburgh"—one reason why the Great Depression would hit it with devastating force.

---

[1]The elements refused to serve Daniel Webster Hixson's stubborn optimism. The drought of 1919 extended into 1922, and countless farmers and cattlemen in the West and Southwest were ruined by it.

The starting salary offered to the headmistress was $3,500 annually, more than most college deans of women were earning. Fringe benefits included a cost-free apartment at the school, cost-free board, and all expenses to educational conferences. These details appealed to Elma. But there was something else which made the prospect ahead attractive to this lifelong suffragette. She saw a chance to change this "finishing school" into a pioneering institution where young women of "breeding" could be educated for the emergent new world of "equal rights" and civic responsibilities for women. For now the congress had adopted the Nineteenth Amendment guaranteeing nationwide suffrage for women, and every sign said that it would be swiftly ratified.

Elma's application for the post as the head of Hosmer Hall was handsomely backed by faculty members of Columbia's Teachers College. In swift sequence, she was invited and went to Saint Louis, was interviewed by the trustees of the girls' school, was offered the post, and accepted it. She then went on to Fergus Falls to help her aging father sell his home. A few days after her arrival, a tornado hit Fergus Falls with fierce fury, but luckily the Hixson home, with Elma and her father in it, lay a bit to the side of the tornado's path and was spared. The consequent shortage of houses made the home easy to sell, but added nothing to Elma's resources. Not a penny was to be had from the Montana homestead, and the rent money from the house she still owned in Minneapolis would be drained off in the cost of moving to Saint Louis and maintaining herself there until her salary at Hosmer Hall began. Thus she could promise her son only a few extra dollars if he joined the training class at the National City Bank—but subject to the condition that he let his brother live with him in New York. Benton said yes, and accepted the bank's offer.

The decision called for a change in his management of a project which promised, in his own mind, to make him rich. A New Yorker named Carey had conceived of a college calendar pad which would mark the red-letter days of each school's academic year—athletic contests, dances, examinations, vacations. He needed a student to take charge of the project at New Haven. The one chosen would get a percentage of the unit selling price of twenty-five cents, but his real profit would come from commissions on the advertisements he got from local merchants for display in the pad.

Yale's placement bureau recommended Benton to Carey. The pair met; Benton was offered the local franchise, accepted it, and promptly recast Carey's format in line with some ideas of his own. The calendar would have drawings, jokes, and sayings to amuse the student market. Moreover, in an early sign of what was to be Benton's lifelong sensitivity to nomenclature, he gave an appropriate name to the item he meant to sell. It was:

YALE UNIVERSITY TICKLER
THE OFFICIAL UNDERGRADUATE DATE PAD

He had to invest $45 of his own money on business stationery, calling cards, stamps, and other office items in order to launch the venture on a professional basis. But he figured that the payoff would be $400 in clear profit. By mid-June, he stood a little in awe of his initial success. After calling on only one-half of the New Haven merchants who were on his list of advertising prospects, he had promises from four-sevenths of those he had called on. But after he was picked for the National City Bank's training class, which was to start on 1 July, he saw he would not have the time to solicit the remaining advertising he counted on, and also get the *Yale Tickler* ready for the printer. He needed a partner to finish the job, and he found one in a classmate. The deal was that the latter would get one-half of all profits on condition that he remain in New Haven, tidying up whatever remained to be done after Benton left for New York.

Elma Benton's own design for brotherly living between her two sons flowed from a decision she had previously reached about another matter. She noted that while the age difference between the boys was eighteen months, by 1919 the difference in where they stood in their schooling had widened to four and a half years. Dan was plainly in a psychological trap at Shattuck, and since he lacked Bill's traits, it was unlikely that he could break out of it unaided. The older son could rail at being afflicted by real or imagined injustices, yet find in all the blows a vision of the victory he meant to win. Or he could run into a stone wall, yet find by another route a prize that was not part of his conscious design. The younger son, on the other hand, stopped where he stood in a moment of defeat. He was not lacking in native intelligence, or in personal charm. He was much beloved by everyone who knew him. The trouble lay in his focus of attention. He was devoted to a life in the field—to dogs, hunting, animals of every sort—and girls. Something other than a military school was needed for a youth of this kind, and as Elma canvassed the alternatives, she discovered the existence of Holderness, an Episcopal school in Plymouth, New Hampshire, with a student enrollment of around forty boys. After much correspondence and a visit with its rector, Reverend Lorin Webster, she was convinced that in this small and highly personalized school Dan could get a new lease on life.

In the spring of 1919, Elma enrolled Dan for admission to Holderness in the fall term. And as a part of her plan, she sent the youth to New Haven in June, preliminary to moving with his brother to New York for the summer. The two brothers had not seen each other for almost a year. When they were united in New Haven, Bill's big brother protectiveness—and his acute embarrassment as a socially ambitious Yale man—spilled over in a report he sent to Elma in Saint Louis:

> Dan showed up here in a shiny and worn green suit. It is about all he has to his name, and that suit is all wrinkled. He didn't have a straw hat. He is virtually without a change of shirts, ties, underwear, and he has no pajamas. Now that college is over, there have been some big sales here. I spent $10 of the little money I have, buying Dan some shirts and the other things he absolutely needs. We will be sharing the one pair of pajamas I have. Mother, Dan absolutely has to have some suits before he goes to school in the fall. I don't think he has to get them right away, for I have two suits—and they fit him better than they do me; so that we will have one suit apiece while we are having the third suit pressed. The bill for pressing is going to run into money. But it is absolutely essential that we make a good appearance. It is a recommendation anywhere and nothing looks worse than a poorly pressed suit.

The two boys had a first cousin who was living in New York, Mrs. Margaret Clark Williams, Aunt Harriet Benton Clark's daughter. Margaret, then on the staff of the *New York Herald*, was about to move to Utica, where her husband Howard was to be the local agent for the National Cash Register Company. Her cousins arrived in New York on the eve of her move, and it was through her connections that a job was found for Dan in the mailing room of the American Lithograph Company at a starting salary of $14 a week.

This hopeful start of life in New York was quickly overcast by troubles in living arrangements. The National City Bank main-

tained a clubhouse where its trainees could live, and Benton had
secured special permission for his brother to share a room with him
there. But room and board would have to be paid for in advance,
and Benton's salary from the bank would not be forthcoming until
the end of his first month of work. All the two brothers had between
them was $50, and an emergency appeal to their mother yielded
only $10, the extent of what she could spare. So ended the prospect
of club life. Instead, the two brothers moved into an $8-a-week room
for two in a bedbug-infested YMCA on 125th Street. They could
spare only another dollar a day each for food, and they were often
hungry. Both boys rapidly lost weight, Dan losing twelve pounds
after only a few weeks in New York.

Little food and the bleak YMCA were but two of the many factors
which made the month of July 1919 a low point in Benton's life. He
was the youngest member in the training class at the National City
Bank, and while he quickly made friends (for life) with William and
Tom Joyce, two youths from California, he was cut off from the
rest by the fact that he did not live in the clubhouse. Then, the calendar pad business had taken an ugly turn. Ten days after Benton
went to New York, his partner back in New Haven wrote to say that
he was leaving for Maine and would not return until early September
and would then complete his share of work on the project.

There had been no further soliciting of New Haven advertisers,
no makeup of the pad, no approach to printers for bids on the printing. Nothing. Benton protested to his partner, but to no avail. The
vision he once had of clearing $400 in profit evaporated. Merely
to salvage his original $45 investment, Benton spent nights on end
in his oven-hot YMCA room, writing letters to New Haven merchants, printers, and Yale authorities, all bearing on matters related to the calendar pad project.

There was also his brush with a near-disaster of another kind. He
had met a pleasant girl in New York but couldn't afford to take her
anywhere except for a walk in the park or to "an 11¢ movie." When
he kissed her one night, she said to him breathlessly, "When do we
tell mother?" "Tell mother what?" he asked. To which she replied,
"We're going to get married, aren't we?" The budding romance died
on the hook of the question mark. After that, Benton found his
entertainment in listening to "Bolshevik" stump speakers harangue
125th Street crowds about the world's evils, and about the coming
revolution which would set everything right. Or occasionally he and

Daniel would stand at Grant's Tomb looking across the Hudson River at the bright lights of the Palisades Amusement Park, wondering if some day they would get there; they never did.

The lowest recorded point in Benton's life in New York that summer occurred on a night when he was invited by William Joyce to meet four of his own friends who were then in the city. The effect of the encounter led to a volcanic eruption in a letter Benton wrote to his mother the next day:

> The four fellows were all about my own age, and every single one of them had been overseas. They had all volunteered right out of prep school, except one, and he went after his freshman year in college. Oh, Lord, how I felt out of it, and I suppose that is the way I will feel the rest of my life.
>
> You did not know what you were talking about, nor did the whole family, and I often feel very like cursing at everybody who even mentioned to me that I oughtn't to go. I feel it is a lot my own fault, though, for I should have told everybody to go to the devil and have gone anyway. I was plenty old enough to decide for myself, and that is what I ought to have done, instead of listening to this darn peace talk and wailing of Aunt Mary and everybody else.
>
> The men I am meeting every day always take it for granted that *I* was in the service the way everybody else was. They are always talking about the war, and I never can even listen with a clear conscience. . . . I seem to have reached a place where I feel very unsettled and do not know what on earth to do with myself. The war made me very restless, anyway, and I sometimes feel that the height of my ambition would be to see the whole world, and become an educated bum. I know I think I would be a great deal more satisfied at work this winter, earning my own way, than I would with your borrowing money at the bank to put me through college. I feel so darn inefficient anyway. Yet I really do not look forward to spending my life in an office. I seem to crave excitement, especially since I missed out on the war, and I can't get over my great restlessness.

Life turned a little brighter when the mail one day brought him a check for $3.50 from *Judge* magazine, then a leading humor magazine in the nation. He had sent it four jokes that had been previously refused for publication by the *Yale Record*, and one of the four had

been accepted. Life took a still brighter turn when he was transferred to the investigation department of the bank. "In this department," he noted for his mother's benefit, "you get a knowledge of
the whole bank. I am getting more interested in banking all the
time." This was followed toward the end of August by an announcement to his mother that he had "definitely" decided on a career in
banking. If so, what did she think about his not returning to college
but continuing to work for the bank? Also, what did she think about
the comparative advantages of working for it in South America,
Europe, or Asia? "The place of work awaiting you," Elma answered
caustically, "is back at Yale. Moreover, if you are restless to see
the world, you can see more than 5000 years of it by going with Dan
on Labor Day to visit the Metropolitan Museum."

By now there had been a fundamental change in the relationship
between the two brothers. When they were first thrown together in
New York in a miserable room and had barely enough to eat, old
temperamental differences revived old spats. Dan assailed Bill for
being "too damned bossy." Bill assailed Dan for being sloppy, care-
less, indifferent to the fact that his shoes were not shined or his
fingernails cleaned, and caring only for dance hall girls. But as the
summer wore on, a changing relationship was mirrored in the older
brother's report to their mother about how "thrilled" and "proud"
he was because Dan had earned a salary increase from $14 to $15
a week, how "lovable" he was, and how he had "been improving all
summer." At leave-taking time on 20 September when Dan left for
the Holderness School, the brothers parted on a mutually affectionate note.

Benton's farewell from the National City Bank itself was also on
a happy note. He was told that the bank regarded him as the outstanding boy in the training program and would await his return
the next summer for another training period. The wind in the compliment filled the sails of Benton's pride, and one of the first things
he did when he was back in New Haven was to change his academic
plans in order to major in economics while minoring in English. This
meant concentrating on courses in banking, finance, accounting,
and transportation. The National City Bank expected this of him,
and Benton dutifully complied with the expectation—to his bitter
regret in later life, when he was a strikingly successful businessman.

For the new school year Benton had two new roommates. One
was Dana Clark, the son of the clergyman who had been the pastor

of the First Congregational Church in Minneapolis in which Professor Charles Benton had been the first deacon. The other was Hervey Clark of Santa Barbara, California. In reporting this development to his mother, Benton said that he was "crazy" about both boys, and went on to amplify some of the reasons why. Dana had been class orator the previous year, and his duty had been to make a speech when the Yale fence was given over by the sophomores to the freshmen. It was "the sign of the most popular man in the class, to be elected to this position." Hervey, meanwhile, was the circulation manager of the *Yale Daily News*, "which is a big honor." In fact, said Bill, "being elected Class Orator is one thing, but I take my hat off to anybody who can make the Yale Daily News." There was but one small flaw in Dana. While he was partly earning his own way, "he hated to do anything which might lower his prestige." In evidence of this there was the matter involving the *Yale Tickler*. After much *Sturm und Drang*, Benton had managed to get the calendar pad published. "I offered Dana a chance to sell these desk pads last night, and he wouldn't take it. I went out and sold 66 in an hour, which would have made $3.30 for Dana." All in all, however, he felt he could not have two better roommates.

Suddenly, however, there was a crisis in connection with selling the calendar pads. Dean Jones had established a rule forbidding all organized student canvassing in the dormitories of the college. When Benton learned of the rule, he went to see the dean in the hope that an exception could be made in the case of the *Yale Tickler*. But the dean said no. He explained that feelings were bad enough between the town and the students. If he let students drum up business in an organized way inside the dormitories when he wouldn't let the townspeople do it, there would be even worse feelings. Did the rule, Benton asked, "forbid student salesmen from hawking their wares in front of the dormitories?" No. Did the rule "extend to Sheffield Scientific School?" No, Sheffield was out of the jurisdiction of Dean Jones.

The double negatives charted the course Benton steered through the crisis. He found some hungry students in the college who were willing to sell the *Yale Tickler* in front of the dormitories, and he also organized a force of hungry students for a door-to-door canvass in the Sheffield dormitories. He did not clear the $400 profit he had once anticipated, but neither did he have to declare himself bankrupt. The venture netted him $100, with a psychic bonus on the side. His classmates, who were fast hardening into the mold of a money-minded generation, could not help noticing how Benton had converted an airy idea into dollars. "The other night," Benton reported to his brother, "a fellow offered me $10 cash for all the money I ever make over $500,000. I think I will take him up, because I haven't got one chance in a million of ever making that much money. He only offered me 50¢ for all I ever make over a million, but that does not sound so good to me."

Meanwhile, Benton was buoyed by the reports he had from his mother in Saint Louis. Everything in her previous life seemed to find fulfillment in her new work. She was overjoyed by the students, their parents, and the school trustees, who understood and approved of what she meant to accomplish. She was also delighted with the new friends she had made among faculty members at Washington University in Saint Louis. There was also a happy note in the letters exchanged between her sons. "If you can graduate this year," the older brother wrote the younger one, "try to plan on taking the Yale College Entrance Exams, and only if you fail them, go to Dartmouth. I would like more than anything to have you down here at Yale next year. I feel I could help you a lot if you came. I have written mother about your meeting me in Boston for the Harvard game, and I have got seats for it. It comes off in the middle of November, and we will have a big party." Dan, in reply, said he was enthusiastic about Holderness. He had made many new friends and was having no trouble in his classwork. It looked as though he might make the football squad, and he was not a bit homesick for Shattuck. He was grateful for his brother's help and interest.

On 13 October, a shattering letter from his mother in Saint Louis sent Bill to Holderness. Dan was in the infirmary of the school with what had been diagnosed in a preliminary way as a brain tumor. The older son was to move the younger one to the Boston General Hospital for an examination by Dr. Harvey Cushing, the noted brain surgeon. In Holderness itself, Bill found his brother propped up in bed and in cheerful spirits. "I can see two of you," Dan called to him gaily. But his words were followed by a whispered aside from the attending nurse. "I fear," she said to Bill, "that your brother is never going to get well."

Later Dan was shifted to a mobile bed and, with Bill by his side, was moved into a baggage car on a Boston-bound train. Dr. Cushing had been alerted to their coming. Soon after their arrival at the Boston General Hospital, he diagnosed the case not as a brain tumor but as encephalitis, a form of "sleeping sickness" that was first recognized in epidemic form toward the end of the war. The mortality rate varied greatly with the virulence of the strain of virus or bacteria that was the infecting agent, and with the age and physical condition of the afflicted person. Benton was reluctant to leave his brother among strangers, but after he transmitted the medical report to his mother, she directed him to return to New Haven to continue his studies. She would be coming to Boston to move Dan to the Washington University Hospital in Saint Louis, where he would be placed under the care of her newly made friends on the medical faculty.

With his return to New Haven, Bill kept up a cheery flow of letters to his brother, carefully spacing them so that Dan would receive special deliveries on Sunday "in order to break up the monotony of the long day without any mail." He was able to report that he had at last been elected to the board of editors of the *Yale Record*. He felt the next issue would be a "wonderful number," and would send Dan a copy as soon as it came out. He was "cracking" most of his studies "fine," but was almost failing Spanish. At the recent Princeton-Yale game, special trains ran from New York and there were mobs in the city—fifty thousand people must have come in. "I wish you could have been here to see the crowds, but you will be a part of it some day, so you should not worry."

The cheeriness was the antithesis of what he felt.

Elma and Dan reached Saint Louis in the first days of November 1919, but the doctors in the Washington University Hospital could do nothing to break the grip of the sleeping sickness. The youth would rally briefly, hold his own, and then lapse into a coma. "I am worried about Dan all the time," Benton wrote his mother on 23 November, "and every day I don't hear from you, I feel more so. I don't believe there is another woman in the world like you, who can do as much and go through as much." Four days later he added:

> If anything happens to Dan, Mother, and we are left all alone, you must plan to live with me just as soon as I graduate. I don't see why you shouldn't come abroad with me if I go with the bank, and there is every sign that that is what I am going to do. You might not like to, and if so, I must plan to do something else. For if we are all alone, we ought to be together. I am very busy these days, and I am thankful I am, for every

time I stop, I think about Dan and his lying unconscious there, with your going through so much anxiety and trouble. I feel I ought to be in St. Louis with you, but I do not know that I could do any good. It is just so terrible being way off here and not knowing what is happening there, or how you are getting along.

Good-bye, Mother dear, I hope that God will bless you at this time, and take care of us all.

There was one more note written a few days before Benton left for Saint Louis to be with his family at Christmas:

I can hardly wait until I get home. I want to see you and Dan, and I know that Dan will improve steadily now that he has started. It was terrible for a while when he was unconscious and did not even know you. But now I know he is going to be all right.

The seeming turn for the better was, in Dan's case, the last upward leap of a candle flame before its extinction. The youth died in the last days of 1919, running a fever of 108 degrees.

6

Chairman of the Board

Benton was back in New Haven a week after classes began in January. He was nervous and unsettled. He was also uncertain about his future. The National City Bank had just sent him a pamphlet about the training course for the summer of 1920. Should he continue with it or not? If it meant that he eventually would be sent to South America—at the recently reduced starting salary of $1,500 a year—did he really want to go into banking when this would entail a three-year separation from his mother? "More and more," said he in a note to Elma, "I hate the idea of leaving you to hibernate for three years in South America. Fifteen hundred dollars a year seems to me a very small salary, too. I guess it is the best I can get, though. I am trying now to do as much work as possible in order to forget that Dan is dead. But I've put his picture in the back of my watch and I find myself looking at it constantly."

As the weeks passed by, Benton had something else to report to his mother. The eleven members of his class who were members of the board of editors of the *Yale Record* were about to elect officers to manage the magazine for the year ahead, starting in March. Benton prophesied that "the fraternity men will try to control it all, as they always do in the dirty politics the college abounds in." The prophecy was right, but the intrigue failed because of the outgoing 1920 board chairman, Harry Wanger, the brother of Walter Wanger, later of motion picture fame. Harry was not enrolled in Yale College, but in Sheffield Scientific School. He had not been bothered by being excluded from a fraternity because he was Jewish. But rewards made on the basis of caste instead of merit bothered him greatly. He took a firm stand on the proposition that Benton was *his* choice and the only logical choice to be the new chairman of

63

the board because he had earned the right in free competition. Harry used all his residual powers as outgoing chairman to make the point prevail. The result went by telegram from Benton to his mother on 3 March:

HAVE JUST BEEN UNANIMOUSLY ELECTED CHAIRMAN OF THE BOARD FOR NEXT YEAR WITH TEN VOTES FIRST ISSUE OF OUR BOARD OUT MARCH 31 PRETTY HAPPY TONIGHT

A few days later, Benton was elected to Zeta Psi fraternity and was quickly initiated. But on "Tap Day," he would be passed over and not elected to a senior society like Skull and Bones. He lacked a spokesman from the *Record* to be his sponsor.

Benton faced a serious problem with the first number of the *Record* to be published under his direction. "The best man for drawing," so he informed Elma, "was on the outgoing board and we are going to miss him a lot." He felt that the textual material would be all right, but it was "the art that makes the magazine." The "best man for drawing" was Reginald Marsh.[1] Benton, while "heeling" for the *Yale Record* used to write gag captions for Marsh's paintings. The artist, even then, specialized in painting "taxi dance halls," starting with the one on Chapel Street in New Haven, which was frequented by Yale students. Marsh turned in an uncaptioned painting of the place at a time when the *Yale Record* was preparing its "baseball number." The caption used was Benton's contribution: "Foul Ball."

Marsh belonged to the class of 1920, of which Henry Luce, Jr., was also a member. He had left the *Record* in line with a tradition whereby the outgoing board retired en masse in February of their senior year, and he refused to contribute anything further to the magazine. Benton, determined not to lose a good artist to tradition, violated custom and code and offered the artist $50 a month if he continued to submit drawings to the *Record*. Marsh accepted the proposal, and was forced to paint hard for his money. Benton, thinking ahead, laid by a stockpile of his drawings for use in the next year, following Marsh's graduation in 1920.

It was the John Held, Jr., era. The "He-She" jokes in the *Record*

---

[1] By 1935, Reginald Marsh's paintings were to hang in at least fifteen museums, including the New York Metropolitan Museum, the Chicago Art Institute, the Whitney Museum, and the Detroit Art Institute.

reflected it, and they led to a summons to Benton to report to Dean Jones, who was sharply critical of what the magazine was printing. An example of bad taste cited by the dean happened to be a caption which Benton had written for a Marsh drawing. Beneath the drawing of a boy and girl seated at opposite ends of a sofa were the lines: "He: Have you an hour to spare? She: Yes. He: May I kiss you good night?" "Do you think your mother would approve of that joke?" asked the dean. Benton boldly answered yes. "Well," said the dean as he slammed his desk, "I cannot control the *Yale Record*, but I can control you. You put a stop to this kind of stuff or you will be expelled from the College."

Benton at that time did not feel ardently enough about the freedom of the press to invite the martyrdom of being fired in defense of the First Amendment. He returned to the *Record* office, called in the ninety heelers, and told them that henceforth things would be different—at which, the heelers named his board "The Purity Board." Going further, Benton got a certain Professor Bangs, a young English instructor, to act as censor. But the professor seemed to view his job as ceremonial and never censored anything. Benton himself was not so blasé. An off-color quatrain appeared in the "exchange" columns at the back of the magazine where jokes were printed from publications like the *Harvard Lampoon*, the *Princeton Tiger*, and the *Cornell Widow*. The *Record* was already in print when Benton caught sight of the verse for the first time. He had the heelers clip it out, and the issue was distributed with a little hole in the back of each copy.

After Benton's election as chairman, several new notes cropped up in the reports he passed on to his mother. One concerned Professor John Berdan, with whom he was studying English composition in a class known as "daily themes." Berdan took a fancy to Benton, but rode him hard. "He tells me," Benton informed his mother, "that my possibilities as a writer are good, but that I am wasting them on superficial forms." Further, under Berdan's influence, he had been "suddenly overcome with a thirst for learning, and particularly literature. I am losing all my interest in economics courses," he added. "I can't understand the reasons why except for the fact that the professors who teach them are a sorry lot."

The second new note concerned a rumor that had more lives than a cat. Grandfather Daniel Webster Hixson had finally been forced to move to Los Angeles where he was living with Capitola. Edwin still clung to the Montana homestead despite the ruinous drought in 1919 and the slim prospects of bringing in any kind of crop in 1920. But he was suddenly excited by a tale that geologists suspected oil beneath the parched soil around Zurich. As Elma owned the homestead next to his own, Ed asked her to urge Bill to soak up all the geological lore Yale possessed. It would come in handy when there was an approach by the oil companies—say "within a few weeks' time"—in order to buy outright or to lease the lands Ed and Elma owned. But Bill, the soaring optimist at the onset of most new business proposals, was not swept off his feet this time. He wrote his mother in the spring of 1920:

> I can't get very excited about the oil outlook. Uncle Ed ought to realize I could learn nothing about oil in a few weeks. If there is oil there, these geologists will find it out for us soon enough. I can't take much stock in the possibility, however, for the country would be flooded with prospectors and capital, property would have a high speculative value, and everything would not run so normally. I hope you aren't planning to do anything about it. We can't lose by waiting. I am not very excited by the prospect of wealth, anyway. The only reason I wish we were wealthy is that it would give me—or both of us— the opportunity to study at the European universities, which I would deeply love to do.

They were to wait, and wait, and wait.

The third new note was about the *Record* itself. Benton was breaking new ground in circulation. Sales of the *Yale Record* in years past had been largely confined to the students on campus and to a few alumni subscribers. Benton, however, wanted a magazine whose contents would justify its being distributed on newsstands along the New Haven–New York axis and, if possible, beyond. More circulation meant more advertising. More advertising meant more revenue, and a greater return to him personally, since as chairman he shared in any earnings.

Before his one-year tenure as chairman was over, his board brought the *Yale Record* to a point where it had by far the largest newsstand circulation of any college magazine in history up to that time. Its total paid circulation each two weeks was six thousand. Issues often ran over one hundred pages, and copies were available in such elegant places as New York's Plaza and Biltmore Hotels. Its profits in Benton's year as chairman of the board were $25,000, and the example of this success reportedly inspired the launching in the next year of a new national magazine, *College Humor*, which digested individual college magazines devoted to humor.[2] The time Benton spent on *Record* business meant less attention to his studies. Besides, his interest in economics and in a banking career had flagged. Yet when the school term was over, he felt he might as well spend the summer of 1920 working again in the National City Bank's college training course.

During his second tour at the bank, Benton was spared some of the hungers of the year before. His salary of $100 instead of $80 a month enabled him to live in the new boardinghouse the bank had acquired for its trainees in Brooklyn Heights. Here he made new friends, and also renewed and deepened his friendship of the previous year with William and Tom Joyce. He also came frighteningly close to being blown to bits at 12:01 P.M. on 16 September 1920, when a bomb concealed in a cart placed in front of the Morgan bank on Wall Street exploded. He had walked past the bank on an errand only a few minutes before and was a block away when the bomb went off. Even so, the blast hurled him against a wall and the impact left him senseless. When he recovered, he rushed back to the Morgan bank and helped remove the dead and the injured before the police arrived.

A week later, Benton was back in New Haven to start his last year at Yale. Again his work on the *Record* absorbed his energies. The magazine was winning high praise from his classmates, and this only made his mother's silence all the more jarring. "You never write me a darn thing about what you think of the *Record*, how to improve it, or anything," he wrote Elma in the late fall. "The fact that I've built up the largest college circulation in America seems to mean nothing to you. You are always bawling me out for my extravagances and other things, but you never give me any credit for the least thing I try to do. I often think you would just laugh off any-

---

[2]Still later when Benton was about to graduate, *College Humor* as well as the old national humorous magazine, *Life,* both offered him jobs at $50 a week. He declined because he had no high confidence in his talents as a professional humorist, or high hopes for the field itself as a life work. He said his most famous line, publicized from coast to coast was, "In the spring a young man's fancy lightly turns to what the girls have been thinking about all winter."

thing creditable I try to do. It makes me so completely and utterly discouraged sometimes that I think I'll pass out." Elma Benton still did not compliment her son. Neither did Professor Berdan. The latter remained sharply critical of Benton's English compositions.

But there was more to Benton's last year at Yale than work on the *Record*, or for Professor Berdan or on the economics courses in which he had lost all interest. Now, instead of knocking on dormitory doors selling calendar pads, he was welcomed through those doors for a special reason. His head for mathematics and for "figuring percentages," had accounted for his success at cards even when he was a Shattuck cadet. He had gone back to card-playing during the summer of 1920 in order to escape the boredom of National City Bank work, and he kept on playing cards at Yale in order to escape the boredom of his courses in economics. Auction bridge, the postwar successor to whist, was the rage at Yale. Benton soon excelled at it, and indeed in later life he called it the only thing he ever really mastered. He was solicited as a partner or opponent by other student addicts, many of them in the Sheffield Scientific School. He thus spent many hours in the Sheffield dormitories with bridge-playing youths who vaguely had in mind careers as civil engineers, architects, and mining engineers. One of these, destined to cross Benton's path in later life, was the gifted Ralph Ingersoll, who would be a mining engineer, a managing editor at the *New Yorker*, a central figure for a while in the publishing empire of Henry Luce, Jr., and the creator and publisher of the shortlived newspaper *PM*.

In his last year at Yale, Benton also rekindled his interest in debating, won a place on Yale's intercollegiate debating team, and became better acquainted with a classmate and a teammate, Robert Maynard Hutchins. What Hutchins's contemporaries at Yale today recall of him as a Yale student was his physical splendor. He was tall, lithe, graceful, perfectly proportioned, and had flawlessly sculptured features. As an ambulance driver on the Italian front during the world war, he had been decorated for valor by the Italian government. In addition, his classmates knew that he was among the leaders of his class in academic standing. They knew that he had marked gifts as an orator (and elected him class orator for 1921). The rest was mystery. He could fell an adversary with a single stroke of his ironic wit; yet he looked at the world through eyes flecked with ineffable sadness. Here was a young man clearly marked for "success"—who conveyed a sense that his life must be one of atonement. For what? For life itself? The war? Some episode in it? No one knew.

A joint membership on Yale's debating team against Harvard led to more than a casual relationship between Benton and Hutchins and partly accounted for their post-Yale friendship. But perhaps more important was the similarity in their family backgrounds. The father of each had attended Yale. Each father had prepared for the clergy and had served as a clergyman for a while. Each father had left the clergy to take an appointment with a college— Hutchins's father at Oberlin, and Benton's at the University of Minnesota. Benton's father, coming from a missionary family, had been brought up in Asia Minor, while the period of service Hutchins's father had put in at Berea College in Kentucky was very much in the missionary tradition and spirit. Benton and Hutchins were both born and brought up in the West. Both had transferred to Yale late, Hutchins entering as junior from Oberlin. Both found the Yale curriculum extremely easy, and both tended to be bored by it.

Hutchins, however, had discovered that he did not have to spend his senior year in the College but could spend it in the Law School with credit for a bachelor's degree. It was to be his general conclusion in after years that his formal education began at the age of twenty-one when he started to study law. "I do not mean to say that I knew then that I was getting an education," he said. "I am sure the law professors did not know they were giving me one—they would have been shocked at any such insinuation. They thought they were teaching me law. They did not teach me law. But they did something far more important; they introduced me to the liberal arts."

Benton later mulled over one point of difference between himself and Hutchins as it was brought into focus by their debate against Harvard about the merits of the closed shop—a debate which Yale lost. "I spoke as number two man on the Yale team," Benton recalled, "and Bob Hutchins, as Yale's star orator, was the number three or anchor man. Harvard conceded our entire case almost from the outset, and proceeded with a lot of 'buts.' It was then the job of the Yale team to prove that since Harvard had conceded our case, we had won the debate. As the number two man, I threw away my prepared manuscript and pitched into Harvard. Bob, in the number three position, went ahead with his beautifully prepared speech and proved the case beautifully—the very case which Harvard had conceded. I wanted to win by making the most of Harvard's weakness. Bob, indifferent to Harvard's weakness, wanted to persuade the audience about truth itself."

On Benton's twenty-first birthday, in 1921, there was a birthday box from his mother, along with a check and the usual letter of advice. Elma was in no way disappointed that he had abandoned all thoughts of becoming a banker. She had hoped all along that he might go into a proper career, like teaching or scholarship. "Billie," she said when it was apparent he would not, "if you won't do something respectable, won't you at least be a lawyer?" On the other hand, if he had no immediate interest in studying law, the best thing for him to do upon graduating was to go to work in some sort of business. In reply, Benton surveyed his standing in the New Haven world, and found it far different from the earlier day when he looked about and saw how the wicked prospered and the ways of the righteous were set at naught. "I feel very happy, now, Mother," said he; "it is a wonderful peaceful existence, with all my friends, and with few worries. I will never be able to let you know how grateful I am to you for my course at Yale. It is something I shall always have, and always remember as a wonderful experience. This year has been particularly happy, for I have become well acquainted with my class and everything has gone smoothly."

He had other comments to pass along to his mother in the final months before he graduated. In public finance he was learning to make out an income tax, but it would be "a long time before that would worry me." Then again, he had just read *The Age of Innocence*, and was very impressed with the phrase, "the suppressed eloquence of the inarticulate." Benton imagined "that we all feel that way," only he felt it "very keenly." He had produced "some great lines" of his own in an essay he wrote for "Johnny Berdan's class," but felt that the essay as a whole was "too rambling, with no proper division of paragraphs." The same trouble plagued all the things he wrote. He was relying "on the individual cleverness of the lines and phrases and sacrificing coherence and unity." While his "lines were getting better," there was no change for the better in the qualities where he was "weak."

He had another ground for regret. Back in the fall of his senior year, he had been told by the registrar at Yale that he would be elected to Phi Beta Kappa if he maintained the existing average of his grades—though his old trouble with languages brought him a 61 in second-year Spanish. But then, in his senior year, his boredom in his economics major was reflected in his middling performance on examinations, followed by middling grades. Professor Berdan's high opinion of Benton's promise as a writer was offset by the middling grade he gave him in English composition. Even so, Benton might have reversed the current were it not for the time he spent editing the *Record*, playing bridge, and debating.

When the list of members of his class who made Phi Beta Kappa was published, it included Hutchins. Benton was the second man "off the list," and he consoled himself with the thought that he had not missed making it by just one place. He was, however, gratified to report to his mother in mid-May 1921 that in the class voting he had "received a half dozen votes for Most Original, and a few for Most Brilliant." There were even two for "Most Likely to Succeed." He added, "A lot of the voting was very humorous, but it seems I have a few admirers or whatever you would call them." Elma was disappointed by his failure to make Phi Beta Kappa, but she wore the "Owl Charm" he had sent her as a memento of his chairmanship of the *Record*. It was a silent compliment, the only one of any kind she ever paid him.

There remained the question about what he would do once he graduated. His outlook in the twenty-one years of his life had been so deeply stamped by the punch press of genteel poverty that upon his graduation, if he had been offered a firm contract at interesting work at $5,000 for the next twenty years, he might gladly have signed it. It would have been almost twice as much as his deceased father had earned at his peak as chairman of the Romance Language Department of the University of Minnesota.

Business was in a recession in the spring of 1921, but many large corporations had asked Yale's bureau of appointments for the names of prospective graduates who might qualify for jobs with them. Benton's name seemed to carry a blanket endorsement by the bureau of appointments, and he couldn't decide which offer he should accept. Once more his mother helped make up his mind. Howard Williams, his first cousin by marriage, had urged Elma to persuade her son to come to Utica to work in Williams's local sales agency for the National Cash Register Company. The starting salary, to be sure, would only be $35 a week, and his duties at the outset would be "to look after the office." But he should bear in mind that the National Cash Register Company had a glorious past, and a bright future. There was no telling how fast and far Benton could rise in its structure. Besides, he would not have to live with strangers if he came to Utica. Other members of his family, led by his Aunt Harriet Benton Clark, were now living there, and he could doubtless find his bed and board under their roof.

After many exchanges in this vein, his mother finally urged Benton to accept his cousin's offer and see how matters worked out. She had a special motive for doing so. She had accidentally discovered in his account books entries for certain small sums of money representing gambling winnings and losses. These, in her view, were the wages of sin, and she would not have him earn or lose any more wages that way—as might be the case if he went on his own, unsupervised, to work in a big city like New York. In Utica, Aunt Harriet—"Aunt Hattie"—would watch over him and would not tolerate the slightest sign of a Faustian deal with Satan. Benton agreed to comply with his mother's directive, but he also struck a note that would eventually undo the agreement. "I may be making a big mistake by going up to Utica," he wrote her in May. "I have had some good chances to go into advertising, and if I could develop into a good copywriter—well, I'd be set for life. Advertising is now in a slump and it's a good time to go in—you're there when the business stages a comeback."

In June 1921, Arthur Twining Hadley presided for the last time as president of Yale at the events of commencement week, and his last important address, the baccalaureate, was titled "The Race That Is Set before Us." In this last charge to graduating seniors, he said:

> Gentlemen of the graduating class: We have spent these last years together in a place where for more than two centuries men have consecrated their lives to the service of others; where teachers have worked hard for small worldly reward; where they have been more concerned to follow out the truths of science and philosophy than to gain ease and comfort, where men of distinguished talents and eminence among their fellows have been making an honest effort to follow the teaching of our Lord Jesus Christ according to the measure of their understanding. Out of their self-sacrifice has grown a spirit of self-sacrifice. By their example, even more than by anything that they taught in the classroom, men have been prepared to render public service in church and civil state.

What he had to say was true enough of the Yale men who belonged to the generations of Benton's grandfather and father. It would be true again of the Yale men of the generation of Benton's own sons. But it was false—save in the case of a handful of very distinguished students—when applied to the members of the Yale class of 1921 who sat before him.

The kindest thing that could be said about them was that they had absorbed some information. They had not received an education. No love of learning had been instilled in them. They were not more concerned with the truths of science and philosophy than with a life of ease and comfort. They were not stirred by a spirit of self-sacrifice, caught from their professors. They were not prepared to render public service in church and civil state. They were as sorry a lot of disoriented money-minded young men as ever slid in or out of Yale. They were Gertrude Stein's "lost generation."

The climate of the times, caught in F. Scott Fitzgerald's *This Side of Paradise*, was strictly anti-intellectual, and it involved students at Princeton and Harvard as well. The great goal of many graduates was Wall Street, to be a broker or a bond specialist or an investment banker. None had respect for the handful of fellow graduates who had achieved any academic distinction. Indeed, the "proper pose" they were expected to strike was that they themselves had achieved "success" without studying and simply because of their native intelligence. Some in later life would "discover" themselves, and give a good account of themselves in "the public service." But too many were destined for the melancholy distinction of amounting to nothing in particular.

2

PREVIEWS

7

Sales—and Advertising

In Utica, Benton spent fifteen dreary months working for the National Cash Register Company. But he sensed then, and more clearly in retrospect, that he was getting an introduction into American business society and methods available at the time to very few men with college backgrounds. This was because the NCR sales organization—the greatest "specialty sales" organization that had ever been developed—was then at its full and finest flower, thanks to its founder, John H. Patterson, the "father" of what Patterson himself called "scientific salesmanship."

The twenty-one-year-old youth out of Yale met the seventy-eight-year-old Patterson only once, when the old man got off the train at Utica with his family en route to the Adirondack Mountains and young Benton met him at the station to facilitate his passage. Yet before Patterson's death—which was imminent—the impact the man had on Benton is suggested in the later claim by some of Benton's own business associates that he absorbed many sales and business maxims from Patterson. Nor was he alone in doing so. When Benton took over the *Encyclopaedia Britannica* at the end of 1942, he was told by Louis Schoenewald, the sales manager: "There is nothing we ever do in Britannica, or nothing any other specialty sales organization ever does, which John H. Patterson did not do first." Benton agreed. So much so, that he made a practice of giving to his top associates in the Britannica company a copy of a biography of John H. Patterson. A word about Patterson's life.

Patterson was a successful coal merchant in Dayton, Ohio, when in 1884 he acquired the basic patents on a crude cash register that punched holes in appropriate columns on a strip of paper. There was no demand for the device; in five years, a total of only one hundred registers had been sold. Selling in those days consisted of maintaining a regular contact with the trade, and the salesman was merely the personal medium—"the drummer" through whom the contact was made. His job was to build up his circle of "contacts," to cultivate personal goodwill as the representative of a manufacturer who made what the market demanded. His principal qualifications were personality and a knowledge of the buyer's idiosyncrasies and requirements. The salesman was expected to be a good mixer and a glib talker. Armed with a catalog, he would sell scores or hundreds of products simultaneously. His chief asset was his circle of acquaintances, and he often relied on his ability to take the circle with him if he changed employment.

In Patterson's special case, since there was no demand for his product, there were no salesmen to push it. He had to begin from scratch in creating a wholly new kind of business organization. In the list of Patterson employees whom he fired or who left him in disgust because they couldn't stand his autocratic ways were many future "captains of American industry"—men like Thomas J. Watson of the International Business Machines Corporation, Hugh Chalmers of automobile fame, C. F. Kettering of General Motors, and Henry Theobald of the Toledo Scales Company. What they learned from Patterson was the modern art of creating and stimulating mass public acceptance and demand for products hitherto unwanted or unknown.

Indeed, all modern selling of specialty products—such as scales, typewriters, business machines, and sets of books—is based on the system which Patterson originated applied to the specific selling problem posed by a specific product. The system was summarized in his three "golden" words: "Analyze! Visualize! Dramatize!" He taught his men that "the eye is ten times faster than the ear," and, in line with this, he taught them to make a drama of everything. Patterson set the pace: he hoisted the American flag over his Dayton factory—"in honor of the first NCR salesman who made his quota of sales for the year."

Patterson realized that he could best build a stable and permanent sales organization if his selling agents felt that they were in the cash register business for themselves. That meant guaranteeing a specific territory to a selling agent, and restricting him to it until he was shifted, promoted, or fired. It meant teaching the selling agent that he was not through with a customer once he had sold him a cash register—that if he maintained close contact with the customer, and continued to service his needs, old customers were likely to be the best new customers. It meant providing selling agents with a "primer" and a "book of arguments" demonstrating the "right" and "wrong" approaches to a prospect. It meant the creation of "training schools" where the old "natural born salesmen" could be retrained in "scientific" methods related to their work, and where new salesmen would receive that scientific training before getting a guaranteed territory.

Before Patterson put selling agents in business for themselves, the "straight commission" was the badge either of a man selling an item of questionable worth or of a neophyte who couldn't get a better job. The salesman who had won his spurs received a salary. If it occurred to him that he would make more money on the commission basis, he knew that his employer would not give it to him anyway. Patterson broke this pattern of thought. He slowly convinced his salesmen that, in the specific territories they were being guaranteed, their earnings would depend wholly on their own efforts. There would be no slash in the rate of their commissions if they succeeded beyond ordinary measure. The more the salesmen made, the more Patterson made. "If you will sell a million dollars in a week," he would say, "we'll hire a brass band to bring your commission to you."

Benton was to adopt the same view in his own enterprises. He also followed Patterson's assault on the ancient dogma of thrift and frugality, which meant paying as little as possible for service rendered in any department. Patterson, to the irritation of his fellow manufacturers, and labor union leaders as well, did the opposite, overpaying almost everybody that he paid at all. Philanthropic sentiment had little to do with the practice. Rather, it was the product of a realistic analysis of human motivations. He was after exceptional service, and he felt that the most immediate and practical way to get it was to pay more than the same service could command elsewhere. The obviously overpaid man would make extraordinary efforts to hold his job, knowing that he could not make as much money elsewhere. But the man who was paid at or below the market rate would have no such incentive.

As a master psychologist and pioneer in the development of incentives of every kind, Patterson not only had his salesmen in mind but their wives as well. Every week new folders from Dayton would

descend on his sales force glistening with glamorous products—
silverware, furniture, diamonds, automobiles—which were to be
had by salesmen who forged ahead in the various competitions that
were always being staged within the organization. The salesmen
took the folders home and their wives prodded the salesmen to ever
greater efforts. It remains to be said in this connection that Patterson was the inventor of the "point" or "quota" system for the sales
forces of modern industry—in his case, to estimate the demand for
cash registers, to guide factory production, and to spot the salesmen of great or no ability. Aside from the rewards in the form of
prizes won, the direct financial rewards to an NCR salesman could
be very great after he got a "big-time" territory, and the rewards
were widely publicized within the organization to stimulate the ambitious. The agency head in Los Angeles was earning $175,000 a
year. The one in Chicago had earned $250,000 in 1920. The New
York territory, with its many thousands of small merchants, was
the best in the country, and many NCR agents had accumulated a
capital of millions.

There had been rules in the Patterson organization not to hire
anyone under twenty-five years of age, or anyone who had gone to
college. The rule against college graduates, however, had been
broken when Howard Williams himself was employed, and the latter
in turn broke both rules when he hired Benton. Benton himself was
not aware of the problems this would pose for his ambition when he
reported for work in Utica on 1 July 1921. He had heard about the
rewards awaiting NCR salesmen. So now, just as he concentrated on
making the crack squad at Shattuck, and chairman of the board of
the *Yale Record,* his new goal was the acquisition of a great NCR
agency of his own.

In Utica, he became a paying boarder in the home of his cousin
Howard Williams, which was also the dwelling place for Aunt
Hattie and her youngest daughter, Beatrice. Another of Aunt
Hattie's daughters, Miriam, with her husband, Zenas Potter, lived
across the street. Seeking a kind of escape, Benton took to reading
an hour of poetry every day, and trying to write it as well. Poetry,
however, could not make up for his negative reactions to Utica as a
city, or for his keenly felt lack of friends his own age who shared his
interests. Utica itself typified Sinclair Lewis's *Main Street* just as
did all the other dreary towns in the Mohawk Valley; and the members of its Rotary Club—the select group to which all aspiring

young businessmen hoped to belong—typified what Sinclair Lewis would portray in *Babbitt*. "I am frank to tell you," Benton wrote his mother when he had been in Utica for a short while, "that I do not like this town. It is terribly dumb and uninteresting. You will probably grin a sardonic smile at that and say it is good for me, but I am emphatic when I say that this deadly monotony eats into my spirits something terrific."

The only male friend his own age whom he found in Utica—and kept in the years following—was Richard Balch, who was eventually to be a Democratic candidate for lieutenant governor of New York, and for three years state Democratic chairman. In 1921, however, he was living in Utica in very modest circumstances with his widowed mother. Her father, however, was a person to be reckoned with. He had come to Utica at nineteen as a penniless immigrant from England and had stuck to the same work routine for fifty-four years. Now eighty-three, he was one of Utica's wealthiest men and the owner of a fishing tackle factory. His grandson, and heir apparent, had gone to work at $24 a week in his grandfather's plant after graduating from Williams College in 1921. But not even the friendship Benton formed with Balch, or with Catharine McKeown, the daughter of one of Utica's leading citizens, was enough to offset his dislike of the city itself.

At first, in his words, he was put in charge of "running the office." He swept the floor every morning at 8 A.M., handled the clerical and accounting work, and demonstrated the machines to prospects who wandered in. All the while he gobbled up mounds of NCR literature in preparation for the hour when he would be given a territory where he could sell cash registers in his own right. But there was an early setback. An NCR training school was due to start in New York on 1 September, but Howard Williams felt that Benton was both too young and too new with the company to qualify for it. To offset the disappointment, Benton was given outside responsibilities in addition to his office work—installing cash registers that had been bought from other salesmen in the agency, starting new bookkeeping systems for the buyers, and showing them how to balance their accounts. Benton did this for some men's stores and then for a garage and, in his eagerness to find the bright side of the bleak life he was living, felt that he was contributing to his education by learning the clothing and garage business "cold."

Through correspondence with his former classmates, he learned that few were making more money than he, and few saw any prospect of increasing their earnings for some time. All, however, had "high class jobs" with banks, brokerage houses, or with the prestigious industrial corporations. "My own job by contrast," he wrote his mother, "is utterly plebeian. I've been in all the dives in town, have dealt with all the bootleggers, and whatnot. It is not at all uplifting." But he had something to add which set him off from many members of his own generation: "I do not give a darn for the so-called white collar jobs, if one can be more successful in a low brow job. Whether one can be or not is the question." He added something further: "I feel that the next thing I will try will be advertising. It is what I wanted to get into to begin with. Only you insisted on Utica. I feel I would be much happier in New York."

He continued to be unsettled in his mind as 1921 drew to a close. But then two developments simultaneously cheered him up and complicated the decision he felt he must make about whether or not he should stay with NCR. One development concerned Catharine McKeown. He was seeing Catharine twice a week, and her father intimated that he would be pleased to have young Benton as a son-in-law. The second development was the word from Howard Williams that an NCR training class would be held in Dayton in February 1922, and that he meant to send Benton to it. With these new variables to weigh, Benton went to Saint Louis to spend Christmas with his mother, and to talk about his future. The son talked only in passing about Catharine McKeown. But he talked a great deal about other prospects he faced, including the idea of going to New York to try his hand at advertising. Elma, on her part, urged him to stay with Howard Williams and the NCR agency until at least July 1922, which would round out a full year. Then, if he still wanted to leave the agency, he should consider entering Harvard in the fall of 1922, in order to study law. It was left at that.

While Benton was en route back to Utica, a letter had been delivered to his mother's address in Saint Louis. The writer was Catharine McKeown in Utica. Elma, thinking the letter was meant for herself, automatically opened it. She realized her error when she saw the salutation, but her eye carried her on through the first paragraph before she stopped. What little she read aroused her alarm that her son was headed for a marriage with the girl. She used all of her command of English to blast him for a "flirtation" whose ultimate consequences he was in no position to meet. Benton, approaching his twenty-second birthday, at last replied with a Declaration of Independence:

> You have mentioned very often how much I owe you, and how much you have given up to put me through college, and what my responsibilities should be. I realize all that, Mother. I suppose that in your eyes I am a gamble which has turned out bad, about like your mining stock. But I hope to make money in the future, and if you will send me a note for the approximate amount my education has cost, I will sign it and endeavor to pay it off with the first money I can ever get hold of. That is a trivial part of the obligation, but perhaps if I paid the actual money back you would let me decide a little more as to how I might be allowed to feel and act. For you do not know me and own me as you did when I was 3; and, Mother, it seems that it is utterly impossible for you to understand how I feel, think, or look at the world in general. But you know there is nothing I could not do for you, or to please you. I would not marry a girl you disapproved of, but you make me feel tied hand and foot. I think you would deprive me of the privilege of thinking for myself. My judgment is undoubtedly immature, but so is everyone's at the same age, and there are certain things that a person at that age must rely on his immature judgment to decide. But you try to push me so, and rush me into thoughts which are so utterly contrary to my whole outlook on life.

The umbilical cord was about to be cut. A man was about to be born. Benton would continue to revere his mother, to seek her counsel, respect it, be eager for her word of approval, exceed beyond ordinary measure the attentions loving sons give their beloved mothers. But he would no longer be dependent on Elma for the way he used the gift of life itself. For good or ill, most of the critical decisions he would henceforth make would be solely his own—though they flowed from the foundation of things his mother had earlier set in place.

The NCR training class in the offing was meant to start at the end of February 1922 with a week in New York, followed by four weeks at the company headquarters in Dayton. Benton was in a fever of anticipation. The class would give him a chance to catch the eye of the principal officers of the company. But on the eve of the day he was to leave, he was told he could not go. He was being assigned a regular territory in Utica but was to cover it as a one-third-time salesman—with all that this meant in commissions, "points," and "quotas." The remaining two-thirds of his time he was to spend as before, tending the office.

It was a hard blow, yet it seemed to make him all the more fiercely determined to show what he could do as a salesman without the training that was denied him. His territory was mainly the "dives" in Utica, but he made headway with the bootleggers and "foreigners" where others had failed. In fact, he soon outsold some of the other salesmen in the agency, but not his cousin Howard, and his record helped pull the Utica agency "over the top" of its quota of "points" to make it "the leader" in the Northeast Division of NCR.

John H. Patterson had just died, and his son Frederick had inherited the company and succeeded him as president. To launch himself in his new role, Frederick promised a special, secret prize for the month of March 1922 to all salesmen who exceeded their quotas. The prize proved to be a pair of heavy gold cuff links from Tiffany's with the recipient's initials in blue enamel and, engraved on the back, "President's Prize, March 1922." Benton earned a pair, for his very first month in his territory, and their acquisition was a high point of his young business life. Further, aside from the commissions he proceeded to earn regularly, the share of his sales that went to the Utica agency itself soon exceeded his salary for "running the office." Howard Williams held out the hope that in view of his kinsman's success as a salesman, the Northeast Division manager would surely use his good offices to get Benton into the next NCR training class scheduled for September 1922. After that would come money, fame, and power.

Benton's success as a salesman did not come easily. It meant long, lonely, and dreary hours of pounding the streets of Utica far into the night to track down prospects to whom he could make a "presentation." It meant rebuffs nineteen times out of twenty. It meant going over the same ground with the same prospect a dozen times before a sale was closed. It meant moving through days and nights without seeing any of his friends. It meant ripping every suit he had lugging cash registers into the store from the Dodge truck in which he delivered them. It meant tearing his hands handling incoming shipments of cash registers. It meant frequent physical weariness.

It was an experience Benton did not forget later when he was the leader of the Britannica company, with its many thousands of men selling such "specialty" items as the *Encyclopaedia Britannica*, the Great Books, and other sets of books in the Britannica family. Those who succeeded, Benton felt, as he placed himself in their shoes, deserved every cent of the generous financial rewards the best of them got.

On his twenty-second birthday Benton received his traditional letter of greeting from his mother, with a check enclosed. She renewed her offer to support him through a three-year law course, in the event he decided to become a lawyer. The offer dominated all the exchanges with his mother in following weeks. Benton felt he could do well in law, but was it worth three years? Weren't the odds good that if he did well in law, he could do so in business without spending those three years, and all the money it would cost his mother? Wasn't the law, he asked, "just another form of the selling business"? On the other hand, if he went into business, what business was there that wasn't "just another case of cash registers, cash registers, cash registers all the time"? What could he do in business that wouldn't drag him "back into a terrible rut" like the one he was in?

In the meantime, he had learned that getting into Harvard Law School was absurdly easy. If he would show up on opening day with his Yale diploma, he would be admitted. But what would happen when he got out of law school, at age twenty-five? He saw himself starting work in some law office at a salary less than he was earning selling cash registers. His commissions were rising rapidly; he often earned $100 in a week and he had been able to save $400 in Utica. He liked the sense of independence the little nest egg gave him, and he did not look forward to being put on a monthly allowance by his mother while he was studying law.

Despite his continuing indecision, he went so far as to tell Howard Williams that he planned on leaving Utica in the late summer. Williams urged Benton to stay and, in addition, informed Mr. Pearson, the Northeastern Division manager of the NCR, that the company was in danger of losing Benton. This brought Pearson to Utica for a fatherly talk with the restless youth. He told Benton that he had all the makings of a great salesman. He was bound to get a good agency of his own and have a bright future with the NCR company. But, said Benton, when would he actually get an agency of his own?

The answer was that he would get one after he passed through the NCR training school and had made a record. Well, said Benton, would the division manager recommend him for the training school that was to start in September? Regretfully no, said the manager. According to company rules he would have to wait until he was twenty-five years old. The manager subsequently had a change of heart and agreed to make the recommendation. But if this was a triumph for Benton, it came too late. He had thought so much about another plan, and had become so committed to it emotionally, that this time he turned the manager down.

In August 1922 he said his goodbyes, and promised to write to all his kinsmen in Utica, to Richard Balch, and to Catharine McKeown. Then he left for what ostensibly was to be a brief vacation before proceeding to Cambridge and the Harvard Law School. In New York, the parents of William Fleming, a Yale classmate, were away for the summer, and the refugee from NCR had a free bed in their suite at the Sherman Square Hotel on West Seventy-third Street and Broadway.

Benton, on the day of his arrival in New York, for the first time in his life defied his mother's explicit wishes in a major matter. He called on the Yale Club's employment bureau to see if any jobs were available in the advertising business. Before the week was out he had knocked on the doors of countless advertising agencies. His qualifications were a year as chairman of the board of the *Yale Record*, and a little over a year selling cash registers. On the Friday which ended the week, he called at the small New York branch office of the Chicago-based advertising agency of Lord and Thomas. He was interviewed by the New York manager, thirty-seven-year-old Frank Fehlman, and hired at $25 a week as Fehlman's personal assistant.

Benton, elated, wrote his mother that he had a job with the biggest and most successful advertising agency in the country, with such Chicago accounts as Quaker Oats, Pepsodent toothpaste, and Palmolive soap. Elma compressed into a single sentence her profound dismay over the fact that her son had not got to Cambridge. "Dear Billie," she wrote him, "I am sorry to hear that you are going to go into a business that says, 'Palmolive soap is a good soap.'"

One more detail. Howard Williams himself would eventually enter the same sort of business after a very successful career with NCR.

In the latter organization, he eventually became the vice-president in charge of all export business the world over, and representing about 40 percent of total sales. Then he went to the advertising firm of Erwin, Wasey and Company as a partner of Louis R. Wasey, one of the leaders of the advertising business in his day. After Wasey's death, Williams achieved control of the agency, where he was succeeded in the presidency by his son, David. The father and son eventually sold the company to one of America's largest advertising agencies—the McCann Erickson Company, one of whose clients is now Encyclopaedia Britannica, Inc.

New York in the early 1920s had more advertising agencies than Chicago, but it was Chicago where the best advertising was being generated. "Madison Avenue" in New York did not become a synonym for advertising until the late twenties, in the wake of two developments. One was the rapid acquisition by Wall Street bankers of independent manufacturing companies throughout the country. The other was the rise of radio. As control of the companies came to be centered in New York, advertising accounts were often transferred there from Chicago or elsewhere, and, as a result, many gifted men trained in the West also came to New York and virtually took over the advertising business.

Many of the most gifted had at some point been trained in the earthy "Chicago school" of advertising, and many of the valedictorians of the Chicago school were trained at Lord and Thomas, whose head and sole owner was Albert D. Lasker. Lasker, an imperial, imperious, exciting, excitable, and at times wacky genius, was to the advertising world of the early twentieth century the same sort of protean force that John H. Patterson was to the world of sales management. Young Benton would not meet him directly until 1928. But the emanations from the man even before that time, like those from the remote figure of Patterson, were to help round out the education Benton needed before he started a business of his own.

Benton started to work in the New York office of Lord and Thomas in straitened circumstances. His salary was about one-quarter of his total earnings when he left Utica. Moreover, his pocket had been picked on the New York subway, he was living out of a suitcase as the guest of Fleming's family until he could find a reasonably priced place to live, and he yet had no clearly defined place in Lord and Thomas. He had hoped he would be assigned work as a copywriter. Instead, he was placed outside Fehlman's office, dependent on him for daily assignments. Some were "thrilling"—like getting Harry Lauder to endorse "Good Old Scotch Brew," or like going to a New York movie studio and finding a director and cameramen to film an advertising stunt for Autostrop razors. He also took advertisements to clients to get their approval, and he had to learn the arguments. He went with Fehlman on some of his solicitations. Often he had nothing to do. He could have been dropped from the organization without a ripple. Yet he felt that the job was "wonderful" and that it offered him a "remarkable opportunity," especially since it gave him a chance to educate himself in America's most successful advertising agency.

In Fehlman, moreover, he had an older friend who was anxious to help him cut three to five years out of the advertising route to riches. Fehlman, who had not previously worked under Lasker in Chicago and had not developed the latter's respect for copywriters, discouraged Benton from doing copywriting work as a form of training in advertising. His own plan was for Benton to become acclimated to the business generally, and then take to the streets in soliciting accounts. A good copywriter, he explained, could work for years and not earn more than $5,000 annually. But if Benton "landed accounts," he would be earning $15,000 a year in quick time. He would also be in a position to profit from the fact that the "account executives," not the men on the "creative" end of things, ran all advertising agencies. Fehlman's advice on these matters was dutifully recorded by Benton and passed along for judicial review by his mother in Saint Louis.

Like other young men who had come to New York and whose lives centered in the Yale Club and other places where the young meet the young, Benton was rarely invited anywhere, rarely saw older people outside the office, and had no sponsorship and no connections. These were the young who led respectable lives with the interlude of an occasional affair, worked hard at their jobs, often at night, drank very little and only at parties, and sought personal advancement. As one of these, Benton began to wear a stiff collar and bought a new suit. His outlays exceeded his weekly income of $25—an income that remained the same for five months. He justified his spending on the ground that he was in a business where "appearances" count a great deal, though this meant saving money on food the hard way. He budgeted a dollar a day for meals, breakfasting on a five-cent Sportsman's chocolate bar. He would debate each day whether to spend seventy-five cents for lunch and twenty cents for dinner, or vice versa. When he was through with work at the office, he would go to the Yale Club where the dues were only $15 a year for the first three years out of college. He more than used up the dues in stationery, in nightly reading of the newspaper, and in constant use of the club library. Then, having finished writing "the letter" and reading "the paper" in the best clubman's sense, he would slip down into Grand Central Station where for twenty cents he would get a glass of milk and a sandwich. He was hungry all the time, until he received a $10-a-week raise in January 1923. He often said later that this was the greatest financial advance of his life.

In the Christmas season preceding this landmark event, Elma came east to visit her son, their first meeting in a year. Elma's own work in Saint Louis had been going well. She was modernizing the physical facilities and upgrading the faculty of Hosmer Hall. She had become an important figure in the cultural life of Saint Louis, was in wide demand as a speaker, and was regularly quoted in the newspapers. Her salary had recently been raised to $5,000 a year, with another increase in the offing. Elma, who had often spoken to her son about "the history of failures in the family," had plainly broken the pattern. Since she remained determined that he too would break it, it was as much as an inspector general as a mother that she visited him at Christmas time. As usual, she had virtually nothing to say to him directly that could be construed as a compliment. But in her letters to Aunt Hattie and to the other members of the family in Utica, she revealed her pleasure in the results of the inspection, covering the progress in his work, the opinion other people had of him, the way he was rationing his money, and the cultural uses to which he was putting his evening hours.

Yet Elma had been back at Hosmer Hall only a few days when the family along the Utica–New York–Saint Louis axis was shaken by charges about "Billie the Gambler." One evening at the Yale Club two friends asked young Benton to play bridge. They found a fourth in the card room, who later turned out not to be a member of the club but had somehow procured a visitor's card. Walking to Broadway after the game, the visitor proposed that Benton play bridge with him three evenings a week—against poor players the man knew. The stakes would be high, but the man would cover all losses and would guarantee that Benton would win $300 a week. Benton refused the offer and later reported the episode to the secretary of the Yale Club. He also told the story to a youth from Utica who was temporarily sharing his $9-a-week room. Soon afterward the youth returned to Utica and repeated the story to one of Benton's kinsmen. In the course of repetition, it came to appear that Benton was earning $300 a week by gambling. Since this was many times his regular salary, the fact that he was winning more than he was earning made him in the eyes of his Aunt Hattie nothing better than a "common gambler."

She wrote him a stern letter of admonition, saying in the end, "Billie, beware, come back, take refuge with the God of your fathers who alone can save from self-hood and sin, for the wages of sin is death." Benton, in a fury, sent the letter to his mother, and a storm of letters and copies of letters raged within the family. For twenty days the mails were filled with charges, countercharges, innuendos, circumstantial evidence, demolitions of that evidence, direct testimony, and cross-examination. There were no face-to-face confrontations. It was a writing family, and all the surge of fear and anguish ran its course on paper, until the storm subsided. The truth came out and everyone's confidence in "Billie" was fully restored.

Did Benton ever acquire "the frame of mind of a gambler," as his aunt seemed to fear? The answer is yes and no. He became an expert bridge player—and he played for money. But he quit playing bridge when he married, though not for that reason alone. Benton quit because the gambling in his life turned to other areas which offered a greater potential for gambling, areas of very high risk in business which promised high rewards or complete ruin.

The $10-a-week raise which Benton got at Lord and Thomas meant the difference between penury and comparative affluence. He now had enough to eat and could occasionally take a girl to a movie or buy a ticket for a second-balcony seat in the theater. Meanwhile, he was making new friends among young men like himself and deepening other friendships begun at Yale. One of his Yale friends was Walter Schleiter, an excellent athlete and tennis player who walked off with many honors at Yale, from Phi Beta Kappa to membership on the junior prom committee. Beginning in the summer of 1923, Benton would share a basement room with Schleiter on East Thirty-eighth Street. Another friend from Yale whom Benton saw regularly was Reginald Marsh, the former artist for the *Yale Record*. Marsh was then working for the *New York Daily News* drawing daily a full vertical column illustrating and rating vaudeville acts. He got free tickets to the vaudeville theaters, and Benton often went with him.

But of all the young men Benton saw much of during this period, the one who was to be his closest friend for life was Galen Van Meter. Their acquaintance dated from the time Benton was a senior at Yale and Van Meter, covering Connecticut for the Moon Motor Company, would come by and play poker with him and other students. In 1922–23, while trying to find a niche for himself on Wall Street or in an advertising firm, Van Meter was also courting Janet Mackey and would eventually marry her. In early 1923, however, his short financial rations made the courtship a touch-and-go affair.

So it was also with William Benton and Helen Hemingway. Helen, a direct descendant of Yale's first student, Jacob Hemingway, was then a senior at Connecticut College for Women. She had first met Benton when she was a freshman there and he a junior at Yale. He had been her "blind date" escort at a dance at the Gateway School, a distinguished private school for young ladies in New Haven from which Helen had graduated. There were subsequent meetings and exchanges of letters between them, and in her last year at Connecticut College, while Benton was at Lord and Thomas in New York, he had been Helen's escort at her senior dance. It was one of only two times he ever escorted a young lady to a college dance. He never had the money—or the girls—for a more extensive social life.

It was while he was at Lord and Thomas in 1923 that Benton described Helen in a letter to his mother as being "a remarkably fine girl who would make a wonderful teacher for you. She is very steady." He added that Helen had decided to wait another year before marrying a young man in his own Yale class whom she favored, and in the interval planned on teaching high school in Lakeville, Connecticut. Helen's mother, he said, was very happy at this decision. He added prophetically: "Personally, I doubt whether she will marry him at all."

Shortly before Benton's twenty-third birthday, Fehlman delighted him by presenting a prospect involving a chance to become a kind of founding father for a proposed chain of quick lunch restaurants to be known as "Blue Kitchens." In contrast to the "quickies and dirties" which used unknown goods in quick luncheons, Blue Kitchens would use only nationally known products served in clean, attractive lunchrooms. Herbert Cohen, the general manager of Lord and Thomas in Chicago, was closely tied to the venture, as were some of the country's leading merchandisers including W. B. Ward of Ward Baking Company, Adolph Liebman of "Scotch Brew," Otto Stahl, a leading packer of high-grade meats in the East, and the Dairymen's League. All had major stock interests in the company. Fehlman was secretary and treasurer but had no time for bookkeeping details or other clerical matters. If Benton would take on this assignment by posing as his "confidential secretary," Fehlman would try to get him ten shares of preferred stock for $1,000. A down payment of $250 was required within thirty days. Benton also would get an option on $4,000 in additional stock.

"Now, Mother," Benton wrote Elma informing her of what was afoot, "this looks like a very good chance, and I ought not to pass it up considering the men back of it, the soundness of the idea, etc. I know you haven't got $1,000 lying around loose, but I believe it worth a good deal to get it. And I wish you'd loan it to me. $250 March 1, and $750 at a date somewhat later. So I want to know if you'll back me up in it." She couldn't and wouldn't. It sounded too much like some of her father's get-rich-quick schemes. Benton tried to change her mind. He cited the "Big Men" in on the proposition—not the kind to invest their money blindly. His own friends on Wall Street reassured him that this was "a chance in a lifetime."

Elma did not change her mind, though she loaned him $100. Benton turned to a friend who loaned him the remainder he needed to meet the initial down payment on the ten shares of stock being held for him. He later had a fugitive moment of delight when he was made an "original incorporator" and a "classy figurehead" member of the board of directors. He met with all the "Big Men" involved in the venture. Then he was asked to resign as a director in order to make room on the board for W. B. Ward of Ward Baking. Benton subsequently paid in full for his ten shares and subscribed to still more. How could he go wrong in the company of "Big Men" like Leibman, Stahl, Cohen, and Ward? Wouldn't they surely support Blue Kitchens because a great and successful chain of such restaurants would prove to be marvelous outlets for their products? All the rational arguments supported the investment, and Benton was an insider. But the company failed. Benton lost every cent he had invested in it; and proportionate to his own resources at the time of the original investment, it was the greatest financial disaster Benton ever suffered.

Meanwhile, the "personal elements" in his employment at Lord and Thomas, represented by his dependence on Fehlman's goodwill, suddenly changed with a change in Fehlman's own position. Albert Lasker, who since 1921 had been spending most of his time in Washington as the chairman of the War Shipping Board, decided to move Fehlman to Chicago, though he would retain the title and authority of eastern manager. Mark O'Dea, a copywriter and a favorite of Lasker, came from Chicago to handle "production" in the New York office. Next in the line of authority was the thirty-six-year-old Louis H. Hartman, who had recently been hired by Fehlman on a gamble that was to pay off handsomely. It was to be through Hartman that the fabulously profitable Lucky Strike cigarette account came to Lord and Thomas.

On the eve of Fehlman's departure for Chicago, he told Benton in private that he wanted him to remain in New York where he could send Fehlman "confidential reports" on how things were going in the office. He should continue to service two small accounts that had been turned over to him. Most importantly, he should resist any effort O'Dea might make to convert him into a copywriter. Instead, he should at once step up his efforts to solicit accounts.

Benton, in passing this news on to his mother, had mixed reactions to its implications. He said he knew his future eventually lay in the selling end of the advertising business but felt that he was not ready for it yet. He was "too young looking." He "was not well versed in the business," and he "didn't know enough of the Lord and Thomas story." But the advantages, as he saw them, were these:

> First, it is a great opportunity if it is possible for me to get the business. I can build a bigger place for myself and my earning power will increase faster that way than any other.
>
> Second, I have the confidence of knowing I have a great organization behind me. I am firmly convinced that any account I do land will get better advertising, copy and service, than they could get any place else.
>
> But, oh Mother, it's a big job of which I am somewhat afraid. More men have failed at soliciting agency business than any other form of selling. So wish me luck. I wish I had more confidence, but I rejoice in the opportunity. It will be up to me to go out on my own and dig up prospects. God knows how or where.

Lacking experience, young Benton used his powers of rational analysis. He studied the *Saturday Evening Post* and the *New York Times* and tore out advertisements he thought were inferior. He then called on the New York advertisers in question and asked why they wouldn't let Lord and Thomas, with its superior skill in advertising, prepare ads for them. There was nothing wrong with his logic, but he failed to take one factor into account. He didn't realize that the firms running inferior advertising did not understand advertising. He didn't realize that he was criticizing the men in the firms who were responsible for their advertising—men who did not like Benton's brash, youthful criticism. He didn't understand that an enterprising young man could get ahead in advertising if he had cooperative clients to teach him what he should know—or to interpret successfully his new ideas and viewpoints.

In addition to the difficulty Benton had in soliciting advertising accounts was the awkward position in which he found himself because of the relationship between O'Dea and Hartman, his own immediate superiors in the New York office, and Fehlman in Chicago. From the outset, Benton got along well with Hartman, who urged him to look upon Lord and Thomas as no more than a training school for starting his own agency. Nothing of this spirit was present in Benton's initial relationship with O'Dea. He became a "bouncing ball" between Fehlman's absentee management and O'Dea's wish to organize and run the New York office as he saw fit. Benton was no sooner started on some project for O'Dea than Fehlman in Chicago pulled him off for a different one.

Meanwhile, Benton composed his first ad. "Even though I don't believe I shall set the world on fire writing copy," he wrote his mother, "I think I shall do fairly well, and it is a wonderful opportunity to study under Mr. O'Dea. There could be no better teacher. I really imagine I shall write copy more and more." Soon afterward, he wrote a half-page ad for the *Saturday Evening Post* for the Autostrop razor. Triumphantly he wrote his mother that "Mr. O'Dea was very pleased. He called me in to congratulate me and to encourage me further."

In anticipation of his emergent new life as a copywriter, Benton sold for $15 the typewriter his mother gave him in 1914 and bought a new one. Toward the end of August he approached O'Dea and thanked him for the chance to write advertising copy. But what was the likelihood that he would be given an opportunity to write advertising copy full time? "He said," Benton reported, "that he has been afraid to assign me more work because I'd no sooner get into it when Fehlman would, or might, write me from Chicago and

send me into Pa. for two weeks or something. Then I'd drop O'Dea's
work. I thought for a while that I was free of the cross-fire between
these two men. But I am not. I have two masters and I can't serve
both of them."

He instinctively felt that the way to learn advertising was by
writing copy. This seemed impossible at Lord and Thomas because
of the conflict between Fehlman and O'Dea. So he began to apply for
a copywriter's job at other agencies. One of these was the George
Batten Company. Its founder, Mr. Batten, was no longer alive;
the agency was slipping, but it was still the fourth largest in the
nation after N. W. Ayer, J. Walter Thompson, and Lord and
Thomas. Benton wanted to get into its trade and industrial department. But when the job did not come through by 1 October, the
date he had set for leaving Lord and Thomas, he accepted another
job at the Charles W. Hoyt agency, whose head was the father of
Winthrop Hoyt, a friend of Benton at Yale though in a class behind him.

Like many New York advertising men of the day, the elder Hoyt
felt the best preparation for the business was through experience
in selling, and young Benton was put to work with a Hoyt client
which manufactured bathroom fixtures. His sales territory was the
hardware stores along Avenue A and the Bowery. He had been at it
for four weeks when a call from the George Batten Company offered
Benton a copywriting job at $50 a week. He felt guilty about leav-
ing Hoyt but took the Batten job for the discipline in copywriting
he could get only with a bigger agency.

Any new employee hired by the Batten agency was required to
hand in his resignation effective three months from the day he
started to work. The agency could then accept the resignation at
once, without giving the employee time to hunt another job. "Good
for them," Benton said in describing the custom to his mother. "But
it is kind of tough on the employee. What I'd do if I were out of a job
at the end of three months, I don't know." He would not be out of
a job for the next five years, at which time he would know precisely
what he would do.

8

Shooting Star

The George Batten Company, like most old-line New York agencies, was controlled by the "account executives," often former publishing salesmen who knew little about the creation of advertising. The men who thought "intellectually" about the matter were generally in the copy departments, but when the copywriters clashed with the account executives, the copywriters were usually the casualties. The Great Depression was eventually to change the system by changing many attitudes of the clients.

Benton didn't fully understand the system when he was hired, and there wasn't much he could do about it anyway. He was the youngest, newest, and lowest paid of the twenty-five copywriters, and the trade and industrial department to which he had been assigned was a place of solitary confinement. It prepared copy for trade and industrial publications, window displays, and direct mail broadsides, booklets, and letters designed to persuade merchants to buy products for resale. Copywriters who "counted"—insofar as any did—were in the consumer department, where the "highest type of copy" was prepared for newspapers and magazines in order to persuade people to buy the product for their own use.

During Benton's three-month probationary period, he found that despite his economies there was a $10 gap between his income of $50 and his outgo of $60. So he put a want ad in *Printer's Ink:* "For sale, cheap, a copywriter in a big national agency who will work nights at cut rates." The result was a client who became a lifelong friend. This was Robert Goldstein, who then owned a small printing company which also published the *Juvenile Magazine* for department stores. Benton spent two nights a week writing ads and direct mail circulars that helped bring in new business for Goldstein.[1] He received $25 a week for this, which added 50 percent to his pay— and kept him from spending money on the nights he was working.

On 13 January 1924, Benton was told that the resignation he had submitted when he was hired by the Batten agency was not accepted. The management hoped he would "be with them for a long time." But, as he informed Elma, he doubted whether he wanted to be with the company for a long time, since he found the work less interesting than he thought it would be. Besides, he was having difficulty writing satisfactory copy. He knew what was wrong with his texts, but not how to set them right. After mulling matters over, on the last day of February he submitted his resignation to the Batten agency in order to go to work for Goldstein as a $100-a-week salesman and promotion man. When Arthur Brashears, his "group head" at the agency heard the news, he took the matter up with William Board- man, the vice-president in charge of all copy, who had never once spoken to Benton in five months. Now Benton was called into his presence and told that advertising agencies were the new road to fame and fortune and that the young man would be a fool to leave it. Further, Batten was an "aristocratic agency" where "culture" counted. The agency liked highbrows, and highbrows like Benton were hard to attract to the business. "I convinced myself of my own importance," Benton reported to his mother, "and as a result am not leaving. I have told Bob Goldstein the news. I will continue to work for him on a free lance basis at $25 a week, and I get a raise of $1,000 a year from Batten's. It's a poor way to get a raise, but I should worry. They're in business to buy men as cheaply as they can. In any case, I am going to work much harder in the future."

He did indeed work harder at Batten's, hammering out copy eight hours a day. The yield was submitted to Arthur Brashears, who painstakingly taught him how to cut the first paragraph, cut adjec- tives and adverbs, put in periods, make transitions. Benton learned much from this able teacher but still was not wholly reconciled to

---

[1] In later years, beginning with Benton's thirty-fifth birthday, Goldstein at intervals would publish a book of birthday greetings to Benton from his circle of friends. The successive volumes, of which the latest was published for his sixty-fifth birthday, chart his widening interests and record the fact that the friends he made at every stage of his life remained friends through all the passing years.

the work itself. In a searching self-analytical letter he wrote Elma, he confessed that he was "often filled with indescribable longings." Then he explained:

As I sit at my desk turning out copy on oil ranges, Elliott Fisher machines, etc., it all seems so futile. I am helping no one. Not even myself very much, except that I am further developing a style of writing and an ability to express myself. As I read of the Teapot Dome scandal in Washington, I have an overwhelming desire to go into politics. But not as an ordinary politician. Rather as a Ramsay MacDonald, whose life fascinates me, and whose personality stands out in his picture and in his writings.

There are great things to be done for the laboring classes in this country. The enthusiasm of helping do them has filled me ever since my debate on labor unionism while in college. There is no question about it but the next hundred years will see tremendous changes in our social organizations. Yet I am torn between two desires. The desire to enter body and soul into a cause in which I believe, is retarded by my desire to make money and put myself into the luxuriously living class. The second desire seems the easier to fulfill. I know how to go about it, and it is the accepted thing. The first desire is so lacking in "concrete ways and means" that, knowing not how to start, I only think of it by fits and starts.

To be a leader in a political movement of new thought and new ideas is a great ambition. I shall never fulfill it on the track I am now. Sometimes whole ideas sweep on me. Other times, they are only half formed. But always they keep coming. I am really cursed with abilities along too many lines and with outstanding ability at none. I can write well. But only ordinarily well. I have little imagination. I shall never be a great writer. I can sell well. Perhaps salesmanship is the best thing I have developed in myself to date. I can sell myself exceptionally well. People whom I first meet form a higher opinion of me than is really justifiable.

I can talk to groups of people well. I proved that in college. There are many—like Bob Hutchins—who are better. But they are better orators. There was no one in either Carleton or Yale who was as good as I in rebuttal—or in the ability to analyze another's arguments and successfully combat them, speaking extemporaneously.

I can do detail work exceptionally well. I like it. And my memory is good. I really am a kind of jack of all trades and master of none. I absolutely lack any leaning toward science—except, as you know, my ability in mathematics. But I am not interested in how an automobile works. Or in the why and wherefore of radio. I am a terrible procrastinator. I have difficulty making up my mind. And then I am never sure I'm right. Yet, dealing with facts outside myself, I can decide quickly and well what should be done. It is about myself that I procrastinate.

This is a letter of ego. But I know myself is interesting to you. Perhaps if I write you these things as I think them you can help me decide more wisely.

The introspective mood dominated his letters as his twenty-fourth birthday approached. At Shattuck, he and Phil Works had agreed that by the time they were twenty-four they would be married. "I realize," said Benton in a note to Elma, "that marriage is the central experience of life, and I should think of it that way for myself." He didn't as yet. All his friends seemed either to be married or engaged to be married. "But for some reason, I go out of my way to avoid meeting girls. Besides I can't afford it." Still, he was seeing Helen Hemingway now and again, and all the people to whom he had introduced her thought she was a "knockout." There was a chance that she might be going abroad for a year, but he didn't know how he really felt if it should turn out that he would not be seeing her again. And so on, back and forth.

In the second week of April, the introspective mood suddenly vanished. One day after the regular Wednesday copy meeting, where copywriters and executives were addressed by speakers "dragged in from every place," Benton lunched with another copywriter, Elizabeth Woody, a Wellesley graduate, beautiful, intelligent, and emotionally complicated. Benton jokingly told her that he would like to address one of these meetings. He felt he could give a better talk than most he had heard. No copywriter, except two or three from the consumer department, had ever spoken at these weekly gatherings. It was an idle conversation, with a major sequel which Benton related to his mother:

A week ago last Friday the man who was supposed to speak this Wednesday called it off. Elizabeth suggested to the man arranging the programs that I be asked. He didn't take her very seriously but spoke to me about it and I jumped at the chance. The chief O.K.'d it and there I was on the program.

I elected to talk on the way Lord and Thomas wrote copy. The firm of Lord and Thomas is like a red flag to a bull in George Batten Co. It was a very delicate subject. It was further complicated by the fact that a terrific argument was raging, and is still, about whether we should not do work a good deal more like Lord and Thomas's. I deliberately precipitated myself into the midst of the battle.

I spent every minute between a week ago last Friday and last Wednesday preparing my talk. The big day came. I was quite nervous. I guess I was the youngest person of the sixty or seventy people in the room. Applying old Patterson's principles (at the National Cash Register Company) about the eye being stronger than the ear, I had something like nineteen exhibits (comparing Lord and Thomas advertising and Batten advertising) and I had a big pad of paper to work on. I started in following my speech as I had written it. But I did not follow it very long. As I expected, before I'd been going five minutes they started to ride me. One vice president walked out of the room. But it was at the extemporaneous repartee that I made my points. A lot of people disagreed with what I said, but everyone agrees that I can talk. Everyone knows me now. One vice president fell on my neck afterward. Ever since there have been excited groups discussing the speech.

I'm boasting a lot, am I not?

Unfortunately, the day of the speech several meetings were on and two clients were in town. The four biggest executives of the company were not there to hear me. They have heard so much about it, however, that it looks as if I shall have to redeliver it to them. Which will be an unprecedented thing. The eventual outcome of it all may be that I shall be transferred into the new business department. Which will be still more unbelievable. Or I may get fired. Or have to quit.

Benton had not exaggerated the likelihood that he would be fired or have to quit. He had told the account executives in the audience:

"Albert Lasker of Lord and Thomas knows a whale of a lot more about advertising than you do, and Albert Lasker's agency is a whale of a lot better than the George Batten Company." Nor did he soften his approach when he faced the board of directors, which included "the four biggest executives," even when one of them, a Mr. Busser, waspishly said to him before he started: "You look like the young man in the International Correspondence School ads telling all the old men what to do." Yet Busser's colleagues were sufficiently impressed with what they heard to lift the young man over the hump of anonymity in the firm and start him upward. Within a week's time, he was given his first chance to write "consumer copy" for a mouthwash called Odol that was to be handled along the lines Benton had advocated in his speeches. More changes followed, including management shakeups that soon cleared the way for Benton to step into empty managerial shoes.

"I have many friends here," Benton informed his mother, "but I also have many enemies, due to my talk and sudden prominence. I may still be fired. But I'm not worrying much. There's no use. I can easily get another job."

He was more serious about another matter. The 1924 presidential election campaign was underway, the first national election in which Benton was old enough to vote. The Republican candidate was the incumbent president, Calvin Coolidge. John W. Davis was the Democratic nominee, chosen after a bitter deadlock between Al Smith and William Gibbs McAdoo. There was also Senator Robert M. La Follette, Sr., the nominee of the Progressive party and a hero to old Grangers and Populists like Daniel Webster Hixson, Benton's grandfather. Benton carefully read the speeches of all the candidates, and, after weighing their words, solemnly made his first political commitment by joining the Yale-for-Davis Club. "Davis," said he in a note to Elma explaining his decision, "is the best man, while Coolidge is the 'silent man' because he has to cover up a multitude of sins."

Late that fall, while the campaign to pick a president to lead the nation was at its height, Benton was made a "group head" in the trade and industrial department in the Batten agency to replace Arthur Brashears, who was promoted to consumer copy. Soon afterward, he was urged to accept a proposed transfer to the Chicago branch office with enlarged duties. He evaded the proposal without too much difficulty, only to be pressured to accept a proposed transfer to Batten's Boston branch. In addition to the "laying on of hands" by Mr. Emerson, the head of the Boston branch, three other pairs of hands were involved in the intended blessing. They belonged to William H. Johns, the aging head of the Batten firm; Mr. Boardman, the head of all copy; and Mr. Page, the head of the "new business department." At Yale, Benton would have thought himself in Heaven if a single finger had tapped him for Skull and Bones. Now, however, he politely but resolutely shrugged off all the approving hands that blessed him in terms he didn't like. In a memo addressed to Johns, Emerson, Boardman, and Page, he made it clear that before he would move to Boston he would move out of Batten.

He was playing from strength. Lou Hartman of Lord and Thomas had recently pressed him to take a $4,200-a-year job writing copy under O'Dea, with none of the earlier troubles he had experienced. "It's bad to go back to a place you've left," Benton subsequently observed to Elma, "but I'm pleased that Hartman and O'Dea want me. It's something to remember in case Mr. Johns gets too resentful over my refusing to go to Boston." Further:

> The time has come to let Mr. Johns and the other company executives in the Batten agency know that I am very concerned over myself, over my future, and over my rapid advancement regardless of my youth. I never intend to make any emotional appeals to an employer. I never intend to cry about how I need more money because I have to support a wife and ten children or a widowed mother. My approach will always be: "I am worth more money. If I'm not, don't pay it to me, or even fire me. If I am, fork it over." I personally feel I'll more often gain respect by the latter attitude than by the former. As I go along, Mother, I realize more and more the general incompetence of most men in business.

At the end of 1924, Benton's new resolve to march at the head of events brought its new reward. In another shakeup, Boardman had been fired and displaced as head of all copy by Maurice Collette, who had been with the organization since 1908. The temporary head of Benton's department was shifted elsewhere, leaving a vacancy to be filled. Benton was the youngest of the twelve men in the department, and the others, from the standpoint of length of service, had a stronger claim to head it. But a majority of the executives of the company, impressed with his energy and talents, induced Mr. Johns to shelve his annoyance at Benton's sidestepping Boston and to make him head of the trade and industrial department.

The various members of Benton's family were informed of his new job, which made him the leader of eleven subordinates. Among the replies he received, one from his Aunt Mary Benton was full of advice on how to be a leader and inspirer instead of an autocrat. And she informed her nephew that Aunt Hattie was on her way to Syria "to pick up the heritage of love"—which meant looking over conditions at the Benton School in B'hamdoun, Lebanon, founded in memory of Benton's missionary grandparents. In the years that had passed since the founding of the school, successive members of the Benton family had contributed to its support. Now that her nephew had a new job, and a salary increase, would he wish to contribute to the support of the school?

Before answering, he wrote to his mother for advice:

> I haven't much sympathy with Aunt Hattie's visit, though I suppose it is all right. If the school is going along satisfactorily under its present support, if you think I ought to put in my contribution, let me take Aunt Mary's place on the roll. Let her keep her money, as she needs it so, and I'll give mine instead. Do you think she'd agree to that? I'd rather give the money to her indirectly, than to the school.

His mother's advice was that Aunt Mary, despite her straitened circumstances, would be crushed if she could no longer contribute something to the Benton school. It was best to let her reduce her contribution but still give something, with Benton making up the difference. He agreed, and assumed half of Aunt Mary's share by contributing $90 a year, which he soon increased to $180. It was his first important "philanthropy."

Benton was now earning $5,000 a year—less than several men working under him—but, as he proudly noted, equal to his mother's salary. It was his intention to save at least $1,000 a year, for he still had his $25-a-week client on the side. His savings plan, however, fell apart. First, he induced Walter Schleiter to move with him out of their dark and airless basement quarters on East Thirty-eighth Street and into a tiny two-room apartment on West Fortieth Street that had some sunlight. There would be an extra cost in furnishing the place, but at least they could start living like human beings instead of moles. Then he loaned half his savings to his friend Galen Van Meter, who finally had a position with a Wall Street firm that he liked. His prospects seemed bright, but he was momentarily short of cash, and this was an embarrassment, since he was now engaged to marry Janet Mackey.

In venturing to be a "leader and inspirer instead of an autocrat" in his new job, Benton moved in measured steps. "My aim," so he informed his mother, as though he were Marshal Joffre talking to Marshal Foch, "is to weld the men in my department into a unit. Everyone else in the Batten agency is working at cross purposes, fighting his own little battles. If I can get all the men really strongly behind me, I shall become quite a power in the office." He gently replaced two older section chiefs with young "Benton men." He then bound the personnel of the department to his own fate by showing that he was willing to risk his own job by fighting for his subordinates. But this was not enough. "I am now putting up a fight for better personnel," he informed his mother. "I am trying to get the company to plan on hiring boys out of college, instead of trying to save $5 a week on a salary by taking some high class office boy. I hope to put this over." And so he did.

He was soon entrusted with the responsibility of hiring new copywriters for the company. He insisted that an on-the-job training school for copywriters be created within his own department. This was done, and Benton was made the head of it. He insisted also on a manual to guide copywriters along lines more advanced than those of Boardman, the departed chief of copy. This was agreed to, and Benton wrote the manual. "I am beginning to decide my judgment is unusually good," he informed his mother in mid-February 1925. "That is an inheritance I've received from you. It is remarkable how poor people are at analyzing things and reaching an obvious conclusion. I see it every day in business."

His increased work underlined the need for an assistant. He had interviewed many young men and had chosen one, to start work on Friday the thirteenth. The young man asked for a more auspicious starting date, and that was the end of him. Benton looked askance at anyone who took superstitions seriously. Ironically, the young man's superstition affected the course of Benton's own life, for he finally chose a young assistant who had been referred to him by Yale's job placement bureau. Benton, in reporting the event to Elma, had this to say about the aide he was breaking in:

He has had very little experience, having just graduated from Yale last year. He is in the right business, as he was captain of the golf team at Yale, and is from one of the oldest New England families—from father to son his forebears have been editors of the Springfield "Republican" for over 100 years. He is engaged to the daughter of the Vice President of the Fiske Rubber Company, and has many connections which will prove of enormous benefit. He is either going to be a tremendous success in advertising, or a tragic failure. (His girl won't let him go onto the newspaper, as it means working until one or two in the morning for the rest of his life.)

The nameless young $25-a-week assistant was Chester Bowles. In the passing days, "Bill" Benton and "Chet" Bowles grew closer to each other, and by the last week of March there was the first sign of a gestating idea about a Benton and Bowles team. It was augmented a few days later by the idea of adding the older and more experienced Maurice Collette to the combination. Two letters Benton sent his mother mark the onset of the plan—and its first miscarriage:

March 23, 1925

Chet is most likeable, and is already popular with all the boys in my department. Next summer he is to marry Judy Fiske. His father-in-law to be has remarked to him: "I see no reason why you shouldn't have the Fiske Tire Company account someday." The Fiske account is somewhat similar to a gold mine. Tonight at dinner Chet was talking to me about the possibility of our going into business together in four or five years, with the Fiske account to run on. If such a thing works out, it is like finding a fortune. It may work out, too, but four years from now is difficult to predict.

April 8, 1925

Chet and I went up to Springfield last week. Either Chet had exaggerated Mr. Fiske's optimism, or else Mr. Fiske had changed his mind. He vetoed the idea of a new agency at this time. He found the selling job with the other executives in his company much bigger than he had thought it was. He decided it would be easier to sell George Batten than it would "Collette, Benton and Bowles." He advised us to try to bring the account in to Batten's, and if we wanted to a couple years from now, then there was plenty of time to try to put the new agency idea over. (I don't know whether I would do that. I rather doubt it.)

Last week I went over the whole thing with Mr. Johns and Mr. Page. They are, of course, highly keyed up over the possibility. I am to figure very decidedly in the solicitation, and, if we get the business, I may be the representative on the account. A big job. Mr. Fiske said, "I would give many thousands of dollars to have the chance at the Cadillac account that you have at the Fiske advertising account." Mr. Fiske is going to recommend us, but he is in no position to jam us down the throats of his sales and advertising managers.

Benton correctly estimated Mr. Fiske's position. There was no Fiske account to be had either by the putative advertising firm of "Collette, Benton and Bowles" or by the George Batten Company— or later, by Benton and Bowles. But the matter started Benton and Bowles to thinking of themselves in terms of a team, while the chimerical Fiske account and other, more tangible things spurred Benton's rise in the Batten agency. He had inherited the trade and industrial department in bad shape, but within a year he had straightened out its accounts and personnel and had turned an operating deficit into a profit. He had worked on solicitations and had spoken at advertising, direct mail, sales, and other conferences.

In the spring of 1925, he was ready for a further step upward in the Batten hierarchy, facilitated by Maurice Collette, whom he had thought of as the senior member of a future "Collette, Benton, and Bowles." Collette now reciprocated Benton's compliment. He wanted Benton to become his main assistant in the copy and service department while continuing in direct charge of the trade and industrial department. Mr. Johns, the president of the Batten agency, had to give his approval, but Collette volunteered to get it. "That would really be quite a promotion for me," Benton informed his mother. "I would be stepping into a job which can be built up to God knows where. The salary limit is much higher than in the job I now hold." The shining prospect ahead, if realized, seemed to be connected in his thoughts with the idea that he would be financially situated to get married. But to whom? Benton jumped to a word of self-analysis about his own memory, and from there jumped to a postscript devoted to a certain girl. "My strong forte," said he, "is not my memory. It is nowhere as good as Dan's was, in remembering things that happened long ago. I remember the logic of situations, the reasoning and principles behind the things I saw or did, but not the details." After that he added:

> P.S.—Helen Hemingway of whom I've often written you, returns after a year in France this coming August. She is one of the finest girls I've ever known. She graduated from Connecticut College in 1923, President of the Christian Society, etc. In 1923–4, she taught French in a Connecticut high school. You couldn't find a better, nicer girl, more of a leader, than Helen. Do you think you could use her next year? She might be interested. I have no idea that she would, but she'd be a real find!

Collette came through with Mr. Johns, and Benton was raised in rank and salary effective 1 June. At the same time, Bowles introduced Benton to a private world previously unknown to him. This was the Baltusrol Golf Club, located at Short Hills, New Jersey, where Benton encamped for most of the summer months as a junior member, while commuting to work in New York. He had never before seen such a collection of affluent people assembled in one place. Bowles's aptitude for golf brought him in intimate touch with the Big Men in the club who were golf addicts, while Benton's status as a duffer made him ashamed to get out on the links. His skill at bridge, however, equalized the distance between himself and the Big Men who were bridge addicts.

Helen Hemingway, meanwhile, returned from Europe in late August. She passed through New York en route to New Haven without seeing Benton, but found time for a phone call, and it was arranged that they would meet in early September. On the eve of their scheduled reunion, however, Benton passed through a crisis in his life. The reasons, unrelated to Helen, could have meant his not seeing her again if the turmoil had resolved itself differently.

On Thursday, 21 August, Benton received a telegram from a friend in Miami, Russell Hoye, Yale '18. Hoye had been one of the young men who had swooped down on Florida and its land boom, like birds in search of golden worms. Now, he telegraphed, he was very well located with the Miami Advertising Company, and the company needed a $250-a-week copywriter. Was Benton interested? The salary was more than twice what he was earning at Batten. So he wired for more information about the financial condition of the

Miami agency, and whether it would give him a contract for a year. The next day a telegram from Miami referred him to people in New York who could assure him about the company's financial soundness. When the proposed contract arrived in the mail on the following Monday morning, Benton took it to a lawyer and was told it was valid. If he joined the Miami Advertising Company, he would draw $250 a week for a year just as long as he reported for work.

That noon, he submitted his resignation to Mr. Johns. Johns, dumbfounded, urged Benton to take a day to think it over. So he did, but he was still of a mind to resign when he saw Johns the next afternoon. The latter now spread out a batch of Florida newspapers showing Benton the "cheap" real estate copy he would be expected to write; then he said: "Are you an exceptional copywriter? I don't think you are a genius. And, if you aren't, you don't want to stick to copy work. You want to be here with a big executive job ahead of you." Benton still held to his decision, and his resignation was finally accepted.

That night, he talked his decision over with four older men at the Baltusrol Country Club. All advised against it. One, Bill Williamson, sales manager of a Wall Street brokerage house, was particularly emphatic in arguing against the move, saying: "You are a fool to leave. Every year you stay with Batten's is worth thousands of dollars to you in prestige. This you sacrifice if you go to Miami. You now enjoy the respect of the men here at the club. They know you have a fine job with a fine company. But what of Miami? We all have hundreds of ex-Miamians, so to speak, apply to us for jobs every year. They are the ne'er-do-wells, those who may settle down in later life and make a success, but the odds are against them."

The revelation stopped Benton's precipitous lunge down the primrose path. The prodigal returned. He called on Mr. Johns Wednesday morning, contritely confessed his error, said that he had consulted several older men, and all had advised him to stay at Batten. It had taken him several days to get a clear view of the situation, but now that he had "passed through a crisis," he felt it would "mark a turning point" in his "way of thinking." He got up to leave, but was stopped by Johns, who said: "I have been looking over the payroll, Mr. Benton. I have decided to increase your salary to $7000 a year. There are at least two men in your department on more of a salary than you are. You have done well and should be the highest paid man in the department. Furthermore, you have made a real monetary sacrifice in not going to Miami. I recognize it, and want to compensate you in some measure. I don't believe you'll get another raise for some time. But I know you won't expect it."

In relating all this afterward to Elma, Benton, still a little dazed, observed that with his outside job with Goldstein, he would be making $8,300 a year at least. "That is a great deal of money," he continued. "Things change rapidly. I should save $4,000 or so during the next year." Assorted postscripts to this report extended from the end of August to mid-October 1925.

> I have paid off all my debts, and don't owe a cent to anyone. I hope that the days of "being broke" are over for me. I feel as if I started on the road to financial independence. It is a great feeling.

> I am very glad that you liked your gold wrist watch. It afforded me great pleasure to give you such a present. I honestly didn't expect to for many years to come. So my pleasure is doubled because of the early date.

> Secretly, I'm quite proud of the Benton School. The School will have my support, though never to the exclusion of things which in my estimation are more worth while. Aunt Mary is one of those things. She is quite a remarkable woman.

> You'd better start hunting a wife for me. I have my bachelor-hood thrown up to me all the time. All the boys in my department are married except one, and he is getting married in six weeks. I sit alone on a solitary pedestal, the best able in the lot, financially, to support a family.

> Helen Hemingway is coming through the city this weekend. I didn't see her when she got in from Europe, as she took a train right out. I'll be glad to see her. She is a charming girl.

In mid-October 1925 a note from his mother rocked Benton back on his heels. She had just been to a doctor, and some sort of chronic disease was suspected, perhaps heart trouble.

The note marked a new turn in the mother-son relationship. "You have always been the one to lecture me," he wrote her; "now my turn has come to lecture you." He wanted her to spread the work load instead of trying to do everything herself. The best executives, said he, "had the least to do themselves." A subsequent report about her condition led him to add: "Your common sense has always been so far above that of most people, that I have never questioned it in regard to yourself. Aunt Mary questions it. And now that you are having trouble with your health, I question it also. I don't know whether one who has been as strong and active as you can realize a new day has dawned." If the doctor thought it would help, she should quit Saint Louis at once and spend the rest of the year in California. If the doctor approved and her own interests drew her to Europe, she should plan on going there. The costs of the trip would be his gift to her. If she wanted to move to New York, she could live with her son. Financial considerations should play no part in her decisions. "You know," said he, "I can easily send you whatever you need to live on. *And I'd love to.* There is nothing would please me so much as to feel I was working for you. You had that feeling about me and Dan. You can understand the same feeling in me. I never will, financially or in any other way, be able to repay you for all you have done for me."

In mid-December agency business took Benton to Chicago, and he went on to Saint Louis. He found his mother had not cut back on her work, and he was disturbed by the way she looked. So he again urged her to consider the various proposals about the future he had sketched in his letters. Her disinterest prompted an afterthought on his part when he returned to New York. "While you think you will be happiest if you keep your work at Hosmer Hall," he wrote Elma, "there is absolutely no need of your trying to save money while you stay at Hosmer. Stay there because you like it, not because you are achieving independence. Get yourself a maid. If your present income isn't sufficient to cover expenses, call on me. If you feel any easier, I will start a ten-year endowment fund for you so that you will have the money you want by that time, guaranteed you, or we'll make it five years."

His mother declined the proposal and argued that there was no real cause for concern. By the end of January 1926, as if to prove that she had completely recovered from her malaise, she journeyed east for a teachers' convention in Washington, D.C., and then to New York for a reunion. Benton had asked Helen Hemingway to come down from New Haven to meet his mother. Everything could have gone wrong between the powerful older woman and the shy younger one. Nothing did. Each was happily impressed by the other. The only trouble was with Benton himself. Elma left for Saint Louis feeling that her son didn't know the true state of his heart. However, since Helen and her own mother were due to move from New Haven to New York in early March, Elma assumed that he would be seeing the girl more often.

Not long after she was back in Saint Louis, Elma collapsed and was bedridden for several months. "I hope," her alarmed son wrote her, "that you aren't too old, or too proud to listen to the advice I have been trying to give you about how to arrange things so that you can take it easy." Yet when Elma was allowed to move about, she again plunged into her work at Hosmer Hall, along with that of the many civic committees of which she was a member. She slowed down only in mid-June when she came east to spend the greater part of the summer of 1926 at a seaside hotel in Madison, Connecticut, where her son joined her on most weekends.

Meanwhile, at the Batten office, Benton passed through another spasm of complaining about the advertising profession generally, and about the Batten agency specifically. He had increased the business of the trade and industrial department by 40 percent while the business of the agency as a whole had increased by only 10 percent. His success, he felt, was largely due to the kind of young men he hired or helped train as copywriters. Some, in fact, were to become major figures in modern American advertising. First there was Chester Bowles. Then there was Ted Bates, whom Benton engaged to succeed Bowles as his personal assistant when Bowles was assigned to the writing of copy. Bates, in time, would found his own agency and would make it one of the largest in the world. There was also J. Sterling Getchell, who had been with Lord and Thomas before Benton hired him for Batten. Getchell would later found a highly successful agency of his own, but its boundless promise came to an end with his untimely death while he was still in his early forties.

Also during this period, Benton came to know two young men who were to have a direct or indirect effect on his future career in the advertising business. One of these who worked with Benton at the Batten agency was Charles Mortimer, later president of General Foods. The second was Bayard Colgate, heir apparent to the dominant interest in the Colgate Company, one of the largest advertisers in the nation and at that time a Batten account.

Since it seemed to Benton that he would be staying with the Batten Company for some time, he decided to end his living arrangement with Walter Schleiter and to move into a place of his own. The one he found was an apartment in the Hotel White at Thirty-seventh Street and Lexington Avenue, an eleven-block walk from his office. Yet what he called his "homeloving instincts" still stopped short of marriage.

Seven years had passed since he had first met Helen Hemingway. Now that she was living in New York, he was seeing her at least once a week—and was regularly confiding the ambiguous aftereffects to Elma: "Helen," so he wrote in mid-December 1926, "is the best company a man can have. I doubt if I could ever do better in finding a wife. I believe I'll stop seeing Helen in the next few months. If I don't, it's marriage."

Suddenly, after a New Year's Eve party given by Chet and Judy Bowles, Helen gave Benton a piece of news which he passed on to his mother: "She says that she has made up her mind to go to France. I am at a loss when I think that I won't see her anymore. I can't understand what she's up to. She says that there is someone in France she met the year she was there, and is now going to marry him and settle down in Tours." On his twenty-seventh birthday, he added a perplexed postscript: "I have been seeing Helen despite what she told me on New Year's Eve. But she is serious about going to France. Someone was up to look at the apartment that she and her mother were renting. I don't understand this French business at all. My guess is that she won't marry that man."

He was judging the matter on the basis of the many goodbyes and reunions that had marked his relationship with Helen since the first of her goodbyes had been uttered the previous New Year's Eve.

On his own part, he could not cite financial reasons for withholding his own marriage proposal to her. His finances took another bright turn when Mr. Johns raised his salary to $10,000 and offered Benton a "partnership" in the agency, along with fifty shares of stock valued at $10,000. Though he had been with the agency only a little over three years, if he accepted Benton would head the "third line of defense" at Batten. The second line was headed by Collette and Robley Feland, who were his seniors in age by thirteen or more years, and the "first line" was headed by Johns and four other aging top executives, some of whom were soon due to retire. In the normal course of things, therefore, Benton might look forward to becoming the president of the Batten agency. Further, the block of stock he was offered, when it paid for itself from dividends, would increase his income by from $2,000 to $3,000 a year. The additional increments of stock he would get as the existing stockholders retired and turned their holdings back to the company would prospectively mean $30,000 to $40,000 a year in stock dividends by the time Benton was forty.

Johns's offer was not unfettered. If Benton accepted the stock, he would be bound by a provision not to go into the agency business for a period of five years after he voluntarily left Batten. This might make any change difficult because only in another agency could he capitalize fully on his experience. "This means," he wrote to Elma, "that I would be casting my lot with George Batten Company, while still a very young man. The company can make men financially independent, but it does not make them millionaires. My income should be excellent, but the dreams of great wealth vanish into the limbo." But if he left Batten, it would probably be for a business other than advertising, for he doubted whether another agency would present opportunities as great as those he currently faced. In the end, he accepted the stock offer. He became the youngest "partner" in the history of the Batten agency, and took the "partner" role so seriously that the results eventually spread havoc on all sides.

He was still riding high in his new role when his mother finally agreed to take a year's leave of absence from Hosmer Hall. She came east for a vacation with her son in the early summer of 1927, and in mid-August sailed for Europe. This was the first time since 1914 that the Atlantic Ocean separated the mother and son. But the emotional jolt of this particular separation was increased three months later when Helen Hemingway actually left for Europe.

Benton felt bereft—and defensive—for having maintained a relationship with the girl for so many years, only to see it come to nothing. He appealed to his mother for some "understanding" of his behavior. "Girls take marriage much more calmly than men," he wrote Elma in the course of reporting on Helen's departure. "To them, marriage is a natural and pre-ordained function, no more to get excited about than breakfast. To men it is a tremendous event, to be pondered and decided slowly. Girls think about marriage much more than men, before they are engaged, because they look forward to it as the inevitable. Perhaps that is why men, in their unpreparedness, get more excited about the event when it is upon them." And he added: "Janet Van Meter says she doesn't see how I'll ever get married because I'll never find a girl whom I think is the equal of my mother. Yet all the girls I have ever been interested in—Cordelia,

Catharine, and now Helen—are those who most closely resemble you in many of their personal traits."

If he was clear in his mind about that one matter, he was increasingly unsettled in his thoughts about the Batten agency and about the advertising business itself. Where the agency was concerned, he joined in a plan which envisioned the formation of a four-man consortium to buy out the stock of Mr. Johns. The other members of the consortium were to be Collette, Robley Feland, and Sterling Getchell. All felt as he did that Johns was a drag on the agency and that he could serve it best by retiring as president. Johns, however, saw the case differently and backed away from the proposal—even as Benton hesitated to back into a proposal of marriage to Helen Hemingway.

Helen did not marry "that man in Tours," but settled in Paris, where she was working in the fashion industry. She and Benton resumed their correspondence, and Benton felt drawn closer to marriage but still couldn't take the final step. He appealed to his mother for help, saying that it was "unusual in itself" that Helen was the only girl he had "ever really considered marrying." He had "become more self centered, more selfish." Perhaps if he didn't "marry now," he never would. This was one matter, however, which Elma declined to decide for him. She had visited Helen in Paris in April, and afterward wrote Benton a prose poem in praise of the girl, but stopped short of telling him directly what he should do with respect to marriage. "You have not helped me much with Helen," Benton complained in a reply. "I am still at sea but I must sail for one shore or another."

Someone else helped make up his mind.

On the evening of 1 May 1928, after a bridge game at Galen Van Meter's apartment on Fifty-fifth Street, Gene Tracey, who had sat in the game, walked with Benton part of the way back to his hotel. Gene had recently been divorced after three and a half years of marriage, and in the course of the walk Benton voiced his regret that his friend had married a girl, only to see it all end in a divorce. Tracey snapped back: "I don't agree at all. I'm not sorry I married her. Marriage is the natural state for a man. I took my chances and they didn't work out. Why don't you have the nerve to get married?"

Benton thought about this when he walked the rest of the way alone. When he got to the White Hotel, he wrote a letter to Helen proposing marriage. Then he was afraid he wouldn't mail it if he waited until morning. So he walked out and mailed the letter. He then thought he was being unfair to Helen, since she would not know that he had mailed the letter. So he walked to the nearest Western Union cable office and sent her a cablegram: "In letter just mailed four most important words are, Will you marry me?"

He later learned that the landlady of the boardinghouse where Helen was living in Paris telephoned her when the cable arrived, read its contents over the phone, and asked in French: "Are you content?" Helen was content. "Read it again!" she exclaimed. She accepted the proposal of marriage and would soon return to the United States in the company of her cousins, Mr. and Mrs. William Walsh of Litchfield, Connecticut.

Another piece of news was a little slow in reaching her. Five days after she had received Benton's cabled proposal of marriage, he was fired from the George Batten Company. Why? The cause was rooted in Benton's old complaint about how the company was "slow as molasses," a complaint based on the growing gap between the strength of the advertising copy Batten was turning out, and the agency's weakness in soliciting new business and in handling what it had. In a single week in early February it had lost four accounts with aggregate billings of one million dollars.

It was Benton's feeling that the advertising firm of Barton, Durstine, and Osborne, located in the same building with Batten, was successful in soliciting new business, but was producing "lousy" ads. Why not merge the two agencies so that the strength of one in producing high quality advertising copy could be reinforced by the strength of the other in getting business and in management? The idea seemed so logical that he sent a hail of memos to Johns to drive home the argument that the Batten Company simply had to merge with Barton, Durstine, and Osborne. Collette associated himself in writing with Benton's views.

But pride was stronger than logic. On Saturday morning, 5 May, Johns called Collette in and fired him in five minutes. Benton was called in next. This took a little longer. After two hours he fired Benton on the charge of "disloyalty" to the Batten agency. "I told Johns," Benton later recalled, "that he had made me a so-called partner in the agency and that the proof of my loyalty to him was that I wanted to make Batten a successful company. In fact, I should have been given a million dollar check as a 'finder's fee' for being the man who came up with the idea of the merger of Batten and BD&O."

He was given a week to clear up his work and clear out. But since he had been summarily fired instead of resigning, he was freed from the clause in the contract barring him for five years from working for or starting another agency. At lunch on the Saturday he was fired, Benton discussed his plans with Sterling Getchell and Chester Bowles. He was now determined to start his own advertising agency, but first he wanted further experience at the management end of things. "There are plenty of hazards in this business from the clients," Benton observed. "Why also accept the hazard from bosses inside the agency?" Sterling Getchell immediately volunteered to join Benton, and Bowles added: "Let's go in together."

Collette was reemployed, but only at the price of having to make a humiliating speech that Monday before all the principal people in the Batten Company. Benton, however, refused to humiliate himself as the price of being rehired, and in this he had the backing of a revolutionary movement in the copy department. It had been his vain practice beforehand to buy a ten-cent carnation en route to work and to wear it in his lapel. The men in the copy department now sported carnations for the rest of the week in a symbolic gesture of solidarity with their banished chief. The Jacobin gesture was not lost on Johns, nor did he miss the meaning of other developments. Frank Presbrey, the head of a large New York advertising agency at the time, telephoned him to ask what had happened at his agency —since seven copywriters from Batten had applied to him for jobs in a single day. In the interim, the ablest of the copywriters, Sterling Getchell, had printed little cards reading inelegantly: "Aw Nuts." He gravely left one on each executive's desk, and then walked out for good. A job was waiting for him at the J. Walter Thompson agency.

Faced by such internal discontent, Johns entered into the very negotiations Benton had urged on him at the price of being fired. In July, a merger brought into being what is now the giant firm of "BBD&O"—Batten, Barton, Durstine, and Osborne.

There was a comic footnote to this. Just before Benton was fired, he had hired one Charles Brower for the Batten copy department, but left no record of this fact. Brower checked in a week later, asked for Benton, and was told that he was no longer around. Referred to someone else in the firm, Brower said, "Benton hired me and I quit my job and here I am." He was asked: "And what did Benton agree to pay you?" Brower subsequently confessed that in answering the question, "I gave myself my first raise." He did a little more than that as time went by. He became the president of BBD&O.

Benton, on his part, returned his stock to the Batten Company, and received for it about $5,000 in accumulated dividends. He was not lacking in new job offers, but he felt that Lord and Thomas was the best place quickly to get the experience he wanted in the management end of the advertising business. Over the five years that elapsed since leaving that agency, he had kept in close and friendly touch with its executives. When he now informed them of his "availability," he was promptly offered and just as promptly accepted a job as assistant general manager in the Chicago home office of the firm.

During the time he spent in the New York office, in order to get a "feel" of the people with whom he would correspond from his own base in Chicago, he also attended to the details bearing on arrangements for his wedding, honeymoon, and the disposition of his New York apartment. And at four o'clock, 12 June, in the Saint Regis Hotel, with two hundred guests present, with Galen Van Meter as the best man, and with Elma Hixon Benton looking on, Helen and William were married. The minister was the Reverend Stanley Kilbourne, the Episcopal minister who in 1913 had helped get Benton into the Shattuck School on a choir-singing scholarship. He was another of the many people out of the past with whom Benton had kept in touch through nights of letter writing.

After the wedding, Bill and Helen left for a three-week cruise to Jamaica, and then back to the States and on to Chicago, where they arrived on 8 July. The private world facing Helen had become a topsy-turvy one even as she was being fitted for a bridal gown. Yet she calmly accepted the change as though it was the most ordinary experience a young woman could know. So it would be in the abrupt changes lying ahead for the Bentons in their life together. The bridegroom, despite his agonizing indecision in the years before, had chosen brilliantly in this daughter of a long line of Connecticut Yankees. He had chosen intelligence, laconic humor, honesty, generosity, and a dignity of style which springs from an inner elegance.

Benton was determined to save toward the capital needed to start his own advertising business. In Chicago, the Bentons settled into an inexpensive two-room apartment in the 300 block of Webster Street.

Helen busied herself with making the place comfortable, while Benton wrote his mother: "I am becoming more settled in matrimony. Helen is better suited to me than any girl I would ever have met, and we are very happy. I am reading aloud to Helen, 'John Brown's Body,' by Stephen Vincent Benet, a boy who was in college with me. A 350 page poem telling the story of the Civil War. I think you would like it. We are leading a very, very quiet life. Doing absolutely nothing. The only excitement I get is in business, which is not good." He presently had more than his fill of excitement in business, thanks to Albert Lasker, the head of Lord and Thomas.

Albert Lasker once defined an "administrator" as being "somebody without brains." What he liked—and rewarded in his own eccentric way—was stimulation, ideas, and originality. The organizational structure of Lord and Thomas featured a board of directors that never met. A succession of "presidents" had no effective power of command over their own subordinates; Lasker was forever making end runs around his "presidents," to decimate their subordinates or to raise them (briefly) to summits of glory. There were many men who were hired to be heads of various enclaves within the agency. They often found that someone else had also been hired to do their assigned jobs. The chaos generated by this system of dual proconsuls led to resignations, firings, and new hirings on what seemed to be a six-month cycle. (Frank Fehlman, Benton's original employer, had been a casualty of the process.) Yet, despite the chaos, in 1928 when Benton joined the Chicago office of Lord and Thomas, the agency was in its greatest years as the pacesetter in American advertising.

Benton did not meet Lasker for three months after starting to work as assistant general manager. He later learned that an important point in his own favor when he was hired was not his previous association with Lord and Thomas but the fact that he had been fired by the George Batten agency, for whose head Lasker had a profound "professional contempt." William H. Johns and his associates used to solicit business by stating that Batten spent almost all its commissions on client services, retaining for itself only around 2 percent. Lasker, by contrast, used to solicit business by stating: "I've made a million dollars a year or far more ever since I was 26 years old. Do you want a smart man to work for you?" And he insisted on keeping 10 percent of the 15 percent in commissions. It was something Benton would echo later, when he would brashly tell prospective Benton and Bowles clients: "Whatever J. Walter Thompson charges, we charge more."

At Lord and Thomas, Ralph L. Sollitt, the general manager, was Benton's immediate superior. Their personal relations were excellent: The two men and their respective wives had a standing biweekly social evening which they spent in reading plays. Benton's thoughts, however, remained centered on his friends in New York. When one of them, such as Gene Tracey, visited Chicago, joy was unconfined. Sterling Getchell, by now working for J. Walter Thompson, also came to Chicago, anxious to talk about Lord and Thomas, and still more anxious to talk about a Benton and Getchell advertising agency. Twice he and Benton met midway at Toledo for a weekend discussion. There was also a telegram from Charles Mortimer, who wanted to leave BBD&O, and Benton sent a letter introducing him to the head of the New York office of Lord and Thomas. There were also long, newsy letters from Bowles, working at BBD&O but full of plans for a future Benton and Bowles combination.

Then again, there were letters from Galen Van Meter and from Bill Williamson of Baltusrol days, now partners in a Wall Street firm. They had a $15,000-a-year job waiting for Benton, after the 1928 presidential election. The victory of Herbert Hoover provided a new jet of steam for the upward surge of the New York stock market. Van Meter and Williamson, like many other men on Wall Street, were ebullient; each expected to make $100,000 in the year ahead, and they urged Benton to join them around the gravy bowl.

Benton (who had voted for Al Smith) might have been tempted, but at that moment he was tied to Lord and Thomas by a major project that Lasker had put in his charge. Colgate, a former Batten account, had merged with the Palmolive Company, a Lord and Thomas account. Would each of the two agencies retain its former account, or would the advertising also merge into a single account? Lasker had an idea.

Though Lord and Thomas was the world's largest advertising agency, it then had no research department, reflecting Lasker's built-in contempt for research, especially of the statistical kind. "Research," he thundered, "is simply something that tells you that a jackass has two ears." Nonetheless, in the autumn of 1928, the Colgate-Palmolive merger forced Lasker to dissemble his contempt for research. He sent for Benton—it was one of their earliest meetings—and said to him: "I know the Palmolive people too well to ask them for the Colgate account, but I want to show that I am interested in it. Which means that I want you to make a survey on the problems growing out of the merger."

"What kind of survey do you want?" Benton asked. "What shall I survey?"

"I don't give a damn what you survey," Lasker answered impatiently. "All I want is the biggest one ever made."

Most advertising agency surveys of the time took the form of market research. This meant determining, for instance, the number of drugstores in Des Moines, and how to get one's products displayed in their windows. But now that Benton was ordered to produce something colossal in size alone, he poured his energies into his assignment. He put the entire copy department of Lord and Thomas to work framing elaborate questionnaires, not for drugstores but for consumers. Copywriters were sent to the suburbs for a house-to-house canvass of consumers to get a feel for the subject they were to think about. Palmolive and Colgate, for example, both produced packaged soap flakes—Super Suds and Kwiksolv. If one brand was to be withdrawn from the market in consequence of the merger, what were the consumers' preferences? The questionnaire covering the laundry soap field was distributed to trained teams of interviewers across the nation. When all the returns were in, Benton translated the results into mathematical symbols and some two hundred charts whose meaning could be grasped at a glance.

The project was a day-and-night grind for Benton, seven days a week for sixty days. The final ten days were the hardest he had known in his eight years in business. He worked almost around the clock, with no more than a four-hour nightly break for sleep and with but one break during the day—a lunch at his desk. Though exhausted at the end of the assignment, Benton proudly felt that he may actually have produced what Lasker was billing as "the biggest survey in the history of the advertising business."

The finished survey was a foot thick, in four morocco-bound gold-embossed volumes. These Benton carried through the barricades of three doors, each with its sentinels, guarding the inner citadel where Lasker had his office. He laid the volumes on the latter's desk.

Five minutes later, Lasker sent for Benton. "Magnificent!" he exclaimed, pointing to the height and width of the survey. He had not read it and did not have to. While Benton had been slaving over statistics, Lasker had won the Colgate account on his own. "At least," said Benton, "these are the most expensive bindings your money can buy." Lasker jumped to his feet, slammed his hand on the gold embossing, and exclaimed: "Well, I assume your survey is as good on the inside as it looks on the outside!" Though he gave no further sign that the survey would have any bearing on the Lord and Thomas campaign for its new client, Lasker felt that the survey's author deserved his day in the sun and scheduled a whole day for Benton to present and explain his two hundred splendid "consumer research" charts to the heads of Lord and Thomas and the Colgate-Palmolive Company. The charts were a smash hit with the Colgate-Palmolive executives, who were given to understand that the charts would help Lord and Thomas in handling their account.

Benton became a key man on the account, subordinate only to Lasker and his general manager. Advertising copy may or may not have been written with the research findings in mind. The findings themselves were only rudimentary. In later years, however, Dr. George Gallup generously observed that Benton's new if stumbling approach to advertising consumer research entitled him to a place among its modern "fathers." Benton himself did not at the time sense that he was being a pioneer. Nor did the Colgate-Palmolive executives. The year 1928–29 was a boom year, and Benton's survey seemed to add an extra dimension to the hoped for boom in their own business.

No part of what had happened changed Lasker's own attitude toward research in advertising. He still detested it "on principle." But with the attitude of a man wearing a clothespin on his nose, he put Benton to work on similar surveys for other accounts. Along with this went a special assignment after Bayard Colgate, the heir apparent of the Colgate family, moved with his wife to Chicago. Benton had seen him occasionally in New York when the Batten agency had the Colgate account. But as no one in the Chicago office of Lord and Thomas knew the young man, Ralph Sollitt assigned Bayard to Benton as a "major client responsibility."

The arrangement was to the liking of the Colgate heir. He knew few people in Chicago. He seemed to be in the family business mainly from a sense of duty, and he welcomed Benton as someone with whom he could share a few interests other than toothpaste. Besides, his wife, Ann, who had been miserable over the move to Chicago, found in Helen Benton someone who made life in the Windy City a little more pleasant.

Benton's salary by the end of 1928 had been increased to $15,000 a year, and the dividends on the Lord and Thomas stock he had been given brought in an added $7,000 a year, for a total income of $22,000. There would presently be another raise in salary to boost his earnings to $25,000—or a doubling in six months of what he had earned at Batten. Yet he was gearing himself all the while for a change. Thus in early January 1929, he went to New York with Helen to meet friends with whom he had previously been discussing various joint plans by letter. In New York he was offered a partnership in Pedlar and Ryan, a young New York advertising agency whose principal client, Lee Bristol of Bristol-Myers, was one of his friends. A similar offer came from the advertising firm of Charles Hoyt and Company in which his Yale friend Winthrop Hoyt was dominant. But the partnership prospect that interested Benton the most was that with Chester Bowles, who had been the first to broach the idea of a partnership early in the Batten agency days. "I feel certain," Benton explained to his mother, "that I will never meet anyone with whom I am more congenial than I am with Chet. He is the one person I feel certain will stick to the spirit of any partnership arrangement we agree upon."

To their meeting in New York, Bowles brought Charles Mortimer, who had a new job in the advertising department of the Postum Company—the cornerstone of what would soon be General Foods. Although General Foods would embrace some twenty brand names and Mortimer himself eventually would become its head, in early 1929 he was still too new in his job with Postum to make more than a modest promise to Benton and Bowles. He would intercede on their behalf with Ralph Starr Butler, advertising manager of the Postum Company. A small piece of that one account would warrant the launching of a Benton and Bowles agency.

With this target to aim at, each of the three returned to his own base of action. The task of making the first "presentation" to Butler fell to Bowles, since he was near the seat of decision in New York. Benton, in Chicago, suggested improvements in the presentation. He was himself under the strain of a new consumer research survey he was doing for Lord and Thomas, this one for Kotex. He was also under the strain of a stock market loss. He had hoped to save

$12,000 by the end of the year in Chicago, but he lost $3,000 on an investment in Colgate stock. The most he now could hope to have at the end of the year, once he had met the expenses of settling into a New York apartment, was $6,000. Still, he made a quick emotional comeback from the stock market loss. For as he informed his mother, now back at Hosmer Hall, his decision about whether to stay in Chicago would not be governed by any fear of failing to succeed elsewhere. It would be governed by his decision about where the best business opportunities—"and the most happiness for Helen" and himself—were to be found.

On the eve of Benton's birthday in 1929 he received a telephone call from Charles Mortimer in New York. Postum's advertising manager had responded enthusiastically to Bowles. Bowles had "sold himself as an advertising man, and Butler liked and appreciated him." Further, Bowles was submitting his "presentation" to Taylor, Postum's sales manager. The chances of getting something out of the Postum account "were easily fifty-fifty."

Like other imaginative young men on Madison Avenue, Benton had been increasingly drawn to the potentialities of radio as a new medium for advertising. At the National Cash Register Company, he had been taught by "old Patterson" that the "eye is 100 times more powerful than the ear." Long pauses in a radio broadcast of the Harvard-Yale football game, for the announcer to absorb what was happening, led Benton to conclude that the eye was a thousand times more powerful than the ear. With that, he began to wonder how radio advertising, which worked through the ear, could acquire the qualities of immediacy associated with advertising that worked through the eye. The question was never far from his mind, and, in the final months of 1926, he had drawn up a radio advertising plan for the executives of the Batten firm. "It seemed to go over big," he wrote his mother afterward, "and we are to go ahead with further ideas and estimates. If my ideas land a big account for us, it will be quite a feather in my cap. We are especially interested in landing the account of the National Broadcasting Company, the kings of the air, because that account would make us the leading authority, among agencies, upon radio advertising." He would have to wait until he had an advertising agency of his own to put across his ideas, and the result was something more substantial than a feather in his cap.

During the late 1920s, Benton's friend Gene Tracey was becoming a specialist in the new and rapidly developing radio industry. In 1929, Tracey told Benton that, with the backing of the Lehman Brothers investment banking house, he was in the final stage of putting together a fifty-million-dollar merger of radio tube companies soon to be known as the National Union Radio Corporation. Tracey would be one of its principal executives, and he wanted Benton to be its advertising manager. It would mean for Benton several hundred thousand dollars within a few years, since he would get stock in the enterprise by buying it at the banker's price.

Benton played for time in the hope of hearing more from Mortimer about the Postum account. He thought that in any case he would ask Tracey if he could take on the advertising of the National Union Radio Corporation on an agency basis, instead of being tied directly to the structure of the enterprise. "With this account," he wrote to Elma, bringing her abreast of developments, "plus Postum's, we will start off with a rush that will resound in every agency in the country. I am so steamed up about the possibilities that I quiver with every step I take." He admitted in a postscript that both ideas could "flop." But he would not be worried if they did. If two such possibilities could develop in such a short time, it could not be long before a "real thing" would hit him "squarely in the nose." He was sure that his next move would either take him into his own agency or out of advertising completely and into a new field.

In early May he went to New York to meet with Bowles and Ralph Starr Butler. It was time for Benton to tell Sollitt what was in the wind. Sollitt was distressed to learn that the young man was seriously considering leaving Lord and Thomas but respected his wish to do so. However, would a sharp raise in salary, plus another two thousand shares of stock, induce him to stay? The answer was that factors other than money weighed heavily in the balance of the decision Benton would be making.

The meeting in New York with Bowles and Butler went well, as did a follow-up one in Chicago between Benton and Butler. Butler made no pledges but said the chances were "ten to one" that Benton and Bowles would get at least one of the many accounts he controlled. At the same time, there was an encouraging word from Tracey. The proposed merger creating the National Union Radio Corporation was a "98% certainty"; Benton and Bowles could have the advertising account. The "immediate and substantial" billings on this one account would give the agency its "living" for the balance of 1929, even if they failed to get any new accounts. And what if everything fell through that Benton had been counting on? He still felt that he and Bowles "could make a go of things" and should form a team "without regard to any business in immediate prospect."

His mind was made up, and he proceeded to tell Albert Lasker directly what he had previously told Ralph Sollitt. Benton had sensed, correctly, that Lasker "despised anyone who worked for someone else, and secretly admired the man who left him to start his own business." Nonetheless, Lasker tried his best to get Benton to stay. He offered to make him the European manager of Lord and Thomas with headquarters in London and branch offices all over the Continent. Lasker would give Benton the Colgate-Palmolive account for all of Europe and pay him $40,000 a year. If he would stay in Chicago, Lasker would double his income from $25,000 to $50,000 a year. "Why, Mr. Lasker," Benton responded laughingly, "do you mean to tell me I have been worth $50,000 a year to you while you have been paying me only $25,000? I thought I was being overpaid. But I see now that you've been taking *my* money!" Lasker was momentarily speechless. "Well," said he when he finally found his tongue, "I don't blame you for wanting to drop out and look us over. The urge to get into one's business is not to be denied."

A key factor in the gamble Benton took was Helen's attitude toward it—and him. If he wanted to branch out on his own, she was all for it, though she knew that until the firm of Benton and Bowles took root, the Bentons would have to live at a "five and dime store" level. They had secured, sight unseen, a flat of two rooms and kitchen in a new apartment building at 50 East Tenth Street in New York, and the $150-a-month rental was twice what they were paying in Chicago. But there would be no money for anything except for bare necessities, given the way the new firm of Benton and Bowles would be financed.

Many of Benton's friends had offered him capital loans in exchange for stock or a percentage of the profits in the projected new advertising agency, but the offers were refused for a reason Benton later explained: "Why should a young man give away a large part of his brain power, motive power and manpower to pay for initial capital? Why not work harder, spend less, and get along without the extra money, even if it means a slower start?" No one but the two partners invested in the founding of Benton and Bowles. The total capitalization was $18,000. Bowles put in $13,000 of which $4,000 was a loan to Benton, and the latter added $5,000 of the $6,000 he had saved in Chicago. The books thus showed a $9,000 capital investment for each partner.

It meant that Bill and Helen, out of their $6,000 savings in Chicago would have only $1,000 left for living expenses until such time as Benton and Bowles would be in a position to pay salaries to its partners. The way the matter eventually worked out, neither drew a cent out of the firm for a year. To stay alive during that period, Benton had to borrow $1,000 from each of three friends: Galen Van Meter, Gene Tracey, and Arthur Hurd. Helen understood the impending need before it became a reality. Yet far from looking longingly at the lush salary offer of $50,000 made by Lasker, she was prepared "to take in washing" if necessary to help Benton get started in a business of his own.

Benton never "goldbricked" in a job he was about to leave. He always worked full blast right up to the last minute, and in this case even more, as he wound up the complex survey he had made for the Kotex account. He stayed an extra six weeks, working twelve to sixteen hours a day. The Sollitts and the Colgates, the two couples who made up virtually the whole of the social life the Bentons had in Chicago, gave them a farewell party. So did the office staff. "No company could have treated me better or given me a more splendid send-off," Benton informed his mother. "It was quite a contrast between the good wishes, sincere and genuine which I received from the broadminded men at L&T—and the nastiness at Batten's."

Of all the parting salutes, the one Benton cherished the most came from Dr. Ernst Mahler, the Vienna-born expert in cellulose chemistry who had invented both Kotex sanitary napkins and Kleenex and was the chairman of International Celucotton Products Company. The major consumer research survey Benton had recently completed for that company was in Dr. Mahler's mind at the exchange of farewell handshakes. "Young man," said he to Benton, "I hate to see you go. I consider you the world's greatest authority on the sanitary napkin." This remark was a diverting contrast to some observations Benton found in two letters waiting for him in New York upon his arrival, following a motor trip east with Helen.

The first letter was from his Aunt Mary, then in B'hamdoun,

Lebanon. She had been kept informed of her nephew's progress in Lord and Thomas, and of his move to New York. She knew little and cared less about advertising and she was perhaps the last person on earth who would be impressed had she been told that her nephew was "the world's greatest authority on the sanitary napkin." Yet when she heard through Elma that Benton was leaving Lord and Thomas to start an advertising agency of his own in New York, she wrote from B'hamdoun to congratulate him on his "courage in facing the challenge of a big city." She had something else on her mind. She wished him great success—and hoped his success would mean that he could take care of a matter she put to him as follows:

> Few things in my life have made me feel more deeply the reality of spiritual things as the reality of life itself in all its forms—great or small. I feel it keenly here in this little village, and in the little Benton School. Don't let's falter or waver in keeping this little school alive. It is tremendously worthwhile. I wish you could see it all and feel the devotion of this village to the memory of my parents'—your grandparents'—consecrated lives. That devotion inspires and fills the feeling of the people for the school and for our family. In being here I have felt in a very peculiar way as if I were representative of all of us. How often they say how much they wish other members of the family might come! Of no one more do they express the wish than of you, Billie, though they know of you only because of what Hattie and I have told them. Yet they look for your coming because you bear the Benton family name, your grandfather's name, and stand for the young generation.

The second letter awaiting Benton in New York was from his grandfather Daniel Webster Hixson, now eighty-six, living in Los Angeles, and in his own words "going strong." He warmed to his subject by observing that he had voted in "17 presidential elections," that the first vote was cast for Abraham Lincoln, and that he was now the last survivor in Co. C of the 303d Iowa Infantry. Then he came to his grandson's new venture. He had heard that Benton was "engaged in a big enterprise" and would be very busy until he got on a solid footing. He was not worried about the state of his grandson's soul. All he wanted to do was to strike a warning note about the state of his grandson's pocket, based on a half-forgotten experience from the past: "I think of the time when Ben Irien stood you and Dan on your heads and captured your two knives that your Uncle Ed had presented you with. Don't let anybody stand you on your head."

9

B&B

The idea of eventually "retiring from business" was fixed in Benton's mind even before Benton and Bowles had a single client signed up. When the firm was formed Bowles agreed to buy Benton's stock if Benton and Bowles prospered, so that Benton would be at liberty to "enter other fields." This was a verbal agreement, but Benton's confidence that Bowles would honor the pledge was one of the reasons why he chose Bowles as a fifty-fifty partner—though Benton was much farther advanced in the advertising business. Bowles later said that he did not hesitate to enter such an agreement because he felt the day would never come when Benton would want to leave business. "At that time," he recalled, "and for a long time afterward, I misjudged him completely, or rather, I misjudged the extent of the influence his mother had in shaping his fundamental outlook on life."

Benton and Bowles opened for business in a $6,200-a-year office at Forty-second Street and Lexington Avenue, on 15 July 1929. That week, the Wall Street indices reached a peak never regained until World War II. Only a handful of squint-eyed prophets could see that the stock market was headed for the great crash, and not even the dourest pessimists could begin to imagine what the Great Depression would be like. Benton himself later remarked that if he had had any idea that, three months after the firm of Benton and Bowles got under way, the American economy would seem to be about to expire, he might have lacked the courage to go into business on his own. "A man," said he, "is often fortunate because he can't foresee the future."

Ralph Starr Butler, the advertising manager for what had become General Foods, was a believer in the "young man" theory of business—even before the great crash forced other executives to look for sources of fresh ideas. In taking a chance on the combination of Benton and Bowles, he gave them two accounts, Hellman's Mayonnaise and Certo, a pectin extract used in making jellies. The advertising for each brand amounted to three to four hundred thousand dollars a year, and the commissions to Benton and Bowles were estimated at around one hundred thousand.

The immediate problem, however, was for the agency to finance a staff and stay alive until the firm received its first commissions. Benton had borrowed $30,000 from a bank, and in March 1930, shortly before the first commissions were due, the bank asked him for a financial statement. He produced one showing that Benton and Bowles was insolvent, even when all its secondhand furniture and fixtures were valued at full purchase price. The firm managed to pay off the loan in midsummer, but this was the low point in its financial history. It faced many problems after that, but the main problems were those incident to expansion.

It is beyond the purpose of this narrative to detail everything that happened at Benton and Bowles. It is enough to stress five key elements in the early success of the company, beginning with the fact that the economic crisis forced corporations to reexamine their advertising policies and to welcome new ideas. New ideas brought creative men to the fore in place of the old-line account executives. This was true not only of men like Benton and Bowles. It was true of other young men who had been originally trained as copywriters. Now they founded their own advertising agencies or were put in key positions in existing agencies—and they have continued to dominate the world of advertising to the present day.

A second element in the success of Benton and Bowles was Benton's introduction into New York of the consumer research surveys he had accidentally devised at Lord and Thomas in Chicago. The surveys, despite their rough shape, gave client prospects the hope of being more "scientific" in deciding how to sell and advertise in a market with drastically curtailed consumer purchasing power. Because of the shoestring financing of Benton and Bowles, there was no money to hire a staff to conduct the original surveys, and the foot work was largely done by Bill and Helen Benton and Judy Bowles. It was Benton who then translated the results of the interviews into charts and advertising plans to be presented to clients and prospects, with Bowles doing most of the creative work in the actual preparation of the advertising.

The surveys still make fascinating reading, as exemplified by one General Foods ordered when considering a merger with the National Biscuit Company. Since the survey reached no conclusions and made no recommendations, Benton titled it objectively: "Some Aspects of the Biscuit Business." "Some aspects" turned out to be a book-long report with two hundred charts, all of which made the point that the biscuit business was infinitely subtle, romantic, challenging. When General Foods backed away from the merger it was contemplating, Benton used the knowledge he had acquired about some aspects of the business to solicit the advertising accounts of both the National Biscuit Company and the Loose-Wiles Biscuit Company. He came close to getting the latter, but not close enough.

Special surveys made for Lehman Brothers brought the firm of Benton and Bowles the account of the Adolph Goebel Company, a manufacturer of prepared meats such as frankfurters, and the account of the Helena Rubinstein Cosmetic Company. But these were short-lived. The Goebel Company, caught in the depression, felt it could not afford to maintain its advertising. As for the other account, it had been secured while Lehman Brothers still controlled the company after Helena Rubinstein sold it to the public at the height of the boom. Then when the depression knocked down the price of its shares to a few cents, Madame Rubinstein turned around, bought back a controlling interest in the enterprise, kicked out the banker's representatives, and, for extra measure, dismissed Benton and Bowles as the advertising agent for the firm. To the loss of these two accounts originally secured through Lehman Brothers, there was added the loss of the account of the new National Union Radio Corporation, in which Lehman Brothers also had an interest. The loss in that case was due partly to the fact that the corporation was badly battered by the depression, and partly because of a corporate shakeup which brought in a new management with its own preferred advertising agency.

These were costly losses in time and energy in the early years of Benton and Bowles, when the short-handed partners could least afford wasted motions. But the losses were offset by gains in a different area. The fact that the vastly respected Paul Mazur of

Lehman Brothers was willing to use "youngsters" like Benton and Bowles to handle the advertising of companies in trouble, companies in which the bankers had a major interest, enhanced the standing of Benton and Bowles in the eyes of men such as Colby Chester, the head of General Foods. More about this later.

The surveys Benton introduced into the New York advertising world remained an eye-catching novelty for two or three years. They later dimmed in importance when Raymond Rubicam, the creative head of one of the most admired newer agencies of the day, thought of turning to the academic world for help. At Northwestern University on the edge of Chicago he found a young sociologist named George Gallup, who was perfecting techniques for polling public opinion. Rubicam engaged Gallup to conduct surveys for his agency, and the practice slowly spread to other agencies, altering the whole character of the advertising business. Benton, in retrospect, was critical of his own failure to think of turning to university-trained scholars. "My failure," he said, "seems all the more odd since I was quite literally born into the academic world. Yet it simply had never occurred to me that anyone at any university was working on any project of any kind that had even a remote bearing on what I was doing in business."

The third and fourth elements in the success of Benton and Bowles were closely related to the rise of the radio. Benton had learned in Chicago that the new medium, barely touched by the old advertising agencies, offered vast scope for inventive new advertising format. Aided by the sensational success of the "Amos 'n' Andy" show, he converted Bowles. Both were equal to the task of invention. In fact, once converted, Bowles became one of the most brilliantly imaginative men in the history of radio up to that time. So much so that Benton and Bowles soon emerged as the leader of the revolution in radio advertising, and in doing so came to dominate radio entertainment in the mid-1930s.

Benton, however, did not confine his thoughts only to the relationship between his agency and radio. In March 1930, at the request of Paul Mazur, he prepared a long memorandum on radio broadcasting in general, and the direction its development *should* take. It was crammed with suggestions which were radical at the time—and still are. Among others, Benton suggested that there should be different kinds of broadcasting networks specializing in different offerings. One, for example, would offer music all the time—an idea later expressed in FM radio, and in Benton's own subsequent invention of "subscription radio." He suggested that radio advertising should be sold as in magazines; the networks instead of the advertising agencies would do the programing and would sell advertising "spots" in the programs. This idea was eventually to find expression in "commercial" television in Great Britain, and increasingly in television in the United States. When these and other suggestions were presented to Paul Mazur back in March 1930, he pronounced them "sensational," and showed the Benton memorandum to David Sarnoff, the head of NBC-RCA. Nothing more was heard from Sarnoff on the subject. Yet one can trace from this memorandum Benton's interest, continuing to the present day, in trying to change the structure of radio (and later television) as an instrument of mass communication.

Precisely because the firm of Benton and Bowles was a laboratory for novel experiments, with a measure of failures as well as spectacular successes, it attracted some of the ablest young men then working in American advertising. Several left well-established positions with larger agencies in order to share the excitement at Benton and Bowles. They gave the firm a reputation for invention and versatility, both illustrated in the presentations made by the firm in bids for new business.

Many associates saw a fifth element in the early success of the agency in Benton's exceptional physical capacity to carry a heavy work load over many months, and his tenacity in pursuing any objective he set for himself. Like other young men on Madison Avenue, he dreamed of getting a *big* account—then defined as a million dollars a year or more in billings—at a single stroke. But the way he actually won his objectives was by nibbling off a small account from a large one serviced by a major agency, then expanding the nibble into biting off the whole account. His success in winning business away from old and large agencies—and his later success with other enterprises at which big companies had faltered or failed—lent credence to a theory he advanced:

Every great corporation is struggling with many failures buried down in its soft underbelly, failures which are waiting to be developed by enterprise and initiative, or failures waiting to be competed with by men who have initiative and original ideas. If I were again a young man, therefore, and if my aim was to get rich, I would look for the soft underbellies of the big corporations and begin to compete with them at that point. I am not talking about big corporations that have monopolies like the Commonwealth Edison Company. You don't compete with monopolies when you are a young man, even though you try to create and own them when you get older. But as a young man, I would look for the soft spots in the business structure of the great non-monopolistic corporations, and start my own business in one or another of these areas.

Nine months after Benton and Bowles had been launched, the firm moved into new quarters at 5 East Forty-fifth Street. The Great Depression was hourly cutting deeper into the life of the nation. Benton felt, however, that now that his agency was receiving its first commissions from its billings on the General Foods accounts—along with a small account through Bowles's connections with the Squibb Company—it had weathered the worst. At the same time, his thoughts about his personal life found expression in a letter he wrote to his mother on 31 March 1930:

This is my last day in my 20's. Quite a gripping thought.

I am wondering again about my choice of a business or profession. Advertising by no means completely satisfies me. It is too transitory, ephemeral, unsubstantial. But I am sure I far prefer it to the law, toward which you tried to head me. The law, it seems to me, is even less constructive. Certainly but few lawyers are really productive. The one advantage of the law is that it might have led into politics, which I am sure I would thoroughly enjoy.

Most of my thoughts about myself today, as in all days, are fixed on the future. Even in such thoughts I do not project myself far ahead. I think about "next year" often; seldom about "where do I go from here?" I believe our agency will be reasonably prosperous, perhaps very much so. My problem within a few years will very probably be to find men to bring into the firm who can buy me out and carry on the business. For such thoughts as I do direct to the distant future, five or ten years removed, revolve around my retiring from business with an income of $15,000 or $20,000 a year to devote myself to some other form of activity. Just what form, I can't decide, and the lack of a definite objective may slacken my pace.

Well—there's lots of time to decide. Maybe you'll get some
bright ideas—I haven't had time to think about the subject for
two years and probably won't for another two or five.

He had other things to think about beginning in July of that
year. First he learned from Helen that, if all went well, he would
have an heir in February 1931. "Hope to raise a big family," the
expectant father excitedly wrote Elma. At the same time, he expressed his concern that his mother might further impair her health
trying to guide Hosmer Hall through the economic depression which
drastically curtailed student enrollments in the school. "You ought
to plan on retiring by no later than the end of the school year
ahead," he observed. "Our business is now in sufficiently good shape
so that I can buy an annuity for you which will be ample for as long
as you live. You can give up the school any time you want to. You
have done so much for me, it's about time you let me look after you."
The advice and the offer, once again, were shelved at the receiving
end.

Meanwhile in anticipation of the birth of a child, the Bentons
moved into a more spacious apartment located on Ninth Street.
Here, among other things, Helen converted an extra room into an
office for her husband. The expected child, a son, was born on 13
February 1931, and the father's first reactions underlined his preoccupation with brand names—even in the case of the infant. Thus
to Elma:

> February 17, 1931
>
> No name has as yet been decided on, and we haven't talked
> about names much. Helen seems to favor the name Charles
> William, partly because it was father's name. I have absolutely
> put my foot down on having any Juniors in the family. In fact,
> I have decided that there are about fifteen good names, all of
> which are perfectly all right and none of which makes much
> difference. George, Ralph, Robert, Thomas, Henry—what
> difference do the names make anyway?

> March 5, 1931
>
> Do you know what lay behind the selection of father's name
> Charles? Was this a family name? Where did it come from
> anyway? Probably the William was taken from his father.
> Somehow Charles seems a hard name to handle. I don't like

Charlie very well and Charles sounds too darned dignified. Too
darn dignified for a seven pound mite of a human being.

Year after year dropped away, and still the father pondered the
question of names until at last, thirty-three years after Charles was
born, Benton appeared to have reached a definite conclusion about
at least a few things. "I am named after my grandfather, William,
whom I do not resemble," he wrote Charles seemingly out of the blue,
"because I take after my mother. You were named after your grandfather Charles William, whom you do not resemble, because you
take after your mother."

After the birth of Charles, despite the creation of an office in the
Ninth Street apartment, Benton generally arrived early in the
morning at Benton and Bowles, where a crush of middle-aged unemployed advertising men were applying for jobs, along with a
crush of bright young men fresh out of Harvard, Yale, and Princeton. Once he had moved through the gauntlet of their despair, he
would work steadily until 7:00 in the evening, mostly out of the
office. Arriving home, he would play briefly with Charles, then dine
alone with Helen. Promptly at 8:30 P.M. he retired to the office in
his apartment, where he dictated rapidly into an Ediphone a sustained stream of suggestions, comments, criticisms and complaints.
At 1:00 A.M. he stopped and went to bed. The only regular break in
this standard routine was between 7:30 P.M. on Saturday and 3:00
P.M. on Sunday, when he did not work.

During one of Benton's few dictating sessions in his Benton and
Bowles office, Edward V. Hale, a Yale classmate working at the
agency, pushed open Benton's office door and found him dictating
at top speed. Benton looked up at his friend, nodded, and continued
dictating—until Hale pointed a finger at him and at the Ediphone.
"Put down that lethal weapon!" he cried. The Ediphone, Benton
admitted, sometimes was a lethal weapon. It could plunge cutting
words into souls. Sometimes justice was on his side, sometimes on the
side of his victim. In any case, the secretaries who transcribed the
dictation and the office managers who routed the memos felt they
could tell at what hour of the night each memo had been dictated.
In the early evening his dictation tended to have an easy conversa-
tional tone and if meant to perform a surgical operation on an associate would first sedate him with injections of compliments and
thanks for small things. But as the night wore on and Benton began

to fight the clock in the face of unfinished work, the anesthetizing compliments grew less frequent, and, by midnight, vanished. He rarely disliked anyone personally, at least not for long. Yet his critical memos sometimes bore down painfully hard on the nerves of his associates.

The knowledgeable women he chose as his office managers— Bertha Tallman in Benton and Bowles days, and Anne Cronin today in his New York headquarters—sometimes stalled the routing of his more lethal memos until they were sure that his past-midnight sharpness was his firm conviction the next morning. In response to their questions, he occasionally softened or discarded a midnight assault.

Apart from the factor of weariness, the brusqueness which sometimes marked Benton's words to his associates may have been conditioned over the years by the manner of his correspondence with his mother. They could say sharply caustic things to each other without bringing into question their mutual devotion. This habit of mind made for moral fearlessness in Benton. But it also made for hurt feelings among business associates. Transposed later into a political context, it once led Benton's friend and adviser, Mrs. Anna Rosenberg (now Mrs. Paul Hoffman), to tell her plan to help Benton's political career. She would place in his Senate office a discriminating agent who would censor every syllable he spoke or wrote.

In early 1931, the deepening depression, a drought, and an encounter with Senator Robert M. La Follette, Jr., all stirred in Benton the memories of his own early poverty, the bleak Montana homestead, and the political loyalties of his grandfather Daniel Webster Hixson. He wrote his grandfather about the meeting with Senator La Follette, and the grandfather in turn wrote back to say how pleased he was that Bill had come to know the son of "Fighting Bob" Sr. "That is the winning crowd if this country is to continue," he said. "Big business can't do anything about the economic crisis. Certainly big business and the newspapers hollering that everything is all right won't do it. Big business forced the money out of the pockets of the masses and now they complain of over-production because people can't buy. What will the harvest be? I fear very troublous times ahead."

Other signs of the times were visible to Benton personally when in the early summer of 1931 he went to New Haven in early June for the decennial reunion of his Yale class. Of an original 250 members in Yale '21, less than 60 members attended the reunion—a commentary on the fact that few could afford the cost of a trip to New Haven. Significantly, too, unlike former reunions, there were no longer any clusters around the heroes of undergraduate days or those who had made "killings" in stocks and bonds or those who had gone to work for the most prestigious banks and corporations. The star of this reunion of Yale '21 was Robert Maynard Hutchins, Benton's debating teammate at Yale. In the decade that had passed, Hutchins had taught for a year and a half in a preparatory school, married Maude Phelps McVeigh, a talented artist, returned to New Haven at age twenty-three to become the secretary of the Yale Corporation while completing law school. He was subsequently appointed to the law faculty and went on to become the youngest dean in the history of Yale's law school. Then in 1929, at the age of thirty, he became the president of the University of Chicago. By 1930, he was presiding over the launching of the "New Plan," representing a basic change in the content, organization, and administration of undergraduate education. With the help of his friend, Professor Mortimer Adler, whom he had brought to Chicago from Columbia, he was also beginning his march toward a goal that was nothing less than a sweeping revolution in American higher learning.

At the decennial reunion of Yale '21, Benton's estimate of Hutchins had little to do with the latter's growing impact on the world of higher education. What interested him far more was the fact that Hutchins was the only member of the class who had attained national renown far beyond the limited kind attained by, for example, the theatrical producer Jed Harris. It was already being said of Hutchins that he was one among several young men under forty who had "a good chance of being President of the United States some day."

Benton himself was on the threshold of a major development in his own line of business. It began with an error of judgment General Foods had made at the time it bought Hellman's Mayonnaise. Mayonnaise, a perishable product, was distributed by truck, and the distributors were small locally owned and locally run businesses. General Foods, however, worked to develop a direct-to-store truck delivery system, modeled on the Standard Brands system used to deliver Fleischman's Yeast. To this end, the company bought the small distributors along with Hellman's Mayonnaise. Instead of benefiting from the skilled management of local distributors, therefore, it now had to rely on salaried employees. Also, as Benton saw clearly because he used to ride the delivery trucks in Brooklyn as part of his "surveys," the whole distribution system was disintegrating. He thus began to write strong reports about the whole matter, and the reports soon reached Colby Chester of General Foods and his top associates.

Shocked by what they read, they were prodded into making independent inquiries which massively confirmed the truth of what Benton had to say. Then they got in touch with the Gold Dust Corporation, the owner of Best Foods. While Hellman's was the largest distributor of mayonnaise east of the Mississippi, Best Foods was an even larger distributor of the product in the extensive, salad-eating region from Kansas City west to California. Colby Chester and his associates at General Foods made a deal whereby they turned over the Hellman business to the Gold Dust subsidiary, Best Foods, for a 30 percent stock interest in the latter company.

Benton, who had set in motion the forces which produced this result, had reason to be alarmed by his own effectiveness. There was a clear and present danger that the take-over would mean that Benton and Bowles would lose the Hellman account. Benton hastily called on Colby Chester to explain the predicament, and the latter did more than just sympathize with the young man. Chester called on Randolph Catlin, president of the Gold Dust Corporation, and urged that Benton and Bowles be retained as the advertising agency for Hellman's after its sale to Best Foods. Catlin replied: "You know a lot more about advertising than we do and have had much more experience with it than we have. If you recommend Benton and Bowles, we'll take them as our agency and give them the entire account of Best Foods." This included Nucoa, the leading oleomargarine, then made out of coconut oil. Following his meeting with Catlin, Chester happily called Benton and told him to go over to Best Foods and pick up what was lying in wait for him. This was the only piece of business Benton and Bowles ever got through a middleman. But the agency did so well with it that Jay Gould, the president of Best Foods, became an enthusiastic supporter of Benton and Bowles, and the enthusiasm spread throughout the Gold Dust corporate structure—and back into General Foods. Gold Dust later gave the advertising agency the account for the Standard Milling Company, the third largest flour company in America. All told, Best Foods and other Gold Dust products amounted to two million dollars in billings in addition to the General Foods Certo account.

The second step in the new development in Benton and Bowles business was foreshadowed in September 1931 when Colby Chester entrusted Benton with a highly sensitive special mission. General Foods was disturbed by the impact of chain store private brands on its own brand-name products, such as Maxwell House Coffee, Minute Tapioca, Walter Baker's Chocolate, Post Toasties, Log Cabin Syrup, and so on. Many of these products in predepression days had been sold at wide profit margins on the strength of demand created by their enormous advertising. But as the depression grew worse, chain stores such as A&P hammered away much harder with their private brands at greatly reduced prices. The first reaction of brand-name manufacturers was to maintain or even increase advertising appropriations, but as the inroads of the private brands on the consumer market grew, Colby Chester asked Benton to visit the heads of the fifteen largest manufacturer-advertisers in the grocery field. He was to get them to agree to a meeting to discuss their common problem of chain store competition. Many of the manufacturer-advertisers Benton was to visit did not know each other. They had never thought of themselves as an "industry" selling through the grocery trade. The flour-milling industry had its trade association, the soap and canning industries had theirs, but there was no overarching general group.

Benton's assignment meant four weeks of travel around the country, featuring among other things the "thrill" of a twenty-five-hour transcontinental flight from Chicago to San Francisco. These flights were but two years old and were still considered "dangerous." But as Benton wrote to his mother afterwards: "I expect to die young, and shall always feel that the exhilarating life I have led is well worth the shortened years. No form of dullness could be of value merely because of added longevity. To be worried is to be active. All the creators in life have spent most of their time worrying." He was particularly pleased that the trip to the Pacific coast, his first by any mode of transport, gave him a chance to bring gifts to his grandfather, to his aunt, and to other kinsmen. He also brought some knowledge back with him which had thus far escaped the notice of most easterners. In California, he saw his first super-

market, his first pineboard drugstore, his first drive-in restaurant—
merchandising innovations which were to sweep from California
eastward to the Atlantic coast.

In discharging his mission for Colby Chester, Benton brought
the fifteen leaders of brand-name grocery items together for two
meetings and acted as general secretary of the group. From Benton's standpoint, the results of the discussions were less important
than the fact that Chester, by entrusting the mission to him, was
again emphasizing his high regard for the advertising firm. There
could be a tangible payoff in future accounts for Benton and
Bowles, a prospect which materialized on Benton's thirty-second
birthday when he was asked to come to the General Foods office to
meet with Ralph Butler, the advertising manager, and Clarence
Francis, the sales manager.

The two men put a question to Benton. They were prepared to
offer him roughly half of the General Foods billings then being
handled by Erwin, Wasey. But did he think Benton and Bowles could
do justice to an influx of business which would almost treble the
size of their agency? The billings included Maxwell House Coffee,
Walter Baker's Chocolate, and Post Toasties. The other half of
the General Food billings, except for the Certo account which Benton and Bowles already had, was then in the hands of Young and
Rubicam. When Benton candidly answered that he didn't think his
agency was ready as yet to do justice to all of the Erwin, Wasey
accounts, Butler and Francis advanced an alternate plan, involving
Atherton Hobler.

Hobler had a 20 percent partnership interest in Erwin, Wasey,
besides being the agency's principal representative on the General
Foods account. If Hobler were brought into Benton and Bowles as
a partner on mutually satisfactory terms, the young agency might
be strong enough to handle all the new business in prospect. Hobler,
an older and very experienced man, would bring many stabilizing
elements to Benton and Bowles. At the same time, he could do a
better job servicing the General Foods accounts he was handling
at Erwin, Wasey, by being emancipated from the troubles he was
having with his two senior partners in the latter agency. Saying
all this, Butler and Francis made one more point clear to Benton.
If he and Bowles balked at the proposal to make Hobler a partner,
Benton and Bowles would still get half of the General Foods business under discussion, but Francis and Butler were prepared to

marry Hobler to some other agency, with a "dowry" of the other half of Erwin, Wasey's five million dollars in General Foods billings. Thus Butler and Francis put all their cards on the table. Subsequently, after visits with Hobler, Benton responded favorably, as did Bowles ; a deal was consummated and Hobler joined Benton and Bowles with a full one-third partnership.

During the partnership negotiations, Hobler was told nothing about Benton's hopeful plan to retire from the advertising business some day, or of his verbal agreement with Bowles in 1929 about buying him out when the time for retirement had arrived. Should Benton have told him during the negotiations, instead of waiting until December 1934? The question was to become the subject of a major dispute between Benton and Hobler. In 1934 Hobler was sharply critical of Benton's lack of çandor back in the spring of 1932, and he had a very strong case. On the other side, however, there were respectable reasons why Benton could not reveal his future hopes when he was negotiating the partnership arrangement. He barely knew Hobler at the time. Moreover, he faced in him a potential rival at General Foods. If he revealed that he was thinking of retiring some day from Benton and Bowles he would undermine the stability of the firm's existing relations with General Foods. Further, how could he say with certainty that his personal plans for the future were more than the hopeful dreams of a young man who had just turned thirty-two? How could he know, amid a deepening depression, that he would in fact reach a point where he could make those hopeful dreams come true? Whether he could make the decision to retire rested in large part on the future stability of the firm, and this he could not prejudge.

Soon after Hobler joined Benton and Bowles and the five million dollars in additional General Foods billings was placed in the hands of the firm, the partners jointly made a startling recommendation to General Foods: that its advertising appropriation on Maxwell House Coffee be greatly reduced—along with the price of the product—in order to make the price more competitive with the growing private brands of the chain stores. They recommended that most of the reduced budget be channeled into the relatively new medium of radio. General Foods accepted the advice, which was carried out with spectacular results for all parties concerned.

For Maxwell House, Benton and Bowles launched a pioneering full-hour radio show, "The Maxwell House Show Boat." It quickly

CAVALIERS

Benton's maternal grandparents, Daniel Webster Hixson and Helen Orr Hixson, with their son Edwin, about 1875.

PURITANS

Benton's paternal grandparents and their children at Hubbardston, Massachusetts, in 1869. *From left:* Charles (Benton's father), Harriet (Aunt Hattie), Reverend William Austin Benton, Edwin, Loanza Goulding Benton, Mary, and Henry.

FATHER
Professor Charles William
Benton, about 1900

Billie Benton, about five years old

MOTHER
Elma Hixson Benton in 1906

CHOIRBOY

Benton, *at left of second row*, with the Holy Trinity Choir

CAPTAIN

Benton, *front row center*, as captain of a Shattuck School scrub football team

The Montana homestead about 1915. Beside the porch is the hogshead in which young Benton dragged water by stoneboat from a spring.

Billie, *left,* and his brother Dan

Benton in his "crack squad" uniform at Shattuck

Benton's mother and his wife, with
young Charles, in Honolulu in 1936.

The William Benton family near the end of his Senate days. *From left:*
Louise, Charles, John, Mrs. Benton, Senator Benton, and Helen.

Benton dictating in the library of his home in Southport in 1943. A colleague once challenged him to "put down that lethal weapon." (Photograph by Herbert Gehr, LIFE Magazine, © Time Inc.)

The Bentons and their son John in Moscow, 1955

became the greatest radio hit since "Amos 'n' Andy," and won an important place in the history of radio advertising because of its many innovations, now commonplace. At the time, however, they were bold inventive strokes. They included the first use of live audiences and the first cueing of audiences with placards reading "LAUGH" or "APPLAUD." The "commercials" were also something new. Previously, during "a pause for commercial announcement," a voice "from the sponsor" would read a few paragraphs of advertising. "Show Boat" changed this. The actors drank coffee, smacked their lips, and tinkled their cups to give listening audiences around the country an acoustical substitute for what their eyes could not see. This device to enliven the commercials culminated in the "singing commercial." Within a year after the "Maxwell House Show Boat" went on the air, sales of Maxwell House coffee increased by 85 percent. The show itself for several years held the first place in the ranking of radio programs, providing the model for two other hit shows which Benton and Bowles launched—Fred Allen's "Town Hall Tonight," and the "Palmolive Beauty Box." These three, all going simultaneously when Benton retired from the advertising business, were three of radio's four shows with the largest audiences.

While there were bright developments for Benton in his business interests, in 1932 there were successive sorrows in his family life. He and Helen wanted more children, but there had been a miscarriage. The consequences were not known to them at the time, but no children other than Charles would be born to them. Their two daughters and younger son would come through adoption.

Also in 1932 Benton's grandfather Daniel Hixson died in Los Angeles. The last letters of this Civil War veteran who had voted for Abraham Lincoln were volleys of verbal cannonballs at another Republican president. In Hixson's impassioned view, Herbert Hoover's floundering response to the Great Depression had left "the defenses of the Federal Union wide open to the destructive gallop of the Four Horsemen of the Apocalypse." On that embattled note the old man breathed his last. Fifteen hundred dollars represented what was left of the original Orr estate that had come under his own mismanagement when his wife inherited it. Of his three children, who divided the estate, Edwin in Seattle and Capitola in Los Angeles could not afford the trip to Burlington, Iowa, where he was to be buried. Elma, closer by in Saint Louis, arranged the last rites.

Out of her $500 share of the estate, she bought Benton a wrist watch—his first—as a posthumous remembrance of his grandfather.

Late in 1932 it seemed that Elma herself would be taken away by death when she suffered an acute heart attack. Benton flew to Saint Louis to impose his will on her as decisively as she had once imposed hers on him when he refused to go back to Shattuck. His object was to get his mother "out of school." He told her that the earnings of Benton and Bowles, which had doubled over what they were in 1931, enabled him to create a fund for her use. She could do what she liked with her own savings. But the fund itself, based on 10 percent of his own Benton and Bowles stock, would produce enough dividends to keep her in comfort and build up a sizable estate at the same time. Should the dividend payment drop, he would make up the difference from his own pocket. She must swallow her pride and accept the arrangement. She was making a vice out of her brave and desperate attempts to keep a costly institution like Hosmer Hall going when the depression made it impossible for formerly affluent parents to send their girls to expensive schools. She could not create sources of tuition herself. She was digging her own grave by attempting the impossible. Her health was in a perilous condition, and she owed it to herself and to the school to take a year's leave of absence to regain her strength and to decide if she ever wanted to return to Hosmer Hall.

Elma was still full of fight, but this time it was her son's will that prevailed. When his mother was well enough to move about, he sent her to Florida for the winter. In the spring he brought her back to New York for a stay before she sailed to meet Aunt Mary Benton in Majorca, then on with Mary to Spain and England. Benton had already begun quietly to contribute to the support of Aunt Mary, whose eyesight was failing, and the European trip was his gift to her as well as to his mother. The two ex-teachers, each with her own physical affliction, still made perfect traveling companions because of the lively intellectual interests they shared. It was on this trip that Elma decided not to return to Hosmer Hall.[1]

Meanwhile, there had been the 1932 presidential victory of

---

[1]What she had meant to the depression-plagued school became clear after she resigned. The trustees in 1935 voted to close the doors of Hosmer Hall for good, and they gave its very valuable property and installations to Washington University in Saint Louis.

Franklin D. Roosevelt, the final collapse of the old order, Roosevelt's inauguration, and the advent of the New Deal and its reforms. Benton still regarded himself as a "political independent," but just as he had voted for Davis and Smith in 1924 and 1928, he had voted for Roosevelt in 1932. His reports to his mother in Europe were full of enthusiasm for Roosevelt's experiments in trying to "rebuild the social system on a saner, more just basis." The reports were also full of predictions that Roosevelt's almost universal popularity and support would be short-lived. "Within another month or six weeks," Benton observed to Elma in a note of 1 September 1933, "we will begin to see Roosevelt splattered by the mud that will be hurled at him plentifully and vigorously." His historical importance "is likely to be buried under a lot of criticism, trouble and general commotion."

Indeed Benton's principal clients at Benton and Bowles would be at the forefront of the "criticism, trouble and general commotion" in opposition to Roosevelt and the New Deal.

Elma's replies from Europe were in a different vein. After years of toil, skimping, and saving in order to meet family needs, she found it hard to believe that her "extravagant" son had really placed her on easy street. It seemed all the more improbable when she contrasted her own leisurely trip through Europe with the mental pictures she carried with her of the depression-stricken scenes she had left behind in the United States and saw duplicated in the poverty of Spain and England. More, it seemed downright immoral that her son had arranged matters with his bank so that his mother in Europe could automatically draw from it any amount of money she wanted. The prudent and moral thing for her would be to continue, as before, to watch her nickels, else she would be left destitute when "Billie the Provider" had his inevitable great fall.

This sense of impending financial doom grew more acute with each succeeding letter to her son. He could only calm her down by outshouting her:

December 3, 1933

The thought of your worrying about the sums of money I have placed at your disposal absolutely makes me sick at heart. If there is one thing above everything else which I want to do, and which gives me pleasure in my business, it is the feeling that you can live in real comfort, on a scale far better than you ever expected. I want you to stay at better hotels, to entertain more freely, to see if you can figure out ways to double the amount of money you're spending. If you can do that comfortably and pleasantly, I'll take more pleasure out of it than almost anything else. And I'll feel better about the results which have come to me personally in the building of this business.

December 15, 1933

What the devil am I doing all this work for anyway? Why should I work nights and weekends in a blue fever in an effort to keep our business successful and growing—and in doing all this really be making a tremendous sum of money, tremendous at least judged by any standard in the Benton family heretofore—why should I be doing this, I repeat, with you worrying about $50 and living on an average expenditure of about $125 a month? It turns my blood cold to think of your denying yourself anything, when I have repeatedly begged you to take full advantage of what I have arranged for you financially. I am sacrificing nothing. Why, then, do you insist on denying me the right to find some pleasure in my work because that work provides the means for making life more pleasurable for you?

The "tremendous sum of money" Benton alluded to, grew out of a doubling in 1933 of Benton and Bowles earnings of 1932—which in turn were double what they had been in 1931. For in addition to its new accounts with Best Foods and General Foods, it had enlarged its standing with Bristol Myers by securing from that source the Sal Hepatica account in addition to the previously secured account for Peterman's Insecticide. Many other companies offered their accounts to Benton and Bowles only to be rejected because of a policy that was then unique in American advertising. Benton and Bowles chose to concentrate on a few food and drug accounts whose products had a market even in a depression and which promised high average billings per client. Benton astonished a U.S. Steel representative by turning down his account, saying, "Your company looks big on Wall Street, but Bristol Myers looks a lot bigger to me." His words had a flippant ring, but Benton and his partners knew that high-quality advertising made little difference to U.S. Steel, but was a life and death matter to Bristol Myers. If the latter company grew and prospered because effective advertising had been prepared for it by Benton and Bowles, then the agency would grow and prosper proportionately.

An accumulation of detailed knowledge about the food and drug business, moreover, was the equivalent of money in the bank for the Benton and Bowles agency. It could be drawn on at will, whereas many small new accounts in many fields would have meant time and energy lost in learning the ABCs of each product; also, by limiting itself to a few advertisers in the same general area of business, Benton and Bowles would not need a large staff. It could offer financial inducements that could attract to the agency's relatively small staff some of the most talented men in American advertising.

The place even attracted—for a different reason—no less a figure than Sinclair Lewis, who applied for a job with the firm as a $100-a-week copywriter. Benton was delighted to meet an author who by now had published *Main Street, Elmer Gantry,* and *Arrowsmith.* But he assumed that Lewis had in mind writing a book on the advertising business, and he said no to Lewis's job application. "I don't want to be the Babbitt or Gantry of your next work," Benton explained. The relationship between Lewis and Benton, however, did not end there.

By the end of 1933 the organization of Benton and Bowles was as follows: Benton was president while Bowles and Hobler were vice-presidents. Benton's newly acquired "first assistant" was James Adams, now a senior partner in Lazard Frères. His "second assistant" was Ted Bates, who was brought over from BBD&O when Benton and Bowles got rolling. The Benton and Bowles copy department was under Walter O'Meara who had left the Chicago office of J. Walter Thompson when Benton had spotted his ads and sought him out. O'Meara had sold his Chicago home at a loss in order to join in the excitement at Benton and Bowles. He subsequently became the highest-paid copywriter in America, and a distinguished historian and novelist on the side. There was also William Baker from BBD&O, and Robert Lusk, who had been the advertising manager of Macy's. Both men were to have successful careers in advertising, with Baker, and later Lusk, becoming president of Benton and Bowles, both men serving with Hobler, who became chairman of the board.

All these men fitted in well with Benton and Bowles's unique policy of concentrating on a handful of food and drug accounts. What little danger that policy entailed was removed a day before Thanksgiving in 1933. The previous March, Bayard Colgate, who had assumed the presidency of the Colgate-Palmolive-Peet Company, brought "the camel's nose of Benton and Bowles into the tent" by recommending the agency to E. H. Little, then executive vice-president and sales manager. Ed Little gave Benton and Bowles a new account, Cashmere Bouquet Soap, and Benton worked to make it a wedge that would open the way to other accounts. This meant months of special surveys, presentations, letters, telephone calls, and many evenings with Colgate-Palmolive executives. It also meant gnawing questions about the wisdom of concentrating so much time and sales work on just one company, without assurance that anything would come of the effort.

But the day before Thanksgiving, Benton, Bowles, and Hobler were called to Chicago by Colgate-Palmolive-Peet. They were given the accounts for Palmolive Soap, Super Suds, Octagon, Crystal White, and Peet's Granulated—about two-thirds of the company's total billings. Added to Cashmere Bouquet, they now had all the company's soap business. The drug products such as Colgate's Ribbon Dental Cream and Colgate Shaving Cream were still in the hands of Young and Rubicam. Since one-half of all General Foods billings were also still in the hands of Young and Rubicam, Benton and Bowles split with its competitor two of the largest advertising accounts in the country. It would not be long before the case would be altered, for Benton and Bowles soon picked up the drug accounts of Colgate-Palmolive-Peet when that company became the only big-time advertiser to entrust the advertising for all of its many products to one agency. The agency's size doubled once more.

In writing to his mother about these developments, Benton said:

> I remember your distress when I went into the advertising business, and your low opinion of Palmolive soap. But now that you as a stockholder in Benton & Bowles are going to prosper with us, perhaps you will be a bit more forgiving about Palmolive soap. Anyway, for your personal use you can choose any one of the many other soaps made by Colgate-Palmolive-Peet.
>
> This new account not only tremendously increases our volume and our profit but also gives us a far more stable business. No business is ever too secure which relies largely on the favor of one manufacturer. But today we have a splendid spread be-

cause our business at the top becomes divided between two large advertisers, with about 20 per cent or 25 per cent of our business spread among four other clients.

Then Benton informed his two partners and other principal associates that he was nearing the point of retiring from business. His associates did not take him seriously, even though he gave them a memorandum stating his intentions and terms. As Bowles was to write him seven years later: "Hobe [Hobler] and I didn't really think that you would leave. I knew that someday you intended to leave the business, but I didn't think it would come so soon, and particularly not at that time, and I am sure that Hobe had no real idea that you had any such plan. He had a strong suspicion, in fact, that what you really wanted was a larger share of the business." For the moment, it was felt that what Benton needed was a good long vacation, after which he would return refreshed to the field of advertising. Yet even as this was being considered, complications set in which slowed down for more than a year the timing of the vacation— and Benton's plans to leave the agency.

It was plain to Benton that what he planned for himself depended in part on a growth in Bowles's capacity to join Hobler in assuming the leadership of Benton and Bowles. Bowles had concentrated on the "creative end" of the agency, while the actual management had devolved upon Benton. "It was Bill," recalled Walter O'Meara, "with all his energy, honesty, imagination, and tactlessness, who was always the fall guy whenever a rough decision had to be made."

Bowles's powers of leadership, like much else about him, were to flower, especially after his first marriage came to an end and he was remarried to Dorothy Stebbins of Boston, a Vassar graduate who was keenly interested in social service work. But at the time Benton first began to talk seriously about getting out of Benton and Bowles, Bowles still seemed unformed. In fact, his long absences from the firm for reasons of health made it impossible for the Bentons to pursue their plans for a vacation in Europe in 1934.

There was a second complication. If Benton was to get out of the firm, Bowles and Hobler had to gain confidence in their own powers and in the talents of their many gifted associates who were in the process of expanding their own responsibilities. These associates, in turn, had to know that, even without Benton around, their own continued association with Benton and Bowles promised them a secure and personally profitable relationship. The clients also had to be persuaded that the firm was so solid and versatile that the removal of Benton from the picture would not affect its topflight performances in boosting sales by the special touch the agency brought to the different advertising media.

Bowles, for example, had become a master of the "situation copy" used in comic strips to advertise Colgate toothpaste. Walter O'Meara and a collaborator, Maitland Jones, invented the radio soap opera "Young Doctor Malone" to promote the sale of Post Bran Flakes. It was O'Meara who also came up with the idea of the radio soap opera "Portia Faces Life" to promote a Colgate product that was in trouble from the standpoint of sales. These talents, plus those which made the "Maxwell House Show Boat," Fred Allen's "Town Hall Tonight," and the "Palmolive Beauty Box" three of the four most popular radio programs on the air, would not be removed if Benton left the scene. Indeed, it would be argued that by the departure of Benton, with all his impatient ferment, the company could gain more for the long haul from the aura of stability and permanence that enveloped a man like Atherton Hobler. Benton and Bowles had become almost overnight the largest single-office advertising agency in the world, and in 1936 it was to rank sixth in total billings after the old-line agencies with branch offices in Chicago, San Francisco, London, Montreal, and so on.

Benton's share of the profits anticipated for 1935 would give him a year's income of more than $250,000, with as much or more in prospect for 1936. Few Americans had any such earnings during the depression. Benton's income warranted the decision he and Helen made in 1934 to buy a country place in Southport, Connecticut, in anticipation of a more leisurely life. A contrast to the life they looked forward to living could be found in two of Reginald Marsh's paintings which they were to buy at $750 apiece in the course of furnishing their home. One would be *Coney Island Beach 1935;* the other, *Marines in Central Park.* Marsh's work already was hanging in fifteen of the largest museums in the country, but Benton was surprised to learn that he, personally, was the first "private collector" ever to buy one. Why no one else? "The paintings are too shocking," Marsh explained. "They remind people of what they see in Macy's and on 14th Street and in the subways. They aren't pleasant on the walls. But just wait until they are old-fashioned. Wait until they do not remind the owners of the current scene. Then they will be popular. When they are old-fashioned like Daumier and Hogarth—people will want them and will buy them."

At a later date Marsh came out to Southport to paint portraits of the Benton children, and remarked to Benton: "Do you know that the WPA is giving $100 a month to artists and that they can paint anything they want? Sometimes I wish I could get a deal like that." To which Benton replied: "Go ahead. I'll be your WPA. Paint anything you want for me and bring it in, once a month and I'll give you $100 for it." On this basis, some twenty Marsh paintings were delivered to Benton in a three-year period.

Still later, after Marsh's death, his lawyer suggested a partnership between Benton and Marsh's widow, Felicia. Benton agreed to purchase half the paintings remaining in Marsh's estate, and for $18,750 he acquired hundreds of Marsh works. While alive, Marsh never earned more than $5,000 a year from his work as a painter, though he augmented his income as much again by teaching at the Art Students League. Yet he was prophetic about the value his work would acquire after his death when the realistic people he chose to portray were no longer part of the live daily experience of prospective buyers of works of art. Benton's Marsh collection is today probably worth a million dollars or more. He never thought of it as an "investment," but found pleasure in giving away Marsh paintings to museums or the philanthropies in which he was interested.

Though it anticipates the future, this is the place to add a word about how another continuing friendship from the past led to another unanticipated financial gain. The person involved was William Joyce, who had been a fellow trainee with Benton in the National City Bank. Bill Joyce and his brother Tom had eventually returned to their home in Pasadena, California, but Benton over the years had kept in touch with them. In July 1935 on a business trip to the west coast, he called on Bill Joyce and persuaded him to come along on a weekend holiday in Mexico. Joyce was flat broke, and Benton played host to him. In Mexico, among other things, they talked about a company Joyce was trying to develop to manufacture a new style of casual shoes for women. The venture could succeed with very little added capital, but the depression made it difficult to raise. In fact, said Joyce, he had come to Mexico only in the hope of being able to extract $5,000 from his host for investment in the shoe company. The investment was made. The Joyce Shoe Company, refinanced with Benton as its second largest stockholder, took root and flourished. Ten years later, Benton sold his stock in it for $125,000.

At the end of 1934, when Benton and Bowles, following through on the soap business it secured from Colgate-Palmolive, acquired the drug business as well, Benton again formally notified his partners that he wanted to sell out and leave Benton and Bowles within the next year. Bowles and Hobler again vigorously protested, saying that the firm would fall apart if he left. Just as vigorously, Benton protested that nothing of the sort would happen. But largely at Hobler's insistence, he agreed to an experimental four months' absence to see what would happen while he was away. E. H. Little of Colgate-Palmolive agreed to the proposed absence, but he wanted Benton to defer his departure in order to work on a campaign for Colgate's toothpaste. Benton pitched in and helped to develop one which had its origins in a casual chat with Atherton Hobler. Hobler suggested adopting an idea in Listerine advertisements about bad breath. In the adopted form, it came out that Colgate Ribbon Dental Cream not only cleaned your teeth but freshened your breath. The campaign based on this idea was to run for at least twenty years and carry Colgate to the biggest sales in the history of toothpaste, at better than $50 million a year.

When everything had been prepared for this long-lived advertising campaign, Bill and Helen left for Europe in the spring of 1935, where they joined Elma, and the three of them went on to the Middle East and paid a sentimental visit to the Benton School at B'hamdoun. Here, as Aunt Mary had prophesied back in 1929, Benton was royally received by the villagers as the grandson of the man who had saved their town during its hour of peril in 1860. The Bentons then returned to Italy, where Elma was to remain for several months to study Italian. Bill and Helen went on together for three weeks in Paris and another three in London.

It was a far different Europe from the one Benton had seen twenty-one years before. His observations about it appear in a memorandum he wrote in April aboard the ship taking him home from England, a memorandum intended for his clients. The salient point in it was his conviction that Europe was rushing pell-mell toward another war. Benton had heard much talk in United States business circles that Hitler's intentions were peaceful; that even if he was bent on war, he couldn't wage it because of his lack of strategic materials and an unfavorable balance of trade; that the

French, behind their Maginot line, were invulnerable; that the British had a knack for "secret diplomacy" which would rescue Europe at the last moment from impending disaster. To Benton now, all this was nonsense.

The French people are riven from within. They almost universally believe their precarious and shaky government to be corrupt, and the belief cuts deep into their willingness to sacrifice for France itself. . . . The English traditionally hope for the best, play for time and postponement after postponement, expecting somehow by avoiding unpleasant reality as long as possible to muddle through. . . . So Hitler takes advantage of the internal weaknesses of his erstwhile enemies. . . . Give the German factories and the German army two more years of day and night work and without doubt Germany will again be the most powerful country in Europe.

It is a mistake, I believe, to attach too much importance to the financial situation as a deterrent to war. We are likely to forget that Germany between 1914–18 fought four years without real financial power, without much outside financing. Yes, and with very inadequate supplies of raw materials and food. "Don't be fooled by the German trade balances," the purser on our Hamburg-American ship told me. "Every ship going into Germany groans and staggers under its load of war materials—zinc, copper, and other supplies not produced in Germany—1,500 tons of copper on my last ship from San Francisco—and this heavy importing is throwing the trade balances out of line."

Europe is indeed like unto a powder box with fuses running out in all directions, surrounded by small boys playing with matches. It is my feeling that with war in Europe will come a speed-up of Socialism and Communism. Even under present conditions of peace, all through the world capitalism is on the defensive and almost with its back to the wall. In time of war, remember, centuries of change can be packed into a year or two. What happens in Europe will throw up in the United States major political issues to a degree and with a speed beyond any we have known.

There was but one note in the memorandum which the future did not bear out. "I believe," said Benton in conclusion, "that America will keep out of the war." Why? His answer had in it the echo of the disillusioned post-1918 idealist who believed that America got into World War I for no valid reason whatever. "We will keep out of the war," he explained, "because we will turn a deaf ear to foreign propaganda, to slogans about freedom of the seas and American property rights." Benton would learn better after he passed through his America-First Committee days—and the shock of Pearl Harbor—and began to understand America's place in the world as clearly as he understood the Europe he saw in the spring of 1935.

10

Disengagement

Despite the forebodings of his partners, Benton and Bowles ran smoothly while Benton was away. On his return, between work on new advertising campaigns, a drawn-out and painful round of negotiations began in earnest around his determination to quit the firm. Bowles was the man in the middle. He could not forget the verbal agreement of 1929—that Benton could quit with a good price for his stock when he thought the time had come. Bowles could not forget that they had started the business 'together and had lived through its early problems, and that Benton had several times given due notice of his intention to leave. At the same time, Bowles had an obligation to Hobler, who, when he became the third partner in 1932, was unaware of the hopeful boyish understanding of 1929 between the two original partners. Bowles could not expect Hobler and other associates to look with favor on too liberal a settlement for Benton's stock. The cost of retiring it would be a heavy charge on the future earnings of the firm even if Benton and Bowles survived Benton's exit.

In the end, subject to a number of conditions, the matter was resolved in Benton's favor, almost solely because of Bowles's firm stand. He said if Benton wanted to leave he had a right to do so even if the firm did blow up—which he did not anticipate. He never tried to back away from his original commitment to buy Benton out. Another partner, less strict in his code of personal honor, might have told Benton that the time was not yet and that the risk was too great. Benton himself later said that he was not sure that any other friend he ever had would have so scrupulously lived up to the original oral agreement he made with Bowles.

On 30 December 1935, Benton turned back all his stock to the firm. He had not publicly resigned, nor had all the fears ebbed that if he left the agency might as well write its epitaph. Now the Bentons went to Nassau for two months on another experimental absence. Again everything went smoothly while he was away, though some potentially explosive client-agency relationships needed handling with the utmost care when he returned. In any case, on 1 April 1936, his thirty-sixth birthday, his resignation from Benton and Bowles became official. Twelve days later a memo announced the event to the office staff. A release to the trade papers went out the same day, stressing that Benton was giving up advertising "in order to devote his energies to interests outside the advertising agency field." It added some further details. Bowles had become chairman of the board, Atherton Hobler was president, and all the other officers—Walter O'Meara, James Adams, Ted Bates, Robert Lusk, and William Baker—remained in their vice-presidential posts.

The release was soon picked up by the New York metropolitan press and by the wire services, and traveled the length of the country in the form of a "gee-whiz"—though apocryphal—story. When Benton graduated from Yale in 1921, went the story, he said he was going to "make a million dollars" in business by the time he was thirty-five. Then he would "retire." Now, despite the Great Depression, he had achieved his million-dollar-goal at age thirty-six. And now he was quitting business, precisely as he had said.

The story, half true, titillated depression-dogged readers. It also missed the real story, for the text of the Benton and Bowles release did not mention the terms of Benton's sale of his stock to the firm. Had the terms been known, his decision to leave the agency would have been revealed as a gamble few people would risk at any time, much less during a Great Depression.

Benton's stock was divided into six equal blocks. Payments would be made in six annual installments beginning in 1935 and extending through 1940, with the price for each block to be five times the average earnings on the same amount of stock during the previous three years. If the firm disintegrated, Benton's return on the stock would be negligible. Only if the firm prospered would he receive a high return. Combined with his savings, his $100,000 capital accumulated in the firm, his investment in his home and his insurance, his assets would total around a million dollars. Under this plan, even after leaving the firm—Benton would have a material stake in helping it prosper.

Another element in the settlement cast a long troublesome shadow. To "validate" the sale of the stock, he gladly bound himself never to return to the advertising agency field, which he never regretted. But at the same time he sold his name to the firm in perpetuity, for his former associates did not want to wake up one morning to find themselves in competition with a newly formed William Benton and Company. Benton later blamed his lawyers for not having advised him to sell his name only for five or ten years, by which time the agency would have been either firmly established or out of business. Yet the sale of his name was partly due to Benton's imprecision about the career he meant to pursue after quitting advertising. He knew he wanted a career outside of business, but where? He meant to "look around." His only immediate commitment was a trip around the world with Helen, to start after the 1936 presidential elections.

As it turned out, the connection of his name with a Madison Avenue firm kept alive the memory of Benton as an advertising man. He was to spend in a variety of other fields many more years than he had spent in advertising; yet no matter what he did or how he did it he always had to buck the suspicion that he was just another Madison Avenue phrasemonger.

The matter of the name was a mixed blessing also to Atherton Hobler, who was particularly insistent that Benton sell his name in perpetuity. He has said that if he had had any idea that both Benton and Bowles would one day "go into politics" he would himself have changed the name of the firm. For as the two men in time got into the thick of political fights on a national scale, to advertisers who mistakenly thought the pair still were connected with Benton and Bowles the firm itself may have been politically suspect.

Leaving the firm meant an immediate sharp drop in family income to the Bentons—from $250,000 a year to a return of around $15,000 on the investments Benton expected to make (less the 10 percent of the stock he had placed in trust for his mother). If things went well, the yearly income might double or even triple. For the moment, however, no one could really be certain that things would in fact go well. Yet the one person who cared the least about the immediate reduction of family income to a fraction of what it had been was Helen Benton. She welcomed her husband's decision to get out of the eye of the business hurricane in which he had worked since their marriage. She asked only one thing of him. She was tired of his absorption in commercial radio programs, and she made him promise that he would never listen to them again. Except for the public service programs with which he later became involved, he kept that promise and extended it to include television as well. When he left the advertising business, he slammed the door behind him and rarely so much as looked at an advertisement again.

Benton, however, could not abruptly turn his back on clients like Colby Chester of General Foods and his top associates, Clarence Francis and Ralph Butler, who had sponsored Benton as a young man. Nor could he ignore E. H. Little and Bayard Colgate of Colgate-Palmolive-Peet, or Randolph Catlin of Best Foods. Benton looked up to these clients, had ample reasons to be grateful to them, and counted them among his closest friends. In fact, Benton's high regard for his clients and prospective clients had once brought a reproach from Bowles as the partners were talking about Benton's years as a cadet at Shattuck. Bowles broke in to say: "Bill, you spent so much time saluting at Shattuck, that you still salute anything and anybody sitting at a desk behind a frosted glass door with his name on it."

If so, the clients' reciprocal regard for Benton became evident when he resigned. If several of them, or even Little alone, had threatened to take their accounts elsewhere, Benton might have been forced to reconsider his decision. His clients, however, were not unsympathetic with his intentions and wanted to give him a break. It was just as important for Benton as for Bowles and Hobler that the principal clients stay with the firm, so that it could pay the yearly installments on Benton's stock.

In fact, his clients wanted to help plan his future, though their good intentions threatened to entangle him in flypaper. The principal clients of Benton and Bowles were Republicans, strongly opposed to Roosevelt in the forthcoming presidential election. Moreover, they were involved in an effort to make Governor Alf Landon of Kansas the Republican nominee. It therefore occurred to Colby Chester and to other client-friends, that they should promote Benton for the post of publicity director of the Republican National Committee, now that he had no advertising business to look after. They were certain—too certain—that they could swing the job for him, and they wanted him to join them at the Republican National Convention in Cleveland where the deal could be sealed. Benton, confiding his own feelings about the matter in a note to his mother, said: "I am no Landon man. I personally have always been for Roosevelt, and am secretly sympathetic with the Democrats and with President Roosevelt's policies. I can't offend my clients by flatly refusing their offer. But it means that I have to walk a wary course between what they expect me to do, and the direction of my personal inclinations."

On a Monday morning in the third week of April 1936, Benton arrived at his office in Benton and Bowles full of uncertainty about his future. His "wary course" on Colby Chester's political proposal had not yet been charted, but he had promised Chester he would talk to some Republican leaders like Eugene Meyer in Washington and Joseph Pew in Philadelphia.

This was the April Monday on which Benton received a telegram, a special delivery letter, and a stack of telephone messages from Chicago—all initiated by Robert Maynard Hutchins. At noon Hutchins walked into the office—spoke about the Walgreen case— offered Benton the job of secretary of the University of Chicago— was turned down flat—asked Benton at least to consider coming to Chicago to survey the university's problems and to suggest approaches. Benton's answer to the last proposal was "I'll think it over."

A few days later, in line with his promise to Colby Chester, Benton went to Washington to meet Eugene Meyer, the owner of the *Washington Post*. Benton had never met anyone like Meyer, and the experience was an eye-opener. Here was a Republican, Yale '93, who had been among the main financiers of the copper, automobile, and chemical industries, and yet had contributed greatly to the development of public finance as the head at various times of the War Finance Corporation, the Farm Loan Board, the Federal Reserve Board, and the Reconstruction Finance Corporation. A wealthy and public-spirited publisher with a phenomenal success record in business, he thought most businessmen boobs or bores.

The two talked about Robert Maynard Hutchins. Benton did not fully understand the revolution Hutchins was leading in higher education, but Meyer did, and heartily endorsed it. Indeed, the following year he transferred his daughter Katharine from Vassar to the University of Chicago to expose her to Hutchins's influence. He snorted at the Walgreen charges about communism at Chicago just as he snorted at charges of radicalism at the London School of Economics, where he sent his only son to study under Harold Laski.

On the central purpose of the visit to Washington, Benton made no commitments to Meyer about the Republican National Committee job that was being urged on him. He agreed to keep in touch, and possibly to attend the Republican Convention in Cleveland to "see what happens." On the way home from Washington he stopped off in Philadelphia to see Joseph Pew, a rich and powerful right-wing Republican boss who was in politics for reasons of business. Pew asked Benton to undertake a "get out the vote" effort for the 1936 Republican cause, but the latter demurred on the ground that he was not as yet in a position to assume any responsibilities in connection with the Republican cause.

If Benton could be politely evasive with Joseph Pew, the tactic would not work with Robert Hutchins. Hutchins knew the main reflexes of the man he was after, and he began to play on them when Benton got back to New York. He began with a telephone call from Chicago. Hutchins, at the Chicago end, said that he had been thinking about Benton's objections to public relations and fund-raising work for the University of Chicago. If that is all he had had in mind for his friend, then Benton was quite right in balking. But there was far more important work awaiting him. He could interest himself in the academic work of the Business School or in the university's extension school or with its night courses for working students. There were two other things in which Benton had expressed interest—the development of radio, and the creation of films for educational purposes. There were endless tasks that clamored for the kind of help Benton was uniquely qualified to provide. But as these prospects could not fully be explained over the telephone, Hutchins was asking a delegation from the board of trustees to call on Benton in New York. A date in late May was set, and the delegation arrived on schedule.

The delegation consisted of the president of the board of trustees, Harold Swift (Swift and Company, the packers); John Stuart (head of the Quaker Oats Company); and Edward L. Ryerson (chairman of Inland Steel). The three were also Republicans of varying hue, but none was a Liberty Leaguer. They were deeply attached to the University of Chicago and were anxious to help Hutchins achieve his aims in higher education.

The delegation looked Benton over as they talked to him about the problems and plans of the university and defined the present and anticipated duties of its secretary. Benton uncovered some of the grounds for his uncertainty. He did not explain the charade he was acting out with some of his Republican former clients. But when he touched the subject in passing, the three trustees, despite their Republican party affiliations, surprisingly dismissed it as of little consequence. They saw no reason why Benton should waste himself on the Republican National Committee when there was really important work to be done on behalf of one of America's three foremost universities—and thus on behalf of higher education generally. In parting, the delegation seconded Hutchins's suggestion that Benton come to Chicago for a visit.

Benton wrote to Hutchins the next day in a mood to do some bargaining. He said he had been looking toward a period of a year or more, immediately following his departure from business, in which he "hoped to have a good deal of time to search after that ever elusive perspective on oneself for which most of us eternally grasp but never reach." Would Hutchins weigh an alternative to "a 100 percent move to Chicago." Would it be possible to do "a really constructive job on a part-time basis"? He could come to Chicago for sixty or ninety days to study the background and the broad outlines of the problems to be faced. Then he would try to write a basic plan of procedure. With a plan formulated and agreed upon, perhaps he could come to Chicago, for a month or so, to supervise and correlate the major activities launched in line with it. Benton added: "Your remarks about the Business School, and your Extension Courses, greatly interested me and I am sure there is a chance for much really constructive thinking and work in that direction. Unless there is in the background at least a potential promise for getting involved in that kind of work in the future, I wouldn't consider going into the educational field at all."

Soon afterward, Benton went to Chicago for two days of sustained talk with Hutchins and various trustees he had not previously met. He came knowing very little about the character of the University of Chicago, its history, its place and influence in American life. He had not stopped to think about what a university is, or should be. He had never before seen Hutchins on his home ground, or had more than a vague notion about the scope of his work. Benton's Chicago visit did not result in a blaze of light upon such matters. But he saw more clearly than ever before that Robert

Hutchins, his former teammate at Yale, was an exciting person to know, and that there was no telling where an association with him would lead.

Hutchins himself was about to publish four lectures he had recently given at Yale under the title *The Higher Learning in America,* a volume of no more than one hundred pages that remains to the present day a landmark critique of American education and a prescription for reform. Many books in a similar key were written after October 1957 when the Soviet Union's first artificial satellite precipitated a new concern about the quality and aims of American education. Hutchins said it in 1936, and he reviewed his thesis for Benton's benefit on the occasion of the latter's visit to Chicago.

Hutchins's thesis was that the central aims of higher learning in America must be indivisibly connected with democracy. But, said he, American universities were falling all over themselves in a hysterical desire to be of service to the people moment by moment, keeping up with every turn of the news and establishing departments in deference to the latest fads. Instead, he wanted the university to do what it alone of all institutions in a democratic society could do. It should study first principles, concern itself with the timeless truths about man as man, cultivate the intellectual virtues, provide an understanding of both the past and the present in the light of which things absolutely new could be examined. The university could thus permeate society with men who shared a common fund of knowledge, who could transcend vocational specializations, and who could thus lead in the discussion and resolution of common problems.

A restructuring of higher education was a necessary corollary of this view. In Hutchins's design, people capable of learning from books would receive a general education beginning in the last two years of high school and extending through the first two years of college. Within this four-year unit, the curriculum would be uniform for all students. It would consist of the greatest books of the Western world and the arts of reading, writing, thinking, together with mathematics, "the best examples of the processes of human reasoning." A bachelor of arts degree would be granted to a youth who successfully passed his examinations for this four-year unit of study, and the whole of the curriculum would have in view the preparation of the graduate for intelligent action in any field of endeavor, particularly for the endeavors falling to him as a citizen.

The intellectually gifted graduates would go on to higher learn-

ing in a university, which would be held together by a unifying principle. Unlike the medieval university whose unity was derived from
the central place assigned to theology, the university in American
democracy would derive its unity from metaphysics—meaning the
science of principles and causes. The university would not provide
specialized training in the professions. The latter function would be
relegated to outlying institutions offering such practical experiences as the professions themselves could not or would not give.
Moreover, the accumulation of data or the advancement of the em-
pirical sciences would also be relegated to other institutions. The
university itself would have one purpose only: to expound in a coherent fashion the nature of the world and the nature of man.

Hutchins's views had been expressed at the University of Chicago
long before they took the form of lectures delivered at Yale. Indeed,
they had whirled in controversy over the Midway—oversimplified
as the battle of "facts versus ideas"—in which students as well as
professors either sided with Hutchins or resisted him. Either way,
the University of Chicago in that hour took education seriously and
by contrast made Harvard and Yale seem to be sleeping.

As for Benton personally, it would take some time before he
grasped all the nuances of what Hutchins had in mind. Yet in his
two days in Chicago, what he absorbed from the excitement in the
air made him want to keep one foot over the threshold of the door
Hutchins had opened to him. Before returning to New York, therefore, he volunteered to pursue an idea of his own. He would conduct
a Benton and Bowles kind of "consumer research" survey, with the
University of Chicago as the product. The survey would be confined
to three groups of people in the Midwest—businessmen, nonaca-
demic members of the general public, and newspaper editors—who
would be asked what they thought about the university. If really
helpful information were secured from these groups, similar surveys
could be made among other groups, such as alumni, teachers, high
school students, and so on. The idea was simple—and radical. No
university had previously used such techniques to determine the degree of "acceptance" or "sales resistance" to itself. Hutchins enthusiastically urged Benton to go ahead with the proposed plan,
and in this he had another object in view. He guessed that Benton,
by undertaking a specific job for the university, would become
deeply attached to the institution.

In New York, Benton enlisted the aid of the Benton and Bowles consumer research staff, and the questionnaire they prepared about the University of Chicago was ready for testing by the time Benton left for the Republican Convention in Cleveland. He was still under pressure from his well-meaning client-friends to take the job as publicity director of the Republican National Committee which they felt they could easily get for him. In Cleveland itself, however, he managed a graceful exercise in evasion and escape. He learned that Hill Blackett, a partner in a leading advertising firm and a personal friend of Governor Alf Landon, was an active candidate for the very job Benton was trying not to get. So he called on Blackett in his hotel room and said: "Hill, I will do everything in my power to support your bid for the job provided you never ask me to do one single thing for you—and I make this condition because I am for Roosevelt."

The deal was sealed on those terms. Benton then went to work on his financially influential client-friends. He argued that Blackett, because of his friendship with Governor Landon, combined with his personal abilities as an advertising man, was the logical choice as publicity director for the Republican campaign ahead. The client-friends finally agreed and swung their support behind Blackett's bid for the job. As it turned out, however, they were not as all-powerful as they had seemed. Other forces within the party were strong enough to block their drive, and it was not until a month after the convention that Blackett finally got the publicity assignment. When Benton informed Hutchins about these developments and added for extra measure a doleful note about the state of the Republican party, Hutchins replied:

I wish you'd stop worrying about the Republican party, which is beyond redemption, and concentrate on education which may yet be saved. The most hopeless element in the G.O.P. is my old pal, Frank Knox [the publisher of the *Chicago Daily News*, who had been named in Cleveland as Landon's running mate for vice-president]. If you let your wife see him, she'll never want to come to Chicago. And I am very anxious to have her come.

I am pleased that H. Blackett has the job. The more money he makes the more we can take away from him. He is a graduate of the U. of C., and it's about time he did something handsome.

I am eager to have you do the survey which is now in progress, and still more eager to have you come to Chicago for as
long a time as you will. When you get here you should stay.
It will be a damned sight more interesting and important than
trying to make Frank Knox into a statesman. I can promise
you that.

With one apologetic exception, Blackett did not ask Benton to do
anything for the Republican National Committee during the 1936
campaign. Nor did the Benton and Bowles clients maintain their
pressure to that end. As Benton's attendance at meetings of the
agency grew more infrequent, the clients gradually got used to dealing with Bowles, Hobler, and their associates. And as everything in
the agency moved along smoothly, concern over Benton's departure
diminished.

By mid-September, Benton and Bowles interviewers had finished
a succession of surveys testing views about the University of Chicago. The findings were discouraging. At a time when the university
was rated by experts as one of the leading institutions of higher
learning in America and in the world, only 50 percent of the alumni
said they would send their children to the university. In the city of
Chicago, only 25 percent of the general public said that if they
were in a position to give to a university a hypothetical gift of millions of dollars, they would give it to the University of Chicago.
Only 38 percent of all professional and businessmen polled in the
Midwest said they would give that same hypothetical gift to the
university—despite the preeminence of its professional schools and
despite the impact on the economy (among other things) of the scientific work done at the university.

The findings, though discouraging, affected Benton like a call to
arms. Though he was not yet ready to bind himself to the university
in a formal way, he now wrote Hutchins to say that he could come
to Chicago with Helen around the first of October for several weeks.
He would gather material for his report and question the trustees,
faculty members, and Chicago civic leaders. Then he would go home
to Southport and write a report on ways and means for dealing with
the university's problems in public relations. Hutchins answered
with a bravo.

While still in New York, Benton pursued two matters that were of
interest to him even before his first visit to Chicago but that were

further stimulated by what he learned on his visit. He had already fastened on radio broadcasting and educational talking pictures— neither of which had been exploited for educational purposes—to change the university's public relations picture for the better. During his first visit to Chicago, he learned that the university's administration and faculty had more experience with both, and more interest in both, than any other institution of higher learning in the nation. For example, the prospects for radio's further development were emphasized by a Crossley Report he saw concerning the University of Chicago's pioneering "Round Table" radio program.[1]

The "University of Chicago Round Table," which was to become for two decades the leading radio discussion program in the United States, had begun very modestly on 1 February 1931, when three professors sat around a card table before an old "target mike" at WMAQ, the *Chicago Daily News* station. The subject they talked about was the Wickersham Commission report on prohibition. Two years later, NBC began carrying the program once a week in an offering to network stations, which relatively few carried at first. But the program gradually became popular; the professors it featured talked well without a script. With the coming of the New Deal, they had a great deal to talk about of interest to a great many people, and so, by the early fall of 1936, the "Round Table" had a national audience. According to the Crossley Report which Benton saw, the program drew 23 percent of all those who were listening to the radio at the hour the discussion was broadcast. This was a phenomenally high figure, considering that the program went on the air at 12:30 P.M. on Sunday, just when millions of Americans were either homeward bound from church or were drawing up their chairs for Sunday dinner. It was all the more phenomenal since it suffered from technical flaws that were no longer tolerated in commercial radio broadcasts. It had no producer, no preparation, no budget, no format.

Benton's personal strength in the medium of radio was very great. He was well and favorably known to the leaders of the networks, and he hoped to convert this fact into a source of support for an expansion of the university's efforts in the field of educational

---

[1]The title "Round Table" was derived from the name given to a special luncheon-discussion round table in the faculty's Quadrangle Club—special in the sense that it was reserved by custom for senior professors and administrators, and distinguished guests of the university.

radio. While still in New York, therefore, and before leaving in October for Chicago, he discussed the matter with William Paley, president of CBS, and with Niles Trammell, then vice-president of NBC and later its president. Both men told him that the networks would be glad to give the University of Chicago more time on the air provided the proposed new programs sounded promising. It would be very difficult for the networks to refuse time, so Benton assumed, if the programs were indeed good.

The prospects involving the use of educational talking films were more remote and complicated. In the era of silent films, movie magnates had dreamed of profits from educational films, but the dream always eluded them. Small companies were formed to make educational films. Confused between motion pictures for entertainment and motion pictures for the classroom, they produced a hodgepodge that often was neither entertaining nor closely related to the teaching of a particular subject. Instead of quick profits there were quick bankruptcies.

In 1929 the leviathan AT&T decided to enter the new field of "talking" educational films. Western Electric, an AT&T subsidiary, then manufactured motion picture sound projectors, and felt it owned basic patents. But because there were no good classroom films in sound, schools would not invest scarce funds in the purchase of sound projectors. Western Electric tackled the problem by creating a subsidiary of its own, Electrical Research Products, Inc.—or ERPI—which became the first major unit anywhere to produce and distribute instructional sound motion pictures. In 1932 it occurred to ERPI officials, led by Colonel Frederick Devereaux, that acceptance of its classroom films might be increased if they were produced in collaboration with educators. Discussions between Colonel Devereaux and his friend Beardsley Ruml, then dean of social sciences at the University of Chicago and a professor of education, led to a five-year contract between ERPI and the university. ERPI provided the financial and mechanical resources of picture-making. The university provided the professors, with their knowledge of subject matter and pedagogical methods, and put its "imprimatur" on the completed films.

By 1936 thirty-six films had been produced for use in the university's New Plan survey courses in the biological and physical sciences given to freshmen and sophomores. The films had also been introduced into some high schools and even elementary grades with astonishing results. When a test group of schoolchildren was exposed to the films, they scored between 40 and 60 percent higher in achievement in their schoolwork than a control group that had not been exposed. On the basis of these findings, Hutchins had told Benton during their first meeting in Chicago that if educational talking pictures were properly developed, they could mean a potential advance in educational techniques that was perhaps equal in importance to the invention of the printing press and certainly as important as the advent of the textbook.

At the same time, Benton learned that AT&T wanted to sell its ERPI subsidiary and get out of the educational film business entirely. So now, on the eve of his return to Chicago, he sought out Colonel Devereaux to ask the reasons why. Devereaux advanced a number of secondary reasons to account for the desired sale. It was left to Benton to guess, and to guess correctly, what the real reasons were. AT&T had but recently withdrawn from the business of manufacturing projectors for talking pictures, after it learned that its patents were not valid. Denied the prospects of royalties on the projectors, it had lost interest in the production of educational films. Second, in all the schools in America there were only one thousand projectors for talking pictures, and the absence of special budgets for audiovisual materials constricted the market. Further, because so few films were available—and, more critically, because there was no real distribution system for the few that had been produced—there were no inducements for school systems to invest in talking motion picture projectors. Finally, the schools which had bought sound projectors were asking for more films, and more of a particular kind, than the ERPI subsidiary of AT&T wanted to produce. For example, they were asking for films in the social sciences which the company wanted to avoid altogether, since it feared that it would be accused of "trying to spread propaganda through the school system." Here, to sum up, was a vicious circle—and a great long-shot opportunity for someone with vision and courage to break out of the ring.

Benton at this time was still not ready for any formal connection with the university, and he was well along in his plans for a year-long trip around the world with Helen, beginning in late January 1937. To this end, he had already turned over to Lehman Brothers about $175,000 of his capital, to be invested in stock, for a fee. Benton was eager for his trip, and particularly to visit India.

Walter Schleiter, his Yale classmate and his New York apartment-mate in the early 1920s, had made India his main base of action for the previous decade. He had often urged Benton to come for a visit and promised him an enjoyable and instructive time. But first, there was the report to write for the University of Chicago's board of trustees, and the trip to Chicago in order to gather the necessary material. Benton, his wife, and their five-year old son, Charles, arrived in Chicago on 1 October 1936. They took a suite at the Shoreland Hotel, and a place of work was found for Benton in the university's Social Science Building.

11

The University—and a World Trip

Benton, newly arrived in Chicago with a report to write, needed a guide to the university's activities. He asked one of the first men he met, Paul ("Pete") Russell, a celebrated football player at the university during his undergraduate days and now a devoted trustee of the university and a respected Chicago banker: "Who knows the most about the university? Where can I turn for guidance and insight?" Russell answered: "What you are looking for is John Howe. He's a handsome young fellow in the publicity office who devotes himself only to the university—and the girls who attend it. Go after him. Get him."

John Howe, an alumnus of the university and a versatile student leader as an undergraduate, already had behind him a decade of work in the university's publicity office. Aside from being handsome, he was bright, kindly, self-effacing, and a professional writer of marked ability. Nothing as yet, however, had spurred him to use his talents beyond the routine of his assignment as the No. 2 man in the publicity office. The No. 1 man was William Morgenstern, laconic, uncorruptible, overworked. Chained to an office budget of $10,944 a year which covered everything from salaries to paper clips, and under siege from all sides every time the university was touched by a bad news break, Morgenstern found it impossible to engage in any except low-key public relations efforts.

When Benton called on John Howe, his first question was: "What goes on around here? Will you please write a memorandum for me?" "How much time do I have?" Howe asked. "Twenty-four hours," Benton answered. The memorandum turned out to be the first quick summary ever made of the kind of work university faculty members did. John Howe gave a hundred examples, about fifty drawn from

170

the past and the rest contemporary. He did not expect any of this to be printed. But that was because he was new to Benton's way of doing things. Benton reasoned that the trustees themselves didn't know the range of the research performed at the university. So he published, in an appendix to his own report, John Howe's list of examples. He wanted the trustees to share his own excited discovery that there was a minimum of five hundred research laboratories on the campus and the ways in which the university's many distinguished faculty members, past and present, some of them Nobel Prize winners, had advanced human knowledge.

One of the first things that caught Benton's eye in Howe's memorandum was an item about Professor Nathaniel Kleitman's study of sleep. He questioned Howe about it and somehow construed the answer to mean that Kleitman hoped some day to cut two hours out of a normal night's sleep. With Howe, Benton rushed at once to the scientist's laboratory. "Why, John," said he, "gaining those two hours a day would practically amount to doubling my creative life. Those would be *golden hours*. Most of a man's waking hours are taken up with routines—bathing, eating, answering the phone, etc., etc. Few men have more than two hours a day free for creative effort—wholly free hours. If Kleitman can tell me how to get two more, what a gift it would be!" He was disappointed when the professor explained that he was not ready to promise such a gift.

Benton was disappointed again when he met Dr. Arthur Holly Compton, the Nobel Prize winner in physics. Compton, who would be Benton's neighbor in Chicago the next year and who was to become a close friend, began to explain to him the then science-fiction dream of atomic energy. "The time will come," said the physicist, "when we will be able to propel a ship across the Atlantic on no more than 5 cents worth of fuel." "When?" Benton asked eagerly. "Oh," said the physicist, "in about a hundred years." "But we'll all be dead by then!" Benton exploded. Compton nodded his head serenely, while Benton wondered how anyone could be so patient about so great a hope deferred for so long.

But there was a practical piece of research which Benton personally was well equipped to perform for the university—research on Mr. Charles Walgreen. In the course of the Walgreen case, some of Chicago's leading businessmen blasted the drugstore chain owner for being wrongheaded in making charges about "communism at the University of Chicago." One in particular who did so was Edward

Eagle Brown, Walgreen's own banker. Also, while the investigation of the charges was underway, Professor Charles Merriam, chairman of the university's Political Science Department, had reasoned with Walgreen privately. But there had been no follow up by the university on the ground which Merriam was trying to cultivate.

Benton, learning this, felt that his own identity as a former advertising man who had specialized in drug accounts might make for a worthwhile meeting with Walgreen. He talked over the prospect with Charles Pearce, president of the International Celucotton Products Company, whom Benton had come to know in 1929 at Lord and Thomas when Pearce was president of Colgate-Palmolive-Peet. Pearce, who knew Walgreen well, not only urged Benton to see him but also called the owner of the drugstore chain and arranged a meeting with him the next day.

When this had been arranged, Benton met with Hutchins to tell him about what was in prospect. "What can I do to fix up the feud with the university?" he asked. Hutchins instantly replied, "Get him to give some money to the university."

When Benton met with Walgreen the next morning, the latter said he was greatly disturbed over the way his withdrawal of his niece from the university had blown up a storm that damaged it. This had not been his intent. "After all," said he to Benton, "I know the university is a very great institution and I am merely trying to point out a small flaw in it, but nobody from the university has wanted to talk to me about it in that light." The conversation went on for two hours, but when Benton was on his feet preparing to leave, he cast his hook. "Mr. Walgreen," said he, "the university is a private institution and it depends for its sustenance on the support of men like you. If you think there is a small defect in the university, you would do well to consider trying to help it correct that small defect. If you don't think American institutions are stressed in the teaching program as much as they should be, the university would welcome your support in strengthening its program in American institutions. Why don't you give the money to the university to help the university correct the defect which you feel is in it?" Walgreen thought a long minute and then said, "I would be glad to consider this." Whereupon Benton promptly replied, "I will ask President Hutchins to drop around and see you in the morning."

Hutchins followed through. The next morning he called on Walgreen, and it required only that one session to lay the basis for what eventually became the Charles R. Walgreen Foundation for the Study of American Institutions, designed to "forward the development of good citizenship and the improvement of public service." Walgreen eventually contributed $550,000 to its creation while the Rosenwald family of Chicago quietly added $250,000 to its funding. The Chicago newspapers which had been pummeling the university were momentarily stilled by Walgreen's benefaction. Walgreen not only became devoted to Hutchins but emerged as a hero in the eyes of the university community. To the trustees and those faculty members who knew of his role in the matter, Benton appeared to be a magician.

But he did not stop there. Of all the Chicago newspapers that were hostile to the university, the most powerful was the *Chicago Tribune,* published by Colonel Robert McCormick. McCormick had some very strange views, but from a purely technical standpoint, he produced one of the best-written newspapers in the United States, with the best advertising department, the most energetic circulation department, and probably the best sporting pages. All this helped him dominate Chicago and he was determined to have his way with the things he liked or hated. He had decided to hate Robert Maynard Hutchins, and for five years Hutchins was never once identified by name in the *Chicago Tribune.* As a nonperson to Colonel McCormick, Hutchins, when he had to be alluded to, was called only "the President of the University of Chicago."

Benton decided to call on McCormick to talk over university public relations problems. Once again, his identity as the former head of Benton and Bowles stood him in good stead. His experience in handling difficult clients did the rest. Colonel McCormick took a personal liking to his caller and, as a sign of it, agreed to Benton's suggestion that he meet with Hutchins, the nonperson. The meeting took place in late December; Hutchins called it "a crossing of the Rubicon." The sequel was to be a *Chicago Tribune* editorial which astonished trustees and the whole university community, as well as other readers familiar with McCormick's vendetta against Hutchins and the university's "New Deal professors." The editorial, published as Christmas approached, praised the university as Chicago's most priceless asset and as its greatest ornament. Here was another seeming Benton miracle.

Benton paused in his work in Chicago long enough to fly to Southport on election day, 3 November, to vote for FDR. Early the next day, before returning to Chicago, he dictated a hasty note to Bowles setting forth some "professional" judgments about the way the campaign had been conducted, the decline in influence of newspapers, and the rising influence of radio, "provided the candidate knows what to say and believes what he is saying."

He also dashed off a letter to Colby Chester, venturing some "professional" views about the management of the campaigns. A passage in that note contains the germ of an idea, which was to be cultivated by Benton at the University of Chicago and in which one can see the remote antecedent of what was to become the Committee on Economic Development. Benton observed that "the important and urgent angle" in the election result "concerned business." He recalled in this connection that "a couple of months ago," Lewis H. Brown, president of Johns Manville, had talked to him "about the need for a major propaganda job for American business." To this Benton added:

> If I understand Lew correctly, he conceived this was a counter-irritant to what he called "subversive influences." It was my view that such a program might boomerang. Before launching such an activity, shouldn't business develop a constructive program on problems like unemployment, social security, etc.? I remember telling Lew that business should prepare itself constructively to cooperate with Roosevelt on his re-election, that this seemed to me to be an important viewpoint regardless of the candidate elected, that with Roosevelt's re-election the need was much the greater. I for one would gamble on this, particularly in view of the fact that there is hardly any other road for business with a better promise of successful turnings.

Shortly before Thanksgiving, Benton finished collecting his raw material in Chicago and returned to Southport to write his report. Instead of a memorandum it turned out to be a full-length book, which he finished on Christmas Eve. When he got the galleys from the printer, he sent a set to Hutchins for any changes he felt were necessary. Hutchins made only one change—a new opening sentence reading: "A report such as this, to my knowledge, has never before been written; surely never before for any university."

Benton had made no concessions to august academic utterance, far from the madding crowd. The titles of the three opening chapters, for example, used terms drawn from the world of prizefighting.

Thus the first chapter, titled, "Weighing In," gave the background of the report. Next came a chapter titled "The Purse," on the theme that "public relations to most universities is just a fancy name for money raising." The following chapter, "The Gate," recognized the importance of wealthy donors to the university but argued that over a long period a friendly "general public" was even more important.

Then Benton shifted to the idiom of the advertising world. In a chapter titled "The Basis of Appeal in Public Relations (or the Sales Story)," he analyzed the university as Benton and Bowles would analyze a product before planning an advertising campaign. What is a university? What is unique about the University of Chicago? How does the work done on its campus relate to the problem of existence the individual American faces in his daily life? In answer, Benton provisionally defined the university in terms of its "public service" and its contribution to the "general welfare."

> One way to develop a business is to find out what the public wants, then to deliver that product. Another way to develop a business is to start with your own idea of a product, often far in advance of what the public thinks it wants, then go out and sell the public that it should want your product or service. Often this is the harder way. But often it leads to the development of the most profitable business. The second way . . . must be the way of any university that would be great.

There was an echo here of what he had known about the history of John H. Patterson and the National Cash Register Company. The connection was made clear in a chapter titled "The Sales Resistance." "Ever since the days of John H. Patterson," he wrote, "the smart sales manager has trained his men not only in their sales story, but has also forewarned them of their sales resistance. Further, he has coached them on how to meet it." In the case of the University of Chicago, the "sales resistance" appeared in the findings of the three surveys Benton had initiated in the summer of 1936. He enumerated the charges they brought to light, then took up one by one the human instruments that could serve the university's public relations. In separate chapters devoted to each—Hutchins, the trustees, faculty, students, alumni—he analyzed what they were not doing to promote the university's cause, and what they could and should do.

His treatment of Hutchins's role was the longest of all. "Mr.

Hutchins in the public view," Benton wrote, "is the University, just as Henry Ford is the Ford Motor Company, and President Roosevelt the Democratic party." He went on to compare education to an enterprise in which millions of people regarded themselves as stockholders. Hutchins, however, was a rarity among university presidents, since he persisted in talking about the need for educational reforms and thus upset the vested rights of stockholders. Yet should Hutchins try to make himself as conventional and comforting "as Queen Mary's hat"? The answer was no. If he shunned controversy, he would stunt the talents that could carry him to the heights of leadership and make him "the kind of man to whom people turn in times of crisis." Everything Hutchins said and did should revolve around education—the problems confronting all education and specifically those of the University of Chicago. He should continue vigorously to espouse reform in education and should crusade for the university idea.

Benton's recommendations about what the faculty could do for public relations further developed an idea he had previously voiced in different form to Lewis Brown and Colby Chester. There should be created at the university a forum where businessmen could meet with leading professors in order to discuss practical problems of common interest.

> The recent election may have paved the way for this. If there is to be greater freedom of thought and expression, and a more liberal public attitude, let the University try to capitalize on its experience and background. Try to turn what has been a public relations liability into a public relations asset. Invite business men in groups to the University to discuss short-term and long-term business legislation, and possibly social implications of major legislation passed since 1932 or impending. This might become an annual series of three or four meetings. Such correlation on legislative and social questions between business groups and the Faculty might provide a convincing demonstration to the former of the need in society for the latter.

In a chapter devoted to radio broadcasting and films as media for influencing the public, Benton observed: "If the great universities do not develop radio broadcasting in the cause of education, it will, perhaps, be permanently left in the hands of the manufacturers of face powder, coffee and soap, with occasional interruptions by the politicians." But, "If Mr. Hutchins is correct in anticipating a great future development in public education, not of the vocational type but along cultural lines as working hours shorten, this is a natural field for radio broadcasting. It makes for equality of opportunity for everyone. As printing and books did originally, so can radio in the decades to come."

Most programs offered by the networks and billed as "educational," said he, were not only mediocre but bad, neither of much interest nor of educational benefit. To his "amazement," he discovered that "some Benton & Bowles programs have been classified by the networks as 'educational.' " The University of Chicago was in the strongest position of any of the great universities to seize the educational opportunity offered by broadcasting, to develop that opportunity, and "selfishly to capitalize upon it." How and why? "The City of Chicago was one of the three important originating points for radio programs." The university itself was "one of the few in the nation with a faculty equipped in background and in scholarship to seize the opportunity in broadcasting." It also had a running head start because of its broadcasting experience of the last several years with the "University of Chicago Round Table," the first and only regular radio program of controversy.

Benton also had many suggestions for educational films, and ERPI in particular. He strongly cautioned against the university's developing a motion picture company of its own. Rather, its future in the field should depend on a contractual arrangement with an outside group. He also urged a shift in emphasis away from making films for colleges exclusively, to making educational talking pictures for use in secondary and elementary education. Here the need and the market were the greatest. Here the university could do the most good. He suggested that the university inquire into the possibility of getting a foundation to buy ERPI.

Benton, always sensitive to "brand names," went on to say that he was depressed by the name of the University of Chicago. It conveyed a picture of a municipal college and not one of the great privately endowed institutions in the land. It also identified the university with any unfavorable publicity about the city of Chicago. "In my opinion," said Benton, "the name of the University, more than any other factor handicaps it in taking its rightful place in public opinion alongside Harvard, Columbia and Yale. If the University had originally been named 'Harper University' [after its first president], its public reputation today would be greater, and its public relations problem easier."

Northwestern University in Evanston, north of Chicago, had an irrevocable state charter exempting it from taxes. There had been off-and-on discussions about a merger between it and the University of Chicago. Benton observed that if the merger occurred, it would not only give the University of Chicago a chance to win perpetual tax exemption but also a chance to acquire a new name. Said he:

> Northwestern is a far better name than the University of Chicago. I for one like its association with our frontier, our pioneering past. Such a concession to Northwestern might achieve the merger. In public relations, this concession is in fact an advantage if the merger commends itself on other counts. Mr. Hutchins suggests the possibility of an entirely new name for a merged institution. But Northwestern, with a new Faculty and Administration, would take unto its name a new significance and through its new association would begin to be a new name almost immediately.

Would all the new forms of public relations work Benton outlined, and the additional personnel they required, justify the increased budgetary cost? "I have never seen an institution with a promotion opportunity that seemed comparable," he answered after giving $75,000 as a working figure for an anticipated budget increase he felt would be necessary. "Business must spend money to make money, and the University faces the same problem." He therefore disagreed with the implications in Hutchins's remark that "$75,000 is ten fine professors." The implication was true only if the money was unwisely spent. "The issue, however," Benton wrote, "is whether the $75,000 a year may not raise $750,000 a year which in turn is 100 good professors." If the plans he had recommended were sound, said he, then the money put behind them should prove productive beyond a doubt. But if the plans were unsound, or were ineffectually handled, then it was "much better to put the money into the professors."

Only fifty copies of Benton's report were printed. They were numbered, and bore the author's admonition that "the book be kept strictly in the hands of him to whom it is issued." There was too much controversial material in it, much that would embarrass the university in potentially hostile publicity through the press and radio. The admonition was respected. Indeed, most of the copies were later reclaimed from the trustees, and all of them were supposed to be. No part of the text surfaced publicly until the spring of 1962 when the *College and University Journal,* the magazine of the American College Public Relations Association, published large excerpts from it with the introductory comment: "This book—the first comprehensive public relations program ever developed for an American university—is not simply an historical curiosity. It is an amazingly accurate primer of college public relations in 1962."

The numbered copies were sent to the trustees in advance of their scheduled meeting on 3 February 1937. Benton, however, could not be present at that time. He was due to leave on 23 January for his trip around the world. But in those days anything agreed to between Hutchins and Harold Swift, the chairman of the board of trustees, was agreed to almost automatically by the rest of the board. Hutchins and Swift had a plan, and they were certain the other trustees would approve of it, since the latter had already been impressed by Benton's successful dealings with Charles Walgreen and Colonel Robert McCormick. They proposed to offer Benton an appointment as vice-president of the university, starting in the fall of 1937. According to a plan Benton had suggested, he would spend six months of the academic year on university work at a salary of $10,000, and, for the remaining six months, he would be free to pursue other interests.

The plan became a direct offer to Benton. He accepted it, and on 18 January circulated a memorandum to the Benton and Bowles staff informing them of his decision. Two days later, in a note to Hutchins, he observed:

> A man who sets out to sell an idea to himself, even if the original setting out isn't deliberate, may come to with a start and discover that he is doing an amazingly fine job.
>
> That seems to be what happened to me in the last few days when I tried to explain to Chet Bowles and others just what I am up to in moving to Chicago and towards education.
>
> If I tend to emphasize my interest in educational broadcasting, and in educational moving pictures, and if I tend to minimize my functions as the Middle-Western King of Money Raisers, I know you will excuse me for that.

Because perhaps I have not seemed as enthusiastic as I might, in some of our past discussions, showing what is perhaps a natural hesitancy at the thought of such a change of life, I wanted to drop you this note today to tell you that my enthusiasm is mounting rapidly, and, I believe, will continue to mount from now until next October, when I join you in Chicago.

The trustees of the University of Chicago, impressed by the scope and ideas in Benton's report, did the expected on 3 February. They confirmed him as one of the university's two vice-presidents. The other was Frederick Woodward, who was due to retire in 1938. It was assumed that Benton would succeed him at that time as the only vice-president of the university. He would then be regarded as the "academic" vice-president primarily, while attending to the other major general duties that would devolve on him as Hutchins's main assistant. The assumption that the appointment was not for promotion or fund-raising was to be modified for various reasons.

The Benton trip around the world resembled a pincer movement. Helen, with her mother-in-law and Charles, then age six, voyaged through the Panama Canal and then on to Honolulu, where a house had been found for them by Lorrin Thurston, publisher of the *Honolulu Advertiser* and a classmate of Benton's at Yale. Helen then went on to Singapore to meet her husband, who had previously reached India by way of the Atlantic, the Mediterranean, and the Suez Canal. After Singapore the two journeyed together through Asia to Peking, back to Honolulu, and then home. They were away seven months in all.

On the eve of his departure for the Far East, Benton had secured letters of introduction from Hutchins. In addition, Eugene Meyer of the *Washington Post* and Mrs. Ogden Reid of the *New York Herald Tribune* armed him with press credentials. Since his *Yale Record* days, Benton had published nothing under his own name in a newspaper or magazine, and he knew nothing about the rules of journalism, not even the simple mechanics of filing a story. Nonetheless, his trip around the world did result in a newspaper story. It also resulted in his most humiliating experience, of which Benton later said: "I remember it with shame, and I remember it often."

The prologue to the experience went back to 1935 when the Bentons, then in London, met Webb Miller, the head of the United Press in Europe. Miller had won acclaim as a foreign correspondent by circumventing the censorship of the British raj in India to inform the world about Gandhi's passive resistance campaigns. Miller proudly carried a cigarette case signed by world figures like Lloyd George, Clemenceau, and Gandhi, and, of these, Gandhi's was the prize signature. The Indian leader did not give autographs and had many times refused one even to his valuable friend and ally, Miller. Gandhi finally gave in and told the American correspondent that he could have the signature on condition that Miller never again carry cigarettes in the case—this because of the Hindu taboo against tobacco. Miller agreed, and the case was always empty.

Benton saw the cigarette case and heard the story when he met Miller in London. He was intrigued and irreverent. In anticipation of his retirement from Benton and Bowles and the trip around the world, he bet Miller a hundred dollars that he too could get Gandhi's signature. In this way the stage was set for the "most humiliating experience" of Benton's life.

When Benton reached India in early 1937, he was astonished to learn that in the preceding five months, Gandhi, who was staying at his ashram at Wardha, had not been visited by any reporter or any European. He was also astonished by the scornful indifference of the European colony in India toward Gandhi personally, and toward the passive resistance movement of the Congress party. The measure of the matter was brought home to him after he met Madame Sarojini Naidu—a Gandhi supporter, a celebrated poet and orator—who took Benton to the great Congress party rallies in Bombay. He could not take in the whole of the vast sea of people of which he was a part, yet it seemed to Benton as he looked around that he was the only "European" present.

Benton, meanwhile, had shown Madame Naidu his newspaper credentials and had spoken of his eagerness to meet Gandhi. She said that Gandhi was in urgent need of understanding in the United States and that she would try to arrange an interview with him on condition that Benton write a story about it. Madame Naidu thus proceeded to write and then telegraph Gandhi. But after days went by without a reply, Benton felt that nothing would come of the matter. So he left Bombay to tour the country, proceeding in a northerly direction that would take him to the Khyber Pass. At a New Delhi stop, however, he canceled his plans when he received a wire from Madame Naidu saying that Gandhi would see him. He boarded a train for a thirty-six-hour ride to Wardha, and the rest of the story, as Benton told it, went like this:

On the morning of my arrival I was shown the Gandhi-inspired activities of Wardha. There were students studying agriculture. There were students doing their hand weaving. There were students making a coarse, brown, thick, heavy wrapping paper. I bought a sheet of that paper for an anna and put it in my pocket. An anna was then worth 2¼ cents, while the average wage for common labor in Wardha, a city of 20,000 and further advanced than the villages, was 1½ to 2 annas daily.

Gandhi was seated cross-legged on the floor when I was introduced to him. But he grasped my hand firmly like any good Tammany politician. "You'd better sit over there," he said, motioning to a varnished box six feet in front of him. The box, about half the size of an orange crate, was the only article of furniture in the room.

Our talk at one point turned to American public opinion, and its attitude toward India. "It's a prevalent idea in America," I said, "that India requires England for defense. Without the English, would there not be civil and religious disturbances? As the Congress Party is successful in driving the English out of power in India, will India fall prey to someone else? Or, for that matter, how will Congress deal with the native princes right here at home?" Gandhi answered: "These are gross superstitions. They have been propagated for years. Stories and statements of such dangers are hopelessly exaggerated. I know that many English people sincerely believe them; there you have the power of such ideas often repeated."

He then began to talk freely about a subject close to his heart—his great movement to improve the lot of the Indian villager or farmer, who constitutes 85 percent of India's total population. "Progress is slow," he observed, "but you must remember that our work is new. We started with nothing but faith. Only faith. Today knowledge is added." I then asked him where he got the money for keeping his students in Wardha and for conducting his political activities. He came back at me, saying: "What are you going to do with the money you get for writing this story?" It had never occurred to me that I would be paid for what I might write. "You might add a third ingredient to progress," he continued. "Give us part of the money you make when you sell your story." To which I replied: "You think that if faith plus knowledge are potent, faith plus knowledge plus capital are more so." Gandhi cackled, "Yes, yes," in a full laugh.

Before I gave him a direct answer to the question of what I was going to do with the money paid me for the article I might write, I asked him whether he had ever seen an American movie. "No, no, I haven't," said he, laughing again. "Now there's a good story for you. Do what you can with it. I've never seen a moving picture." Had anyone ever brought a movie to him? He again laughed and answered no. I then explained to him that my question had not been asked in jest. In the talking moving picture, cheaply made and shown with low cost portable projectors, lay a method for greatly speeding up the reaching of India's illiterate millions with the story of village uplift. I added that any monetary contribution of mine would be earmarked for making such an experimental moving picture.

At the end of my interview, I told the Mahatma how much it had meant to me. Then I asked him for his autograph. He froze. I saw that I had made a most unhappy mistake. I was embarrassed, but didn't know enough to stop. I plunged on. I pulled the sheet of village-made paper out of my pocket and said: "Mahatma, I bought this paper this morning especially so I could take your autograph on it back to the United States." He rose from his cross-legged position on the floor, turned his back on me and said bitterly: "Even that does not tempt me." I was totally humiliated by the rebuke. It was the first autograph I had ever sought, and I never have asked for another.

On the train from Wardha to Calcutta, Benton wrote an article about the visit with Gandhi. Much of the foregoing appears in it, rounded by observations about village life, and about Mr. Mahadev Desai, Gandhi's faithful secretary for twenty years. Desai had served six or seven years in jail, not far behind the Mahatma's record, and this fact had prompted Benton to ask him how he liked the English. "I like them," he said. "They've been very considerate to me, twice. They know how close I've always been to the Mahatma and twice they've let me share the same cell with him, once for a year and a half." The reply was in Benton's mind when in 1937 he wrote the final paragraph of his story:

> As we plod homeward on the train, I try to picture the tens of thousands in India who speak of their years in jail with pride. And tens of millions more will cheerfully face jail, mutilation or death at a nod from the 63 year old political-saint who makes of whatever village he occupies the most important town in India, and of whatever mud hut or room, one of the most important in today's world.

Benton didn't know what to do with the article after he had finished it. He sent it by mail to the head of the publicity department of Benton and Bowles, who on receiving it sometime in April also didn't know what to do with it. He submitted it to three or four magazines, all of which turned it down. The editors failed to grasp the newsworthiness of the first visit any writer had made to Mahatma Gandhi in five months. Finally the Benton and Bowles publicist turned the article over to the North American Newspaper Alliance, and the story ran in newspapers with a circulation of some five million. The *New York Times* carried it with photographs on the front page of the second section of the Sunday *Times*, predecessor to the current "News of the Week" section.

When the Bentons returned to their Connecticut home in September, Benton found a fifty-dollar check awaiting him from the North American Newspaper Alliance. He endorsed it to Mahatma Gandhi, and sent it off to the Mahatma's secretary, Mahadev Desai, with a note telling Desai that he still wanted the Mahatma's autograph and reminding him that the Mahatma had asked Benton what he was going to do with the money for the story. Now that he was turning over the check for it, he wanted in return not just an autograph but an autographed picture.

As a last desperate chance, Benton meant to recover the canceled check from the bank, with Gandhi's signature on it—though he doubted that Webb Miller would call this bona fide. Months went by without a reply from India. Benton was about to inquire about the check, fearing that he had gone too far in asking for an autographed picture. But then, at last, there was a letter from Desai reading:

The Mahatma doesn't have any pictures. This is why it had taken me so long. He's never had a picture taken. But I finally secured a picture from one of the newspaper agencies. Here it is with his autograph. I hope you don't mind if I'm in it too. I'm walking right behind the Mahatma, and, incidentally, I have always wanted a full set of Eugene O'Neill's plays.

As the object of such a high-level "squeeze," Benton admired its deftness. He sent off the plays. Later, during World War II, Gandhi's autograph ceased to be so rare. More adjusted to Western ways, he gave autographs to American GIs stationed in India. It remains to be added that Benton never collected the bet from Webb Miller. Miller was killed in London when he accidentally stepped in front of a speeding express train during an early wartime blackout.

3

THE
NEW
ADAM

12

University Life

When Benton resigned from Benton and Bowles, he felt that the long and complex contract covering his sale of stock covered almost every imaginable disaster. Moreover, when he turned over the first payment on that stock for investment by Lehman Brothers, he felt he was doing what prudence called for. He realized that he knew very little about any business except advertising, and it seemed only sensible, therefore, for him to turn his capital over for management by a respected investment firm.

What he did not foresee was the recession in the United States which was to begin in August 1937 and worsen in the following months. While he was still on his world trip, the New York stock market suffered a sharp decline. Benton's personal loss amounted to between 10 and 20 percent of his total anticipated liquid capital from Benton and Bowles—if his contract paid off. Suddenly he saw himself in the future, at age fifty, no better off than the broken men who had daily crowded the Benton and Bowles waiting room in a desperate middle-aged search for employment.

"The more I thought about the matter," Benton recalled, "the more stupid I felt. Here I was allowing an 'investment counsellor' to take my hard-earned money and put it into U.S. Steel, and then sell out from U.S. Steel, and then put it into U.S. Steel again. Whose stock am I buying when I buy U.S. Steel? Perhaps the stock of the president of the company, or one of the directors who knows much more about the company than I do. . . . And when I sell, perhaps I'm selling to the president of the company or one of the directors who knows much more about the company than I do—and who is smartly buying. No, this is a fool's game." He made up his mind that he would buy a business of his own and would set its policies while hiring someone to run the operation. The precise nature of the business to be bought was undefined, but the principle of "natural selection" he set forth as a guide to his own search, and as a guide to friends whom he asked to help him in the search, was a carry-over from his experience in building Benton and Bowles by winning advertising accounts away from major agencies. The business to be bought might well be a failing part of a great corporation.

His stock market losses and his search for a new business opportunity took nothing away from the zest he brought to his tasks at the University of Chicago. The university's trustees had warmly endorsed his report, and Benton soon discovered that despite the previous understanding that he would *not* be a vice-president for promotion and development, he had no choice except to help Hutchins carry out the public relations recommendations in the report. His principal experience, after all, lay in that field, and Hutchins by conscious or subconscious design channeled Benton's work toward matters where his background could be most helpful to the university.

In the first hour of the first morning Benton reported for work as a university vice-president, Hutchins gave him a copy of a report prepared for young Nelson and Laurance Rockefeller by a Wall Street engineering firm. It concerned the proposed sale by the AT&T of its Electrical Research Products, Inc.—or ERPI—the pioneer in educational talking motion pictures. Since ERPI had a contractual agreement with the University of Chicago, the two Rockefeller brothers had sent a copy of the report to Hutchins, and the latter in turn put a question to Benton. What could be done to help the Rockefeller brothers acquire the film company? What was to be done with it if they actually bought the company?

The question led to a number of meetings in New York extending over the fall of 1937 and early 1938. In attendance were Nelson and Laurance Rockefeller, Benton, Hutchins, Beardsley Ruml, Wallace Harrison, and Ernest Hopkins, the president of Dartmouth and a board member of the Rockefeller Foundation. While John D. Rockefeller, Jr., in the end vetoed the prospective purchase of the film company by his two sons, the round of discussions marked the onset of a fruitful friendship between Benton and Nelson Rockefeller. It also fully exposed Benton to the force of Beardsley Ruml —or "B"—who was to play a major role in his life.

Ruml once described his mental state as one of "dispersed attention." His ideas sounded, and often were, outlandish. Yet, in their startling simplicity, they often accomplished what experts had ruled impossible. Ruml, no farm "expert," had originated the Agricultural Adjustment Act of the New Deal. No "expert" at philanthropy, he led a revolution in the life of foundations. No tax "expert," he would originate the revolutionary Ruml "pay-as-you-go" tax plan of 1945.

When he was twenty-seven years old, he had been propelled into a central position at the head of one of the Rockefellers' great philanthropies, the Laura Spelman Rockefeller Memorial Fund, with a $74 million endowment. The traditional objects of Rockefeller philanthropy had previously been medicine, sanitation, laboratory research, and university buildings. Ruml, against the initial opposition of veteran Rockefeller advisers, decided to spend a large part of the endowment on the social sciences. The result brought new life to the social sciences in America. In 1930 Ruml had resigned from foundation work in order to accept from Robert Maynard Hutchins an appointment as dean of the social sciences and professor of education at the University of Chicago. But he soon discovered that there was a difference in his effectiveness when he no longer had endowments to go with his ideas. In 1934, therefore, he resigned from the university to become treasurer of Macy's department store in New York, where new challenges awaited his free-wheeling mind. Maude Phelps Hutchins said he had "exchanged ideas for notions." Ruml said he had exchanged frustration for futility, and to help combat it he maintained his interest in the University of Chicago.

After John D. Rockefeller, Jr., vetoed the purchase of ERPI by his two sons, Ruml advanced a new idea harking back to his experience with the Laura Spelman Rockefeller Memorial in launching what became the enormously successful *Parents' Magazine,* which published in popular form the results of research into child behavior. On his initiative, the memorial fund allocated funds to four universities so that they could buy two-thirds of the stock in the proposed magazine ; the remaining third of the stock went to George Hecht, the magazine's promoter and publisher. Ruml thereby had joined philanthropy and educational leadership with private initiative and enterprise. With this precedent to draw on, Ruml now proposed that the General Education Board of the Rockefeller Foundation be asked to grant $4 million to a group of universities which would form a corporation to produce and distribute educational

motion pictures and other visual aids to education. The first move
of the proposed corporation would be to buy ERPI films. If the
corporation materialized, it was proposed that Benton manage the
enterprise in the six months of the year he would not be devoting to
the University of Chicago.

Hutchins, Nelson and Laurance Rockefeller, Ernest Hopkins,
and Benton embraced Ruml's idea, and Benton was asked to prepare a memorandum for submission to the General Education Board
in support of the $4 million request. Benton's best efforts at writing
advertising copy went into the text. He stressed the need for a production goal of more than four hundred films. "Unless films are
available," he wrote, "schools are not warranted in purchasing pro-
jector equipment. Without films, courses cannot be intelligently reorganized, nor can teachers be trained." A large percentage of the
$4 million would go, not to operating or research, but to producing
"a film library which will constitute a capital asset for at least a
decade." Further, the corporation would correct existing conditions whereby school superintendents were offered "odd lot" films
on subjects mostly "out of key with the regular classroom curriculum." Guided by a committee of distinguished educators, production
would start in selected fields of instruction according to age groups.
The films would be produced in sequences so that the student could
see the whole of a subject unfold coherently.

The corporation would not presume to determine the subject content of the films. "Such an effort," Benton wrote, "would be resented
by educators better qualified to undertake it. The objective of the
corporation, and of its pictures, would be to set up standards for the
improvement of teaching procedures. The corporation assumes that
a subject worth teaching is worth teaching better." Moreover, it
would speed up changes in content, with the agreement of leading
educators. It would offer school boards and superintendents "the
instruments, in the form of pictures and correlated material,
through which teachers can adjust themselves to new requirements
in the curriculum."

The participating universities would share equally in 60 percent
of the common stock. But, said Benton, taking a leaf from Ruml's
experience in financing *Parents' Magazine,* 40 percent of the common stock should be "set aside for the directors to use as an incentive for merit." Although "profit possibilities, at best, were many
years removed," the possibility seemed sufficient to provide an incentive. The management plan was devised "to combine the advan-

tages of the profit objective with those of a straight philanthropy, and to avoid the disadvantages of both."

The memorandum was a comprehensive analysis of every aspect of educational films and visual aids as of 1937. Its submission to the General Education Board of the Rockefeller Foundation led to a round of meetings in Chicago and New York until finally, in the spring of 1938, the members of the board of the Rockefeller Foundation spent an evening looking at ERPI films. John D. Rockefeller, Jr., was again present, and again brought his veto into play. Benton, for one, was not prepared to let the no stand as the last word. He approached his friend Henry Luce with a proposal for a joint venture whose object would be the purchase of ERPI films and the development of educational talking pictures. This approach also ended in a no. Luce had backed away from the proposal because, said he, an eleven-page memorandum prepared for him by the treasurer of his publishing empire "proved" that classroom talking pictures were at a dead end. Benton was not so easily swayed. After five years of watchful waiting, he would eventually acquire ERPI films, and after still more years of effort, would fulfill all the prophecies about classroom talking pictures which he had made in his 1937 memorandum to the General Education Board of the Rockefeller Foundation.

Benton was formally presented to the faculty of the University of Chicago as the featured speaker at its "homecoming" dinner, toward the end of October 1937. Hutchins introduced him as "the model professor's son" and went on to tell how much money that son had made before walking away from the advertising business. When it was Benton's turn to speak, he went out of his way to set his audience straight about his interests. He told the faculty openly, as he had often told Hutchins privately, that he had no interest in coming to the University of Chicago just to publicize the place. There was no intellectual challenge in such work. His real interest was in other things that could have enormous educational impact— for example, the educational uses of radio and motion pictures. He did not add that he was also interested in doing some teaching, principally English—and in the Law School. He had had a good deal of experience in the advertising business teaching young men to write, and he knew of no group that needed such training more than lawyers.

Benton's experience at the University of Chicago elevated the tone and range of his reflections, but he remained a man for whom ideas took on meaning only when related to practical action. Informed critics approved. Before the academic year 1937–38 was out, Frederick Woodward, the "senior" vice-president of the University of Chicago, was saying publicly that Benton could "accomplish more in a shorter time than the combined efforts of any ten men" he knew. The Nobel Prize winner Dr. Arthur H. Compton was saying that he "never knew a man who could absorb more complex information in as short a time, and *correctly.*"

Robert Hutchins, to be sure, could be playful at Benton's expense. He was quoted as having said: "Don't try to understand Bill Benton in human terms. He is not a man. He is a phenomenon." When the laughter subsided, Hutchins made a more sober estimate. He found Benton a loyal and generous friend, a selfless ally in a fight, a resourceful associate of high intelligence, and a courageous and honest man. Indeed, even when Hutchins used Benton as a foil for laughter, a tribute of some kind was almost invariably part of the sally. So it was, for example, as late as 1963 when he publicly said:

> Administrators, politicians (not campaigning), and butchers are likely to be more virtuous than professors, not because they want to be but because they have to be. One odd confirmatory fact is that those whose business it is to lie, such as advertising men, are often scrupulously honest in their private lives. For example, Senator William Benton, founder of the firm of Benton & Bowles, used to say that he had to be honest on Madison Avenue because if he wasn't, word would get around that Benton was a crook and he would be ruined. When he retired from the advertising business he became vice president of the University of Chicago, whereupon he was prompted to say, "Look at these professors. What harm would it do them if word got around that they were crooks? They are all on permanent tenure!"

Hutchins continued:

> The general moral tone of academic life was once handsomely demonstrated at a University of Chicago faculty meeting. It was a solemn occasion. Two hundred full professors had assembled to discuss whether the bachelor's degree should be

relocated at the end of the sophomore year, giving it and other degrees a meaning they had never had before. The faculty debated this proposition for two hours without ever mentioning education. The whole discourse concerned the effect of the proposed change on public relations and revenue. Mr. Benton, fresh from Madison Avenue, stormed out of the assembly shouting, "This is the most sordid meeting I ever attended in my life!"

The main body of the university's faculty, meanwhile, was hard put to fit Benton into its scheme of things. He was well liked as a person, but he posed a problem of identification to many members of the faculty. Most of them were specialists at something. He wasn't. Most of them stuck to one thing all the time. He didn't. He was not one thing at one time in one place all the time. He was always on the move, with six different irons in six different fires in six different places, fanning all the fires simultaneously.

He was also a puzzle because when something struck him as sensible, he said or did it, regardless of how odd it might seem to others. He once flagged down a commercial airplane that was beginning its ascent off a runway, causing it to wheel about and taxi to a stop so that the pilot could learn what the trouble was. The trouble was that Benton had missed his connection and wanted to get aboard the plane, which he did. It was sensible to him to walk, traveling bags in hand, into the middle of the street and, finding no taxis available, to stop a private car and say: "Excuse me, I'm in a great hurry. Will you take me to Grand Central Station?"—to which the flabbergasted driver could only answer, "Of course."

Benton also seemed strange because he actually did what was rational. Once when he was flying to New York, he sensed that there was something seriously wrong with the plane. He had previously written to Helen that he was making that particular trip by train instead of by air. Now he wasn't sure whether the plane would reach its destination. In that moment, he decided to write a note to Helen, explaining what he was doing on the plane, and also bidding her a tender goodbye. This done, he walked up and down the cabin looking for a place to put the note where it wouldn't burn if the plane crashed. He spotted a spittoon, lodged his farewell note in it, and returned to his seat to await developments. The only thing Benton feared in the world was pain, and if the plane was going to crash, there would be no pain, just death. So why worry? He felt he had done all that a farsighted man could do who dearly loved his wife and wanted her to know that in a moment of maximum peril she was uppermost in his mind.

The pilot put the aircraft down at an emergency landing field short of New York, and the fact was announced to the passengers. Benton moved swiftly toward the exit door of the plane. He reasoned that there would be only one taxicab at a field so small. If so, he meant to get it. Another passenger, unknown to Benton, had much the same idea. When the door of the plane was opened, the two men made a dash for what in fact proved to be a solitary taxicab. They reached the vehicle in a photo finish and agreed to share the cab to New York. En route they discovered that each knew of the other. The stranger was Orson Welles, whom Benton and Bowles had used as "The Voice" in a detective-mystery radio show. Welles told Benton that the regular checks he had received from the advertising agency were a sustenance and a joy to him in the lean years before he won stardom on the stage and screen. Later, when he met Helen, he told her that what Benton, in writing his farewell note, meant to do was to explain why he was in the *wrong* accident.

Faculty members at the University of Chicago came to delight in these Bentonisms. But one audience in Chicago taught Benton a lesson he never forgot. Soon after he became vice-president of the university he was invited to address a black-tie dinner of the Chicago Bar Association. He worked hard on his speech and had Hutchins and Frederick Woodward, both former Law School deans, read it over. Benton had geared the opening of the speech to a "free association test." He had listed a number of words and had asked the Benton and Bowles research interviewers to determine the instant reactions of a cross section of the public to them. This, he felt, would illuminate public attitudes. The word "alderman," for example, led to an association with "fat men"; "Supreme Court," to an association with "old men"; and "lawyer" all too often led to an association with uncomplimentary phrases like "watch out," or, "second-story man," or "Philadelphia." He meant his words to be taken humorously, including this passage:

> If you accept the theory that every man wants a job and nobody wants to work, where are those two conditions more ideally combined than in the practice of Law? All you have to

do to become a lawyer is to put your name on the door and you have a job. By contrast, look at the sad lot of your poor manufacturer. If his plant shuts down for two years, he can't go around boasting of his prosperity. But if a lawyer doesn't make much of a go at it, he can sublet his office to some promotion scheme, get its name written on the door under his, and then he's a corporation lawyer.

Most of the members of the audience accepted these remarks in the playful spirit in which they were made. Benton's main point was to discuss the greatly improved curriculum of the university's Law School, which was designed to turn out lawyers who would bring a higher professional standard to the practice of law. But he misjudged the sensitivity of those in the audience who would brook no implied criticism of their profession. The moment he was through, two or three members of the audience jumped to their feet to protest that they had not come to a Bar Association dinner in order to be insulted. "I learned a valuable lesson from the experience," Benton has said. "You can't kid a professional group. You can't kid the boys who've given their all in order to be lawyers." But this did not lead him to avoid mentioning the shortcomings of future special audiences. In a speech to a body of educators, during his early days as a University of Chicago vice-president, he said:

A depression can liquidate the rights of railroad bondholders. The automobile manufacturer can assassinate the carriage maker. No depression or new idea is yet in sight which can change the habits of educators or liquidate the vested rights of teachers and professors. Some rich men, we hope, get through the eye of the needle. So with educational pioneers. Some get through. But few are chosen to make the effort. The mortality rate is high. Thus few university presidents try to pioneer. And of the few who do, few try very long. Most settle back and become alumni greeters, glad handers, ornaments for their institutions, social lions, money raisers. But what about important or fundamental educational innovations? Nothing is done.

In the fall of 1937, Benton's friend William Paley, the head of the Columbia Broadcasting System, asked Benton to give three fifteen-minute radio lectures. For all his radio advertising background, Benton had never spoken over any network. CBS at this time put out a little magazine called *Talks* in an effort to show the Federal Communications Commission that it was indeed interested in "public service." Benton's talks were to be published in that magazine, and he sweated over their preparation. His theme was the "Education of a Businessman," and under the cover of this title he ventured to do two things simultaneously: to promote the University of Chicago, and to answer those businessmen who thought of professors as the sinister or lunatic "Brain Trust figures" portrayed in the cartoons of anti–New Deal newspapers. The tenor of his remarks appears in this extract from the first of the talks he gave:

> In business where I spent the first fifteen years out of college, I discovered that the pioneer has an easier job than in the arts, the professions and the social sciences. The businessman has a God to whom he can appeal who will answer all his critics. That God is money. If he makes money, his pioneering will receive the plaudits of the business world. Yet even with a sure fire incentive and a definite yardstick there doesn't begin to be the pioneering spirit in business which you might suppose.
>
> In contrast to all this is the revolutionary work quietly being done in universities. Not long ago, the element U-235 was first identified by Professor Dempster at the University of Chicago. As a result, research engineers at General Motors might double the efficiency of combustion engines; engineers at General Electric might double the efficiency of the dynamo; but it is highly unlikely that any industrial research engineer would have hit upon U-235, which, I am told, has brought us a big step closer to the era of atomic power. And the overwhelming majority of the great scientific discoveries upon which modern industry rests can be traced back to university laboratories.

An incidental by-product of those CBS talks was to launch him on what could have been a full-time career as a writer. His speeches were spotted in *Talks* by "Missy" Meloney, the editor of the Sunday newspaper supplement *This Week*, which then boasted the largest circulation in the United States. "Missy" Meloney wrote to Benton asking, on the strength of his speeches in CBS *Talks*, if he would consider writing for her magazine what she called "Page 2 editorials," "inspirational" pieces of the type produced by one of her favorite writers, Bruce Barton.

Benton told "Missy" Meloney he would be glad to do some articles for her, provided he could do them about the University of Chicago. She was alarmed by the suggestion but said she would welcome a chance to look at a sample. Instead of one, he sent her three, each dealing with a piece of key research work being done at the university. She bought all three, sent him a check for $750, and asked for more. He was overwhelmed. He knew he could write advertising copy and earn hundreds of thousands of dollars. He did not know he could write "Page 2 editorials" for *This Week*—and get $750.

Since he was not yet engaged in any activities of central importance at the university, within thirty days he turned out seventeen articles, with the object of placing them in various publications. He combed the university for ideas. One of these grew out of his own constant search for ways to do and devour more things in a shorter space of time. In this way he was attracted to the pioneering experimental work being done by Professor Guy T. Buswell of the Department of Education in speed reading. Buswell had developed machines to photograph the movement of people's eyes as they read. He discovered that poor readers read a word at a time, whereas good readers read a phrase at a time, and superb readers read a full line or a sentence at a time. He invented a technique to teach phrase reading or even full-line reading, thus reducing the total number of eye movements.

Benton, once disappointed that Professor Kleitman could not promise to reduce by two hours the sleep he needed, hoped again to find a time-saver by learning to read faster. When he mentioned this to Hutchins, he was not impressed by Hutchins' reply that he was wasting time reading the wrong things—that the way to save reading time was by knowing what were the right things to read. Benton called on Professor Buswell, who, after testing his eyes, reported that he read with normal rapidity. "I know that I read with normal rapidity," Benton said. "But can you make me read faster? I've simply got to read faster." Buswell smiled as he said, "I can try, I might be able to improve your reading by 5 percent or so." Benton was delighted. Once a week for the next six months, he went through a drill in Buswell's laboratory in the hope of earning a 5 percent return in time on the time he invested in trying to save time.

Benton drew on this experience to write an article which the *Reader's Digest* bought, marking his introduction to that magazine. Then one day Bruce and Beatrice Gould, the editors of the *Ladies'*

Home Journal, selected five of the seventeen articles he had written in his thirty-day rush and alternated them over the next year with editorial page articles by Dorothy Thompson. Other articles out of the seventeen were bought by *This Week.*

In the years ahead, Benton was to write more than 170 major magazine articles and 3 books. He would also write millions of words for speeches and for about 900 radio and television programs, though writing itself was to be but a relatively minor aspect of his life.

He had first signed his articles "William B. Benton." But the magazine editors often spelled out his middle name so that the author became "William Burnett Benton." One day, he learned from Chester Bowles's secretary at Benton and Bowles that the people in the office who knew him as "Bill Benton" and saw the various articles asked her: "Is this *our* Mr. Benton?" Benton passed the incident on to his mother, who responded with a piece of advice: "The British don't use middle initials. A man who amounts to anything is known in England by one name, or at the most by two names, and most surely he doesn't need three names. You should drop the middle initial and name. Get rid of it." And so he did. He abandoned the "Burnett" originally given him out of deference to the wealthy cousin, William Burnett, in the hope that the latter might remember his namesake and bequeath him $5,000 for a college education. But William Burnett had failed to do this. Now William Burnett Benton, potentially "rich" in his own right, dropped the "Burnett," without malice. In the same spirit, he further shortened his name so that his signature on all documents became "Wm. Benton."

One more change occurred early in Benton's association with the University of Chicago. Because the Bentons wanted children but were unable to have more of their own, they were drawn to the idea of adopting an infant girl. They talked the matter over with Hutchins, who called their attention to The Cradle in Evanston, Illinois, a pioneering institution devoted to the placement of infants for adoption. The daughter of Dr. Frederic William Schlutz, the noted head of pediatrics at the University of Chicago's Medical School, had adopted three children through The Cradle, and all three were flourishing. Hutchins therefore urged the Bentons to seek Dr. Schlutz's advice.

Dr. Schlutz encouraged them and volunteered to inquire about adoption prospects and to examine them physically and mentally. Shortly thereafter he informed the Bentons that he had examined two infant girls at The Cradle, one ten weeks and the other six weeks old, and that the Bentons could confidently adopt either baby. While the Bentons and the doctor were en route to The Cradle to choose between the two, Benton suddenly suggested taking both babies instead of just one. The doctor agreed, as did Helen when she saw the infants. And so it happened. The older of the two girls was named Louise Hemingway, joining the name of Helen's cousin with her own family name. The younger was named Helen Orr after Benton's maternal grandmother.

Soon after the adoption of the two infants, the Bentons moved into a home on Woodlawn Avenue—across the street from Dr. and Mrs. Arthur H. Compton. Not a large place, it was adequate for their needs and was only three or four blocks from the heart of the campus.

When Benton was working for Lord and Thomas back in 1928–29, Chicago had not been too happy a place for Helen. Her vision of the city had been restricted by the narrow circle of bosses and clients in which her husband moved, and his concentration on Lord and Thomas to the exclusion of virtually everything else. But now, once settled with her family in the University of Chicago neighborhood, she expressed surprised pleasure at her new life. That her husband's earned income had dropped from $250,000 a year at Benton and Bowles to $10,000 a year as a half-time vice-president of the university in no way diminished her pleasure, nor did his recent losses in the stock market. What she valued far more in her new life was what she underlined in a note to her mother-in-law:

> Living here is like living in a very delightful "village." I didn't know I'd like it so much. It's a great pleasure to be able to walk. Charles calls Bill at 7:30 each morning. They dress together and then Bill walks to school with Charles, after which he continues on to his office. There is none of the old frenzied rush to catch the commuter train, or a scramble for a solitary taxi, or any hectic tinkering with a stalled car. We've been invited several times to dinners and in every case we have been able to walk. Everybody has been very cordial. It's not unusual to have dinner at one professor's home and then move on with your hosts to the home of another professor and to

join with several members of the faculty there, in reading and acting out a play. I have found this kind of entertainment far more amusing and pleasurable than the old round of bridge playing in which I was trapped when Bill was in Chicago working for Lord & Thomas. We've enjoyed every single evening we've had with people in the University community.

But in addition to the community social life, Benton was soon busy on many fronts to promote the university's interests—so much so that his six months at the university became, in practice, about ten months.

Typical of the promotional ideas Benton conjured up for the university was a brochure titled "Great Men," about the university's endowed professorships. Each left-hand page showed a large picture of the donor of the professorship. (In the "academic" language Hutchins taught Benton in the late 1930s, a "donor was a rich man who preferred professors to racehorses.") On the right-hand page were pictures of the great professors who had held the chair, with the story of their work to benefit mankind. The text suggested that further chairs might be endowed at $250,000 each, earning immortality for the donor through the work of the men of learning who would hold them. One prospective donor who received the brochure wrote Hutchins saying: "Dear Bob: I've received your booklet. I take it that all I need to do in order to become a great man is to give the University $250,000." Hutchins replied with a characteristically pithy one-sentence letter: "Give us the $250,000 and it will make you feel great."

The University of Chicago contributed to Benton's own education and to his own future contribution to the education of American businessmen. Though Benton had majored in economics at Yale, his real education in the subject began at the University of Chicago in the fall of 1937 when he was exposed to one of the most distinguished groups of economics professors in America. The preceding fall, he had heard one of them, Paul H. Douglas, attacked by a rich and powerful university trustee for producing a study of the Samuel Insull utility empire showing how that empire had been built at the expense of unwary investors and how it was headed for a collapse. "But Professor Douglas was right, wasn't he?" said Benton to the hostile trustee. "Yes, he was right," the latter replied, "but he shouldn't have done it anyway!"

The episode made a deep impression on Benton, and when he did his three CBS broadcasts in the fall of 1937, he wove the story into one of his speeches. He praised Paul Douglas—whom he had yet to meet—for the precision and courage marking his prophetic studies about the Insull empire, and pointed to him as an illustration of how a social scientist is supposed to perform. Douglas called Benton the next day to voice his thanks for the kind remarks. This was the first contact between the two men. They were drawn ever closer in passing years and were to be on the same side of controversies over one issue after another when both served in the United States Senate.

Other noted economists on the faculty in the fall of 1937 who became friends of Benton were Jacob Viner, Frank Knight, Henry Simons, Theodore Yntema, and Neil Jacoby. A later addition was Theodore Schultz, a farm economist who was forced out of the University of Iowa after angering the dairy farmers of the state by opposing their drive to tax oleomargarine out of existence. These economists often disagreed among themselves, and Benton began as a respectful eavesdropper on their disputes when they met at lunch at the "round table" in the faculty's Quadrangle Club at which everyone was welcome. He read their books, which introduced him to economic concepts he had never thought about before. Some startled him. For example, since he had devoted many years to building up brand names through his advertising agency, he was shaken when Henry Simons told him how a truly successful effort in that direction could only lead to monopoly—indeed, that all advertising was an instrument of monopoly power. In time, however, Benton found his own voice and became an active participant in the discussions among these professional economists; and he sought to adapt their views to the business milieu with which he was familiar.

A related part of Benton's education grew out of his responsibility for the university's "Round Table" radio program. Soon after he arrived at the Midway,[1] he persuaded the Alfred Sloan Foundation to contribute $50,000 a year for the improvement of the program. This made a vast difference in the quality of the "Round Table" broadcasts and their promotion. It was now possible to hire a production director and a research director. The latter, Richard M. Scammon, who was to be the U.S. census director under President John F. Kennedy, provided each participant with

---

[1]The campus is nicknamed after the boulevard on which it is situated, Midway Plaisance, the former Midway of the Columbian Exposition of 1893.

a hundred-page "background memorandum" a week before each program. It was now possible to pay the participants modest fees and to invite experts from almost anywhere the director chose. Indeed, the "Round Table" itself moved about the country and eventually even abroad. A printed transcript of each discussion, with illustrations and suggestions for supplementary reading, was made available to listeners at ten cents a copy. The number of stations carrying the program doubled and tripled, and the "audience rating" steadily rose to make the "University of Chicago Round Table" the most influential discussion program on the air.

The formula called for two participants who were "experts" on the day's topic, and one "non-expert." Benton was frequently cast as the "non-expert," but he diligently did his homework on Scammon's background memorandums, spending as much as fifty hours poring over them and supplementary materials. Often on the night before a Sunday broadcast in which Benton was to take part, he would keep at his homework until the approach of dawn. Fearing the impending encounter with two experts in a given field, he would carefully write out things he expected to say—and seldom used in the end. Debating and sparring with experts may have made for a compressed kind of education, but it prepared him for his Senate years when he was a frequent participant in radio and television panel shows.

Much of the talk among the economists in the fall of 1937 and early 1938 was centered on the recession and the apparent faltering of President Roosevelt's recovery program. Benton had a natural interest in the theme, since he had lost so much of his liquid capital in the 1937 stock market decline. In addition, on the New Year's Eve which ushered in 1938 he met one of the most energetic and acute political critics of Roosevelt's management of the economy, Governor Philip La Follette of Wisconsin, son of "Fighting Bob," and brother of Benton's friend Senator Robert M. La Follette, Jr.

Bob Jr. and his wife Rachel had invited Bill and Helen Benton to Madison for that New Year's Eve. There the Bentons met Philip La Follette, who had recently launched a revised "progressive" party, convinced that the Republicans were hopeless and that the Democrats under Roosevelt could not do what was needed for genuine economic recovery. The new party harked back to "Fighting Bob's" 1924 campaign for the presidency as a Progressive, and even further to Teddy Roosevelt's Progressive or Bull Moose party of 1912. Over this holiday La Follette pressed his views on Benton, who, while not entirely convinced, did bring to the La Follette brothers a legacy of respect for "Fighting Bob," inherited from his own grandfather Daniel Hixson.

Of his relationship with the La Follette brothers at this time, Benton later said:

> I promised $5,000 to the two of them to be spread over two or three of their campaigns. I argued that they would do well to try to get money by subscription—instead of operating one campaign at a time, to try to sign up people to give them money consecutively over several campaigns—to pledge to do so. They were very skeptical about the proposal, and of course they were quite right. One campaign at a time is as far as a politician can look when it comes to raising money. But my gift to them was my first significant political contribution and in line with my resources at that time, before most of the payments from Benton & Bowles had come to me, it was a big one. . . . For years I remained friendly with Bob La Follette, but though I kept in touch with Phil, my relationship with him was not close. It was snapped off by the war from which he emerged as a major supporter of General Douglas MacArthur for the presidency.

As Benton thought about how much he was learning in his conversations with the University of Chicago professors, an idea he had first touched on in 1936 in conversation with Lewis Brown, president of Johns-Manville, began to take on more specific form. He had repeated the idea to Colby Chester after the 1936 election and had touched on it in his report to the university trustees. He believed that the business and academic community, and ultimately the nation, could benefit from a systematic exchange of views between leading businessmen and university economists.

In the early spring of 1938, Benton asked Lewis Brown to help arrange a series of two-week summer seminars in economics for the presidents of America's one hundred largest companies. "Only the presidents will be invited and admitted," Benton said. "You provide the presidents. I'll provide the economists." Brown fell in with the idea, and tried to help out. Nothing came of it in time for the summer of 1938, but it was agreed that work on the project would begin again that fall with the next summer in mind. Many things, however, happened in the interval both to delay further work and to recast its form when work on it was eventually resumed.

Benton rounded out his first half-year at the University of Chicago in April 1938 and moved with his family back to Southport, where he remained until July. His mother, who had spent much of her time traveling the world over, settled in an apartment on New York's Riverside Drive. She had become reconciled to the physical comforts her son made possible, and now, in late July, as Benton boarded a ship for a month's trip to Europe with Walter Schleiter, she pressed into his hands an affectionate bon voyage note. The tenor was so unusual that Benton wrote her as soon as he reached England: "That marvelous note of yours thrilled me all across the Atlantic. I've memorized it. It's much the nicest love letter I've ever received."

The trip to Europe was both for pleasure and business. His *Reader's Digest* piece about Professor Buswell's work in speed reading had been well received. DeWitt Wallace, the *Digest's* owner and editor, interested in Benton's background in radio, suggested an article contrasting the government-controlled British Broadcasting Company with the so-called American system of broadcasting. The *Reader's Digest* would pay the expenses of a trip to England to gather material. When Benton agreed to Wallace's terms, he expected to deride the BBC and praise American broadcasting. He discovered in London, however, that an honest article might do the reverse. BBC newscasts and other aspects of its broadcasting were superior to those in America. But to say this would risk losing the friendship of leaders of American broadcasting, just when he was trying to get them to use the University of Chicago faculty in order to develop high-quality public service programs. Since he would not lie about the BBC, yet could not tell the truth about many facets of its superiority, he abandoned the article project. He turned to another matter growing out of a letter of introduction from Governor Philip La Follette to Sir Robert Vansittart, permanent undersecretary in the British Foreign Office.

Hectic diplomatic moves were then underway which would presently lead to the Munich conference. Before his call on Vansittart, Benton had met a number of highly placed British civil servants who believed in the theory of "peace in our time" based on an "understanding" with Hitler. "If we can come to terms with the Nazis," a leader of the British government told Benton directly, "this will mean peace for twenty years." Vansittart strongly disagreed. Indeed, for this reason he was soon to be removed as permanent undersecretary, made a lord, and assigned an honorific but impotent "advisory" post in Foreign Office work.

At his meeting with Vansittart, Benton said that after leaving London he planned to go to Stockholm for a holiday. Vansittart urged him to go to Berlin instead, saying: "Berlin is now the most important city in the world. What is happening there is more important than what is happening anywhere else." The passion of Vansittart's words sent Benton to the German capital, where, if he could not understand the nuances of diplomacy, he understood too well the lewd meaning of the yellow park benches set apart for Jews. "I didn't stay in the city long," Benton later recalled. "But I was shocked by what I saw, and the experience is to this day one of the most searing in my life."

Benton was back in Chicago when the Munich conference was held on 29 September 1938, and Britain and France yielded to Nazi demands for the Czech Sudetenland. Five days later the news that Eduard Beneš had resigned as president of Czechoslovakia turned Benton's thoughts toward certain facts. Between 300,000 and 350,000 Czechs lived in Chicago, making it the second largest "Czech city" next to Prague. Further, Thomas Masaryk, the noted professor of sociology who had led the struggle for the rebirth of Czechoslovakia as an independent state in 1918, had once taught at the University of Chicago; when a monument was raised to him in Chicago, it was placed on the Midway at the east end of the university campus. Still further, Beneš had studied under Masaryk at the University of Prague, and later had become his chief political lieutenant and, in 1935, his successor as president of the Czech Republic.

With all this in mind, Benton got in touch with Hutchins, then in the East, to suggest that Beneš be brought to the University of Chicago as a professor. Hutchins endorsed the idea but asked about funds for the Czech leader in case he accepted. Benton volunteered to find the answer. He called on Charles Walgreen, by this time a Hutchins admirer and a firm friend of the university. He was no less kindly disposed toward Benton—who now asked his approval for the use of Walgreen Foundation funds to bring Beneš to the University of Chicago. Benton did not know how much time the Czech leader might wish to spend at the university, but if it were only one quarter every year, the sum of $5,000 would be offered. In any case, said Benton, Beneš above all men could speak with authority on democratic institutions like those in America and could contrast them with the totalitarian forces which were tightening their grip on Europe.

Walgreen immediately gave his consent to the proposal, and Benton's next problem was to get in touch with Beneš. He first tried the State Department, only to be told that it might take a month to find the Czech leader. Not content to move at the pace of grazing sheep, Benton called on the publisher of the *Chicago Daily News*, Colonel Frank Knox, whose friendship he had been courting for the university. Knox cabled his chief correspondent for central Europe, M. W. Fodor, who was headquartered in Prague, to locate Beneš. Within twenty-four hours, Fodor not only found Beneš but had his acceptance of the university offer.

Beneš's arrival in Chicago caused a great stir in the city and at the university. Benton would eventually see him often in private, besides attending some of the seminars where the self-exiled leader accurately forecast the timetable of the successive steps Europe would take on its road to war. But the frequent meetings with Beneš occurred only after Benton had recovered from an illness extending over an eight-month period.

At the start of the fall term in 1938, he had felt in excellent health, but one day began to run a fever of 105 degrees. He was rushed to Billings Hospital, where his case was diagnosed and treated as pneumonia. But even after his temperature was brought down, he continued for eight weeks to run a low-grade fever. He became a scientific curiosity to leading doctors at Billings, who daily subjected him to new tests. Opinions differed about what was wrong with him. Dr. Schlutz, the pediatrician, had a strong opinion of his own—"You had better get your husband out of that hospital," said he to Helen, "or those doctors will kill him with their tests." Still bedridden at Thanksgiving, Benton read on the front page of the *New York Times* that a new drug called sulfanilamide had just arrived from Germany and was being tested at Johns Hopkins University. When he called the item to the attention of his doctors, one of them telephoned Johns Hopkins, and soon a dose of the drug was shipped to Billings, where it was administered to Benton. He was told that he might be the first person west of Johns Hopkins on whom the new sulfa drugs were used. He awaited the scientific effects with great interest, and within a week's time, he was ready to leave the hospital to convalesce in Palm Beach, Florida.

His hope of being able to resume his duties at the University of Chicago, after a few weeks in Florida sunshine, continued to be deferred week after week. Impatient at wasting so much valuable time trying to get well, he finally, at the suggestion of his Chicago doctors, placed himself in the care of a Dr. Nichols, a graduate of the University of Chicago Medical School who was practicing in Miami. "You sound," said Dr. Nichols when Benton called on him and related his medical history, "as if you've had undulant fever along with pneumonia." A test resoundingly confirmed this suspicion. The medical experts in Chicago had missed what was wrong. A doctor in an area where undulant fever was endemic had spotted it.

In the final stages of his recuperation, Benton was in an automobile accident. "I was lucky that I didn't cut off my head," he wrote to Bowles from Palm Beach. "I was pitched headlong through a nonshatterable glass window, leaving a hole the size of the seat of your chair. A broken thumb and a broken rib, plus an hour and fifteen minutes on the table for seven stitches in my head. I owe a debt of gratitude to the fellow who invented nonshatterable glass. But I didn't even know that you could go through it like that! Did you?" After hinting that Bowles might go after an advertising account for nonshatterable glass, Benton issued some direct advice. "If you're ever going to have an automobile accident the time to have it is while you are laid up anyway. It's just as easy to be laid up on two counts as one."

It was early June 1939 before Benton returned from Florida to Chicago by way of his Southport home. He was free of the fever that went with pneumonia, but not of the fever of his temperament. His troubled conscience about his eight months' absence from the University of Chicago goaded him into trying to make up for the lost time by doing everything at once. "I have been on a regular merry-go-round since my arrival," he wrote his mother; "just one thing after another." He added that he was spending "too much time on Chicago's football problem, on a projected alumni campaign, on a Fiftieth Anniversary celebration," and on other things that didn't particularly interest him. What did interest him were the continuing opportunities the university provided to enlarge his horizons. Fragments from his letters to his mother written during a single week from Chicago tell part of the story.

"At the Friends of the Library Dinner, I introduced Mr. Giuseppe Borgese, the author of *Goliath*, the best book on Italian fascism." "I attended the School of Business dinner for alumni, at which I said a few words." "Phil La Follette spoke at International House. I went to dinner to hear him. He gave an excellent talk. Then he stayed overnight with me at the Shoreland." "I am dining with Mr. Borgese." "Last night Colonel Knox, the 1936 vice-presidential nominee for the Republican party, gave a dinner for Phil La Follette and about eight other men. I took Dr. Hu Shih, the Chinese Ambassador in Washington. It was intensely interesting with La Follette, Knox and Hu Shih, all sounding off on foreign and national problems." "I am giving a dinner for Colonel Knox and some of the people of our faculty, to discuss the general economic situation." "I dine tomorrow with Harold Swift and meet with Congressman T. V. Smith afterwards." "I went to hear a moving picture producer lecture on 'Motion Pictures As An Art.' The producer was a flat-head. He has one fair idea, however. . . . Yes, in most ways this is a most interesting spot for me."

13

Muzak, Publishing, and Politics

Since the stock market break of 1937, Benton had been on the look-out for a business to invest in, but not until mid-1939 did he finally find a venture that appealed to him. He was in New York, and Beardsley Ruml invited him to breakfast to meet an American soldier of fortune named Allan Miller.

Table talk in Ruml's apartment brought to light something of Miller's buccaneering history in the world of finance and some of Benton's background in advertising. But the conversation found its cutting groove when Miller dwelt on his involvement in "wired music." He had formed a British firm, Rediffusion Company, to exploit his idea. It called for stringing wires into British homes and installing loudspeakers carrying BBC radio programs and others that the company chose from among programs originating with European stations. Home subscribers to the service paid the company a shilling and sixpence a week. Benton asked why people would pay that fee seemingly in perpetuity for what was really a radio set by another name. Miller's answer offered three points: no static came over the loudspeaker; people enjoyed the sense of having a private broadcast wire of their own; and subscribers didn't have to lay out all at once the whole cost of a radio set.

Miller's interest in "wired music" led him to invest in an American firm named Muzak. He now owned one-third of its common stock, representing an investment of about $75,000. He explained that in the late 1920s, the North American Company, a billion-dollar utility holding company, had conceived of bringing music into the home over electric power lines and had formed a subsidiary, Muzak, for this purpose. A lavishly financed experiment had been launched in Cleveland to prove the merit of the plan, but the depression, technical difficulties, and the need of costly booster stations put an end to the dream of launching Muzak nationally through electric light companies. Muzak itself, despite some money-losing subsidiaries of its own, lived on, selling music by telephone wire in New York City to restaurants, hotels, and other places that wanted music but could not afford live orchestras—all of which won the enmity of James C. Petrillo and his American Federation of Musicians. Muzak also owned a recording studio in New York. Under a patent from AT&T, it produced its own records in what was known as "high fidelity vertical cut," the needle vibrating up and down instead of the conventional side to side. This offered top recording quality, and only Muzak used it. The telephone wires which carried Muzak reduced the quality, but it was still far superior to that of the shellac phonograph records in common use. Some fifteen "distributors" in other cities provided a similar wired service and paid Muzak a 10 percent royalty. Muzak's New York studio was also available for a fee to other interests who had recordings to make.

There was another aspect to Muzak's business. When the North American Company began to pour money into Muzak, the fear that ASCAP might shut off the supply of music led agents of Muzak to the main music publishing houses of Europe. They bought the rights to virtually all the great classical music still under copyright. Muzak then formed a subsidiary company known as Associated Music Publishers, or AMP, which rented performing rights to this music to symphony orchestras and collected rental or license fees of various kinds. Arturo Toscanini, for example, would spend a week or two in AMP offices drawing on its library of music to block out his annual concert schedule.

Muzak also had formed the Associated Program Service, APS in the trade, to prepare musical programs for rebroadcast by radio stations. The APS service consisted of a basic "library" of five thousand tunes, with one hundred new selections a month plus a script service. The radio station could take the script from the mails and the discs from its files and go right on the air, adding local commercials in the spots left empty for the purpose. Finally, Muzak had acquired from Warner Brothers a small radio production company which wrote and recorded soap opera programs for sale to radio stations.

This miscellany was presided over by Waddill Catchings, a former senior partner of Goldman Sachs, and a man who had a flair for showmanship. Catchings had been flattened by the great crash of 1929, but he still had many influential friends. Among these were the Warner brothers on whose board he still served. Another was Harrison Williams, the head of North American. Catchings owned one-third of Muzak's common stock; Warner Brothers also owned a third. Potential control over Muzak remained with the North American Company, because it retained $500,000 in preferred stock.

Miller, after telling Benton about the development of Muzak, seemed suddenly smitten by a great idea. Would Benton be interested in one-third of Muzak's common stock so that the enterprise could benefit from his experience and contacts in advertising? He might persuade advertisers to rent Muzak's New York studio. Later Benton was to discover a stronger motive behind Miller's show of interest. With Catchings and Warner Brothers owning two-thirds of Muzak's common stock, Miller had no real say in running the company. He was effectively disfranchised. If he could persuade Catchings to persuade Warner Brothers to sell their stock to Benton, Benton and Miller could jointly control the company. This could give Miller a much stronger position in its affairs—if he could control Benton.

Benton said that the general proposition did not interest him. The investment was small, however, and he felt he understood and could contribute to the business. At the end of the breakfast meeting, it was understood that Miller would consult with Catchings about bringing in Benton and ask if Catchings would approach Warner Brothers about selling their one-third of Muzak's common stock to Benton.

Catchings was persuaded that Muzak could profit from Benton's advertising experience. He won Warner Brothers to that view, and they agreed to give up their common stock. Benton would be paid $15,000 a year to help Catchings expand Muzak's operations, and he and Miller would put up another $30,000 each. The new money would build a record processing and pressing plant to supplement the studio Muzak already owned. This would give the studio a package extending right through to the record—the final product—and should make its services easier to sell.

Years later, looking back on the circumstances that made him a partner of Miller and Catchings, Benton observed: "The picture of me not long out of the advertising agency business in association with these two old-time speculators and financial experts is rather amusing." He could afford to think it "rather amusing" at that time—for he emerged from the experience with a personal gain of more than $4 million. It was not at all amusing in the beginning. His lawyers, Davis and Gilbert, looked with disfavor on his initial involvement in the enterprise and, a year or so later, strongly warned him against an even deeper involvement.

Benton soon saw that his inexperience in corporate management and finance had led him, in the case of Muzak, to acquire little more than a sharecropper's interest in a dust storm. Nothing was right. The organization had no coherence and no central direction. Its divisions either drifted or worked at cross purposes. Though the company was virtually insolvent, Waddill Catchings drew $60,000 a year as president, occupied an expensive suite of offices in the Chrysler Building—and occupied his thoughts with other matters. He was fascinated by the bands in Muzak's recording studio, spent much of his time at recording sessions, but showed little interest or capacity for the executive operations of the company. Allan Miller wished to see Muzak made profitable. But as he was based in London and was more a financier than a business manager, he could contribute little on the executive end of things.

If there was any fortunate element in the picture it was that Benton was free—because of his half-time arrangements at the University of Chicago—to come to New York regularly to attend to Muzak business.

In many friction-laden meetings with Catchings, Benton argued that Muzak would remain a trifling hodgepodge if its salesmen confined their approaches to hotels and restaurants and sold Muzak as a substitute for the live music these establishments might yearn for. Like the music that cigar manufacturers had played to Cuban workers while they were rolling cigars, Muzak should be described as "music that is *not* to be listened to." It should be sold that way to banks, department stores, barber shops, doctors' offices, hospitals, and other places where no music of any kind had been used before. Catchings scorned the argument.

One day Benton was in New York meeting with Catchings and learned to his surprise that Muzak had just been installed throughout the National City Bank's Forty-second Street branch. This was the bank where he had been in the college training class during the summers of 1919 and 1920. As Benton later recalled:

I went at once to see the manager, and he recognized me as a former trainee as I walked through the door of his office. In answer to my questions about Muzak, he had a story to tell. "I live," said he, "at the Hampshire House where Waddill Catchings lives, and we have Muzak. You know that a lot of our people in the bank have to work at night and it's pretty dreary being up under the electric lights—much like a prison. The department head where checks are processed, and who works at night, came to me and asked for a radio. I didn't like the idea of a radio with its talking. So I put in Muzak. The people in the department liked it. Then the other departments asked for it. Then still other departments. Finally, everybody in the bank wanted it. Now I have it installed throughout the entire bank. Come, I'll show you."

The tour of the bank confirmed Benton's repeated argument that Muzak could and should be sold not merely as a substitute for live music. He was particularly struck by his visit to the "personal loan department," where people came to borrow $300 or less—and came back only when they were in default on their payments. Here Benton asked a young receptionist, "How do you like Muzak?" She liked it, and added, "You know, it makes this place less gruesome." It was to be an important phrase.

The next day an embattled Allan Miller came to New York and met in private with Benton for some plain talk. He was displeased with Waddill Catchings's performance as president of Muzak. He had hoped that with Benton's help things could be changed for the better but now realized that no one could change things for the better until the root of the trouble was dealt with. That is what Miller meant to do. If Benton was not prepared to join with him in firing Catchings, he would buy Benton's common stock in Muzak and pay well for it. Since the ownership of that stock would give Miller control of Muzak, he could then proceed to remove Catchings from the presidency.

Apart from the financial inducements Miller was offering, Benton's own rapidly maturing antipartnership approach to business made him sympathize with the motive behind the offer. Yet he refused to dispose of his stock to Miller, whatever he offered for it. He said he could not forget that he had acquired the Warner Brothers common stock through Catchings. If he now resold it, it would appear that from the very beginning Miller had used Benton to get control of Muzak at Catchings's expense. If the setup was to be changed, it should not be done behind Catchings's back but with his direct knowledge and participation.

His refusal to sell set the stage for a three-cornered session among Miller, Benton, and Catchings. Benton had never in his life witnessed a clash like it. He was in the middle while the two old-timers tested each other in hand-to-hand combat. Miller took the initiative by bluntly stating that he was disgusted and proposed to clear out of Muzak. He was therefore prepared to sell his common stock for $100,000—a sum Miller said was roughly equal to what by this time he had invested in the company. Would Catchings buy it? He could not. He didn't have the money, and he couldn't raise it. In the end, the deadlock between the combatants was broken when Benton spoke up coolly to say that he was prepared to buy Miller's stock at the asking price of $100,000.

Miller and Catchings agreed. But Benton's lawyers, Davis and Gilbert, reacted to the news of his offer as though he were on top of the Empire State Building preparing to jump. It was bad enough that he had recently lost so much of his capital to misguided investments in the stock market. It was reckless in the extreme to pour into a highly risky venture like Muzak so great a proportion of the remaining capital he had or was due to receive from Benton and Bowles.

Benton, however, would not retract his offer. He told his lawyers to close the deal. He realized that there were risks, but he was interested in the challenges and opportunities the business presented; they were more important to him than the possible dangers. He remembered the remark of the young receptionist in the National City Bank's personal loan department— Muzak "makes this place less gruesome." The land must be full of other places that Muzak could make "less gruesome"—given the right sales approach. He was buying Miller's stock not on the past record of the company, which was dismal enough, but on his confidence in what he could do with the company in the future.

After Benton acquired control of Muzak, he tried for a full year to work in harness with Waddill Catchings as president. But Catchings continued to oppose Benton's ideas. In the hope of getting more hauling power into the company, Benton engaged his old friend Gene Tracey to work in the New York offices as a part-time sales manager. But Tracey let Muzak slide in favor of other matters. There was a change for the better when Benton prevailed on Bertha Tallman, who had served Benton and Bowles as a kind of "expediter and traffic manager-in-chief," to work for Muzak. She was an exceptionally intelligent, imaginative, and devoted woman who made a profound impression on anyone who ever worked with her.

In addition to the acquisition of Bertha Tallman's services, there was another potential change for the better when Catchings agreed to let Benton give his own sales pitch to Muzak's New York salesmen. There were six of these, and they worked under a $100-a-week manager. In a meeting with the salesmen, the manager told Benton that Muzak was in 80 percent of the hotels and restaurants in New York which were potential customers, and that this was the ceiling of the market because there would always be 20 percent that could not be sold or whose credit was not good. The manager laughed at Benton's view that Muzak could be sold to other places that were not the traditional users of music—banks, hospitals, department stores, and the like. Benton interrupted to ask the six salesmen if they agreed with the manager's view, and five did. The one who, like Benton, saw the opportunities, was a young man named Dudley Earl who had worked for Muzak for six weeks. Shortly, the other salesmen were fired and Dudley Earl was made sales manager.

This only served to exacerbate relations between Catchings and Benton. There was then a mutually agreed upon divorce and mutually satisfactory barter deal. Benton, despite his keen interest in radio, was not interested in Muzak's radio program production division. He did not want to produce soap operas in competition with producers that might rent Muzak's studios. Catchings, on the other hand, was interested in the division. In exchange for Catchings's common stock, therefore, Benton gave the radio production part of Muzak to Catchings, plus $2,500 in cash. As a result, Catchings found an extraordinary new and natural outlet for his gifts of showmanship. In the next few years he succeeded brilliantly and reaped handsome financial rewards as a producer of radio and then of television shows. Later, too, Allan Miller sold his Rediffusion Company to a large utility firm in Great Britain, and retired with a large fortune.

The deal with Catchings meant that Benton in three bites had gained all the common stock of Muzak at a total cost of $132,500. The North American Company, in addition to its $500,000 in pre-

ferred stock, was also entitled to certain royalties. Dividends at
7 percent had accumulated and were due on the preferred stock.
Moreover, the holder of the preferred stock had the right to elect
one member of Muzak's board of directors and for many years this
member was Herbert C. Freeman, the principal financial officer of
the North American Company. Of his relationship with Freeman,
an Englishman, Benton said:

> We got along exceedingly well. He wanted nothing for
> North American except to protect its $500,000 preferred
> stock investment. He understood the problems that I was faced
> with—and he understood them with sympathy. He was the
> highest type of financial officer who develop through our top
> crack accounting firms, so many of which stemmed from En-
> gland. Many of the financial gyrations of the company re-
> quired the approval of Mr. Freeman. Many men would not
> have given the approval. He gave me his confidence and sup-
> port and approved everything and ultimately got his $500,000.
> I have every reason to be deeply grateful to him. He was a
> model director, always constructive and generous with his time
> and advice.

Muzak's potential growth was slowed down first by the defense
program and then by America's entry into World War II. After
V-J Day, when restrictions on telephone wires were lifted and raw
materials became available, the enterprise began an expansion into
countless cities with many new outlets—factories, elevators, buses,
airplanes. To direct this expansion work, Benton found a new president for Muzak in the person of Harry Houghton, a Canadian-
born advertising man recommended by Raymond Rubicam.

At Yale, Benton had come to know only a few members of the class
ahead of him. One of these was Henry Luce, Jr., whose family background, like Benton's and Hutchins's, featured clergymen and missionaries. In the passing years, Benton and Luce had developed a
resilient, "slam-bang" friendship that mixed elements of personal
affection, professional respect, one-upmanship, and mutual irritation.

A number of Benton's friends were key figures in the growing
Luce publishing empire: Russell ("Mitch") Davenport, a Yale
friend; Tom Matthews, Benton's roommate at Shattuck, who had

become managing editor of *Time;* and Roy Larsen, a neighbor at Southport. There was also Ralph Ingersoll, former managing editor of the *New Yorker* whose star was now rising in the Luce organization. In the summer of 1936 when *Life* magazine was in the final months of gestation, Benton had been among the first outsiders to whom Luce and Ingersoll showed the dummies of the format. Ingersoll on that occasion had brought along a cameraman—*Life*'s first employee—who took pictures of the men poring over the dummy. Two of the photographs, inscribed by Luce and Ingersoll, led Benton to begin a collection of newsworthy photographs which in a few years literally covered his office walls.

Benton had seen little of Ingersoll in the three years after the pictures were taken showing the huddle around the dummy of *Life* magazine. But on a day in the fall of 1939, Ingersoll invited him to cocktails. On arrival, Benton was delighted to find a third person at the party—Laura Kean Hobson who had been with Benton as a young and low-paid copywriter at Batten. Now she was the chief writer of promotion ads for *Time* magazine and was known to be one of the most gifted writers in the genre to be found in America.

Ingersoll told Benton that he was taking leave of the Luce organization in order to start a new type of newspaper in New York City. "We are turning to you," Laura Hobson cut in to say, "to find out how to raise the money." Benton couldn't answer this, but he had a question of his own. Had anyone prepared a statement explaining why another New York newspaper was needed, the form it would take, the reasons for investing in the project, and the grounds on which a profit could be expected? Ingersoll, in reply, handed him a sixty- to seventy-page document, and Benton promised to read it on the train home to Southport.

In this reading, Benton felt that the text failed to make a convincing case why prospective stockholders could reasonably hope to make money on their investment. But where the text touched on editorial content and format, it was often eloquent, and electric with new ideas. Benton raced through dinner in order to get at his dictating machine. He rattled off seven single-spaced pages of comment to Ingersoll.

Two days later, Ingersoll arranged another cocktail meeting with Benton and Laura Hobson. Benton was now urged to write the fund-raising document for what became the newspaper *PM*. He first refused, but then agreed. His interest had been aroused by Inger-

soll's vision of a new kind of newspaper. While he asked no compensation for writing the fund-raising document, it is unlikely that
the prospect of getting some stock for his work eluded him. On his
return to Southport that evening, Benton worked through the
night, and by dawn had a fund-raising document of twenty-nine
handwritten pages. These were typed in the morning and sent to
Ingersoll, who accepted the text without changing a word. The
effort came to be known as the "Blue Book," for its binding between
blue cardboard covers. Most of the editorial ideas in it were Ingersoll's. The presentation was largely Benton's, as were the arguments dealing with financial and business appeal to prospective investors.

The "Blue Book" stressed among other things that the newspaper
would have large, easy-to-read type and would be better and more
interestingly written than any contemporary newspaper. Stories
would be printed continuously, and news, arranged in departments,
would appear in the same place every day. There would be lavish use
of color, maps, photographs, and diagrams. The newspaper would
also have innumerable features not to be found in any other publication: shopping reports on bargains; menus based on food sales
and daily market reports; the first complete, intelligent guide for
radio listeners (a Benton idea); information about housing bargains; and so on.

Like the highly successful *Reader's Digest* at that time, the newspaper would carry no advertising—would be free of the pressure
said to lead editors and writers to "censor themselves 1,000 times
for every one time" they are censored by their advertisers. "We
know for whom we are working," said the "Blue Book." It is "the
good people who pay us five cents a day for our paper. Later, when
they also know for whom we are working, we expect to solicit and
profit from certain types of advertising. If we achieve the substantial circulation we expect, publishing history shows that advertisers
in plenty will inevitably follow. Thus advertising can and will be
sold, but only after we achieve circulation success. Circulation is
the heart of the problem, for with this, at a five cent price, we don't
even require advertising and are independent of it. The advertising
will be *plus* revenue and *plus* profits." It was estimated that the
newspaper could break even with a 200,000 circulation, with
profits rising to $7 million a year on a circulation of 1,000,000.

Benton neither helped Ingersoll in personal approaches to investors nor did he buy any of the stock. He felt that the venture was much too speculative for the condition of his own financial resources at the time. When the capital stock had been raised, however, Ingersoll gave him one thousand shares of *PM* common stock in recognition of his work in writing the fund-raising "Blue Book." After that, it seemed that Benton's future connection with *PM* would be confined to little more than the role of a man in the bleachers cheering the home team. But in February 1940, when he was vacationing in Palm Beach, Florida, he was unexpectedly visited by Ingersoll, who urged him to come to work for *PM* on a part-time basis.

After reviewing his responsibilities to the University of Chicago —and now also to Muzak—Benton finally decided that all could be managed simultaneously. He would concentrate on *PM* for the crucial months immediately before and after its first publication date, set for 12 June 1940. Then he would return to the Midway in October to concentrate on University of Chicago matters until May 1941. Ingersoll agreed to the proposed schedule, and Benton signed a contract to consult with him on creating a sales and promotion operation for *PM*, "including the staffing of same and determining the policies under Ingersoll's direction." He would complete the job by 15 July 1940, and from then until October first, he would "take no responsibility, but would be available for consultation."

For services rendered, he would have Ingersoll's personal commitment to recommend to the board of directors that he receive three thousand shares of common stock from the fifty thousand set aside for employees, plus $7,500 in salary and $2,500 in expenses. The compensation would not be contingent on anything that happened after 15 July, though it was hoped that "*PM* will want Benton in some permanent capacity, at present completely undefined, and that Benton will want to accept such permanent responsibility." The press announcement would make plain that Benton was still a vice-president of the University of Chicago but could work for *PM* under his half-time agreement with the university.

Benton joined *PM*'s board of directors and went to work on promotion and circulation problems. The circulation manager was Harry Feldman, a brave and honest man who talked like a Damon Runyon character and had been president of the local newspaper deliverymen's union. He was around five feet ten inches in height and weighed about 230 pounds—all muscle. He had needed it to

survive the gangster-ridden circulation wars of the past when he
was the city circulation manager of Hearst's New York *Evening
Journal*. Benton rode the delivery trucks, met their drivers, talked
to newspaper distributors and to people who ran newsstands.
Crowds seemed to part before Feldman, and newspaper venders
would rush forward to grab his hand. With Feldman as the teacher,
Benton, a university vice-president, was educated in the raw and
exotic world of newspaper circulation in New York. What he
learned in his "cram course," he soon put into a harshly realistic
memorandum to Ingersoll and *PM*'s executive committee.

> Theoretically [he began], editorial content should be the
> major determining factor in a newspaper's success. Practi-
> cally, this is not true. The editor, generally speaking, rates
> about fourth in the newspaper hierarchy—below the publisher,
> the business manager and the circulation manager—and often
> below the advertising manager as well. . . . The second man in
> power and influence on most papers is either the business man-
> ager or the circulation manager. . . . *PM*'s distribution presents
> a problem not resolvable by any ordinary efficient business
> approach. Our circulation operation may require substantial
> capital outlay; it will require close collaboration with City
> Hall and the Police Department; it may require an editorial
> crusade in *PM* itself; and since our revenue will accrue solely
> from circulation, this becomes our most difficult problem dur-
> ing the months to come. If the editorial operation is the heart
> of the paper, the circulation operation is the lungs and intes-
> tines.

There followed a detailed analysis of how the hostility of the
existing evening newspapers would bar *PM* from using existing distributing agents and make it virtually impossible to find space on
the city's twelve thousand newsstands. Benton hoped to solve part
of the problem by ordering twenty-five hundred special metal stands
like those Emory Thomason of the *Chicago Times* had used. But
there were other problems. Suburban agents changed their minds
about handling *PM* under threats from the circulation managers
for the *News* or the *Sun*. Plainly, *PM* had to find small distributors
in outlying territories, or finance young men trying to establish
their own businesses.

The key figure in New York distribution was Max Annenberg,

the circulation manager of Joseph Patterson's *New York Daily News*. Benton had paid a New York newspaperman $500 to go to Chicago and to dig into Annenberg's career in that city, where he had first made his reputation in the circulation wars between the *Chicago Tribune* and the Hearst newspapers. The research in Chicago provided the background for the portrait Benton drew in his own memorandum of a brutally ruthless competitor. It was Annenberg, said Benton, who was "largely behind the present activities aimed at *PM* in sending the word out to distributors not to handle *PM*."

To get around this menacing man, Benton recommended that several things be done. Home subscriptions, especially in the outlying districts, should have a first priority of *PM*'s circulation efforts, and home subscriptions should be solicited by direct mail. Moreover, in a two-week trial, *PM* should attempt to cover between six and seven thousand newsstands through its own delivery trucks, at an estimated cost of $7,500 weekly. If the circulation did not hold up after two weeks, the scope of the newsstand effort should be sharply reduced in proportion to circulation, and in line with a schedule set in advance. Out of town, *PM* should move into only those territories where it could secure representation at a reasonable cost.

As publication day approached, it appeared that *PM* would have in home subscriptions one-half of the 200,000 circulation estimated as the break-even figure. But before *PM*'s first number was actually printed, Benton dined with Louis Weiss, the lawyer of both Marshall Field, a major investor in *PM*, and Ralph Ingersoll. He told Weiss that he had grave doubts about *PM*'s power to survive. Benton also had a personal reservation. Under his contract, he had been paid $7,500 in salary, but at Ingersoll's request he had used this salary to buy common stock. The way things were going, however, if he wanted to reclaim the $7,500 in cash, it seemed highly unlikely that he could find a buyer for his stock. "Don't worry," Weiss said; "I think I can guarantee you that the purchase money of $7,500 for your common stock will be forthcoming."

After two weeks of publication, Benton had a candid talk with Ingersoll. He told him that *PM* had not turned out as it was meant to be. It was but a "distant cousin" of the newspaper described in the "Blue Book." He wanted to resign from the board and cash in his common stock. He also wanted to cash in the one thousand shares of common stock given him months previously for work on the "Blue Book." Ingersoll agreed that Benton was entitled to the $7,500 in cash but did not feel that he should be asked to redeem the stock. Moreover, Ingersoll hoped Benton would remain a member of the board of directors for the summer, until he could be replaced without creating a stir. "I was so relieved," Benton later recalled, "at the thought of getting back my $7,500 in cash, that I hastily agreed to keep the 1,000 shares he'd given me." The stock he retained presently lost all value except as a memento.

While Benton foresaw disaster for *PM*, he did not expect it to happen before the summer was out. He therefore agreed to remain on the board for another two months, but he never attended another board meeting. He had been one of the first to join Ingersoll on the *PM* project, and he was the first to leave it when he saw where it was heading. For the common stock he had turned in, Benton soon received a check for $350 more than the $7,500 he expected. The check came from a law firm he had never heard of. Only afterward did he learn that the money for the stock purchase had come from Marshall Field via Louis Weiss's law firm.

In retrospect, it appeared that Marshall Field, early in *PM*'s history, was interested in acquiring control of the newspaper. His overt move to that end came at a time when its circulation dropped to 31,000 while its debts falling due exceeded by far any funds on hand. Field then let it be known that he was ready to invest $800,000 in *PM* in return for full stock control of the newspaper and all its assets. Under the terms of his offer, he would pay twenty cents on the dollar in order to buy all the preferred stock, but the common stock would be worthless. Some of the investors angrily threatened lawsuits if Field's conditions were accepted by a majority of *PM*'s directors. Benton was instrumental in heading off the threats by telling the disgruntled investors that even at the twenty cents on the dollar being offered for their preferred stock, they should get down on their knees and thank Marshall Field for bailing everyone out of a messy situation without further embarrassment to all concerned.

Much later, in the spring of 1941 to be exact, Benton learned that Field's interest in the newspaper business went beyond *PM*. The two men were lunching together in Chicago and talking about such matters as *PM*, whose bills Field was paying, and the University of Chicago, of which he was a trustee. The university was still being roughed up periodically by most Chicago newspapers, though Benton's efforts with Colonel Frank Knox of the *Chicago Daily News* and with Colonel Robert McCormick of the *Chicago Tribune* had greatly eased the blows. That there were any blows at all bothered Field greatly. Now at lunch, he suddenly said to Benton: "I'm sick and tired of seeing the University of Chicago pilloried by McCormick and his kind. Why don't I start a newspaper in Chicago? How do I do it? Will you look into the matter for me and tell how to go about it?"

Benton welcomed the surprising assignment. He was certain that Hutchins would share his own conviction that nothing could better serve the needs of the University of Chicago than to have a strong, friendly newspaper on its side. He was not slighting the role of the *Chicago Times*, which, alone among Chicago newspapers, had steadily backed the university. But its launching in 1929, as an afternoon tabloid, had coincided with the onset of the Great Depression, and most of its troubles stemmed from that fact. Its publisher, Emory Thomason, seemed to be holding the *Chicago Times* together only with chewing gum and baling wire.

Benton went to see Thomason, whom he had first come to know back in 1936 in connection with the Walgreen case at the University of Chicago. The publisher had supported the university valiantly even when Walgreen withdrew his advertising from the *Times*. A self-sustaining friendship had developed between the two, and it had been natural for Benton to seek Thomason's advice about *PM*'s prepublication problems. Thomason, in turn, was fascinated by *PM*'s "Blue Book" and observed that he would like to have the person responsible for its final form as one of his own stockholders. Benton in time accepted the implied invitation. After he received the $7,850 for working for *PM*, he used the money to buy eleven hundred shares of *Chicago Times* stock at 6½, representing around 1 percent of the outstanding stock.

When Thomason was told what Marshall Field had in mind, he said: "Well, that's the end of the *Chicago Times*. I'm just hanging on by a hair." The two men continued to talk. "There's just one way for Marshall Field to accomplish what he has in mind," Thomason suggested; "I'll have to sell him the *Chicago Times*, and he will have to move the *Times* into the morning field as a tabloid. That's where it belongs. Field will then also have to buy an evening newspaper. That means the *Daily News*. He will then have a morning and an evening paper—the *Chicago Times* and the *Daily News*. It's the only way to compete with the *Chicago Tribune*."

The remark was based on sound business sense. The *Chicago Tribune* was a morning paper and did not have an evening paper as well. Thus if Field moved the *Chicago Times* into the morning field and owned the evening *Daily News*, he could offer advertisers special bargains. This would give him a competitive advantage over the *Tribune*, the strongest rival in the newspaper world. Further, Field could publish both newspapers in one plant, with obvious savings. Benton asked what it would take to buy the *Times*. Thomason, in reply, first revealed that he owed the International Paper Company $3 million. He felt, however, that he could settle the debt for $1 million, provided Field was very discreet about his own interest in buying the *Times*. Thomason could then turn over to Field a controlling ninety thousand shares of the *Times* at $30 a share. The arithmetic here worked out to a debt-free sale of the *Times* for $3.7 million.

All this had an honest ring in Benton's ears, and he subsequently arranged to go with Thomason to New York for a meeting with Field. In introducing the two men, he said to Field: "Here is an experienced man who will tell you how to get into the newspaper business in Chicago. I trust him." The Chicago publisher proceeded to outline his thoughts, and Field responded by saying that everything he had heard made sense. "But," said he, "suppose I buy the *Chicago Times*, how do I get the *Daily News*?" Benton had been mulling over the question; "Frank Knox and I are good friends," he cut in to say. "I'll go right down to Washington to see him. He's about seventy, with no children. How can he know whether he'll ever be back? He ought to sell." Field urged Benton to follow up, and he was soon on his way.

Benton's relationship with Knox, starting in 1937, went beyond trying to get Knox's *Daily News* to be more sympathetic toward the University of Chicago. Though the age difference between them was almost thirty years, the two men made congenial companions on "after work" occasions. So it was even after Knox went on leave from the *Daily News* to become secretary of the navy in the Roosevelt cabinet. In the spring of 1941, for example, Knox boarded the yacht at the disposal of the secretary of the navy and sailed to Palm Beach where Benton was vacationing, just to play golf with him for ten days in a row.

Benton sensed that Knox loved the pomp and circumstance of his cabinet post. Moreover, his one-time friends in the Chicago Club, along with many of the key advertisers, bitterly resented his action as a former Republican vice-presidential nominee in accepting appointment as Franklin D. Roosevelt's secretary of the navy. As Benton saw matters, Knox might welcome the chance to escape having to return to the hostile ring of Chicagoans who could make life uncomfortable for him.

Knox received Benton cordially in Washington, and behind locked doors Benton explained his purpose. Without mentioning a prospective deal between Marshall Field and Emory Thomason, he told Knox about Field's general interest in starting a new newspaper in Chicago, "As part of his plan," said he, "Marshall wants to buy your interest in the *Daily News*. Will you sell it to him?" "I don't know whether or not I want to sell the *Daily News*," said Knox; "I'll have to think about it. But if Marshall Field decides to come to Chicago in the morning newspaper field and compete with the *Chicago Tribune*, I'll print the paper in my plant." The offer owed nothing to brotherly love. Knox had a money-eater on his hands in his costly printing plant. Nothing would suit him better than to have Field as a blind angel who would pour vast sums into the treasury of that plant—all for the privilege of bearing the brunt of the battle against Knox's own competitor, the *Chicago Tribune*.

Benton went back to New York and made his report to Marshall Field. Up to this point he felt he had done his best as Field's friend. His one selfish interest in the venture was the University of Chicago's welfare. "It seemed to me," Benton later said, "that I had faithfully and fully answered Marshall's question about how to get into the newspaper business in Chicago. But then I made a serious blunder." He explained that he should have urged Marshall Field to engage a professional for the hard bargaining that still remained to be done. He was sure that under the threat of Field's entrance into Chicago, and Frank Knox's very weak personal and financial condition, the stock Knox owned in the *Daily News* could be bought. Knox was just jabbing for an advantage. "But," said Benton, "I overestimated Marshall's capacity to follow through on his own—though later on, he showed great business ability and staying power when he was forced to bring it into play. In the opening moves, however, he did not know how to use his strength in dealing with Frank

Knox. I was guilty of another serious oversight. I didn't realize that Marshall at the time could be easily influenced by his friends, and often they were friends who were deceived themselves or didn't have his best interests at heart."

Benton left for a springtime vacation in Florida, assuming that he had done all he could to get Field's project underway. A month later, he touched base in Chicago and boarded the Twentieth Century Limited for New York. At Harlem, when the morning newspapers were brought aboard the train, a brief item in the *New York Times* caught his eye. Marshall Field—so he read—was going to start a newspaper in Chicago. It would be called *"The Sun,"* and would be a standard-size paper in the morning field. It would be printed in the plant of the *Chicago Daily News*, and Silliman Evans would be its publisher.

It was the reverse of everything Benton had thought would happen. When the Twentieth Century Limited pulled up in New York's Grand Central Station, he bounded off the train and rushed on to Marshall Field's office nearby at 250 Park Avenue. He burst in on him with a massive question: "Why?" "Well, Bill," Field explained, "after you left for Florida, my friend Charles Cushing took me to lunch with Silliman Evans, his friend from AEF days, and the owner of the *Nashville Tennessean*. They persuaded me it would be undignified to buy a tabloid like the *Times* in order to compete against the *Tribune* in the morning field. Cushing urged me to employ Evans and go into the field with a standard-size paper, and of course I told him about the proposal Frank Knox made to you. This is why we shall print in the *Daily News* plant. I have hired Silliman Evans at $3,500 a week. Emory Thomason looked old and tired compared to the young and vigorous Silliman Evans. Silliman, he's a wonder."

Benton was heartsick when he heard Field's explanation through to the end. Knox now had no financial inducement to sell Field the *Daily News*. Further, by going off to Florida before Marshall Field "had been set up in the right way" with his newspaper project, Benton felt that he had neglected the interests of a friend, the interests of the University of Chicago, the interests of the city of Chicago.

Later in the year, when the *Sun* hit the streets of Chicago, it was hit almost at once by the blow that fell at Pearl Harbor. Under the best of managements, it would have been hard to start a newspaper from scratch with so little preparatory time. It was still harder during the war with everything in short supply—qualified personnel, newsprint, and transport. But in Benton's view, these natural causes for trouble were multiplied by people like Knox, Cushing, and Evans "who saw in Field's innocence and kindness, and his enormous wealth, an open invitation to exploit him."

Each new sign of the terrible financial and personal beating Field was taking was another running sore on Benton's conscience. He ceaselessly thought of how much trouble Field could have been spared if only he, Benton, had stayed close by to help consummate the plan first outlined by Emory Thomason. Sometime in 1944, when Field had lost untold millions in keeping the *Sun* alive—he had already sloughed off *PM*—Benton could hardly contain his own feelings in the matter. He asked Field to join him for a drink at the Chicago Club and there put a passionately felt question to him: "Marshall," said he, "are you going to give up on the *Sun* and chuck it overboard?" Field responded quietly, but firmly. "Bill," said he, "my son, young Marshall, is on Navy duty out in the Pacific. He wants a newspaper in Chicago. For his sake, I'm going to keep at this if it takes every penny I've got."

Eventually Field had to take the first step that Emory Thomason, back in the early spring of 1941, had said would be necessary to make a success of his Chicago newspaper venture. He bought the *Chicago Times*, merged it with the *Sun*, and made the *Sun-Times* a morning tabloid in competition with the *Tribune*. His son, Marshall Field IV, took the second step. He bought the *Daily News* from John Knight who had previously bought the controlling interest in it from the estate of Frank Knox. Marshall IV thereby had the morning and evening newspapers Thomason had envisioned for Marshall III.

How much money had swung on what Benton felt was his own failure in 1941 to guide Marshall III into the course that was ultimately followed? In 1962, when Marshall III was no longer alive, Benton suggested to Marshall IV that the difference in cost to his father had been between $30 and $50 million before he came out on the right side of things. The suggestion went unchallenged.

Benton unexpectedly got a windfall from all this. The time was 1946. Emory Thomason had died, and Benton was serving in Washington as an assistant secretary of state. He was on Capitol Hill one day attending to some official business when he was called to the telephone. Richard Finnegan, the editor of the *Chicago Times*, was at the other end, speaking from Chicago. "Bill," he said, "do you remember when Emory died, you told me I could have your stock in the *Chicago Times* any time I wanted if I had good use for it?" Benton said he remembered. Finnegan responded: "I'd like to buy it. Marshall Field is buying the paper and he wants it." Benton agreed. He later learned he would get $60 a share for the eleven hundred shares of the *Times* stock he had bought at 6½ with the $7,850 he had salvaged from *PM*. This would come to $66,000, which Benton badly needed at the time. Fate seemed to have held it in reserve as balm for two virtuous failures—one in connection with Ralph Ingersoll's *PM* idea, and one in connection with his suffering conscience about his involvement in Field's Chicago missteps.

Toward the end of his life, Field himself was spared any need to be remorseful. Out of his costly blunders from one publishing venture to another he built Field Enterprises, which Benton called "the finest privately and personally owned publishing company in the world." Moreover, Benton felt that he had contributed indirectly to the acquisition by Field Enterprises of *World Book*—today one of the most profitable book companies in the world and pressing the *Britannica* for first place in gross volume of books.

When Benton acquired the *Encyclopaedia Britannica* early in 1943, he wanted some people with experience in book publishing to serve as members of his board of directors. He first approached his friend Harry Scherman, the president of the Book-of-the-Month Club. Scherman said he could not serve, but recommended Max Schuster of Simon and Schuster, who did join the board. Schuster was startled to learn what went on in the encyclopedia business, "Good God!" he exclaimed; "this is the finest book company in the world!" About this time, Marshall Field wanted to find a profitable publishing house to merge with his *Chicago Sun* to offset its heavy losses. Purchase of Pocket Books, 48 percent of which was then owned by Simon and Schuster, led Field to Max Schuster. The latter's observation as a *Britannica* board member subsequently led him to urge Field to acquire the Quarrie Company, which owned *World Book*. Field Enterprises' profits from *World Book* alone were estimated in 1966 to be as high as $20 million before taxes.

Back in the spring of 1940, Benton was drawn into a bizarre project involving Sinclair Lewis, Robert Hutchins, and the 1940 Democratic vice-presidential nomination. Sinclair Lewis had but recently met Hutchins, was greatly taken by him, and decided that

he should be vice-president of the United States under President
Franklin D. Roosevelt. Moreover, in the course of the Chicago visit
he let it be known that he meant to go to Washington to push the
idea among Democrats. Benton who was in Chicago at the time, met
Lewis, heard of his plan, and had grave doubts about what the
novelist would do. Benton told the rest of the story like this:

> I didn't know much about politics but I greatly mistrusted
> Sinclair Lewis wandering around Washington on any such
> mission as this. I went with him. We talked to many of the lead-
> ing intellectuals in Washington. I suppose most of them were
> too incredulous to let us know how incredulous they were. The
> conversation I most vividly remember was the one with Su-
> preme Court Justice William O. Douglas. He said to me flatly,
> "Your friend Hutchins could have had the vice-presidential
> nomination of the Democratic party for the asking, if he had
> accepted the chairmanship of the SEC when Roosevelt offered
> it to him at the time I resigned the chairmanship to go onto the
> Supreme Court. But by turning it down, he forfeited his
> chance."

There may have been a great deal to this, but that was not
the end of the matter. Later, while the 1940 Democratic Convention was getting under way in Chicago, Harry Hopkins
called on Hutchins at his home on the University of Chicago
campus. The oldest Hutchins child, Franja, was then about
fifteen. She opened the door of her home, peered up, saw Hopkins standing there and said to him: "Who are you and what
do you want?" Hopkins replied: "I am Harry Hopkins and I
have come to offer your father the vice-presidential nomination
of the Democratic party." Hopkins and Hutchins were on the
telephone that night with Roosevelt. What was said? I don't
know. But there must have been something in the wind concerning the vice-presidency, since important elements at the 1940
Democratic Convention were uneasy and resentful about the
nomination going to Henry Wallace.

A more substantial enterprise which was to absorb Benton's
energy began in the late spring of 1940 after a meeting of the University of Chicago board of trustees had adjourned. One of the
trustees was Paul Hoffman, an alumnus of the university and the
president of the Studebaker Corporation. Benton had never before

fully taken the measure of the man, but as he headed for the door with Hutchins, Hoffman called after them: "Wait a minute. I want to talk to you two." They stopped. "As a trustee of the university," Hoffman began when he was abreast of the pair, "I think the time is here when our universities must try to do something about the state of the nation. This university has economists and other scholars whose knowledge isn't being applied for the good of the country. What can be done about it?"

Then he drew in broad strokes a picture of existing economic conditions. The economy was being stimulated by war orders from abroad and the beginnings of America's rearmament program. But there remained the unsolved question of how to achieve high levels of employment and production under normal conditions. "This is a problem for university scholars," Hoffman continued. "What they know about it, and the best things that businessmen know, should be merged. If the University of Chicago is to live up to its responsibilities, it should not merely try to accumulate knowledge about society and government, it should apply this knowledge to major practical problems before it is too late. As things stand, patriotic and ignorant businessmen attend Chamber of Commerce meetings and advocate policies which if followed would destroy them and all of us."

Hutchins was surprised by the implied charge that the University of Chicago in nearly fifty years of its life had done so little to better the state of the nation. Yet he and Benton promptly accepted Hoffman's challenge to seek ways for the university to do more to help better the current economic picture. Benton, moreover, was pleasantly startled to hear Hoffman advocate what he himself had been groping toward during the year before he fell ill in October 1938, when he had proposed to Lewis Brown that an educational union be formed between economics professors and corporation presidents. Before the day was out, Benton was on the move to see what could be done to advance the idea he now shared with Hoffman.

In working out the details, Benton turned for help to a University of Chicago faculty member who had become an after-hours companion. This was Harold Lasswell, who had pioneered in the study of public opinion and propaganda and who had raised Benton's sights far beyond the range of Madison Avenue ideas. Lasswell was not concerned with advertising. He was concerned with the question of power in all its forms—political, economic, military, social, cultural, religious. Who, he asked, gets What, When, and How in various societies? To get at the answer he began to apply to group political behavior a number of concepts drawn from the field of psychology and psychoanalysis. This led him to study the subject of psychopathology in politics, particularly as it appeared in the genesis and practices of communism and fascism. He looked long and hard at these worldwide disorders of the political mind, hoping to find in them the terms for a program of preventive medicine that could help maintain America as a free society with equal opportunity for human dignity open to all.

Lasswell welcomed the opportunity to work with Benton on the particular project that had begun in earnest with Paul Hoffman's challenge. The name given the undertaking was the American Policy Commission. In mature form, it called for lining up not a hundred corporate presidents as Benton once hoped but fifteen to twenty "literate" businessmen willing to devote time, effort, energy, and money to the task of clarifying their own minds and those of their fellow citizens about the major alternatives of national policy for a free society. Chosen for their "understanding instead of their name value," they would not be a shifting group of men like the *Fortune* "Round Table," nor, like it, a "mechanical representation of interest groups" brought together to talk off the top of their heads. The same group of men would meet four to six times a year in two- or three-day sessions devoted to the study and discussion of public policy questions, all learning as they went along. With them would work a staff of social scientists appointed to or drawn from the University of Chicago faculty. All members of the American Policy Commission would prepare themselves in advance of meetings by reading the memorandums specially written for the purpose by the academic staff. Experts in any subject under discussion would be brought in from business, government, and the universities. The conclusions of the business and academic group would be published every six months. On a case-by-case basis, they would set forth the ways in which the gap between knowledge and public policy could or should be closed in the interests of a free society.

With the plan of action in mind, a select list of businessmen was compiled, representing likely prospects for membership on the American Policy Commission. Most were personal friends of Benton and Hoffman. Hoffman approached some of these, and introduced Benton to others. But it was Benton who carried the main burden of finding and recruiting fifteen to twenty "literate" businessmen who would be willing to join and had something to contribute to the educational work of the commission. What this entailed would be more than a year and a half of organizational effort—writing, talking, flying around the country, between his other work on many fronts.

The kind of men he and Hoffman approached and who eventually agreed to become members of the American Policy Commission included Thomas B. McCabe, the head of the Scott Paper Company, who would become head of the Federal Reserve Board in 1949 ; R. R. Deupree, the head of Procter and Gamble, and the chairman of the Business Advisory Council to the Department of Commerce ; Clarence Francis, the head of General Foods and a former advertising client of Benton ; Ray Rubicam, the advertising man who had been Benton's principal competitor for General Foods ; Beardsley Ruml ; Paul Mazur ; Marshall Field ; and Henry Luce. In addition there was Ralph Flanders, a Republican, a flinty Vermont toolmaker, and a Boston banker. Flanders, in time, would become the first chairman of the Committee for Economic Development's Research Committee, of which Benton was to be the vice-chairman as well as the vice-chairman under Paul Hoffman of the CED as a whole. Later, as a Republican senator from Vermont, Flanders would escort Benton onto the floor of the United States Senate when the latter was to be sworn in as a Democratic senator from Connecticut. Still later, when Senator Benton tried to persuade the Senate to condemn Senator Joseph McCarthy of Wisconsin, it was Senator Flanders who took the lead after Benton's defeat and was largely responsible for the ultimate censure vote.

Benton's work on the American Policy Commission ran concurrently with his service as one of three official consultants to Nelson Rockefeller, the newly appointed Coordinator of Inter-American Affairs. The other two consultants were Dean Robert G. Caldwell of the Massachusetts Institute of Technology and Henry R. Luce.

Benton had been seeing Nelson Rockefeller regularly from the time they first met in the fall of 1937 in connection with the plan to buy ERPI films and then with the equally futile bid to create—with Rockefeller Foundation money—a corporation to produce educational talking pictures. Apart from his spontaneous personal liking for the man, the cultivation of Rockefeller's friendship was in

Benton's line of duty as a vice-president of the University of Chicago. The Rockefeller family seemed to be trying to move out of its half-century role as a chief source of benefactions to the university. The university was trying to prevent this and wanted one of the Rockefeller brothers to join the university's board of trustees. John, the oldest, was ineligible, since he was the chairman of the Rockefeller Foundation. Nelson, the second oldest, was the logical person to continue the family's link with the university, and in a sense he became Benton's "client responsibility."

Nelson Rockefeller's appointment as Coordinator of Inter-American Affairs at the age of twenty-nine had been recommended to President Roosevelt by Mrs. Anna Rosenberg (now Mrs. Paul Hoffman), who was then, as she is now, one of the most remarkable women in American life. Born into a half-Jewish Hungarian household in the Austro-Hungarian empire, she had come to the United States with her family as a young girl. She got her start in politics as a high school student in the Bronx selling Liberty Bonds during World War I. Later, as a protégée of Mrs. Belle Moskowitz, whom many people credited with being the political brains of Governor Al Smith, she met Franklin and Eleanor Roosevelt and became their intimate friend and collaborator. President Roosevelt wanted to make her secretary of labor or to send her to Moscow as United States ambassador. Other political leaders in New York City urged her to seek the Democratic nomination for mayor or United States Senator. But she declined these promising proposals and chose instead to concentrate on building the very successful firm of Anna Rosenberg Associates, which specialized in labor-management problems and public relations. In 1942, however, when the American defense effort got underway, she closed the doors of her firm to become, by appointment of President Roosevelt, the manpower commissioner of New York. It was in this work that she won the admiration of General George C. Marshall, the United States Army chief of staff, whose faith in her was later graphically expressed when, at the outset of the Korean War, the general, now secretary of defense, recommended that President Truman appoint her as assistant secretary of defense, the first woman ever to hold such a post.

It was in the 1930s that Anna Rosenberg had first emerged in a special relationship to America's "Princes of the Blood." One of her clients was Macy's department store. Beardsley Ruml was then its treasurer, and with his continuing interest in the Rockefeller family, he introduced Anna to them. They became her clients, and through him she met Jock Whitney and Bill Benton, who also became her clients. Through Benton she met Marshall Field, who became a client until his death. Anna fawned on none of them. She scolded them, coaxed them, warned them, encouraged them, guided them toward public service, and used her many political connections to open the doors for them. In this way, she introduced Nelson Rockefeller to President Roosevelt, and his appointment as Coordinator of Inter-American Affairs followed.

Benton met Anna Rosenberg when he himself became a consultant to Nelson Rockefeller. Subconsciously inclined to judge women according to how they compared with his mother's talents and character, he quickly joined the circle of her admirers. As Benton later recalled:

> It was clear to me from the outset that when Henry Luce, Dean Caldwell, and I met with Nelson Rockefeller as his "official consultants"—and when Anna was present—she was the most potent consultant of all. The rest of us could advise him on certain technical points or could help him recruit the personnel he needed. For example, I secured for his Latin American program the services of James Young and Don Francisco, two very able men drawn from the advertising world. But we were all relative strangers to Washington, except for Anna. She alone could recast our advice in political ways that would win acceptance from the President, the Congress, the bureaucracy and the press. We would have been lost babes in the Washington woods without her.

As Nelson Rockefeller's work expanded, so did the number of his official and unofficial consultants. And it was in this way that Benton met and became a close friend of a man whom he was to describe as "one of the finest products the American business community produced in modern times." This was Will Clayton of Houston, Texas, who would be the assistant secretary of commerce to Secretary Jesse Jones and who later would be assistant secretary of state for economic affairs. "While Anna Rosenberg could instruct us in the ways of Washington," Benton said, "there was no one to instruct us in the ways of Latin America until the day Nelson Rockefeller brought Will Clayton up from Houston to join in on our meetings. From

the moment I was introduced to him, I saw the living embodiment of
the old Scotch saying: 'Where McGregor sits, there is the head of
the table.' Will Clayton first looked us over in his quiet way. Then
he listened to us patiently. Then he spoke up to tell us what Inter-
American affairs were all about, and what we might do to contribute
to them in a useful way." It was out of these sessions that Nelson
Rockefeller put together a program—confined by statute to the
Western Hemisphere—which made him the "grandfather" of many
of the programs Benton himself was to extend around the world
after he became assistant secretary of state for public affairs.

Benton, as always, kept his mother abreast of what he was doing.
It was not just a matter of lifting all economic worries from her
shoulders. It was not just a matter of settling her in a comfortable
Riverside Drive apartment with a maid to do all the housework and
cooking, and with a nurse in attendance as well. These details could
be arranged by a check made out to her, or by a secretary. What he
continued to give her was sustained personal attention. When he
was away from New York and could not visit her, he arranged for
friends in the city, or those who were passing through it, to drop in
on his mother for a dinner or a visit. And always, always, through
the frequent letters he wrote her, there ran the language of a devoted son: "I think of you constantly." "I'll catch an earlier plane
so that I can get in an extra hour with you." "It's wonderful to
think of you so much improved, taking your walks, going to mati-
nees, entertaining." "I wish you were here to write that speech for
me which I promised to give Friday night." "When I don't hear
from you, I want to reach for the nearest phone or catch the first
plane out of here to make sure that everything is all right."

Elma, for her part, was not awed by the fact that her son was
moving among the "makers and shakers" in the New York–Chicago–Washington triangle. Though he was now past forty, when
she felt he fumbled or backslid in any small or great matter, she
still let him have it squarely between the eyes. In the spring of 1941,
for example, he sent his mother a newspaper clipping concerning his
work with Nelson Rockefeller. Elma in her own reply ignored everything except one point. "I see you quoted as saying: 'Cultural relations between the American republics.' It sounds very awkward," she
tersely wrote him, " 'between' refers to two. You should say 'cul-

tural relations among the American republics.' " Again, if her son felt that he was managing many things with great aplomb, his mother let him know that he was being harum-scarum. "I think you can easily improve your files," she wrote to him at the University of Chicago. "You are constantly sending me letters that I think should be filed."

She reserved her sharpest barbs for her son's pre–Pearl Harbor involvement with the America-First Committee. Benton himself, in retrospect, found it hard fully to explain that involvement. He was no pacifist, and he detested every aspect of fascism and nazism. Nor was he a Roosevelt hater. In 1940, he flew from Chicago to Southport on the eve of the election for the express purpose of casting his ballot for FDR and not for the Republican presidential candidate, Wendell Willkie. "Willkie," so Benton wrote to Henry Luce after the election to explain his own vote, "thinks politics is a matter of charm and personality. Roosevelt knows it's a life and death business."

Yet the fact remains that Benton and, although it is easily forgotten today, many other people with bona fide liberal credentials did support the America-First Committee directly or indirectly. Among them were such distinguished citizens as Norman Thomas, Philip Jessup, Faith Baldwin, Harry Emerson Fosdick, Philip La Follette, Chester Bowles, and Robert Maynard Hutchins. All these were deeply concerned with the preservation of civil liberties in the United States. All recalled how those liberties had been battered in the United States during and immediately after World War I, and they feared a repetition of the experience if America were drawn into a second war. "Fortress America" had a special meaning for them. They felt that if the United States strengthened its society from within, it could face the world—even an Axis-dominated part of the world—with an example of democracy at its best; and the force of the example by itself would somehow work for the liberation of people who were voluntarily or involuntarily caught in the camp of the totalitarians. Their implicit assumption seemed to be that America actually had a choice to get into the war or stay out of it. Hence Roosevelt must be prevented from choosing to get into it or from moving in that direction. They did not see that events themselves were in the saddle. And they were eventually surprised when it was not by the route of Europe, on which their attention was focused, and not by free choice, but by the route of the Pacific and a surprise attack by the Japanese that America was plunged into a world war.

Elma Benton from the very beginning disapproved of her son's association with the America-First Committee, but she compressed her strongest blast into a letter she wrote him the day after Pearl Harbor. "There are many nice people at large," she observed, "who will be behind bars like the Englishman Mosley before this war is over. There is nothing creditable in failing to give the last full measure of devotion to your country when her life is at stake, no matter what might be thought of the many factors that brought her into the present situation. I think that if there were any way of determining what brought you in touch with that America First crowd, maybe it is to your credit. I fear it is a case of Old Dog Tray getting into bad company. Your mother did not raise you that way." She had something else to add: "I have an unhappy feeling that you are maladjusted at present. Your will is not your own. Hutchins is marching to a certain doom, and you are being dragged along to it by him." She wanted her son to break the chain of that close association and was even ready to see it done by having Benton go back to Benton & Bowles at anything or nothing a year, since Bowles had left the agency to become the Connecticut director for the Office of Price Administration.

> Tell Robert Hutchins [Elma said] that either Chet or you ought to be with the business and that it seems under the circumstances that Chet is of more use to the government than you can be. . . . You have had a valuable experience in Chicago. There is nothing to gain by staying there. You have a God-given opportunity to leave. You have to have three homes. You can't afford it. If Robert Hutchins were discharged you might feel that you must stand by him. This is the time. You have put yourself in a very ugly position because of the America First connection. I shall always consider Robert Hutchins responsible for that.

It was one of the few times in her long life that Elma, the daughter of a Union soldier who had been a sharpshooter at Vicksburg, missed hitting the bull's eye. It had been more a case of Benton persuading Hutchins to speak out in support of the America-First Committee's position than the other way around. It was also the only time in her long life that Elma ever advised her son to contract out of what she felt was a character-testing situation. Ironically, the advice came at a moment when Benton, unknown to himself, had set in train a sequence of events which were to tie him tightly to the University of Chicago generally and to Hutchins personally. More about this after a transitional chapter.

14

Rule Britannica

In November 1941, Benton had completed four years as part-time vice-president of the University of Chicago. His initial hope of concentrating on academic work had been largely diverted into the kind of public relations work which Hutchins thought would be most useful to the university. Many of the ideas in the book Benton wrote for the trustees in 1936 had been carried out with good results, and in Benton the university had an effective ambassador to the business community and to the Chicago press. But Benton himself felt that after five years of association with the university he had failed to advance in any major way on two fronts which were of central interest to him—the development of radio and of talking pictures for educational purposes.

His use of the $50,000 annual grant from the Alfred Sloan Foundation had greatly improved the quality and enlarged the audiences of the university's "Round Table" broadcasts. In the "Human Adventure" broadcasts, originating at the university and dramatizing strategic episodes in the advancement of human knowledge, he had shown that a radio program could be instructive *and* entertaining. Still, by his own standards, and considering the "personal muscle" he once wielded in the radio industry, he had fallen far short of his initial hope that the university's resources could bring about at least a minor revolution in broadcasting in "the public interest, convenience and necessity"—to use the key phrase in the law establishing the Federal Communications Commission.

The university had the courage but lacked the money to underwrite such a revolution. The great foundations had the money but lacked the courage. The radio networks were inclined to evade appeals to back educational broadcasts "in the public interest, convenience and necessity," and the career of the "Human Adventure" program was a case in point. CBS, to its credit, had given the program a trial run during the summer. But when its popularity had been proved, CBS knocked it off the network as the fall approached. William Paley, with disarming candor, said he did not want to get stuck with a popular program on a free-time basis—as NBC had already been stuck with the popular "Round Table" broadcasts. "Human Adventure" was rescued only when the smaller Mutual network picked it up.

Benton had even less to show with respect to his early hope that the University of Chicago could dramatically improve the quality and quantity of educational talking pictures and relate them directly to courses taught in elementary and secondary schools. Every time he tried to acquire ERPI films for the university or for a group of people working closely with the university, he found himself in another dead-end street. He seemed to live the truth of Beardsley Ruml's remark that "in a university setting, what you want to do is important, only you can't do it, while in business what you want to do is unimportant but you can do it."

Still, despite his gnawing sense of failure, Benton in the four-year period before November 1941 served the university in ways which went beyond the work described above. Because he continued to look at the world of higher learning through "naive eyes," he was often the first to hit upon critical issues to which wise men were blind. He would then formulate the issues succinctly and compel the university administration to consider its own position with respect to them. Thus he was the first person at the University of Chicago—and perhaps one of the first at any American institution of higher learning—who recognized an emerging major question: How would government research, development, and training programs affect the universities participating in them?

As late as mid-November 1941, or three weeks before Pearl Harbor, the percentage of federal funds embraced by university budgets was miniscule. At that time, for example, Dr. Vannevar Bush, the head of the government's newly formed Research and Development Committee, had only $17 million to distribute to all universities and industrial corporations doing government-contracted research in the physical sciences, and only $3 million in the biological sciences. Also at that time, John W. Studebaker, the United States commissioner of education, had only $17.5 million to underwrite college courses to meet the shortages of engineers, chemists, physicists, and production supervisors. Yet minute as the figures and the programs were, they were large enough for Benton to see the great issue they pointed to.

He had spent the second week of November in Washington, interviewing fifty leading officials at different agencies, hoping that they might tell him how the University of Chicago could best be used to promote the defense effort. On 14 November, he paused long enough to write a memorandum addressed to Hutchins and to key trustees. He observed, to start with, that the natural scientists at the university were already at work on about twenty government research projects totaling $250,000, and the number of projects was increasing. Most were highly confidential, all were in the natural sciences, and some helped carry the university's overhead. But the university did not know whether it was doing all the research work it should in a time of crisis, or what it was best fitted to do. Benton then posed the real issue:

> The implications of present government research and training projects are of paramount importance to us and to all educational institutions. The University of Chicago faces important questions on policy. *The government activity in research and in training is the wave of the immediate future. We must decide how aggressively we wish to try to swim with this wave and ride it. In riding it, the character of our institution may change.*
>
> We are compelled on patriotic counts, even if we disregard the financial incentive for the University, to collaborate when the government comes to us and seeks our collaboration. Our choice comes in whether at this time, impelled either by patriotism or by our financial needs, we should more aggressively seek government research funds and training projects. Should we assume a far more active role of self-promotion, instead of the relatively passive role heretofore? I am here assuming that our role should be more active, the extent of greater activity as yet undetermined.

He then related how he had called at the Navy Department, the War Department, the National Research Council, the Department of Commerce, the Office of Government Reports, the Office of Defense Health and Welfare Services—all in order to determine what the government might need from an institution like the University of Chicago. Nothing he heard made any sense. The only bright spot was his meeting with the budget director, Harold D. Smith:

> I told Mr. Smith [Benton continued in his report] that I had come to him to see if he could set up a plan regularly to provide us and other universities with information on the allocation of government expenditures in education and research. Mr. Smith said significantly: "I have been sitting here expecting you." He implied he'd been wondering why I, or someone on a similar mission, hadn't reached his office months ago. Mr. Smith said he hoped leadership could be developed among the universities taking "a larger view" than, he implied, anything Washington has seen thus far. He asked whether such leadership could not, through the presidents of a few leading universities, *initiate a concerted effort on the part of the universities to dig into the whole government effort from their point of view.* "No one will do this digging," said Mr. Smith, "unless the universities initiate it."
>
> Mr. Smith specifically proposed that the universities should look into the administration of Dr. Bush's $20,000,000: "With this vast sum being spent on research by the government, how can the distortion of the universities be prevented?" Mr. Smith advised, "Don't gripe, but study this program constructively. The policy on federal aid to higher education must be clarified. The field should be studied to 'conserve' the resources of the universities."

Benton, at the end of his memorandum, rephrased the paramount question: "How should the grants-in-aid be handled in the best interests of the country and the universities?" He followed this with twenty-two specific questions and proposed answers, including his proposal that "the Federal Government should set up a board to allocate funds for university research, similar to an independent foundation." There was also his proposal that the university "should aggressively seek to place its men on Washington committees" which were then favoring the scientists in the eastern universities to the neglect of those elsewhere in the nation.

In time, everything Benton had foreseen came to pass. The University of Chicago itself was soon represented in force on all the key scientific committees of the war effort. Tens of millions of dollars of federal funds soon began to flow into research projects on the Chicago campus. At war's end, moreover, when the veil of secrecy was drawn back, the university's Metallurgical Laboratory emerged as the single greatest—and most troubled—hero on the scientific front of the war effort. It was in that laboratory, under the direction of Dr. Arthur H. Compton, that physical scientists from the faculty of the university—and those attracted to the university by Compton and by Hutchins—had built an atomic pile beneath the west stands of Stagg Field. Here, on 2 December 1942, they achieved the first sustained, controlled production of atomic energy, and the way was open for the development of the atomic bomb.

The University of Chicago's key role in wartime science was a far, far cry from the conditions which prevailed when Benton wrote his memorandum of 14 November 1941. But the melodramatic changes in the picture at the university, and at other leading universities caught up in the massive federal financing of research, only lent added force to the questions he had raised as an early prophet in Babylon.

In late November 1941, Benton read a memorandum from W. K. Jordan, general editor of the University of Chicago Press, who had just attended two related meetings. The first had been held in New York City, where a distinguished group of scholars had joined David H. Stevens, vice-president of the Rockefeller Foundation, to "consider the desirability and practicability of preparing a new edition of the *Encyclopaedia Britannica*." Jordan observed that all the scholars agreed that a new and completely rewritten edition was in order. But each time "the difficult problem of cost and distribution" came up, Stevens made it plain that he was giving no assurances that the foundation would support the project financially. At Stevens's request, Jordan had called a meeting in Chicago of some twenty members of the faculty to get their views about the *Encyclopaedia Britannica*. Their reaction echoed the sentiments that had been previously voiced in New York. The scholars criticized the quality of the *Britannica* and favored its being rewritten quite literally from *A* to *Z*.

Benton, finding these views in Jordan's memorandum, was taken by surprise. He had never before been even faintly aware that scholars of national repute had a low opinion of the *Britannica*. As a boy, when he looked at the ninth edition arrayed on the shelves of his father's study, he was certain that the *Britannica* ranked only behind the Old and New Testaments as a source of revealed truth. At Shattuck, he was awed to learn that a fellow cadet personally owned a set of the *Britannica*. When he saved his first $100, as a hungry $35-a-week copywriter, his first purchase was a bed from Macy's basement; the second was a set of the *Britannica* in fake green leather.

To hear at the age of forty-one what respected scholars had to say about the *Britannica* was as jolting as if he heard it said that the Sermon on the Mount was the work of a novice copywriter on Madison Avenue. Still, Benton did know something about the history of the encyclopedia. The *Britannica* was not a philanthropy awaiting someone like the Rockefeller Foundation to underwrite the costs of improving its quality. First issued, beginning in 1768, by "a Society of Gentlemen" in Scotland, the *Britannica*, after many ups and downs in the British Isles, was now the property of Sears, Roebuck and Company. The Chicago-based mail-order house had first become involved in the finances and operation of the *Britannica* during World War I. Then, after financing the fourteenth edition of 1929, it had acquired full ownership. Having invested millions in it, Sears now maintained a respectable interest in selling the *Britannica* on the market.

After thinking about this new problem for a while, Benton persuaded Hutchins to go with him to a luncheon with General Robert E. Wood, the chairman of the board of Sears, Roebuck and Company. Benton had become an intimate of the general in the course of work for the America-First Committee of which Wood was the acting chairman. Hutchins, for his part, had known Wood intimately for more than a decade, describing him as his "favorite General," or as "the most respected businessman in Chicago," now that Julius Rosenwald was dead. At the luncheon the three men talked only briefly about the *Britannica*. General Wood revealed that in 1928, Julius Rosenwald, the founder of Sears, had tried to interest the University of Chicago in producing the fourteenth edition of the *Britannica* and offered to underwrite the full cost. The offer had been rejected. Subsequently, Rosenwald had approached Harvard with a similar offer, but Harvard also refused. There was one more significant disclosure. Sears sold nearly one-half of its sets of the *Britannica* to people whose annual income was $2,500 or less. They were the most eager for knowledge for themselves and their children.

A few days after this luncheon, Benton asked Hutchins to consider the possibility of inducing Sears to make the *Britannica* an outright gift to the university. This could bring great tax savings to Sears, while ownership of the *Britannica* could enhance the university's prestige and the scholarship of the university would improve the quality of the set. Hutchins, in reply, thought it best to wait until the directors of the Rockefeller Foundation at an impending meeting decided whether to lend financial support to a wholly new edition of the *Britannica*. The meeting, held on 29 November, made clear that the foundation was an unlikely source of funds.

That is how matters stood on Sunday, 7 December 1941. Benton was at home listening to a "University of Chicago Round Table" radio broadcast dealing with the problem of the American railroads when the announcer cut in with the news flash that Pearl Harbor had been bombed. With this shock, Benton's outlook on America in the world arena was radically changed. At the instant of the news flash, he knew that the America-First Committee must bury itself. He put in a call to General Wood, but learned that Wood was out of the city on business and was due back in Chicago on 9 December.

On the ninth, Benton lunched with the general at the Chicago Club, where they discussed how best to end the life of the America-First Committee.[1] They had settled the matter by the time coffee was served, and Benton changed the subject. "General," said he, "don't you think it's rather unsuitable for a mail-order house to own the *Encyclopaedia Britannica*—and isn't it even more unsuitable in wartime?"

"Yes," the general snapped. "We should never have acquired it to begin with." He agreed with Benton's intimation that the ownership of the *Britannica* could even be an encumbrance now that the United States was at war.

"Does it make any money?" Benton hesitantly asked.

"Yes," said Wood. "It will turn the corner this year and should earn about $300,000." Though this meant profits before taxes, the figure surprised Benton. Everything he had previously heard about the *Britannica* from Wood and other sources led him to assume that the *Britannica* was still a splash of red ink on Sears's ledgers.

"Well, General," Benton said when he rallied from his surprise,

---

[1] General Wood had already volunteered his military services. The committee's files were to go to the library of Stanford University, where Herbert Hoover, an unflagging supporter of the committee, headed the board of trustees.

"you know that universities don't have money to buy businesses. Why don't you make a gift of the *Britannica* to the University of Chicago?"

The general looked hard at him but said nothing. Benton felt nearly as embarrassed as he had in India when he had asked Gandhi for his signature, and the latter had bitterly turned his back. His question to General Wood was straight and crude and fast, and he feared the general felt he was being taken advantage of. The general wordlessly stamped down the big winding staircase of the Chicago Club. Benton followed him to the checkroom where the two men picked up their hats and coats, then walked out of the door leading to the street where Wood's chauffeur drove up and the general got into the car. He had said nothing for perhaps two full minutes. Suddenly he leaned forward from the seat to break the silence. "All right, Bill," he said, "I'll give you the *Britannica*." Then he grinned, waved his hand, and directed his chauffeur to drive off.

Benton wanted to jump the distance between the Chicago Club and Hutchins's office on the Midway. Arriving by conventional means, he burst into Hutchins's office and exclaimed: "Call General Wood immediately and tell him Bill Benton has just arrived in your office and says you [Wood] have just given the *Encyclopaedia Britannica* to the university. See what he says." Hutchins usually could improve anyone's phraseology. This time, however, he repeated Benton's words to the syllable when he reached Wood on the line.

When the general returned to his own office, he had asked for the *Britannica*'s balance sheets and was studying them when Hutchins called. "Of course," Wood said, after verifying the offer, "I didn't mean that we would give you the cash and receivables we have in the corporation. I'm sure Bill understands that. Nor can we give you our inventory—our present stock of books and books being printed. You'll have to come up with about $300,000 for this inventory. But the rest of it—the plates, the copyright, the goodwill, everything else is yours as a gift to the university."

Later he added two points that touched on the heart of the gift. To help the university succeed in the enterprise, General Wood told Benton that he would propose to Sears's directors that all new receivables for five years be financed by the Sears, Roebuck bank. Second, for five years or until one year after the war, collections on the receivables for a university-owned *Britannica* would continue to be made through the six hundred or more Sears credit managers in stores scattered all over the country.

But was the university and its board of trustees prepared to accept the gift? If they did, then aside from the $300,000 needed to buy the existing inventory, how much working capital would be required for operations? Experienced men felt that a minimum of $750,000 in working capital would be needed, and perhaps more than that. It was Benton's judgment that the financing could be handled easily with $250,000. Yet even if he were right, where was that amount to be raised—on top of the $300,000 required to buy the *Britannica* inventory? The search for funds to acquire and finance the *Britannica* was thus interwoven with the question, yet to be answered, about whether the University of Chicago would accept General Wood's generous offer. Benton felt, as did Hutchins, that if the money could be found, the university would welcome the gift.

Before pursuing this particular matter any further, Benton had to bring to a close something else besides the America-First Committee. On the weekend following Pearl Harbor, he went to South Bend for a visit with Paul Hoffman regarding the American Policy Commission. Over the preceding eighteen months, Benton had invested great amounts of his time, energy, and money in getting the commission organized. But in the course of his conversation with Hoffman, the two men agreed that the bombs which fell on Pearl Harbor had also killed the plan for the commission. They felt that, with the nation at war, the kind of businessmen they had recruited for the commission project would be too busy with war work to have any time to spare for educational meetings with economics professors. The judgment erred on the side of pessimism. Their commission idea would spring to life again, and then thrive in the transfigured form of the present-day Committee for Economic Development.

Soon after his return from South Bend, Benton began what he described as a career as a "professional beggar"—all in connection with his search for people who would be willing to put up the money that would enable the University of Chicago to acquire the *Britannica* on General Wood's original terms. This career lasted a year. At one point in it, Benton was prepared to give up everything to attend to an unfinished piece of psychological business carried over from 1917–18 when he had missed World War I. In the spring of 1942 as he neared his forty-second birthday, the War Department offered to make him assistant military attaché in London, with the rank of colonel. Days later, during a visit to the Washington office of his friend Colonel Frank Knox, then secretary of the navy, Benton mentioned the London appointment. Knox's first answer was a soft laugh; Benton countered with an earnest argument. "Frank," said he, "I think I'll be able to write the best reports ever written by a military attaché in all history!" The secretary, laughing louder, asked, "But who would read your reports?" He told Benton to go back to the University of Chicago and apply himself to its great opportunities to be of service to the war effort. The decision was a tough one for Benton, but he later turned down other opportunities offered him by the army, including a major role in training personnel for military government in the conquered territories.

Benton's efforts to find financing for a university-owned *Britannica* began with a January meeting in Washington with Lessing Rosenwald, then a "dollar-a-year man" for the War Production Board. He seemed a logical choice as the first person to turn to for help in raising the funds needed to buy the *Britannica*'s inventory, and for working capital. Not only had his father, Julius Rosenwald, acquired the *Britannica* for Sears, but the Rosenwald family ranked only behind the Rockefellers as the largest donors to the University of Chicago, and Lessing was a trustee of the university.

Rosenwald received Benton courteously, and then politely put a damper on his hopes. He said that nobody could make a financial success of the *Britannica*, and he would be most unhappy if the university acquired it. If it were to be published at all, it might have to be by a world congress or by the Library of Congress drawing on a government subsidy. His key objection—and Benton recognized its force—went back to the circumstances in which Sears came to finance the *Britannica* during World War I.[2] The government had then prohibited installment selling of any object, including books. The *Britannica* had been crippled by this ruling, and to save it from disaster, Sears had temporarily taken it over. No one knew for certain whether in World War II the same governmental ban on installment buying of books would be imposed. If it was imposed, said Rosenwald, where would the University of Chicago be if it operated the *Britannica?* Adequate sales volume to sustain the needed press runs could only be achieved by installment selling, since the great

---

[2]Sears helped finance the company, bought it in 1920, sold it back to its publisher, financed the fourteenth edition, and ultimately reacquired it as that edition appeared in 1929.

group of middle-income families which wanted the *Britannica* could not afford cash.

Benton reported Rosenwald's crucial objection to Hutchins, but met it with a sanguine prediction : installment sale of *Britannica* sets *would* be permitted. "When people find they can't buy automobiles and refrigerators," he wrote Hutchins, "they may buy the encyclopedia they always wanted." In this, however, he had no official assurances whatsoever that wartime installment buying of books would not be banned. To the personal friends in the publishing business whom he subsequently asked to help the university acquire *Britannica*, the words "risk" and "uncertainty" loomed so large that they blotted out any glimpse of the word "profit."

Among those who felt this way were men who could scarcely be accused of having weak nerves. They included Henry Luce, Jr., Harry Scherman of the Book-of-the-Month Club, the Cowles brothers of the Cowles publications, Albert Lasker, DeWitt Wallace of *Reader's Digest*, and George T. Delacorte, Benton's former client at Benton and Bowles who published scores of magazines and Dell Books. All were risk-takers of a high order and had profited enormously from their clear-headed boldness. Yet all doubted that the *Britannica* could be made a publishing success, especially in view of the possibility of a wartime ban against installment buying of books.

Of all the publishers Benton approached for money and leadership, Colonel Robert McCormick of the *Chicago Tribune* was the only one who felt that the *Britannica* could be successfully published from a financial standpoint. McCormick, however, would not give the University of Chicago any gifts. Also, he agreed with Henry Luce on one point—he didn't like the name *Encyclopaedia Britannica*. Luce himself had said that the name implied parochialism—a product "made in England" for the English—and very few such products "would look so hot in the decades immediately ahead." Benton fired back a hot reply. He said that not one person in a thousand associated the name *Britannica* with Great Britain. *Britannica*, with some "150 years of promotion behind it," said he, had "become in the English-speaking world, the generic name for an encyclopedia. It was one of the best-known trade names in the world, compared to which Coca-Cola, Chevrolet, and Kodak were passing fancies."

While Benton encountered successive rebuffs, General Wood did what he could to help the university acquire the *Britannica* on terms which grew successively more generous. He had candidly warned Benton—as Lessing Rosenwald had done first—that the government might put a ban on all installment sales. Indeed, General Wood urged Benton to go to Washington to secure approval of the *Britannica's* installment selling policy, and in early May he did so. He talked to Marriner Eccles and M. S. Szymczak of the Federal Reserve Board, to Beardsley Ruml, Sidney Weinberg, and Leon Henderson, then head of the Office of Price Administration. None could give him a definite answer. But he came away from Washington feeling more strongly than before—on instinct alone—that installment sales of encyclopedias would not be officially curtailed. This gave him a second wind in urging his highly solvent friends to put up the money the university would need to acquire the *Britannica*. The results, as before, were a succession of rejections.

His campaign took a new turn when he received a critically important letter from General Wood. "If I were in the place of the University of Chicago," the general wrote to him on 3 June 1942, "I think I would take a chance on *Britannica*, as I believe the risk is small, and such an opportunity will not occur again. As far as Sears, Roebuck & Company is concerned, I am sure that the combination of circumstances in making this offer will not occur again. We can do it only because this year we have excess profits taxes. Next year we will continue to have the excess profits taxes but it is problematical whether our profits will be above our base."

The question now became whether the University of Chicago—in the absence of an outside benefactor—should use its own funds to acquire the *Britannica*. So far, there had been no formal notification to the University of Chicago's board of trustees of General Wood's offer. Benton, however, had been in constant touch with key trustees. He sent Harold H. Swift, chairman of the board, copies of all important correspondence with the general. He was in frequent contact with Paul Russell, an important trustee and prominent Chicago banker. He also consulted frequently with Herbert P. Zimmerman, an especially important trustee, since he was president of R. R. Donnelley and Sons, the firm that printed the *Encyclopaedia Britannica*.

At a meeting of the full board of trustees held on 11 June 1942, Hutchins formally presented the details of General Wood's offer. He also presented the salient points of a memorandum from William

B. Harrell, business manager of the university, estimating the amount of new capital that would be "required to finance the *Encyclopaedia Britannica* if taken over by the University." On the basis of General Wood's latest offer, this estimate "was not less than $250,000," as against Wood's new and drastically reduced estimate of $50,000 and Benton's revised estimate of $150,000. But Harrell went further to discourage the trustees. He emphasized that additional capital of $425,000 would be necessary to "provide a reasonable margin of safety" in order to cover operating contingencies such as a possible decline in sales or a change in the length of time Sears would be willing to finance accounts receivable and handle collections.

The official report to the trustees touched off months of meetings and discussion—"The Great Debate," Benton later termed it. But even as the proponents and opponents squared off, Benton, in response to a request from Hutchins, prepared a comprehensive document that anticipated everything that was to be said on all sides of the debate. "I don't think this is a simple case of pros and cons," Benton began softly. "One pro may be worth a hundred cons and vice versa." He listed the risks. "We are sure to be criticized for our editorial management. If we stick to the 'annual revision plan,' which I emphatically favor from what I know about it, we'll be criticized by scholars throughout the world for not bringing out a new edition. If we bring out a new edition, this new edition will be criticized, as new editions always are. They never can live up to 10,000 expectations. Then again, we shall have some criticisms of our 'commercialization' of the University, particularly in respect to the *Encyclopaedia*'s installment selling methods."

In stronger accents, Benton continued:

> The big risk is that we might lose money. The University isn't experienced in operating such a business. . . . I think the University, conscious of this risk, should do its best to protect itself by the management set-up provided for the *Encyclopaedia*, and by the instructions given that management by the University's Board of Trustees.
>
> The major chance is the chance for profit. We need the money and this seems to me to be a highly respectable way to get it. I agree that there is risk involved in trying to get it. But the University takes far greater risks all the time, and is so

accustomed to those risks that we forget we are taking them. We have the risk of our investment in common stocks and bonds—and on this risk we can lose more money any day between the opening and closing of the market than we are likely to lose on the *Encyclopaedia* in a year. Then when we add the risks involved in the *Encyclopaedia* our total risk is increased only imperceptibly. Yet our chance of profits is enormously increased. The *Encyclopaedia* may earn $300,000 this year. Thus, as in all business propositions, we must weigh the risks against the possible profits. To me, the risks are relatively small in comparison to the chance at profits.

Beyond possible financial gain, Benton cited another kind of profit. "The University," said he, "is in business to serve the public and it seems to me that improving the *Encyclopaedia* is a suitable [public] service. This is another reason for taking it over." He didn't mind looking a gift horse in the mouth. It was part of his and Hutchins's responsibility to do that. But he didn't think anyone should question the motives of General Wood or Sears, Roebuck in making the offer. "Of course, the General has handled this with an eye to his friendship for you and me," wrote Benton to Hutchins. "It seems to me that the profit figures of the *Encyclopaedia Britannica* demonstrate this. . . . I concede that the teeth in the mouth of this horse are not solid gold. On the other hand, the glint that you see in those teeth is gold. The teeth are at least gold-filled." In concluding with a strong recommendation in favor of accepting the gift, Benton said: "I do not think we should delay too long in accepting it. In fact, I urge speedy consideration of the gift, and enthusiastic acceptance of it, with the full knowledge that the University is taking onto its shoulders a perpetual headache, a headache, however, with the promise of a golden cure which, God knows, is lacking in most of the headaches to which you and I are thoroughly accustomed."

As the weeks went by, the trustees remained undecided about whether the university should use its own funds. Some of their objections echoed exactly what Benton had anticipated in his own memorandum to Hutchins, and these were passed on to General Wood when Benton and Hutchins met with him in the last week of November. The general now said he would not "give, sell, or transfer the ownership of the *Britannica* unless [he was] satisfied that the new control was in the best interest of the *Encyclopaedia.*" Nor would he have offered the *Britannica* to the University of Chicago specifically, were it not for Hutchins's and Benton's presence there. "Of course," he continued, "Sears, Roebuck must officially give the *Britannica* to the university. But I am really giving it to you boys." Then turning to Benton directly, he said: "If you'll interest yourself in the *Britannica* and go to work on it, you can build it into a big business. This is a five-million-dollar gift. Please tell that to your trustees."

He added the offer of a safety net. If the university took over the *Britannica* and if the business operation went bad within the first year, Wood would consider working out an arrangement so that at the option of the trustees, Sears would take back the property. But he stressed that an earlier offer he had made on behalf of Sears— namely, a $50,000 cash gift to the university toward the working capital the *Britannica* would need—would be held open only until 1 February 1943, when Sears's fiscal year ended. This deadline also applied to the offer of the *Britannica* itself.

On 1 December 1942, all that Wood had said—save for the complimentary reference to Benton and Hutchins—was duly reported by Benton in a memorandum to the trustees' joint committees on instruction and research, and on business affairs. Benton added something else of importance which had occurred to him for the first time during a protracted talk with Sherman R. Fuller on the same afternoon as the meeting with Wood. Fuller, who was the comptroller of the Britannica company and a veteran Sears executive who had the general's full confidence, told Benton that he had been studying the many different estimates of various people about the actual amount of working capital the *Britannica* would need for its operations. Now, on the basis of "revised and clarified figures," he had concluded that $100,000 would be sufficient. If so, in the light of the $50,000 gift Sears offered to make toward working capital, the University of Chicago would only have to advance another $50,000. "My opinion is," Benton informed the joint committees of the board of trustees, "that the Board should provide the additional $50,000 and accept the property." However, said he, the financial need probably could not be limited to that precise amount. The trustees should be prepared to advance another $150,000 if required.

In the same memorandum to the joint committees, Benton presented "An Alternative Proposal," which he had privately discussed with Hutchins and Harold Swift after his conversation with Fuller, when the idea was born. If the trustees were not prepared to provide the $50,000 indicated—and it was Hutchins's strong feeling that they were not—then Benton offered personally to finance an amount "up to $100,000" toward the university's acquisition of the *Britannica*. As "the heart of this proposal," he suggested a system of royalties to the University of Chicago in exchange for its editorial advice, consultation, and imprimatur. On the basis of existing operations, said Benton, his alternative plan, if accepted, promised the university an annual yield "in excess of $100,000" besides giving the university "the benefit and prestige involved through its imprimatur on the *Britannica*."

On the day the joint committees met, Benton conveyed to General Wood the details of the alternative proposal he had made. "If you are prepared to accept this alternative," Benton wrote, "you will note that I have decided that it is advisable for me to put in $100,000 for working capital, rather than the $50,000," which the general had suggested should be forthcoming from the university's trustees. The additional working capital would give Sears greater assurance that its notes on the payments for *Britannica* inventories would be met. Benton went on to say that if the university trustees accepted the alternative, he would follow a suggestion of Hutchins and Harold Swift and take a stock interest in the company and become its chairman. "My motives in this alternative proposal are mixed, as you can well imagine," said Benton. "However, apart from my interest in the *Britannica* and in the University, which as you know, is the most important interest I have, I would not be prepared to risk $100,000, a very substantial sum for me, unless I thought, over the long pull, it was a fair risk." He would "of course expect to agree that there be no dividends of any kind on the stock until all the notes to Sears had been paid off." [3]

The $100,000 in capital was indeed "a very substantial sum" for Benton at the time. Of the payments received on his stock in Benton and Bowles, after his heavy 1937 loss in the stock market, he had invested $132,500 in acquiring Muzak, which had begun to feel a wartime pinch. There had been the heavy expenses of maintaining homes in Southport and in Chicago, along with substantial out-of-

---

[3] Actually there have been no common stock dividends for twenty-five years.

pocket expenses incurred in the earlier effort to organize the American Policy Commission. Benton now had turned in all his common stock in Benton and Bowles and the last capital he had left in that enterprise was $100,000 in preferred stock, which had been paying him dividends of $30,000 to $40,000 a year, on which he had largely been living. The preferred stock was now due to be paid off, and it was this $100,000 that he was prepared to advance to finance his proposed alternative way for marrying the University of Chicago and the *Britannica.*

Benton's offer met with no immediate response from the joint committees. But on 9 December 1942, the day before Benton was to make a further report to the full board of trustees—and a year to the day after General Wood's original offer—the general phoned him to say: "Bill, I have great news for you. My treasurer has discovered that it would be more profitable from a tax standpoint for Sears to give you the inventory rather than sell it to you." The proposal entailed a withdrawal of the earlier offer by Sears to make a $50,000 contribution to working capital. But as Benton promptly informed Hutchins, the new offer represented "a much better proposition." General Wood will "give us the whole thing, lock, stock and barrel. No notes and no payments for inventory."

Benton included this information in the oral report he gave to the trustees. In general, what he had to say duplicated his report of December first to the joint committees, wherein he set forth the alternative plan by which he would personally advance $100,000 to facilitate the acquisition through a separate corporation affiliated with the university. However, he put to the board three possible procedures under which the university itself could still acquire full ownership of the *Britannica.* First, said he, the university could put up $100,000 for working capital, with the understanding that an additional $50,000 might be required. The advantage here was that it opened the possibility of ownership and operation of the *Britannica* by the University of Chicago Press, with tax exemption on profits. Second, ownership of the *Britannica* could be vested in three trustees, as had been suggested by Paul V. Harper, a member of the board. Third, the *Britannica* could be set up as a separate corporation with an independent board of directors but owned by the university (and paying corporate taxes).

At the end of their meeting, the trustees adopted a resolution declaring their interest in "the proposed publishing project if a suitable vehicle for it can be developed," and Harold Swift was authorized to appoint a special committee "to study and report." Herbert P. Zimmerman was named its chairman, the other members being John Nuveen, Joseph C. Beaven, Laird Bell, Paul V. Harper, and John Stuart. The committee met several times over the next month, for day-long sessions, pondering the case for and against the offer, and reexamining all records and memos bearing on the issue.

Meanwhile, on 30 December, General Wood sent Hutchins in itemized detail the terms of the proposed transfer. In the gift, he wrote, would be assets totaling close to $705,000, including $376,-000 owed the American company by the British company; [4] $90,000 of accounts receivable in Canada; $225,000 of inventory in the United States; $3,050 in prepaid taxes; and copyrights, good will, trademark, and plates, carried on the company books at $1.00. Sears would assume accrued liabilities and would keep the "trade receivables," described as bookstore and government sales. Most vitally, Sears would continue to finance and handle at cost all collections on installment sales for at least five years.

On 14 January 1943, two weeks before the 1 February deadline set by General Wood, the university trustees gathered at a special meeting called by their chairman, Harold Swift. Herbert Zimmerman announced that his special committee recommended that the gift be accepted because of "the educational merit of *Britannica*, the possibility that the property may continue to earn substantial profits, and the prestige value of *Britannica*." At the same time, his committee had rejected the plan to have the university advance any capital or retain 100 percent ownership and management responsibility. It had approved the alternative plan whereby Benton would put up his own $100,000 as working capital, with his personal assumption of risks and management responsibility, and with the stock interest suggested by Hutchins and Swift.

The formula for the stock distribution was geared to an earlier idea of Beardsley Ruml for *Parents' Magazine*, for which he had secured financing from the Rockefeller philanthropies. In brief, stock ownership control of the *Britannica* would be divided so that Benton initially would own two-thirds of the stock, and the univer-

---

[4] The $376,000 item was not a solid asset, since the British company, in the midst of the war, had neither assets nor money to repay the American company; the item was carried on the balance sheet because potentially it offered tax advantages in the future.

sity the remaining third. However, the university at any time during the next seventeen months had the option of returning to Benton $50,000 of his $100,000 investment, thus taking control of the *Britannica* corporation by stepping up its stock ownership from one-third to two-thirds, leaving Benton with one-third. With this plan, said Zimmerman, "better management is likely to result" and, for at least a year, a decision could be postponed on "whether the University shall invest any funds in the project, without handicapping operations in the meantime." By a majority vote the special committee recommended the latter proposal, Zimmerman informed the trustees.

Now that working capital was assured and the university was spared the need to make any investment, the trustees accepted the recommendation. Even the members who were most skeptical at first —and who were still inclined to look upon Benton's action as rash and risky—now came forward to express their thanks to him.

On 1 February 1943, official contracts relating to the transfer were signed by the various parties concerned—officials of Encyclopaedia Britannica, Inc., Benton and his wife, and Harold Swift on behalf of the university. The stock division and royalty schedules Benton suggested were set up to give the university liberal advantages, along with the right to withdraw its imprimatur if "the educational and scholarly standards of the *Britannica* publications" slipped and were not rectified within eighteen months after a notice was served calling for a correction. Even if the imprimatur were withdrawn, royal payments were to continue for at least five years afterward.

In the stock transfer, Sears turned over all its shares in Encyclopaedia Britannica, Inc., to the university. By the terms of the contract between the university and Benton, the latter, in exchange for providing $100,000 for working capital and assuming responsibilities for running the company, received two-thirds of the common stock, with one-third going to the university. It was soon discovered, however, that the shares in the corporation were not entirely common stock but a combination of preferred and common stock. It was then decided that the university should take all the preferred stock, while surrendering the common stock to Benton.[5] Accom-

---

[5] The preferred stock which the university retained was entitled to $875,000 priority in case of liquidation, to one-third of any dividends, and was convertible into one-third of the total authorized common stock.

panying provisions preserved the spirit of the original agreement—namely, that the university's preferred stock represented ownership of one-third of the company and that at any time before 1 July 1944, for $50,000 and without interest, the university had the option of buying half of Benton's stock, thereby giving the university two-thirds ownership and leaving Benton with one-third and an investment of $50,000.

There were other provisos designed to protect the interests of the university. For example, neither Benton nor his wife could dispose of more than half of their stock without first offering it to the university, thus insuring that control would again be open to the university, if it chose to exercise this option. A further safeguard of the university's interests was a provision that if Benton were ever to receive an offer from a third party for all or part of his stock, no deal could be made without notifying the university of the offer. The university then had the right to acquire the stock on the same terms arranged with the outside party. Benton also agreed that three of the nine directors of Encyclopaedia Britannica, Inc., should be university trustees nominated by the university. In addition to Benton himself, the new board members included Hutchins, Paul G. Hoffman, and John Stuart, as the directors representing the University of Chicago, plus M. Lincoln Schuster and Henry Luce, Jr., directors chosen by Benton to strengthen the board with experienced publishers, and Beardsley Ruml.

After these details were agreed to and implemented, Benton wrote a long letter to Harold Swift. Now that he was charged with the responsibilities of Encyclopaedia Britannica, Inc., said he, he would strive to make it a thriving company. He promised that changes deemed essential to retain and improve editorial standards of excellence would be instituted, and he reminded Swift that the university had the right to withdraw its imprimatur from the encyclopedia if such standards declined. "If the *Britannica* venture does not work out successfully for the University," wrote Benton, "I shall carry the responsibility and may lose $100,000. If it does work out successfully, the University can acquire two-thirds of the stock ownership, leaving me with a minority interest which, as business experience indicates, is often of little value in a corporation run for the benefit of the majority owners."

When everything was in order, Hutchins summoned the university faculty to a meeting in Mandel Hall to explain the significant details of the contract between the university and Benton. He described the events of the preceding months during which Benton had tried to persuade the university to become the full owner of the encyclopedia company. He cited the possible financial and educational advantages that would accrue to the university as a result of this gift. He then explained how Benton, after his fruitless attempts to persuade various influential and affluent persons and the university trustees themselves to put up money for working capital, had come forward with his own $100,000 for this purpose. "Vice-President Benton," Hutchins concluded, "has become the victim of his own propaganda."

Benton took over the *Britannica* on 1 February 1943, as "owner," publisher, and chairman of its board of directors. Some of the top editorial and business executives he inherited were skeptical about the event. Except for Elkan Harrison ("Buck") Powell, president of Encyclopaedia Britannica, Inc., and Louis C. Schoenewald, the company's sales manager, few among them had known anything about the long negotiations for the transfer. Some now said privately that if the University of Chicago were to dominate the organization they would seek employment elsewhere. Others were eager to cooperate. But the fearful inherited employees soon found that their various fears were groundless. The editor of the *Britannica* since 1930 was Walter Yust, a former newspaperman and literary columnist for a Philadelphia newspaper. Benton, at their first meeting voiced admiration for Yust and the *Britannica* and added: "Call me, Bill. I'll come up with a lot of editorial ideas. I always do that. I get about five hundred ideas a week and if one or two of them work out I feel I've had a successful week."

One of Benton's ideas—acted upon—was to expand sharply the use of university faculty and graduate students in the encyclopedia's continuous revision program. A senior advisory faculty committee was formed of some of the university's leading scholars, and in the ensuing months, graduate students were selected to become what were termed "Britannica Fellows." Expert readers were also found at other schools to help check all articles under their assigned classification, to spot errors of fact or outdated information, and to suggest necessary revisions on which scholars should be asked to write new articles.

In line with his policy of upgrading *Britannica*'s quality, Benton created the first board of editors the *Britannica* had in modern times. The board was headed by Hutchins, and foremost among its members were the University of Chicago professors Robert Redfield, Richard McKeon, and Ralph Tyler—respectively, authorities in anthropology, philosophy, and education. Later the board was to include Beardsley Ruml; Governor Adlai Stevenson; Geoffrey Crowther (now Lord Crowther), the noted editor and publisher of the *London Economist;* Stanley Morison, British Academician famed as historian of the *London Times* and world's leading typographer and calligrapher; the philosopher Mortimer Adler; and other leaders of thought in America and England. They were to meet four times annually with Yust and his managing editor, John V. Dodge, to discuss policies and procedures ranging from the introduction of major new articles to specific improvements in the methods of continuous revision, to the feasibility of publishing reading guides for encyclopedia owners.

What Benton wanted was not only a "hunt and find" encyclopedia of facts or, in Hutchins's phrase, "a piece of printed furniture." He was prepared to invest heavily in the board of editors in order to attract and hold the kind of men who would make the many volumes of the *Britannica* a "congress of teachers" from the world over. He wanted the volumes to be a kind of world-girdling university, coherent, well organized, but without walls—a meeting place for the brains of the world, an agent to synthesize the knowledge they possessed, to disseminate that knowledge to everyone. There would be many shortfalls between the ideal and the real in Benton's concept for the board of editors. Yet he dreamed on, and enlarged it beyond the *Britannica* to include the vast proliferation of products and activities that would flow from the interlocking companies he was to create. He often said that the *Britannica* was the only corporation with which he has ever been connected that could seriously talk "about one hundred years from now."

Soon after Benton became the head of the *Britannica,* he branched out in new directions, beginning with the negotiations that led to the acquisition of ERPI classroom films. But before coming to this matter, it is necessary to go back in time in order to deal with developments on a different front that have been bypassed to get on with the *Britannica* story.

15

The Economics of a Free Society

In January 1942, the Department of Commerce addressed itself to the question of what would happen after the war to the vast new forces of production generated during the war itself. Could business plan jobs for demobilized veterans? Would individual companies take into account the demand for new products, new competition, new developments in aviation, light metals, plastics?

In answer to these and other related questions, it was proposed that the department's Bureau of Domestic and Foreign Commerce under Carroll Wilson should create an independent committee of public spirited business leaders who would stimulate and help direct a broad investigation of postwar private investment opportunities —there being "no other organization, public or private prepared to take the lead." The Department of Commerce would provide a technical staff and act as a connecting link between public planning in government agencies and the private planning the cooperative efforts would encourage. But to guarantee "the impartiality of the research" and forestall any criticism that the effort was just another New Deal venture in "socialism," the department would not become deeply involved in the committee's work. Once formed, the committee would be on its own. Within the department, the working name for the proposed committee was the Institute of Business Enterprise.

In April 1942, Benton was in New York on Muzak business when he received a telephone call from Paul Hoffman, who told him about the proposed institute. Hoffman went on to say that Marion Folsom, treasurer of Eastman Kodak and head of the Economic Policy Committee of the Business Advisory Council to the Department of Commerce, was about to submit a report about it to the secretary of commerce, Jesse Jones. Hoffman did not know what the report would recommend, but he wanted Benton to see Folsom and find out. Perhaps here was a chance to breathe life into the idea of the American Policy Commission they had been forced to abandon a week after Pearl Harbor.

Benton went to see Folsom, whom he had never met, at New York's University Club. Folsom seemed to be thinking of a small organization with a budget under $100,000, geared to the propaganda task of exhorting businessmen to prepare in advance for the employment, sales, and production opportunities that would come with the end of the war. Benton agreed that plant-by-plant propaganda was needed, but, as a former advertising man, he felt that planning by business should be based on something more than exhortation. It should be based on a foundation of knowledge of the kind the American Policy Commission had been conceived to provide.

Folsom's plans, said Benton, left out research into long-range policies that could foster maximum production and full employment after the war. Could the business community plan for high postwar employment without regard to whether the economic climate favored business expansion? Who should study the formulation of postwar policies that could help bring about a favorable climate? Was this a responsibility of government alone? Couldn't a new pattern of policy making be established by business itself? In sum, said Benton, the proposed Institute of Business Enterprise should have one part to do the necessary propaganda work Folsom had in mind, and on a far bigger scale. But it needed another part to provide an intellectual base, research into long-range economic policies.

Benton came away from the meeting with a sense that Folsom, in his report to Jesse Jones, would not favor the idea of joining the propaganda side of the proposed institute with the American Policy Commission idea of fundamental research. He conveyed his impression to Hoffman, and the two men now agreed that the problem merited a hearing from Owen D. Young, chairman of the board of General Electric and one of the few respected big businessmen in America who was a Democrat. It had been rumored that Young would be asked to head the proposed Institute of Business Enterprise; if so, something might be gained by trying to win him over to their view. When they called on Young, he confirmed the fact that he had been asked to head the institute, but he said he was going to decline on the ground that the post should be filled by a younger man like Hoffman or Charles Wilson, president of General Electric. He added that he liked the idea of having the institute undertake the kind of long-range economic research his callers had in mind. However, while Benton and Hoffman wanted the organization confined exclusively to businessmen, it was Young's view that it should be a tripartite organization, one-third business, one-third labor, and one-third government.

In early June, when twelve leading businessmen, one from each Federal Reserve district, met in Washington with Jesse Jones, the secretary of commerce voiced his strong opposition to the tripartite concept. Labor, said he, could make its own postwar plans. If other segments of the community wanted to make plans of their own, no one was stopping them. What he personally had in mind was a natural joining of big and small business and industry to deal with "the promotion of commerce after the war, the restoration and continual enhancement of America's standard of living, and the efficient, effective employment for these purposes of all persons able and willing to work." The secretary then appointed a committee to organize the institute. Its chairman was Undersecretary of Commerce Wayne Chatfield Taylor, and other members were Paul Hoffman, Marion Folsom, Thomas B. McCabe, R. R. Deupree, and Eric Johnston. Arthur Kudner, the New York advertising executive, was to serve as the publicity consultant.

Jones had not yet heard of the Benton-Hoffman proposal for fundamental research into long-range economic problems. His thoughts for the institute were still confined to the idea of the so-called field program designed to exhort businessmen to plan ahead for peacetime production. And it was on this basis that he negotiated the terms of an agreement with the Chamber of Commerce and the National Association of Manufacturers in order to secure their cooperation with the Institute of Business Enterprise. The two old-line organizations posed as apostles of the free enterprise system. But they also liked their monopolies and plainly did not want to face in the postwar years a new organization that would compete with them for the minds and voice of business. As the price for wartime cooperation, Jones agreed that, once the war was over, the Institute of Business Enterprise would be dissolved. All of this was an unwritten "gentlemen's agreement." Benton's apprehension, however, was aroused when he belatedly heard about it. The agreement would cause trouble later on because it was unrelated to the organization which actually evolved.

The organizing committee which Secretary Jones had appointed to launch the institute eventually settled on a new name—the Committee for Economic Development—and cast about for a man to head it. Owen D. Young, when approached, formally declared himself unavailable and urged that a younger man be selected as chairman of the CED. When the matter was discussed at an organizing committee meeting, Paul Hoffman, who was present, momentarily left the room to take a telephone call. He returned to the meeting to discover that the other members had nominated him chairman of the CED. He accepted the nomination on condition that Benton be nominated vice-chairman. This was agreed to by the committee, subject to ratification by Jesse Jones. Benton in turn laid down a condition: he would serve as vice-chairman under Hoffman only if an economic research group was incorporated into the structure of the CED on an equal footing with the projected field program.

Jesse Jones had wanted an independent entrepreneur in a key role in the new organization, one without a Wall Street or "big business" label. He readily approved the choice of Benton as the CED's vice-chairman. When Hoffman and Benton met with Jones, Hoffman explained that Benton would not agree to serve in the indicated capacity unless objective research into public policy was made an integral and coequal part of the CED's work. Jones asked, "Well, boys, what would you study?" They answered with concrete examples of how some existing policies of labor, business, agriculture, and government—along with a hodgepodge of federal tax laws—combined to work against high levels of peacetime employment and production. "All right, boys," the secretary said; "your idea sounds practical to me. Go ahead." Hoffman pressed the advantage. He emphasized that the CED should be prepared to spend as much as 50 percent of its budget on the research program, and to give it a full 50 percent weight in its organizational setup. "All right," Jones repeated. "Go ahead."

"It was," said Benton afterward, "our easiest sale." The idea, born earlier at the University of Chicago for the American Policy Commission, now was to be realized in a national businessmen's organization born in the Department of Commerce.

Benton himself later joked about the way he had become the vice-chairman of the CED. "I was cast in the role," he would say, "as a small businessman—not as vice-president of the University of Chicago. After six years of pretending to be an educator, I was distressed to discover that I hadn't fooled anybody. I had wrapped myself in a sheepskin, but I was still a wolf."

Benton revealed his enthusiasm for the task and for his chairman in a letter to Paul Hoffman in July:

> I am going hell-bent trying to get all I can cleaned up preparatory to this new proposed venture of ours. I need hardly tell that, month by month, I get more enthusiastic over your capacity for leadership. The great hope of this program revolves around yourself. You know that I will do everything I conceivably can to be of assistance, and to carry responsibility for you. . . . Part of the problem in the next year or two or three on the CED plans, is to build you up in the right way. That will come anyway, but if you sometimes see my undercover hand pulling a string or two, don't be critical.

The wolf in sheepskin was in and out of Washington every week of the summer of 1942. Wayne Chatfield Taylor, the undersecretary of commerce, made appointments for him with some forty or fifty Washington men of power Jesse Jones felt should be told in person what the CED was all about. Sometimes Taylor accompanied Benton, sometimes Paul Hoffman when he was in town. Just as often, Benton would be on his own.

Much of Benton's time, and of Hoffman's when he was in Washington, was also spent in screening countless men until forty-five were chosen as the core of the CED, eighteen trustees, a research division of fifteen, and twelve regional chairmen for the projected field program. Each of the forty-five men had to be approved personally by Jesse Jones. This meant long hours for Benton in going over lists of prospects with Jones, but he felt that the final results more than justified the procedure.

> Jesse Jones [he said] was the best judge of men I've ever known, and his choice of the forty-five men is the best job of selection in my memory. Some of the people we picked were soon lost to the CED because Roosevelt appointed them to official posts in the war effort. Two or three of the original forty-five later quit when the CED came under bitter attack. In Southern California, the Chamber of Commerce was so

aroused that it held a secret meeting accusing the CED of being a left-wing, communist-infiltrated organization; and the president of the Chrysler Corporation speaking before the Detroit Economic Club claimed that Paul Hoffman, Eric Johnston and Beardsley Ruml were the three most dangerous men in the country. But even the people who quit never denounced CED. Their faithfulness in this respect was largely a tribute to Jesse Jones' skill in judging character.

By 10 July, it was agreed that Ralph Flanders would serve as chairman of the Research Division—the transfigured form of the American Policy Commission. Marion Folsom would be chairman of the Field Development Committee—the committee for propaganda to stimulate postwar employment. Clarence Francis, head of General Foods, would serve as chairman of the Finance Committee, to raise an initial budget of $250,000 but on a very broad basis. It was also agreed to accept Secretary Jones's offer to release Carroll Wilson from the Commerce Department to act as executive secretary of the CED. At the same time, Scott Fletcher, a skilled sales executive Hoffman borrowed from his Studebaker Corporation, would direct field operations under Folsom's committee.

Benton was deeply immersed in all organizational details but the aspect of CED which was his special concern was the Research Division. In addition to the chairman, Ralph Flanders, the roster of these presently became: Chester Davis of the Saint Louis Federal Reserve Bank; William L. Batt of SKF Industries; S. Bayard Colgate of Colgate-Palmolive-Peet, chairman of the NAM Committee on Postwar Planning; Donald David, dean of Harvard's Graduate School of Business Administration; Max Epstein of General American Transportation and a trustee of the University of Chicago; Harry Scherman of the Book-of-the-Month Club; Eric Johnston, the new president of the United States Chamber of Commerce; Beardsley Ruml; Charles E. Wilson of General Electric. Hoffman and Benton were ex officio members, with the latter ex officio vice-chairman.

At the same time, Benton recruited and organized an advisory board of eight university social scientists to assist the Research Division. Among the members were Sumner Slichter of Harvard, who was named chairman; Dean Robert Caulkins of the Columbia University School of Business; Neil Jacoby, of the University of

Chicago; Harold Lasswell, formerly of the University of Chicago and subsequently the director of war communications research of the Library of Congress; William I. Meyers, head of the Department of Agricultural Economics at Cornell; Theodore W. Schultz of the University of Chicago; and Ralph Young, of the University of Pennsylvania. Here was a group of eminent scholars, respected by their colleagues and at home in the world of practical affairs.

The critical position to be filled was that of research director for the professional staff that was to serve the Research Division. Some fifty people in all were recommended to Benton, and he interviewed many of them. The choice narrowed down to five and then to one: Professor Theodore Yntema of the University of Chicago, later to become financial vice-president of the Ford Motor Company. Yntema's name had cropped up on virtually all the lists of recommendations Benton had received, but he hesitated to urge the choice because Secretary Jones, as well as Donald David of Harvard, had dropped the hint that "there was too much of the University of Chicago" in the shape the CED was taking. The hint could just as well have been dropped that there was also "too much Benton and Bowles," since at least three of Benton's former clients were part of CED. Nonetheless, Yntema was chosen because of the unanswerable argument Benton voiced in a letter of 20 August addressed to Ralph Flanders:

> I have leaned over backwards on the question of the Research Director because of Secretary Jones' early question as to whether, in view of my connection with the University, we should pick a member of our faculty for this post. Both Paul Hoffman and I have been sensitive to the charge of favoritism and, frankly, speaking for myself, I would prefer selecting a man from some other University. However, Yntema is commended far more frequently than any other person in the country and I think it's unwise to hesitate any longer in trying to get him. He is a guarantee that our research work will be conducted in an objective way.

To the same end—objectivity in research—Benton was eager for Beardsley Ruml to serve in the Research Division. But when Ruml was approached, he asked to see the bylaws of the CED. Told that none existed, he said he would not consider a committee membership until there were some he could read. Until that moment,

Benton had never read any bylaws for anything. But now he set out to write some for the CED at what he thought would be a sprightly pace. Instead, he was forced to produce ten drafts before he had a text which the trustees of the CED approved. "I shudder to think of what might have happened if we hadn't gone through the laborious process of these ten revisions," Benton wrote Ruml afterwards. "As a result of the hard work the Committee will simply have to produce something worthwhile in order to live up to its bylaws."

He had good reason to "shudder." Before working on the bylaws, he had been blind to the many ways in which the CED's research work into public policy could have been corrupted. The bylaws, unique in the history of American business organization, safeguarded the CED against the vice of "kept economists." They gave a free but responsible rein to the independent judgment of professional economists and were the guardian of the CED's "conscience." They provided a system of checks and balances with two central objects in view: first, to make sure that each research project would be approached "from the standpoint of the general welfare and not from that of any special political or economic group"; second, that each project would bear directly on public policies designed to create an environment for "the attainment of high and secure standards of living for people in all walks of life through maximum employment and high productivity." In line with these objectives, there would be a thorough review and full discussion of the scholarship of all materials before anything was published under the imprimatur of the CED. There were also provisions safeguarding the rights of dissenters to make their own views known. This expressly granted "right of a dissenting footnote" was a new innovation in American business thought—and Benton, for one, was to avail himself of that right frequently in the years ahead.

Beardsley Ruml was sufficiently pleased with the bylaws to join the Research Division, and to bring to it the full benefit of his original mind—with important consequences for the nation itself. Once chosen, all the businessmen and the professional economists on the CED's Research Committee battled the difficulties of wartime travel to hold bimonthly meetings "to bridge the moat between the ivory tower and the market place." These unpublicized meetings were intensely hard-working seminars which generally began on Saturday morning and extended to the following Sunday afternoon, with no Saturday evening off for relaxation. Professional papers made available to the participants for study well before each meeting provided a frame for the things talked about. No quarter was asked or given in a swirling battle of ideas. The professional economists learned from the businessmen. The businessmen learned from the economists. Dogmas on either side were often left in ruins after a weekend meeting, and a beginning made on worthier objects of belief.

Early CED research had indicated that if a high level of postwar employment and prosperity was to be attained, production would have to be increased some 30 to 45 percent over what it had been in 1940, while the number of new jobs would have to be increased by ten million. This meant a postwar gross national product of around $150 billion, with jobs for fifty-three to fifty-six million people. It also meant that employers must be stimulated to plan not only for conversion from war to peacetime production but for expansion. Yet with the recent depression still fresh in memory, figures of this magnitude seemed like a midsummer night's dream. So it seemed to Senator Robert A. Taft, the Ohio Republican, when, because he was on Jesse Jones's list, Benton and Hoffman called on him to explain the work of the CED. Benton, speaking of this encounter with Taft, later said:

> Taft brushed aside the CED studies showing that with the coming of peace, we must achieve a productivity of around $150 billion if we were to avoid substantial unemployment. He flatly said that it was impossible for the U.S. economy to attain a national output of over $100 billion, and he added for good measure that Alfred Sloan agreed with him.
>
> We then put a question to him. If he was right that $100 billion in productivity was the optimum, how did he propose to deal with the dangerous levels of unemployment that would inevitably follow? "Oh," said he, "I have that all figured out." Paul Hoffman and I hung on to the edge of our chairs. "We can handle the problem," he explained, "by prohibiting women from working." I was astonished that this passed as a serious thought from a man reputed to have one of the best minds in the Senate.

Paul Hoffman was even more deeply shaken by the answer. Hoffman was not vindictive. But it was from this encounter that one can date the onset of his determination to do everything within his per-

sonal power to prevent the presidency from ever falling to Taft.
The determination was to be reinforced by other experiences in the
years leading up to the 1952 Republican presidential nominating
contest in which Hoffman was to emerge as a leader of the successful
drive to secure the party nomination for General Dwight D. Eisenhower.

Elma Benton, meanwhile, had thought that she had lost the
Montana homestead because of nonpayment of taxes on it. But
then she discovered by accident that she might yet retrieve it. So
many people had been driven off their Montana homesteads by the
ruinous drought of 1918–22 that the state had "forgiven" the payment of delinquent taxes to induce the afflicted homesteaders to
stay on the land and begin paying current taxes. Now, Elma
learned, the payment of back taxes for only one year would satisfy
the obligation. She promptly sent the state authorities the money
needed to clear her title—it was not much more than $30 or $40—
and the land was hers again.

Thus Elma regained as an inheritance for her son an arid stretch
of American earth that recalled the lean years in the Benton fortunes. Benton did inherit the homestead, and with it the old rumor
that oil was located somewhere beneath the soil. An agency of the
federal government, acting on the mistaken assumption that the
land had irrevocably reverted to the public domain, had built a dam
across one of the coulees that cut through the property. The land
itself was still worthless, but the water conserved by the dam attracted the attention of a cattle rancher who wanted access to it
for his herd. The rancher offered Benton $1,200 for the property,
and the sale was made in the mid-1940s. Benton, however, retained
the oil and mineral rights, and transferred them to his oldest son,
Charles, as a link with the past. Charles himself later collected
another $1,000 or more by granting prospecting rights to an oil
wildcatter in Havre, and thus the hope for oil rolled on into a third
generation.

In 1942, two changes occurred in the Benton family, one bringing
joy, the other sorrow. The first change was the addition of another
son, John, adopted, like his sisters, from The Cradle in Evanston.

The second change was the death of the remarkable woman whose
profound influence had done so much to shape the lives of her son.

Elma had closed her Riverside Drive apartment on 1 August and had come for a visit to the Benton home in Southport. On her arrival, she took to her bed and was in and out of an oxygen tent for the next eight weeks. Two days after Benton returned to the University of Chicago on 1 October, Elma Hixson Benton died, as though she had willed it that way.

Her son, as if to shut out the fact of his mother's death, seemed to pour even more energy into his work. He was engaged in launching the CED, and trying to acquire the *Britannica* for the university. Shortly after he had taken over the *Britannica* he learned that Electrical Research Products, Inc., was still available. It still led the nation in classroom films, though its annual sales were only around $300,000. To Benton, nothing seemed more logical than for Encyclopaedia Britannica, Inc., to acquire ERPI. He dug out the long memorandum he had prepared five years earlier for the Rockefeller Foundation and read portions to his *Britannica* associates. Nothing had changed, he emphasized, to cause him to revise the main conclusion he had reached in the spring of 1938: that educational talking pictures were a "potent and largely unexploited medium, perhaps the most striking opportunity for public service in the field of education today," and that it should "be seized by those whose primary interest is the welfare of the American educational system."

In March 1943, Benton began intensive talks with Arthur Page, vice-president of AT&T, and Kennedy Stevenson, financial vice-president of Western Electric, the AT&T subsidiary that owned ERPI. Eight months later, the talks culminated in a purchase agreement. The terms were complex, because the *Britannica* lacked the money to buy ERPI outright; in fact, it had to pledge its assets and credit in order for the deal to go through. By 5 November, however, the encyclopedia company was the new owner of ERPI at a cost of $1 million payable over the next decade (during which another $1.5 million was spent in building and developing the film company), and the name of the new subsidiary was changed to Encyclopaedia Britannica Films, Inc.

The acquisition was capped by a beau geste from the Eastman Kodak Company. Eastman, which had produced silent educational films in the 1920s and '30s, had previously seen its own sales decline under the impact of the talking films. Now, with Marion Folsom arranging the details, the Eastman Company gave the University of Chicago and the *Britannica* its library of some three hundred silent films and withdrew from the field. The library had little inherent value, but the end of Eastman's involvement with educational films left Britannica Films, tiny as it was, the largest enterprise in this sphere of business. Thus, one of the hopes Benton had brought to the university in 1937 advanced a step toward fulfillment.

At the same time, Benton sounded a warning for the university trustees similar to the one he had sounded in his 1937 memorandum to the Rockefeller Foundation. He said that while profits from the film company would be welcome, they should not be expected for at least ten years so that the company could be developed. He hoped the university would "use its resources and knowledge to develop an educational tool which expands the range of material available to the teacher as no other device can do." It was also his hope, during the decade of development, to produce enough films to support a national sales organization—since only through salesmen could the schools be persuaded to buy sound projectors and use the films. Since no profits were expected for ten years, there was no royalty arrangement between the university and the film company. Benton, however, lost little time in creating a board of consultants for Britannica Films. With a membership drawn from the ranks of educational leaders, the first chairman of the board was Hutchins, who continued in that post in subsequent years except for a nine-year interval when Governor Adlai Stevenson served as chairman. Other members of the original board were Professors Mortimer Adler and Ralph Tyler of the University of Chicago; George Shuster, then president of Hunter College; Anna Rosenberg; and George Stoddard, then president of the University of Illinois. Clifton Fadiman, the literary critic and editor, was added at a later date.

As Benton anticipated, the film company faced a long, hard, and rocky road ahead. But following a decade of struggle, a strategic turn for the better occurred when Benton moved Maurice B. Mitchell from Muzak into the presidency of Britannica Films (and later into the presidency of the Britannica Company). Mitchell brought to the film company a drive, imagination, and judgment that enabled the firm to surmount many difficulties and financial hazards. Through Mitchell's close collaboration with Benton, Britannica Films would become by far the largest and most respected educational motion picture producing and distributing organization in the world. From its original role as the pioneer in classroom talking pictures, it would expand across the whole spectrum of the audio-visual field. Its present catalog includes not only two thousand films, but filmstrips, language tapes, single concept "film loops," overhead transparencies, records, texts, classroom study pictures, and complete systems of educational materials representing innovations in both teaching techniques and the expansion of knowledge. Robert Maynard Hutchins may not have been hyperbolic when he said that the impact of Britannica Films on American public education promised to be greater than the impact of Harvard and the University of Chicago combined.

While the purchase of ERPI was still under negotiation in the summer of 1943, a favorable turn in the war picture quickened the pace at which the CED prepared policy papers on major questions the economy would face with the coming of peace. It also underlined the need for a continuous fund-raising campaign to support the scholarly studies and reports of the CED Research Committee. Benton, as usual, was deeply involved in both matters in addition to traveling around the country exhorting business groups to reconsider the character of the free enterprise system. The leitmotif in all his talks was that the free enterprise system was nearing a testing hour that would decide whether it could in fact be free and at the same time be the servant of economic security and economic opportunity. The more he talked about the matter, the more he felt the need for an expository statement that would crystallize certain economic tenets for CED members. The felt need in turn induced him to start work on an essay to which he gave the title: "The Economics of a Free Society: A Declaration of American Business Policy."

In August 1943, just after Benton had started this work, he was invited to join Eric Johnston on an unusual wartime visit to Great Britain. Until that time, few Britons and Americans had talked about business—the ordinary, everyday business on which the economic future of the two countries was going to have to depend. Wartime travel restrictions had curtailed contacts between their respective businessmen. Now that the smell of eventual military victory was in the air, however, it was timely for the businessmen of Great Britain and the United States to consider a question about the future. Could the wartime collaboration between the two countries be converted into peacetime economic collaboration?

The question was being discussed quietly in advanced sectors of British and American opinion, when Lord Halifax, the British ambassador to Washington, invited Eric Johnston, the president of the U.S. Chamber of Commerce and a CED trustee, to visit England and meet with leading businessmen of the United Kingdom. The same invitation was extended to Paul Hoffman, chairman of the CED. When Hoffman regretfully declined, Halifax and Johnston jointly invited Benton as vice-chairman of the CED to take his place. Benton welcomed the role of substitute. A visit to Great Britain would give him a chance to learn how and if British businessmen meant to achieve high levels of production and employment after the war. He could see what Britain looked like physically after four years of war. And, the visit would give him an opportunity to inquire into the condition of the British subsidiary of the *Encyclopaedia Britannica.*

Benton had by this time logged one million miles in air travel. But perhaps because he was heading for a theater of war, a note of 2 August, written on the eve of his departure, had the tone of a last will and testament. Addressed to Paul Hoffman, it dealt with the CED and with Hoffman's role as its chairman. Benton said he feared CED was not being courageous enough and might prove to be "an NAM with a facelift." It was spending too much time on "public relations" angles because of its fund-raising and not enough time on the "product" itself. Indeed, it seemed to be compromising itself on leading issues. Benton then got down to cases:

> Paul, you and I have spent most of our lives selling products. I will admit that my perspective on selling ideas has changed somewhat during my years at the University of Chicago. I think I take a longer range viewpoint after six years in Chicago than I did before. I've learned a good deal from watching Bob Hutchins. Bob often loses an immediate sale and runs counter to the immediate opportunity—shooting at the long range chance. I'm not claiming that you and I should model ourselves on Bob. He's a special fellow in a special field. I merely mention him because there may be a moral to be learned from Bob, applied to CED.
>
> I believe that we need the intellectual and liberal forces of the country behind us. I think we can get them. I would rather

have them for the pull of the next two or three years than
money in the pocket right now. I would rather operate on a
$600,000 budget for the next year, with the right ideas prop-
erly keyed for the long pull, than I would on a $1,200,000 with
fuzzy ideas. The $600,000 with the right ideas will grow. The
$1,200,000 with fuzzy ideas will shrink.

Benton then suggested that for the long haul it might be a "great
thing" for the CED if certain leaders in American business openly
came out against it. Indeed, if only the CED were developing the
right "product" for the long haul, he hoped that it would be attacked. If the CED was to have the right friends, it needed the right
enemies, because the right enemies breed the right friends.

Paul [he continued], you have the most remarkable chance,
through your leadership of CED, of any man I know anywhere
in the country. You cannot be all things to all business groups.
I think you must make a choice. The Committee may do a
bigger job, in the coming year, going along the way we're going, sticking to the general story we've developed thus far,
avoiding the controversial issues which confront us. . . . But
the next year is a short year. The big chance for the Committee
is over a much longer period. And to a much greater extent
than I think you realize, the big chance for the Committee re-
volves around you personally. You are the Committee more
than you know. You yourself are our product. You are the
Committee as you walk down the street.

I believe that you personally will be more effective as a leader
of ninety-five percent of American business than you can ever
be if you aim at one hundred percent. I believe that you will
be more effective politically, that CED will come closer to
achieving its objective. I think Ralph Flanders and you and I
and others need to put a great deal more time into our research
program. We are not doing justice to it—and our research
program is our major long range choice. . . . Our chance is literally tremendous. Almost everybody wants us to do better than
we can possibly do. CED's chance is intimately involved with
your personal chance. I don't know anybody who has a greater
chance than you have to make a major contribution to the next
ten years. But to live up to that chance we must be prepared

to take some raps from "the right" if we are to maintain and hold our position with the great middle group who will prove our long term strength.

The "last will and testament" being mailed, Benton left for England with Eric Johnston. At the London airport, where they were met by Lord and Lady Riverdale, they were handed a printed program twenty pages long. Each page marked a day of the visit; virtually every morning, noon, afternoon, and evening of their twenty days was to be spent on tightly scheduled interviews with handpicked business and governmental leaders in London, Manchester, and Liverpool.

Benton, as always, carried a notebook which he filled with jottings about people and places—whom he met, where he went, what he saw, heard, said, thought. These jottings recorded his discoveries about key differences in the outlook of British businessmen as against American businessmen of the CED type. The first of these differences popped up the first day at the end of a lunch at the Savoy that Sir Harry Brand gave for sixty leading British businessmen. Eric Johnston spoke, and was briskly applauded for his eloquence about Anglo-American concord and postwar cooperation. Then came the question period—and the voice of a kill-joy. Next to Benton sat Lord McGowan, the self-made and self-reliant chairman of Imperial Chemicals, one of the most powerful companies in the world. As a member of the board of General Motors, McGowan was a frequent visitor to the United States, and he was also under indictment by the U.S. Justice Department for violating U.S. antitrust laws. Now he stood up and spoke his mind: "I see no hope of collaboration between British and American business," said he, "unless the United States repeals its Sherman Anti-Trust Act. Can we in England look forward to that?"

Johnston let the question alone, noting that it touched on a subject of special interest to Benton. Benton, invited to deal with McGowan's challenge, was prepared for it. At every meeting of the CED's Research Committee, he had joined Beardsley Ruml in a vain plea that the committee must study the problem of monopoly in the American economy, if for no other reason than to make clear the CED's distinctive character. Further, two weeks before leaving for England, he had spent many evening hours reading material about cartels in preparation for a "University of Chicago Round

Table" radio broadcast on that topic. By chance, much of his homework came from the Department of Justice files and dealt with the chemical industry—including Lord McGowan's Imperial Chemicals.

Benton now responded that there was no chance whatever that the antitrust laws would be repealed—that no congressman would openly support a proposal for repeal—that there was no cleavage on the point between Democrats and Republicans. The American people, said he, instinctively felt that the concentration of too much economic power in too few private hands must ultimately throw the management of the economy into governmental hands. American antitrust laws expressed the intent of the people to keep the nation's future economic development in private hands.

The response agitated the audience, and Lord McGowan spoke for the dominant mood in rebuttal: "Unrestricted competition," said he, "is no longer a method which generally commends itself. The alternative road is by cooperation and agreement." That meant regulated prices, production, and the allocation of markets—Imperial Chemicals did not compete with DuPont in the United States. McGowan added that "internecine competition and eventual chaos were the fruits of a system of unrestricted competition." He had therefore recently proposed in the House of Lords that all private international trade agreements should be registered with the government, which would thus approve and control them. In the following days it became clear to Benton that Lord McGowan spoke for a majority of Britain's leading businessmen. They stoutly approved of monopoly as a business device, and they could not understand why there were antitrust laws in the United States when there were none in Great Britain or Europe.

Other British business attitudes about relations with government came into focus when Benton and Johnston returned to London after their first week of visits to other English centers of commerce and industry. A large formal luncheon had been arranged for them, presided over by Oliver Littleton, then in charge of British war production. Seven other members of the British cabinet were present, and special cars brought down leading businessmen from Glasgow, Liverpool, Birmingham, and Manchester. Johnston spoke, and in the colloquies that followed, he and Benton reacted with astonishment when told that English businessmen expected their government to step in with funds and government-appointed directors in order to save from bankruptcy any company that was a substantial employer of labor. Nothing of the sort, said Johnston, with support from Benton, could happen in the United States.

Why, Benton asked himself, would a nation of nineteenth-century risk-takers—in India, China, and the world over—become so committed to security? Part of the answer seemed clear to him. Britain was still climbing out of the depression when it was hurled into war. Programs to cope with the two successive crises entailed a high degree of centralization, and British businessmen had grown used to a system where risks were also centralized in the government for the sake of their own security. The war, moreover, placed most of Great Britain in the front lines where survival and security took precedence over all other things that count in life. Benton also realized that the businessmen he talked to were in the main Conservatives. Why should they fear their government as a business partner? They had always been a potent force in the government, and they prized security because they had had it in partnership with their government in prewar years.

Still, he was not entirely satisfied with this answer. There was a missing element, and at last he felt he'd found it during a dinner in Liverpool. He sat between a Lieutenant Colonel Buckley, chairman of the Liverpool Gas Company, and Sir Sidney Jones, a senior partner of the Blue Funnel Line. "You know, Mr. Benton," said Colonel Buckley, "Sir Sidney's firm began with only £50,000 in capital [$250,000], yet it now operates over eighty ships." His tone was that of a man who scarcely expected to be believed.

"When was the firm founded?" Benton asked.

"Only eighty-odd years ago," Colonel Buckley replied.

Benton silently compared this with Eric Johnston, who started business in Spokane with $2,500 and in twenty years pyramided it into four companies employing 1,700 people. He thought of his own start in business in 1929 with $5,000. "Colonel Buckley," said he, "your comment suddenly makes clear for me a major difference of outlook between our two countries. You British believe in *capital*, we believe in *capitalism*. You think capital is more indestructible than we do. With us, individual initiative comes first. Capital, which underwrites and rewards enterprise, comes second. You put capital and security of income first. You are astonished because a large Liverpool company can develop in eighty years from £50,000. We would be astonished if a large Chicago company had that much capital eighty years ago, or even if the company existed at all."

Johnston and Benton had relatively few chances to talk to British labor leaders. Yet those they met echoed, in a labor accent, the views of British businessmen. They made common cause with business leaders in furthering monopoly practices, on the straightforward theory that when the time came to nationalize industry, it would be easier for the government to take over monopolistic big business, like McGowan's Imperial Chemicals, than fragmented competitive business.

The emphasis on nationalization was squarely put to Johnston and Benton by Professor Harold Laski, a member of the Labour party's executive committee and one of its chief theoreticians. The occasion was a Benton-arranged "University of Chicago Round Table" broadcast among the three men. This was the first such broadcast to originate outside North America in the twelve-year history of the "Round Table," and the bomb shelter studio deep underground in the BBC was made available. Most of the explosions, however, came from rapid exchanges among the three participants in the clash of ideologies—and metaphors. A fair sample of what listeners heard went like this:

MR. BENTON: I would like to ask you, Laski, assuming that you are in a position of authority in this country—say, you are the prime minister—just what you would do in applying the principles you have been advocating to the economy in England?

MR. LASKI: The first things that I should want to do would be to nationalize the banking system; to nationalize the land; to nationalize mines and power and transport. They are the first big bite that I would take off of this particular cherry.

MR. JOHNSTON: I would say that was taking a bite out of the cherry and ruining the whole cherry.

MR. BENTON: Or swallowing it anyway. . . . Laski's social democratic purpose is substituting a group of state monopolies for private monopolies and he ultimately aims at one giant monopoly to absorb the economic system. . . . The hope of the American economy, in my opinion, for inventiveness and improvement rests around the imagination of [its] nine million enterprises and, of course, the millions of others yet to be born.

Mr. Laski: I think that you have dreamed the wrong dream. Is that what you hope? I doubt its realization.

Mr. Benton: Dreams or nightmares. I think that Laski wants to amputate the arms of the patient because it has the itch.

Mr. Laski: So far as your amputation is concerned, may I point out respectfully that the Venus de Milo is the result of an amputation.

Mr. Johnston: Yes, but she was a cracked girl, and is that the kind of girl you like?

Mr. Laski: Well, it would be a better world if every girl looked like the Venus de Milo.

Mr. Benton: I have heard of the Venus de Milo's figure and her profile is famous, but I still prefer my girls with arms that they can use.

To Laski, the views voiced by the American visitors about the relationship between government and the economy seemed so reactionary that, in a syndicated column he later wrote for publication in the United States, he said that compared to Johnston and Benton, Winston Churchill was a left-wing radical.

A better by-product to the encounter with Laski was a meeting with David Lloyd George, the former head of the Liberal party, who as prime minister had led Great Britain in the decisive years of World War I and its immediate aftermath. Laski had recently visited the eighty-year-old veteran of world politics, then living in retirement in Surrey. In speaking to Benton and Johnston about the event, Laski quoted Lloyd George as saying to him: "You write history and I have made history. In writing history always remember one thing. All politicians are mysterious, but in the final struggle for ultimate power, all politicians are malignant." The tale prompted Benton and Johnston to ask their hosts if it would be possible to see Lloyd George, and it was arranged.

"You Americans," Lloyd George said to them when they met, "can look around you and see on all sides what individual enterprise has contributed to your economy and you will want more of it, not less, after this war. But many of you Americans make a mistake when you come to England in thinking that there is any basic difference between our Conservative party and our Labour party. Both

parties look forward to a rapidly expanding role for the state in
the economy. The Conservatives are reconciled to it and think they
can control it. Labour is pledged to it. Only the Liberal party has
stood against it."

Then speaking of himself, he said: "As I look back on it, I think
I made a mistake after the last war. We Liberals mistrusted centralized state planning and state control. We resisted it. If I had
to do it over again I'm not sure I'd resist what seems now to be an
irresistible trend here in England. But you Americans will resist.
Good for you." And he concluded: "You in America and we in England may think we share the same basic social and political objectives. I'm not sure we do. Each country will have to go about working toward its economic objectives in its own way. You will have to
work them out in your own way, we in ours, and your way cannot
and will not be our way, nor our way yours."

When Benton got back to New York, he had a long talk with
Henry Luce in the Yale Club, centered mainly on the impressions
he had gained in England. Luce, always sensitive to journalistic
nuances, recognized a "beat" in what he heard. He urged Benton
to write an article for *Life* about the attitudes of British businessmen—a subject that had gone virtually unreported in the American
press after five years of war. Benton agreed, and his article appeared under the title "Business in Britain." He also wrote an article on the subject for the *Saturday Evening Post* and delivered
many speeches on it before CED groups around the country. In the
Life article in particular,[1] Benton made a prediction that was "un-
thinkable" to most Americans in 1943. England, said he, was "not
so much interested in opportunity for the individual and in abun-
dance on a high level as it is in security, even on a low one." If so,
then the outcome of England's first postwar election would not be,
as most Americans felt, a Conservative party victory in reward
for Churchill's wartime leadership. It would be "the inevitable return to power of the Labour party." Few readers could believe this
startling prediction in the late summer of 1943, though it came
true two years later.

In the fall of 1943, Benton's arrangements with the University of
Chicago were changed under the pressure of multiplying demands

---

[1]The article was reprinted in five installments in a British financial paper,
headed "The Amazing Impressions of Mr. Benton."

of the *Encyclopaedia Britannica*, the impending purchase of ERPI, CED, and his many other involvements. Effective as of 1 October 1943, Hutchins and the trustees agreed that Benton would give the university three instead of six months of his time and would work it out by coming to Chicago for one week out of every month for the length of the year. He would retain the title of vice-president and would be paid $5,000 annually instead of $10,000. Indirectly, of course, he would be devoting far more time to the university, since it had a major stake in his making a success of the *Britannica*. Benton's salary from the Britannica Company was fixed from the outset at a modest $7,500 a year.

At about this time *Britannica* embarked on a side excursion that was to have a costly career. "Buck" Powell, the president of the Britannica company, was a University of Chicago graduate, a veteran top manager at Sears, and a frustrated painter. In 1943 Powell proposed that leading American artists be commissioned to paint illustrations for various *Britannica* publications, especially the new *Britannica Junior*. A number of paintings were commissioned and others purchased, to illustrate particular articles. After the paintings had been reproduced for the publications, they were hung in the corridors of the *Britannica* offices. It soon occurred to Powell that the paintings already on hand should be augmented and put to a new use. "Why not," he asked at a board meeting, "complete the survey of what is going on in this country, of what twentieth-century American painters are doing? We could get the best of the work of other Americans and build a collection of contemporary painting—and we could then send it on tour. It will serve two purposes. It will bring art to people who might never take the trouble to see this kind of work, and it will have promotional value for the Britannica company."

Powell assumed that the Britannica company was headed toward excess profits tax brackets and that most of the costs of the pictures would be paid for in tax write-offs. More specifically, he assumed that this project could be charged off to editorial and advertising expenses, as had the paintings purchased to illustrate *Britannica* articles. Benton apparently neither approved nor disapproved of the venture. But when the art project was far advanced, he did persuade himself that there was some merit in the idea. The collection of American artists would help dramatize the fact that the

Britannica was not British but American owned, and that the promotion of the *Encyclopedia Americana*—the only encyclopedia that could be remotely said to compete with the *Britannica*—falsely conveyed the implication that while it was American the *Britannica* was British. "I was just rationalizing," Benton later confessed. "The truth is that many businesses made grievous errors in the name of the excess profits taxes."

Once the decision had been made to go ahead with Powell's idea, the question arose which twentieth-century American artists should be represented in the *Britannica* collection. Artists like John Steuart Curry, Grant Wood, and Charles Burchfield seemed obvious choices in addition to artists like Thomas Hart Benton, whose painting *Boom Town* had been purchased to illustrate the article on petroleum in the *Britannica*. But to make the final selections as comprehensive and fair as possible, a questionnaire asked two hundred leading artists, museum directors, and art dealers to nominate artists. Art experts believed that the resulting list was the best cross section of twentieth-century American painters whose contributions could most logically "sell American art to Americans." Some painters created new works; others sent paintings which they had done earlier but which they felt would represent them at their most typical; and there were many works from artists who had died. By April 1945 when the Collection of Contemporary Paintings sponsored by Encyclopaedia Britannica, Inc., premiered at the Art Institute of Chicago, its 121 paintings represented all twentieth-century styles and schools.

The collection was exhibited in forty-five major cities, with attendance running into millions. Editorialists and art critics praised the company for stimulating interest in American art. Indeed, the show brought new and needed prestige to American art, aided the reputations of individual artists—and, as had been hoped, helped to spread the name of its sponsor. Harry Salpeter, the respected art critic, commented wryly, "If you reserve a small margin of your mind for the credit line, you will be doing no more for one of the leading cultural institutions of the English-speaking world than you do for the manufacturer of a dental cream through whose enterprise the humor of Bob Hope is made available to you." This pioneering enterprise by the Britannica company was to be widely copied by other American corporations like IBM and Johnson's

Wax. So far, so good. The unhappy sequel for *Britannica* will be told later. A different matter, for chronological reasons, falls in place here.

In the fall of 1943, Bill and Helen Benton enrolled in the "fat man's" course, an evening seminar in the great books which Hutchins and Mortimer Adler conducted for University of Chicago trustees and other Chicago business leaders and their wives. Adler and Hutchins, who called Adler the "Great Bookie," had collaborated on the Midway in an undergraduate version of the discussion group, making it the most exciting intellectual offering at the university. It was no less exciting for the eminent citizens in the "fat man's" course.

Benton, however, in preparing himself for the discussions, found that it was not easy to get his hands on the great books. Many, to be sure, were available through one publisher or another—if one had time to ferret them out. Many were also available in a library— if one had time to go to a library, and if someone else was not reading the single copy on hand. To Benton, all this seemed to be a conspiracy against his time. To put a stop to the evil, he proposed to Hutchins and Adler that the Britannica company had an obligation—and an opportunity—to publish a set of the great books. Hutchins and Adler, being bold entrepreneurs in their own special realm, immediately embraced the proposal.

When Benton put the same proposal to men at the business end of the Britannica company, they were highly skeptical. They observed that a large percentage of the books could be bought in Modern Library or other editions, often for less than a dollar a copy. Why should the public pay Benton a price estimated at six dollars a book for Homer, Machiavelli, Tolstoi? Most people needed and wanted the information they could find in encyclopedias, and were willing to pay for it. But would people pay for ideas, even great ones? After all, Dr. Eliot's "five-foot shelf" of the classics was doing very badly.

Benton was not put off by the arguments. He *wanted* to publish the great books. He felt the sets *could* be sold. He was not proposing to sell books, but education. Even if he should be proved wrong, the cost could be supported on the same ground that the *Britannica* art project could be supported. That is, since the company appeared to be moving toward excess profits tax brackets, the costs of the project could in the main be absorbed by a tax write-off. It was a plausible argument, destined to be proved wrong. Under the so-called installment method of accounting, which he had inaugurated at the Britannica company, profits were reported only as the installments were collected. The company would never reach excess profits levels.

In what seemed to be a bright, devil-may-care spirit, Benton gave the go-ahead signal for the project and, in the course of a follow-up conversation with Hutchins and Adler, added a suggestion. His suggestion grew out of his own lack of time and the eyesight he would have to expend on a vast amount of reading if he wanted to learn what various authors had to say about a particular idea. "We need," said he, "some kind of allure that will induce people to take the great books off the shelves and actually read them to find out what they want to know. Why not some kind of index?" Adler was as agile a student as he was a quick-minded teacher. He had long been thinking about ways to make readily accessible and in an orderly way the insight and understanding contained in the great books. Now he pounced on Benton's suggestion and quickly expanded it. "An index of ideas, of great ideas!" he cried. "We can get up an index that will help the average reader learn about topics in which he is especially interested. It will save the student and the scholar unnecessary drudgery before his thinking starts, and it will show that the thinkers of the past have something to say to the present. A man won't have to read through all the books to find what he wants to read about. He can turn right to it in book after book— whether the subject is democracy, or astronomy, or love, or any of the other great ideas."

Benton, Hutchins, and Adler were now in delighted accord. The index was to be something that never existed before, and a new name had to be coined for it, just as the words "lexicon" and "dictionary" and "encyclopedia" had to be coined when these reference works first came into being. The word invented by Adler was "Syntopicon," derived from Greek roots, the literal meaning being "a collection of topics." The persistent problems men have tried to solve, the fundamental questions they have discussed, the whole range of subjects they have thought about—these were to be the topics constituting the inner structure of the great ideas. The *Syntopicon* would be an aid to reading, an instrument of research, and a stimulus to thinking.

Hutchins was to be the editor of the Great Books, now copyrighted and capitalized, and Adler the associate editor. But to aid in setting up criteria for choosing the volumes, an editorial council was formed of men distinguished in the world of education for their interest in teaching from the Great Books. They included John Erskine of Columbia University, one of the pioneers in the study of notable writings of the ages; Mark Van Doren, the poet and teacher; Stringfellow Barr and Scott Buchanan, who had made the Great Books the center of the curriculum of Saint John's College; Clarence Faust and Joseph Schwab, leaders in the reforms then under way at the University of Chicago; and the great humanist Alexander Meiklejohn, one of the principal proponents of liberal education for young people and adults. After much debate within the editorial council, 443 works by 73 authors were finally chosen for inclusion in the set itself, and the works were divided into four main groups—poetry, fiction, and drama; history and social science; natural science and mathematics; philosophy and theology.

Adler, in addition to being the associate editor for the set, was to be the editor of the *Syntopicon* proper. The budget for the Great Books project as a whole was $500,000. But in the original estimates, it was felt that the compilation of the *Syntopicon* would require a small staff, an appropriation of only $60,000 and about two years' steady work. It was on that basis that Adler began work in October 1943 with a handful of helpers in two cellar offices near the university. First they drew up a list of four thousand basic ideas. Adler then spent months whittling away at the list, decreeing which topics should be discarded, which might be incorporated with others. More than a year after the time that had been deemed suficient, he finally pared the list to manageable size—102 major ideas from "Angel" to "World" subdivided into 3,000 subtopics. Then began the steady task of reading through the 443 works by 73 authors, from Homer to Freud, from Virgil to Marx, and finding the pertinent references to each of the ideas and subideas.

Before the project would be ready for publication, Adler's staff would fill a rambling graystone building with fifty indexers and a clerical force of seventy-five. The 163,000 references they made to the Great Books, assembled under 3,000 topics, would represent 400,000 man-hours of reading, and some 900,000 decisions about dropping or changing references. Far from the $60,000 originally budgeted, the *Syntopicon* would cost in excess of $1 million, added to another $1 million spent on the Great Books themselves. The whole project became notorious throughout the book trade as

"Benton's Folly." Yet those who laughed first were not to be those who laughed last.

In November 1943, after the launching of the new ventures involving the Britannica Films company and the Great Books, Benton took a close look at the CED. In his view, the order of priorities shown by the Research Division in issuing its first major policy statement, with another pending, was wrong. He felt the priorities reflected an excessive desire to avoid dealing squarely with subjects that might offend powerful business interest groups. He spent three weeks trying to reorient the work of the Research Division, and, as if in a postscript to the earlier letter he wrote Paul Hoffman before leaving for England in August, he wrote him another impassioned letter on 1 December.

Benton began by saying he hoped that the CED would identify itself with the "equity-enterprise sector" in American life, in contrast to the "debt-monopoly sector." American business desperately needed an identifiable "equity-enterprise sector," or at least it lacked an articulate one. The CED, he continued, was "now moving out in the political arena," which posed a public relations problem quite different from the problems of an advertising and selling campaign. "In politics, the problem is usually persuasion by contrast, and not by affirmation, as in advertising." But was the CED aware of this distinction now that it was "coming into the crucial stage in its development"?

Benton answered his own question by saying to Hoffman:

> CED's first major public statement through the Research Division, on termination of contracts, featured an angle of selfish interest to business. Our second proposed major statement on taxes, will feature another angle of selfish interest to business. It's traditional for business groups to yap about taxes, and thus, our critics can say, we are running true to form for a business group.
>
> Suppose, as a contrast, our first statement had been on jobs for soldiers, our second on monopoly, our third on economic power. Yes, we would have trod on some toes. Yes, we would have made some enemies. Yes, we would have flushed other critics into the open. But wouldn't we have positioned ourselves much better with labor, the politicians, and the public? Isn't

that where our real job lies—*not* with certain business groups which thus far have made us timid? Wouldn't we be in a stronger position for the long pull without the support of some business groups who might be openly critical?

Now that we are heading into our tax presentation, we will be further stamped as a business-pressure group, concerned with business first, rather than the public first. I don't think we will be as effective on taxes as we would be if we first demonstrated we are in fact dedicated to the public first (through, let us say, a newsworthy statement on monopoly). The tax studies will please business, yes, but if pleasing business was our objective, we might have left the job up to the NAM and the U.S. Chamber to begin with.

Benton returned to the theme again and again for the remainder of the war. In one frustrating matter, however, he finally won a breakthrough in the fall of 1944. Since midsummer of 1943 he had been trying to produce a document stating the basic economic tenets of the CED—or what he felt they ought to be. No writing chore in his life proved more nerve-wracking. He produced forty-four successive drafts for submission to the eight members of the research advisory board as well as to the fifteen members of the Research Division. Back would come comments and criticisms, making a pile six to twelve inches thick. He would spend more days preparing another draft, and much of the manuscript would have to be reviewed again. In the fall of 1944, however, his forty-fourth draft was unanimously approved. There was also a unanimous agreement to publish it as the CED's first "Supplementary Paper," thus carrying the imprint of the organization but not identified as an official declaration of CED policy. Henry Luce read the document and wanted to publish it immediately in *Life*, but was persuaded by his editors that it belonged in *Fortune* instead. There it was published under Benton's title: "The Economics of a Free Society: A Declaration of American Business Policy." It was credited as a CED document, and the rapidly growing organization sent reprints to its two thousand community chairmen for local distribution to and discussion among the CED's fifty thousand members. It had an immediate impact on public opinion and remains to this day the document most often reprinted by the CED, in response to demand, and the one with the largest circulation of all CED reports except those on current research work.

Part of the 1944 impact could be ascribed to the appearance of the pamphlet at the height of the presidential campaign. Further, it was the first, full-scale, *coherent* response from high business circles to the "economic bill of rights" set forth by President Roosevelt in his annual message of January 1944. But above all, here, as in no other single document to be issued at the time by a major business organization, there was synthesized much of what the New Deal years had to teach a thoughtful citizen who wanted the "security" that the political order could provide, and the "opportunity" that a freely competitive economic order could provide.

"The Economics of a Free Society" was divided in two parts, a statement of twelve propositions and a text amplifying them. Benton began by asserting that the common good was superior to the economic interest of any private group—that the economic system is a tool for achieving the common good, and in a free society it is shaped, maintained, and modified by the free choice of the whole community. From there he moved on to assert that the people through their government must devise and enforce rules that will encourage private, voluntary enterprise. Rules to prevent practices that stifle competition, hold back growth, and check a rising standard of living. Rules to allow wage earners to combine for collective bargaining—but not to stifle technological progress or unduly limit access to jobs. Rules that can help foster a climate in which new, small, and independent business can be conceived and born, can grow and prosper. More adequate government skills, meanwhile, would have to be devised "to help stabilize the economy against the effects of the business cycle." Businessmen must rid themselves of "hostility to evolution and change" in the responsibilities of government in the discharge of its proper function.

Prolonged and severe depressions as the result of which millions lose their savings and their jobs, cannot be accepted as natural and irremediable phenomena. . . . Constructive policies respecting taxation and public expenditures (including expenditures for public works), intelligent handling of the national debt, and enlightened control over credit and money can greatly retard or prevent excessive swings of the business cycle. The American people . . . through their federal government . . . have wisely provided in the past, and should continue to provide in the future, a program of social security—unemployment insurance and old-age pensions—for the benefit of those who are unable to work or, if able and willing to work, are for any reason whatever unable to find sufficiently remunerative employment to protect themselves against want. *Such individual protection against hazards should be extended as rapidly as practicable.*

Yet, said Benton, the economics of a free society no longer stopped at America's shores. After the war, "the maintenance of high levels of production and employment in the United States will be one of the most important influences contributing to prosperity and peace throughout the world." That means that the United States must learn how to import, as well as export, if the economies of other countries were not to be disrupted and if the United States wanted to be paid for what it sold. Within the framework of its own free enterprise system, it must also learn how to deal with those countries that have other economic systems.

There is nothing in all the horrors and suffering of war that gives anyone the right to believe that victory will produce utopia or anything like utopia. All victory will do is remove certain specific dangers. The process of making war may or may not increase the capacity of men to cooperate. A major part of the problem after the war is to replace fear and discouragement by hope and initiative.

New products and services that only wait for development— they are everywhere around—will beckon men on to renewed exertion. America stands at the gate of an age of plenty. The key is in our hand. A system of free enterprise, based upon the principles herein set forth, can act as the provider as well as the safeguard of democracy.

Benton had come a long distance in his thinking since the day in 1936 when he visited the University of Chicago fresh from Madison Avenue.

In the months of trouble Benton passed through before the publication of "The Economics of a Free Society" was approved, he had no trouble with the economics of the *Encyclopaedia Britannica*. In happy contrast to the situation during World War I when the encyclopedia was almost ruined financially because of the ban on installment buying, sales of the *Britannica* rose steadily during World War II—as they did for most encyclopedias. Thousands of people who had always wanted a top-quality reference work now found themselves able to afford and acquire it—in part because there were no new automobiles or washing machines to buy. Exempted for strict governmental credit regulations, encyclopedia makers tightened their monthly payment terms and still secured more customers. Only paper shortages and insufficient printing and binding facilities prevented a more rapid increase. Sales and profits mounted.

Benton assumed that if the *Britannica* thrived, the University of Chicago would exercise its option to gain control of the enterprise, buying back one-half of his common stock for $50,000 and leaving him the minority stockholder with a $50,000 investment. The university's option was due to expire in mid-1944, and the trustees had to decide what to do about it. Benton learned of their decision while lunching at the Chicago Club with two trustees, John Stuart and William McCormick Blair. Speaking in the name of the board, they told him that the university would not take up its option.

"Why not?" Benton asked in surprise. "Hasn't everything been working out even better than anyone anticipated?"

That was the point. The university was delighted with the existing arrangement, with the revenues it had already received, and with the fact that Benton was responsible for running the company. Under the 1943 agreement, $300,000 had already been paid to the university in royalties. If business continued as well as it had, that level of annual payments in the years ahead would constitute a virtual endowment of vast proportions.

The university's decision confirmed Benton's position as the two-thirds owner of the Encyclopaedia Britannica Company. A new contract was signed in October 1944. It stipulated, as Benton suggested, that for two years after his death the university would have another chance to control the company by buying up to 50 percent of the stock plus one share, the price to be "the fair value thereof." Such a price would be handled by arbitration if it could not readily be agreed on. The time limit was later reduced to one year after Benton's death and still later, early in 1957, by which time the university had received many millions in royalties and could anticipate many millions more, the option was canceled by mutual agreement.

In November 1944, or a month after Benton and the University of Chicago signed a new contract regarding the *Britannica*, he gave explicit form to an idea he had been thinking about since early 1942.

Before America's entry into World War II, many owners of apartment houses in New York subscribed to Muzak as an inducement to the rental of empty apartments. But when the apartments were filled during the war, many landlords canceled their subscriptions, since they no longer needed Muzak as a come-on. It occurred to Benton that he might be able to sell Muzak directly to tenants much as Allan Miller's Rediffusion Company did in Great Britain. A survey of two apartment houses that had canceled Muzak confirmed Benton's hunch. Sixty-seven percent of the tenants interviewed said that they would be willing to pay five cents a day—or the cost of a newspaper—in order to get Muzak back.

Meanwhile, Muzak had developed a patented device to jam a radio broadcast with an unpleasant singing noise which could be filtered out by a special unit attached to the radio receiver.

Further, Muzak had been working closely with Major Armstrong, the developer of FM, and in fact had programmed his experimental FM station. The apartment-house survey set Benton to thinking about the use of FM stations instead of telephone lines, with Muzak's patented device preventing nonsubscribers from listening free. From there he moved on to what he called "subscription radio," the forerunner of the misnamed "pay television."

This was the time when the Federal Communications Commission opened FM licenses. Benton decided to apply to the FCC for licenses to three such stations in New York, and he worked out his programming ideas in consultation with Victor Ratner, a former vice-president of CBS. Each of the three stations would be specially programmed. One would carry just Muzak or background music for the home. The second would carry dance bands and vocalists so that young people could get the equivalent of the "Lucky Strike Hit Parade" at any time of the day or night, merely by snapping a button. There would be no talking on either of these two stations. All the talking—sixteen hours a day of it—would be reserved for the third station, and it would not be the kind of talk that the regular networks might carry. Instead, there would be morning programs for the preschool child so that a mother could put a child in front of the radio and go about her own work. There would be programs for the International Ladies Garment Workers, for stamp collectors, for stargazers, for those who wanted to learn Spanish, for lawyers interested in hearing leading law professors interpret Supreme Court decisions. There would be programs of special interest to countless minority groups. The general editorial principle would be that of the Sunday *New York Times*—except that nowhere, either on the "talk" station or on the other two, would there be any advertising plugs or commercials.

Benton was convinced that he could develop a vast business in New York City with his three FM channels by charging subscribers only five cents a day, or $18.65 a year. Nonsubscribers would be kept from listening by the unpleasant jamming noise which would be broadcast along with the programs, but which would automatically be eliminated by the special apparatus Muzak would attach to the FM radios of subscribers. He figured that operating costs for the two music channels would be relatively modest. They could draw on Muzak's record library; the material could be used over and over again not only in New York but in other cities to which Benton might extend his plan for subscription radio.

By November 1944—after spending $75,000 in preparatory work—he was well enough along in his planning to incorporate companies called Subscription Radio, Inc., one in New York and one in Chicago, and to apply to the FCC for license rights to three FM channels in New York. In his application, he proposed to let other broadcasters use the Muzak attachments and programs for a small royalty so that he would not have a monopoly. Benton's plan, when disclosed, alarmed the great commercial networks, who referred to the Muzak jamming device as a "pig squeal." The leaders of NBC and CBS, for example, both feared that the success of an audience-sponsored subscription radio would threaten the financial life of the advertiser-sponsored networks. Benton replied that he was not threatening anyone. He was merely inviting everyone to engage in some good, old-fashioned competition in the much talked about "American way." If subscription radio provided programs the public liked, commercial radio remained at liberty to compete for that audience approval, or it was free to lose it.

Besides being objected to by the commercial networks, Benton's plan for subscription radio was attacked on 12 November 1944 by the radio editor of the *New York Times*, who claimed that the whole idea did violence to the concept of "freedom." The charge and Benton's reply published in the *Times* on 3 December were the opening skirmish for what was later transformed into a raging and still unresolved battle over "pay television."

Said the radio editor of the *New York Times:*

> The pig whistle injects a poll tax on radio—the payment of
> a fee in order that the public might enjoy what is already free
> and their property—the air. This is hardly a liberal concep-
> tion of the "freedom to listen." [This could open] the doors to
> a whole series of exclusive squeals, each representing a differ-
> ent fee to the listener. [It] seems an undemocratic means to a
> generally desirable end.

Benton replied in part:

> Freedom is too big a word to be bandied about or to be
> assumed as something which is the exclusive responsibility of
> anybody—whether networks or newspapers or broadcasters
> or advertisers. "The air" may be free. But broadcasting cer-
> tainly is not. It must always be paid for somehow. Under our
> present system, people pay for radio through their purchases
> of radio advertised goods, all listeners having to submit to the
> interruptions of commercial announcements. In a few in-
> stances, such as the city-owned WNYC in New York or the
> educational stations here and there throughout the country,
> they pay for the broadcasting through taxes or subsidies.
>
> In no instance is the broadcasting "free." It is only a ques-
> tion of differing methods of payment. We propose to give the
> listener, for the first time, the opportunity to pay for some
> radio programs directly rather than indirectly. It is hardly
> a question of which particular method is "right." Each, we feel,
> has its place if the public chooses to support it. If we do not
> fill a real need, that will soon be decided for us by the public. . . .
> It is the way that built our economy. Certainly there is nothing
> in legal theory and very little in tradition that makes broad-
> casting solely a venture for advertising. . . . We are simply
> offering listeners an additional choice of programs. And the
> greater the choice, in actual fact, the greater freedom of the
> air.

Benton's fight for subscription radio was abruptly terminated
for reasons which grew out of a new job he undertook.

4

=====

THE
PUBLIC
MAN

16

Clear It with Byrnes

In February 1945 Benton had been a member of the United States delegation to the Chapultepec Conference to coordinate Latin American and United States approaches to the forthcoming United Nations Charter conference in San Francisco. Suddenly, in April, Franklin D. Roosevelt died; the nation rallied to the new president, Harry S. Truman; the Atlantic war was over; the Philippines had been reconquered; Japan was under blockade; and the United Nations Charter conference was underway.

Benton was disappointed when he was not asked to serve on the United States delegation to the San Francisco Conference. Since 1940, he had done more work with Nelson Rockefeller on Latin American matters than any other private citizen. He now read press reports that the United States leaned heavily on Latin American support at San Francisco and that Rockefeller, now assistant secretary of state for Latin American affairs, was playing a key role in coordinating United States and Latin American stands.

Rockefeller himself had urged the appointment of Benton to the United States delegation. But the White House had specified that United States delegates to the San Francisco Conference should be chosen on a bipartisan basis with an eye to the help the delegates could render in winning Senate approval for the United Nations treaty. And Benton had no base of political strength.

Benton sympathized with the reason but even more with himself. "You must understand something about Bill," a close associate explained in a different connection. "If he suddenly found himself on the right hand of God, judging souls and dispensing justice as their cases passed in review, his first reaction would be one of awe: 'Imagine me, Bill Benton, sitting on the right hand of God!' But after ten minutes had passed, he would point to a soul, and taking God into his confidence as a colleague in the judicial proceedings, would exclaim: 'Now this is an absolutely fascinating case!' " Many "absolutely fascinating" cases were to be decided in San Francisco, and he felt personally bereaved at their being decided without the benefit of his counsel.

Meanwhile, CED business brought an invitation to Benton to call at the White House along with Paul Hoffman. This was the first time he had met a president of the United States face to face. President Truman, it seemed, wanted to stop the guerrilla war that had dogged FDR's relationship with the business community, and he also wanted support for the "full employment" bill that Senator James Murray of Montana had introduced into the Senate back in January 1945 to give legislative expression to Roosevelt's economic bill of rights. Would the CED help out on both counts? Hoffman and Benton, chairman and vice-chairman of the CED, answered that they had been trying to help all along, without waiting to be asked for it.

Truman then broke into a half-hour lament that he had not wanted to be president, was not qualified to be the president, and therefore shouldn't be the president at all. He seemed not to notice that even as he declared his disability, he was *acting* like a president. Benton would eventually grasp that central truth about Truman and become one of his most steadfast admirers. But when he left the White House at the end of the introductory meeting, he was of a mind to quote Scriptures to Hoffman: "If the trumpet gives an uncertain sound, who shall prepare himself for battle?"

The CED's relationship to Senator Murray's full employment measure had merged in Benton's mind with his fears for the future of the CED itself. The basic concepts of the bill were in line with those in "The Economics of a Free Society." The bill, in its own words, was designed to "establish a national policy and program for assuring continued full employment in a competitive economy through the concerted efforts of industry, agriculture, labor, state and local governments, and the federal government." It explicitly stated—for the first time in American history—that the federal government had a positive duty to foster free competitive enterprise and the investment of private capital, and the right to "useful, remunerative, regular and full-time employment of all Americans who were able and seeking work." With equal explicitness, it did not guarantee specific jobs to specific workers, or guarantee individual markets or profits, or guarantee government determination of prices, wages, or output. But it proposed a mechanism that would make the president and the Congress directly responsible for maintaining a climate in which the private enterprise system could better provide full employment.

The CED itself took no official stand on the measure. But from the moment the text of the bill was made public in January 1945, it had in Benton an energetic apostle working among businessmen to win their support for the measure. Paul Hoffman and other leading spirits of the CED's Research Committee—Ralph Flanders, Beardsley Ruml, and Harry Scherman—testified as individuals before House or Senate committees in support of the measure and suggested ways for strengthening it. A proposal by Hoffman led to the formation of what is now the President's Council of Economic Advisers, similar to a provision in the Full Employment Act which created the Congressional Joint Committee on the Economic Report. In opposition, spokesmen for the U.S. Chamber of Commerce, NAM, Farm Bureau Federation, and the Committee for Constitutional Government, denounced the full employment bill as "a communist creation of the Communist-sparked CIO-PAC." It was a plan for "the government to move in and destroy economic freedom by taking over the management of business." Talk of "full employment" was nothing but "primitive drumbeating" by persons who were convinced that "the capitalistic free enterprise system was on the way out."

Such clichés sounded insane to Benton. But if the CED was to speak for a saner point of view, the CED itself had to stay alive. That was the rub. It was threatened by sudden death for a reason which went back to the time when the idea of the CED was first put forward. It will be recalled that, initially, the CED was to organize and direct a city-by-city propaganda effort exhorting businessmen to prepare in advance for postwar conversion. The U.S. Chamber of Commerce and the NAM—who wanted no rival business group on the scene they had so long dominated—demanded and got a gentlemen's agreement as the price of their cooperation: CED was to disband with the coming of peace. But this agreement had preceded the decision to establish the CED Research Division as a coequal partner of the Field Development Division, and there was no supplementary or collateral understanding that the CED's Research Division should also be abolished at the end of the war.

Still, some of the bureaucrats in the U.S. Chamber of Commerce and the NAM advanced the thesis that the gentlemen's agreement should apply to the Research Division as well. The CED met that argument by proposing to the Chamber of Commerce that it accept $500,000 from the CED, together with the talents of Scott Fletcher, to merge the Field Division into the Chamber of Commerce and thus strengthen the latter organization. The offer was rejected. The Division, with all the vital energies it had generated under the skilled chairmanship of Marion Folsom, was doomed. But the central idea of the Research Division—to provide systematic educational exchanges between businessmen and professional economists and to write reports on public policy—had been in Benton's mind since the 1936 presidential election and had engaged his and Hoffman's active interest. To allow the Research Division to be killed off when it had not been incorporated into the concept of the "gentlemen's agreement" was to Hoffman and Benton too much to ask of any gentleman.

During the war years, the Research Division had dealt chiefly with the problems of postwar transition. But V-J Day found it involved in or contemplating major studies about a number of long-range economic problems central to the future of the free enterprise system. If this work was to be cut off, who would speak for businessmen in other than the stale slogans sounded by those who were attacking Senator Murray's full employment bill? Indeed, if the Congress eventually passed the bill, there would be an even greater need for the kind of work the CED's Research Division had in view. It would be needed even more to help study, formulate, and publicize policies that bore on the goal of full employment—fiscal and monetary policies, labor-management policies, farm policies, antitrust policies, foreign economic policies, and so on.

The fight for the full employment bill and the fight to keep alive the CED's Research Division could thus be viewed as two fronts of the same war. In the end, Senator Murray's measure, as amended in the legislative process, became the Employment Act of 1946, and even the NAM and the U.S. Chamber of Commerce finally accepted it as "made in America" and not in the Kremlin. As for the CED's Research Division: the CED's trustees in late 1945 voted to extend its life for three years so that its planned projects could be completed. Later on, it was discovered that the Research Division had developed a powerful constituency of its own in the American business community. It could not be killed off merely to accommodate monopolistic interests of the old-line business organizations. Instead it became the whole of what is now the CED.

One more note bears on yet another change in Benton's relationship to the University of Chicago. Robert Hutchins had always wanted to free himself from time-consuming fund-raising and administrative business, in order to concentrate on educational policy. His efforts in this direction had led to years of abrasive conflicts among the trustees and faculty. But in the spring of 1945 an agreement was reached for a reorganization of the university's administration which went into effect on 1 July, when Hutchins became the chancellor of the university. The office of president remained the administrative workhorse, and the post went to Ernest Cadman Colwell. Other organizational changes and growing administrative responsibilities required the creation of a new group of vice-presidents, and this meant that Benton had to relinquish his quarter-time post and title as vice-president. He became "The Assistant to The Chancellor," to spend one week a month in Chicago for a total of three months a year.

Hutchins, perhaps fearful that Benton would be offended by the change, placed heavy emphasis on the word *the* in the title "The Assistant to The Chancellor," and put Benton's name immediately beneath his own on the letterhead of their office stationery. Far from being offended, Benton had his hands full with other projects and was privately considering whether to remove himself altogether from the university's administration. The decision came in August with a summons from James F. Byrnes, who was to be, in a new sphere of life, a new teacher to Benton.

The struggle to govern in Washington is a struggle between what the written law says and what the political climate allows; between the power of tenure and the power of causes; between the power of massive organization and the power of well-placed individual men; between secretive power and noisy power; between the power of expert knowledge and the power of passionate ignorance; between the naked will for power and the power that lies in self-abnegation.

All that Benton didn't know about Washington and would soon begin to learn the hard way, James F. Byrnes had mastered in the course of a Washington career that began in 1911 when he was a newly elected congressman. He had moved on to become a senator, legislative leader of that chamber, Supreme Court justice, and in World War II the "assistant president" in charge of all war agencies on the home front. Byrnes had hoped to be chosen Roosevelt's vice-presidential running mate in 1944, but when that nomination went to Harry S. Truman, he dutifully did his campaign chores for the Democrats and attended to his government business as assistant president. Then, in February 1945, he went with Roosevelt to the Yalta Conference, and at his request returned to Washington in advance of the rest of the president's entourage to give restive senators a preliminary report of what had happened.

In March 1945, knowing that victory in Europe was in sight, Byrnes resigned as assistant president and director of war mobilization and reconversion and went home to Spartanburg, South Carolina, physically exhausted. He explained to FDR that he did not want to end his many years in public service as a peacetime bureaucrat in a rapidly shrinking reconversion agency. Fred Vinson, the director of economic stabilization, succeeded Byrnes, and Chester Bowles, in reward for a solid performance in the difficult post of national OPA director, to which he had been raised from a Connecticut OPA post, succeeded Vinson.

With Roosevelt's death, Byrnes agreed to accept President Truman's appointment as secretary of state. However, in order not to lessen the prestige of Secretary of State Edward Stettinius, who was heading the United States delegation to the San Francisco Conference, it was agreed that a public announcement of the change would be withheld until the conference had developed a United Nations charter.

Most political secrets in Washington have a shorter life than the mayfly. The imminent appointment of Byrnes set a record in secrecy. It lasted about a month before even the most "in" of the "insiders" got hold of it. Nevertheless, Benton, still an "outsider," guessed the secret soon after he received a telephone call from Hutchins in May 1945. "We've got it!" Hutchins said from Chicago, and Benton knew that he meant the atomic bomb. Hutchins also had a request to make of Benton, a request growing out of the agitation among some of the University of Chicago scientists who had worked on the bomb in the Metallurgical Laboratory, the scientific heart of the Manhattan Project. In the initial stages of their work, few were under any strains of conscience. They had been dealing with basic scientific questions and, in the words of Enrico Fermi, had turned out a "great piece of physics." Moreover, when they thought about the military implications of their work, they viewed it as insurance against Nazi Germany's developing its own atomic weapons, for it seemed certain to many of them that Germany's scientific community was capitalizing on its great prewar lead in nuclear physics. But with Germany out of the war, could any further work on the bomb be politically and morally justified, since it was known that the Japanese were in no position to develop atomic weapons? The Chicago scientists knew better than anyone else that they had uncorked a bottle and released a djinn with fantastic destructive powers. Some among them were passionately determined to recapture the djinn and seal it up again before it could do any harm.

One of the most passionate of the scientists was Leo Szilard, a physicist who had come to the United States from his native Hungary. Back in 1939, it was Szilard who got Albert Einstein to write a letter to President Roosevelt which set in train the American program to develop an atomic bomb as a preventive measure against any Nazi success in the same field. Now, on 25 March 1945, at a time when United States pilots were being trained for the first raid with atomic bombs, Szilard again approached Einstein. He explained the vastly different global situation. He indicated in broad outline alone—since under the security rules Einstein was not entitled to know any details—the possibility that the United States might initiate an atomic-armaments race. He asked Einstein, as in 1939, once more to sign a letter intended for President Roosevelt. Szilard attached his own memorandum arguing that any momentary military advantage the bomb might bring to the United States would be offset by grave political and strategic disadvantages. The letter and the enclosure were mailed to the president.

After that, silence. There was no reply before Roosevelt's sudden death on 12 April 1945, and no indication that the new president, Harry S. Truman, had seen the letter—or even understood what the atomic bomb meant.

It was decided that a committee of three scientists—Szilard, Harold C. Urey, and Walter Bartkey, speaking for others among the Chicago group—should try to call on President Truman personally. But how to get an appointment with him? The committee discussed the matter with Hutchins, who recalled that Benton and Paul Hoffman had recently been summoned to the White House by President Truman. Thus the call to Benton, the cryptic words, "We've got it," and a pointed follow-up comment. It was urgently necessary for Szilard, Urey, and Bartkey to see President Truman.

Benton promised to try to help, and called Truman's appointment secretary, Matt Connelly. The president's schedule left no room for him to see the scientists, but he said they should talk to James Byrnes in Spartanburg. The White House alerted Byrnes to their coming, and after a flurry of Benton-Hutchins and Benton-Connelly telephone calls, the scientists met with Byrnes in Spartanburg on 28 May. Benton himself knew that the bomb was a certainty, but he could only guess the purpose behind the visit of the scientists with Byrnes. However, he assumed that President Truman would not have sent the scientists to Byrnes unless the latter was about to return to government service. If so, there was no post other than secretary of state which could tempt him back to Washington. Harry Hopkins's control of the State Department through Secretary Stettinius must soon be terminated.

When he was in fact appointed secretary of state, James Byrnes faced an uncharted world of power and diplomacy. So did everyone else, including his chief aides in the State Department. The lineup of these, as announced or about to be announced by the end of August, was as follows:

First there was Dean Acheson, who during the war was assistant secretary in charge of congressional relations and international conferences and who was brought back as undersecretary a week after he had retired. Next in line was the department's counselor, Benjamin V. Cohen, an original New Deal "brain truster" who had served Byrnes as general counsel of the Office of War Mobilization and Reconversion. After Cohen came William L. Clayton, assistant secretary for economic affairs. Clayton, who had previously served as assistant secretary of commerce under Jesse Jones, had moved into the State Department during the Stettinius regime and was a holdover from it.

The fourth top post—assistant secretary of information and cultural relations—was vacant. It had been held by Archibald Mac-Leish, who had just resigned. MacLeish had been in charge of some one thousand employees in the State Department library, the archives, the beginnings of the Cultural Relations Department, and a special section dealing with all the nongovernmental organizations in contact with the department. All these, however, would presently be hit by a tidal wave of new people upon the issuance of an executive order of 31 August, which assigned to this post the responsibility for eighty-five hundred Office of War Information employees, thirty-five hundred people in Nelson Rockefeller's Office of Inter-American Affairs, and the Office of Strategic Services. Even without the OSS they represented more than half the employees of the whole State Department.

Next in line in the State Department hierarchy was the post of assistant secretary for administration. As of 31 August, it was filled by Frank McCarthy, a former personal aide to General George C. Marshall, who had recommended him to Byrnes. McCarthy, however, was to survive but a few months in the State Department and would be succeeded by Donald S. Russell. James G. Dunn was temporarily retained as assistant secretary in charge of European, Far Eastern, Near Eastern, and African affairs; but Nelson Rockefeller, assistant secretary for Latin America, became a casualty of Byrnes's takeover. Rockefeller had been at his best under the White House umbrella as coordinator of inter-American affairs. Here, his powers of analysis, imagination, and decisiveness had a free scope. But in the State Department as assistant secretary of state for Latin America, the Foreign Service made life uncomfortable for him. He had too many ideas which, though good, didn't fit the cozy rut of Foreign Service thinking. Its officers fought him at every turn. He fought back, lost out, and was summarily fired in the last week of August.

Benton, still an outsider, understood little about the kind of infighting that could make a casualty of Rockefeller. He admired his abilities and credited him, justly enough, with being the "father" of United States information and cultural exchange programs. Besides, Rockefeller had first introduced Benton to Anna Rosenberg and Will Clayton, two people whose friendship loomed ever larger in his life.

Anna Rosenberg's wartime work for the government had been performed at a financially substantial personal loss. Once she had shut down her New York public relations firm, she had no income other than her government salary. She had not only used up all her savings in meeting various expenses connected with her wartime work but had gone into debt. She said nothing to her friends about her straitened condition. Moreover, because of her attachment to President and Mrs. Roosevelt, and her unqualified commitment to the war effort, she would not ask to be relieved of her assignment. In July 1945, however, when the war in Europe was already over and victory in the Pacific was in sight, she resigned her governmental post to reopen her New York firm. When Benton at that time accidentally learned that she didn't have two dimes to rub together, he moved, without her knowledge, to set matters right. He reminded Nelson Rockefeller that the Rockefeller family used to pay Anna Rosenberg $6,000 a year as a consultant but had not been able to do that while she had been in the government. If Nelson Rockefeller would now give her $12,000 as a two-year advance on that retainer, Benton would do likewise on behalf of *Encyclopaedia Britannica*. She would then have $24,000 to pay her debts and open up her office, with Nelson Rockefeller and Benton as her two clients. Rockefeller needed no persuading. "Of course I'll do it," he said immediately. And he added: "Anything I've achieved in Washington I owe to Anna." This last, in Benton's view, was a generous sally which spoke well of Rockefeller's character. "What Nelson owed to Anna," he later said, "was an introduction to Washington, and gratitude for the sound advice she gave him. But what he achieved in Washington—and it was a great deal in the face of great odds—he owed to his own natural abilities."

Since office space was almost unobtainable in New York in those days, Benton got his old friends at Benton and Bowles to squeeze out of their own quarters at 444 Madison Avenue a suite of offices in which Mrs. Rosenberg could resume business. She began to prosper mightily, earning yearly retainers many times larger than the sums which Benton and Rockefeller had initially advanced to put her back into business again.

Toward the end of August, when all the reshuffling in the State Department was underway, Benton, then in Connecticut, received a call from Chester Bowles in Washington. "I have just been offered a job as assistant secretary of state," said Bowles, "and I've turned it down. This is Archie MacLeish's old job, plus a scheduled takeover of the OWI, OIAA, and OSS. I have recommended you to Jimmy Byrnes, and so have Ben Cohen and Will Clayton." He briefly explained that the post meant consolidating the big wartime information agencies within the State Department and launching a new peacetime information program. "Get ready for a phone call," he added, "and make up your mind whether you want the job or not." Byrnes did call a few hours later, and, on 31 August, Benton flew to Washington to see the secretary of state.

En route to Washington Benton formulated nine reasons why he wasn't the man for the job. There were also some reasons for accepting it. First of all, he knew that in his wife, Helen, he had an ideal partner on the stage of the national capital. In earlier years when Benton was in the advertising business, it was said that Helen was the "ideal wife" for the head of an advertising agency. Then, at the University of Chicago, where Helen was a kind of one-woman Red Cross, comforting faculty wives who bore the wounds of their husbands' vendettas, it was said that she would be "the ideal wife of a university president." She was by far the most popular faculty wife in the Chicago academic community, a fact which gave rise to one of the most graceful compliments Benton paid her, without her knowledge.

The circumstances were these. One day in New York, Marcellus Hartley Dodge, the senior trustee of Columbia University, took Benton to lunch at the Racquet Club to ask if he was willing to be considered for the presidency of Columbia.[1] Dodge disclosed that other men under consideration were Dwight D. Eisenhower, Edward Stettinius, and Eric Johnston. Benton said that he didn't think he personally was qualified for the post and recommended Robert Hutchins for it instead. When the lunch was over, Dodge added a postscript to their conversation: "Mr. Benton, I am greatly surprised that you don't think you have a single qualification to be president of Columbia." To which Benton replied: "Mr. Dodge, you misunderstood me. I didn't say I didn't have a *single* qualification. I do have one. My wife. She was born to be the wife of the president of Columbia University." Similarly, in August 1945, Benton knew that if Washington beckoned, Helen was born to be the "ideal wife" of a high official in the State Department.

There was another reason for accepting the post Byrnes was offering. Benton was now in his second month as the assistant to the chancellor of the University of Chicago. It occurred to him that

---

[1]At an earlier date, Benton had turned down an offered appointment as president of the University of Minnesota.

anything he could do for Hutchins could just as well be done on a purely personal basis. Even if he cut his official administrative ties to the university, close ties with Hutchins and with the university would necessarily remain because of their association with the *Encyclopaedia Britannica*, Britannica Films, and the Great Books project. And Benton could no more divest himself of these three projects than he could of his own skin.

In a moment of rigorous self-analysis, Benton said that while he had "soaked up the intellectual atmosphere of the University of Chicago like a blotter put to ink," he had "never remotely done justice" to the opportunities the university gave him "to reeducate himself" from the ground up. "By the time I came to the university," said he, "I had lost the patience necessary to master hard intellectual assignments. I was trying to do too much in too many different directions, my reach constantly exceeded my grasp, and the result made for a superficial intellectual performance. I wholly lacked the capacity and the dedication Hutchins and Adler had to seek knowledge for its own sake. I would listen to their discussions of ideas about ideas, but I came alive only when I saw the practical application of their abstractions."

This practical bent of mind, as he understood it, provided the grounds for another reason for accepting the State Department post. In August 1945, while the world was agog over the birth of atomic energy, the University of Chicago was the one place where more knowledge of the subject was to be found and where its implications were being more thoroughly discussed than anywhere else on the globe. Indeed, soon after the Japanese surrender, the university's atomic scientists had called in their colleagues elsewhere for a thorough review of what their discovery meant for the world's future. Benton had not been able to get to Chicago for the three days of sustained talk. But he had a full report from John Howe, who had attended all the sessions of the scientists. Everything Benton heard came to a head in one point: there was an urgent need to close the great gaps between the stark meaning of atomic power and the public's lack of insight into how that power had drastically changed conventional relations among nations. Benton therefore felt that, as an assistant secretary of state, he could be of help in bridging the gap between the specialized knowledge of the atomic scientists and the popularization of that knowledge in all its staggering practical implications for American conduct in the world arena.

There was yet another reason for saying yes to Byrnes's offer. As a consultant to Nelson Rockefeller, Benton had been fascinated by the State Department and by the potential powers of an assistant secretary in it. The department, as constituted at that time, was very small, and each of its four "legal" assistant secretaries seemed equal in importance to most members of the president's full cabinet. Moreover, from the telephoned description Benton got of the post being offered him, it was clear that the work which went with it had no peacetime precedent in American history. From a purely administrative standpoint, it would be enough of a challenge to consolidate, pare down, and give peacetime coherence to the wartime information agencies he would inherit. The larger challenge was that he would be expected to formulate and launch an information and cultural exchange program in direct support of America's foreign policy—in a world where people had suddenly become as frightened of America's power as they were dependent on it to reconstruct their war-shattered lives. To a highly competitive man like Benton, the more novel a problem seemed to be, and the fewer the precedents for dealing with it, the more he was attracted to the possibility of making the problem obey *his* will.

But then, to offset these reasons for saying yes, there were the nine reasons why Benton felt he was not fit for the post. One of these reasons stemmed from Benton's insight into the way he affected his subordinates in an organization. He drove himself hard, with all the throttles pulled way out, but he did not stop to think that all his subordinates were not similarly disposed. He was constantly erupting with new ideas, but he did not stop to think that his subordinates could be confused regarding the ideas they were to take seriously and those which they were to ignore. And when they wrongly pursued a random idea, thinking it to be of central importance, while neglecting one to which Benton himself was deeply attached, he could explode in anger. "I am often unfair in my relations with subordinates," Benton once said in acknowledging these defects within himself. "More of them would quit if they didn't have some respect for me, but few hold me in any great affection. Indisputably, I lack tact, and this is a serious fault. I alibi my bluntness by calling it 'candor.' Some of my associates get used to it; at least they know where I stand. But I overdo my tactlessness."

He could get by with "overdoing" it in a business organization where he was the boss, free to hire, fire, reward, or censure his subordinates. In the State Department, however, he would be dealing with people entrenched in positions and points of view which were protected by a subtle system of offensive-defensive alliances. They would not take kindly to Benton's ramrod thrusts. On the other hand, Benton was not at all sure that he could really get anything done in the State Department if he stopped to weigh the nuance of every word he spoke before it passed his lips. He felt that every man pays some price in weakness for the strengths he has and that the weakness, paradoxically, is often a point of strength carried to excess. He could only be as he was. He could say plainly what was on his mind in direct response to a challenge, but he strongly doubted that this style would please his prospective colleagues and subordinates in the State Department.

There was a second major reason for saying no. Nine years had passed since Benton had left the advertising business. But no matter what he did, and no matter what new interests he pursued, he had found that many people refused to credit him with being anything more than a "Madison Avenue huckster." He was always the man who was going to do a "slick advertising" job in a project, not because he was deeply committed to the project itself, but because "slickness" was his stock in trade. He had encountered that reaction at the University of Chicago, in his work with Nelson Rockefeller, and in his work with the CED. If he took the State Department post, his old association with Benton and Bowles would again be recalled, and it would be said that he had been engaged as assistant secretary of state to do a "slick promotion job" for the department. This talk would harm the department and any program with which he was connected.

Yet another major reason for saying no was Benton's pre–Pearl Harbor association with the America-First Committee. Unlike Chester Bowles, whose name, beginning with the letter *B*, was the first on the committee letterhead, Benton was not listed at all. Moreover, his total financial contribution to the committee had amounted to a meager $100. Yet he had put a great deal of time and energy, ghost-writing, behind-the-scenes leadership, and even two assistants, into the committee's work. Pearl Harbor and the war years had changed his whole outlook on America's role in the world, and there was no trace left in him of the prewar "isolationist." Even so, if he accepted the State Department post, his background with the America-First Committee would surely come to light, and he felt that it could lead to the kind of embarrassment which would disqualify him for a role in helping to shape and direct United States foreign policy.

At the outset of his Washington meeting with Byrnes, Benton said that he had in mind nine reasons for refusing the appointment. "*Only* nine?" Byrnes asked. "If I had a little more time," Benton answered, "I would think of a lot more." He then cited his background with the America-First Committee and was astonished by Byrnes's reaction. "Instead of being the great handicap you think it is," said the secretary of state, "it is a positive asset. I can tell you from first-hand knowledge that before Pearl Harbor, between 80 and 90 percent of the members of the Congress had varying degrees of open or secret sympathy with the America-First Committee."

Byrnes also knocked down Benton's objections growing out of his identity with Madison Avenue. He said that no one in the nation was really trained to take over the unprecedented "peacetime" propaganda job the State Department faced. He felt that Benton, with his thirteen years of experience in the advertising business, had as good a background for it as anyone else. But at this point, Benton cut in to correct the secretary of state. His background in the advertising business, said he, could prove helpful only in the purely technical aspects of the job. His more important preparation for the work ahead was the knowledge he had absorbed in his eight years at the University of Chicago and his five years of work with Nelson Rockefeller on Latin American matters. All the political, economic, diplomatic, military, sociological, and cultural problems he had been introduced to on the Midway were now the paramount problems of the United States and of the world. This, and not the experience on Madison Avenue, was his major preparation to be assistant secretary of state in charge of information and cultural exchange programs.

When Benton paused for breath, he knew that he had swung away from all his reasons for saying no, and was saying yes. Byrnes knew that too. Without further ado, he "verbally" appointed him an assistant secretary of state, two days before the signing of Japan's surrender on the battleship *Missouri*. It was understood that the appointment would be announced on 5 September, when President Truman would send Benton's name to the Senate for confirmation.

There was more to the first meeting between Byrnes and Benton. The secretary had asked Benton to assume responsibility for the press division of the Department of State. But he explained that the most immediate problem was both defined and complicated for him by an executive order President Truman had just signed and was ready to issue on that same day, 31 August. This was the order transferring to the State Department the employees of the OWI, OIAA, and the OSS. By 31 December 1945, the eleven or twelve thousand employees of the OWI and OIAA had to be reduced to around three thousand and consolidated into an interim International Information Service for incorporation into the State Department itself. No estimates as yet had been made on the extent of the reduction of OSS personnel, then believed to exceed twelve thousand.

The employees of the wartime information programs included some of the most gifted men and women in the field of American communications. But when wartime manpower was at a premium, many "undesirables," including people sympathetic with Soviet ideology, had found places in the information programs, and particularly in the OWI's overseas branch. Benton must not only reduce drastically the size of the agencies he inherited, but before incorporating the residue into the State Department on 1 January 1946, he must get rid of individuals known within the OWI to be either Communists or Communist sympathizers. Yet in reducing the information agencies to a fourth of their wartime size, he must try to retain the services of the very talented people in the OWI's overseas division who were now eager to go back to the private jobs waiting for them in the communications field.

Nor was this all. Benton must plan a permanent United States information program congruous with the 31 August executive order, which called for a continuous presentation to the world of a "full and fair picture of American life and of the aims and policies of the United States government." Further, he must supervise the formulation and execution of United States policies in "reeducating" occupied Germany and Japan. He must make plans bearing on the American position for the forthcoming meeting to charter UNESCO. He must deal with the radio industry, wire services, press, and the motion picture industry, whose representatives were already working among their congressional friends to exacerbate deep and natural suspicions of anything smacking of government peacetime "propaganda."

Finally, and most critically, he must educate the Congress and the country on the reasons why the United States government in a radically new world had to engage in a peacetime information and cultural program, not in competition with private enterprise but in supplement to it. Depending on whether he succeeded or failed in this particular matter, he would succeed or fail in a matter indivisible from it. Specifically, all wartime activities, except Nelson Rockefeller's Latin American operation, had derived their "legal" life from executive orders. The Latin American operation alone stood on the legal foundation of a congressionally enacted statute. If an effective worldwide United States information and cultural program was to be launched on a permanent, peacetime basis, only "the consent of the Congress" expressed in a statute could insure it continuity in policies, functions, personnel—and funds. But to get the Congress to enact the necessary law, the Congress must be persuaded that the program itself was necessary and was not competitive with privately owned media of communications.

17

Hurricane in the State Department

Benton was no sooner out of Byrnes's office on 31 August than he whirled into a hurricane of activity preparatory to becoming assistant secretary of state. With the housing shortage in mind, he called Nelson Rockefeller. "Nelson," said Benton, "you've just been fired this week from the State Department, and I've just been hired. Tell me, what are you going to do with your home in Washington?"

Rockefeller took no offense at the rather ghoulish approach. On the contrary, he said that while he was still using the home, he could move out if Benton wanted it. That was agreed to. "Do you also want the five servants and the chauffeur?" Rockefeller asked. Yes. "One more thing," said Rockefeller getting into the spirit of things. "What are you going to do for places in school for your four children?" Benton confessed that the problem had not occurred to him. "Well," said Rockefeller, "you'd better think of it because it's the toughest problem you face in Washington." Silence. "However," Rockefeller resumed, "you can have the places of my children in the Friends School." One telephone call, and a thoughtful friend at the receiving end, settled the details for family living in Washington.

Then Benton called Hutchins, informing him of the decision. Hutchins was all for it, though it meant severing Benton's increasingly tenuous connection with the University of Chicago. Other university friends, however, were not so sure that Benton had made the right decision. One of the skeptics was Professor Charles E. Merriam, the chairman of the Political Science Department and a man wise in the ways of Washington's infighting. "If I know Bill," said he, "in three weeks' time they'll be blaming him for the Japanese attack on Pearl Harbor."

Benton also wrote to John Howe, who had been his assistant at the university since their first meeting in 1936. He told Howe, who was now married, that he wanted him in Washington, but didn't feel it was right to kidnap him from the university. But Benton would welcome Howe as his personal assistant if he ever decided on his own to leave the university. Was there anything he could do for him in the meantime? After Howe read the letter and talked it over with his wife, Barbara, a University of Chicago graduate, he called Benton to tell him that there was indeed something he could do. Benton could arrange to have him come to Washington right away. Thus, on a "leave of absence" arrangement with the university, Howe moved to Washington and into the State Department as Benton's personal assistant.

On the day of his appointment as assistant secretary, Benton attended to some other details. Secretary Byrnes had asked a young man in the department to show Benton the office he would occupy in the State Department building. It turned out to be a huge corner office with a beautiful balcony. Facing the White House and the Mall, it had been the office of the secretary of war in the old days when the building was called "State, War and Navy." It lacked nothing in the way of "status" symbols. But it lacked one utilitarian object without which Benton could not work. "Where is the dictaphone?" he asked after a quick glance around the room. The startled young man replied: "Why, Secretary Benton, no one ever has had a dictating machine in the State Department!" "Well," Benton snapped back, as if to brush aside a vision of quill pens, parchment and sealing wax, and couriers mounted on horseback, "there is going to be a dictaphone in here right now. Get me one."

Also on the first day of his verbal appointment, Benton engaged a suite at the Statler Hotel as his base of operations until the Senate acted on his appointment. From one day to the next, he worked far into the night questioning people whose wartime operations he would inherit and meeting his future principal colleagues. There were meetings with men like Elmer Davis, the wartime head of OWI, and his deputy, Edward Klauber; Davis was exhausted, near a breakdown, yet his interest in the fate of the OWI in its new location in the State Department was deep and unshakable, and he was to be an ardent Benton supporter. In the course of meetings with other men, warning notes were sounded for Benton about the problems he faced. "It is a great jump," Archibald MacLeish told him, "when a man goes from civilian life into government. But even after a man is thoroughly acclimated to life in government, it is an even bigger jump into the State Department. And you, Bill, are making the two jumps at the same time." The same note was obliquely echoed by the State Department's new counselor, Benjamin V. Cohen. "Many good men come and go in the State Department," said he to Benton, "but the State Department goes on forever."

While Senate confirmation of his appointment was still pending, Benton tidied up his private business interests. He resigned as chairman of the board of the *Encyclopaedia Britannica*, Britannica Films, and Muzak, and he asked Beardsley Ruml, a director of the *Britannica* and Muzak, to watch over certain of their operational aspects. Then, as a two-day-old "verbally" appointed assistant secretary, Benton learned that the CBS radio network was balking at the peacetime use of its facilities for government shortwave broadcasts overseas—this, on the ground that the government could preempt commercial markets the network meant to exploit. Benton saw that he was in for a hard fight in trying to change this attitude. At the same time, he knew that his plan for subscription radio, unveiled in November 1944, had upset the networks. This in turn raised the prospect that the networks might hit hard at the government information programs he would be directing—in order to cut him down for reasons of private business. To make himself a smaller target in the battle ahead, he withdrew his applications before the Federal Communications Commission, and the action was to kill off his idea of subscription radio.

And if he had kept his applications before the FCC? What then? Paul Porter at the time was the FCC chairman, but when he left the government to return to private life, he indicated that Benton had "the FCC in a corner." Benton had argued that he needed the three FM stations in order to compete with and combat the monopolies of the giant networks. The FCC recognized the force of this argument, and, said Porter, "if the three applications had not been withdrawn, there was little doubt but that the FCC would have felt compelled to approve them." If so, and if Benton had followed through with subscription radio, it is conceivable that the pattern of American broadcasting, starting with radio and extending to television, might now be different. In any case, Benton soon learned that his costly withdrawal of the applications was a futile sacrifice. CBS was no more ready to cooperate with a United States information program than it had been before he made his sacrificial move.

On 5 September, the day Benton's name was sent to the Senate for confirmation, Secretary of State Byrnes left Washington with his principal advisers for the first meeting of the Council of Foreign Ministers in London. While Byrnes was overseas, Benton was caught up in a swirl of things that had to be handled on an ad hoc basis in a race against time. The arrival of John Howe from Chicago meant that Benton now had a trusted aide on whom he could unload many chores and who could also explain "pure Benton" to State Department people who had never met that kind of thing before in their lives.

Someone else helped to explain Benton to the Senate Foreign Relations Committee when he appeared before it for his confirmation hearings. Benton expected major assistance from Senator Robert La Follette, a committee member. But La Follette said nothing. On the other hand, Senator Theodore Green, who never liked Nelson Rockefeller's Latin American program, attacked Benton indirectly by attacking that program. The badgering went on for some time, until Senator Arthur Vandenberg, the ranking Republican member of the committee, cut in with a comment. Vandenberg had been an active sympathizer of the America-First Committee before Pearl Harbor, and his knowledge of Benton then had been renewed in connection with CED work. He now stopped the badgering by telling the committee members: "Last week I was talking to a man who said to me, 'all roads in the United States these days lead to Bill Benton.' I move for his confirmation."

The deed was done, and the fact that Vandenberg made the motion for confirmation helped establish an intimate relationship with the senator which Benton enjoyed throughout his own service in the State Department. In a comment on his own conversion to "internationalism," Vandenberg once sighed and said: "Oh Bill, how much simpler my life was when I was an isolationist."

Benton was confirmed by the Senate and sworn in on 16 September. The next day he met for the first time the reporters who regularly covered the State Department.

The department's press office was in charge of Michael J. Mc-Dermott, a twenty-year veteran of the department and a man wholly devoted to it. Many people, however, didn't like the way the office had functioned in the past, and secretary Byrnes had told Benton on 31 August that he was free to fill the press post with a man of his own choice. A Benton-McDermott luncheon meeting had followed, but no heads rolled once McDermott explained the difficulties of his post. He was not a public relations man. He was a straight press man. He was thus caught in the cross fire of reporters who "wanted to know," and State Department careerists who "didn't want the reporters to know." Benton felt that he couldn't find a better person to handle the straight news, and he decided to keep McDermott and help him with his occupational hazards in the department.

Benton's meeting with the State Department reporters on 17 September came at a time when the London Conference was well into its second week, and the relationship between the press and the department wore an air of crisis. Byrnes had agreed with the Russians, British, and French to keep secret everything passed among them at the conference. Yet while the American secretary of state stuck to the agreement and would not reveal to reporters what was said, other countries proceeded to hold "background" briefings for the press. American reporters, frustrated by the tight-lipped Byrnes and other members of the delegation, turned to the English and French, and even the Russians, to learn what was going on. Bitter complaints flowed from reporters in London to their editors in the United States—and from them to Washington reporters. Benton's telephone kept ringing with complaints. He was responsible for press relations; couldn't he do something?

At his first meeting with the press, Benton read a prepared statement bearing on the nature of his assignment and the wartime agencies which had been placed under his direction. Most of the points he made now seem axiomatic. But, at that moment, he was a new peacetime gale blowing through the corridors of the department. The development of modern means of mass communication, said Benton, was a wholly new factor in the conduct of foreign affairs. Peoples in all parts of the world were being brought into direct contact with one another. Inevitably and increasingly, foreign relations would be conducted in the open under popular pressures. Friendships among world leaders and diplomats remained important, but they no longer sufficed. The great stakes of diplomacy now involved the winning over of "peoples" as a precondition for winning over leaders. It would be dangerous for the United States in particular to ignore this development. Benton explained:

> The war has dramatized once more the superlative economic strength of the United States. The advent of atomic power,

with American science in the forefront of research, means that we have become—temporarily at least—the most powerful military nation on earth. Such strength could easily generate suspicion and dislike abroad. Thus we face one of the great challenges of our history. Morally, spiritually and intellectually we must rise to the responsibilities inherent in our economic and political strength. And we must make clear to all the world that we propose to use our strength, and the force of our example, constructively and in the interest of the well-being of all mankind.

If America were to do this, said Benton, it must strive to interpret itself abroad through a program of education and cultural exchange. The taint of special pleading or of what goes by the name of "propaganda" must be avoided. The objective must be a clear understanding of our democratic process. We ourselves must come to know the other peoples of the world. "Our processes in foreign relations," Benton concluded, "must be exposed to the insights of the common man: his conscience and intelligence must be drawn into the State Department."

When he was through, the listening reporters did not pause for as much as a cough before they began firing at their enemy— "secrecy." A sample of the barrage went like this:

Q. Mr. Benton, you made a statement and you did not qualify it. "Foreign Relations are being conducted in public to an accelerated degree." I think some people might challenge you on that. Take the Yalta, the Potsdam and now the London Conference. . . .

A. If I put in qualifications, I would say over the years, over the decades. It seems evident so far.

Q. There have been charges that often we don't have the information that possibly the American people are entitled to. We are available here at the State Department to learn about those things, and I thought unquestionably you have some positive ideas about making that information available to us.

A. I have positive ideas growing out of my whole background that the more information that can be made available, and the faster it can be made available, the better.

Q. Mr. Benton, from the days when you were a common man did you make any observations on government policy which you thought were wrong that should be corrected?

A. As an ex-common man, twenty-four hours ago, I felt that there was a great need to open up the Department of State to my gaze and the gaze of others like me and to liberalize the viewpoint of the Department of State from the standpoint of its dealings with the public through the media of communication.

Q. Do you think you will be able to retain a touch of that for a while?

A. Now that was my feeling day before yesterday, but I am learning already, and the extent to which it will be my feeling day after tomorrow I am not going to speak about right now.

Toward the end of the interview, Benton explained that Mc-Dermott would remain in charge of the press office, adding that he was "trying to figure out a way to get him a raise in pay." Benton then brought up a sore point of his own. He emphasized that he had severed all connections with Benton and Bowles almost ten years previously. He had sold his name to the firm along with the common stock, and his association with the University of Chicago exceeded by one-half the number of years he had spent with Benton and Bowles. Thus the stories and editorial comments about his appointment in which he had been labeled an "advertising executive" were factually wrong. Then he mentioned the companies from which he had just resigned—Encyclopaedia Britannica, Inc., Britannica Films, Muzak and its five affiliates, and Subscription Radio. The tag end of the transcript reads:

Q. What Radio is that?

A. Subscription Radio, which is a happy idea now sadly dead. I killed it.

Q. Mr. Secretary, you might need a raise as well as Mc-Dermott if you keep this up. (Laughter)

Mr. Benton: Thank you so much.

Two years later, this press conference joke about his needing a raise would not be a laughing matter.

Benton told the reporters—and meant it—that his whole life made him a partisan for freedom of information. He now had to make the government deed match the personal word. He felt that, apart from the special problem that had come to a head at the London Conference, information could be properly opened up to the reporters by making prudent changes in the department's security classification system—top secret, secret, confidential, restricted, and unrestricted. He turned the problem over to John Howe, in the vain hope that a quick agreement could be reached within the department on proposed changes, which Byrnes could then approve when he returned from London.

Howe discovered the heart of the difficulty. After sitting in on interminable and futile sessions of a departmental committee formed to consider changes in the security system, he told Benton that the security classifications were but a secondary cause for the excessive secrecy that riled the reporters. The real cause was that the department lacked an "official spokesman" who would do what McDermott seemed powerless to do: give reporters essential "background," while waging a day-by-day, issue-by-issue fight for the release of information the careerists locked up, often for no valid reason. Benton pressed this point of view on Byrnes after the latter returned from the London Conference.

While Byrnes was away, Benton cabled him only twice. First, he told Byrnes that he wanted to do something about the fact that the word "propaganda" was being associated with "information," and thus with his own work. No matter how nobly conceived any information program was, and no matter who administered it, it was always open to the charge of "propaganda" in the pejorative meaning of the word. He added that unless Byrnes cabled back an objection, he meant to call himself "Assistant Secretary of State for Public Affairs"—a name Benton borrowed from Canada, where a wartime cabinet minister had this title. There were no objections from the secretary of state. The title chosen stuck to Benton—and to all his successors in the post, though their responsibilities were to be reduced to only 10 percent of those he had carried.

The second cable grew out of the proposed transfer of the OSS to Benton's jurisdiction in the State Department. The wartime head of the OSS, General William ("Wild Bill") Donovan, was anxious to see the organization he had built converted into an important peacetime activity. Because Benton was expected to take it over in addition to everything else, he asked Benton to spend several days with him in the OSS headquarters. At the end of the exercise, Benton was thoroughly instructed in the operations of the organization— but not persuaded. He told General Donovan and Assistant Secretary of State Frank McCarthy that he wanted no part of the OSS.

Its spy operations and "black propaganda" wouldn't mix with the "white propaganda" Benton was expected to conduct.

The cable to Byrnes developed the argument against mixing "black" and "white" propaganda, and when a typed draft of it was ready, Benton showed it to a State Department veteran on his staff, saying: "What comment have you to make on this? You have been working in this field." The veteran gasped at the language and line of argument, then in a quivering voice said: "Mr. Benton, you are not yet completely conscious of the fact that you are moving into a spot which is the sanctum of the qualified phrase." The cable went off as originally written, proposing the formation of an intelligence system within the Department of State that could operate wholly apart from the "political" and "regional" desks and from Benton.

In his early days in the State Department, Benton was the subject of a *Life* profile written by his Chicago friend Milton S. Mayer and titled, "America's Number One Number Two Man." It summarized Benton's nonbusiness life since 1937—a life of being vice-president or vice-chairman to number one men like Robert Hutchins, Nelson Rockefeller, Paul Hoffman, Eric Johnston, and now James Byrnes. But the title of the *Life* profile did not make clear that when Benton took hold of a project he thought worthwhile, he was no number two man dancing in attendance on a number one man. He spoke his mind firmly and could not, in fact, serve as number two to any man who did not want an unfettered exchange of opinion to govern their relationship.

His manner, unfortunately, sometimes turned away people who would otherwise have been his intimates. One of these in the State Department was Undersecretary Dean Acheson. Mutual friends of the two men saw that they shared many character traits. Both were strong-willed, had uncommon analytical powers, were devoted to the public service, had a great taste for battle, and neither frightened easily. Both seemed to be at their best in the thick of a good fight. Besides, they were both descended from clergymen—and, like many sons of clergymen, enjoyed the pleasures of the senses as well as the pristine ones of the spirit. They should have made as companionable a team in the State Department as Benton and Hutchins made at Chicago. Instead, they became—and remained—irritating mysteries to each other. They became—and remained—wholly out of phase with each other and ill at ease in their personal relationships.

The first brush between the two occurred at a State Department staff meeting while Byrnes was still in London. Acheson, who was presiding, read a powerful and moving draft statement about how American foreign policy would be conducted in line with the late President Roosevelt's views—all interlarded with praise for FDR. As the "new boy" in that department, Benton held back when Acheson asked the staff members what they thought of the draft text. Everybody thought it was fine. But then Benton spoke up. "I think it's lousy," he said tartly.

The staff members froze. Acheson allowed himself a rare show of the middle-class emotion of surprise. "What's wrong with it?" he asked.

"You've been listening too much to Truman run himself down," said Benton. "He's the President now, not Roosevelt. This statement should deal with President Truman and not with a president who is dead." Acheson, a logical man, hesitated, then agreed. The statement was rewritten. But the episode did not promise a happy relationship between the undersecretary and the new assistant secretary.

Byrnes returned from the London Conference knowing he was in for protracted haggling with the Russians over a postwar settlement—and that this would keep him out of Washington and the United States for long stretches of time. He would not be in a position, therefore, really to run the State Department. His chief aides would have to backstop him within their assigned spheres of responsibility. They would also have to fight their internal battles, sending up distress signals only in case of absolute need.

In a way this situation enhanced Benton's standing with Byrnes. The two had spent but a few hours with each other before the secretary left for London, and apart from the two cables previously mentioned there had been no other messages from Benton. The returning secretary of state nonetheless found that the assistant secretary he had left to fend for himself was quite ready to take full responsibility for anything in his purview. He also found that Benton was in battle on many fronts; the air around him rang with the moans of assorted victims. But he was making swift progress toward the December goals that had been set for him. Byrnes thus began to unload on Benton many tasks that would not normally go with his office, and to support him in virtually everything he wanted to do on his own—though Benton could not always do as much for Byrnes as he would have liked.

One shortfall occurred in connection with Byrnes's desire to make

a nationwide broadcast about the meaning of the London Conference. The date was set for 2 October, and Benton asked John Howe
to follow through on the necessary details. Howe got in touch with
the Washington offices of the various networks and the Washington
independent station, WINX, asking them to get together and recommend a time for the secretary's broadcast on a basis open to all.
They were given twenty-four hours to come to an agreement. When
no agreement was reached, Howe set a time for the broadcast and
reported that CBS and NBC each refused to carry Byrnes's talk
unless it was given to them exclusively.

Benton was now drawn into the picture. He was sympathetic with
the general problem the networks faced. If they did not protect
themselves from the demands of government agencies and from the
desire of public and political figures to secure maximum access to
the air, they would be exposed to requests for time which were not
warranted and which were not, in fact, in the "public interest, convenience and necessity." Yet he also strongly argued that the NBC
and CBS demands for exclusive right to any broadcast except one
by the president did not square with "the public interest" in the
case of a speech such as the one Secretary Byrnes meant to make
on his return from London. Its content made it one of the more important public utterances since the end of the war, and he felt that
it merited an all-network hookup. CBS and NBC, however, refused
to see things that way. Benton, being forced to choose between them
in order to get maximum coverage, gave the exclusive to CBS—
which led the smaller networks, Mutual and American, plus station WINX in Washington, to charge him with discrimination.

Immediately after Byrnes's speech, Benton entered into an extended and vigorous correspondence with CBS and NBC on the
principle involved. He said that the "all or nothing" policy of the
two major networks put him and the State Department in an unfortunate position of either failing to give Secretary Byrnes adequate coverage for a major speech or, alternately, refusing to permit coverage by the smaller networks and independents. The two
major networks would not budge, though Benton continued to
hammer away at them. More about this later.

In the interval between Byrnes's return from the London Conference and his departure for the Moscow Conference of Foreign
Ministers, Byrnes agreed to several pending matters which Benton
put to him. One concerned the OSS. It was agreed that a separate

intelligence section should be created within the department to eval-
uate all incoming information. As eventually created, the unit was
first headed by Colonel Alfred McCormack of Greenwich, Connecticut, a lawyer who had served with great distinction in the War Department's G-2 section. But in the State Department he ran afoul
of the Foreign Service "desk men" who were used to making their
own evaluations of intelligence data. After a valiant, six-month
battle ending in frustration, McCormack felt compelled to resign
from the department. "I've learned the difference between the War
Department and the State Department," he once told Benton with
a sigh. "In the War Department you submit a paper and it will come
back to you the next day marked: 'This is impossible!' In the State
Department, you submit a paper and get it back with a dozen nota-
tions from Foreign Service officers all saying: 'This is wonderful!'
But then, nothing happens."

Throughout McCormack's battle in the State Department, Benton had been on his side. This made for a kind of "blood covenant"
which lasted over the years, to Benton's own benefit when he became
active in Connecticut politics. McCormack, though a Republican,
emerged as one of his most steadfast supporters.

Byrnes also approved a second proposal—that concerning the
appointment of an "official spokesman" for the State Department.
Byrnes said that if the "right man" could be found, he would have
the "official spokesman" in for breakfast each morning he was in
Washington to review late developments, to decide what could be
disclosed to the press that day, and what should be released later.
The "official spokesman" would also go with the secretary to future
international conferences where he would hold "background briefings" for the press in line with the British and Russian practices
at London.

Benton's search for the "right man" proceeded along with his
efforts to liberalize security classifications. The man he sought
must be tough, intuitive, precise, deft, discreet. He must have the
confidence of the secretary of state, the department careerists, and
the press corps. These traits are rarely joined in one man; yet Benton, with the help of John Howe, drew up a list of some thirteen
people, mostly newspapermen, who in their view possessed most of
the required qualities. James Reston of the *New York Times* was on
the list, as was Edward R. Murrow of CBS, Seymour Berkson of
the INS, Joseph Phillips of *Newsweek*, and John Gunther of Inside

Everything. The thirteen were serially offered the post of "official spokesman" in the State Department. Not one would touch it.

The time-consuming search had but one concrete result, which set a precedent for the future. In February 1946, when Byrnes led an American delegation to the Paris Council of Foreign Ministers, on Acheson's recommendation and with Byrnes's approval, Benton appointed Charles E. Bohlen to go with Byrnes as the "briefing officer." Bohlen's performance as official spokesman for the American delegation won Byrnes's admiration, as it later would that of General George C. Marshall when he became secretary of state. It was one of the factors in Bohlen's eventual appointment by Marshall as State Department counselor, and his later appointment to ambassadorial posts of increasing influence.

There was less delay in firing pro-Communists in the work force Benton inherited, while saving for his program persons who were falsely charged with pro-Communist sympathies. "The operation, concentrated in the fall of 1945, was not perfectly done," said Benton, years later. But it was done well enough so that by the time the work force of twelve thousand had been slashed to the thirty-one hundred men and women who were transferred into the department, not one of the transferees was ever picked up as a Communist; rather, the Communist problem proved to be more serious among the one thousand employees whom Benton had inherited inside the department than among the transferees from the war agencies. Yet in slashing the war agencies by 75 percent, he had to maintain the morale of the best of the men he wanted to keep on the job to help him plan a permanent information and cultural exchange program. It was hard to convince them to trust to the president's and the department's determination to make of this work an important peacetime activity. They could see thousands of fellow workers being fired, and they read in the daily papers about mounting attacks on the proposed program by members of the Congress and by spokesmen of the communications industry.

Through all of this, Benton felt that the wartime information agency workers had not been given the recognition due them for loyal and often valiant contributions to the war effort. Those who remained in government service, and those who left it voluntarily or were severed from it, had come under a blanket indictment as "pinkos" and "draft dodgers." Benton tried to right this wrong. He noticed that General Brehon Somervell, who had been in charge of the supply services of the army, seemed to pin a medal on practically every colonel under him who left the Pentagon. Benton tried to get some decorations for the men in the OIAA and in the OWI—the latter agency having had a higher mortality rate overseas than the navy. Yet the only man for whom he could get a medal was Elmer Davis, the wartime head of the OWI. The committee on medals flatly refused to give one to Nelson Rockefeller. Much less would it consider awards of any kind to rank-and-file members of the information agencies, although some had been decorated for bravery by commanding generals in the field.

To right this wrong, Benton made up certificates of merit for employees of the wartime information agencies. In issuing these, on his own and without clearance from anybody, he wanted to give the OWI and the OIAA alumni something to hang on the walls of their future offices. The simple gesture went unnoticed by Washington. Yet the certificates of merit became the connecting links among members of an "enlightened Mafia," all loyal to Benton's purposes. And what a Mafia it was—gifted reporters, editorial writers, columnists, book publishers, novelists, dramatists, screen writers, and radio broadcasters. When these former employees of the wartime information agencies resumed their peacetime careers, the certificates bound them to Benton's program. He, in turn, had in them a strategically placed private army that might be drawn into the fight for the basic legislation he was interested in. Without their help, it is almost certain he could not have prevailed in his protracted effort to win congressional approval for the Smith-Mundt Act, cornerstone of the present-day United States Information Agency.

It remains to be added that Benton later helped the State Department prepare legislation, approved by the Congress in July 1946, enabling the department to create its own medals, as was true of the military. In the order of medals created under this legislation, the highest is the Distinguished Honor Award. In an amusing twist of fate, Benton was to become the beneficiary of his own idea. In late 1967, he was given the Distinguished Honor Award—the forty-sixth recipient in its history. Two other men were given the same award at the same time, Governor W. Averell Harriman and Ambassador Henry Cabot Lodge.

Benton's first direct encounter with Congress came in early October 1945. The forum was the House Appropriations Committee, and the cause was urgent. His agency needed money to maintain its operations even at a drastically reduced scale until the authorization for the 1946–47 budget was made. To come within hailing distance of his roughly estimated figures, Benton had to get safely past many obstacles. One was Clarence Cannon, the Missouri Democrat who was chairman of the House Appropriations Committee. But his real problem was the awesome one-man hatchet brigade represented by Congressman John Taber, the senior Republican on the committee and a man who prided himself on his talent for ruthlessly cutting back or eliminating requests for appropriations.

Before Benton went up to the Hill to face Taber, Secretary Byrnes filled him in on some background facts. Byrnes and Taber had been "principal fixers" on prewar budgets, with Byrnes representing the Senate and the Democrats and Taber representing the House and the Republicans. In effect, the two men had bargained and decided between them what the major appropriations would be. Therefore, while Benton was at his side, Byrnes telephoned Taber and delivered an assist characteristic of him. "John," said he, "I am sending up to you a fine and capable young man named Bill Benton. He is my new assistant secretary of state. I want you to know that I *personally* stand behind him. I want you to treat this able young man sympathetically and fairly."

Benton had been a reluctant slasher, but the slashing did him no harm when he told the Appropriations Committee generally, and Taber specifically, how swiftly he was cutting back on the wartime agencies he had inherited. Many of the slashes were against his personal judgment, but he had to carry out an order to cut down, carry on, and plan at the same time, in line with the total United States need as interpreted by the Bureau of the Budget.

At one point Benton tactically retreated, as a prelude to a counterattack. He wanted to adapt shortwave radio to the permanent peacetime uses of the government, because radio, not subject to censorship at national boundaries, was the best way to get at the 75 percent of the earth's population who lived under some degree of censorship, blackout or dimout, particularly on news. Benton put the key question to the Appropriations Committee when he spoke of shortwave radio as an instrument for information and education:

What is to be done with it? It is expensive; one-third of the entire cost of the Government's information work is represented by the programming and operation of short-wave radio and its relaying by medium-wave. It is troublesome in the sense that the responsibility for any radio programs is troublesome, especially in the hands of a government department. It is generally unprofitable for private industry, since there is no way of assuring adequate revenue from listeners abroad or sponsors at home; and in any case, only 13 of the 36 transmitters now in use in the United States were in operation at the time of Pearl Harbor. All the rest were built for or by the Government. To scrap these new transmitters, 18 of which are owned by the Government, and to stop programming them at once, would not seem intelligent from the point of view of the future national interest.

Benton went on to stress that a "great national interest" was involved here and that it was also "one of the most complicated problems" in the field of government. He said he meant to study the matter carefully and would return to the Congress with his recommendations. He did not reveal the ideas that were already buzzing around in his own mind—and that soon would find expression in legislation. But until the indicated study and recommendations were made, said he, he would have to conduct the operation of short-wave radio "on a reduced scale, with fewer languages, fewer hours on the air, and fewer employees."

It was at this time that the shortwave radio program came to be called "The Voice of America," and the question of who really originated United States overseas broadcasting, and who gave it that name, was to run through Benton's correspondence for twenty years. As late as the 1960s he was still trying to nail down for posterity the truth about these two matters. Benton had credited Nelson Rockefeller with being the grandfather, with his Latin American broadcasts. Edward R. Murrow, when he was the head of the United States Information Agency, dated the first use of the phrase "Voice of America" from OWI broadcasts in 1942 out of London, but credited Benton with popularizing the phrase after V-J Day and applying it to the total worldwide broadcasting efforts of the United States. Edward Barrett, one of the later heads of the postwar information program Benton began, was inclined after many exchanges of letters to accept as correct what Benton wrote to Murrow on 2 March 1962:

As far as I have been able to learn, the phrase "Voice of America" was not used in the United States until the war was nearly over. I'm told the phrase does not appear in the New York Times index until June 1945, although the phrase "OWI broadcasts" does.

Many (though by no means all) of the OWI's broadcasts to Europe were introduced with a version of the phrase, and I'm sure you'll remember the broadcasts as they were carried in England. John Howe reports hearing them in French and Italian in this country, with "Yankee Doodle" as the opening theme, and an announcer saying "This is the Voice of the United States of America coming to you from across the Atlantic Ocean."

I had been in the State Department for some weeks before I had ever heard the phrase, "Voice of America." This had never been applied to the total output of either war agency. One day in my office I was looking at the program schedule of the former OWI broadcasts from London [which had become State Department broadcasts]. I saw the name applied to some of the newscasts, "Voice of America." The name struck me as a very good one. I was seeking some way to dramatize our radio output. The Navy was trying to steal our frequencies. Others, such as your friend Earl Gammon [of CBS] were trying to kill off the broadcasts. I slapped the name "Voice of America" onto the entire output all over the world.

Benton's decision in the matter put the overseas broadcasts into America's domestic headlines, because the phrase "The Voice of America" had dramatic appeal to the press. It also appealed to Secretary Byrnes, who soon thereafter greeted Benton with a laughing question: "How's your Voice today?" Benton, however, ruefully admitted that in his desire to publicize the project he had given the relatively feeble broadcasts too big a name. More than that, he privately agreed with General David Sarnoff of RCA, who, on returning from a trip to Europe in 1946, responded to a group of ship reporters: "Bill Benton's Voice of America? It's just the Whisper of America!" Thus the phrase was to play its own part in getting the kind of publicity Benton would need for his program.

Benton made a good personal impression in his first appearances before the House Appropriations Committee in October 1945.

Months of hard work, however, lay ahead before he won the dollars and cents he needed, and still more months before he could get the Congress to enact legislation to authorize his program, which was meanwhile provided for only by the executive order of 31 August 1945.

A first move to secure the enactment of the requisite law dates from late September 1945. A draft bill was prepared in Benton's office to authorize what was already being done in a limited way under the cover of the executive order, and to authorize on a world-wide scale what existing law authorized in the limited case of the information and cultural exchange program applied to Latin America.

The draft bill authorized an extension into the world arena of United States activities such as shortwave broadcasts; the exchange of students and professors; the maintenance and servicing of American information libraries abroad; a daily wireless bulletin carrying to United States diplomatic missions the full text or extracts of important official announcements; a documentary service to supply United States missions, by mail, with background material, biographical sketches, and information about life in America, together with a limited service of still photographs from government sources; photo exhibits, displays, and filmstrips for noncommercial use in foreign countries; the continuation of the bimonthly illustrated magazine *America* in the Russian language for distribution in Russia, where private foreign magazines were barred; the acquisition, adaptation, and scoring in foreign languages of newsreels and documentary films about the United States for noncommercial showing to foreign audiences; on-the-spot work by a small staff of information officers at sixty-two United States missions; the translation of American technical and other books into foreign languages; and the detailing of many types of United States government officials for temporary service to other governments.

When the draft bill was ready, Benton persuaded Representative Sol Bloom of New York, chairman of the House Foreign Affairs Committee, to introduce it into the House. This he did in October 1945, and the measure was referred to his committee. The committee held two weeks of hearings and spent several more weeks refining the bill, but finally reported it out unanimously. Under congressional procedures, however, it could not come before the Congress for a vote until approved by the traffic-managing Rules Committee. The Rules Committee kept the bill bottled up from one month to the next, and, with no legislative sanction for his program, Benton was to see how easily it might die through reduced appropriation. He had initially asked for $25 million. The Bureau of the Budget had reduced this to $19 million. A House appropriations subcommittee had further reduced it to $10 million—$3 million of it for liquidation costs of the wartime information agencies. This left only $7 million for actual operations—which plainly meant that short-wave broadcasts would have to be eliminated. The House and the Congress as a whole, however, had yet to approve all these proposed cuts in the budget appropriations for 1946–47. With the handwriting on the wall hardly in his favor, the current operations of Benton's program continued to be financed by the unexpended authorized funds of the wartime agencies he had inherited. There matters stood for several months.

Meanwhile, of the many other matters that needed attention, one grew out of a Senate speech made on 7 September 1945 by Senator J. William Fulbright. Fulbright, like Benton, was a relative newcomer to the Washington scene. While reflecting on how much he himself had learned in England and the world as a Rhodes scholar, he sensed that the Congress was of two minds about student exchanges. It wanted to promote them but didn't want to draw on Treasury funds for the purpose. At the same time, in a different direction, Fulbright feared that the divisive "war debts" quarrels following World War I might recur. In a synthesis of the foregoing considerations he proposed to serve the cause of learning, thrift, and peace in a single program by financing student exchanges with foreign credits frozen abroad from sales of World War II supplies. He thus introduced a bill, characteristically brief, authorizing "the use of credits established abroad for the promotion of international good will through the exchange of students in the field of education, culture and science."

The Senate quickly approved the bill. Just as quickly, Benton saw in it a chance to extend on a global scale the formula of United States cultural exchange programs hitherto confined to Latin America. In the House, however, a companion version of the bill ran into trouble, and Fulbright asked Benton for his help in saving the measure. Benton in turn brought Will Clayton into the picture, since he carried great weight with the House members who opposed the bill.

The sequel can best be told here. After a year of effort, the measure was finally approved by the House, and President Truman signed it in the summer of 1946 as Fulbright and Benton looked on. When the ceremony was over, Benton drafted a press release saying that the State Department would presently announce the composition of the *Fulbright* Board provided for under the *Fulbright* Act, and that the board would then appoint *Fulbright* fellows. Fulbright was taken by surprise. Without Benton's long-standing devotion to "brand names," it had never occurred to Fulbright that his own name would be attached to every aspect of the exchange program. In the press releases flowing from Benton's office, which administered the program, the word "Fulbright" was prominently underlined with the result that Fulbright was to become perhaps the best-known United States senator around the world, and his name a synonym for the words "education" and "cultural exchange."

The charter conference of the United Nations Educational, Scientific, and Cultural Organization (UNESCO) was due to start in London on 1 November 1945. Since its work lay within the field of Benton's responsibilities, it was automatically assumed that he would be the chairman of the American delegation. Instead he confined his own role to that of vice-chairman and appointed Archibald MacLeish as chairman. "Now I've seen everything," Secretary Byrnes exclaimed. "I've been in Washington for almost four decades, and this is the first time to my knowledge that any man in government has ever been appointed one of his predecessors to be the head of anything." Benton, however, was pursuing his own logic. He knew that he would be personally responsible for the actions of the delegation whether or not he was its chairman. Also, because his own work in Washington was so demanding, the American delegation would have to precede him by a week. He would need an effective stand-in chairman, and MacLeish was the ideal choice. He was a world figure, eloquent in both French and English, a noted poet, and had won the Distinguished Service Cross for battlefield valor in World War I.

In choosing the members of the American delegation to the London Conference, Benton told Byrnes that he wanted Mrs. Eleanor Roosevelt as one of the delegates. He was unaware of the ill-will between the two while Byrnes was serving as assistant president to Roosevelt, nor did Byrnes say anything about it to Benton. "In my presence," Benton later recalled, "he picked up the phone and called Mrs. Roosevelt so that I could listen in. The device, which he often used with his subordinates, spared him the need to send them a subsequent report. When he extended to Mrs. Roosevelt my invitation to join the American delegation, she said: 'UNESCO isn't right for me. I suggest that you take Dean Mildred Thompson of Vassar with you. She's interested in education, and will greatly contribute to UNESCO. What I would like for myself is an important role in the United Nations itself.' Secretary Byrnes promptly promised her that he would work out such a role. He kept his promise, and Mrs. Roosevelt was presently injected into the United Nations, where she greatly distinguished herself."

Besides Benton, MacLeish, and Mildred Thompson, the American delegation to the UNESCO Conference included Dr. Arthur H. Compton, the Nobel Prize winner in physics who was now chancellor of Washington University of Saint Louis; Representative Chester E. Merrow (R., N.H.), of the House Committee on Foreign Affairs; Senator James E. Murray (D., Mont.), chairman of the Senate Committee on Labor and Public Welfare; and Dr. George Shuster, then president of Hunter College. They were accompanied by an equally distinguished group of advisers and technical experts.

Before leaving for London, the delegation reached one crucial decision that bore the imprint of an argument Benton advanced. He agreed that it was important to have continuous and close international contacts among scientists, teachers, and learned societies. But he could not accept the prewar assumption that these men alone through their scholarly association could bring about mutual understanding among their respective nations. That assumption lay at the heart of the Institute of International Cooperation, a League of Nations predecessor to UNESCO with restricted interests and small membership. If increased international understanding was to be the prime objective of UNESCO, then masses of people had to be reached by modern means of mass communication—newspapers, radio, and motion pictures. This radical concept, unknown to the Institute of International Cooperation, was a by-product of Benton's work in advertising and then at the University of Chicago. The American delegation would weave the idea into the working plans, and then into the fabric of UNESCO.

In one respect, Benton was carried away by his own enthusiasm when he envisioned a worldwide UNESCO radio network which would teach people how to read and write, make accessible certain basic cultural materials, teach farmers how to be more productive. He came to see that from a political and United States standpoint, no such radio network could work satisfactorily if it were managed by an international organization in which Communist-bloc countries participated. But at its inception, the idea of a worldwide radio network had a dramatic appeal. He repeatedly stressed the point that UNESCO's goals should be broader than the narrow goals of intellectual cooperation among scholars and learned societies. Benton thus became the root source of what is now UNESCO's deep involvement in the area of mass communications. And his dream of broadcast education is now being urged on member nations by UNESCO agencies in terms of television as well as radio.

The London Conference lasted for eleven days. Forty-four nations were represented, but the quality of the delegations varied from country to country. The British, for example, sent what seemed to be a second-string team. On the other hand, French intentions to regain in the cultural field a leadership they could not then wield in any other, were signaled in the composition of its impressive delegation, headed by former Prime Minister Léon Blum. The power of decision, however, often lay in the American delegation—which placed Benton in a key position.

The question of a suitable name presented difficulties from the beginning, since no single word described in all languages the field of the new organization. The solution finally adopted was necessarily a list of adjectives, rather than a single comprehensive characterization. Thus on the motion of the United States delegation, the word "scientific" was added to "educational" and "cultural," mainly in the hope that science could form the bridge over which the West could pass in conversation and dialogue with the USSR.[1] No one was wholly satisfied with the title. "One trouble in thinking and talking about this proposed organization," Benton said, "is that the contraction into its initials, UNESCO, makes it sound like something wrapped in cellophane."

Beyond the question of a name, the London Conference attached

---

[1]Many in London felt that the world of science should have its own independent United Nations organization, unfettered by education and culture.

great importance to the preamble of the constitution it was framing. It was felt that a new international organization, starting on work without international precedent, had a duty to state the reasons for its existence and the principles it would steer by. The preamble, as finally adopted, was largely the work of Archibald MacLeish, though MacLeish later said that he had taken from a speech by Prime Minister Clement Attlee of Great Britain half of the much quoted opening sentence of the preamble: "Since wars begin in the minds of men, it is in the minds of men that the defenses of peace must be constructed." The rest of the preamble reflected the then prevailing view that "mutual understanding" among nations could somehow by itself remove the grounds for war.

Meanwhile, the conference was agitated by the question of where UNESCO was to be headquartered. It was Benton's feeling, strongly shared by the rest of the American delegation, that the new organization should be thought of as a new start in international collaboration. Neither its location nor its personnel should necessarily relate it directly to the Geneva-based League of Nations. At the same time, Benton felt that the seat of an international organization dealing with cultural matters should be in a center of world culture and that, in view of the problems created by the war, it should probably be in Europe.

The point at issue was settled in a "smoke-filled room" where Benton met alone with Léon Blum. Blum urged Benton to support the choice of Paris as the permanent seat, and the latter agreed subject to a proviso about this and two other matters. Uppermost in Benton's mind was the question of how far the French would go in their efforts to dominate UNESCO, and whether France might go Communist. He felt the latter question would probably be decided one way or another within five years. For that reason—and also to keep open an avenue for maneuver in the event France withheld full cooperation—he agreed that the seat for UNESCO would be Paris for *five* years, at the end of which time the question of relocating the permanent seat would be reopened. Conversely, he got Blum to agree that the biennial sessions of UNESCO's General Conference should be held at places other than the permanent seat, the location to vary from conference to conference. He also got Blum to agree that the director general of UNESCO would not be French.

Unfortunately, there was a failure to incorporate these three provisos into a report to the State Department, and no formal record

exists to substantiate them. Moreover, none of the provisos with-
stood the eroding force of time and events. Paris became UNESCO's
permanent home. The biennial sessions of UNESCO's General Conference are now always held in Paris, because the secretariat is there
together with all the permanent delegations assigned by member
countries to UNESCO. The director general of UNESCO today is
a Frenchman, though his election was opposed by the United States.

While the UNESCO Conference was still in session in London,
Benton went to Berlin for two days in line with his responsibility to
oversee "the reeducation of Germany and Japan." [2] He first called
on Robert Murphy, the State Department's senior political adviser
at the headquarters of General Lucius Clay, the commander of the
United States occupation forces. Murphy, an experienced diplomat
who had held assorted posts of great difficulty during the war years,
was one of the best products of the Foreign Service and a model
held up for its members. He met but once with Benton, a nonprofes-
sional in charge of a new and highly controversial area of work.
After that, he was unavailable as a source of help. It seemed to Benton that the standoffish attitude of the State Department's senior
political adviser at the general's headquarters clearly reflected the
hostility of State Department professionals to the postwar invasion
of the department by the personnel and activities of the wartime
agencies.

Benton, for his part, was primed to contest various decisions
General Clay had made in the fall of 1945 in matters bearing on the
United States information program. "The OWI," said Benton in
drawing up his bill of particulars, "had a large and powerful radio
station in Berlin. But Clay closed it down because the Russians
didn't like it. We had a powerful newspaper in Berlin, with something like 300,000 daily circulation. But he shut it down because
the Russians didn't like it. He gave Radio Luxembourg back to its
original owners; yet this had been one of our most powerful voices
in Europe. I was to have my troubles with him a few months later

---

[2]Benton later sent important educational missions to both countries to report on the problems of their reeducation. "This sounds rather amusing today," he said. "Certainly we contributed little if anything to Germany's
alleged reeducation. As to Japan, I think our efforts were more productive.
George Stoddard, the President of the University of Illinois, whom I appointed as chairman of the Japanese delegation, picked the woman who
became the tutor to the young prince who is now heir to the Japanese
throne."

over the Munich transmitters. His policy in my area, in the early months after the war, was weak and wrong." Benton admitted that other United States government officials were making mistakes of their own in assessing the Russian intentions and that all officers in the field worked within the broad frame of policy directives they received from Washington. Yet in Benton's view, General Clay, exercising his power of on-the-spot decision, was making many unfortunate decisions in spheres which were Benton's responsibility. "I strongly felt," Benton said, "that America's interest, and not the feelings of the Russians, should determine what America did in all aspects of its information program in occupied Germany and elsewhere."

He had hoped that a frank conversation with Clay about disputed points at issue would lead to a meeting of minds and to a coordination of efforts. But when he called at Clay's office, he was kept waiting a very long time before the general had him ushered in. To make matters worse, Clay showed little interest in Benton's views and treated him brusquely. Benton was already in an embattled frame of mind, and after ten minutes of talk, he rose from his chair, picked up his hat and said with some feeling to Clay: "General, as assistant secretary of state, I am responsible for our propaganda and information policy and for the reeducation of Germany. I did not come all the way to Berlin to be insulted by you." Then he left the room. As he proceeded down the hallway outside, he heard the sound of running feet behind him and wheeled about. He was being pursued by General Clay. The general apologized for his earlier manner. He explained, truthfully enough, that he had been working around the clock without letup. His nerves were frayed. This was something Benton could understand. He was in the same condition.

The two exhausted men both calmed down. They returned to Clay's office and talked for two hours. Benton questioned Clay closely about the proposed reeducation of Germany,[3] and got in reply Clay's defense of his closing the OWI newspaper in Berlin and

---

[3]Clay had no ideas on the reeducation of Germany and Benton had very few. Benton later visited with Major John Taylor, then supposedly in charge of the reeducation of Germany (and later deputy director general of UNESCO, president of the University of Louisville, and now in charge of educational television channel 11 in Chicago). It was Benton's conclusion at that time that the symbol of the army's attitude toward this key subject was the way it relegated the reeducation of Germany to a United States Army major so far down the line he could hardly be found.

returning Radio Luxembourg to its owners: Clay felt he had to try to get along with the Russians, and these points seemed less important to him than to Benton. They did not talk about Radio Munich, because Benton himself at that time had not decided on direct broadcasts to the Soviet Union; no one had even thought of such broadcasts. But the control and use of Radio Munich by Benton was to set the stage for another clash with Clay, albeit at long range.

Following the unproductive visit to Germany, Benton returned to London for the rest of the UNESCO Conference. While there, he called on William Haley, then the head of BBC. Haley was subsequently to become Sir William, and the editor of the London *Times* until 1967 when Benton brought him to Chicago as editor in chief of the *Britannica*. In the fall of 1945, the "Voice of America" was leasing a number of BBC transmitters, and in discussing this arrangement with Haley, Benton asked him why the British (like the Americans) were not broadcasting to the Soviet Union in Russian. "The Russians broadcast to us in English, and also to you," said Haley dryly. "They say they want to cooperate with us on our kind of democracy—which favors freedom of speech and freedom of information. They ask us to reciprocate by cooperating with them on their kind of democracy. In their kind, they do not believe in freedom of speech and do not want us to broadcast to them." The bite in the dry remark forced Benton to consider the matter more fully, with consequences to be described later.

Back in Washington after the UNESCO Conference, Benton transmitted to Secretary Byrnes the formal report of the United States delegation and attached to it for public release a note of "serious warning" to the many groups throughout the country interested in UNESCO not to "overestimate" what had "so far been accomplished." UNESCO was still only a document. It would remain a piece of paper "if it is starved for leadership or funds, if it is bypassed when governments try to deal with knotty problems, if it is kept as a sort of ornamental cabinet in the hallway of the UN." He then created a five-man committee to formulate proposals regarding the way in which UNESCO could use mass media to further international understanding. The five were Edward W. Barrett, editorial director of *Newsweek* and formerly the director of the OWI's overseas branch; Thurman L. Barnard, vice-president of the Compton Advertising Agency and formerly the executive director of the OWI's overseas branch; Don Francisco, vice-president of the

J. Walter Thompson Advertising Agency and formerly the assistant coordinator of the OIAA; Ferdinand Kuhn, Jr., formerly chief of the London bureau of the *New York Times*, later deputy director of the OWI and director of the interim International Information Service; and John Hay Whitney, formerly the motion picture chief of the OIAA, and the chairman of the board of Selznick International Pictures.

At the same time, Benton had to steer the UNESCO enabling legislation through the Congress. The legislation was eventually approved by an overwhelming vote in both the House and Senate, though it set Benton back in one respect. It specified a National Commission on UNESCO, and Benton had hoped this would be confined to thirty members appointed by the president (meaning the secretary of state). However, the teachers' union and the National Education Association, together with others, feared that they would not be represented on a small commission. So they persuaded the House Foreign Affairs Committee to enlarge the commission membership to one hundred, of whom sixty would be representatives of national organizations. The UNESCO enabling legislation as enacted by the Congress contained that feature, and with negative results which Benton foresaw. The sixty representatives tended to be trade association secretaries or their counterparts, while the size of the commission diluted the responsibility of the individual members.

Benton nonetheless persisted in trying to find able people for the places that were subject to direct presidential appointment. In particular, he wanted a middlewesterner and a strong leader to be the chairman of UNESCO's National Commission. Dr. Milton Eisenhower, who had had a distinguished prewar career in the Department of Agriculture and was serving as president of Kansas State College, fitted the job description perfectly—aside from being General Eisenhower's brother. Benton secured his appointment as chairman and promptly made him the subject of the usual publicity buildup on a national scale. The hundred-member commission, however, because of its composition, never became a significant national force—though Benton kept trying to make it one.

18

Power of Survival

Secretary Byrnes returned to Washington from the Moscow Conference on Saturday noon, 29 December 1945. He had been through a grueling experience, and he felt the American people should know what they faced in the world arena as Russian strategy emerged. The best way to get the message across was through an all-network broadcast which he wanted to make the next day. It fell to Benton to arrange the details, and once again he ran into the old problem of CBS and NBC, the two major networks, each insisting on handling the speech on an exclusive basis or not at all. If the smaller networks were cut out, that was the price they would have to pay for being small. Benton argued with the major networks through the remainder of Saturday and well into Sunday, and in the end, he had his way. Byrnes's report to the nation on the Moscow Conference was opened up for all networks to carry.

Benton, however, was not of a mind to let well enough alone. Immediately after New Year's Day 1946, he released to the press the backstage history of his encounters with the CBS and NBC rule of "all or nothing" applied to Secretary Byrnes's major speeches. Then he drew his conclusions on the matter:

> It is my belief that the industry should examine its present editorial practices. I should be able to offer all such important speeches by the Secretary—speeches which were not originated by any network or sponsored as special features by any network—to all networks or stations interested in carrying them, in line with the editorial importance of the speech. I should be able to do this on a basis which will result in satisfactory coverage for the speeches—and, in fact, for maximum coverage.

The industry itself, in its own best interest, so it seems to me, should examine its practices—so that such procedures become possible, so that they are easy to apply and so that the rules and the consequences are understood by all.

The issues of the weekend, which took so much time on the part of so many people, both in government and in industry, seem to me to require rather rapid clarification. I hope I can assume that, at least insofar as Secretary Byrnes's speeches are concerned, the action of NBC and CBS on Saturday evening, in reversing their past policy, has established a new policy for the future.

Washington politicans and bureaucrats, generally awed by the radio industry, were not used to hearing talk of this kind about it. Benton, who knew the industry as an insider, refused to be awed. His "client" was Secretary Byrnes—and the national interest. He felt that CBS and NBC were dead wrong in their proposed treatment of his client, and he saw no reason to dissemble. He would soon be doing the same in a bigger fight with two other powerful institutions—the Associated Press and the United Press.

With Byrnes back in Washington, Benton was able to report that he had met the target date and completed the tasks assigned to him under the directive of 31 August. He had reduced the twelve thousand wartime personnel he had inherited to thirty-one hundred. He had matured his plans for a permanent cultural and exchange program. The enabling legislation for UNESCO was passing through the congressional mill.

He also had some problems to report. First, it was necessary to position his remaining personnel within the State Department, and to do so within the framework of the new Foreign Service legislation then being drafted within the department. Second, the "Bloom bill," which would place his information and cultural exchange program on a legislative foundation, was still bottled up in the Rules Committee of the House and thus had yet to come before the chamber as a whole for a vote. Third, the program was threatened by drastic cuts in its appropriation requests for the budget year 1946–47. Byrnes was too pressed for time before returning to Europe to lend any immediate help, and Benton had to make out as best he could on his own—in the face of formidable hostile forces.

As has been implied, part of the radio industry was opposed to shortwave overseas broadcasts by the United States government in time of peace. The industry feared that these broadcasts, aside from taking away the international commercial markets it intended to exploit, would provide a precedent for the government to establish an American domestic version of the BBC. In addition, there was the hardening opposition of the United States wire services to a government information program. During the war, the AP, UP, and INS had contracted to provide the OWI and the OIAA with news for dissemination around the world. After V-J Day the high volume of wordage was sharply cut. Some went into ten-minute daily broadcasts by the "Voice of America." Some also went into a daily bulletin to United States foreign missions around the world for use in their local information work. Yet despite the drastic reduction from the wartime levels, the managers of AP and UP complained. It was one thing, said they, to provide such news as a patriotic duty in time of war. It was quite another thing to do it when the war was over. If they provided Benton's program with their services, they would not be able to sell their news to the foreign press, which, they said, could get much of the same news free of charge by monitoring the "Voice of America" or from United States embassy bulletins. More importantly, they feared any connection with the government, having seen the foreign news services of Italy, Germany, Russia, France, and even England become official mouthpieces for their governments at the cost of their objectivity.

Benton contended that his information program was in no way competitive. Nor would the United States government try to influence the wire services in any way. He repeatedly stressed that the main burden of informing the world about the United States had to be carried by the wire services, and the radio, film, and publishing industries. He was, in fact, the last person on earth to compete with the wire services or to stand in the way of any private agency trying to earn an honest dollar in the communications field. The government program was designed to fill the gaps no private agency was filling, or could afford to fill. Most of the news the wire services were providing the government was used where there were no AP or UP outlets, no newspapers, or where newpapers could not afford AP or UP services, or where by local custom—as in the Middle East— newspaper editors demanded payment for the news stories they printed instead of paying for them.

The points at issue had been the subject of many private exchanges between Benton and the heads of the wire services in the months following his appointment as assistant secretary. In line with these exchanges, Roy Howard, who was responsible for the United Press, a Scripps-Howard offshoot, came to Washington to press on Benton the reasons why the latter should discontinue his bulletins to State Department offices overseas. Benton regarded Howard as a personal friend and greatly respected his abilities as a journalist, but was singularly unimpressed by what he said on the occasion of the Washington visit.

"Roy," Benton asked him at the start of a rejoinder, "is it true that you do not have a single UP outlet in Iran?" It was true. "Well," said Benton continuing, "do you object to our sending the speeches of the president of the United States through our diplomatic pouch to Iran so that the American ambassador in Iran and his staff will be informed about what the president is saying?" Howard, startled, blurted out: "Of course not!" Benton pressed on. "Do you object to our sending the text of the speeches by air mail?" Howard by now foresaw the *ergo* at the end of the syllogism, but he had to agree that he did not object. "Then," said Benton, "if we deem them to be important, why can't we send them by wire? How can you possibly object? You do not send the full text of a president's speech even to Germany, Britain, and France, where you have many clients, or to Latin America, where you have more. Aren't our ambassadors entitled to the full text? Why then do you tell me that the State Department has no right to cable the full text of the president's speeches to our ambassadors?" Howard was embarrassed, but still did not agree. The dispute was unresolved and continued to simmer undercover a while longer—until it exploded in the open because of a precipitate action of the Associated Press.

The AP was being operated by Kent Cooper, a close associate of Colonel Robert McCormick of the *Chicago Tribune* and many other like-minded publishers. In a seeming consequence of this connection, the AP in early 1946, without advance notice, announced that it was canceling its contract to provide the State Department with its wire service. The UP followed by pulling out its own wire, though its managers seemed to have a guilty conscience about doing so. They told Benton that if they didn't pull out their wire, they would give AP a competitive advantage with potential customers for news, since the AP would tell them that the UP was "corrupted by being in bed with the government." Benton observed that the INS, directed by his friend Seymour Berkson, was the weakest of the three wire services, but it kept its wire in the State Department—as did Reuters, the English service.

Secretary Byrnes was back in Europe at the time the foregoing actions were taken by the AP and UP. Benton was on his own in responding to the case. In a press release he noted that the AP, while refusing to sell its news services to the United States government, sold the same services to the Russian government, thereby allowing the Russians to feature, in worldwide Communist propaganda, stories of United States rapes, lynchings, and social violence culled from AP dispatches. He gave expression to his feelings in a fiercely worded condemnation of the news agency.

Many people felt that he had blundered seriously—that the case should have been handled sotto voce. To Benton's surprise, the *New York Times* printed his denunciation in full. When he next saw Arthur Sulzberger, the publisher of the *Times*, he asked why. "I personally ordered this printed," Sulzberger answered. "I knew that this was of great importance." It was a straw in the wind indicating that at least part of the press was waking up to the potential controversy in establishing a peacetime governmental information program. The AP took the blast as a warlike act and was primed to respond in kind but held its fire until Byrnes returned from Europe. On his return, the secretary of state got Benton's version of the story and responded by saying that he admired Benton's courage and felt the condemnation of the AP was justified. Nor did he waver in this view when the president of the AP, Robert McLean, publisher of the *Philadelphia Bulletin,* called on him a few days later to lodge a protest. Byrnes arranged for Benton to be present. "Mr. Secretary," said McLean, "no man in history has ever spoken about the AP as has Mr. Benton." Benton laughed. "You haven't heard anything yet," he shot back. "I have many other most unpleasant things to say about your organization." Byrnes once again backed his assistant secretary, and McLean got no satisfaction out of the interview. The AP would presently marshal its forces for an intended all-out assault on Benton and his program.

Meanwhile, Benton was engaged in some fierce bureaucratic infighting, first with the War Department and then with the Navy Department. He had brought from London the idea of starting "Voice of America" broadcasts to Russia by way of the powerful Munich transmitters, then silent but controlled by General Clay. In line with this idea, he sent an able young engineer to Germany to study the technical aspects of the problem. The findings were encouraging. Though the transmitters were originally beamed toward the Balkans for Hitler's propaganda broadcasting, at a small cost they could be shifted to beam into the USSR, and for only $135,000 they could also be programmed in Russian for a year.

Benton, without further discussion, announced that he was going to initiate the Russian broadcasts. Then a deadlock developed. General Clay refused to give up the Munich transmitters. To break the deadlock, Benton asked Dean Acheson to arrange a meeting at the State Department with Secretary of War Robert Patterson and Secretary of the Navy James Forrestal. Once the meeting got underway, Acheson had business elsewhere, and Benton was on his own in an argument that grew increasingly bitter. Patterson insisted that Clay must be supported at all costs in his decisions in the field. Benton insisted that decisions should be overruled when they were inimical to America's highest interests. Forrestal initially sided with Patterson but then swung over to Benton's view. At that point, Benton said to Patterson: "I want you to send Clay a cable directing him to turn the Munich transmitters over to me." Patterson answered: "I will do it only on your order." "All right," said Benton; "the State Department gives you the order. I will write it in a way that will indicate you are doing this against your will." The cable he drafted for Patterson's signature went something like this: "You know that I want to support you in every way in your policies in Germany. But the State Department has demanded that I order you to turn over to Benton the Munich transmitters. I do this reluctantly. His engineers will arrive to beam them to the Russians to begin the Russian broadcasting." The cable was sent off as drafted. The transmitters were turned over to Benton for use in his program, and the Russian broadcasts were soon launched.

Subsequently, the navy tried to take away all the broadcast frequencies of the "Voice of America" for its own use. But with the help of Charles Denny, chairman of the FCC, Benton blocked the admirals. The navy was forced to retreat—with honor, but without victory.

In February 1946, Byrnes invited Benton to make a late afternoon cocktail call at his Shoreham Hotel apartment. This was unusual. All their previous meetings had been in an official setting. But after Byrnes mildly anesthetized his visitor with two huge slugs of bourbon, it turned out that the secretary of state had something other than chitchat on his mind.

Byrnes explained that he would be leaving the next morning for the Paris Conference of Foreign Ministers, and from the looks of things, might not return before the fiscal year ended in July. He was therefore telling Benton to take charge of his own legislative and budgetary programs on Capitol Hill. If he did not get them approved, the worldwide United States information program would be out of business.

Benton replied that he knew only a handful of people in the Congress and was unprepared, ill-equipped, and without the time for congressional relations. Besides, the general responsibility for getting his program through the Congress lay with Undersecretary Dean Acheson. When Byrnes said that Acheson, for all his brilliance, lacked the impact on the Hill to put the program over, Benton observed that Don Russell, Byrnes's law partner and protégé and the new assistant secretary of state for administration, was specifically assigned to handle State Department legislation. Byrnes revealed that Russell had been asked to handle Benton's legislation but had declined to do so. Benton later put the matter as follows: "Byrnes was telling me in his own way that unless I successfully did what he said I had to do, I might just as well get out of Washington—or settle back into a postwar State Department version of Archie MacLeish's old job, plus UNESCO and the press department and a few trimmings."

When Benton asked the secretary of state how to go about doing what was expected of him, Byrnes had two general pieces of advice. "The first thing to do," said he, "is to find out who the key man is in the specific legislative matter you are interested in. Go see him and try to get his support for what you want to do. At the same time, ask him who the number two man is and go see him—and ask who is number three. Then report back to number one and number two, and ask all of them who number four is. Keep the shuttle movement going back and forth until you've contacted everyone who needs to be contacted." Second, Byrnes advised Benton to abandon hope of help from anyone in the department, but to secure his own aide or aides for full-time work on congressional liaison. A former newspaperman familiar with the Hill would be effective.

By the next morning, Benton decided that the suggested former newspaperman could be even more effective if he had a southern accent, not only for the benefit of southerners, but also for Republicans in the North—since the man would sound like a conservative ally. The search for a person of this description began at once, while Benton on his own acted on the other piece of advice Byrnes gave him. When he asked the State Department who the key man was on the Rules Committee responsible for bottling up the Bloom bill, he was told it was Representative Eugene Cox, a conservative Democrat from Georgia. Benton now called on him and the two-hour meeting proved fruitful. Cox respected wealth and power, and he was impressed with Benton's background as a successful businessman and as a former CED vice-chairman who had close connections with the leaders of large corporations.

At the end of the meeting, Cox laid his political prejudices on the table. He explained that he had blocked the grant of a "rule" permitting the Bloom bill to come to a vote in the House mainly because of his very low opinion of the House Foreign Affairs Committee, which had unanimously approved the measure. Nobody on the committee, said he, amounted to anything except two Republicans—Representatives John M. Vorys of Ohio and James W. Wadsworth of New York—though he conceded that he might cast about "one-quarter to one-half of a vote" for James Richards, a fellow Democrat and Georgian. As for the rest of the members, they had no standing in the House. Cox then added that he had distrusted the State Department, and especially Benton's end of it, because of reported Communist infiltration. But now that he had met Benton and had seen that the department's information and cultural exchange program was in the hands of a sober, successful businessman, he was of a mind to be more kindly disposed to it.

Cox introduced Benton to House Speaker Sam Rayburn. Benton thus found himself at last full-fledged in the heart of influence in the House. From that time on, he worked closely with Rayburn, but made sure of Cox's continued support. He liked Cox personally even in disagreement, and he tried to do favors for those of Cox's friends who had "problems" with the State Department.[1]

For Benton, the number one man in the Senate was Arthur Vandenberg of Michigan, ranking Republican on the Senate Foreign

---

[1]Benton even lost $1,700 playing poker with Cox one night. Recalling the loss, Benton asked plaintively: "What more can a man do for the State Department?"

Relations Committee, who had "moved" the confirmation of Benton's appointment as assistant secretary of state. Since then, Benton had been working closely with Vandenberg, but after February 1946, he made a practice of entering the senator's office through the back door at least once a week, to consult with him personally (or with his son) and to work out agreements on various State Department matters. Together, for example, they largely worked out the percentage of United States contributions to United Nations agencies. "Regardless of all the statistics," Vandenberg had told him, "I think we should stand fast on the proposition that the United States will not contribute more than one-third of the budget to any of these United Nations agencies." The way Vandenberg said things ought to happen was the way they generally did happen.

On the Democratic side of the aisle in the Senate, Benton began to work closely with Senator Carl Hayden of Arizona after a suggestion from President Truman. In the absence of Secretary Byrnes, Benton often had to talk to the president about his problems. During one such session, Truman said: "I am going to commend you to Carl Hayden. He can be of more help to you than any other Democrat on the Hill. He's the most effective man in the Senate." Then, in the Byrnes fashion, President Truman had Benton listen in when he telephoned Hayden and said to him: "I am going to send Bill Benton up to see you and I want you take care of him. I commend him to you without reservation. Do anything you can for him." Hayden did so on appropriations bills and much else. Benton, now getting into the swing of things, added a refinement. As one of his congressional liaison officers, he employed a Hayden protégé, Darrell St. Claire, who had a southern accent (and who became chief clerk of the Senate, its second highest appointive office). In this indirect way, Senator Hayden's office became Benton's command post for operations in Capitol Hill, since St. Claire made Hayden's office his own headquarters.

While these sources of support were being developed on Capitol Hill, Benton in early March 1946 made a long-overdue trip to Hollywood at the invitation of his friend and wartime collaborator Eric Johnston, the new president of the Motion Picture Association.

Along with the radio networks and the wire services, the motion picture industry had its own reasons to suspect the government's information program. The film makers in Hollywood had found after V-J Day that the export markets which used to provide the margin of profit on a number of their films were being denied them by foreign governments, partly because of foreign exchange problems and partly for internal political reasons. Benton was aware of these problems, and he had actively encouraged Will Clayton, assistant secretary of state for economic affairs, to support the film industry in matters related to the overseas distribution of its products. Film industry leaders knew about Benton's intervention on their behalf, were grateful for it, yet remained suspicious of his information program. They feared that in the name of improving America's "image" abroad, he might favor censorship, even to the point of preventing maximum distribution of some of their films in a foreign market that was already shrinking.

Since becoming assistant secretary of state, Benton had engaged the leaders of the film industry in long-distance parleys by letter and had met with them in Washington. In this, he had leaned heavily on the advice of John Hay Whitney, who during the war had headed a motion picture liaison office established in Hollywood by Nelson Rockefeller as part of the Office of Inter-American Affairs. The society had offered the film industry advice on how to reduce the risk of offending Latin American audiences, and Whitney had suggested to Benton that the various Latin American precedents for bringing the film industry into a better working relationship with the United States government's information program could be extended on a worldwide basis.

Benton was prepared to do what Whitney had suggested, and after his four-day visit to Hollywood a bargain was made, under Eric Johnston's auspices, with the leaders of the film industry. The Inter-American Affairs Hollywood office would be closed, and its library of films and research material would be turned over to the Motion Picture Academy. The State Department would cooperate with any film producer who wanted to avoid giving needless offense to foreign people anywhere. The Motion Picture Association under Eric Johnston, as the agent of the film industry itself, would supervise an enlarged system of voluntary control. A special deal was made with the newsreel companies. They would continue to score in foreign languages and would turn over newsreels wanted for foreign distribution by the State Department. But whenever a newsreel company found it commercially profitable to distribute its products directly in these countries, the State Department would remove itself from the picture. The same arrangement applied to documentary films and short subjects. Thus Benton, guided by his friends John Hay Whitney and Eric Johnston, came to terms with the film industry.

Still, the most critical battle Benton faced in the spring of 1946 was to get his information and cultural exchange program the operating funds it needed. And it was on this front that he was attacked by the AP in reprisal for his earlier denunciation of it. The AP, with the reluctant assistance of the UP, sent agents all over the country to call on members of the American Society of Newspaper Editors in order to persuade them to pass resolutions at their annual meeting in April condemning Benton and his program.

When Benton heard what was going on, he got in touch with John S. Knight, who owned the *Miami Herald* and now controlled the *Chicago Daily News*. "Knight," said Benton, "was a great newspaperman and beyond that, he was a gentlemen." He also owed Benton an undischarged personal debt. In the closing months of the war, some ASNE representatives had visited the Soviet Union and had invited three representatives of the Soviet press to pay a return visit to the United States. The three were Konstantin Simonov, the journalist and playwright; Ilya Ehrenburg, the brilliant Soviet apologist; and Major General M. R. Galatkianov, the editor of *Red Star*, the Soviet military newspaper. But by the time the three Russians were due to arrive in the United States in the fall of 1945, wartime Soviet-American relations had begun to sour. Knight called on Benton in the State Department to ask if the department would rescue the ASNE from its embarrassment by taking over the Soviet visitors. Benton immediately said yes, and did welcome the Russians, entertaining them at a luncheon in Blair House. Knight was grateful. "When I heard about what the AP and UP were up to," Benton later recalled, "I told Jack Knight that it would be grossly unfair if he permitted the ASNE to condemn me and my operation without hearing my side of the case. He agreed partly for reasons of simple justice, and partly because I held his I.O.U. in the case of the three Soviet writers. He arranged for me to appear as a speaker in the ASNE program."

Benton always looked back on his appearance at the ASNE convention as his single most important action as assistant secretary of state. He knew he could not get the ASNE to censure the AP or the UP, and that he could not get the organization to pass a resolution on the spot to support the government's information and cultural exchange program. But he pitched his appeal to the "judiciousness" which legend ascribes to newspaper editors and which the editors themselves like to feel they have. He told them it would be unfair to condemn his program without investigating it, and he demanded that they appoint an investigating committee.

The impact of the unexpected speech disrupted the plans for a resolution condemning Benton and his program. Some highly respected editors in the ASNE had disagreed all along with the action of the AP and the UP. These included George W. Healy of the *New Orleans Times-Picayune*, who had been with the OWI, Ralph McGill of the *Atlanta Constitution*, and Wilbur S. Forrest of the *New York Herald Tribune*. McGill and Forrest had taken a trip around the world investigating the OWI and had learned its importance to American foreign policy. Now, amid the buzz caused by Benton's speech, men like them moved quickly and rallied enough shaken editors to their side to carry a motion to appoint the kind of investigating committee Benton had demanded.

The AP and the UP did not resume their wire services to the State Department, which continued to rely on INS and to a lesser degree on Reuters. But two larger objects had been won which were not part of Benton's design. The ASNE, which had seemed ready to condemn and perhaps destroy his program, swung around to support it in a highly favorable report issued by its investigating committee. Second, Benton's willingness to fight the AP and the UP gave pause to the radio industry. CBS had tried, often surreptitiously, to kill the information program. NBC, like the motion picture industry, showed a greater breadth of outlook. But the fight with the AP and the UP and its outcome left no one in doubt about Benton's will for battle—and it also left the radio people uneasy about the extent of his strength. They were not willing to test it in a head-on clash.

It was one thing to prevent the program from being destroyed by private interests. It was another to get the Congress to appropriate the funds needed for the information and cultural exchange work. Benton went everywhere and met with anybody who could be of help. He needled, wheedled, complained. With the graceful help of his wife, he gave countless expensive dinners in their Foxhall Road home. Previously, in his first months in Washington, he had arranged such dinners at which the principal officials in the State

Department met for the first time University of Chicago atomic
scientists who spoke about the implications of atomic energy—and
who lobbied for civilian control of its further development. Now, in
his Foxhall home, he brought congressmen together with experts
who spoke about the importance of the United States information
and cultural exchange program. His main hope for a restoration of
the funds cut by the House Appropriations Committee was pinned
on the Senate appropriations subcommittee, where he could count
on the behind-the-scenes help of Senators Vandenberg and Hayden.
In his own testimony before this committee, there was no trace of
the Madison Avenue young man paid to write "Palmolive soap is a
good soap." Benton's language had the resonance of passionate personal conviction when he told the subcommittee:

> The proposition I'm here to discuss is peace. . . . It is said
> that we live in one world. If this is so, it is one confused, igno-
> rant and suspicious world. Confusion, ignorance and suspicion
> are not a hopeful setting for peace.
>
> The program for which I speak is designed to replace the
> confusion, ignorance and suspicion that exist throughout the
> world about the United States—the world's greatest economic
> and military power—with clarity and understanding.
>
> We request no money for building "good will" indiscrimi-
> nately, or for "selling America," or for propaganda. This is
> not an advertising program, though many American corpora-
> tions spend two or three times as much annually as we propose
> in this budget. The program covered by the budget includes no
> elements of psychological warfare, no so-called "black" propa-
> ganda, and no secrecy. It deals only in facts. Its purpose is to
> gain understanding for America, as America actually is, and
> not even as we hope America may some time be. . . .
>
> There is a logical question that should be asked by you—and
> answered. It is: "Can't people in other countries get adequate
> information about us without a Government program of the
> type the State Department proposes?" The answer is a plain
> and unequivocal "no." Without a program like this, they can-
> not get it, they do not get it, they will not get it.

Beyond this, Benton appealed to the enlightened self-interest of
the leaders of the companies in the shortwave broadcasting field,
which meant enlightening most of them about where their self-

interest lay. The leaders were Brigadier General David Sarnoff, chairman of the board of RCA, the parent company of NBC; William Paley, president of CBS; Philip D. Reed, chairman of the board of the General Electric Company; Walter Evans, vice-president of the Westinghouse Electric Corporation; and J. D. Shouse, vice-president of the Crosley Corporation. Except for Sarnoff, the others somehow overlooked a self-evident fact. The House cuts in Benton's appropriation requests, by ending the "Voice of America" broadcasts, would financially hit the companies whose shortwave facilities were being used under licensing arrangements.

In the first week of May 1946, Benton brought these men abreast of what an end to government shortwave broadcasts implied. He also posed a question. If the government stepped out of the picture, could their own companies sustain, unaided, an adequate information program to be broadcast over their shortwave facilities? General Sarnoff, for one, replied by sending Benton a copy of a statesmanlike memorandum he had written to Secretary of State Cordell Hull as far back as January 1943. The memorandum, said he, still represented his central conviction—namely, that America's postwar interest would require "no less than $15,000,000 or $20,000,000 a year for international radio activities." Sarnoff had gone on to add: "It does not seem that international broadcasting with all its national and international implications constitutes a field for private competition, or even if it did, that it represents a field with adequate commercial revenue to provide the very large sums needed to render a public service of genuine world magnitude."

The four other executives studded their written replies with reminders about the need to settle the unresolved question of whether the future of shortwave broadcasting should be entrusted to private or governmental hands. They naturally favored private hands. But until that question was settled, they felt it would be a disaster for the future development of shortwave radio itself if governmental shortwave broadcasts were abruptly stopped because of budget cuts by the House Appropriations Committee. Moreover, the alarmed captains of the broadcasting industry went beyond writing letters in this vein—letters which Benton promptly circulated where they might do the most good. They arranged for Benton to meet the leading radio commentators, who gave a luncheon for him in New York. They, too, were startled at the thought that the government might discontinue international broadcasting, and their views on the subject soon were heard on the airwaves of the nation.

By mid-May, Benton felt that he could win his fight to restore the budget cuts, provided the administration strongly and openly supported his efforts. Its failure to do so up to that point underlay a general feeling among Democrats in the Congress that the administration itself was not deeply concerned with the prospect that the information and cultural exchange program might wither away. Benton wanted President Truman to know about this attitude, and he asked Undersecretary of State Acheson to make it clear to the president that his stand could very well determine what the Senate appropriations subcommittee finally did. In a memorandum to Acheson, Benton observed:

> I feel this issue is not only of vital importance to the country, but to the President and his administration. I am asking for one cent to every five or six dollars requested for the armed services, yet in this program is one hope, however faint, of less likelihood of need for the armed services. It is the hope in the President's speech of last Saturday. Surely one-fifth of one percent is very little with which to back such a hope. In retrospect, in view of what has happened in the world since last December, I am frank to state that I regard the $19,000,000 as far too little. Other countries have stepped up their expenditures rapidly, and England and Russia are spending far more than this.

The memorandum, followed by Benton's direct appeal to Truman, was projected against the backdrop of a world picture that was becoming increasingly bleak. Russian military pressure on Iran had led to a bitter confrontation between the Soviet Union and the United States. General George C. Marshall had been dispatched to China in the vain hope that he could settle the growing conflict between the Chinese Nationalists and the Communists. The United Nations Commission on Atomic Energy showed its incapacity to arrange for the international control of atomic energy. Soviet tirades against the United States had stepped up in scope and fury. Winston Churchill had delivered his "iron curtain" speech at Fulton, Missouri, and at the Paris Conference there were more Soviet tirades, only minimal progress in some directions. and retrogression in others.

A brief adjournment of the Paris Conference toward the end of June enabled Byrnes to come back to Washington. After a quick sounding on Capitol Hill, he called Benton in to say rather breathlessly: "You have won a mighty friend; Gene Cox is a mighty man. He controls forty votes!" Benton's cultivation of Cox had paid off. Cox, who had bottled up the Bloom bill in the Rules Committee for many months, now allowed the measure to come to a vote on the floor of the House, where it was to be overwhelmingly approved in mid-July.

Meanwhile, Benton's work in countless places inside and outside the government—backstopped by the help inside the government he got from President Truman and from Senators Hayden and Vandenberg—paid off in another vital matter. He had won over practically every member of the Senate appropriations subcommittee which dealt with State Department matters, and they were disposed to restore the cuts made by their House counterparts. Now, at the end of June, at an executive session of the Senate subcommittee where Benton was present, Secretary Byrnes provided the final thrust—"Bill Benton's news broadcasts in Russian to the USSR only cost $137,000," he said, "but they are worth the full $19 million-plus which he's asking for his entire program." The appropriation passed the subcommittee unanimously and the Senate by a large majority. The senators stood firm in conference committee with members of the House—who had already been softened by the public pressures Benton had generated. The conference report agreed with the Senate. The appropriation was overwhelmingly approved by the House as well as the Senate, and the seemingly impossible was achieved. All the cuts were restored to the $19 million level set in the first budget requests. The "Voice of America" had been saved. The manner in which it was saved was to be recalled in the fall of 1947 when Benton resigned from the State Department and his subordinates presented him with a six-panel screen of letters received from all over the world by the "Voice of America." The screen bore the inscription: "To Bill Benton, without whose valiant fight there would have been no Voice of America."

Benton now had the appropriation, but he only had half the basic authority he needed for the government's international information and cultural programs. He had the House-approved Bloom bill. He still needed Senate approval for the same measure, bearing the Senate name of the "Thomas bill," after its sponsor, Senator Elbert Thomas, a Utah Democrat. Byrnes, meanwhile, had returned to Paris. The Senate was watching the clock. After a brief hearing, the Senate Foreign Relations Committee under the chairmanship of

Senator Tom Connally voted out the Thomas bill. It was now imperative to get the measure to the floor of the Senate for a vote before the Seventy-ninth Congress passed into history. What happened in that specific connection will be told after another matter,
hitherto bypassed, is dealt with.

Toward the end of the war, there had been a resurgence of interest
in the reform of the Foreign Service, often for contradictory reasons. Career officers wanted to improve their own welfare as a guild.
They also wanted to restore and safeguard their prewar functional
monopoly in foreign affairs—broken into by wartime employees in
the OSS, the OWI, the Board of Economic Warfare, and the OIAA,
who had not "come up the hard way" by passing Foreign Service
examinations before they were thirty-one years old. Other sources
of opinion agreed on the need to liberalize Foreign Service salaries,
allowances, and promotions.

Still others were concerned over ways in which the Foreign Service, which had played only a secondary role in the war, could be
revitalized and reorganized for the new world born during the war,
and so they asked, Should all key persons devoting full time to foreign relations be brought together in a unified Foreign Service?
Should the clear division continue between an elite corps of careerists and a non-elite body of agents? If the groups were to be drawn
together, should men and women enter the Foreign Service only from
the bottom—or laterally as well?

A clear sign of how the Foreign Service wanted these questions
answered could be seen in early 1945 when Selden Chapin, a senior
Foreign Service officer, was simultaneously made director of the
State Department's Office of Foreign Service and head of the department's Committee on Foreign Service Legislation. The other
members were also career Foreign Service officers. It could be pre-
dicted that such a committee, provided it could have its way, would
be mainly interested in protecting and strengthening the guild interests of the career Foreign Service. The early drafts of the legislation that emerged from this body confirmed the predictions. The
drafts, however, had to be reconsidered after Will Clayton, as a
newly appointed assistant secretary of state for economic affairs,
brought with him into the department the economists of the Board
of Economic Warfare, which he had inherited. They had to be reconsidered again after Benton was appointed assistant secretary

of state for public affairs, with an executive mandate to integrate the OSS, OIAA, and the OWI into the department.

Benton, from the first days of his appointment, saw the connection between the content of a proposed Foreign Service bill and the quality of the people he could thereafter recruit. He wanted to guard his employees and his program against discrimination and neglect within the general Foreign Service framework, for he knew that most Foreign Service officers saw in his staff a dubious and unassimilable group. Its members, assembled during the war, included newspapermen and women, magazine and radio writers and editors, and an odd lot of persons chosen for specific linguistic abilities, or intimate acquaintance with particular skills or countries. Abroad, most of them had worked in establishments separate from the diplomatic missions. Within the Foreign Service, the deep-seated suspicions about such individuals remained very much alive after the war.

The picture was somewhat different in the case of Will Clayton, assistant secretary for economic affairs. Economic activities had been carried on by the State Department and more determinedly by the Department of Commerce even before the war—though after 1941, they were greatly expanded through BEW, and Clayton's staff was largely recruited from the transferees. Some of the older Foreign Service officers continued to lament the importance attributed to loans, trade agreements, aid programs, and the like. Some "political" officers at home and in the field continued to treat the economists as junior partners. Still, economic functions had been reluctantly accepted as an unavoidable and permanent part of the State Department, and the economists themselves were often veterans of bureaucratic wars. Although the Foreign Service bill had meaning for them, it lacked the critical importance it had for Benton's people, who were fighting to survive. Will Clayton personally sided with Benton, and since his personal prestige was very high within the department, as it was everywhere else in Washington, his strong and unfailing support was of great importance. Benton in effect carried Clayton's proxy in his pocket.

Donald S. Russell, as assistant secretary of state for administration, brought a special point of view to the Foreign Service bill. His chief interest was to protect Secretary Byrnes and to avoid any harmful clash between the secretary of state and the Foreign Service officers. Russell thus came under the influence of Selden Chapin, whom he encouraged to resume work on the Foreign Service bill and to prepare a text agreeable to the career Foreign Service. By 2 March 1946, the Chapin draft was ready for clearance within the State Department.

When Benton read the hundred-odd pages of the draft, he saw in it a firm decision to underwrite the concept of a protected and privileged career Foreign Service, managed and controlled by a special group within the Foreign Service itself and largely oriented to world conditions before World War II. There could be no lateral entry into the Foreign Service from any other groups or agency. Entry could be made only by the traditional route of examinations designed, given, and graded by the Foreign Service. As in the past, no one, however experienced, could enter the Foreign Service unless he was under thirty-one and could pass a set of examinations traditionally geared to young men who had just graduated from college. Benton himself spent four hours one night taking self-administered examinations of this kind and decided he couldn't rate a grade of over 40 percent at the most. After that, in a staff meeting on the subject, he asked the State Department counselor, Benjamin Cohen, whether he could pass the *bar* examination. Cohen, the author of many pieces of legislation, admitted he couldn't unless he went back to school and was drilled all over again.

During the most critical phase of the drafting of the Foreign Service bill within the Department of State, Secretary Byrnes was out of the country at various foreign ministers' conferences. Even when he was in Washington, he was too taxed by the urgent and substantive issues of foreign policy to think much about the mechanics of administration. He doubtless felt that in Donald Russell he had an experienced aide of unquestioned loyalty, whose judgment in administrative matters could be accepted at face value. Thus when Russell advised Byrnes to approve the details of the evolving draft bill, the secretary did so—even though the practical effect was to weaken his own power to be master of his household.

Meanwhile, Undersecretary Acheson kept himself several degrees removed from department work on the Foreign Service bill. He agreed with a Benton contention that the extremely detailed provisions of the proposed bill would impair the secretary's power to control the Foreign Service. But he apparently felt he could not support any proposal for administrative flexibility greater than that agreed to by his superior, Byrnes, on the advice of Russell. To challenge that agreement would imply that the secretary had been unaware of the danger to his own powers involved in the draft bill. In any case, given the intimacy between Byrnes and Russell, the secretary of state most likely would back Russell in any disagreement with Acheson.

Benton had no inhibitions. On 11 April, at a departmental staff meeting where Acheson presided and where Chapin and his four aides presented their draft for approval, Benton spoke his mind. "Unless the draft is changed in accordance with my wishes," said he, "I will go to the Hill and testify against it, and this will assure its defeat." Acheson seemed convinced not only that Benton meant it but that he had enough friends on Capitol Hill to defeat the measure. "You will have to make your peace with Mr. Benton," Acheson said to Chapin and his aides; "otherwise you will have no bill."

Chapin was forced to yield, and his men met with Benton to thrash out the major and minor points in dispute. Benton was armed with proposals for more than a hundred changes, and most of these were accepted. Not only were they designed to open up the Foreign Service to the great world outside the prewar guild but they proposed direct benefits to the Foreign Service itself, beyond any benefits which Chapin was willing to sponsor. This included perquisites, privileges, residence requirements in the United States, rotation in the field, special treatment for hardship posts, and so on.

The main structural proposals Benton made, which were agreed to by Chapin, were as follows: The restrictions which barred entry into the Foreign Service to people over the age of thirty-one would be ended. Lateral transfer into the Foreign Service would be permitted after a time of service in any other government agency, and on the basis of performance records and general fitness instead of the old-style academic examinations. A new category of officers, known as the Foreign Service Reserve—or FSR—would be created for people who did not wish a permanent career in the regular Foreign Service. Members of the FSR would be eligible for diplomatic and consular commissions, and the names of people qualified for the FSR would be included in the lists submitted to the president of persons recommended for appointment as career ministers. Other proposals bore on the composition of the Board of Foreign Service, the Foreign Service Institute, and the qualifications for the director of the Foreign Service itself.

When Byrnes briefly returned to Washington from the Paris meeting of the Council of Foreign Ministers, Benton told him that he had worked out his difficulties with Chapin over the Foreign Service bill and wanted it put through. Byrnes had had no time to read the draft bill. But as he consistently backed subordinates who had won his confidence, at Benton's request he called Senators Connally and Vandenberg while Benton sat in, and asked their help in securing quick passage. Acheson testified for the State Department at the House hearings. Benton did so at the Senate hearings. The measure was reported out favorably, and the Congress enacted it into law.

After President Truman signed the Foreign Service Act of 1946, he spoke of the need for a further strengthening of the Foreign Service. At the same time, he listed the major improvements which he felt would flow from the 1946 act. Ironically, more than half the designated improvements were those Benton had successfully fought for within the department.

There were to be two epilogues to this experience.

Beginning with his appointment as assistant secretary, Benton had written countless magazine articles to drum up public support for the information and cultural exchange program. He felt that as an official in the State Department he could not accept payment for these articles, though there were then no rules—as there are now—to prevent it. So, despite his rows with the Foreign Service, he contributed all his earnings from the articles to a scholarship fund for children of Foreign Service families. After he left the department, all money from his writings continued to go into the fund, as it does to this day. The fund is known in the Foreign Service Association as the "Benton scholarships."

The second epilogue occurred in 1949. Benton was then two years out of the State Department and was surprised by a letter from the Foreign Service Association asking him to be an honorary member. In accepting the compliment, he asked how many other honorary members there were, and what were the perquisites. He was told that there were two other honorary members, both of whom had spent their lives in the State Department: one for thirty-odd years had helped Foreign Service officers get through customs, and the other signed expense checks in the accounting department. The perquisites consisted of an invitation to all Foreign Service Association affairs and a free life subscription to the *Foreign Service Journal*. It was odd company to share, and not much in the way of bounty to enjoy. But Benton assumed that by 1949 the Foreign Service had come to the belated conclusion that in his struggle with it in 1946 he had been trying to promote the interests of the Foreign Service as a united whole.

By the time the Seventy-ninth Congress was ready to adjourn, Benton could look back with satisfaction on his role in securing the passage of not only the Foreign Service Act but the Fulbright Act, the UNESCO enabling legislation, and the House-approved Bloom bill. To round out his legislative program, he still needed Senate approval for the Thomas bill, which was the Senate's version of the Bloom bill. Once the Foreign Relations Committee had reported out the measure favorably, it was imperative to get the chairman, Connally, to bring the bill before the full Senate for a vote before the session adjourned. Benton asked Undersecretary of State Acheson to prod Connally in the matter because he had reason to feel that, if the matter came to a vote, no more than five senators would be against it. Acheson apparently did not ask Connally to give priority to the measure; the bill was not called up for a vote before the Congress adjourned; and all the months of work Benton had spent on the matter were now of no avail. To get the basic legislation which he needed to support his information and cultural exchange program, he would have to begin all over again when the Eightieth Congress convened in January 1947. This would be a Republican-controlled Congress and there would be a new secretary of state; the two factors would each work in different ways to complicate Benton's efforts.

19

The Great Art Scandal

On Connecticut's voting lists, Benton was a registered Independent, as were roughly one-third of the voters of his state. He had always supported Democratic presidential candidates but had taken no aggressive partisan role in state and local politics. In the nominating and election contests of 1946, however, he was especially interested in what happened to two party figures. One was Senator Robert La Follette, Jr., of Wisconsin, a Republican. The other was Chester Bowles, of Connecticut, a Democrat. In different ways they would have a profound effect on Benton's future.

Nine days before Wisconsin's Republican primary in 1946, La Follette and his wife, Rachel, came to Sunday dinner at the Benton home in Washington. At one point the host raised blunt questions about press reports of political developments in Wisconsin. La Follette was being strongly challenged for the Republican senatorial nomination by a young Marine Corps veteran named Joseph McCarthy. Benton asked why La Follette was staying in Washington. Why wasn't he in Wisconsin fighting off the challenge? "I've been in the Senate representing Wisconsin for twenty years," the senator explained wearily, "and if the people at home have decided they don't want me, then I'm ready to quit."

Benton urged him to reconsider this fatalistic attitude, and La Follette then said he had to stay in Washington to lead the fight in the Senate for the La Follette-Monroney bill to reorganize Congress. The La Follette-Monroney bill eventually became law, but the nation was to pay a heavy purchase price for it. Robert La Follette, by not campaigning, lost the Wisconsin Republican primary by five thousand votes to Joseph McCarthy.

On the Democratic side, Chester Bowles in his first open bid for

365

an elective office was, most fortunately for him, also a casualty of the nominating process. He was anxious to secure the Connecticut Democratic nomination for governor, but the state convention turned him down. Not the least of the reasons was the failure of Connecticut's Democratic Senator Brien McMahon to support him. McMahon, who feared and disliked Bowles, later was to confess to Benton: "I should have let Bowles get the Democratic nomination for governor in 1946, so that he would have been killed off for good." It turned out that the Republicans swept Connecticut as they did Wisconsin and the country so that they even won control of the Senate (and the House as well). With a few saving exceptions, the Republican "class of 1946" that was elected to the Senate at that time—James P. Kem (Missouri), Zales N. Ecton (Montana), Harry P. Cain (Washington), George W. Malone (Nevada), William E. Jenner (Indiana), and McCarthy—was probably the worst lot of senators ever injected in one shot into the upper chamber. One of the exceptions to this dismal crew was the newly elected Republican senator (and former governor) of Connecticut, Raymond E. Baldwin.

In the days immediately after the election, Benton was too busy to worry over what the incoming Republican Congress might do to his program. A year had elapsed since the constitution of UNESCO had been adopted at the London Conference. Now, UNESCO's first general conference was to meet in Paris in November 1946 to become "operational" with an action program formulated by a preparatory commission. Benton was inundated by program suggestions, but his main personal interest continued to be in reaching the world's people through the media of mass communications. The ways and means had been spelled out for him by the committee he had appointed under the chairmanship of Edward W. Barrett. Further, Benton's approach to UNESCO's administration and financing followed from his views about the functions of the organization—and from Senator Vandenberg's advice to hold the total UNESCO budget to $7 million a year, with the United States contributing one-third. It was Benton's view that, since UNESCO was a novel experiment, its initial budget should be small—that the organization should not try to run before it learned to walk.

As the chairman of the United States delegation, Benton had a supporting staff of forty people, one-third of whom happened to have a University of Chicago background. Some delegates, such as

Archibald MacLeish and Arthur H. Compton, were veterans of the 1945 London meeting. Among the new recruits were Milton Eisenhower, Anne O'Hare McCormick of the *New York Times*, Charles S. Johnson, president-elect of Fisk University, and, significantly, Chester Bowles. Benton had long felt that Bowles's preoccupation with domestic affairs had kept him from involvement in the vast challenges of foreign affairs. He persuaded his old friend, "unemployed" at the time, to begin to expose himself to the shape of things abroad, and the Paris meeting of UNESCO was an available vantage point to start the learning process. Bowles went along, and the consequence was a decided quickening of his interest in foreign affairs.

After the UNESCO meeting Benton confessed an error of judgment to Secretary Byrnes. But in doing so, he spotted a tendency which would become starkly clear in future years. Most of the American delegates had assumed that UNESCO "was above politics" and that they were on their way to "an educational, scientific and cultural conference." In Paris, however, Benton quickly learned that he and his delegates were attending a "political conference of the first order." The governments which came out of the war politically and economically weakened "saw in UNESCO an instrument for developing leadership in other fields. As the older empires dissolved, the struggle opened for the empire of ideas." Because it dealt with ideas, UNESCO presented itself "as a hotbed for politics," even though Russia boycotted the conference, as it had the one in London a year earlier.

With UNESCO now headquartered in Paris, it became clear that the French anticipated steady infiltration of French personnel and ideas. In Paris as at London the year before, the French chose their most distinguished citizens as delegates. Léon Blum was again at their head. Other French delegates were carefully picked to reflect the various political and intellectual groups in France, thus to insure continuing political support for UNESCO. Further, the Bank of France was getting a creditor's claim on UNESCO by financing it until the various member governments came forward with their prorated contributions, and the delegates were the objects of lavish personal attention.

The cold war had intruded on the work of UNESCO, though the Soviet Union had yet to join the organization. Benton reported that Communist Yugoslavia, a UNESCO member (still "Stalinist" in its Communist line), was the real spokesman for the Soviet Union. The first speech of the leader of the Yugoslav delegation made this clear—and it led to a clash with Benton. The Yugoslav had denounced the so-called scientific humanism enunciated by Dr. Julian Huxley of England as the proposed philosophy of UNESCO. This philosophy, said the Yugoslav, did not allow for dialectical materialism. Benton, in reply, stated that "UNESCO does not believe and cannot believe that peace is to be obtained through the intellectual and cultural subjugation of the world by any single political philosophy or through the conversion of the world to any single religious faith." UNESCO was founded on the belief that "neither the forced unification of the world, nor the forced standardization of the world of the mind can give men peace, but only a world democracy of the mind as well as the spirit."

> Cultural democracy [Benton continued] implies cultural integrity, as true political democracy implies the freedom of the person and his personal integrity and self-respect. The cultural democracy which UNESCO proposes is a democracy of mind and spirit in which every culture shall be free to live and develop in itself and in the great community of common culture. Free men do not fear ideas; free men are not afraid of thought; free men are eager to confront the differences and rich varieties that life presents, and to determine for themselves the things they take as true. This, from the beginning, has been the path of freedom.

Between the French and the Communists, Benton took note of a change in Great Britain's approach to UNESCO. The British delegation to London in 1945 had been a second-string team, but the one sent to Paris contained renowned figures in the arts and sciences. The British, frustrated by United States domination of the London meeting and piqued by the eminence of the French, this time sent David Hardman, parliamentary undersecretary of the Ministry of Education, and John Maud, later knighted and now Lord Redcliffe-Maud, whom Benton described as "one of the most able, effective, personable and hardest-working men" he had ever met.

The issue of who would be UNESCO's director general overshadowed the Paris Conference and the deliberations of many of its subcommissions. Benton had scoured the United States for an American candidate for the post, once Archibald MacLeish declared

himself unavailable. At one point, he had spoken to the French ambassador, Henri Bonnet, about the necessary qualifications and was
told that it wasn't "imperative" for the candidate to speak French
but that it was essential. This drastically reduced Benton's range
of choice. He settled on Francis Biddle, former solicitor general and
attorney general, and one of the judges at the Nuremberg trials. He
approached Biddle, got his expression of interest, then followed this
by getting President Truman's approval.

"I went to Paris hoping that because it was widely felt that an
American should be director general, I could put over Biddle,"
Benton later recalled, "only to run into a most unusual situation
with my own delegation. The members did not face the fact that they
were attending a political conference of the first order. They took
the position that Francis Biddle was a 'politician,' and they asked
why I was advocating a 'politician' for a top role in education, science, and culture. Though I continued to work for Biddle's election,
I lacked support from within the American delegation. Many of
the members swung behind John Maud's advocacy of the candidacy
of Dr. Julian Huxley—whom he had been instructed to elect. After
extraordinarily skillful political maneuvering by Maud, a two-week
deadlock was finally broken when Julian Huxley was elected. I
worked out a deal which limited his tenure to two years."

At one stage of the UNESCO Conference, it was agreed to recess
for forty-eight hours. Benton decided that he could use his time by
flying from Paris to Moscow. He cabled his desires to General
Walter Bedell Smith, the American ambassador in Moscow, who
promptly sent his plane with its crew of five to facilitate the trip.
Benton proposed to ask the Russians if they were going to fill the
seat held open for them on UNESCO's executive board. If not, he
proposed to have the seat filled by some other country. He also
wanted to explore the possibility of setting up student and professor
exchanges between American and Russian universities. The idea
seemed so suprapolitical that Benton did not dissemble when he
asked the Soviet representatives in Paris to clear the way for a
Moscow trip he wanted to make with his wife, Helen, and Chester
Bowles, who was an alternate delegate. He emphasized that he would
have only forty-eight hours to fly to Moscow, transact his business,
and fly back to resume work at the UNESCO Conference. The clearance was granted—up to a point.

Bowles and the Bentons boarded General Smith's plane and

landed in Berlin on the first leg of the Moscow-bound flight. The Russians stalled them in Berlin for forty-eight hours. First they refused to clear General Smith's plane and said Benton had to proceed by a Soviet plane. He agreed. Then he was told that the Soviet plane had only bucket seats. He said that didn't matter. Finally he was notified that the weather wouldn't permit the plane to land at Moscow. By now, Benton had to admit that he simply wasn't wanted in Moscow. He felt, as never before, the icy blasts of the developing cold war. When he returned to Paris, he sent a coded, cabled question to the American embassy in Moscow. In answer, he learned that the weather had been perfect during the time he was barred from the Soviet capital "because of the weather."

While Benton could not get Francis Biddle elected director general, he won his fight to keep UNESCO's initial budget of "fledgling" size. "By a fledgling budget," he explained in a debate, "I do not mean a helpless bird without wings. I mean a budget suitable for a newly born organization—a budget adequate for UNESCO to carry out its first year's task both competently and carefully." When David Hardman, chairman of the British delegation, denounced Benton's budget stand as "cheese paring," Benton responded with a different metaphor that became famous in the history of the organization. He said that "UNESCO was a pork barrel riding on a cloud." In the end, the delegates approved a budget of only $6,950,000—$50,000 below the maximum figure set by Senator Vandenberg—to launch over one hundred UNESCO projects in 1947. Benton privately told Secretary of State Byrnes that if 10 percent got off the ground in the first year, it would revive his faith in miracles. But he was excited about the possibilities in four programs. One program—and it has already been indicated that he would change his mind about its feasibility—envisioned a worldwide broadcasting network under international auspices. Another projected a worldwide attack on the problems of illiteracy and the establishment of minimum standards of education everywhere. There was also to be an attempt, in cooperation with the United Nations Commission on Human Rights, to reduce the barriers to free communications among people. Finally, in the field of science, UNESCO would try to create an International Institute of the Amazon which would bring together scientists to study the problems of food, disease, and natural resources of a tropical area.

When Benton returned to the United States he spoke of the new-

born world organization in a number of public addresses and magazine articles. He did not overlook the hard rocks that would have
to be scraped away before anything could grow out of the seeds that
had been planted. He was particularly concerned by the long-range
problems the UNESCO Conference had posed for the United States
generally and its UNESCO delegations specifically. He put his
thoughts into a private report he sent to Secretary Byrnes on 12
December 1946, saying:

1. I should have had with me in Paris two or three of our
best political officers. . . .

2. It is none too soon to begin to seek Huxley's successor.
. . . Do we want an American? This is not an abstract question.
It must be discussed in terms of a particular man.

3. We should appoint more younger men, who are on the
make and who are potential candidates for positions in
UNESCO, to our future delegations. . . . With the benefit of
the experience we have just had, the same delegation would be
far more effective at a second such conference. . . . There is
need for continuity in our representation at such conferences.

4. Only seven Latin American countries have joined
UNESCO and their interest in UNESCO is no more than
embryonic. We should learn more about why their attitude is
as it is, and should seek to develop ways in which their interest
in UNESCO can be stimulated. Instructions should, in my
opinion, go to all our missions.

5. It is important at once to begin to forecast the future
development of UNESCO, including a forecast of the political
implications. For example, how would the decision of Russia
to join UNESCO affect its management and its program and
the attitude of the United States towards UNESCO? What
if France should gravitate to Communism, with the UNESCO
headquarters fixed at Paris? I believe that a top political officer
in the Department should now be assigned to such problems.

Benton's note to Byrnes coincided with the adjournment of a
Foreign Ministers' Council meeting in New York. The secretary had
negotiated five peace treaties to the point of signing. He had previously given President Truman a predated letter of resignation
to take effect upon the completion of the work on the treaties. Now,
in a long and friendly chat with the president, he said he wanted to

retire as secretary of state. The president urged him to stay, but Byrnes said he was in earnest about wishing to step down. Truman then asked Byrnes what he thought of General George C. Marshall as a successor. The answer was that the appointment would be splendid and would be well received. The appointment of General Marshall as secretary of state was announced on the afternoon of 7 January 1947.

As it happened, at that same time Benton was treated to a pleasant surprise. The University of Chicago trustees, once his employers, elected him a fellow trustee and invited him to come to Chicago as the featured speaker at the trustees' annual dinner for the faculty. Benton responded on the occasion with a tribute to the university, saying that all the problems of education he had first encountered as vice-president confronted him now on a global scale through UNESCO. Unfortunately, neither the University of Chicago nor UNESCO gave him the education he would need to get along with General George C. Marshall.

After the family warmth of his dealings with Byrnes, Benton was chilled by his relations with General Marshall. Like other presidential appointees in the State Department, he had submitted his resignation to Marshall when the latter became secretary. Two weeks went by and he neither heard a word from the general nor saw him in person. "I ran into Will Clayton," Benton later recalled, "and I asked him whether I was being singled out for this kind of treatment. Will replied: 'Not at all. I sent in my resignation also. I haven't heard a word either. Neither have I seen the General.' " Some days later, Benton heard from Marshall saying that his resignation was not accepted. He was to continue as assistant secretary for public affairs.

Paradoxically, though Benton was in constant touch with President Truman he saw little of General Marshall. The secretary did not even invite him to be present for a discussion with John Taber of Benton's own budget. It was Taber who later told Benton about the meeting. Episodes of this kind helped form Benton's opinion of Marshall—which in retrospect he admitted was severe. He was not opposed to generals in highly sensitive political posts; he felt that Eisenhower or Bedell Smith, for whom he had warm affection, would have made a better secretary of state than Marshall, although his first choice had been Will Clayton.

"Marshall never told me to get out," Benton recalled, "but the general discomfort in my relationship with Marshall made me feel that he hoped I would leave—since he couldn't fire me because of my intimate relationship with President Truman and many members of the Congress. One by one, the ten principal presidential appointees who were in the State Department when Marshall became secretary of state either resigned or were fired. When Ben Cohen, the State Department counselor, told me that he was going to resign, I begged him to stay. I needed him. He was a bulwark of support. But Ben said in his high squeaky voice: 'The General tells me that he wants me to stay but he does not act as if he wants me to stay.' Ben was eventually replaced by Chip Bohlen. I was the last of the original ten to leave.[1] I wouldn't resign until I knew the future of the information and cultural exchange program was assured."

Benton's difficulty in communicating with Marshall was foreshadowed within three days after the latter became secretary of state. A staff aide brought into the department by Marshall issued a general order setting forth "by the numbers," in field manual style, general staff regulations that would henceforth govern all communications to the secretary. All were to adhere to the following form:

First paragraph: the problem
Second paragraph: the recommended solution
Third paragraph: the reasons for the recommended solution
Fourth paragraph: alternative solutions

The general order went on to say that if Secretary Marshall agreed with the recommended solution in the second paragraph, he would initial the memorandum in the upper right-hand corner. Then the person who had addressed him would be responsible for carrying out the solution. The secretary might indicate that he would like to have a follow-up memorandum on some one of the alternative solutions in the fourth paragraph. Further, the writer of the memorandum could attach as many annexes as he liked in reference to any one of the four paragraphs, or any of the various combinations thereof. But the writer was given to understand that he should not expect the secretary to read any of the annexes.

Unfortunately, one of the problems an assistant secretary of

---

[1]"Where Are They Now?" headlined *This Week* magazine shortly after Benton's resignation, over a feature on Byrnes's top aides.

state lived with every day was to discover what was a problem. That raised difficulties with the first paragraph. Next, not every problem had a solution. The most one could hope to do with some of them was to learn how to live with them unresolved. That raised difficulties with the second paragraph. Nor could all recommended solutions proceed on the basis of detailed reasons. The great problems confronting the State Department were "great" precisely because the reasons for doing something and the reasons for not doing it often were equal in strength, and the recommended solution depended more on a "feeling in the bones." But how was one to state all this in the third paragraph?

Finally, in the daily life of the State Department, while some problems had no solution, others had only one solution and no alternatives. So that raised difficulties with the fourth paragraph.

Benton, a skilled professional writer, decided that the army approach was not for him. He also came to decide that Marshall was not for the State Department.

Aside from the troubles with the four paragraphs, troubles came in other forms. Soon after the Republican-dominated Eightieth Congress convened, a number of newspaper stories appeared to the effect that Benton was not getting along with the Congress. In the erroneous belief that the stories were being generated on the Hill, he went to see Representative Karl Stefan (R., Neb.), who was now the chairman of the House appropriations subcommittee dealing with the State Department. Stefan was not beyond subjecting Benton to a hazing now and then. But they had become good enough friends so that Benton could ask him point blank whether Representative John Taber, now chairman of the House Appropriations Committee, was the source of the hostile stories.

Stefan laughingly explained that John Taber wouldn't know how to get such stories into the papers, even if he wanted to—which he didn't. He assured Benton that Taber wouldn't dream of operating in that manner. Later, Benton got the word from John Taber himself when he sat up with him twice until two A.M. drinking a full bottle of whiskey. In vino veritas—Taber said that he hadn't even thought about the kind of stories that were appearing until Benton brought up the subject. He was off on a track of his own. Mrs. Ruth B. Shipley, who was in charge of the passport division of the State Department, had passed along the word to him that during the war she had been ordered by the White House to give passports to many

Communists who had gone to work overseas for the war agencies later absorbed into Benton's part of the State Department. That is what concerned Taber. He believed what Mrs. Shipley told him. Where were these Communists? As for the allegation that Benton couldn't get along with the Congress, well, there was proof to the contrary—the 100 proof whiskey he and Taber had consumed. Taber remembered the telephone call from Byrnes giving Benton a personal endorsement. The endorsement still held as far as he was concerned.

The stories had actually been planted by people inside the State Department who wanted to get rid of Benton and his program. This was standard tactics. One would give a newspaper columnist friend a tidbit of inside information. The quid pro quo was an implied request that a story be printed about Benton's troubles with the Congress. The Republican National Committee took it from there. Benton and his program before long were being earmarked as the number one target for attack by the committee in its preparation for the 1948 presidential election. Several bad public relations breaks in a row made Benton and the whole information and cultural exchange program vulnerable to such attack.

One of the bad breaks over which he had no control came when the United States cultural affairs officer in Moscow publicly announced that he was resigning because the United States was deliberately insulting the Russians. This fanned the smoldering fires of the old charge that the program was riddled with Communists. Ironically, in the previous year, Benton had proposed to Senator Pat McCarran (D., Nev.), chairman of the Senate Judiciary Committee, a means whereby the State Department could better deal with just such a matter. In a private meeting with McCarran—who had long inveighed against the "Communists" in the war agencies that had been absorbed by the State Department—Benton told him that, in the course of reducing the size of these agencies, all known or suspected Communists had been discharged. However, it was exceedingly difficult under Civil Service procedures to get rid of a small number of suspected Communist sympathizers who were still around the department. The kind of hard proof which would stand up under Civil Service regulations and justify a dismissal was not easily come by—even if the attitude of the suspect was made clear by the pattern of his behavior. Benton therefore proposed that a new ground for dismissal—namely, "for the good of the service"—be detailed in legislation. It should empower the secretary of state to dismiss any suspected employee without the need to brand him openly as a Communist or Communist sympathizer. With such a discretionary power in hand, the secretary and his chief aides could better cleanse the department of suspected personnel.

McCarran embraced Benton's idea and sponsored it in the form of an amendment to the State Department Appropriations Act. It was subsequently approved by the Congress and was afterwards used with great restraint by the department in its cleansing operation. Benton never publicly avowed this cooperation with McCarran at the time of its occurrence. Five years later, however, he felt it was worth recalling when he was engaged in his fight against Senator Joseph McCarthy. It would show that Benton had been deeply concerned by the need to wipe out every taint of communism in the State Department long before McCarthy raised his storm about that matter. Accordingly, he wrote Senator McCarran to remind him about the background of the so-called McCarran Amendment to the 1946 Appropriation Act, but McCarran had a convenient spell of amnesia. He remembered nothing at all about Benton's coming to him with the idea that was embodied in the amendment.

A cluster of bad breaks came all at once at a late April hearing of the House appropriations subcommittee under the chairmanship of Benton's Republican friend Karl Stefan. The Republicans on the committee had had an investigator working for weeks trying to dig up information which would embarrass the State Department and Benton. What he dug up, joined to what the subcommittee already had in hand from other sources, was hurled in Benton's face the moment he appeared before the committee to argue in support of his budget requests. Stefan called the meeting to order, and asked the ladies present to leave the room. He then took out from underneath his desk a copy of Edmund Wilson's *Memoirs of Hecate County* and read a passage aloud from it. The passage lacked nothing in the way of prurient interest. "Mr. Secretary," said Stefan to Benton after he broke off the lascivious reading, "would you send to our libraries overseas a book containing that passage?" "No, sir, I would not," Benton answered. "But," said Stefan, "you did." To prove the charge he unfurled what appeared to be a list of books selected for United States information libraries abroad. Wilson's *Memoirs of Hecate County* was on it. There was no denying the fact.

But what Stefan held was not a list of books that were actually sent overseas but an early compilation of possible choices for United States libraries overseas—not yet cleared by the State Department committee which passed on such matters. Actually, the clearance committee had eliminated Edmund Wilson's book from the list that was finally approved. Stefan did not know this, nor did Benton nor John Howe, who flanked him at the hearing. No one knew the truth of the matter until forty-eight hours later. In that interval, though the subcommittee meeting was ostensibly held in a closed session, a member leaked the story to John O'Donnell of the New York *Daily News*, who had a fierce hatred for anything touched by Democrats. He now used his superb gift for plausible distortion in order to report that Benton and the State Department, at the expense of the overburdened United States taxpayer, was peddling pornography around the world in the name of an information and cultural exchange program.

The hearing was reopened to ladies and Representative Stefan sprang another trap that had been baited by the committee investigator. The latter had reported that at 9:15 in the morning on a certain day earlier in the year, he had visited a floor of the Walker Johnson Building—one of the many buildings in Washington which housed operations for the information and cultural exchange program. Though the place normally accommodated 150 employees of the program, the investigator reported that he had discovered only 12 people at work. Stefan turned to Benton and asked: "Mr. Secretary, do you think this is the way to run a railroad?" "Mr. Stefan," Benton replied in all earnestness, "this information you've given me could be very valuable. This is all new to me, and I'll look into it immediately." So he did.

For the next twenty-four hours, he hurled out questions on all sides bearing on the damning report that was already in print. The answers revealed that the day the investigator had dropped in on the Walker Johnson Building was also the day of the worst snowstorm in Washington in a decade. All transportation was at a standstill. Karl Stefan may or may not have known that to be true. Benton gave him the benefit of the doubt. But at least he was having fun needling his friend Benton, for he meant the needle to go straight through Benton and hit its real target, the Truman administration.

The third bad break at the same hearing was the source of the most hilarious fun of all. In the fall of 1945 Benton had inherited, with the Cultural Relations Division of the State Department, a young man now on the art faculty at Yale. Scarcely anybody knew of his existence, or of the scheme that was forming in his mind. He had long felt that the United States government ought to have a collection of American paintings which could be sent abroad. He further felt that a good collection could be selected only by one man. Any jury, said he, reflected the combined conservatism of various members. He had more thoughts. One was that Europeans regarded American painting as a feeble imitation of nineteenth-century French impressionism. Any American collection, therefore, should emphasize the experimental nature of the new American painting. Another thought was that it would be more economical to buy inexpensive paintings than to borrow them from museums because of the costs of insurance and shipment.

The young man got the approval of his superior (today a college president). He also raised the question of how the project could be financed. The superior found that the Benton operation had digested the budgets of the OWI, the OIAA, and the Cultural Relations Division. So now the two art lovers submitted a budgetary request for $50,000 to finance their project. The item rolled along through the unexpended funds carried over from the OWI.

With this uninspected money in hand, the young man proceeded to commission artists and to choose from their works. He chose well, and he was a good buyer. He flattered the leading American artists he approached, and they often sold him their paintings for less than they were worth—all for the patriotic honor and duty of being represented in the first United States government sponsored exhibit of art to be shown abroad under the enticing title "Advancing American Art." By the early spring of 1947, everything was in order and the paintings were sent abroad. Part went to Prague, Czechoslovakia being not yet behind the iron curtain. Part went to Port-au-Prince.

Benton, thus far, did not know the project existed. He had not seen any of the pictures, nor been informed that they had been sent overseas for exhibition. In Prague, the pictures seemed to score an American victory in the propaganda war. Indeed, the Russians were so upset by the American exhibit that they quickly put together a competing exhibit of "socialist realism" paintings, shipped it to Prague, and then sent Russian aircraft over the city to shower the populace with tickets of admission to their exhibit. *Look* magazine saw a story in this hubbub, and its editors proceeded to give a double-page spread to the American experimental paintings, but with a headline that carried a wallop: "Your Money Bought These Pictures." This was how Benton learned of the exhibition and what it contained. He soon learned the kind of trouble he was in for when Senator William Knowland said to him: "Bill, where in the hell did you get those screwy pictures?" The *Look* article had featured Kuniyoshi's *Circus Girl*, a painting done years before of a Parisian tart. The *Look* article attracted the attention of the editors of Hearst's *American Weekly Magazine* with its then enormous Sunday circulation in all the Hearst newspapers. Now, for their "cover story" they reproduced Leonardo da Vinci's *Last Supper* across the top of the cover. On the bottom half, they reproduced Kuniyoshi's *Circus Girl* from the United States exhibit. A top headline asked, "Which Is the Better Painting?" Beneath the experimental work another headline read, "You Are Paying for This."

The immediate consequence was a field day in the Congress. Karl Stefan's subcommittee investigator had secured photographic copies of the United States exhibit in Prague. Now Stefan put one picture after another in front of Benton and grilled him.

> STEFAN: What is this picture?
>
> BENTON: I can't tell you.
>
> STEFAN: I am putting it just about a foot from your eyes. Do you know what it is?
>
> BENTON: I don't even hazard a guess of what that picture is, Mr. Chairman.
>
> STEFAN: How much did you pay for it? You paid $700 for it and you can't identify it. Do you know what this picture is, Mr. Secretary?
>
> BENTON: I would hesitate to pass judgment on any of these pictures, Mr. Chairman.
>
> STEFAN: Do you know what that is?
>
> REP. HORAN: Are you holding it up straight?
>
> STEFAN: It is straight. Do you know what that is?
>
> BENTON: It does have a resemblance to many things that are not fit to mention before this committee. . . .
>
> STEFAN: Would you say that is a seascape or a mountainside?

BENTON: I would hesitate to pass opinion on it. I am afraid the artist wouldn't like it. I think you might ask Mr. Horan. That looks like some of his western country. He might have some judgment on it.

STEFAN: What kind of country?

BENTON: It looks like good country to leave behind you, Mr. Chairman.

STEFAN: Do you know what this is, Mr. Secretary? (exhibiting another picture).

BENTON: I think that is much more recognizable. It seems to me to be a city scene that has very little resemblance. . . .

STEFAN: Look at that, Mr. Secretary (exhibiting). Those are supposed to be human beings in a discussion on a street in the United States somewhere. Aren't you horrified yourself?

BENTON: I would not use the word "horrified."

STEFAN: Well, you are shocked aren't you?

BENTON: No, I wouldn't say I was shocked.

STEFAN: Well, what would you say?

BENTON: I would say "art."

Benton saw clearly that the State Department—assuming the dubious merit of having an art collection—had made a mistake in letting one man select all seventy-nine pictures. "The greatest genius in the world," said he to the committee, "could not select seventy-nine pictures that would appeal to any four of us as all being good pictures." The department, if it was to go in for art, needed the kind of big name committee that had selected the Britannica Collection of American Art which had gone on tour about two years previously.

General Marshall, meanwhile, had another comment. "It must be very good art," he declared, "because I cannot understand it." President Truman also had a comment. In two long private letters to Benton the president criticized the exhibit as "ham and egg art." But he never criticized Benton publicly. In due course, however, someone in the White House leaked this to Drew Pearson, and one of Truman's letters appeared verbatim in Pearson's column.

Benton himself had reacted swiftly to the event. He ordered the exhibits withdrawn from Prague and Port-au-Prince and brought home, for which he was roundly denounced at mass meetings held in New York by outraged artists. In this matter, he was motivated not so much by President Truman's critical letter or by the hulla-baloo in Congress, though such reactions did indeed justify his decision, but by a more pointed reason he could not discuss at the time and kept to himself in the passing years. It was only much later that he explained himself in these terms:

> I discovered that a very big percentage of the artists who had painted the pictures were on the Attorney General's list of Communists. Now I'm sure that a great many were not justi-fiably on the list because my friend Reginald Marsh, who was on the list, was so agitated he came down to see me in Washing-ton. He said to me, "Bill, you've got to get me off the Attorney General's list; I spent three days once in Russia and I hate the Russians." [Marsh at this time did a lot of work for *Life*, traveling through Latin America for them.] I pressed Marsh to discover how he had received this label. He shook his head in bewilderment. Finally he said innocently, "Do you think it can be because I gave some of my etchings and engravings to the *New Masses* to be auctioned off for the Loyalist battalion in Spain?" Reg wanted to see his pictures in print. Because the *New Masses* printed them, he went on the Attorney General's list.
>
> Meanwhile, I had had a report that the most important cul-tural attaché in Prague was the man who represented the Soviet Union. His home was one of the most important salons in Prague. Thus I had a mental picture of the Soviet ambassa-dor to Prague going down to visit the American art collection. I could imagine his saying, "I am glad to discover that so many of the great artists of the United States, as judged by the State Department itself, are fellow comrades of the great Soviet party." Or words to this effect. I had the mental picture of the impact of this on the Congress. This was a final argument to cause me to order the collection back from Prague. I con-sulted with nobody on the decision.

At the height of the furor, John Howe asked Professor Harold Lasswell, then an adviser to Benton, for suggestions on how to handle the problem. Lasswell had sound and pragmatic advice: "There is only one thing to do with the situation; you find a scape-goat." John Howe passed this on to Benton. "You can't do that!" Benton exploded. "How can you maintain the loyalty of your employees if you do a thing like that? I won't criticize anybody or fire anybody." Nor did he. He had his scapegoats, but he never revealed their names. He had known nothing about what they had initiated, but he accepted full personal responsibility for the result, though it embarrassed him profoundly in the department and threatened the integrity of his whole operation. The episode was to have a protracted sequel.

While there were comic sidelights to the art project, the publicity impact on Benton's program was more harmful than any single thing that had hit him since he joined the State Department. It gave the Congress a pretext for slashing his budget requests drastically, and it was only after he pulled every string in sight that the Republican Congress finally authorized $10.8 million for fiscal 1948, less than one-half of the $25 million he had originally asked for.

More importantly, the art project scandal complicated Benton's effort to get a legislative floor beneath his program by a revised form of the deceased Bloom bill. In this matter, Benton had again turned for help to Senator Arthur Vandenberg, who, in the Republican-controlled Eightieth Congress, was the new chairman of the Senate Foreign Relations Committee. Vandenberg, while sympathetic with the information program, felt it unwise to sponsor the legislation personally. "You and your program," he told Benton, "require a lot of time and are hot to handle. I've got my hands full trying to put through the Greek-Turkish aid program and the ratification of the new peace treaties. I can't imperil these efforts by taking on the legislation for the information program as well." However, he suggested that Benton work through two members of the Foreign Relations Committee, Carl Hatch of New Mexico and H. Alexander Smith of New Jersey. He promised Benton he'd give them his support, and he said about Smith: "He must be interested in education since he used to have something to do with Princeton; besides, he's new in the Senate and he hasn't got anything to do on the committee."

Approaches were made to Smith by Vandenberg and Hatch, the latter now one of Benton's friends. Smith agreed to introduce a Senate companion measure to the House bill which Benton was again putting through the Foreign Affairs Committee. It was subsequently sponsored on the floor of the House by Karl Mundt, a relatively new and generally unknown Republican congressman from South Dakota. Mundt and Benton had a common bond as former undergraduate debaters at Carleton College.

Mundt led off on the House side on 6 May 1947, when he introduced "The United States Information and Educational Exchange Act of 1947." Significantly, the word "cultural"—an unappealing idea to the House—was dropped from the title, and the word "educational" was substituted in its place.

It was the first foreign affairs proposal since V-J Day to come before Congress without formal bipartisan support or advance bipartisan strategy meetings of congressional leaders. In making its way on the Hill unaided, it became a kind of litmus paper, registering the acid of congressional prejudices and frustrations concerning the State Department and postwar foreign policy. According to Mike Monroney, the Oklahoma Democrat then in his tenth year in the House, not even the Taft-Hartley bill was more bitterly and lengthily debated in the House. Over one hundred speeches were made about the information program bill. Some, like those of Monroney and Representative Mike Mansfield, supported it. But most of the speeches were by members who used the bill to vent their dislike of something or other about the State Department or American foreign policy.

Strong countervailing forces elsewhere moved against the hostile tide. Thus Benton's cause was materially aided by the investigating committee of the American Society of Newspaper Editors whose 1946 report strongly endorsed the program. The cause was aided even more by a committee Benton had covertly organized to advise him on the conduct of the program and to lobby for the act. The committee was quartered discreetly in a private building and its operating costs were met by Benton personally and by contributions he solicited mainly from Republican friends like Henry Luce and Gardner ("Mike") Cowles.[2] The committee staff alerted former OWI and OIAA employees now in the communications industry. Favorable opinions were collected and published. Draft speeches were prepared for friendly congressmen. Favorable editorials and letters were read into the *Congressional Record*. Support for the bill rose around the House. Karl Mundt steadily slugged away for the measure which later bore his name, and every blow was

---

[2] Benton felt that, given the hostility of a Republican-dominated Congress, Republican support would be less vulnerable if the lobbying operation should come to light.

broadcast across the nation by the supporting network Benton and his friends had organized. Mundt, previously unknown outside his own constituency and hardly known in the House, thus became a national figure—a fact which materially contributed to his subsequent election to the United States Senate.

Benton meanwhile had lined up many formidable witnesses to support the bill before the House Foreign Affairs Committee. He looked outside the ranks of State Department officials for supporting witnesses. General Dwight D. Eisenhower pleaded for the bill, saying that he was "constantly struck by the appalling ignorance that exists throughout the world about the United States." General Walter Bedell Smith, then ambassador to Moscow, cited the extensive scope of the Soviet propaganda apparatus and praised the United States information program for its combating of the anti-American distortions the Soviets were broadcasting. He said he had an "intense personal interest" in seeing the bill enacted, that it was "vitally important to his own mission in Moscow." Smith's predecessor, Secretary of Commerce W. Averell Harriman, stressed the bill's bearing on American foreign trade, then running in excess of $20 billion a year. It was indispensable for United States commercial interests, said he, "to have the world understand America, its life, the quality of its workmanship and the quality of its products."

Benton learned that some congressmen who had been hostile to the bill had gone abroad and had come back converts to the information program the bill authorized. So the staff of his private committee generated articles and editorials urging congressmen to go abroad, to see what the world was like, to judge what other peoples thought about the United States, and to draw the necessary implications for United States policy. Some 140 members of the Congress did in fact travel abroad in the summer of 1947, and the mass hegira was to lead to legislative benefits beyond Benton's immediate interest. Paul Hoffman, the first administrator of the Marshall Plan, was to say that he doubted whether the Congress would have approved that plan but for the great number of congressmen who made overseas trips in the summer of 1947 and saw at first hand the critical shape Europe was in.

Leading the attack on the education and information bill was Representative Clarence Brown of Ohio, an ally of Senator Robert

Taft. Benton spent long hours with Brown, trying to win him over, but it was wasted effort. Benton, however, was not without supporters on both sides of the aisle. While most liberal Democrats defended him and his measure, the most impassioned Democratic speech on his behalf was made by his convert—Representative Eugene Cox of Georgia, the conservative but "mighty man" who "controlled 40 votes." But when the crunch was on, it was Representative Dewey Short of Missouri, a Republican of impeccable conservative credentials, who broke up the hostile Republican attack. Dewey Short had toured the Pacific in the fall or winter of 1946 and brought back some searing impressions which he kept to himself until the height of the bitter debate over the information and education bill was reached in August 1947. To the astonishment of the House, he suddenly sprang to his feet and, drawing on what he had learned in the South Pacific, in fifteen minutes of eloquent oratory—the House boasted no one better at it—proclaimed his passionate support for the bill. Brown's forces never regained the initiative they had held in the bitter controversy. The bill had seemed a lost cause when Benton had it reintroduced in the Eightieth Congress, but late in August 1947 the House approved the measure by a three to one majority. It deserves to be viewed as a Benton victory. General Marshall and others in the State Department contributed nothing to it.

Now came the Senate battle. Hearings under Senator Smith had proceeded smoothly, and a favorable report was issued by his subcommittee, but there was no time to bring the measure to a vote in the Senate before the first session of the Congress adjourned. Every sign said Senate passage was assured as soon as the Congress reconvened in January. Benton, however, was not taking chances. Working closely with Senators Vandenberg, Hatch, and Smith, and Representative Mundt, he helped bring about a ten-man joint Senate-House committee which went abroad to investigate the need for the program contemplated by the bill. All ten of the men chosen were known to favor the bill, but it was felt that exposure to overseas conditions could help keep their attention riveted on the need for the program. Their interim reports from abroad, via press conferences at various stops, reinforced the certainty that the bill would quickly and overwhelmingly pass the Senate as soon as the Congress reconvened. It did. And perhaps because Benton's privately conducted high-pressure publicity and lobbying campaign for it succeeded, no one even raised the question of whether it violated federal law.

Convinced now that the information program was at last to be placed on a secure foundation, Benton, on 3 September 1947, submitted his resignation to President Truman, to be effective on 30 September. His determination to get enacted what would shortly be named the Smith-Mundt bill alone explained why he had remained in the State Department despite his awkward personal relationship with Secretary Marshall; despite the way he had been abused by the Republican National Committee, by part of the Congress, and part of the press; despite his having spent $250,000 out of his own pocket in his time as assistant secretary of state; and despite the dangerous postwar disintegration that had set in with the affairs of the *Britannica*.

In resigning Benton did not feel triumphant. He had been too battered for that. But he was cheered up when President Truman, accepting the resignation, praised his work and took note of the special difficulties he had faced in launching a program without precedent in the peacetime history of the United States. It was a compliment Benton cherished, for he had come to admire Truman as a man and as a president, and his admiration was unqualified. Truman had added that he was pleased that Benton had consented to carry on through the fall by heading the United States delegation to the forthcoming General Conference of UNESCO in Mexico City. General Marshall, despite all intermediate strains, was equally generous in his praise and singled out for special commendation the staff that worked under Benton. Former Secretary of State Cordell Hull wrote Benton to say that he had performed a "miracle," and former Secretary of State James Byrnes told Benton that he had achieved a better record with the Congress in a shorter period than any other man he remembered in his time in Washington.

The outpouring of compliments from all sides inspired Arthur Krock of the *New York Times* to write a perceptive column titled "The Butcher Pinned a Medal on the Calf." Krock observed that "with few exceptions, the news of Benton's resignation was greeted throughout the press and the airwaves by a chorus of praise of his services." The praise was unexpected because "it came from many who still oppose his concept of what is proper government business. But he made a hard, open fight for his State Department projects, got unexpected results from a Congress which regarded him and his plans with hostility." Krock went on to note how many strikes Benton had against him, how many times it seemed that everything was lost, and how many times "some of the most respected public servants and citizens would bombard" the Congress with a "saving cannonade that was partly spontaneous but mostly the result of Mr. Benton's efforts." Now he was retiring "in a rain of compliments that for once were not perfunctory." To which Krock added, "This correspondent feels he can make this report the more objectively because he disapproves of government news services and believes that almost all the rest of Mr. Benton's functions should not be in the State Department."

Part of Benton's pensive attitude about leaving his work in the State Department was reflected in a farewell letter he wrote to General Marshall. He observed that the assignment he assumed at the request of former Secretary of State James Byrnes was largely completed. But then he qualified the claim, saying:

> We have made a beginning, yes. We have taken the obvious first steps. But to any American who understands the goals of our people, and the needs of the peoples of the world, our accomplishments are meager indeed. The security of this nation depends upon an informed opinion at home and abroad, and the truth is that, although we have won such support for the principle, we have not yet aroused the imagination of our fellow Americans to the outlay of brains, energy and dollars necessary to sustain the responsibilities of the State Department in the field of education.

President Truman and General Marshall asked Benton to recommend a successor. Benton urged the choice of Adlai Stevenson, then a member of the United States delegation to the United Nations. Marshall met with Stevenson in New York and offered him the job. Stevenson refused. He later told Benton that he had very much wanted the appointment but that he had said to Marshall: "My wife has threatened to divorce me if I take another job in Washington. I've got to go back to Illinois." Stevenson's wife divorced him anyway after he became governor of Illinois. But for her, he might well have succeeded Benton as assistant secretary of state for public affairs. Benton came up with several more possibilities, but none, so far as he knew, was offered the appointment.

The post went unfilled for about five months, until the State Department made the decision it almost always makes in such a dilemma. It turned to a professional Foreign Service officer, George
Allen, then an American ambassador in the Middle East. He was
appointed to the post, held it for two years, but proved unsuited for
its special demands. The Mark Ethridge committee, created under
the Smith-Mundt Act as an Advisory Committee on Information,
was forced to recommend to the then Undersecretary of State James
Webb that Allen be replaced by someone else. This was done. The
choice was Edward Barrett, a highly respected journalist who had
been one of the principal officials in the wartime OWI and who had
helped Benton formulate ways and means for using mass communications media to promote the work of UNESCO. The information
program then fell under successive short-term leaders until 1961,
when President John F. Kennedy, on Benton's strong recommendation, appointed Edward R. Murrow to head what by then was called
the United States Information Agency (USIA), after its separation from the State Department.

What remains to be told is the protracted sequel to the "art project" which had caused so much trouble. Briefly, after Benton had
submitted his resignation as assistant secretary of state, he spent
several hours with General Marshall reviewing some twenty or
thirty major points of policy which had to be cleaned up. When he
came to the end of the list, he said, "General, in conclusion, I am
going to do you a big favor before I leave the department. As you
know, the artists in New York have held mass meetings in protest
against my decision to recall the art collections from Prague and
Port-au-Prince. They've even threatened a march on Washington.
But I shall tell you what I'll do before I leave the department. I
shall personally declare that art collection surplus property and
throw it on the market." The general was unabashedly relieved.

Twelve months later, an editorial in the *Washington Post* began:
"An interesting sequel has developed to all the Congressional rant-
ing of last year over the collections of American art that were being
exhibited abroad by the State Department." It went on to report
that when the exhibit was sold at auction, private bidders offered a
total of $80,000 for the collection—a profit of $30,000 over the
original cost. (However, the regulations governing the sale of war
assets surplus allowed any tax-supported institution which made a

bid to pay only 5 percent of the bid.) "Obviously the private bidders," the editorial concluded, "who are not in the business to make gifts to the government, thought more of the pictures than the self-appointed critics."

Benton himself, by now no longer in the government, had sent John Howe to the auction with instructions to bid on thirteen paintings. He was to level off at the price the State Department itself had originally paid for them but could go a bit higher. Benton particularly wanted the Kuniyoshi *Circus Girl*, which had been featured in the *Look* story. The government had paid $700 for it, and $2,000 was offered. (One seascape alone brought a bid of $10,000.) Benton, however, didn't get a single painting out of the collection.

The choice items, including a Jackson Pollack and the Kuniyoshi, were bought by the Alabama Polytechnic Institute—for a 5 percent payment of only $100 in the case of the *Circus Girl*. The institute saw in the auction a windfall chance to pick up at a 95 percent discount the nucleus of a Whitney Museum of American Art. And so it did. For several years Benton corresponded with the institute, trying to make a trade for the Kuniyoshi. He even enlisted the help of Senator John Sparkman after Benton joined him in the Senate. But it was all to no avail. "The smart cookie who made the purchase," Benton later said, "remained just as smart as ever." His judgment was subsequently confirmed when the museum directors of America voted Kuniyoshi number two among all modern American artists they most wanted to have represented in their museums.

20

Rue Britannica

When Benton left the State Department, the entire million dollars he had received from Benton and Bowles was gone. He had invested about half of it and spent the rest—$250,000 between 1936 and 1945, and another $250,000 in his two years in the State Department. What assets did he have to show? He had put $100,000 into an insurance policy to give himself a $9,000 annuity at the age of sixty-two—so that he would never be destitute in his old age. He had put $125,000 into his Connecticut home and $75,000 into another home in Phoenix, Arizona. There was $132,500 he had put into Muzak, and the $100,000 he had put into his two-thirds of *Britannica* stock. With the *Britannica* as security, he had developed Encyclopaedia Britannica Films, which he later made a separate company. As Benton said: "I was always confident of my ability to make money, and have always spent my capital when I wanted to spend it—just as if it were income, and I never really differentiated between the two." Within a month after he left the State Department, with no cash and no more stocks or bonds to sell, he began to borrow money from the banks, and heavily. The *Britannica* was in deep trouble.

During his two years in the State Department, Benton had never been out of touch with the *Britannica* and with the broad policy questions it faced. But the State Department job was the hardest and most absorbing job he had known, except for the critical years of the early 1930s when Benton and Bowles was expanding explosively. He couldn't remotely do justice to the affairs of the *Britannica*.

At the time of the 1943 transfer of ownership of the *Britannica*, Sears had agreed that until at least 1948 it would provide credit-

and-collection services through six hundred Sears retail stores with trained and experienced staff. Further, Sears's bank would loan the *Britannica* 90 percent on its orders. But in December 1946, more than a year before the 1943 agreement was to terminate, General Wood, to whom Benton was so indebted, requested the *Britannica* to begin assuming its own credit-and-collections operations. The general tried to ease the transition by transferring from Sears to the *Britannica* a large group of skilled credit-and-collection employees to train workers. After three months, mainly to retain their Sears profit-sharing and retirement privileges, the skilled employees went back to Sears.

All credit-and-collection work was thus centralized under new and inexperienced employees in the Chicago office of the *Britannica*. But it soon became clear that no centralized group of new employees, even if well trained, could duplicate the credit-and-collection operations of some six hundred credit managers spread across the country. By the fall of 1947, the new system was a shambles. There was no follow-through on collection procedures. New orders were accepted from poor or marginal credit risks. Monthly collections dropped by hundreds of thousands of dollars.

More than 90 percent of *Britannica* purchasers bought the set on installments, and the promptness of their payments determined how much money the company could borrow from the banks—now that Sears's bank no longer did the financing. Thus the breakdown in credit and collections compounded a previous costly error in greatly overestimating gross sales of the *Britannica*.

In 1946, "Buck" Powell, the president of the company, had estimated that 1947 gross sales would reach an all-time high of $32 million. He therefore ordered the paper and printing to fill this demand. But by 1947 refrigerators, automobiles, and other durable goods were back on the market, competing for the consumer's dollar, and the sales of encyclopedias began to fall swiftly. It was too late to cut back the 1947 printing orders placed at the R. R. Donnelley Company. By early fall, sales were running at half the estimates. The *Britannica* now owed R. R. Donnelley $400,000, and the arrangement it had inherited from Sears made payments due as soon as paper was bought and the printing begun. R. R. Donnelley, now in its own expansion program, was being hard-nosed in insisting on prompt payment. The *Britannica* had no cash to meet the bill.

Its cash had been eaten into in many ways. There were the heavy costs of redesigning the *Britannica* and furnishing new quarters. The home office force had been doubled. Other costs had been incurred in moving Britannica Films from New York to the Chicago suburb of Wilmette, and in acquiring living facilities for officers. New ventures which never materialized had been expensively explored. Many new ventures had been launched without carefully weighing the immediate hazards—though some later proved profitable.

In addition, the *Britannica* had invested $200,000 in acquiring its art collection and tens of thousands of dollars for its tour of forty-five major cities. When the art project was launched, it had been assumed that its cost could be deducted as an editorial and advertising expense from the 90 percent excess profit tax. It now turned out that the Internal Revenue regulations would not permit such deductions to be made. Paintings did not shrink in value as did, say, a typewriter that could be amortized and charged off in ten years. They could double or triple in value. Aside from the art project, there was the great drain of money represented by the *Syntopicon*, conceived as the key to the Great Books publishing project. Instead of the original $500,000 budgeted for the whole of the Great Books venture, by the fall of 1947 around $700,000 had been invested in the *Syntopicon* alone, with no end in sight.

Many businesses go bankrupt when one crisis occurs at the wrong time. With so many things out of joint simultaneously at the underfinanced *Britannica*, the wonder was that it did not go under. But a greater wonder was that, despite the miscalculations, breakdowns, loss of income, excessive outgo, and the absence of collateral for more bank loans, the only immediate threat to the *Britannica* was one unpaid bill. This was the $400,000 it owed to the Donnelley Company. Benton, however, found no comfort in the fact. He saw that the time had come to overhaul and rebuild the whole *Britannica* enterprise. He had not inherited a well-rounded company: Sears had performed many of the key services—financing, collections, purchasing, manufacturing, legal work. He had inherited only an editorial and sales department.

The many troubles besetting the *Britannica* were brought home to Benton in the month he spent in Chicago between his resignation from the State Department and his leaving for Mexico City to head the United States delegation to the General Conference of

UNESCO. He felt that in some areas, "profligacy was the only suitable word" to describe the major blunders and reckless commitments that had been made. So he asked Harry Houghton, president of Muzak, to come to Chicago to study *Britannica* affairs and help decide how to set matters right.

Houghton proposed drastic steps to Benton while the latter was still in Mexico City. Among others, he proposed that the people working on the *Syntopicon* be given two weeks' severance pay and that all further operations should be stopped. This meant in effect that the whole project would be scrapped, since the success of the Great Books publishing project—and a major distinction between it and the Harvard Classics—was the *Syntopicon*. To be sure, the staff under Mortimer Adler was now far into the project, but there was yet no way to put the material in hand to any coherent use. Thus shutting down would mean no return on the $700,000 so far invested in the *Syntopicon*.

Benton in Mexico City knew that Adler and his people would also be hearing Houghton's advice. He therefore hastily telephoned Adler to assure him that he had no intention of scrapping the project. When Benton finally returned to Chicago, Adler had an alternate plan ready for him. The heart of the problem, said he, was the heavy payroll costs of the indexing. By reducing the number of index editors from twenty to four, the costs could be sharply reduced. The next round of indexing had been scheduled for completion in six months. But with only four index editors, it would take two years to complete the round, and this would entail a further delay in publication until 1952. Benton agreed to Adler's plan and backed it fully.

Benton made other decisions bearing on the *Britannica*'s tightened operation. He arranged for the University of Chicago to accept debentures for the $1 million in royalties due it that year and the next. He approved the sale of extra stocks of paper, which brought in $92,000 in cash. All executive bonuses for 1947 were canceled. Then, to enable an immediate payment in full of the Donnelley bill, Benton secured a personal loan of $350,000 from the banks, which he then loaned to the *Britannica*. He also borrowed an additional $82,000 in order to buy the entire collection of *Britannica* paintings. The purchase price was the average of the valuations three independent appraisers had placed on the paintings. As security for those personal loans, Benton put up his entire stock in Muzak, thus risking almost all he had on his judgment that the *Britannica*'s financial affairs could and would be quickly straightened out.

Meanwhile, there was the problem of strengthening the management of the *Britannica* enterprise. One of its younger men was Robert Conger, who since 1945 had been in charge of manufacturing, processing, and warehousing. Conger was now told to reorganize credits and collections, and he soon proposed that monthly payments for the sets be collected by the division sales offices scattered over the United States instead of by the Chicago office. This put the responsibility in the field, where the sales were made. Letters of instruction to each of the sixteen division managers struck a new note—in the style Benton himself had learned when he was a fledgling in the National Cash Register Company: "You've been salesmen up to now and only salesmen. Now you must be salesmen and executives. From now on you're responsible for collections as well as sales in your areas. The better the collections on the sales your men make, the better the credit risks and the higher your commissions and your net earnings." The new system went into effect with Conger in charge of credit and collections.

Early in 1948, Powell resigned as president and Benton asked Houghton to fill in while they jointly sought a successor. Stringent economies, cautious budgeting, and reduction in staff continued to be the order of the day. By March 1948 enough progress had been made so that the company was able to repay Benton the personal loan he had made to it. He used the money to reduce his bank loans to the $82,000 he had borrowed for the art collection. But he had learned to borrow, and continued to do so for a decade whenever expenditures exceeded income.

The recovery of the *Britannica* was sufficiently advanced to permit Benton to toy with a proposal conveyed to him by Will Clayton on behalf of President Truman. Would Benton be willing to consider an appointment as ambassador to France? Benton, who could speak no French, recalled what Ambassador Bonnet in Washington had told him about a UNESCO director general—it was not imperative but essential that he speak French. When Benton turned down the offered appointment citing the language handicap, he was amused at Clayton's response and assumed it originated with Truman: "The president of the United States can't speak French either, but he thinks he'd make a good ambassador to Paris."

Although he came to regret the decision, Benton nonetheless put the temptation behind him and continued to spend most of his time on *Britannica* affairs. The central need was to find a new president for the company, and the field of choice narrowed down to three people. One of these was Robert C. Preble, then executive vice-president of the Quarrie Corporation, publisher of the *World Book Encyclopedia,* who personally had thirty years of experience in all aspects of the encyclopedia business. Benton saw in him the man he needed, and eventually, in 1949, Preble became the executive vice-president of the Encyclopaedia Britannica company. Houghton returned to New York, and Preble became president within a year. Under his administration, with Benton active as chairman and publisher, the company settled down to a decade of solid growth and achievement.

In the spring of 1948, Benton agreed to a State Department request that he lead the American delegation to the United Nations Conference on Freedom of the Press and Information, which was to be held in Geneva. The topic in both its domestic and international aspects had increasingly engaged his interest over the passing years.

While still in the State Department, for example, he had dealt in passing with the domestic aspects of the matter in connection with the work of the Commission on Freedom of the Press. The commission had its birth in 1943 in an idea of Henry Luce, Jr., and its form was worked out in collaboration with Robert Hutchins. It was agreed that Luce through Time, Inc., would make a gift to the University of Chicago to finance the commission ; the university agreed to administer the project, but neither Time, Inc., nor the university wanted to be responsible for the results. That responsibility would rest solely with the commission itself.

The commission, as formed, consisted of fifteen persons respected for their scholarly attainments. They were to examine the American press—radio, newspapers, motion pictures, magazines, books (and later television)—in the light of a paramount question: Was the freedom of the American press in danger?

By late 1946, the commission had heard much testimony at public hearings and read many documents prepared by its professional staff. But the study then came to a standstill. Luce's advisers were unhappy about the shape the final report appeared to be taking.

He had already contributed $200,000 to the report, but they persuaded him to withhold funds needed to complete and publish it. Hutchins, also unhappy with the shape of the commission's efforts, had to make something out of what had been done. He turned to Benton, who arranged for the *Britannica* to contribute $15,000; the sum made it possible to complete and publish the report in December 1946. Though it was identified with Luce's name, the final version of the commission's findings was largely the work of Hutchins, with Benton entering the picture as a source not only of financial help but of editorial help as well.

The report flatly stated that the freedom of the American press was indeed in danger. The reasons given were many, but chief among them was the fact that a revolution in communications had greatly decreased the opportunities for large numbers of people to express their ideas through the press. Individuals and the public interest alike were increasingly at the mercy of the private agencies controlling the great mass media. If so, what was to be done? A number of modest "reforms" were proposed calling for different kinds of action by the press, the public, and the government. The key proposal was for a new public agency, independent of the press and government alike and financed by private gifts, which would steadily appraise the press and report annually on its performance. The agency, in a sense, would be positioned with respect to the press as the newly formed Council of Economic Advisers was positioned with respect to the national economy.

Except for a few respected editors who praised the report when it was published, it was widely attacked on two grounds: that it said nothing at all, or that it advocated control of the press (though the text itself explicitly repudiated any such idea). That seemed to be the end of the matter—except for Benton's subsequent efforts. It will be seen that at different times and in different ways, he has repeatedly tried to give life to a proposal for a public body which "would reflect the ambitions of the American people for its press," compare "the accomplishments of the press with the aspirations which the people have for it," and "also educate the people as to the aspirations which they ought to have for the press." To this day he continues to try to launch the idea, with particular emphasis on the broadcast media as part of the press.

In 1946, while the report of the Luce Commission was in its final

stages, the international aspects of freedom of the press and information were brought home to Benton daily in connection with his
work as assistant secretary of state for public affairs. It seemed to
him that the gulf between totalitarian and nontotalitarian states
was greater about freedom of information than about economic production and distribution. Since these differences worked to aggravate world tensions, Benton felt that something might be gained if
an international conference were held where totalitarian and nontotalitarian nations would explore possible ground rules for a free
press and the free flow of ideas. The same idea occurred independently to various leaders at the United Nations, and on their initiative the General Assembly authorized a Conference on Freedom of
Information and the Press. The authorizing resolution said that
"the right to gather, transmit and publish news anywhere without
fetters" was an "essential factor in any serious effort to promote
the peace and progress of the world." The conference in Geneva
would meet under the chairmanship of General Carlos P. Romulo,
leader of the Philippine delegation to the United Nations and author of the resolution just cited.

Eighteen months passed between the time when the conference was
authorized and the time it convened in Geneva on 23 March 1948.
In that interval, the world situation had taken a turn for the worse.
Political and economic instability, and restrictions on the free flow
of information, increased. Censorship in some form prevailed among
half the members of the United Nations. Quotas and exchange
regulations impeded the movement of films and periodicals. The
world seemed to be divided into principalities of controlled thought,
and one more country—Czechoslovakia—was thrust behind the
iron curtain after a Communist coup in late February 1948.

Besides Benton in the role of chairman, the United States delegation to the Geneva Conference consisted of three noted United
States newspaper editors—Erwin Canham, Sevellon Brown, and
Oveta Culp Hobby (the former head of the WACs). The other
delegates were Zechariah Chafee, Jr., the Harvard law professor
who had served on the Luce Commission, and Harry Martin, president of the American Newspaper Guild. Hugh Baillie, president of
the UP, later came to Geneva and Benton made him a delegation
member as he did Howard K. Smith, head of the CBS London bureau, and Walter Graebner, head of the London Bureau of Time,

Inc. John Howe went along as Benton's personal assistant. In commenting about the American preparation for the Geneva Conference, Benton later said:

The U.S. delegation was unprepared for the problems we were about to face. The State Department made no effort to help us, and we would have been in an even worse position if I had not taken Henry Luce's advice and made Zechariah Chafee a member of the U.S. delegation. On the boat that took us to Europe, I had the members of the delegation meet for two hours every morning for a "skull session." Chafee was in charge, and he ran the sessions like a professor running a seminar. Without his lectures, the U.S. delegation would have appeared to be biased ignoramuses at the conference. Even with his help, we still had a great deal to learn.

After our boat docked at London, and before I proceeded to Geneva, I called at the British Foreign Office in order to coordinate a joint American-British approach to the conference. In the Foreign Office I for the first time met Hector McNeil of the Labour party who was minister of state under Ernest Bevin, Labour's foreign minister. McNeil was the son of a Scottish carpenter. Under a system where university scholarships are given each year to 100 Scottish boys who stand highest in their examinations, Hector stood 97th. If he had been unlucky enough to stand 101, it is probable that he would have followed his father and would have been a carpenter also. He was a footballer, about five feet six or seven, with massive thick legs and a powerful chest. He was also a man of imagination and audacity, very quick in debate on his feet like so many Britishers. It didn't take Hector very long to discover that the American delegation to the Geneva Conference on Freedom of Information was pretty naive. He had spent eleven years as a newspaperman under Lord Beaverbrook, and he had been up against the Russians many times. He was prepared for them as the leader of the British delegation to the Geneva Conference, and he there added to my education beyond what Chafee had taught me.

The outlook of the American delegation, as developed under Chafee's tutelage on the ship, was expressed in Resolution No. 1, which Benton introduced at the conference. It claimed that freedom

of information was a fundamental right of the people. Hence the
people's right to be fully informed called for national and international guarantees on the right to gather, transmit, and disseminate news anywhere and everywhere without fetters. There must
be a diversity instead of a monopoly of news sources, and organizations of journalists had a moral obligation to safeguard the search
for truth and the integrity of what the press printed.

This statement of general principles did not take the conference
by storm, nor did it develop much of a following. The Indian delegation, with fresh memories of mutual slaughter among Hindus
and Moslems in the India-Pakistan partition, and the recent car-
nage following the assassination of Gandhi, would not accept even
in theory the classic principles of press freedom which the United
States delegates regarded as self-evident. "The people of your
country," said a leader of the Indian delegation to the Americans,
"have enough sophistication to bring a degree of suspicion to the
things they read in the newspapers. This is not true in India. One
false rumor among us, given currency in the press, can cause 10,000
deaths. If you say to us that our people can in time acquire the
skepticism they need, then I answer that in the meanwhile, the price
of unbridled freedom of the press will be paid for in terrible out-
breaks of mass hysteria, violence, destruction of property and loss
of life." On this ground, the Indians urged that any covenant
adopted by the conference contain a provision affirming the right
of government to impose penalties for "the systematic diffusion of
deliberately false or distorted reports which undermine friendly
relations between peoples and states."

Soviet spokesmen also attacked the United States position. This
was Benton's sixth international conference and the fifth delegation
he had headed. But he had never before been exposed to the full
ferocity of a Soviet onslaught. Its delegation, unlike the American
one, had come to the conference armed with long and detailed dos-
siers which purported to support the valid or fanciful allegations
they made concerning the evils of the American press. The only
armor the Americans had was the traditional libertarian concepts
about freedom of the press and information. It was again different
in the case of Hector McNeil, the head of the British delegation.
When Aleksandr Bogomolov, the Soviet ambassador to Paris and
the chairman of the Russian delegation at the Geneva Conference,
leveled a warmongering charge against the British press, McNeil

jumped to his feet. Then for one hour he marched up and down the aisle speaking extemporaneously but brilliantly as he went after the Russians hammer and tong. McNeil made it clear that he was not going to put up with any of their nonsense. Benton decided not to put up with it either.

He was eager to make a strong statement which would put in clear terms the true nature of the intellectual clash between Western and Communist countries. He had a chance to do just that—albeit outside the setting of the conference—when he was invited to come from Geneva to Paris to address the Anglo-American Press Club on 7 April. This was six days after the Soviet military government of East Germany began its blockade of Berlin. In accepting the invitation to speak in Paris, Benton had in mind a speech attacking the Russians—which he was not sure he had the authority to make at the conference itself. John Howe and Joseph Jones of the State Department worked with him on a text. Benton cabled it to the State Department for clearance, indicating that if he did not hear from the department within three days he would assume it was cleared for delivery. When there was no reply, Benton proceeded to Paris and launched his dialectical counterattack, which some observers considered one of the most forceful any American official had mounted against the Russians up to that time in the troubled postwar international conferences.

First he drew a picture of a divided world as it appeared in the context of the Geneva Conference on Freedom of Information:

> On the one side, the Soviet Union, with the small states which echo its views, daily proclaims that the State, the Communist dictatorship, is the source of all good, the purveyor of all freedom—by decrees. On the other side are ranged the representatives of those countries whose people yet dare freely to express their opinions, and to call themselves self-governing men. These hold that freedom of information means primarily freedom from the state, or from any monopoly whatever, public or private. The free are thus face to face with those whose ideology drives them toward the destruction of freedom. This is the stark reality. It is more clearly illuminated with each passing day at the Geneva Conference.

He then paid his respects to the way the Soviet world had corrupted the integrity of words:

Around the clock and in several dozen languages, the Soviet Union proceeds to appropriate, degrade, and bastardize the words which are the hard-earned and world-accepted currency of free men—liberty, equality, fraternity, independence, justice, freedom, and democracy. For these, brave men have died at the hands of tyrants. But now the USSR insists with a thousand amplified voices that repression is freedom, and that true freedom elsewhere in the world is slavery. They insist that the police state is democracy, and that democracy in other countries is dictation by monopoly capitalism.

Benton then took note of a world caught up in a fear psychosis and asked about its source. "I say without hesitation," he answered, "that its greatest single continuing source is the policy of the Soviet Union . . . to deny the Russian people the right to express themselves and to communicate freely with other peoples, and to deny the right of other peoples to communicate with them." The barriers, said Benton, went up to insulate the Soviet citizens from the outside. Then a campaign of hatred was mounted against foreign countries. This was followed by a policy of expansionism that resulted in the seizure and control of neighboring states which might serve as buffers against free peoples. The old Comintern was revived in new dress to press revolution and Communist control in all parts of the world, to preach everywhere that repression is freedom and that this bogus freedom is the wave of the future. Each new people brought under domination became a new frontier for which a new buffer had to be provided. It was like the land-monopolist who wanted nothing except the land next to his. Yet the alarm felt by free peoples in the face of all this was excoriated by Soviet spokesmen at the United Nations, at UNESCO meetings, and at Geneva as "warmongering." And the efforts of the free press of the world to record the process was dubbed "the dissemination of information harmful to good relations among States."

Benton concluded by saying:

The debate and the tactical moves at Geneva thus far offer no hope that the Soviet Union and its satellites can now be persuaded to let down the bars to the free flow of information, and thus to remove the main source of contagious fear. . . . [However,] the conference will help to make clear to men everywhere the nature of the issues involved. Thus it will help to lay a firmer foundation for the freedom to which the world must and will ultimately come, and meanwhile, we trust and hope, will erect a standard to which all honest men can repair.

Benton returned to the conference in Geneva where his efforts to consolidate at least the noncommunist delegations behind the American position were aided by the refusal of the Soviet bloc to budge an inch toward greater freedom of information. He was aided also by the growing realization among the noncommunist delegations that the United States by various means—including the recently enacted Marshall Plan and the recently instituted Berlin airlift— meant to help them protect their freedom and independence in the face of Communist harassment. In the end, except for the "Indian amendment" which was adopted, the United States stand for or against all major proposals was the stand also taken by a great majority of the other delegations, with the six Communist countries in a fixed minority. Beginning in a state of "ignorance," the United States delegation came to master the complex lessons to be learned in Geneva, and, from an American point of view, the conference was an unexpected success.

When it concluded on 23 April, Benton received a cable from Secretary of State Marshall, its tone in marked contrast to Benton's troubles as assistant secretary to Marshall: "The outstanding achievement of the American delegation under your leadership at the Freedom of the Press Conference has made a strong impression throughout the country, notably among publishers and editors. The American representatives at Geneva more than fulfilled every expectation. You have our congratulations and appreciation." This made pleasant reading. The battle, however, was not yet over. The report of the conference was submitted to the United Nations, where it set the stage for a resumption of the clash between the United States and the Soviet bloc. Benton was not a party to that further conflict but had the satisfaction of seeing his Geneva efforts take root among some United Nations delegations as their own "doctrine"—even if some gave no more than lip service to it.

Soon after his return to the United States, Benton was asked to address a luncheon meeting of the Committee on Economic Development, in which he had resumed active work as one of the vice-chairmen. What he said can be read as a valedictory to his experience as assistant secretary of state, and as the leader of the United States delegations to Geneva and three UNESCO conferences. He put a rhetorical question: "In a world where military and economic power seem overwhelmingly important, in a world where the lie sometimes seems stronger than the truth, can the exchange of facts and ideas make much real difference?" And he answered:

> I agree that we cannot resolve today's crisis by today's lesson in the school room, or by tomorrow's international broadcast. Yet it is a fatal error to mistake the immediate necessities of foreign policy for its basic long-range aims. . . . Informational and cultural exchanges can help a little now to reduce some of the world's acute political and economic tensions. Over a period of time they can help a great deal more, if we are persistent, skillful, and imaginative. Given leadership, an adequate budget and time—and by time I mean the discernible future, a generation or two—such exchanges may conceivably build the moral and intellectual solidarity of mankind to the point where war can become unthinkable. Where do we find another chance? Where is there another—anywhere—more promising than this?

The question was left hanging in suspense. (He would not ask it so crisply today.) The 1948 elections were underway, and their outcome created circumstances that produced a new turn in Benton's career.

21

Cold Bath

On the morning after election day of 1948, the newspapers brought Benton eighteen reasons to be pleased with the results. During the campaign, he had sent checks to eighteen candidates for elective office, twelve Democrats and six Republicans. All eighteen won. Most had helped Benton in the State Department, his principal yardstick for contributions. He was paying off political debts, though he had to borrow from the banks to do so. The contributions were what he later learned fell under the heading of "emotional money."

Among the Democrats, Benton made a $2,500 contribution to President Truman—a twelve-to-one long shot in Wall Street betting. Another $2,500 went to Chester Bowles, who won the governorship of Connecticut—a good twenty-to-one shot. There was also a contribution of $1,000 to Adlai Stevenson. Pre-election polls had said he was running for governor of Illinois just for the exercise, but he won by more than 600,000 votes.[1] Then there were contributions to liberal Democrats like James E. Murray of Montana, Clinton Anderson of New Mexico, Mike Mansfield of Montana, and Hubert Humphrey of Minnesota. All won their Senate seats. There were conservative southern Democrats like Representatives Eugene E. Cox and James P. Richards of Georgia, both of whom won. Republicans who had been helpful in his State Department days, and who were remembered with contributions, included Karl E. Mundt of South Dakota, who won a Senate seat, and Walter Judd of Minnesota and Dewey Short of Missouri, who were reelected to the

---

[1]Two weeks before the election, Edward Eagle Brown, president of Chicago's First National Bank, *Britannica*'s bank, had said to Benton: "Your friend Adlai has as much chance to be governor of Illinois as I have to be Pope!"

House, with Short the only Republican congressional candidate in Missouri to win.

To have all eighteen—Democrats and Republicans, liberals and conservatives—come through with victories, was something like an eighteen-horse parlay, with odds at a million to one. It would have been a twenty-horse parlay except that two congressmen who won their reelection contests returned their checks to Benton. One of these was Karl Stefan, who wrote: "I never take out-of-state money." The other was John McCormack, the Massachusetts Democrat, who wrote: "Bill, there aren't any Republicans in my district."

If Benton had been asked the day after the election to make book on the probability that he would himself become a United States senator within a year, he would have upped the odds by several million. When he thought at this time about the political future, he mainly thought about a question put to him by General Dwight D. Eisenhower. The general had been one of Benton's most effective witnesses in testifying in support of his information and cultural exchange programs, and the friendship thus formed carried over to a new setting when General Eisenhower accepted the presidency of Columbia University in May 1948. They often met to discuss the problems he would face in his new post, and Benton drew on his own experience as vice-president of the University of Chicago to chart the terrain ahead. "I remember," he later said, "that I laughed at Ike when he told me he didn't propose to raise money for Columbia; and I remember when I explained that academic 'permanent tenure' was something on the order of what the army had given him all his life."

On the day when Eisenhower was to be inaugurated as president of Columbia, Benton was invited to join him at lunch in his residence on Morningside Heights. When Benton arrived, he discovered to his surprise that instead of lunching in the company of the university trustees, he was the only guest. He was all the more surprised to learn that the purpose of the lunch centered on the question Eisenhower put to him: "How do we elect Paul Hoffman president of the United States?" The idea appealed very much to Benton. He talked the matter over with the general at that and many subsequent meetings, until in time the talk turned to Eisenhower's own presidential prospects. Benton's involvement in that matter will be dealt with later.

In the summer of 1949, Governor Chester Bowles was in Washington on Connecticut state business and met with Raymond Baldwin, the Republican senator from Connecticut. Baldwin had taken the initiative in arranging the meeting. He now said to Bowles: "I want to resign from the Senate and become by your appointment chief justice of the Connecticut Supreme Court of Errors." This was the highest court in Connecticut. Baldwin explained that he found himself in an intolerable position in the Senate. Senator Robert A. Taft and Taft-minded Republicans had stamped him as a "liberal, internationalist, Eastern Republican of the Willkie type." They had refused him the committee assignments he wanted and had sidetracked the measures he favored. Finally, he had headed a Senate Military Affairs Subcommittee investigating charges that the United States Army was guilty of sadism in its treatment of the Nazi SS men accused of the Malmédy Massacre. Senator Joseph McCarthy had associated himself with the charges and, abusing senatorial courtesy and Baldwin's patience, sat in on the subcommittee, hampering and heckling it and the United States Army at every step. Now the mild-mannered Baldwin was subjected to McCarthy's vile abuse.[2]

Bowles replied that he wanted to think about Baldwin's proposal. In any case, it would be several months before the post of chief justice was due to fall vacant.

Afterward, though the matter had to remain a secret, Bowles felt compelled to inform the Democratic state chairman, John Moran Bailey, and Connecticut's Democratic senator, Brien McMahon. Everyone realized that a gain of one loyal Democratic seat in the Senate would be a great gain for President Truman's "Fair Deal" programs, which were in trouble. But suppose Baldwin were actually offered the post he wanted to "resign into"? The Democrat to be appointed to the vacated Senate seat would have to be chosen with an eye to Connecticut politics. The appointee would serve a year—until November 1950. Then, in the opinion of Bowles and McMahon, he would have to agree to stand for election on the same ticket with McMahon and Bowles, and this would affect *their* chances of victory. Further, how was his campaign to be financed? Bowles and McMahon would both be scouring the state for funds to support their own candidacies, and Democratic financial pickings were notoriously slim.

[2]Harry Truman later referred to Baldwin as McCarthy's first victim.

No decision had been reached by the late summer of 1949, when Congress had adjourned. But when the news of what Baldwin wanted to do, and why, leaked out, Bowles felt it best to declare his intentions. He offered to appoint Baldwin not as chief justice but as a justice of the Connecticut Supreme Court of Errors, noting that, if he accepted, within two years' time he would have enough seniority to ease the way to his appointment as chief justice. Baldwin agreed, and it was presently announced officially that he was resigning from the Senate to accept a post as one of the five judges of the Connecticut Supreme Court of Errors.[3]

Bowles's life was needlessly complicated by his failure immediately to name the man he meant to appoint to the Senate after appointing Baldwin to the Supreme Court. He waited three and a half months before reaching a decision. In that interval, it seemed that every Connecticut Democrat above the rank of precinct captain felt that he, she, or a cousin, was entitled to the Senate seat. The pressures they generated battered Bowles from every side. Among the people prominently mentioned for the appointment were Chase Going Woodhouse, a congresswoman; John A. McGuire, a congressman; and two men later destined to play key roles in Senator John F. Kennedy's successful drive for the presidency. One of the two was John Bailey, chairman of Connecticut's Democratic party, a graduate of Georgetown University and the Harvard Law School. In seeking the 1949 appointment to the Senate, Bailey explained to Bowles that he didn't want to run in 1950. He just wanted the honor of having once served a year in the Senate. He valued the lifelong title of "Senator" that would go with such service, along with the lifelong courtesies "of the floor." [4] However, Senator McMahon, himself an Irish Catholic, was opposed to Bailey's appointment as a senator. It would not sit well with Connecticut voters to have another Irish Catholic represent them in the Senate, and the fact that Bailey would not be a candidate in 1950 would deny some other Democrat a Senate base from which to build himself up for that contest. Nor was this all. As Bailey himself had often argued, the choice

---

[3]When Bowles was defeated for reelection as governor, the Republican victor, John Lodge, did not appoint Baldwin as chief justice of the Court. He attained the post only later at the hands of Democratic Governor Abraham Ribicoff.

[4]On the Washington political stock exchange, it is said that any competent lawyer who has once served in the Senate even for a brief period can convert this service into at least $50,000 a year in legal fees from clients.

of a nominee should be made in the light of how much he could contribute to the election of a Democratic governor.

Another man with a claim on the appointment was Abraham
Ribicoff, congressman from the powerful Democratic bastion of
Hartford, which tended to dominate the Democratic party in Connecticut. In 1949, his vote-getting appeal had been tested and
proved only in the first congressional district of Hartford—the
inner citadel of Bowles's own strength. If so, it seemed doubtful that
he could bring any strength to the governor's race beyond the
strength which Bowles could muster on his own. Besides—and this
may have been the clincher—McMahon was vehemently opposed to
Ribicoff.

While Bowles wavered, the passing months of indecision made it
harder for him to say yes to anyone. But in the late fall of 1949,
Senator McMahon made his own preferences felt to an increasing
degree. A Catholic, he wanted a running mate who was a Protestant,
and not too prominently identified with the Democratic party apparatus in the state. He wanted someone who could finance himself
in the campaign without going to the same sources of funds Mc-
Mahon himself expected to tap. He also wanted someone who wasn't
a lawyer. By these criteria, he eliminated Bailey, Ribicoff, and all
the other contenders for the appointment, and he settled on Benton.
Benton had the assets he looked for, and few drawbacks. He was a
Protestant, an independent, a "successful businessman," with a
varied career in the public service, and he could finance the greater
part of his 1950 campaign costs either out of his own pocket or
from out-of-state sources not available to McMahon. With this in
mind, McMahon now did more than merely approve the idea of appointing Benton. He urged it on Bowles. The ultimate decision, of
course, rested with Bowles, as did the ultimate responsibility for its
consequence. Yet no Democratic leader in Connecticut at the time
had anything like McMahon's prestige. His support of Benton was
strong enough to offset other pressures on Bowles, carry the latter
over the hump of his many legitimate doubts, and finally decide him
in Benton's favor.

Benton's name had cropped up occasionally in newspaper speculation about likely appointees to the Senate. But he was unaware
that McMahon favored his appointment, nor was he in touch with
Bowles about any aspect of the matter. Bowles himself knew Benton's mettle better than did most other people. Still, to appoint him

had as many built-in political difficulties as a plan to create a river without banks. True, Benton's Congregational forebears had been among the first settlers of the state, and many Connecticut cities boasted a Benton street or avenue. True, his wife, another eighth-generation child of Connecticut, was descended from the first student of Yale. Yet Benton had not personally settled in the state until he was thirty-two. He had no political niche in Connecticut, no tie-ins with its power blocs, was largely unknown to the voters of the state, and was not even thought of as a "political figure." Worse, on Connecticut's voting registration lists he was not a Democrat but an Independent. Moreover, since Benton had been Bowles's partner in the advertising business, it would seem to many that personal friend-ship was the basis of the Senate appointment. And the mere connec-tion of the names—Benton and Bowles—would by its own echo bring the "Madison Avenue issue" into the 1950 campaign in ways that could harm Bowles's own bid for reelection.

On a Saturday morning in early November, Benton had as a house guest in Southport his new friend Hector McNeil, who had led the British delegation to the Geneva Conference on Freedom of In-formation. He was now a full cabinet minister, the minister for Scotland, though it is questionable whether he welcomed the alleged promotion. The two were chatting about random things when Ches-ter Bowles dropped by on his way from New York to Hartford. On the spot he offered Benton the Senate appointment, confessed the trouble he had had in deciding on it, explained the requirement of standing for election in 1950, and more in this vein. McNeil promptly urged Benton to accept the offer. Benton was compli-mented and tantalized. He also was hesitant.

If he were to go back to government service, said he, he felt it should be in the executive and not the legislative branch of the gov-ernment where he would have to stand for election. He observed that he was trained as a salesman, writer, and publicist, and as a young man he had sold assorted commercial products. But that was not the same as ringing doorbells, shaking hands, and making speeches for votes. The odds against his election in the coming off-year were con-siderable. Even if he succeeded in the short time in transforming himself into a winning candidate in 1950 along with Brien McMahon and Governor Bowles, he would be elected to fill only the unexpired two years of Baldwin's term. In 1952, he would again have to stand for reelection, and as this was a presidential year, on the record in

Connecticut the chances of winning were not great. At best, he faced three long hard years of continuous campaigning. Only if he actually won a full six-year term in 1952 could he settle down and really live up to the potential of a United States senator. But who could say what would happen in the far-off presidential election year of 1952? Thomas E. Dewey had carried Connecticut for the Republicans in 1948. And yet it *would* be something to be a United States senator. It would be something to return to public service, not as a bureaucrat living by the sufferance of his seniors and hounded by congressmen, but as a United States senator.

It was left that Benton, before giving a final decision, would go to Washington and talk to President Truman, Senator McMahon, and Raymond Baldwin. In Washington early the next week, Benton first called on Brien McMahon, who without disclosing his own role urged Benton to accept the appointment and promised him every help in the Senate. The next call was on Raymond Baldwin, who greeted Benton as an old friend and who vigorously insisted that he accept the Senate seat. His attitude is not hard to understand. Had the appointment gone to a partisan Democrat like John Bailey, Baldwin would have been subject to even more bitter criticisms from Republicans for resigning from the Senate. It had never occurred to him that Bowles would consider appointing a man who was not even registered as a Democrat, or who had made his career not in elective politics but in business, education, and the State Department. An appointment of this kind would dampen the Republican attack on Baldwin personally.

Benton then went to call on President Truman. When the president heard what was in prospect, he leapt to his feet, slapped his desk, and exclaimed that being a United States senator was the second greatest honor that could come to any American. He found it incredible that anyone should hesitate about accepting it. When Benton observed that he didn't know how effective he would be as a candidate running for office in 1950, Truman said emphatically, "Bill, you can never learn anything about politics until you run for elective office." Truman then called in David Niles, a carry-over from the Roosevelt administration on the White House staff whose job was to act as a liaison between the president and minority groups. Niles was instructed to take Benton to lunch and persuade him to accept. "Bill!" he said, "just imagine being called 'Senator' for the rest of your life!"

When Benton returned to Connecticut he gratefully accepted Bowles's appointment. As he saw the matter through Bowles's eyes, he fully appreciated the potential for sharp criticism the governor was inviting. Other men like McMahon and John Golden could give their endorsement. Baldwin and President Truman could give encouragement. But Bowles would be left solely responsible for any adverse reactions to the choice of Benton. It was agreed that Bowles would announce the appointment at a Hartford press conference where Benton would be introduced. On the eve of the conference, Benton dropped in at the Fairfield Town Hall to change his voter registration from Independent to Democratic.

Aided by John Bailey, the Democratic state chairman, Benton began to mend his political fences the day the appointment was announced. Though Bailey had wanted the Senate seat for himself, and had most legitimate claims on it, he took the decision in good grace, and he and Benton became close friends. On the day of the appointment, Benton and Bailey called at a Hartford hospital where Abraham Ribicoff was convalescing from an illness. Ribicoff did not dissemble his feelings. "I should have had the Senate seat, and not you," he told Benton, and he had a strong case from the standpoint of political experience and service to the party. Then Ribicoff added a professional note: "Now that you have it, I will cooperate with you."

Another key person vitally interested in the Connecticut Democratic party was Leigh Danenberg, the owner of the *Bridgeport Herald*, the only "independent" newspaper in the state and the only one that consistently supported Democrats for office. The *Herald* was a weekly newspaper, but its Sunday circulation was the second largest in the state, and Bowles had suggested that Benton call on Danenberg. The latter echoed Ribicoff's words. "I was against your appointment," he told Benton, "and I do not think you deserve it. But now that you have it, I will support you." So he did. As time passed, he became Benton's most valued and steadfast journalistic supporter in the state.

The public reaction to Benton's appointment was favorable throughout the state, particularly among editors and businessmen normally hostile to Democrats. This was true of Francis Murphy's *Hartford Times*. It was true of the *Bridgeport Post and Telegram*, edited by the influential George Waldo, an old-line Republican.

Benton and Waldo had in fact been friends for years. It was Benton who had introduced Clare Booth Luce to Waldo, who in turn became Mrs. Luce's strongest supporter in Fairfield County and played a major role in her nomination (by the Republicans) and election to the House of Representatives.

There was some surprise over the gentle treatment Benton received even at the hands of the rigorously reactionary New Haven newspapers owned by John Day Jackson. "Jackson," Benton later explained, "was obsessed by the idea of taxes in general and inheritance taxes in particular. He thought that because I seemed to be a rich man myself, I 'understood' and was 'sympathetic' with his own problem in connection with inheritance taxes. What I really thought is another matter." [5]

Throughout all this courtship of likely Republican critics, Benton bore in mind the fact that it was the Democratic party that now had the first claim on his loyalty. When invited to a luncheon meeting in Hartford with the presidents of the large insurance companies, Benton said he would bring John Bailey along. The insurance company executives found it hard to conceal their astonishment. They played undercover politics to the hilt, helping "friendly" candidates of either party, but it was unprecedented for a United States senator to come among them openly flanked by the leader of the Democratic party apparatus in the state. Benton was not taunting them but showing John Bailey that he "meant business" in his efforts to align himself squarely with the Democratic party, now that he had been appointed to a Senate seat.

Benton dashed off a note to his former Yale classmate Richardson Dilworth, who had been elected treasurer of Philadelphia with a group of reform Democrats. Already thinking about the election he would face in 1950, Benton wanted to know whether he could learn anything from Dilworth's victory. Of his Senate appointment, he added: "I hope I never regret the plunge I am now making. I have led too many lives, and I am sure this will not be my last. I sometimes

---

[5]When Jackson died at the age of ninety-one in the early 1960s, and his estate was filed for probate at more than $60 million, President Griswold of Yale commented sardonically to Benton, "The man didn't leave one cent to charity." Jackson's newspapers took no stand in the 1950 campaign until the day before the election, when they ran a tepid editorial endorsing Benton's opponent. "I shall tell the boys upstairs to treat you gently," Jackson also told Benton in his 1952 campaign at one of their several long tête-à-têtes.

think of Oscar Wilde's 'he who lives more lives than one, more deaths than one must die.' "

Benton also wrote to his former University of Chicago colleague Paul H. Douglas, who had been elected a Democratic senator from Illinois in a stunning 1948 upset of the veteran Republican incumbent, C. Wayland Brooks. By the end of the first session of the Eighty-first Congress, Douglas was being rated by some congressional reporters as the best senator in the upper chamber, and with this in mind Benton wrote: "Paul, I can't remember when any new man in the Senate has made such a great impression on so many people. When I see you, I want you to tell me some of the ways you've done it. In fact, I earnestly hope you will give me all the guidance you can. I'd even like to hope that you might find time to write me a letter with such suggestions as you may have for me, so I can be thinking about them before I reach Washington for the opening of Congress."

The prospect of sudden political death twelve months after he took his Senate seat had its effect on Benton's living arrangements in Washington. With the children, Helen would remain in Southport to keep political home fires burning. He would take an apartment in Washington's Shoreham Hotel and would commute to Connecticut at every opportunity.

In addition, there was the problem of organizing a Senate staff. John Howe, after Benton's resignation from the State Department, had moved to New York to be his principal personal assistant, and was on hand to help with Senate work. On Anna Rosenberg's recommendation, Philip Levy, an experienced young lawyer who had been administrative assistant to Senator Robert Wagner of New York, joined Benton's Senate staff in the same capacity. Others, mostly suggested by Governor Bowles, joined the staff later for tours of duty of differing lengths. They included Donald Herzberg, now on the faculty of Rutgers University; Penn Kimball, formerly on the governor's staff and later a professor at Columbia University's Graduate School of Journalism; Stephen K. Bailey, then at Wesleyan University and later dean of the Maxwell School of Government at Syracuse University; and Stanley Allen, a New Haven reporter and now head of a prosperous Washington public relations firm.

One of the more fortunate decisions Benton made at the outset was to comply with Baldwin's request that he employ the secretaries and clerks who had been on Baldwin's Senate staff. In this way, Benton inherited two thoroughly trained women to oversee the mechanics of his Senate office. One was Elizabeth Rigo,[6] now a secretary to Senator Ribicoff. The other was Catherine Flynn, who had first arrived in Washington in 1934 from Connecticut as Senator Francis T. Maloney's secretary. She subsequently became an "institution" on Capitol Hill, serving Connecticut's senators, Democratic or Republican, with equal fidelity, great competence, and common sense.

In January 1950, on the morning of the day the Senate was to convene, Benton walked into the Senate suite he was to take over from Baldwin to meet the secretarial staff. As he crossed the threshold, his receptionist said, "Senator Carl Hayden has just been here to call on you." Benton dropped his hat and coat on the settee and went at once to Hayden's office.

If the inner club which ran the business of the Senate had any officers, Carl Hayden of Arizona would have been its president—but not because of his manners or his gifts of speech. His manners were as leathery as his face, and his ordinary conversation consisted largely of sour grunts, like a wrestler straining to break a half-Nelson. Some of Hayden's preeminence was due to the fact that he had entered the Congress in 1912 on the day Arizona became a state, was senior to any senator but one, ranked second on the Appropriations Committee, and was chairman of the Rules Committee.[7] Just as importantly, Hayden incarnated the Senate for those to whom it was all the important things of life: a career, a home, a sum of ongoing memories, a laboratory, a studio, a testing ground for character and a courtroom for judging it.

In Hayden's office, Benton first apologized for not having been on hand when the latter paid his courtesy call a few minutes earlier.

---

[6]Later, as a senator speaking in Bridgeport to a largely Hungarian-born audience, Benton was interrupted by a message that President Truman was on the telephone and wanted to talk to him. Elizabeth Rigo was with Benton at the time, and as she was of Hungarian extraction, he brought her up to the stage and explained that he had to take a call from the president but that his secretary would talk to the audience. So she did, with a few sentences or phrases in Hungarian. She was a sensation, perhaps the most effective campaign speech Benton ever "made."

[7]At the time of his retirement in 1969, Hayden had served in the Congress for a total of fifty-six consecutive years, an unequaled record in American history.

Then he begged Hayden to advise him about his opening moves as he took his seat—particularly what to do and what to avoid. As they talked for forty-five minutes, it became apparent that the helper of State Department days was differently disposed toward Benton now that he was a senatorial colleague. Hayden rationed his words as though they were crumbs of bread to be distributed to a city under siege. The most he could bring himself to suggest was that Benton should call on key committee chairmen like Senators Walter George and Edwin C. Johnson. All efforts to get anything more helpful out of him led nowhere.

"Senator Hayden," said Benton earnestly as he rose to leave, "I'm really disappointed that you can't offer me more solid guidance on how to get on with my work as a senator, particularly since you were so helpful to me when I was an assistant secretary of state." His distress jarred loose the senator's tongue. "Wait," said Hayden. "I will give you one piece of advice. Remember this: You can always explain a vote, but you can never explain a speech."

It was a maxim on which Hayden had built the superstructure of his own career. He rarely if ever made a speech in the Senate, and he voted the straight New Deal line for years without arousing any real opposition in Arizona—the state that would soon make a hero out of Barry Goldwater. Yet by his silence and by his New Deal votes, he was, as much as any one man could be, the great benefactor of modern Arizona, which now receives $1.50 from the federal treasury for every tax dollar the state puts into it.

Benton could hardly follow Hayden's advice. Not only was it at odds with his temperament, but he had only one year to make a Senate record for himself. On reflection, Benton concluded that he alone and no one else could set a Senate course for himself that would square with his own makeup and needs. "As an assistant secretary of state," Benton later said, "I could get plenty of advice. As a senator, I could get little or none. Senator Scott Lucas, the Democratic majority leader, never gave me solid guidance. Brien McMahon treated me with friendly and tender care, but with caution. Les Biffle, the Democratic secretary of the Senate, was equally remote though always accessible. I was on my own, in the cold, cold water." No Democrat came to accompany him to the Senate floor, not even Brien McMahon. As twelve o'clock approached on the opening day of the new session, when Benton was to be sworn in, he felt awkward about just ambling alone onto the Senate floor. His closest personal friend then in the Senate was Ralph Flanders, the Vermont Republican with whom Benton had worked as vice-chairman on the CED Research Committee. So he went over to Flander's office, and it was he who became Benton's escort into the Senate. On the way Flanders said: "Bill, I've been in the Senate for four years and I have never yet seen an important issue decided by the Senate on strictly party lines !"

Benton would have liked a place on the Foreign Relations Committee, a logical assignment in view of his experiences in the State Department and at international conferences. But Senator McMahon was on Foreign Relations, and by custom two senators from the same state were seldom members of the same committee. Benton was assigned to the Committee on Government Operations under the chairmanship of Senator John McClellan of Arkansas, and to the Rules Committee under Senator Hayden. When the Small Business Committee was later formed, on the insistence of the Nebraska Republican Senator Kenneth Wherry and with Benton's support, he was also assigned a place on it.

The "cold, cold water" became warmer as time went by. One reason was Herbert Lehman of New York, a brave and sagacious man of broad experience in public affairs who had defeated John Foster Dulles in a special election in November 1949. Though Lehman was Benton's senior by twenty-two years, the bond that was to develop between them was foreshadowed when they stood shoulder to shoulder in taking the senatorial oath of office. "There is only one way to describe my relationship with Herbert Lehman," Benton later said. "It was that of a son to a revered father, and it remained that way in post-Senate years to the hour of his death."

In addition to Lehman, there was an early drawing together between Benton and Senator Hubert Humphrey of Minnesota. The eleven-year age difference between Benton, then fifty, and Humphrey, then thirty-nine, was not great enough to make for another father-son relationship. Yet from its start in the Senate and in the years to come, Benton's devotion to the younger man grew ever stronger in all its aspects of affection, protectiveness, and profound respect. There would come a moment in 1968 when Benton at a White House banquet reached a point in the receiving line where President Lyndon Johnson stood next to Vice-President Hubert Humphrey, and the president, grasping Benton's hand, said wryly

to the vice-president, "Hubert, here is Bill Benton. He loves you—
and I only get what is left over."

Benton himself later wrote of the attitude he formed toward
Humphrey in their Senate days:

> I saw Hubert Humphrey learn about everything more rap-
> idly than any other man I've ever known in my life. We had both
> known hard times in our formative years, and my boyhood life
> in Minnesota and on the Montana homestead had certain re-
> semblances with his life in Huron, South Dakota, and later in
> Minneapolis. But whereas I, by the age of twenty-five had been
> "everywhere" and knew "everything." Hubert had never been
> outside his father's drugstore in Huron. He was still an un-
> educated young man. . . . He went with me on what was his
> first trip to Europe. For dessert at the end of his first lunch
> in Paris, he ordered chocolate ice cream with chocolate sauce.
> I almost threw him out of the restaurant.
>
> With his father's encouragement, Hubert entered the Uni-
> versity of Minnesota as a freshman at the age of twenty-five.
> He had to do many more menial things than I ever did to stay
> afloat at Yale. Yet what he learned as a janitor from a police-
> man neighbor eventually led him into politics in Minneapolis,
> then a haven for gangsters, with a city government rife with
> corruption, and with the Democratic-Farmer Labor party in
> the grip of the Communists. He was elected mayor, cleaned out
> the gangsters, cleaned up the corruption, broke up the hold of
> the Communists, pushed civil rights on a broad front, and be-
> came what John Cowles said was the best mayor in the history
> of Minneapolis.
>
> When he entered the Senate in January 1949, he was en-
> gulfed by the bitter hostility of the southern members, largely
> because he had led the civil rights fight at the 1948 Democratic
> convention which brought about the Dixiecrat walkout from
> the convention. Hubert, at first, made matters worse for him-
> self by attacking some of the conservative southern leaders
> like Virginia's Senator Harry Flood Byrd for their intran-
> sigent opposition to needed social legislation. Once, in the
> 1950s I was sitting next to Majority Leader Scott Lucas in
> the Senate when Hubert was going after Byrd, and Lucas said:

"They despise him." But that was not the final judgment. Hubert, with his mental gifts, energy, and strength of character, communicated his decency as a human being to his Senate adversaries. The southerners might continue to disagree with him sharply, but he dissolved their original animus toward him, and he learned how to convert them into personal friends without sacrificing any of his basic principles. What I saw him do in the Senate I saw him do outside of the Senate time after time with group after group: converting implacable enemies into admiring friends. I told Vice-President Alben Barkley that Hubert Humphrey was by far the ablest and most promising young man in the Democratic party, and that every effort should be made by the party to push him forward—for the sake of the party, and more importantly, for the sake of the nation itself.

Lehman, Humphrey, and Benton generally stood together at voting time on issues before the Senate. Senator Paul Douglas of Illinois usually joined them, as Senator Brien McMahon often did. Other Democratic senators like John Pastore and Theodore Green of Rhode Island, James Murray of Montana, and Thomas C. Hennings of Missouri could often be found standing with them, depending on the issue.

Meanwhile, Benton resumed the Senate friendships he had made when he was in the State Department. One of these was with the Arkansas Democrat, J. William Fulbright. At a lunch during his first week in the Senate, Benton told Fulbright that he was struck by the wit which senators showed in their personal dealings. Even Senator Robert Taft could be witty in private, and from this Benton concluded that the United States Senate must surely be the most humorous group of men who ever met. Fulbright solemnly agreed, subject to a small amendment: "Wit and humor are releases from the grave and terrifying responsibilities carried by a senator. Whiskey is another release which is believed in by many."

The resumption of other Senate friendships made during State Department days reached across the party aisle to include Republicans like Senators Arthur Vandenberg, George Aiken of Vermont, Leverett Saltonstall of Massachusetts, and the newly elected Karl Mundt of South Dakota. There was also Senator Kenneth Wherry of Nebraska, Senate minority leader, senior Republican on the Rules Committee, and a loyal supporter of Robert Taft, the head of the Senate Republican Policy Committee. Wherry was the first undertaker ever to sit in the Senate, and the cheerful way he helped kill off and embalm Fair Deal measures earned him the press gallery sobriquet of "Wherry, the Very Merry Undertaker." He had been chosen minority leader, however, because his fellow Republicans knew he would take honest care of his Republican colleagues.

Ken Wherry [Benton said] was the kind of man who inevitably owns half the businesses in a small town and who inevitably earns the confidence of his fellow townspeople. He can be mayor if he wants to be, the first step to Congress, the governorship, or the U.S. Senate. His outlook reflected his Nebraska background and it was something I understood because of my boyhood in Minnesota and Montana. I was opposed by conviction—and not by party loyalty alone—to virtually every political stand Wherry took. Yet I trusted him as a person. He returned that trust. We had been friends when I was in the State Department and became even better friends as fellow members of the Rules Committee. He went out of his way—as Hayden did not—to save me from some serious blunders I might otherwise have made during the first months I was in the Senate. He won my affection and gratitude.

One of those potential blunders came when the Rules Committee discussed at length the need to improve the acoustics in the Senate chamber. Benton, meaning to be helpful, spoke up to say that he had expert engineers on sound working for him at Muzak. He could get them to examine and improve the Senate's acoustics without charge. Carl Hayden, as chairman, nodded approvingly, but was otherwise silent. Wherry took Benton aside to explain the political facts. "Bill," said he, "I know your intentions are generous. But for God's sake, don't try to be so helpful. Your offer can cause you more trouble than anything you could stick your hand into. No matter how good the results, you will be accused of everything from wrecking the Senate chamber, to a conflict of interest, to plundering the Treasury." Benton confessed his own naiveté, thanked Wherry for flashing the danger signal, and withdrew the offer about Muzak engineers—while Hayden again nodded approvingly and inscrutably.

Aside from friendship, it was the challenge of the Senate itself as an institution which made each Senate day one of excitement that Benton eagerly awaited and avidly prepared for during long nights of homework. He saw the Senate as a place which ceaselessly forced a man to think and act at the top of his form, to bring into play every resource of experience, reason, and instinct. There were substantive problems of infinite complexity. There were problems of tactics, maneuver, and timing. There were problems, especially for a man in the electioneering position Benton faced in 1950, of reconciling a mass of equally legitimate but conflicting claims—the claims of a colleague, of one's constituency, of the nation, of America's allies, of the Senate as an institution, of one's political party and its leaders. Above all, there was the paramount problem of learning how to live with doubt—and yet decide at roll call time.

In Benton's first year in the Senate, before he was forced to face the voters at the polls, there were over two hundred yea or nay votes, averaging more than one a day. Each vote posed a question of "incentives," which led Benton to conclude that a senator is even more susceptible to "incentives" than a businessman. "A major incentive to a senator," he later said, "is an incentive to win support in his home state. The businessman must have profits or he will go broke, and a senator must have votes back home at the polls or he won't be a senator. If a businessman makes a series of bad decisions and then makes a series of good ones, he can still end up with a profit. But a series of unpopular votes, or even one unpopular vote, can cost a senator his business."

Benton reached another conclusion. To a degree not true in other fields, each senator was a consummate individualist. In combination they made the Senate so poignantly human that the place bore no resemblance to the facelessness government is supposed to have. They made it a place of paradox. It was dignified and disorderly, aristocratic and plebeian, harsh and generous, majestically indifferent and sensitive to the slightest breeze. It was a place of swift reactions and of systematic delay, of usurpations and adherence to every letter of the law. It was a place where men of many skills—but little specialization—managed their affairs more like artists than efficiency experts, each man standing alone in the supreme moments of his Senate career. The Senate, in short, combined as nothing else many of the contradictory traits of Benton's own character. Perhaps that is why he came to love the place so—though the Senate itself, when he took his seat, was about to enter one of the most tormented phases of its long history.

22

The People's Choice

Dean Acheson, now secretary of state, with great skill was pressing a policy in Europe which contained the further advance of communism in that part of the world. But his achievement was eclipsed by the march of events in other places.

It was hard for many Americans to believe that Nationalist China, with its many Christian missions, was the architect of its own fall into communist hands. It was easier to believe that China had somehow been "sold out" to the Communists by treasonable men in high places in the United States government. The noxious charge of betrayal was further amplified when the Soviet Union detonated an atomic bomb far sooner than American scientists had expected. Why so soon? The simplistic answer was that traitors in high places had betrayed United States secrets to the Soviet Union. Presently came the conviction of Alger Hiss, a former high official in the State Department, on a charge of perjury in denying complicity in a Communist espionage ring. This personalized the sense of a Great Conspiracy working against the United States. If Hiss, a leading beneficiary of the good things American society has to give its favored children, was found guilty by implication of spying for communism, who in the State Department could be trusted?

Four days after Hiss was convicted, Secretary of State Acheson was asked by a reporter to comment on the Hiss case. His response paraphrased a scriptural reference to rejecting friends in trouble: "I do not intend to turn my back on Alger Hiss. . . . . I think every person who has known Alger Hiss has upon his conscience the very serious task of deciding what his attitude is and what his conduct should be." Many Americans found no real Christian meaning in

Acheson's apparently Christian attitude.[1] Rather, his words reflected President Truman's "red-herring" comments about the work of the House Committee on Un-American Activities, with the shock about the Soviet bomb, and the loss of China to the Communists. It all went to confirm the views of those who believed, wanted to believe, or saw political profit in fostering the belief, that the Truman administration's foreign policy was shaped by men either disloyal to the United States or "soft on communism."

Ten days after the Hiss conviction, there came the president's announcement that he had ordered work to proceed on the hydrogen bomb. And a few days later, in London, Dr. Klaus Fuchs, a nuclear scientist, was brought to trial after having confessed to relaying bomb secrets to Soviet agents.

On the afternoon of 9 February 1950, an airline stewardess on a flight from Washington to Wheeling, West Virginia, greeted a boarding passenger. "Good afternoon, Senator McCarthy," said she. "Why, good afternoon," he responded. "I'm glad somebody recognizes me." Senator Joseph McCarthy of Wisconsin was on his way to make some speeches on the Republican party's 1950 Lincoln's Birthday circuit. His topic was communism in the State Department.

His first audience was the Women's Republican Club of Wheeling. He did not speak from a prepared text, although a local radio station broadcast his remarks. He spoke of "the traitorous actions of those who had been treated so well by this Nation." The worst offenders were "the bright young men who are born with silver spoons in their mouths, most densely nested in the State Department," which, he said, "is thoroughly infested with Communists." Of all the dangerous men, who was the most dangerous of all? "Dean Ache-

---

[1]Benton showed much the same attitude toward Matthew Connelly, Truman's former appointment secretary, after his release from prison for perjury in connection with a "tax-fixing" case. In addition to helping Connelly find a job, Benton worked for a presidential pardon to restore his civil rights. In this matter, however, Benton did not imitate Acheson by paraphrasing scriptures; his methods were more direct. At the Gridiron Club dinner in 1961— so John Bailey relates—Benton cornered Kenneth O'Donnell, President Kennedy's appointment secretary, and urged him to intercede with the President on behalf of a pardon for Connelly. "And listen, Ken," Benton said half in jest but half in earnest. "*You* above all other people—as the president's appointment secretary—ought to have a vested interest in getting a pardon for Matt Connelly. Who knows? You may find yourself in *his* fix some day. As a man of foresight, I should think you would want to establish a precedent that could be cited if ever *you* need a presidential pardon!"

son," said McCarthy, "that pompous diplomat in striped pants, with a phony British accent." He went on to say: "I have here in my hand a list of 205—a list of names that were known to the Secretary of State as being members of the Communist Party and who nevertheless are still working and shaping the policy in the State Department."

While the Wheeling papers reported the speech, McCarthy did better with the press the next day in Salt Lake City. He repeated the substance of his Wheeling speech, but this time charged that there were "fifty-seven card-carrying members of the Communist Party" in the State Department. The day after that he was in Reno. The speech was the same, but he made headlines by wiring President Truman demanding that the White House do something. President Truman and Secretary of State Acheson issued angry denials. More headlines followed. When McCarthy was back in his Senate seat on 20 February, he no longer had to thank an airline stewardess for recognition. That noon he rose in the Senate to announce that he was ready to document eighty-one instances of State Department loyalty risks: Communists, sex deviates, fellow travelers, and other moral lepers. He had covered two desks with documents and he waved papers.

The result was a Senate fracas lasting six hours. The Democratic majority leader, Scott Lucas, challenged McCarthy sixty-one times; Brien McMahon challenged him thirty-four times; and Herbert Lehman did so thirteen times. All demanded names, dates, and factual proof. McCarthy, pawing about aimlessly among the documents on the two desks, responded with blind numbers and said that Secretary Acheson had the names identified by the numbers. It was established later on, that nearly half of the nameless eighty-one were not in the State Department at all. They were in other departments, in private employ, or in places unknown. It was also established later that the list of eighty-one had been taken from the State Department's screening files relating to the discharge of excess employees in the postwar period, augmented by the names of some men who had left the department in 1948 or earlier. The House Appropriations Committee had investigated the same files in 1946 and had found nothing to get excited about. Yet at the end of the donnybrook on 20 February, when Lucas moved for adjournment, McCarthy had raised enough smoke to suggest the presence of a real fire. The Democratic leadership of the Senate concluded that the best way to deal with McCarthy was to authorize the Foreign Relations Committee to conduct a broad inquiry into Communist influence in the State Department.

The actual investigation was entrusted to a five-man subcommittee, headed by Senator Millard Tydings, a lawyer by profession, who had served in the Senate since 1927 and was a high-ranking member in the Senate's inner club. A Maryland patrician, decorated for bravery in World War I, Tydings proudly wore another medal from the New Deal wars of the 1930s. His conservatism was so orthodox and obstructionist that President Roosevelt had tried to purge him—and failed. Brien McMahon also was a member of the Tydings subcommittee, as were two impeccable Republicans, Henry Cabot Lodge, Jr., of Massachusetts, and Bourke Hickenlooper of Iowa.

Benton did not take part in the Senate clash on 20 February over McCarthy's charges. Number 96 in rank among ninety-six members, he was the most junior senator in the chamber, and an appointed one with only six weeks of tenure and no independent national standing. He had yet to make his maiden speech in the Senate, and he felt that the job of bringing McCarthy to bay on the Senate floor should be handled by the established leaders.

Besides, Benton found it hard to believe that anyone could take seriously McCarthy's charges about how the State Department willfully entrusted to known Communists the formulation and execution of American foreign policy. On the basis of recent personal experiences as an assistant secretary of state, Benton recalled his instructions to his subordinates to clean out all suspected security risks or suspected Communists in the OIAA and the OWI before the transfer of these organizations into the State Department. He recalled that to strengthen the secretary's hand in dealing with personnel within the State Department, he had gone to Senator Pat McCarran with an idea, which McCarran later tacked on as a rider to an appropriation act, to get around elaborate Civil Service procedures by allowing the secretary of state to dismiss people "for the good of the service" without directly specifying them as security risks.

If anything, Benton, in trying to position the department and his own program as an object for congressional support, was vulnerable to the charge that he had not been sufficiently interested in "justice" for every individual suspected of Communist sympathies.

He had known that thousands of people had to be fired for budgetary reasons and felt that Communist sympathizers might as well be included. He had used a broadax to conduct a surgical operation, because there was no time or skill for the scalpel, and inevitably there was no perfect justice in the mass firings. On the other hand, as events later showed, McCarthy never turned up a single bona fide Communist on the State Department roster. He used to beg associates: "Give me just one!" But he never got even one, and it is not improbable that Benton's cleanup operation was responsible. In any case, Benton felt it preposterous to accuse the Truman administration of being "soft on communism" when so many of its acts were manifestly designed to thwart the march of communism. He thus concluded that McCarthy must soon overthrow himself by the weight of his patent nonsense. It was the conclusion of a rational man, not yet a political man, and he could not have been more wrong.

About this time, Robert Hutchins had come to a turning point in his life. After twenty-one years as president of the University of Chicago, he was weary with his unending struggle to reshape the university, and to have it serve as a pilot project for reshaping the whole of American higher education. It fell to Benton—and more importantly to Paul Hoffman—to bring him to a new position where he might find the new vehicle for education he was looking for.

At Beardsley Ruml's suggestion, Benton had previously brought Dean Donald David of the Harvard Business School into CED's Research Committee; David subsequently became a director of the Ford Motor Company and a trusted advisor to Mrs. Edsel Ford and her sons; and in late 1949, after the Ford Foundation was created, David asked Benton to act as an intermediary in offering Paul Hoffman the presidency of the foundation. Hoffman by then had effectively launched the Marshall Plan, and Benton went to see him in Washington and to impress him with the proposition that the presidency of the Ford Foundation was destined to become the most important private job in the world. Hoffman finally agreed to quit the government and accept the presidency of the foundation on condition that he could have Hutchins as his associate director. Benton knew that Hutchins was of a mind to leave the University of Chicago. In his continuing role as a go-between, therefore, Benton talked to Henry Ford II, and afterwards wrote to Hutchins on 9 February 1950:

I spent an hour and a half at breakfast with Henry Ford II this morning, and I'll give you more of the background when I see you. Most urgent now is to tell you that he is expecting you to call him and have lunch with him the next time you are in Detroit. You are recommended to join Paul Hoffman in heading up the Ford Foundation but it was felt that you would bring enemies along with you! I assured Henry Ford that no one would have enemies when he had his hands on half a billion dollars. He doesn't seem to realize the enormous impact himself. My own suggestion is that you don't wait too long on a Detroit visit.

Hutchins resigned as chancellor of the University of Chicago to become the associate director of the Ford Foundation under Hoffman.

A new senator can question, advocate, suggest refinements, and vote. He can introduce bills of his own design. But the power structure of the Senate, based on the committee and seniority systems— plus the intricacies of the legislative process itself—generally prevent a new senator from making a great personal splash as the initiator and successful proponent of new legislation.

Aside from the institutional limitations on what Benton could do in his first year in the Senate, much of his work was defined by the need to join other liberal Democrats in support of President Truman's Fair Deal. Their adversaries were Taft-led Republicans often in powerful collusion with conservative southern Democrats—who could distract public attention by outcries against Communist subversion. In many tough votes, however, the liberal phalanx fell apart, and Benton found himself in a minority of a minority. There was, for example, a vote on a $100 million loan to Spain sponsored by the powerful Senator Pat McCarran, chairman of the Judiciary Committee which controlled the destiny of most of the small "private bills" important to senators. President Truman, the State Department, Paul Hoffman, and the ECA—all were opposed to the Spanish loan. Yet in the Senate, among all candidates for election in 1950, only Senators Wayne Morse, Herbert Lehman, and Benton voted against the loan, even though there were signs that it would be used to beat down the remnants of private enterprise struggling in Spain.

Then there was Benton's 1950 vote to uphold a presidential veto of a bill which presumed "service connected" disabilities for any hospitalized Spanish-American War veteran, plus preferential out-patient care in any case. While not many Spanish-American War veterans were still alive, the bill would establish a precedent for the eighteen million United States veterans of all other wars. Benton watched Senators Robert A. Taft and Harry F. Byrd, who posed as the champions of federal economy, knuckle under to the veterans' lobby. Only Benton and two southern senators in secure seats voted to uphold the president's veto. One was Senator Willis Robertson of Virginia. Benton said to him, "Willis, there weren't many of us!" Robertson answered, "We were right, weren't we?" But Robertson wasn't running for election that year, while Benton was.

President Truman had also vetoed a bill providing preferential veterans' seniority to post office clerks joining the postal service anytime *after* the war. All veterans who had worked for the government before the war automatically got seniority credit for their active military service, and the cost of the bill was put at $452 million for the 100,000 veterans who were postal clerks. If the 800,000 veterans who had joined other departments of the government after the war were to be covered later, the cost would run to a billion and a half. The post office clerks, however, were among the most thoroughly organized politically of any group in the country.

Benton was one of only two northern senators running for office in 1950 who cast his vote in support of President Truman's veto. After the vote, the experienced Republican Senator William Langer of North Dakota, crossed the aisle and said to Benton, "Bill, why did you do it? Who is giving you advice? For a man who is running this year, that is the most suicidal vote I have seen in my long career in the Senate. Your vote wasn't even needed. The veto was sustained by two votes. Why didn't you just stay in the cloakroom and only come out if your vote was needed?" Benton disagreed. He had to vote as he saw the issue. Then he added, "But even if the four thousand postal clerks in Connecticut react as you say they will, even if they and their families will be thoroughly annoyed with me for this vote and want to punish me, where will they go? Surely my opponent in the 1950 Connecticut race, a businessman of standing and experience, will also oppose this measure." Benton was wrong. As with every one of the other votes touched on above, his Republican opponent, a businessman of standing and experience, assailed Benton's vote—in this case by letter to the state's postal clerks.

Not until 22 March 1950, two and a half months after he was

sworn in, did Benton deliver his maiden speech in the Senate. On the eve of his speech, Robert Hutchins had been in Washington to talk to Justice Felix Frankfurter, who mentioned the bitter attack being mounted against Secretary of State Dean Acheson and the fact that no one in the Senate had yet come to Acheson's defense. He wondered why Benton in particular had not done so. Hutchins put the question to Benton, who was persuaded that he had a duty to speak out on behalf of Acheson and the State Department, despite past friction and his own newness in the Senate. Benton had been planning to make his maiden speech in support of a resolution he intended to introduce calling for a "Marshall Plan of Ideas." When he rose in the Senate chamber on 22 March, his defense of Acheson served as the takeoff point for the proposal he had in mind. Said he:

It seems to be the irrepressible fate of any foreign office always to live in an air of uncertainty and suspicion—even when it is fortunate enough to have the gifted leadership of a Dean Acheson. . . . In every country the critics of the foreign office are everywhere. They always have been. They always will be. Who has ever heard of a popular foreign office?

These occupational hazards always produce problems. Ordinarily we bear with them if only because we don't know what to do about them. When I served in the State Department under Secretary Byrnes, I saw him suffer from them. I saw General Marshall suffer, and now it is Dean Acheson in spite of the great reforms he has achieved in the Department and the loyal and able key subordinates he is developing. Harrying and tormenting Dean Acheson until he quits his great post is not the way to cure the problems of the Department. You don't cure a man's headache by cutting off his head.

The role for Congress should not be that of the executioner. Indeed, Congress must play a decisive role in foreign policy, but this role cannot be constructive unless Congress aids and counsels the Department in its efforts to take world leadership. Certainly we shall not get the bold and imaginative planning the times require so long as the State Department is forced to cower like a tormented turtle. Remarkable it is how much leadership we have had from the Department, and how effective the Department has been—in view of the climate of hostility in which it has often been operating.

What could the Congress do constructively about foreign policy which it was not doing? "This leads me," said Benton, "to ask my colleagues in the Senate, wherein is America weak?" He answered that it is not in military or economic power, or in diplomacy. Our weakness sprang from a reluctance to accept the basic proposition that the struggle for the minds and the loyalty of mankind was the heart of the conflict with the Communist bloc. Here was an area where America could move boldly, without depending on the Kremlin or without seeking a meeting with Stalin.

Benton then drew on his previous experiences to spell out in detail a six-point program for a "Marshall Plan of Ideas." "Any campaign, even a moral crusade," said he, "requires organization. I propose that the United States now undertake to organize its campaign for men's minds and loyalties on a scale commensurate with the needs and commensurate with the stakes. Fortunately, we have on our side a priceless asset—we have no need to lie."

There were many recommendations in Benton's program for a "Marshall Plan of Ideas." Pressure for worldwide freedom of information should be steadily increased. UNESCO should be provided with effective leadership in order to help the organization make a significant contribution to peace. There must be a fuller development of the activities of the State Department's Office of International Information and Educational Exchange (now the USIA). Democratic education should be promoted abroad, notably in Germany and Japan. Noncommunist nations conducting international information programs should concert their efforts in order to acquire a better understanding of common themes and to increase their joint effectiveness in promoting them. A nongovernmental agency should be created to inspire and guide private American citizens who might use their talents and resources and contacts overseas to further the "Marshall Plan of Ideas."

Benton had not yet accepted a phenomenon veteran senators take for granted—namely, that most Senate speeches are delivered in a virtually empty chamber. He had loaded his text with facts backing up his arguments. He had waited almost three months to intrude on the deliberations of his elders. Yet he addressed row on row of empty seats. His disappointment was expressed for him by his Democratic colleague, Clinton Anderson of New Mexico, a former secretary of agriculture and now a new senator. He loyally stayed in his seat next to Benton through the whole speech. Afterwards he said: "Bill, it's disgraceful that you didn't have all the Democratic

Senators here listening to you. You've got to run in November and they should have all been on the floor helping you. Instead, most of them who are not engaged in committee work are drinking and visiting in Les Biffle's office."

Benton's "Marshall Plan of Ideas" was referred to the Foreign Relations Committee. Long and important hearings were held on it and impressive witnesses supported it, including Generals Dwight D. Eisenhower, George Marshall, and Omar Bradley, and John Foster Dulles and Bernard Baruch. But the press and the nation were not prepared to face its implications. The only practical net gain from the exercise was a film clip of General Eisenhower's testimony that Benton used in a movie made for his 1950 campaign. Otherwise, the "Marshall Plan of Ideas" was swallowed up in a recasting of many lines of American foreign policy following the outbreak of the Korean War.

Meanwhile, the various reports of the Hoover Commission proposing the reorganization of the executive were coming to the Congress through the Committee on Government Operations, of which Benton was a member. Because of his earlier experience in business and the State Department, Benton felt the plans were of high importance, and they dealt with issues of efficiency, which he readily understood. Indeed, he felt that his strong support of the plans would appeal to the Connecticut business community with which he was at that time seeking to develop a rapport. He became the Senate's leading and most ardent advocate of the Hoover Commission proposals. Former President Hoover described him as the main Senate supporter of the commission's recommendations, and the Citizen's Committee for the Hoover Commission ratified that description with a special award for Benton.

But a foretaste of the fate awaiting much of his work in this area came at the end of his Senate speech in support of the Hoover Commission's Proposal No. 1, recommending certain changes in the interrelationship of the Treasury Department, the comptroller of the currency, and the Federal Reserve Board. Many senators, echoing the hostile sentiment in banking circles, spoke against the proposal. Benton alone spoke for it. In formulating his arguments, he had been helped by Marriner Eccles, governor of the Federal Reserve Board, and by Wayne Chatfield Taylor, a former undersecretary of commerce, who had worked with Benton in setting up the CED. When Benton took the floor of the Senate to make the case for Proposal No. 1, he brought to his remarks the conviction of a man who knew that by any ordinary rules of logic, his position *must* prevail. Yet when the vote came, Proposal No. 1 was lost in a blizzard of noes. Only seven senators sided with Benton on the final tally. He was crestfallen by what he took to be a failure in his power of persuasion. But then, almost immediately after the count was announced, Senator Wherry walked across the aisle, placed an arm around Benton's shoulder, and consoled him. "Bill," said he, "I remember my first speech in the Senate. I wasn't running the way you are. I waited a long time before I made it. While I was speaking I knew I was doing very well. I looked around and I saw all the old heads in the Senate like Senator Walter George giving me nods of approving encouragement. But I was just like you when I finished. I didn't have any votes. And, Bill, I remember that when I walked off the floor, Senator Reynolds of North Carolina put his arm around my shoulder and he said to me, 'Kenny, we was with you as long as you was talkin.' "

The only legislation Benton introduced and saw enacted during his one year in the Eighty-first Congress was an amendment to the Mutual Security Act. On the face of the text it seemed unimportant. But it provided a strong political weapon for American foreign policy. It stipulated that the administrators of the Mutual Security Act in purchasing material outside the United States should give preference to plants where the labor leadership was noncommunist. The purpose here was to provide a carrot and a stick that might induce workers in France and Italy, for example, to break free of their Communist leadership—if they wanted the benefit of jobs provided by the overseas procurement of the American mutual security program.

Senator Tom Connally, the chairman of the Foreign Relations Committee, had opposed the amendment. As a matter of principle, he opposed all floor amendments to bills reported out by his committee. More impressively, the amendment was also opposed by Senator Robert A. Taft. Yet despite this formidable opposition, it squeaked through the Senate by several votes. Benton later called on the House members of the conference committee on the Mutual Security bill; they approved the amendment as the House itself eventually did. The amendment was not much discussed in the United States but it became known overseas as the "Benton Amendment." Indeed, at President Truman's request, Benton subsequently (in 1951) went to Italy to help Ambassador Ellsworth Bunker explain it to Italian bankers, businessmen, and noncommunist labor unions. Here he received a particularly warm welcome from the head of Italy's free union movement, Louis Pastore. The latter greeted Benton as a friend from the great home of capitalism, and went on to ask what union he would like to be made an honorary member of. Benton promptly answered, "the musicians' union." He was thinking of New York Local 802 of the American Federation of Musicians, which had continuing relations with Muzak. A suitably embossed card making Benton an honorary member of the Italian musicians' union was soon presented to him in a formal ceremony.

In April 1950, Benton passed his fiftieth birthday. All his life he had been judged by his mother, his relatives, his classmates, his teachers, his employers, his wife, his business clients, his children, his business competitors, his associates in the academic world, his colleagues in the State Department and, briefly, by those in the Senate. But the election he faced in 1950—and that was always at the forefront of his thoughts—was the first time he would be subjected to the judgment by the electorate.

To make himself better known to his sovereign judges, Benton opened an office in Hartford for his constituents, staffed by Bob Claffey and Kay Hart, and generally spent his weekends in Connecticut on a merry-go-round of meetings, speeches, greetings, picnics, clambakes, fish-fries, barbecues, and church dinners featuring vulcanized chicken. Even a quick trip to Italy had a place in this grueling routine. It had become the practice for United States senators to serve as members of United States delegations to international conferences. Benton was asked by the State Department to serve on the delegation to the UNESCO General Conference in Italy in June 1950. He accepted partly because he was a "grandfather" of UNESCO and partly because he felt that UNESCO had become a fallen angel he might help restore to grace. Also there was some promise of a reflex action that might help him a little with Connecticut's voters of Italian descent, a prospect he helped along by an audience with the pope, which was featured in the films prepared for his campaign.

By the time Benton got back to his Senate work in the second week of June, the Tydings Committee investigating Senator McCarthy's charges of communism in the State Department had piled up some 2,500 pages of testimony and documentation. McCarthy could prove nothing. All he could do was to vilify the committee. But then, on 24 June, came the invasion of South Korea by the North Korean Communists, and the decision of the Truman administration to come to the defense of South Korea. That decision was initially cheered by the Senate, the House, and the nation, and one of the by-products of this reaction was a suspension of the work of the Tydings Committee. The cheers, however, were followed by dismay as the ill-prepared American troops, rushed in from Japan, were forced to retreat down the Korean peninsula. Rumblings could now be heard against "Truman's War," in a contradiction of earlier charges against "the Truman-Acheson policy of appeasement."

The Tydings Committee report, or rather the report of its Democratic majority, was finally submitted to the Senate in mid-July 1950, against a background of heartbreak in Korea. It found that McCarthy's charges added up to "the most nefarious campaign of untruths in the history of the Republic." It denied Communist infiltration into the State Department and asserted that the FBI was capable of discharging its responsibilities then and in the future. It found the idea of a "spy ring" in the department preposterous, and it cleared the names of the specific individuals McCarthy had accused of pro-Communist leanings. The vote to accept or reject the majority report divided along party lines. Senator Robert A. Taft, facing a reelection campaign in Ohio and finding McCarthy's fulminations useful, cracked the whip in a Senate Republican caucus. He demanded that all Republican senators vote against the majority findings. McCarthy himself now knew that he could count on the support of his fellow Taft Republicans if he continued his campaign of vilification. While his colleague, Senator William Jenner of Indiana, bitterly denounced Tydings for the "most scandalous and brazen whitewash of treasonable conspiracy in our history," McCarthy, just as bitterly, called the report a "green light for Communists."

At the end of the second session of the Eighty-first Congress Benton cast a vote which he later described as "the vote I most deeply regret among those I cast during my time in the Senate." The issue was the Internal Security Act. Better known as the McCarran Act, it was named after Senator Pat McCarran, chairman of the Senate Judiciary Committee. Himself the descendant of mid-nineteenth-century immigrants, McCarran seemed to hate foreigners. Most immigrants, in his view, were potential Communists, and he proceeded with cruel competence to try to write his view into law.

In the summer of 1950, McCarran introduced into the Senate an antisubversive bill whose stated objective was to protect America against Communist espionage and subversion. But the terms of the bill made it possible to convert a legitimate concern with Communist depredations into a weapon for the harsh and arbitrary repression of unpopular opinions. President Truman moved to counter this danger. On 8 August, he sent to the Congress an administration bill designed to strengthen the nation's internal security but to do so within a framework that squared with traditional concepts of American civil liberties. It was Benton's original intention to vote against the McCarran Act, but he changed his mind for the following reasons.

Senator Scott Lucas of Illinois, the Democratic majority leader, faced an election contest where his Republican rival, Everett Dirksen, had the backing of the *Chicago Tribune*—and the *Tribune* was all for the McCarran bill. To further his own electioneering cause in Illinois, Lucas made a point of not pressing vigorously for President Truman's measure. Instead, he made a private deal with McCarran. The terms meant accepting the heart of the McCarran bill in exchange for the incorporation of several amendments which Lucas drafted but which had no practical value as safeguards for civil liberties.

The next development affecting Benton's position occurred on the afternoon in mid-September when the Senate was to vote on the McCarran measure. Governor Bowles in Connecticut called Benton to say: "Bill, it is beginning to be much talked about in Hartford that you and Brien McMahon are voting on the opposite side of a number of issues and you are both running with me in November. I am not telling you how to vote on the McCarran bill, but can't you get together with McMahon, and can't both of you vote the same way?" Benton at once called McMahon, who said he was going to vote against the pending measure—or, at least, felt he should. At this juncture, Senators Paul Douglas and Hubert Humphrey had a soul-searching conference with Benton. They felt that Scott Lucas's cave-in left them with no alternative except to cast a bitterly unhappy vote for the McCarran Act. They advised Benton to join them in doing the same. So he did. The Senate overwhelmingly approved the McCarran Act; only seven votes were cast against it. Benton afterward never ceased to regret the fact that he had not added an eighth vote to the nays.

President Truman vetoed the McCarran Act. On 23 September the Congress voted to override the veto. Then it adjourned. The fall elections beckoned.

In the 1950 Democratic convention in Connecticut, Benton's nomination for the Senate was opposed by Wilbert Snow, a fine poet and professor of English who had been lieutenant governor and—for eleven days—governor. Snow, a Protestant and a "Connecticut Yankee" like Benton, wanted the Senate nomination himself, and he was backed by some 10 percent of the state convention delegates from the small towns, but the organization opposed him. Snow's bid failed. Benton won the nomination; later, he won and cherished Snow's friendship.

The Republican who faced Benton in the fall contest was Prescott Bush, then fifty-six years old. Benton described him as the model of everything Yale undergraduates of his own and Benton's day had hoped to be. Strikingly handsome, he "looked like a senator." He was managing director of Brown Brothers Harriman, one of Wall Street's most respected firms. He was wealthy and had married a wealthy wife. He lived in a baronial home in Greenwich, New York's most fashionable suburb. He had five children, and one of his sons, a classmate of Charles Benton, played football at Yale. Bush was a Fellow of Yale University, a director of CBS, Pan American Airways, and other corporations. He was also president of the American Golf Association, played golf in the low 70's, and had an excellent Whiffenpoof singing voice.

Benton, preparing for his campaign against Bush, discovered anew the immense asset of his own family. "I want you to know," he wrote to a political ally on the eve of the campaign, "that my children are the most popular children in our community, and if we don't sweep the community 100%—it won't be the children's fault. The truth is that I shall lose my own Republican community by a wide margin, but it would be a great deal wider if it were not for my children—as you will see if you will take them to lunch." In what he had to say about Helen, he sounded like a groom giddy with delight at having just discovered the unsuspected splendors of his bride. He wrote John Bailey to ask if Helen could sit in on a meeting to plan for the campaign. "Helen," said he, "is full of political ideas and I am full of ideas of what she ought to do politically. As you said yourself last night at dinner—she loves politics; and as I said—she has a marvelous talent for it. Do you agree?" Bailey did. He had a trained eye for the natural aristocracy of political talent.

Helen, as usual, brought a laconic humor to her new wifely role. "In the years of our marriage before Bill got into the Senate," she quietly recalled, "he made much of the fact that his father, grandfather, and uncles were graduates of Yale and went on to become teachers and missionaries. Not much was said about my own family. But when Bill, bless him, had to stand for election to the Senate, he toned down the talk of his own family and tuned up the talk about mine. He made much of the fact that I was the eighth generation, in a direct line of descent from sturdy, self-reliant, God-fearing Connecticut farmers—and from the first student of Yale to boot."

Benton made another discovery which was not so pleasant. Running a campaign was expensive. In a letter to Hutchins in July, he noted that he had to raise at least $85,000—which turned out to be about half of what his costs would be. "I think it is fair to say that my opponent will spend three times anything I'll be able to get." He hoped that Hutchins would tap a dozen people in Chicago for campaign contributions. "I hate to impose on you for this," Benton added. "The truth is I hadn't thought of it until Anna Rosenberg told me how tough it was going to be—that I had to use every available channel. I am sure I would have thought of it ultimately, but Anna was ahead of me as she usually is."

Some money came in from Chicago and from Los Angeles and Houston, Texas, where Benton had friends, thanks to Jesse Jones, Will Clayton, and Oveta Culp Hobby. It all amounted to more money than he raised in his own state; Bowles and McMahon were getting the Connecticut money. In September Benton again wrote to Hutchins, with an apology and a plea for another approach to their mutual friends. "What they cannot be expected to know," Benton observed, "is how much money I need, and how weak are my potential Connecticut resources for raising money. Did I tell you John Bailey's wonderful phrase? He said I'd be able to raise no money except what he calls 'emotional money'!" A few days later, there was a happier word to Hutchins, ending on a note of clinical discovery. "I am," said Benton, "getting a most widespread response on numbers of checks, many of which touch me deeply, but of course they are very, very small. Did you know that a $100 check is regarded as a substantial contribution to an out-of-state candidate?"

Yet if Benton had much to learn about the financial costs of electioneering, he also introduced many campaign novelties into Connecticut. One was the street corner political movie, complete with sound track. The films were projected through special boxes mounted on the back of trucks, parked wherever people were likely to stop and look. Among other things, they saw scenes of Helen and the children washing dishes. They also saw clips of various scenes featuring Benton at work in the State Department or the Senate, and with Truman, Eisenhower—and the pope.

Benton was well prepared by personal experience to use radio and television extensively, and to television particularly he could bring a distinctive touch by deliberately calling attention to his own techniques. In numerous public statements he emphasized that television was about to become a critically important factor in politics; Americans, therefore, should know and appraise the ways it could be used. Thus, after developing seven basic formats for a television program, he invited viewers to make their preferences known. Among his formats there was one of Benton being questioned by a group of high school or college youngsters. There was the street corner interview, the reporters' panel, the fireside chat featuring Senator and Mrs. Benton, the set speech by the candidate "on the issues of the day." There was also a prize. Sets of the *Encyclopaedia Britannica* were offered for the best letters written by high school students judging the various formats. The letter writers (and their parents) obviously would have to look at Benton everytime he was on television if they hoped to win a prize.

Above all, there was Benton's campaign use of a helicopter in 1950, when they were still a novelty. Most American helicopters were made in Connecticut, and the vast Sikorsky plant was near Benton's home. One Sunday in early September his two daughters, Helen and Louise, were being confirmed in the church in Southport —and Benton was due at several Democratic picnics around the state. It seemed impossible to be present at all these happenings. But his press aide in Washington had a suggestion. "Why don't you see your daughters confirmed, and then get a helicopter to take you to the picnics?" Arrangements were made at once. A helicopter was rented for $60 for the afternoon—a surprisingly low cost in Benton's reckoning.

The directions to the picnics were for travel by car. From the

air, one road or one picnic looked like another. "Imagine," Benton
later recalled, "my sticking my neck out of a helicopter trying to
identify a Democratic picnic in Lakeville, Connecticut. Neither the
pilot nor I even knew where we were, let alone how to spot a Democratic picnic. We landed at two Republican picnics." The error
proved to be a masterstroke for publicity. The next morning, there
were stories splashed over the front pages of the Connecticut press:
"Benton Can't Find Picnic." "Benton Lands by Mistake with Republicans." "Benton Surprises Republican Picnic." "Whoops!
Wrong Picnic!"

He promptly rented a helicopter for the length of the campaign,
and careful schedules were laid out to make the most of the novelty.
Town committees in places to be visited had large groups of Democrats and other locals on hand to greet the helicopter candidate.
High schools closed down so that children could get a novel lesson
in civics. A further detail involved the services of the engaging John
Benton, then aged eight. The helicopter was built for two but John
could squeeze in between his father and the pilot. He would read
comic books while in the air, but when they landed, John, introduced
by his father "as my button boy," would make his way through the
crowd handing out campaign buttons and pamphlets, always getting pleasant smiles from the ladies.

The helicopter helped to keep Benton in the papers and sustained
public interest in his candidacy. He had to use old and battered
machines, since he couldn't get the new kind which were being sent
overseas by the manufacturers. Three of the machines broke down
in the campaign, and the most unsettling instance was on a Sunday
at a track where car races were being staged before a large crowd.
The helicopter, with Benton and his son John aboard, landed by a
speaker's platform in the middle of the racetrack oval, and at an
appointed time between races, Benton made his speech. Then with
grave dignity, he led John back to the helicopter and both entered
it. The machine couldn't take off. The crowd was vastly amused, but
there was a net gain in more unplanned front-page stories.

Popular legend has it that there is a "Yale vote" in Connecticut.
If so, compared with his Republican rival, "an upstart from somewhere in Ohio," Benton should have had a clear title to it in view
of the many generations of his own and Helen's family who were
educated at Yale. Yet when Prescott Bush resigned from the Yale
Board of Fellows to run for the Senate, the board issued a statement

intimating that the "Yale vote" should support Bush. Hutchins, hearing of this in Chicago, called the statement "the most disgraceful ever put out by any board of trustees of any university" in his memory. More was to come, and when Benton passed the details on to Hutchins in a note of 17 October, he called it "the best anecdote of the campaign." Yale had inaugurated a new president, but neither Bowles, Benton, nor McMahon, as graduates of the College or Law School, or as Connecticut's governor and United States senators, was invited to the investiture ceremony. "I didn't attach any particular significance to this," Benton observed to Hutchins, "until I learned that the invitation to the three of us had been urged, and had been turned down. I just want to tell you that Chicago is not without its advantages."

Even Yale's Whiffenpoofs were used to underline the "Yale vote" for Bush. They flanked him on television three times a week during his campaign. Singing with Yale's Whiffenpoofs, however, was no way to win the CIO vote in Connecticut or any other vote—except the Whiffenpoofs'. This left Bush open to a shaft by Walter O'Meara, the former head of copy at Benton and Bowles. Two weeks before election day, O'Meara, a Connecticut resident, walked into Benton's office and asked for a typewriter. Then he sat down and pecked out a piece of political advertising copy with the headline "Is This a Time for Whiffenpoofing?"

The headline and copy fitted in with a project on which John Howe had been working. To lay the basis for a "testimonial" type of ad, he had arranged a Benton testimonial dinner in cooperation with the head of the Federation of Women's Clubs, a UNESCO associate. Many people, including prominent Republicans such as Warren Austin, the former Vermont senator who headed the American delegation to the United Nations, gave short talks in praise of Benton. Though the excerpts from the talks were ready for use in the ad, the high cost of a statewide printing of the ad stalled the project—until Benton saw O'Meara's copy. He was delighted with it and made O'Meara's question and text the center box of a full-page ad which also featured all the testimonials John Howe had been collecting from Benton's Republican friends. The display was published in all Connecticut newspapers on the Sunday before election day, at a cost of $13,000—which swelled to $20,000 the deficit with which Benton ended his campaign.

At one point Prescott Bush went on the radio and asked where

Benton was getting the money to finance his election bid. Benton replied on the radio the next day: "I'm getting the money from Bush's Republican friends, from coast to coast." There were no more questions. Among scores of Republicans who contributed to Benton's campaign was his own former congresswoman, Clare Booth Luce, to whom he was deeply devoted. Meanwhile, in the course of the campaign, Bush raised the charges of "Korea, Communism, and Corruption." It made a slogan which Republicans elsewhere picked up and amplified in 1950 and more aggressively in 1952.

Beyond this, Bush denounced Benton because the *Encyclopaedia Britannica* was printed in Chicago in the non-union plant of R. R. Donnelley. (Benton had inherited the Sears contract with the Donnelley Company, which had printed the *Britannica* since 1909 and was the only printing plant in the nation equipped to do so.) "Believe a man by what he does and not by what he says," Bush would announce in front of factory gates. "My opponent prints the *Britannica* in a non-union plant." Benton got some unhappy reports on the effect, so he called on the Donnelley people in Chicago for help. They stopped the attack with the help of R. Douglas Stuart, president of Quaker Oats and a leader of the finance committee for the Republican National Committee. Stuart let Bush know that in accusing Benton of being anti-union, he was hitting R. R. Donnelley as well, and the executives of the company regularly contributed substantial funds to the Republican National Committee. "If Bush hadn't abruptly stopped trying to portray me as being anti-union," Benton later said, "he would have walked straight into a booby trap. As it happened, I saw Juan Trippe of the Pan American Airlines, and knowing that Bush was a member of his board of directors, I asked Juan casually, 'Do you do any printing in non-union plants?' He replied: 'Every chance I get.' "

Senator Joseph McCarthy came into Connecticut three times, partly to campaign for Bush and the rest of the Republican ticket, but more importantly to rail against Senator Brien McMahon because the latter as a member of the Tydings Committee had helped to explode McCarthy's charges of "communism in the State Department." His forays in Connecticut, however, in 1950 were stopped by laughter. In New Haven, for example, while McCarthy spoke in a hall seating 6,000 people, the biggest arena in the state, he drew an audience of only 376, and Benton later jokingly said on the radio that "200 of them were my spies." When McCarthy spoke in Bridgeport, he drew only about 200 people, and Benton said over the radio that he had contributed 5 percent of the audience, since ten of the 200 were the Benton children and six of their friends.

In view of the stresses attending Benton's appointment to the Senate in November 1949, what happened to the Democratic ticket in Connecticut in the 1950 election was shot through with irony. Senator Brien McMahon conducted his own campaign, mainly in splendid isolation from Benton and Bowles. He scarcely had to campaign at all. His Republican opponent was invisible, and unreported in the press. Republican headquarters seemed to withhold campaign funds from him in favor of Bush against Benton and John Lodge against Bowles for the governorship. A sense that interests in control of Connecticut's Republican party had deliberately nominated a wraith for McMahon to knock over was reinforced when the state was swept by a flood of letters from doctors to their patients—in one of the most thoroughly organized interventions of the medical profession in a Connecticut election. The doctors endorsed McMahon but went on to choose Bush over Benton, and Lodge over Bowles.

Bowles had been an excellent governor and had tried his utmost to fulfill his 1948 campaign pledges in a wide range of matters such as housing, civil rights, education, minimum wages, administrative reform, and, prospectively, an insurance program to bear the costs of catastrophic illness. Yet some of his efforts—and achievements— aroused the hostility of a number of interests, including liquor dealers, dentists, and schoolteachers. On top of this came the call-up of National Guard units for service in Korea. The result illustrated John Bailey's observation that a governor "runs 100 times the risks of sudden death, compared to the risks a United States senator faces." Bowles was defeated by 12,400 votes. All other Democratic candidates for state office, including a congressman-at-large, were defeated with him. McMahon, however, was reelected to the Senate by some 40,000 votes.

And Benton?

About two o'clock in the morning of 4 November, when the ballots were still being counted, Benton received a telephone call from Les Biffle in Washington. "Bill," said he, "it not only looks like your election may be settled by a few votes, but it may determine whether the Democrats control the Senate." At least two pillars of Demo-

cratic strength in the Senate—Millard Tydings of Maryland and
Scott Lucas of Illinois—had already conceded defeat. About an
hour later, Benton heard over the radio that someone in Washington (who proved to be President Truman himself), had set in
motion the proceedings authorizing United States marshals in
Connecticut to impound all ballot boxes in the state to prevent
tampering. Though 95 percent of Connecticut voting was done by
machine, the 5 percent entailing the use of paper ballots was cast
in small towns which were overwhelmingly Republican. Benton was
a complete stranger to the kind of politics requiring such action
by United States marshals, nor until that moment had he even
known of the existence in Connecticut of federal officers like United
States marshals.

When the tally was completed around four o'clock in the morning, it showed Benton the victor over Bush by a count of 431,413
to 430,311—or a majority of 1,102 votes. He immediately went
on the air and jestingly said that 1,102 votes looked as big to him
as a million.[2] He interlaced this with some emotion-charged remarks
addressed to "Chet and 'Steb' [his wife] Bowles," who were listening in their living room in Essex.

There were demands for a recount. If 552 people in Benton's victory margin of 1,102 had voted another way, Bush would have
won by one vote, and the Senate itself would have been evenly split
between forty-eight Republicans and forty-eight Democrats. But
the matter was quickly settled in Benton's favor, and with his election as the "forty-ninth senator," the Democrats were in control of
the Senate's committee chairmanships. After the election, Beardsley
Ruml wired Benton: "Congratulations on winning by such a small
margin. Now you can give everybody credit for the victory." So he
could.

Who had won the decisive 552 votes? Benton placed his wife first,
then his successful use of radio and television. Next came the helicopter. Then came O'Meara's ad, and a string of other things, including his trip to Italy and his rather gentle treatment by the
Republican press. Benton mentioned another factor, though it appeared more prominently in Prescott Bush's postmortem on the
election. Bush said that what really defeated him was a Walter
Winchell broadcast late Sunday afternoon before the election. In a

---

[2]In the 1960 presidential contest, John F. Kennedy won by about the same
percentage margin.

staccato roundup of contests around the nation, Winchell said that Benton had conducted the cleanest campaign then being waged in the United States. He went on to explain that Benton could have badly damaged Bush with Catholic voters by broadcasting the fact that Bush was the treasurer of the pro–birth-control Planned Parenthood organization. But, said Winchell, he had never used such material and had prohibited his campaign aids from using it. Whether the broadcast won the decisive 552 votes is open to dispute, but it is certain that Benton had no connection with the broadcast or knowledge of what Winchell intended to say until after it had gone out over the air.

For its bearing on a later development, one more detail must be added here. Benton leaned over backwards in accounting for his campaign funds. His legal counsel attached a young lawyer to his campaign staff largely to keep a daily record of each cent received or spent. Unless the source could be named, cash contributions, even of one dollar, were not accepted. This was in marked contrast to the way things stood in Ohio in the case of Senator Robert A. Taft. Taft's campaign manager reported out-of-pocket expenses of $1,529.14 to the Senate Committee on Privileges and Elections. Yet in later testimony before the committee, the manager admitted handling $250,000 in cash which he had not reported. Benton, for one, was to protest strongly against his breezy excuses for not complying with the election laws, particularly because Taft's supporters acclaimed him as a model of integrity. Benton's protests, however, were drowned out by the reverberations of Taft's landslide victory in Ohio and by the power that victory gave him when he returned to the Senate.

The week after the 1950 election, Bowles and his wife went to Bermuda for a rest, and Benton flew down to join them for the weekend. He was depressed by Bowles's defeat, and, as he later recalled, he said to him in Bermuda: "Chet, in 1946 you told me that you wanted to be governor and did not want to be in the Senate. You took the same attitude when you appointed me to the Senate in 1949. But unexpectedly, I've been elected to the Senate and you've been defeated for reelection as governor. The governorship won't be open again until 1954 [because of the newly approved extension of a governor's term from two to four years]. Do you want to run for the Senate in 1952 to succeed me? If you do, I'll step aside, but I need to know. Then I'll do everything I can to help build you up in the next two years. But otherwise, I must keep campaigning for myself."

As Benton recalls it, Bowles replied: "You are the only man in the world who would make that kind of offer, but I still feel the same way. Go ahead on your own. I don't want to go to the Senate."

There was more to the conversation. Benton observed that Bowles had spent his entire lifetime on domestic matters—in business, as head of the OPA, as Economic Stabilizer, as governor. But the politics of the immediate future would be dominated by foreign policy. Would he let Benton solicit the help of Brien McMahon in getting him appointed to an ambassadorial post? Bowles eventually agreed, and Benton asked him what country he wanted to go to. The answer, "India," took Benton by surprise. The discomforts he had experienced during the six weeks he had spent in India in 1937 were still so vivid in his mind in 1947 that, upon leaving the State Department, he had declined even to discuss a possible appointment to be the first United States ambassador to that country. "India!" he now exclaimed to Bowles. "Why the hell India?" Bowles himself had never been there. But he answered the question by forecasting India's future role in Asia and the influence it would wield among other nations who would soon be winning their independence from colonial rule.

Benton subsequently approached Brien McMahon about supporting Bowles for an ambassadorship. McMahon, who had looked upon Bowles as his main rival for the leadership of Connecticut Democrats, pledged his support, and he kept his word. Benton then approached President Truman, not knowing how he would react to the suggestion about Bowles. For in 1948, when the latter was a candidate for the Democratic gubernatorial nomination, he had said on radio: "Perhaps the Democrats can induce General Eisenhower to take the party presidential nomination instead of Harry Truman, and perhaps this would be a very wise thing to do." The statement was made at a time when Benton was in Geneva at the United Nations Conference on Freedom of Press and Information, but on his return, he called on President Truman to disassociate himself from what Bowles had said. Truman showed no sign of harboring any ill will toward Bowles. But now that he had something to give the man, there was a question whether he would withhold it because of a possible suppressed grudge carried over from 1948.

Nothing of the sort, however, proved to be the case. President Truman reacted favorably to Benton's suggestion that Bowles be given an ambassadorial assignment. However, since the post in India was not open, he offered instead to make Bowles the United States ambassador to the Philippines. Bowles asked for time to think about the alternative, but while he was thinking, Secretary of State Dean Acheson sent the incumbent United States ambassador back to Manila. It was not until September 1951 that Bowles got the appointment to India, and then only after Benton had aggressively and belligerently interceded with Secretary Acheson, in what Benton remembers as one of the most unpleasant interviews in his Washington life.

When Benton returned to the Senate in January 1951, he reluctantly gave in to Senator Carl Hayden's request that he give up his seat on the Committee on Government Operations and accept in exchange a seat on the Banking and Currency Committee. The latter committee, along with Rules and Small Business, thus jointly comprised his committee assignments in the Eighty-second Congress. His personal position in the Senate, however, had been greatly strengthened. At a time when the 1952 Republican sweep led by General Eisenhower was still unforeseen, it was believed that in winning his 1950 contest, Benton was in a good position to win again in the presidential election year of 1952. Eight uninterrupted years of Senate service from 1951–60 thus seemed to lie ahead for him.

23

On His Own

When the Eighty-second Congress convened in January 1951, everything seemed made to order for Republicans who subscribed to Senator Taft's policy of attack for the sake of attack.

For one thing, Senators J. William Fulbright and Paul H. Douglas, two of Benton's Democratic colleagues on the Banking and Currency Committee, had been investigating charges of influence-peddling in the grant of RFC loans; their disclosures added the "mink coat," the "deep freeze," and the "five percenter" to the vocabulary of partisan political epithets.

Benton, for his part, had strongly associated himself with the cause of ethics in government and had testified before a Senate subcommittee under Douglas's chairmanship that sought to frame a code of ethics for members of the executive and the legislative branches alike. But from his place on the Banking and Currency Committee, he also sprang to the defense of William Boyle, the chairman of the Democratic National Committee, when the latter was accused of influence-peddling in connection with RFC loans. Scarcely any other Democratic senator stood up for Boyle, and Benton himself never knew whether he was guilty. His defense of Boyle was long and reckless and he was grateful to get away with it. He reacted solely out of loyalty to President Truman and the Democratic party, for he was still self-conscious about his background as an Independent. He admitted he "went above and beyond the call of duty in attempting to defend Bill Boyle."

In the partisan political forum, it made no difference that two Democratic senators unearthed the evidence of laxity in RFC loans, or that high-ranking Republican figures, including the chairman of the Republican National Committee, were as deeply involved in influence-peddling as any Democrats. It made no difference that President Truman finally called in Stuart Symington to clean up and reorganize the RFC. Republicans joined the new disclosures with the earlier investigations by Senator Estes Kefauver into big-city crime syndicates and portrayed the Democratic party as a moral cesspool.

Also, Taft Republicans saw in the 1950 defeats of Senators Lucas in Illinois and Tydings in Maryland convincing proof that their attack policy paid off at the polls. In the case of Lucas, many things led to his defeat by Everett Dirksen: the opposition of the powerful *Chicago Tribune*, reactions to the Korean War, disclosures by the Kefauver Committee about corruption in the Democratic stronghold of Chicago. Lucas himself laid his defeat principally to Kefauver. But the Taftites also credited the Lucas defeat to Senator Joseph McCarthy, who had made some appearances in Illinois to vilify Lucas. More important was the Maryland defeat of Senator Millard Tydings by his Republican opponent, John Marshall Butler. The eye-catching fact here was the way Senator McCarthy and his staff had worked in Maryland to defame the loyalty and patriotism of Tydings in a campaign of outrageous slander. If a Democrat of Tydings's conservatism could be cut down by McCarthy, what liberal Democratic presidential candidate could withstand such an onslaught, with Taft encouraging McCarthy by his silence?

Tydings charged McCarthy with unethical conduct in the Maryland campaign. The charges were referred to the five-man Senate subcommittee on privileges and elections, under the Senate Rules Committee. The Democratic members besides Guy M. Gillette of Iowa, the chairman, were Thomas Hennings of Missouri and Mike Monroney of Oklahoma, and the Republicans were Robert C. Hendrickson of New Jersey and Margaret Chase Smith of Maine. The hearings were held against an uneasy background. The Chinese Communists had intervened in Korea, the United Nations forces had retreated to Pusan, then counterattacked and advanced back to the thirty-eighth parallel. Then came General Douglas MacArthur's increasing tendency openly to challenge the authority of President Truman as commander in chief.

On the morning of 11 April 1951, when Benton read in the newspapers that MacArthur had been relieved of his command, he felt "it was about time." But he was in a minority. The majority roared in outrage. By ten o'clock that morning Senator Taft and other major Republican figures were caucusing in the office of the House minority leader, Joseph Martin. They meant quite literally to destroy the Truman presidency. As a first step to this end, they agreed that MacArthur should be invited to address a joint session of the Congress and that the whole foreign and military policy of the administration should be subjected to a congressional investigation.

On the night of 15 April, General MacArthur was greeted at San Francisco by an emotion-whipped forest fire of idolatrous humanity, a blaze which, feeding on itself, followed him across the country. It reached its crest at 12:30 P.M. on 19 April, when he entered the packed House of Representatives and mounted the dais. He spoke for thirty-four minutes, and thirty times fervent applause broke in on him. In the best Chautauqua style—his voice fluctuating from pianissimo to fortissimo, his delivery from staccato to a sustained legato—he played upon his audience as he presented his differences with the Truman administration. The tumultuous acclaim in the House was echoed in the cities he subsequently visited— New York, Chicago, Milwaukee—when he attacked the Truman administration. In early May, he returned to Washington to testify before the Senate Armed Services and Foreign Relations Committees, authorized to investigate the circumstances surrounding MacArthur's dismissal and meeting jointly under the chairmanship of Senator Richard B. Russell of Georgia. Russell, a leader of the southern Democrats, and a skilled parliamentary tactician, was the antithesis of General MacArthur. He was shy in manner, discreet, suspicious of theatrics, and unprepossessing in appearance. Yet it was he who became the hidden rock against which MacArthur was shattered.

Before the hearings got underway, Senator Fulbright was the only senator who ventured even by indirection to state the administration's case, and he did this by posing some rhetorical questions concerning MacArthur's views about how the Korean War should be conducted. After the hearings were in progress, Benton, in a spectator's seat, felt that someone must put together in a coherent whole the administration's side in its controversy with MacArthur, as its position was being developed by the joint committee —but released piecemeal to the public. Benton nominated himself for the part, and on 8 May, some four weeks after MacArthur's dismissal, he was the first senator to do so.

As he began to speak on the Senate floor, Senator Wherry cut in to ask how much time he would take. "About forty-five minutes," he answered, "unless I'm interrupted." He spoke instead for three and a half hours, the longest speech of his Senate career, for he was not allowed to proceed without interruptions. Once the drift of his remarks became clear, word was flashed to Republican senators, who came rushing out of their offices to give battle. Ten in particular did so, led by Senators William Knowland of California, Herman Welker of Idaho, Harry Cain of Washington, and Francis Case of South Dakota.

Senator Hubert Humphrey was the only avowedly liberal Democrat who came to Benton's support. But Benton got unexpected help from the powerful Oklahoma Democrat, Senator Robert S. Kerr. Not long before, Benton, following the lead of Paul Douglas, had been among the senators who tangled with Kerr over the latter's advocacy of a measure which would serve the interests of the oil and natural gas producers at the expense of consumers. Though the wounds of that earlier fight were still raw, in the controversy over General MacArthur Kerr's support of Benton's stand was directly connected with the plight of the Forty-fifth Division of the National Guard, composed largely of Oklahoma boys. The division's heavy losses in World War II had cost some Oklahoma towns and villages most of their young men. Now the division had been called up for duty in the Korean War, and if MacArthur's plan to enlarge the war prevailed, it seemed certain that the ranks of Oklahoma's young men would be decimated further.

Benton observed at the start of his remarks that he was talking partly from his background "as a retired private in the army,"[1] and partly from his background in the State Department. He also observed that there was no need to remind his Senate colleagues about "the potential difficulties faced by a man in politics when he tries to speak frankly about a great national hero." These potential difficulties—defeat at the polls—explained the reluctance of his colleagues "to speak up" about General MacArthur. "Our national heroes are deep rooted in our emotions, and millions of Americans like to think that these heroes can do no wrong." But the time had come to speak up. "I not only support President Truman's recall of General MacArthur," Benton bluntly told the Senate, "but I telephoned him the day before the announcement,

---

[1]He acknowledged that, as a "retired private" he took "singular pleasure" in what he was about to do.

not knowing what was coming, and urged him to make the move." Further, said he, "No president in the history of the democracy has ever endeared himself to the public by firing an idolized general; but many popular generals have been fired, and I personally hope they will continue to be fired when they push for too much authority and responsibility." President Truman had a clear duty to uphold the Constitution's principle of civil supremacy, and he deserved the gratitude of the country for doing just that.

Who in fact, Benton asked, was best equipped to decide the national security policies of the United States? Was it a general in the field, or the president of the United States? In the course of MacArthur's own testimony before the joint committee, so Benton noted, the general had not only disclaimed knowledge of the issues and questions vital to the conduct of our foreign policy in Europe but had confessed further that he had only a superficial knowledge of the North Atlantic Treaty. Moreover, MacArthur, in an earlier phase of his career, had underlined the primacy of the president in deciding national security policy. In proof of this, Benton read a passage written in 1932 by General MacArthur when he was the army chief of staff under President Hoover: "The selection of national objectives, and the determination of the general means and methods to be applied to them, as well as the determination of the broad policies applicable to the prosecution of war, are decisions that must be made by the Head of State, acting in conformity with the expressed will of the Congress. No single department head, no matter what his function or title, could or should be responsible for the formulation of such decisions."

There remained the central challenge of whether General MacArthur was right in advocating military policies that could lead to a new global war in which the United States and the Soviet Union would be brought into direct collision. In view of the fact that the Soviet Union and Red China were bound by a mutual assistance pact, could anyone safely assume that it would be possible to enlarge the war with Red China without bringing the Soviet Union into it as well?

In answer to this question, Benton observed that two things were new in America's position as a world power. "We are," said he, "in a period of relative war, a half war, cold war, a limited war, in which fighting is only one aspect of our over-all world problem. Economic operations, propaganda operations, diplomatic operations, yielding here, fighting there if necessary—these are the penalties of world leadership which we now face." The second thing Americans had to know was that in pursuit of our aims we could not go it alone, as General MacArthur seemed prepared to do. We depended for our own safety on the willingness of our allies to move in concert with us, and our allies were plainly not prepared to support MacArthur's plan for enlarging the war in the Far East. "If our allies are worried," said Benton, "if we want to keep them as close allies, we must be sympathetic with their dissensions and difficulties. We cannot and must not at this time take precipitate, unilateral action on this crucially important Far Eastern decision. If we do, we would now indeed move alone, and not as a United Nations."

Senator Knowland interrupted to imply that Benton was advocating "appeasement" of Communists. Benton answered with a capsule version of his Paris speech in 1948 about the way the Russians corrupted the meaning of words. Then he traced the history of the word "appeasement" from the meaning it had in pre-Munich days, to the acclaim the word evoked in British and American circles at the time of Munich, and to its present status. "The word 'appeasement' at the time of Munich," said he, "appealed to everyone, because in many ways all of us are appeasers; we must be appeasers to live; we appease our wives, our children, our relatives, our partners, our associates in the Senate, with one little compromise or another, as our way of adjusting ourselves to them or of persuading them to adjust to us. Yet I now fear that this great pre-1938 word may be used in its new sense of abdication or surrender, and used to prevent us from looking toward what should constantly be our goal, a negotiated settlement to put an end to the war in Korea." He concluded with a plea for the utmost caution and patience in handling the Korean crisis.

Later, on 23 June, there was a flare of hope when the Soviet representative at the United Nations intimated that his government was ready to support a Korean cease-fire. But the hope led only to increased bitterness and frustration when the killing went on while the negotiators talked at Panmunjom. The cumulative frustrations were made to order for Senator Joseph McCarthy. He became more reckless, and particularly so in his attack on the Gillette subcommittee which was investigating Tydings's charges that McCarthy had engaged in unethical practices in the 1950 Maryland senatorial campaign. The subcommittee had repeatedly invited McCarthy to testify. Just as repeatedly, McCarthy dismissed the invitations contemptuously or vilified the subcommittee members, claiming that their investigation of his role in the Maryland election was a part of a Communist conspiracy against the United States.

The final report of the five-member Gillette subcommittee was signed unanimously by all three Democrats (Gillette, Hennings, and Monroney) and both Republicans (Hendrickson and Mrs. Smith). They denounced the McCarthy adventure in Maryland as a "despicable back street campaign" and said the tactics he used were "destructive of fundamental American principles." The report also observed that, under the terms of a Senate resolution adopted on 13 April 1950, any senator, whether or not a candidate in an election, was subject to being expelled from the Senate if he was found guilty of having engaged in election practices of the kind charged against McCarthy. In conclusion, the Gillette subcommittee invited the Senate Committee on Rules and Administration to inquire into the conduct of Senator McCarthy since his election to the Senate and to determine whether to initiate action toward expelling McCarthy from the United States Senate.

When the subcommittee's report was published on 3 August 1951, McCarthy tried to brazen it through. "I am not surprised at the criticism of the two Republicans [Hendrickson and Smith] on the Committee," said he. "After all, they went on record as approving the Tydings whitewash and condemning me for getting rough with the Communists. Moreover, I am not surprised that the Democrats on the Committee [Gillette, Hennings, and Monroney] have not learned that the American people just don't like whitewashes. As long as puny politicians try to encourage other puny politicians to ignore or whitewash Communist influence in our Government, America will remain in grave danger."

It was noted previously that in the early months of McCarthy's antics, Benton neither took him too seriously nor imagined that the country would do so for very long. Besides, he was busily engaged with a mass of legislative business that held his immediate interest. The index to the *Congressional Record* for the period of 1950–51 shows that he joined in sponsoring bills, resolutions, or amendments dealing with emergency food for India; Alaska statehood; government machinery to protect civil rights; a more competent civil service; Hawaii statehood; expanded activities of the Department of

Labor; a cabinet department of social security and education; fair
employment practices; home rule for the District of Columbia; an
antilynching bill; interstate forest fire protection; housing preference for Korean War veterans; overseeing administration of overseas agencies; outlawing of the poll tax; strengthening laws against
monopoly; the Saint Lawrence seaway; a Small Defense Plants
Corporation; rules of procedure for congressional investigations;
troops for NATO; assistance to Israel; a cabinet department of
health; a national commission on radio and television. In addition,
Benton regularly commuted between Washington and Connecticut
to keep his home political base in good order for his next bid at the
polls in 1952.

But as the months of McCarthy's fulminations wore on, Benton
became thoroughly disgusted with his outrageous attacks on the
State Department and the people in it who had no one to defend
them. John Bailey, at a later date, would say to Benton: "You were
the only person in the Senate in an ideal position to go after
McCarthy. You had little political background in elective office, and
thus there weren't too many grounds on which McCarthy could
launch an attack on you. You had the money with which to hire
lawyers to defend yourself. And you weren't afraid of defeat because you had plenty of activities beckoning to you if you lost your
Senate seat." All this was true enough. But a well-equipped army
is not necessarily a victorious army; there must also be a will for
battle.

Benton's growing will to battle McCarthy was triggered on the
evening of Friday, 3 August, in the library in his Southport home
where he finished reading the newly issued report of the Gillette
subcommittee. As a member of the Rules Committee, to which the
subcommittee had submitted a call for further action, Benton felt
a measure of responsibility for the fate of the report. Here was a
chance to curb McCarthy, but he feared the chance would be lost.
For one thing, he noticed that the findings of the Gillette subcommittee got very little play in the evening newspapers. For another,
the Senate was in its August dog days, hot, tired, snappish, and
in no mood for any extra stress. Given the lethargy of the press and
the Senate's irascibility, Benton feared that the publication of the
subcommittee's report would not be followed up and its recommendation that the Rules Committee review McCarthy's Senate conduct
to see if there was a case for expelling him would quickly be for-

gotten. He was determined to make something out of the report, but he wasn't quite sure what.

Benton telephoned John Howe, who was spending the weekend at Cornwall-on-the-Hudson as the guest of John Stillman, chairman of the Rockland County Democratic party and a member of the Stillman banking family. In relating what ensued, Howe told the story this way:

> After Benton told me that the Gillette committee report had been issued that afternoon, he read a few passages from it. He said he was going to send the full text to me by special delivery mail. I was to study it the moment it reached me at Cornwall and should call him back to suggest what he ought to do. The report was in my hands the next day and I read it and thought about it. On Sunday, I called Benton at Southport to say that I felt, as he did, that the report's strong language plainly implied follow-up action. My own suggestion was that he should take the floor of the Senate on Monday morning, and with the report in his hand, should call upon McCarthy to resign from the Senate. I realize in retrospect that the suggestion wasn't too bright. You don't strike at the king without killing him. Yet I thought at the time that if Benton limited himself to a one-shot call for McCarthy to resign, it would make a good one-day story.
>
> That Sunday evening, Benton and I, as usual, boarded the overnight train from New York to Washington. But we got on at different times, and didn't meet until the next morning when we had breakfast in Washington's Union Station. The first thing he said to me was: "I'm going to ask McCarthy to resign, all right. But that's not all I'm going to do. I'm going to introduce a resolution in the Senate calling for McCarthy's expulsion." I didn't argue with him. Though he didn't have even the beginning of the language for the resolution, when Benton decides on a course of action, he acts speedily with no waste of motions. By the time we had reached his Senate office, we had agreed on the simplest and most logical form for the resolution. It was to use the exact language of the Gillette committee report, to break down the text into its component parts, and to put a *whereas* before each finding of fact. The *Therefore, Be It Resolved* part would repeat the exact language used

in the Gillette committee report where it recommended a Rules Committee inquiry into McCarthy's conduct as a member of the Senate, in order to determine if he should be expelled from the chamber.

While Howe worked on a draft of the resolution, Benton made no effort to muster support for it from among his Senate colleagues. He felt it would be hopeless to do so and realized that he would have to act alone. He did put some procedural questions to Les Biffle, the secretary of the Senate, and told him he would like to counsel with one experienced and sympathetic Democratic senator. Biffle suggested Senator Lister Hill of Alabama. Hill clarified procedural points at issue and voiced his admiration for Benton's courage in the venture he was about to launch, but he gave no pledge of support for the resolution. Benton's impending action differed fundamentally from the investigation by the Tydings Committee in 1950. That investigation, coming early in McCarthy's forays, squared with routine Senate procedures. Serious charges had been made about an executive department, and a Senate committee was chosen to look into them. This was true of the Gillette subcommittee as well. Its work also squared with routine Senate procedures. A senator had been charged, and a Senate committee had to inquire into the matter. But it was something else to introduce a resolution explicitly calling for the expulsion of McCarthy from the Senate.

In several cases senators-elect had been refused their seats because of election frauds. Several incumbent senators also had been censured by the chamber. But a resolution to expel an incumbent senator for conduct unworthy of a member of the Senate stood virtually on a plane of its own in Senate history. Many men reach the Senate with skeletons in their closets. Even if none exists, an enemy can twist an innocent past episode to make a person appear in league with the devil. On these grounds, plus the fact that they regard themselves as representatives of their respective states, senators tend to disapprove of motions of censure and expulsion. On these same grounds, Benton's attack on McCarthy could be viewed by every senator as a potential attack on any other senator.

Benton himself, it should be stressed, was fully aware of all this. He knew that the Senate would not approve a motion to expel Senator McCarthy. However, he knew well the meaning of the word "dramatize"—one of the "golden words" which "Old Patterson" had taught employees of the National Cash Register Company. Benton also knew from the history of his own swift rise in the Batten advertising agency that a furor deliberately precipitated—even at great personal risk—can often attain an objective lying beyond the bounds of discreet conduct. These two bits of knowledge carried over from the past in a concealed way influenced his tactical approach to the immediate case he faced. Given the certainty that the Senate would never expel Senator McCarthy, he hoped that the Senate might at least be induced to censure the man. This was his real aim. But to attain it, Benton felt he must dramatize the issue of McCarthyism and raise a furor over it—this, by means of a high-pitched motion to expel, taking off from the Gillette report, that could lead the way to a lower-pitched motion to censure. With this in mind, then, Benton took the floor of the Senate in the early afternoon of 6 August 1951—to set in motion a train of events which were to move over a long, tortuous road, until McCarthy's censure was ultimately attained more than four years later, not long before his death.

Benton began by masking his punch. Newspapers of previous days had carried stories about a West Point scandal where ninety cadets were suspended for cheating on examinations. Most of them initially had been recruited for West Point specifically because they were football prospects. They had maintained their academic standing by taking examinations whose questions they knew in advance. Here, in a place synonymous with honor, was the same corruption from big-time football that had induced Hutchins with Benton's help to end Big Ten football at the University of Chicago.

When Benton took the floor he referred first to the West Point scandals and suggested that football be abolished at all the service academies and that the ninety accused cadets be allowed to remain at West Point on probation and subject to strict discipline. "They were," said Benton, "the victims of a vicious system, not its perpetrators." He also urged an immediate investigation of all the service institutions by the most competent people in the academic world, looking toward reorganization of the curriculum, methods of instruction, and quality of the faculty. He pointed out that West Point had been founded early in the nineteenth century to train engineers like Lewis and Clark to open up the West. At that time the country had no engineering schools; now it had dozens with curriculum and faculty far superior to West Point. The need now was for generals and admirals trained to think for themselves about the new world of the twentieth century.

When Benton had spoken his piece about the academies, he was jumped on by Republican Senators Welker of Idaho and Case of South Dakota. "I am not in favor of the long-haired type of education," cried Welker. "I am for vigorous intercollegiate athletics. I am not for the glee club type of athlete, or the medicine ball type of athlete. I like fine, hard-blocking football and the type of athlete who has been identified with General Eisenhower." Benton shot down that thesis by observing dryly that Welker's personal hero, General Douglas MacArthur, "who had stood first in his class at West Point, was not a member of the football squad." Senator Case then observed that "the Battle of Waterloo was won on the playing fields of Eton" and concluded that future officers of the United States were being prepared to win future wars by playing football, since the tactics of football were the same as those of warfare. Benton met this by saying that future officers could be better prepared to meet future demands if they spent four years "studying the scientific subjects around which the military service of the future will be centered." In any event, said he, if Senator Case's theory was correct, "then we ought to have fifty football teams at West Point, and everybody at West Point should have to take football as a compulsory subject and possibly as the first point in his education." Neither Welker nor Case had more to say, and Benton threw off his mask.

"I have heard no comment on the floor of the Senate today," said he, "on another newspaper story of last Friday, which deals with the charge of corruption which strikes very close at home to all of us in the Senate, far closer than West Point or even Annapolis." He then brought up the Gillette report about McCarthy's role in the defeat of Senator Tydings, and read his own resolution, based on the text of the subcommittee's report. "I suggest today," Benton continued, "that the Senator from Wisconsin should at once submit his resignation from this body. That would be an honorable and decisive gesture on his part. Only so could he take the only step now open to him to make amends to the people of Wisconsin, to his great predecessors [the La Follettes] in the seat he now occupies in the Senate, and to his colleagues in the Senate. If the Senator from Wisconsin refuses to resign—and there is nothing in his record to indicate that he will do other than refuse—then I suggest at least he refrain from taking any further part in the activities and procedures of the United States Senate until my resolution has been received and reviewed by the Committee on Rules and Administration, and until action has been taken upon it by the Committee and by the United States Senate itself."

This was no one-day story. It was war. A dozen or more senators came up to Benton afterward to repeat in their own way the sentiments Lister Hill had previously expressed. They admired Benton's "courage"—perhaps thought him a little crazy—but could not back him openly. Indeed, taking all factional groups in the Senate as a whole—conservative and liberal, Republican and Democrat—Herbert Lehman was the only senator who openly came to Benton's support after he introduced the resolution, and he would do so repeatedly in the long months of battle that lay ahead. Senator Hubert Humphrey, like Lehman, might have openly stood by Benton if the latter had requested his help. But there was no such request. Rather the opposite. "Hubert," said Benton to him when the lines of battle were being drawn, "you stay the hell out of this fight." Among Benton's covert supporters, the principal figure was Senator Mike Monroney, the Oklahoma Democrat on the Gillette subcommittee who worked for Benton behind the scenes. Brien McMahon, a member of the former Tydings Committee, also lent backstage support until he was stricken by cancer and died in the summer of 1952.

Individual newspapers and newspapermen were also helpful. Among the former, most important were the *Milwaukee Journal* and the Madison *Capital Times*. Among the newspapermen, there were Drew Pearson, Robert Fleming of the *Milwaukee Journal*, and Herblock, the superb cartoonist for the *Washington Post*. Among the radio and television commentators there were Martin Agronsky and Elmer Davis, who from start to finish consistently battled every manifestation of McCarthyism and tried to reinforce the position of anyone who waged the same fight. The personal cost to Agronsky was notable. His radio program was broadcast nationally but depended on local sponsors in every city where he had an outlet. He lost fifteen such sponsors because of his vocal opposition to McCarthyism. Yet he continued to speak his mind despite the economic pressure aimed at silencing him. Edward R. Murrow, by far the most popular of the radio and television commentators, never really came to grips with McCarthy or McCarthyism until 1953. When Murrow received the Freedom House Prize because of his stand against McCarthyism, Benton did not begrudge him the honor. "I liked to see Ed get the prize," said he, "because he showed great nerve in his important program and afterwards suffered at CBS because of it. Yet I felt that the prize could even more justly have gone to Agronsky. Perhaps the Freedom House jury did not know of Agronsky's earlier stand, or did not think he could fill the ballroom of the Waldorf Astoria Hotel for the annual money-raising banquet—while Ed Murrow could."

Benton had accumulated from various sources mounds of material about Senator McCarthy's noxious activities. But this by itself did not make an indictment. An indictment must have an organization so that each count points to a clear-cut pattern of censurable behavior. In framing such an indictment, John Howe thought the best way to proceed would be to take a series of cases where McCarthy had deliberately lied to the Senate, and to present them all as part of a single whole. The mass of material in hand was sifted until Benton himself settled on ten specific cases supported by hard facts showing where and how McCarthy had deceived the Senate. The ten-count bill of particulars made a twenty-five-thousand-word indictment. While it was being prepared over a two-month period, McCarthy and Benton repeatedly tangled on the floor of the Senate —as they would continue to do for the rest of the Eighty-second Congress. Benton previously had not made a single Senate enemy. He was on reasonably good personal terms even with Welker, Jenner, and Cain. Now he incurred the bitter enmity of McCarthy's Senate friends and opened himself wide to their continuing attacks.

McCarthy himself at once assailed Benton as being "a mental midget," but it was obvious that he was having trouble in getting his hands on any episodes in Benton's private and public life that could be forged into a weapon for attacking him. Driven to inventing evidence in support of his accusations, he charged, for example, that Benton as an assistant secretary of state for public affairs had induced the State Department to buy Encyclopaedia Britannica films for use in the information program. The charge boomeranged when Benton produced proof showing that he had explicitly *prohibited* the employees of the information program from purchasing Britannica films for use in the program and that no such films were subsequently purchased. McCarthy went on to charge that the Britannica Film Company employed Communists who left their mark on the character of the classroom talking pictures the company produced. That charge also backfired when Benton showed that the films McCarthy attacked were scientific films produced by AT&T before Benton had bought the film company. Even so, Benton demanded that his accuser both identify the alleged Communists by name and specify even a single film which showed traces of Communist influence. McCarthy could produce no names and no evidence.

There was one detail of Benton's recent past which McCarthy made much of. It grew out of Benton's advocacy of the Hoover Reorganization Proposal No. 1, which recommended certain changes in the relationship between the Federal Reserve Board, the comptroller of the currency and member banks in the Federal Reserve system.

A mimeographed copy of Benton's remarks in support of the plan had come to the attention of a Salt Lake City banker named Walter Cosgriff, who was a friend of Benton's friend Walter Bimson, the head of the Valley National Bank in Phoenix. Impressed with Benton's arguments, Cosgriff gave Benton $600 from himself and a few more bankers to help meet the costs of having the speech published and distributed. Benton accepted the money, and added $250 of his own to cover the total printing costs. The contributions had not come in a senatorial campaign. The speech was not a campaign document and wasn't even used in Benton's 1950 campaign. In accounting for his 1950 campaign expenses, it had never occurred to him to list the $600 as a "campaign contribution."

Nor did it ever occur to him that the Salt Lake City banker would ever be nominated for a federal office requiring confirmation by the Senate, but so he was. Some time after the 1950 election, he was nominated to the board of directors of the RFC and appeared before a Senate banking and currency subcommittee of which Senator Fulbright was chairman. The banker, at the recommendation of Walter Bimson, apprised Benton beforehand of the prospect, and Benton in turn had spoken frankly to Fulbright on his behalf. "A man," he said, "is coming up before you who was recommended to me by my friend Bimson. I have a special interest in him because he collected money from some of his banker friends in order to help me print and send out my Senate speech in defense of Hoover Reorganization Proposal No. 1. I want you to know of this interest when he comes up before your committee for confirmation." Benton thought no more of the matter.

When the banker came up for confirmation Fulbright asked if he had ever given any money to have a senator's speech published. It was not Fulbright's conscious intention to harm Benton in any way. He may have meant to be playful. The banker admitted that he had given $600 for the purpose indicated. Thus Benton found himself accused by McCarthy of appearing to sponsor a candidate for the RFC post because he was the source of the $600. But that was the most embarrassing item McCarthy could dig up on Benton.

Despite McCarthy's attempts at intimidation, Benton seemed deliberately to enlarge himself as a target for attack by refusing to be silent about a range of sensitive matters. Thus, for example, on 14 September 1951, or one month after he had introduced the resolution to expel McCarthy, he took the Senate floor again to praise Secretary of State Dean Acheson—in defiance of McCarthy and the latter's Senate friends. President Truman had just announced that he was appointing Chester Bowles as the American ambassador to India. Benton, who had worked hard for the appointment, applauded it on the floor of the Senate. Then, in his speech, he went on to connect the work facing Bowles with the achievements of the State Department during the Truman years— including the widely acclaimed Japanese Peace Treaty just concluded.

"I venture to suggest," said Benton to the Senate, "that no group of free nations in the history of mankind faced with such an overwhelming threat to their security ever owed so much to a foreign minister as the free nations of the world owe today to Dean Acheson. His detractors cannot hope to do more than temporarily hide a brilliant leadership seldom achieved by any secretary of state." Benton recalled that at a time when the entire nation still fervently hoped that it might be possible to get along in reasonable harmony with Russia, Acheson "was one of the first responsible men in the Government to discover what getting along with the Russians actually involved. . . . He often stood alone, and without complaint or retort, in the midst of critics who found it expedient to attack him daily—perhaps sometimes as a means of applying balm to their collective conscience, for many of them had hoped for any easy peace, to be established without effort, and they could not stomach their own bitter disillusionment." Yet Acheson's foresight and courage had helped develop the Truman Doctrine, the Marshall Plan, NATO, and led to the strengthening of the United Nations General Assembly to override the consequences of a Soviet veto in the Security Council. Benton then added a climactic note:

> We can say of Mr. Acheson that he has had to take the responsibility for leadership in areas so critical that by their very nature in time of crises and danger, he has aroused the passions of men. My regret is that here in the Senate, his detractors have proved so much more vocal than his defenders. I respectfully suggest that both sides of the aisle are culpable for lack of restraint. I naturally regret that members of my own political party have not stood up more strongly in their defense of Mr. Acheson. This disinclination on their part has in turn generated more and more irresponsible critics. In the field of combat, an army gives heart and courage to the enemy when it flees before his attack, but inspires caution and respect when it holds its ground. It is much the same with criticism and argument over public policy and the men who are charged in the first instance with formulating and executing public policy.

Once again, many senators agreed with Benton privately in his defense of Acheson. Once again, none joined him openly in a personal association with the man who became the fixed target of McCarthy's venom.

In mid-September, Benton, working with John Howe but more importantly with Kenneth M. Birkhead,[2] completed the ten-count indictment of McCarthy, and Benton then read it in an appearance before the Gillette subcommittee. Many of the counts documented instances where McCarthy had perjured himself and had practiced fraud and deceit. None of this, however, carried weight with the Senate. Senators do not expel a fellow senator for lying, even if it can be shown that the lying was deliberate and part of a consistent pattern.

Fortunately, the listed instances of McCarthy's lying included items about his financial irregularities, beginning with the fact that he had accepted $10,000 from the Lustron Corporation, makers of prefabricated housing, to influence housing legislation. Financial irregularity was something the public could grasp, and it was hard for a United States senator accused of it to wriggle his way free if

---

[2]Birkhead, a former aide of Senator Hennings of Missouri, had been assigned to help Benton after the latter demanded assistance from the Democratic National Committee.

hard evidence supported the charge. The mounds of evidence on this point didn't look good for McCarthy. His financial speculation —much of it with funds drawn from financial contributions to his anti-Communist campaign—began to be spread on the public record.

It is worth noting that when McCarthy was eventually censured by the Senate in 1955, it was for his two offenses against the Senate itself: for his contemptuous treatment of the Gillette subcommittee investigating Benton's charges, and for his contemptuous treatment of the Watkins Committee that investigated the question of whether or not he was to be censured for his treatment of the Gillette subcommittee.

Edward Bennett Williams, the lawyer, was later hired by McCarthy to press a lawsuit against Benton. In his book, *One Man's Freedom*, Williams was to contend that his client's contempt of the Gillette subcommittee was accidental. McCarthy, so said Williams, was on a hunting trip when the committee's first telegram inviting him to testify was sent out. However, an invitation to testify had been delivered orally to McCarthy prior to the dispatch of the telegram. Moreover, the hearings, which began on 25 September 1951, extended for over a year during which McCarthy was invited six separate times to testify on his own behalf. He met each invitation with another roar of defiance. He was used to asking questions, said he, not answering them. His refusal to testify was deliberate. Williams also contended that the committee's invitation was merely a request, not a subpoena, and hence was without force. The contention ignored the Senate practice not to subpoena its members and the fact that senators do not ignore requests from Senate committees for testimony. Further, Williams ignored the extent to which McCarthy systematically defamed the Gillette subcommittee and sought to intimidate individual members.

The first to cave in under his intimidating tactics was Senator Margaret Chase Smith, who had earlier drafted the "Declaration of Conscience" which was interpreted as a rebuke to Senator McCarthy after the latter had venomously assailed General George C. Marshall. Benton had hoped that she would be worthy of the acclaim she won for her courage in originating the document, but instead she resigned from the Gillette subcommittee in the late fall of 1951. The reason she gave was that by switching to another subcommittee of the Rules Committee she would be in line for its chairmanship in the event the Republicans gained control of the Senate in 1952. Yet as Senator Hayden explained to Benton, this was a "pigeon hole" subcommittee which never met and was of no consequence to the work of the Senate. Benton felt that Mrs. Smith may have buckled under the fierce pressure generated on McCarthy's behalf by Senator Taft, who worked on her through Republican Owen Brewster, Maine's senior senator, to persuade her to give up her seat on the all-important Gillette subcommittee.

Benton at first failed to grasp how the investigation might be so adversely affected by Mrs. Smith's resignation. He soon found out when her place on subcommittee was taken by Herman Welker of Idaho, McCarthy's closest Senate ideological crony. The new arrangement showed the hand of Senator Taft; Welker had a virtual mandate from the Taftites to block the subcommittee's operations and derail them if possible. He pursued the assignment with such zeal that in the year following his appointment, the subcommittee seemed to be immobile. "It was," said Benton at the time, "like changing the jury half way through a trial." It was worse. The counsel for the defense took a seat on the jury.

Mrs. Smith was not the only member who resigned from the Gillette subcommittee. On a day when McCarthy and Benton were tangling with each other on the floor of the Senate, Gillette came up to Benton for a private word. "McCarthy has just threatened me," he said pathetically. "He says that if I continue to press the investigation of your charges, he's going into Iowa and campaign against me and defeat me." Gillette, facing a reelection contest two years later, did in fact resign from his own subcommittee in the fall of 1952.

The atmosphere during the investigation of Benton's charges against McCarthy can be grasped from a remark made to Benton by Senator Monroney, the one member of the Gillette subcommittee who never wavered. He asked Benton whether he assumed that every night when he left his office his mail would be read and his files searched and photographed. Did he assume at all times that his telephone would be tapped? Benton expressed astonishment, and Monroney answered unemotionally: "Bill, I assume this is true in my case as a member of the Gillette Committee. I therefore think you would be wise to assume that it is all the more true in your case —since you are McCarthy's chief target."

Benton put private telephones into his suites in the Shoreham

Hotel in Washington and the Savoy Plaza in New York so that calls would not have to go through the switchboard. He also warned his chauffeur, a former prizefighter, to be on the watch for people following him. The precautions, however, were no proof against a deluge of scurrilous mail that descended on Benton's office. Nor were they proof against the fact that some of the mail addressed to him was opened by unseen hands before being delivered.

Perhaps the key line of defense which Edward Bennett Williams advanced to explain away McCarthy's contempt of the Gillette subcommittee was that McCarthy's hostility was justified because the committee staff had ordered a "mail cover" on his correspondence. Under a mail cover, the Post Office furnishes a list of return addresses of mail sent to an individual but does not open letters. When the Senate eventually voted to censure McCarthy, it knew from McCarthy himself that such a mail cover had been ordered. It also knew, as Senator Carl Hayden, chairman of the Rules Committee, told the Senate, that mail covers were a customary investigative technique, made all the more necessary by McCarthy's refusal to testify.

In the fall of 1951, while the foregoing events were running their course, Benton was chosen to represent the United States Senate at a meeting of the Council of Europe in Strasbourg. He had another piece of business in mind which warranted the trip. General Dwight D. Eisenhower had by now left the presidency of Columbia University to assume command of the newly formed NATO headquarters outside Paris, and there was a rising tide of speculation in the United States about the prospect that he might be persuaded to seek the Republican presidential nomination. The earlier Eisenhower-Benton talks about "how to make Paul Hoffman president of the United States" had remained a private matter between the two men and was finally lost in the shifting sands of later events. Now, however, en route to Strasbourg, Benton stopped off at the NATO headquarters for a two-hour conversation with the general and to press on him the view that he should consider making a bid for the presidency in 1952, not as a Republican but as a Democratic candidate.

Like other Democrats facing election contests in 1952, Benton had a natural and respectable interest in having the strongest possible contender for the presidency to head the party ticket. Like other Democrats also, he saw in General Eisenhower precisely that kind of contender. But if Benton was not lacking in a motive of self-interest, there was solid and objective merit in the nature of the argument he advanced when he saw General Eisenhower at the NATO headquarters. If the general sought the presidency in 1952 as a Democratic candidate, Benton said, the whole of the Democratic side of the Senate except for Pat McCarran would support him. The Democratic party itself was the party that shared Eisenhower's views on foreign policy, just as the general was in accord with *its* views. As a Democratic candidate for the presidency, and then as president, he would be indebted to no one. On the other hand, if he sought and won the Republican nomination, he would find himself the candidate of a divided party, a large part of which was out of sympathy with the general's aims in foreign policy. He would be confronted by an embittered Senator Robert Taft and the Taft forces who wanted the Republican presidential nomination for themselves; and the general, in the act of winning the Republican nomination over their opposition, would be indebted to a great many people whom he would have to pay off as president.

"When I finished my main line of argument," Benton recalled, "the general got a golf club as he was in the habit of doing when he needed relief from tension. Between shots on the carpet at NATO headquarters, he finally said: 'But how could I explain it to my friends? How can I explain to them that I am prepared to run as a Democrat?' " The friends he had in mind were Tom Watson of IBM and other trustees of Columbia University who were trying to build Eisenhower up as a prospective Republican candidate.

None of these, however, would prove as important to the outcome as another friend of Eisenhower—and of Benton. This was Paul Hoffman, who had been Eisenhower's own first choice for president.

Hoffman, a registered Republican, had promised Benton in 1948 that he would not support Taft if the Republicans nominated him for the presidency. The nomination of Governor Thomas E. Dewey, instead, had spared him the need to make a painful, wrenching break with his past Republican loyalties. As the 1952 nominating contest drew ever closer, and as the Taft forces were once more gathering strength, Hoffman again assured Benton that he would not support Taft. Yet once again he was reluctant to undergo the pain of a break with his Republican friends, and he saw in a Republican nomination of General Eisenhower a saving way out of the need to make the break. This was altogether apart from his personal respect for Eisenhower's capacities, and apart from his conviction that the general seemed to be the only man in sight who could bring harmony to a deeply divided nation. Accordingly, in 1951, Hoffman had twice made trips from America to Europe for the sole purpose of trying to persuade Eisenhower to accept the Republican nomination. And, with an opposite object in mind, Benton in the fall of 1951 twice flew to Palm Springs for the sole purpose of trying to persuade Hoffman to persuade Eisenhower that he should seek the Democratic presidential nomination instead. Hoffman, however, clung to his party loyalty, with a result that General Eisenhower later publicly acknowledged. He said it was Paul Hoffman, more than any other person, who "talked him into" making a bid for the Republican presidential nomination. There was to be a further result, and a deeply ironical one. Hoffman's work in securing that nomination for Eisenhower was to lead directly to the 1952 senatorial defeat of Hoffman's old friend and collaborator, Bill Benton.

But this was in the future.

In the Senate in the spring of 1952, McCarthy's continual derision of the Gillette subcommittee prompted Senator Mike Monroney to introduce a resolution calling for a Senate vote of confidence in the subcommittee. In a matter of this kind, the Senate could not withhold support from its own instrumentality. It voted confidence 76 to 0. When McCarthy saw how the vote would come out, he introduced a resolution calling on the subcommittee to enlarge the scope of its work by investigating Benton, his accuser. In the name of a fictitious even-handed justice, the resolution was approved, and Benton became a defendant.

There was yet another twist to the story. In April 1952, McCarthy appeared on one of Edward R. Murrow's television shows to charge that Benton in his accusations was hiding behind the Senate's constitutional immunity against libel. The next day, Benton rose in the Senate to waive his immunity, thus boldly challenging McCarthy to sue for libel. If McCarthy failed to do so, his charges on the Murrow program would fall flat. Benton then appeared on the Murrow program to announce anew that he had waived his immunity and again invited McCarthy to sue. Such a suit would permit a review in a court of law of the whole of McCarthy's record—a review governed by judicial procedures that would prevent McCarthy from resorting to the obfuscations he was free to practice in Congress. McCarthy did sue—for $2,000,000—and thus Benton's strategy succeeded, with consequences to be described later.

The long and arduous battle against McCarthy cut into but did not divert Benton's attention from his regular work as a senator—and as a candidate for reelection in 1952. In the fall of 1951, for example, the Federal Communications Commission was getting ready to unfreeze nearly two thousand television channels for allocation. To Benton this meant that the "entire future of television—the most extraordinary communication instrument ever devised—was about to be crystallized, and possibly irrevocably crystallized, for generations to come." If so, he wanted the future development of television to be—in the language of the Federal Communications Act—an instrument for "the public interest, convenience and necessity." On 20 October, he introduced a bill that harked back to the Luce Commission on a Free and Responsible Press. Under the bill, the Congress would create and the president appoint a citizens' advisory board on radio-television, which, like the Council of Economic Advisers, would issue annual advisory reports to the Congress, the FCC, the industry, and the public. It would review the year's progress—or lack of progress—in the public service rendered by radio and television and suggest how such public service could best be developed. Like the Council of Economic Advisers, the board in its own sphere would have no other power than the respect its personnel and their findings could command.

Senators John Bricker of Ohio, Leverett Saltonstall of Massachusetts, and Lester Hunt of Wyoming joined Benton as cosponsors. Bricker seemed a strange recruit. He was a dyed-in-the-wool conservative whose Ohio law firm represented large corporate interests, and he was the ranking Republican on the Senate Interstate Commerce Committee, which was responsible for radio and television. "I didn't have to argue with him about it," Benton later recalled. "He signed up at once and never wavered. Perhaps the reason was that he was a trustee of Ohio State University—which owned a radio station. Bricker believed in educational radio. He was tired of seeing it pushed around by the industry. As for Saltonstall's interest, it grew out of the fact that perhaps the most distinguished educational radio station in the country was in Boston, the Lowell station, and he had a genuine and deep interest in the problems of educational broadcasting."

Three days of hearings on the proposal were held in early 1952 before a subcommittee of the Interstate and Foreign Commerce Committee under the chairmanship of the new majority leader, Senator Ernest McFarland of Arizona. A parade of witnesses enthusiastically praised the proposal. Then McFarland adjourned the hearings. Benton tried repeatedly to get him to resume them, but McFarland stalled. In the meantime, the opponents of the resolution mustered their forces and began a counterattack through the organ of the radio-television industry, *Broadcasting Magazine*. The attack became a vicious assault on Benton personally.

Benton alluded to it in a letter to Hutchins. Hutchins, who was about to launch the Fund for the Republic, apparently wanted Benton to make a Senate floor fight in a matter of interest to the Authors League of America. Benton "with great reluctance," begged off, saying:

> I can't take on everything. Seemingly, I've even made a great blunder in taking on television. The good causes which need champions are everywhere, and there is thus a great and urgent need for your Fund for the Republic. I earnestly hope it won't be long before you get going. With the kind of leadership you hope to provide, I and others can move in with major assistance. But what has happened to me on the television fight is a lesson I shall remember—showing me that I can't tackle too many projects, particularly short-term projects, and most certainly in an election year.

The Benton proposal for a citizens' advisory board on radio-television was thus aborted. No source of national influence offset the highly organized pressures commercial interests brought to bear on television, the FCC, and the Congress—pressures that would convert commercial television largely into an instrument for escapist entertainment. Despite his setback in Congress and the discouragement marking his letter to Hutchins, Benton has not to this day abandoned his idea for a citizens' advisory board. He felt that if he had been reelected in 1952 he could have succeeded in getting action by the Congress. McFarland, also defeated in 1952 (by Barry Goldwater), became a legal counsel for RCA, and is today one of the two major owners of a highly profitable television station in Phoenix.

Despite his letter to Hutchins, Benton did not run away from "controversial subjects" as the 1952 elections drew ever closer. There was, for example, his stand in the spring of 1952 on the long-talked-about and long-postponed Saint Lawrence seaway project. The New York, New Haven and Hartford Railroad, a major political force in Connecticut, strongly opposed the seaway, as did many other Atlantic seaboard transport interests, fearing loss of revenue if oceangoing liners and freighters could reach Great Lakes ports directly. This view was backed by the Connecticut Manufacturers Association with an elaborate memorandum opposing the seaway project.

Benton saw that much careful thought had gone into these presentations. But he also saw that a simple truth about Connecticut itself had been obscured by railroad and Manufacturers Association officials. With a farm population of only 3 percent, Connecticut was the most highly industrialized area in the world. Bridgeport, for example, was more industrialized than Birmingham or Manchester in England. Waterbury was "the brass capital of the world," and New Britain its "hardware capital." Benton called these facts to the attention of the opponents of the Saint Lawrence seaway, and told them that he would fight for the project in the Senate. What was good for the country, said he, was good for Connecticut, since Connecticut lived by its exports—not only to markets overseas, but in Wisconsin, Illinois, and Minnesota. What was good for these states bordering on the Great Lakes was good for the exporters of Connecticut. He took that stand in the Senate in his advocacy of the Saint Lawrence seaway project, though the project was again blocked on the ground that it was "just a Socialist ditch." It would be finally approved in the first years of the Eisenhower administration.

In 1951–52, Benton also came to grips with the connecting links between the power of radio and television as media for reaching voters, the high cost of access to the media, and the effects this had on candidates, and ultimately on American democracy. Speaking in the Senate, he said there was a double danger to American democracy because of the high costs of "buying time on the airwaves" for electioneering purposes. It would discourage men of great talent but little wealth from seeking major public offices—which could often go almost by default to wealthy candidates, regardless of political talent. Alternatively, candidates with meager financial means would suffer because they would be forced to spend more time on

Above, Benton and his wife beside the helicopter from which he campaigned for his Senate seat in 1950.
Below, Benton, *right,* talks serious politics with Democratic National (and Connecticut State) Chairman John M. Bailey at the 1960 Los Angeles convention.

Benton and Adlai Stevenson on their 1960 tour of Latin America. (Photograph by John Fell Stevenson.)

Democratic dignitaries at the 1950 Connecticut Democratic convention. *From left:* Senator Benton, Mrs. Eleanor Roosevelt, Senator Brien McMahon, and Governor Chester Bowles.

President Truman signs the Fulbright Act in 1946, as Senator Fulbright, *center*, and Assistant Secretary of State Benton beam.

General Eisenhower supports Assistant Secretary of State Benton in testimony before the House Foreign Affairs Committee in May 1947. In left foreground is Congressman (now Senator) Karl Mundt.

Benton and UNESCO Director General René Maheu visit with President Kennedy shortly before his assassination.

Benton and President Johnson in 1967

A happy moment at the University of Chicago dinner in 1968 when Benton received the first William Benton Medal for Distinguished Service. *From left:* Benton, President George W. Beadle of the University of Chicago, and Vice-President of the United States Hubert H. Humphrey.

"raising money than issues"; then, if elected, they would be forced to "vote their overdue obligations instead of their inner consciences." How was this double danger to be avoided? Benton's proposed solution was for the federal government itself "to finance a limited amount of free well-spotted radio and television time during campaigns for federal office"—as Great Britain did, or as an extension of Theodore Roosevelt's original advocacy of federal financial support for political campaigns. Though his proposal got nowhere, it was to be revived by Benton again and again, as well as by other men.[3]

One more matter is worth setting down here. On 25 February 1952, Senator Pat McCarran and Representative Francis E. Walter jointly introduced into the Congress a sweeping and complex bill changing existing laws on immigration and naturalization. The earlier versions of the bill—one of which Benton had reluctantly supported with a clothespin on his nose—had been stymied. The new version was deeply imprinted by the hysteria and hatreds that had been running through American life since 1950.

On the assumption that large categories of immigrants were potential subversives, or were bent on mongrelizing the United States, the bill set maximum permissible immigration at 154,000 annually. Moreover, since the distribution was to be according to a "national origins" quota system based on the 1890 census—predating the high influx of immigrants from Italy and eastern European countries—the bill discriminated against them in favor of immigrants from northern Europe. At the same time, it established some seven hundred separate grounds to deny a visa or entry papers and gave American consuls broad powers to refuse applicants for a visa. A similar potential for arbitrary administrative judgment was present in the provisions of the act dealing with the deportation of undesirable aliens or the revocation of citizenship.

Senators Lehman and Humphrey led the counterattack on the McCarran-Walter bill. Benton enlisted on their side, as did Senators Pastore of Rhode Island, Douglas of Illinois, and McMahon of Connecticut. These six tried to win Senate support for a substitute measure of their own. Known as the Lehman-Humphrey bill,

---

[3]After the 1968 elections, Benton, in one of several pungent footnotes to a CED document on financing federal elections, angered some of his colleagues by noting tartly that the Republican candidate knew far in advance that he would have ample money even for last-minute television costs, while the Democrat, Benton's friend Humphrey, knew he would not.

it provided that the number of immigrants to be admitted annually would be set at one-sixth of 1 percent of the population of the United States in the latest decennial census; the national origins quota system would be displaced by a more rational and humane basis for granting visas; and where the McCarran-Walter bill allowed no review of arbitrary administration action in visa and deportation cases, the Lehman-Humphrey bill made the Board of Immigration Appeals a strong statutory body and called for a visa review in the State Department as well.

McCarran, as chairman of the Senate Judiciary Committee, never allowed hearings on the Lehman-Humphrey bill. He cut short any Senate debate on his own measure and he led the forces which, on 21 May, beat back an attempt by Lehman, Humphrey, and Benton to substitute the Lehman-Humphrey bill. By a voice vote a few days later, the McCarran bill was adopted, with a few minor amendments Humphrey had managed to engineer after a floor fight with McCarran. After President Truman, as expected, vetoed the bill in strong language, a quick count showed that two extra votes were needed to sustain the veto. But front-page newspaper stories reported that the State Department favored the McCarran-Walter Act, and this fact was cited by McCarran when he demanded that the Senate override the veto.

The sequel, as Benton told it, was this:

> Because of my background in the State Department, and because I had been a defender of Dean Acheson in the Senate, Lehman, Humphrey, and I jointly felt that I was the logical person to call on him to protest the use by McCarran of the claim that the State Department favored his measure. At the State Department, Acheson brought in two or three staff members who dealt with legislation. The discussion was uncomfortable, and one of the three finally said to me: "You forget, Senator Benton, that McCarran is also the chairman of the Senate Appropriations Subcommittee that handles the State Department's appropriation." I was appalled. I asked Acheson a point blank question. Did he have to make a deal with McCarran in order to get through his appropriations for the State Department? Did he have to sell out those of us on the Hill who were trying to defeat the McCarran-Walter bill? Acheson and his men indicated that they felt they had no choice.

Acheson's dilemma was not a pleasant one. Much less pleasant was the consequence of the choice the department apparently felt compelled to make. The Senate immediately overrode Truman's veto and the McCarran-Walter Act went on the statute books. To Benton, it was a personal affront against everything he thought America was meant to represent. But he and Lehman would later organize and finance a private committee to work for a liberal and humane immigration bill. Benton served as an officer of the committee and, in 1965, the Congress approved a new measure including many features resembling the Lehman-Humphrey bill of 1952.

24

On a Half-Note of Triumph

The 1952 Democratic state convention in Connecticut, held on the eve of the presidential nominating conventions, differed in several respects from former state conventions. Recent changes in the law had changed the term of state offices from two years to four, and for the first time there were no state officers to nominate. The only piece of business was the nomination of a United States senator and a congressman-at-large. This time, in contrast to 1950, Benton was nominated by acclamation. And hanging over the convention was the pall of Senator Brien McMahon's illness. The only real lift for the delegates was provided by Senator Hubert Humphrey, who came to the convention at Benton's urgent request.

Humphrey originally was a suspect figure in the eyes of the right-wing Irish Catholic leaders who were the Democratic town chairmen in many Connecticut towns. They knew he was a founding father of Americans for Democratic Action, and that was enough to make him a "pinko." They knew nothing whatever about the way the ADA served as a vehicle for dissident liberal intellectuals in the Republican and Democratic parties alike in their two-front struggle against inert conservatism on the one side and, on the other, Stalinist-oriented American Communists and fellow travelers. Nor did they know anything about Humphrey's personal role in liquidating the bridgeheads the Communists had driven into the Democratic–Farmer Labor party in Minneapolis. It was enough to dismiss Humphrey as a "pinko" and let it go at that. But that was not enough for Benton. He had repeatedly brought Humphrey into the state when it was politically risky to do so. And Humphrey, on his part, had the effect on the Irish leaders that he had on the southerners in the Senate. With nothing going in his favor except his amazing talent and decency of character, he slowly dissolved their animus and won their respect. At the 1952 Democratic convention in Connecticut, he also won their cheers when, in the course of the fifty-eight-minute speech, he brought the delegates to their feet eleven times.

At the Republican state convention, meanwhile, Prescott Bush hoped to be renominated as the party's senatorial candidate. But he suffered from his loss to the newcomer, Benton, in 1950, and was easily defeated by William Purtell, the president of the Connecticut Manufacturers Association—a post which the Connecticut Light and Power Company and other large firms in control of the association often give to ambitious small businessmen to fill for a year or two. The Republican party managers felt that Purtell, as an Irish Catholic and former Democrat and as an intimate friend of Tom Dodd and other Irish Democratic leaders, could draw strength from the normally Democratic Irish who might be disaffected by Benton's fight against McCarthy. Later in the summer, after the death of Brien McMahon, the Democrats and Republicans were both compelled to hold another state convention to nominate their party candidates for his Senate seat. The Republicans turned to the previously discarded Prescott Bush and gave him the nomination. The Democrats nominated Abraham Ribicoff, then congressman from Hartford.

And on the national scene?

Despite the early reluctance of Dwight D. Eisenhower to take the nomination, and after all the frenetic efforts of Senator Robert A. Taft to get it, the first ballot of the 1952 Republican National Convention made General Eisenhower the party's presidential candidate.

Paul Hoffman, having played a major role in persuading Eisenhower to bid for the nomination and in raising money for that cause, was at the heart of the strategy that led to its triumph. He had secured Henry Ford's consent to a three-month leave from the Ford Foundation to work for Eisenhower. At the convention he publicized if not invented the phrase "the Louisiana purchase" to describe the Taft forces' acquisition of southern delegates. The jibe pushed them into a fatal corner. Yet Eisenhower's eventual victory turned to ashes for Hoffman. He had never made an enemy in his life. Now at sixty he was surrounded by them, with Senator Taft in their lead. Reportedly, when Senator Taft and General Eisenhower had their Morningside Heights meeting after the Republican convention, one of the senator's conditions for supporting the general was that Hoffman be excluded from an Eisenhower cabinet.

What Taft began, his friends continued, and they pressed their vendetta against Hoffman beyond politics. They could not stop his return to the Ford Foundation, but they attacked him in ways that eventually made his position untenable. When he resigned from the foundation, Hutchins's position also became intolerable, and he left to head the Fund for the Republic which the Ford Foundation had created and which Hutchins later called "a wholly disowned subsidiary."

On the Democratic side of the 1952 presidential picture, Governor Adlai Stevenson of Illinois had been spoken of by Democratic leaders as a possible nominee, particularly after President Truman declared that he would not be a candidate and made clear that his first choice for the nomination was Stevenson. But throughout the spring of 1952, Stevenson insisted that he was not interested, that he enjoyed his work as governor, and that he meant to seek reelection to the post.

Benton, who had been in close touch with Stevenson during this period, often heard him talk in that vein. In fact, the last time he heard Stevenson say flatly that he neither would seek the presidential nomination nor wanted it was on the morning the Democratic convention opened in Chicago. After Governor Stevenson's impressive welcoming speech to the delegates, Benton rode back with him to the Loop and again listened to Stevenson insist that he meant to run for reelection as governor of Illinois because he had no interest in anything else. The delegates saw the case differently. Amid southern opposition to Senator Kefauver and northern resistance to Georgia's Senator Richard Russell and labor's coolness to Vice-President Alben Barkley, Stevenson emerged as the one man on whom all party factions could unite. He was drafted for and accepted the presidential nomination.

Benton's own campaign for the Senate began when he made two speeches at the Democratic convention in Chicago. Recalling the first, he said:

> In the late spring of 1952, Brien McMahon asked me to nominate him for the presidency at the national convention. I agreed to do this, partly because I had to take Adlai at his

word that he was not interested in the nomination. More importantly, Brien himself never seriously thought about becoming America's first Catholic president, nor did he think that a man from Connecticut could be nominated for the presidency. He never envisaged pulling all New England delegates together in a bloc, as was later done successfully by Jack Kennedy. Brien was after the vice-presidency—in '52, '56, or thereafter. He said to me laughingly: "A guy can't run for the vice-presidency. I've got to be nominated for president." He thought that the next progressive step of the Democratic party with respect to the so-called "Catholic issue" would be the nomination of a Catholic for vice-president. [His political intuition in the matter was confirmed just four years after his death when John Kennedy, supported by John Bailey and Abraham Ribicoff, missed the vice-presidential nomination by not too great a margin.]

In 1952, about a month before the Democratic National Convention, I discovered for the first time that Brien was dying, but he did not know this about himself. I decided to go ahead and nominate him anyway at convention time. How could I tell him that I wouldn't? I owed it to him. I arranged for a direct telephone wire to run from the speaker's platform at the Chicago convention to McMahon's sick bed in Washington. At the end of my speech putting his name in nomination, in a sudden switch-about I withdrew his name and explained to the delegates that McMahon was too ill to accept the nomination. A heart-felt tribute was paid to him by the delegates. I rushed to the direct wire on the speaker's platform in order to tell him about it. His nurse who answered the phone at the Washington end said to me: "He's in a coma. We had the TV set here tuned in but he didn't see you or hear you, not a word of it." Then the nurse interrupted herself: "Wait a minute, here he is wanting the telephone." Suddenly I heard his voice. I told him what happened. "Brien!" I said, "you got a terrific ovation. I've never seen anything like it. It was sensational. They clapped and clapped for minutes." Brien replied: "They did? They did? Whe-e-e-e." I heard the phone drop from his hands to the floor. These were his last words. What a death for a professional politician!

The second speech Benton made at the convention was devoted "to the issues." His spot on the program was arranged by President Truman, Sam Rayburn, Les Biffle, and other party leaders who thought the big television coverage in Connecticut would help Benton in his Connecticut campaign. All wanted him to win his Senate contest. In addition to his speech nominating McMahon, they gave him more than a fair share of exposure to national television. He was no longer an "outsider" in the Democratic party as he had been in 1949 when he was appointed to the Senate.

The issues of "Korea, corruption, and communism" had been raised by Prescott Bush against Benton in 1950. By the time of the 1952 campaign, these terms were so much a part of public talk that even a dull student in political chemistry knew what Republicans meant when they compressed the three issues into the formula $K_1 C_2$. Meanwhile, the Benton versus McCarthy issue had grown so sharp that most people in Connecticut had a reflex reaction when they heard Benton's name. It was not, as in 1950, "Oh yes, he's the fellow who's hustling for votes in a helicopter." In 1952 it was, "Oh yes, he's the fellow who's against McCarthy." Since many of Connecticut's voters were Irish and around 50 percent Catholic, the association worried Benton's camp, and all the more so when General Eisenhower not only failed to repudiate McCarthy but increasingly implied that the Truman administration was soft toward Communists in government.

McCarthy himself had not yet brought his libel suit against Benton to trial, nor would he ever do so. But during the 1952 campaign he twice came to Connecticut to assail Benton before crowds markedly larger than those he drew in 1950. This time the Republicans organized his meetings and lined up behind him. In Benton's own home town, for example, a Republican group raised $15,000 to bring McCarthy into the state. They organized bus caravans to fill Bridgeport's largest hall with a pro-McCarthy crowd, where McCarthy was invested with respectability when Prescott Bush sat on the platform with him. The process was repeated at Waterbury, which is heavily Irish.

Benton did not view any of this in a lighthearted way. But from the tumultuous reception he got in Waterbury, where he appeared right after the McCarthy visit—and from other signs of support from people who had previously shown little interest in his candidacy—Benton felt there was an element of illusion in the shadow of punitive power McCarthy cast before him. It was a view shared by Connecticut's Democratic state chairman, John Bailey. He said at the time that he didn't believe the net effect of the McCarthy issue would make a difference of more than five thousand votes in Connecticut—or maybe as little as three thousand—and he was not at all sure in which direction the net would fall. He expected many Irish votes to turn against Benton because of McCarthy. But Bailey noted that the other 50 percent of the voters in the state were Protestants, or small towners, who "greatly admired Benton for his stand." In any case, Bailey never once urged Benton to trim his sails on the McCarthy issue, but rather proposed that leading Protestant ministers in Connecticut send letters around the state pointing out Benton's great service to the nation in making known the grounds on which McCarthy should be expelled from the Senate.

On 1 October, as Benton's campaign was picking up momentum, he lost the invaluable services of his long-time aide, John Howe, who suffered a heart attack. Penn Kimball, a former Benton aide then working for the *New York Times*, took a leave of absence to fill the gaping hole on Benton's campaign staff.

Many of the things Benton did in 1950 were repeated in 1952, but the helicopter had lost its charm. On television, the best idea Benton had was to use Helen extensively. Otherwise, he later regretted what he called "the daring and even reckless" new ways he expanded on his 1950 ideas about television. Some of his 1952 programs were imaginative and packed a punch, but others offended people whose votes he might otherwise have received. One positive gain was that he learned a profound lesson about television which many professional politicians understood instinctively.

Benton's background in advertising had taught him to view television as a means of attracting an audience and selling a product. His radio efforts at the University of Chicago were concentrated on attracting audiences for programs of intellectual content. But he was slow to realize that the politician must use radio and television not only to attract an audience but in such a way as to offend no part of his audience. One offended person won't hurt much if you're advertising Lucky Strike cigarettes if two people are impressed and go out and buy a package. One offended person in a political broadcast can do you more harm than several voters you win. He can send money to your opponent. He can talk against you. He can take people to the polls to vote against you.

Benton learned these facts the hard way. There were highly placed Democrats in the state who thought he wasn't any good at television, and their views were echoed by people who told them that Benton put on "a lousy show." By contrast, Ribicoff reportedly spent all day perfecting a five-minute broadcast, doing it over and over on film until he had a polished product that offended nobody. Ribicoff's five-minute spot cost two-thirds of a half-hour program, but Benton couldn't resist the bargain of half-hour shows—six times the exposure for 50 percent more money. Ribicoff was better advised than Benton with his freewheeling and sometimes spontaneous programs, though it didn't do Ribicoff much good in the 1952 campaign, since he too went down to defeat.

Four days before the election, Benton received a note from his secretary: "Archibald MacLeish called Senator Benton. They are trying to get Rep. John F. Kennedy of Massachusetts to go on the air attacking McCarthy. They want material on McCarthy. They would also like someone to go up there and help prepare the broadcast." Benton's follow-up instructions went to an assistant: "Senator Benton wants you to call Professor Jerome Wiesner of MIT. Send him Senator Benton's 30,000 words of testimony indicting McCarthy. Tell him to buy Anderson's book [Jack Anderson and Ronald W. May, *McCarthy: The Man, the Senator, the Ism*]. Send him Truman's speech in Bridgeport calling attention to the fact that Ray Baldwin was the first man McCarthy maligned." The speech by "Kennedy of Massachusetts" never materialized, nor was Benton critical of him on that account. "If I were in his place," he subsequently said, "I doubt if I would have made it. At any rate, it was at the last minute, and would have come too late to affect anybody."

On election day, Purtell defeated Benton by 88,000 votes, while Stevenson lost Connecticut by 129,000. Benton was one of eleven— out of thirty-five—Democratic senatorial candidates in 1952 who ran ahead of Stevenson in their own states. And he ran well ahead in a state with a voting machine lever where it was difficult to run ahead of the ticket. The only such machine of its kind in the country, it required the voter first to pull the lever for the ticket (Eisenhower or Stevenson). Then if he wanted to "cut," he had to push two little buttons, one down against the candidate he was cutting and one up for the candidate on the other party he was favoring.

The margin of 41,000 votes by which Benton ran ahead of

Stevenson in Connecticut was subsequently analyzed in detail by politicians and academics, largely to get at the actual impact the "McCarthy issue" had on Benton's fate in his 1952 Senate race. There are statistical studies showing that because of the McCarthy issue, Benton actually gained an extra 5 percent in the total vote cast. Other studies point out that, in addition to Purtell, there were two other candidates for the Senate seat Benton held. The other two—Jasper McLevy and Vivien Kellems—drew a combined 30,000 votes—which might otherwise have been split between Benton and Purtell. If so, the increment going to Benton would have meant that he would have run ahead of Stevenson by 56,000 votes, making it all the more clear that Benton was defeated in his Senate race by the Eisenhower landslide and not by McCarthy's vengeance. Indeed, Windham County in Connecticut, the most Catholic in the state, was the county where Benton made his best run, while Eisenhower made the best run of any presidential candidate in the state's history up to that time. Finally, considering that McCarthy himself in his own 1952 Senate race in Wisconsin was by far the lowest man in the count of votes for the Republican state ticket—his statewide majority was 139,000 while the Eisenhower majority was 357,000—McCarthy appeared to have been reelected primarily through the hauling power of Eisenhower's Republican presidential candidacy.

On election night, when Benton knew he had been defeated for reelection to the Senate, he at once told Helen that he would take the family to Europe for fifteen months so that the children could learn French. (This would begin in June 1953, and for fifteen months Benton would commute between Europe and the United States.) But on election night, he had something else on his mind besides his personal future. Though he was now a "lame duck" senator, he felt he must quickly return to Washington. He must make a last effort before the Eighty-second Congress passed into history to get the Gillette subcommittee report issued.

In Washington a few days later, Benton ran into complications. Senator Mike Monroney, the stalwart of the subcommittee who had steadfastly refused to be cowed by McCarthy's fulminations, was not available. He was traveling in Europe. Senator Herman Welker, who had constantly obstructed the subcommittee's work, felt he had completed his mission and had resigned. So had Gillette, the sub-committee chairman. Thus of the original members, only Senator Thomas Hennings, the Missouri Democrat, and Senator Robert

Hendrickson, the New Jersey Republican, were still in a position to be "active." In the circumstances, Benton turned to the man who had advised him on his first day as a senator, "You can always explain a vote, but you can never explain a speech." This was Carl Hayden of Arizona, chairman of the Committee on Rules and Administration. It was Benton's turn to give some advice. He urged, and finally convinced, Hayden to substitute himself for Gillette. What had thus begun as the Gillette subcommittee now became the Hayden subcommittee—dubbed the "3-H Club" after its members, Hayden, Hennings, and Hendrickson.

The key member, obviously, was Hendrickson, the Republican, since an anti-McCarthy resolution could mean little without his support. Hendrickson was a decent and kindly soul. But there were doubts about the position he would take when a Republican administration was coming to power and when the Senate Republican leadership seemed clearly opposed to his signing a majority report. Nor did McCarthy himself miss the key to the affair. He had vilified Hendrickson's family, and by personal telephone calls threatened him directly with swift vengeance if he signed any report that was critical.

Benton faced another complication in Washington. Senator Hennings had vanished from sight, and all attempts to locate him in the city led to dead ends. Hennings was an able constitutional lawyer, a valiant champion of civil rights and civil liberties, and a bridge between northerners and southerners in the Senate. He might have been a prospective presidential candidate if it were not for his tragic addiction to alcohol. The fact was known in Washington but, under one of the more humane rules of place, was never bruited about.

Benton guessed that Hennings was on a bender and that he could probably be found in New York. So he flew back to that city and presently located Hennings—who was unresponsive to any ordinary plea. Benton refused to be put off. He knew that Drew Pearson was an intimate friend of Hennings and, because of Pearson's own clashes with McCarthy, had a great stake in getting out a subcommittee report on Benton's charges against the Wisconsin senator. Benton relayed Hennings's whereabouts and condition to Pearson, adding that there would be no anti-McCarthy report if Hennings did not sign it and that Pearson was probably the only man who could get Hennings back to Washington.

Pearson lost little time in coming to New York, took Hennings under his care, and sobered him up for the return trip to the capital. In Washington, Pearson also brought Hendrickson together with Hennings for a meeting where it was argued whether there would be a unanimous "3-H Club" report, or a two-to-one split along party lines. Hendrickson finally agreed to sign the report if some criticism could be made of Benton in the parallel investigation the subcommittee had conducted under McCarthy's anti-Benton charges. There was only the fact that Benton in 1950 had accepted the $600 from the Salt Lake City banker. Hendrickson wanted the report to say that the distribution of the printed speech helped Benton's 1950 election campaign and that its costs should have been included in his account of campaign expenditures. Benton was, therefore, allegedly at fault for failing so to list the $600, especially since it came from a banker who was later nominated for a post requiring Senate confirmation.

It was a murky point, but Hendrickson refused to sign the report unless it was included. Carl Hayden informed Benton of Hendrickson's price for signing and asked if he wanted the report issued on those terms. The answer was a categorical yes. "You can say anything about me you want to," Benton told Hayden. "Pick anything concerning me that came out of any hearings and make use of it. The important thing is to get a unanimous report signed, published, and submitted to the Senate before the new Congress convenes."

Thus the $600 episode was cited in criticism of Benton. Also thus, Hendrickson's signature produced a unanimous anti-McCarthy report, issued on 2 January 1953—one day before the Eighty-second Congress expired. One day later would have meant a stillbirth. The report took the form of six questions, many based on Benton's resolution of 8 August 1951. In response to each, the subcommittee unearthed and gave coherence to massive evidence which left no doubt of McCarthy's shabby conduct. McCarthy afterward lashed out at Hendrickson. "Suffice it to say," he told the press, "that he [Hendrickson] is a living miracle in that he is without question the only man who has lived so long with neither brains nor guts."

Despite the "3-H" report before it, Senate courage collapsed when the new session opened. Control was now in Republican hands, and Senator William Jenner of Indiana, a McCarthy ally, inherited the chairmanship of the Rules Committee. Overnight, every available copy of the report disappeared. Almost the entire subcommittee staff was fired, and the report was never brought before the full Rules Committee for action. McCarthy himself, meanwhile, entered the Senate unchallenged. If a single senator on opening day had challenged his right to serve in the chamber despite his reelection, McCarthy could have been denied his seat by a straight majority vote. Once seated, he could be removed only by a two-thirds vote. At least a dozen senators individually admitted to Drew Pearson: "He's got to be challenged, but I'm not the right man for it." There was silence at the crucial moment when McCarthy walked to his seat. No one challenged him. Silence ratified his right to be in the Senate. He was now in a position to enter fully on his reign of terror.

There was one more flare-up in Benton's direct involvement with McCarthy. It is worth saying here that, even at the height of their 1951–52 encounter, Benton never lost personal contact with the man. The strangest of these contacts occurred after Benton had waived his Senate immunity, McCarthy had filed his lawsuit for libel, and after a day-long interrogation of Benton by Edward Bennett Williams, McCarthy's lawyer. That night, while the Senate and press gallery looked on, McCarthy crossed the Senate floor, threw his arm around Benton's shoulder, and said to him: "By God, Bill, you did marvelously today. I didn't think you could possibly be that good. I was certainly impressed." Hubert Humphrey, who was sitting next to Benton, gulped and his eyes popped. Some reporters in the press gallery wondered if the feud was a fraud. Yet McCarthy seemed to view his battles with Benton as part of a publicity game. He seemed to assume that Benton himself would understand that it was a game and would take no offense because of the way it was being played.

Later, after Benton's defeat for the Senate in 1952, McCarthy withdrew his $2 million lawsuit for libel, and it was this action which paradoxically led to Benton's last direct conflict with him. "I cannot find a single person in the United States," McCarthy explained to the press, "who believes Benton's charges, and so I withdraw the lawsuit."

McCarthy's words still hung in the air when John Howe and Benton discussed the possibility of forcing McCarthy to keep the lawsuit alive so that McCarthy would have to give his own deposition under oath. They seized on the idea of producing people who *did* believe Benton's charges against McCarthy, and it was at this stage of their thinking that Harry Scherman, the head of the Book-of-the-Month Club, entered the picture. Scherman, with his long experience in effective advertising, agreed that it would be a good idea to start an organization called "Believers in Benton." He further offered to advance part of the cost of placing full-page advertisements in the *New York Times* and the *Herald Tribune* built around the theme, "We Believe Benton." The copy for the ad was eventually written by Scherman with help from John Howe and George E. Agree of the National Committee for an Effective Congress. The ads placed in New York in the *Times* and *Herald Tribune* carried a coupon for the signatures of people who were willing to testify that they believed Benton; they also contained a coupon to accompany a financial contribution to pay for further ads. The ads in the *Times* and *Tribune* cost $7,000 and produced $20,000 in contributions. After repaying Scherman and other original donors, the balance of the money was used to take half-page or full-page ads in about twenty other newspapers around the country. Only one of these, however, paid for itself, and the "Believers in Benton" ran out of money. However, fourteen thousand signed coupons were on hand. Howe bundled these up and sent them on to Benton's attorney in Washington, but Senator McCarthy and his own lawyer didn't rise to the bait.

There was a private "believer"—John F. Kennedy by name— whose reaction to Benton's battle against McCarthy merits a word here. Kennedy was already a "coming" congressman when Benton served in the Senate; yet apart from handshakes when the two men happened to meet, not much passed between them. Benton's interest in Kennedy didn't actually begin until the latter was elected to the Senate on the same day Benton was defeated. Benton wrote him a note of congratulation, and this brought a reply from Kennedy on 28 November 1952. To a handwritten postscript saying how much he regretted that Benton wouldn't be in the Senate so that they could work there together, Kennedy added: "I have greatly admired your courageous service." There was no doubt in Benton's mind— and even less later on—that Kennedy's admiration for "courageous service" referred to Benton's stand on the issue of McCarthy and McCarthyism. Benton acknowledged the compliment in a letter to Kennedy on 5 December 1952 and went on to add:

At your age, coming from a state which ought to continue to return you for many terms to come, you have a chance to become one of the great leaders of our party and our country. I don't know another man in the country with a more remarkable opportunity than yours. I'm pleased with the word "courageous" in that postscript of yours. The pressures on you will be constant and unceasing, as you know from your experience in the Congress—to follow roads and angles that are not courageous. Yet in your position, with your background, at your age, and coming from your state—I know of no young man—indeed, I know of no man in American politics—who may stand to benefit so much by consistently taking the courageous route—as you. In my opinion this will pay off for you in a most practical and hardheaded sense, as well as in highest personal satisfaction.

As for McCarthy himself: For two years in a Republican-dominated Senate, where he served as chairman of the Permanent Investigating Subcommittee of the Senate Committee on Government Operations, he seemed invincible in his defamations and demagoguery. Thus in February 1954, eighty-eight senators voted funds for his subcommittee. Senator Fulbright stood alone in voting no. Yet McCarthy's end was near. The antics of his assistants, and his own clash with the army, set the stage for the televised army-McCarthy hearings viewed by twenty million Americans each day for almost two months. Always before, McCarthy's accusations, no matter how fantastic, had reflected some dignity when read in print. But before the television cameras, his wanton ways became glaringly plain. Now respectable men in the Senate moved in for the kill.

In the lead on the Republican side was Senator Ralph Flanders of Vermont, Benton's close friend since CED days. On 9 March 1954, a few days after the television hearings had ended, Flanders accused McCarthy of being a "one-man party" and "doing his best to shatter the Republican Party." In the lead on the Democratic side was another of Benton's close friends, Senator Fulbright of Arkansas, who wheeled Democrats into line behind Flanders's two-part maneuver beginning on 11 June with a resolution to strip McCarthy of the government operation subcommittee chairmanship, followed by the action on 30 July when Flanders submitted the crucial resolution of censure.

A few days later, the Senate voted 75 to 12 to create a Select

Committee under Arthur Watkins, a Utah Republican, to consider the charges against McCarthy. The Watkins Committee, comprised of leading Republican and Democratic members of the Senate's hierarchy, unanimously voted censure. Then, on 2 December 1954, following the flashing danger signal the Republicans saw in the recent congressional election which restored the Congress to Democratic hands, the Senate voted 67 to 22 to censure McCarthy on two counts. One was his abuse and contempt of the Gillette subcommittee in its investigation of the original Benton resolution. The second was related to the first: McCarthy's abuse and contempt of the Watkins Committee which investigated his abuse and contempt of the Gillette subcommittee.

It meant the beginning of the end for McCarthy, who, ill with hepatitis, was drinking himself to death. It meant, after a delay of three years and four months, a massive affirmation of Benton's early stand. It also meant a reverse side of the truth Carl Hayden had voiced to Benton about how you can always explain a vote but not a speech. Had there been no Benton speech on 8 August 1951—and a succession of speeches afterward—there might well have been no Senate censure of McCarthy on 2 December 1954. "I believe it to be true," Senator Flanders wrote him soon afterward, "that your preliminary work made my final success possible." "You made it possible for public opinion to come to understand," Wayne Morse of Oregon wrote Benton as if in continuation of Flanders's letter. "Had you not acted three years before results were obtained, it is hard to say how long McCarthy might have dominated American life and politics."

Senator John F. Kennedy had something more pointed to add. Six months before the censure of McCarthy, Kennedy had met Benton at a Jefferson-Jackson Day dinner in Hartford—a result of John Bailey's initiative. Bailey had begun to sense Kennedy's potential impact as a political leader and realized that, if Connecticut elected a Democratic governor in 1954, Connecticut Democrats would be in a position to take the lead in promoting Kennedy as a national figure. Bailey and Kennedy wanted to weld the small New England state delegations into a single bloc with real power at the Democratic convention. In line with this objective, Bailey invited Kennedy to Hartford to address the Jefferson-Jackson Day dinner on 25 June 1954, and he asked Benton to introduce the guest of honor.

Benton used the occasion publicly to strike the keynote of what Kennedy meant to New England. He noted that the guest of honor was the first member of Congress to visit on his own initiative (in 1951) the battleground in Indochina where the French were locked in combat with the forces of Ho Chi Minh. Kennedy was also the first member of Congress to demand that United States foreign aid to France be made contingent on practical methods for promoting the independence of colonial people from French rule. Further, said Benton, it was Kennedy's speech in the Senate in April 1954, "that first dramatized to the Congress the basic differences and dangers to the free world in Indochina." This was a time when the Republican administration was singularly silent on the nature of that conflict.

Benton then addressed himself to the political aspect of his Kennedy theme. "On the domestic side," he said, "our Massachusetts neighbor has made all of New England his constituency." And he continued: "For decades, as all of us know, New England has suffered among other things from a lack of any kind of unified action by its Washington representatives—particularly in the Senate. You've heard of a silver bloc, an oil bloc, a farm bloc, but never a New England bloc. Yet, New England has legitimate aspirations which call for strong national advocacy and leadership. Ladies and gentlemen, I give you a great young Democrat, a young Democrat for New England and for America." The remarks foretold the future road Senator Kennedy was to travel, on his way to the 1960 Democratic nomination.

The part of that road which bypassed the Senate vote to censure McCarthy always led to troublesome questions put to Kennedy. He could explain that he had been in Florida when the vote was taken, recuperating from a near fatal operation on his back. He could explain that if the matter of McCarthy's censure had come up in the summer of 1954, he had been prepared to vote on it. He could also add, when he subsequently assessed the evidence presented and McCarthy's transgressions of the rules of the Senate, that he felt "the censure was a reasonable action." Yet he could not silence the questions or the criticisms, including those which quietly rose within himself.

In his book *Profiles in Courage*, written during his convalescence, he had included one of Benton's remote kinsmen, Senator Thomas Hart Benton of Missouri, the authentic voice of pre–Civil War frontier democracy and a man who had accepted defeat in Missouri after almost half a century at the front of national politics rather than give in to the expansionist demands of Missouri's slavocracy. When *Profiles in Courage* was published, Kennedy's sense of unease over the fact that he had not voted on the McCarthy censure—and his inferential apology on that account—seemed to be present in a letter he wrote on 18 February 1956 to Benton. "It might interest you to know," Kennedy observed, "that I have thought perhaps I included the wrong Benton in my book. As I remember reading an article by Ernest Lindley about what you tried to do against the tide, and if I am still alive, which I doubt, when you are gone, I will see that you are included in a future book."

5

SYNTHESIS

25

From Mother to Millions

It would take another book to tell the full story of what Benton has done between his 1952 defeat for reelection as a senator and the time of this writing. He sometimes quotes Lord Keynes, who, when asked what he would do if he had his life to live over again, answered, "I would drink more champagne." Benton, however, has always been too busy to follow any such advice. His own impact on events, though more subtle than in earlier years, has perhaps been greater since his Senate days than previously. These have been the years when his efforts have centered primarily on the quality and quantity of American education, and of education around the world. These have been the years when his mother, through him, has posthumously written large her own career as a teacher.

All the while, Benton has retained a deep interest in politics, but an interest free of the pathos noticeable in many other former United States senators who can "never go home to Pocatello"—who linger on in Washington as lawyer-lobbyists or who dream of the power they once wielded.

At his defeat in 1952 Benton was only fifty-two years old. He had many business enterprises that could absorb his energy. Moreover, as his financial resources grew, he enlarged the scope of his personal involvement in educational institutions, philanthropic interests, and public service committees. He was still in the Senate when "Benton's Folly"—the Great Books of the Western World—was ready for an unveiling in April 1952. Nine years in preparation, it represented an investment of $2 million. The result was a set of fifty-four volumes totaling 32,000 pages and 25 million words. Fifty-one of the volumes comprised the Great Books themselves, from Homer to Freud. Another volume was a book-length essay by Robert Maynard Hutchins, *The Great Conversation,* of the great thinkers across the ages; it also stressed the vital connection between the Great Books and a liberal education—in college, after college, or instead of college—and their bearing on an understanding of people and society. The remaining two volumes consisted of Mortimer Adler's *Syntopicon,* indexing references to the 102 Great Ideas— from "Angel" to "World"—which appeared in the Great Books.

Each of the 102 Great Ideas was introduced by an essay—written by Adler or in some cases by his associate, Otto Bird—presenting in dialectical form the different views different authors had about a particular Great Idea. Early in this phase of the work, Adler had sent Benton a draft of the first essay, "Angel." Benton had a question: "Why did you begin with it?" Adler explained that "Angel" came first alphabetically. "But where is 'Adultery'?" Benton persisted. "Isn't that a Great Idea?" Whereupon Adler replied: "Oh, you will find that as a subdivision under 'Family.' " Benton accepted the solemn assurance but looked on the essay as a challenge to his old talent as a copy editor. He was not satisfied with the essay itself. He took the draft and spent a night rewriting it. Adler, and not angels alone, may have danced on the head of a pin wondering apprehensively what the outcome would be. But when the redraft was done, it was generally agreed that the editing made the essay easier to read, without sacrificing scholarship to clarity. The effect was felt in the final cast Adler gave to the other essays.

The Great Books were formally unveiled in April 1952 at a dinner in New York's Waldorf Hotel, with many of the subscribers to the Founders' Edition of five hundred sets in attendance. These were the subscribers who had been persuaded by Hutchins and Adler to put up $500 each, to underwrite the first printing. At the dinner, Benton presented a blue bound leather set to the British consul general in New York for transmittal to his sovereign, Queen Elizabeth II. In an accompanying message addressed to Her Majesty, Benton had written: "These books are not of the moment. They are eternal. They do not deal with here and now; yet here and now cannot be understood without them. In them you can find no answers to the urgent problems that face you throughout the Commonwealth and throughout the world. Yet without them, the answers to these urgent problems can never be found." Benton explained to the founders in the audience that he would present a second such set, bound in red, to President Truman at a White House ceremony the following week and would repeat the same words to him. He had something to add. The remaining two thousand sets of the first printing were in a Chicago warehouse, but unbound and would not be put on the market until fall. "I herewith appoint you, the founders, our advance salesmen," Benton said. "I make you honorary salesmen all— but without commissions! Your very presence here tonight earns for you the privilege of giving more support."

Clifton Fadiman, speaking at the same dinner, struck a more lyrical note. "You who have bought the Great Books," said he, "are taking upon yourselves part of a magnificent burden, the burden of preserving as did the monks of early Christendom, through another darkening, if not Dark Age, the visions, the laughter, the ideas, the deep cries of anguish, the great Eurekas of revelation that make up our patent to the title of civilized man."

The presentation of the set to President Harry Truman the following week had a potentially explosive personal and political danger for Benton, who was then battling full tilt against Senator Joseph McCarthy. For his call at the White House, Benton had worn a "Great Book necktie," designed by Meyer Kestnbaum, president of Hart, Schaffner, and Marx, and a member of the "fat man's" class which Adler and Hutchins conducted for Chicago civic leaders and their wives who were interested in reading the Great Books. Imprinted on the necktie were the names of many of the authors of the Great Books, one of which was Karl Marx. When Benton emerged from President Truman's office, White House reporters, who customarily wait in the lobby outside, closed in on him. One of these, a Hearst reporter, focused on the necktie and pointing to it said: "What's on that tie? Marx!" The scent of a political kill in the air was absorbed into laughter when Benton breezily answered: "Yes, Hart, Schaffner, and Marx."

After the Great Books went on sale in the general market, it was expected that some critics would question the choice of the books or of the 102 Great Ideas that had been indexed. So they did. But there was almost universal agreement that the publication of the Great Books with the *Syntopicon* was an event to be compared favorably with the appearance of the first dictionary and the first encyclopedia. This was the reaction of Gilbert Highet, professor of classics at Columbia University, who reviewed the set for the *New York Times Book Review*. Though critical on points of detail, he called the work as a whole a "majestic set" and "a noble monument to the power of the human mind." The books, said he, "are a new and valuable proof of the high level of contemporary American culture, worthy to be set beside our thronged symphony concerts, our uncomfortably but encouragingly crowded art exhibitions, and other activities which are a reverse of 'U.S. materialism.' " In the same key Mark Van Doren called the project "an intellectual enterprise which has no parallel in the history of Western man."

Something else was "unparalleled." Robert Hutchins had secured a quarter-million-dollar grant from Paul Mellon's Old Dominion Foundation in order to make the special Founders' Edition of the Great Books available to about 1,600 libraries around the country. When Benton heard of this "sale," he called Robert Preble, the president of the Britannica company. "Bob," he asked, "what is the biggest order ever written for subscription books?" Preble answered that it was an order for 500 sets of *Britannica Junior,* sold to the Chicago school board at $90 a set. "Well," said Benton triumphantly, "thanks to our ace salesman, Bob Hutchins, I am sending you an order five and one-half times as large." The order by itself underwrote the costs of printing 6,000 sets, 4,400 of them for general sale.

Sales of the novel work went slowly at first. By 1956, however, the ground had been laid to support a concentrated sales campaign for the Great Books set, priced at $300 and available to buyers on the established *Encyclopaedia Britannica* time-payment plan. The increased acceptance of the set in turn led to new publishing ventures related to or inspired by it. One of these was a ten-volume set titled *Gateway to the Great Books.* Hutchins and Adler were its editors. Compiled especially for young adults, the *Gateway* contains short stories, plays, essays, biographies, scientific papers, letters, histories, and material in other literary forms in what has been called "a cornucopia of choice reading." There was also a single volume published annually for subscribers to the Great Books. Titled *Great Ideas Today,* and modeled on the *Book of the Year* for *Encyclopaedia Britannica* subscribers, it explores significant aspects of contemporary problems and relates current thought to ideas contained in the great writings of the past. It became and has remained one of the largest selling books in the United States every year.

Meanwhile, as sales of *Encyclopaedia Britannica* increased, sales of the *Britannica Book of the Year* surged ahead. *The Book of the*

Year, with over a million words of up-to-date information, was automatically mailed annually to all buyers of the *Britannica* itself. In this first year about 80 percent of all new buyers of the *Encyclopaedia* retained the single-volume yearbook and sent in their money to protect their original investment in the set itself, much as a home-owner paints his house. Purchasers of the *Encyclopaedia* who did not retain the yearbook were removed from the mailing list, and while those who retained volumes dwindled in subsequent years, the cumulative sales continued to grow. Like the *World Book of the Year* of Field Enterprises, the annual gross dollar volume sales of the *Britannica Book of the Year* stood on a plane of its own in the publishing business. Thus in 1968, this one volume's gross earnings were $5 million before taxes—and few book publishers earn that much on their total annual output.[1]

As new publishing ventures were launched and expanded, Benton reorganized the corporate structure of his various enterprises. Britannica Films was "spun off" as an enterprise owned by the Benton family and by some of Benton's principal associates, such as Robert Maynard Hutchins and Adlai Stevenson.

Robert C. Preble continued to serve as president of the Britannica company until he retired in 1959. On his initiative, the company expanded Funk and Wagnall's *New Practical Standard Dictionary* into a two-volume *World Language Dictionary*. About half the second volume contained a basic list of some 6,400 English words with their equivalents in parallel columns in six other languages—French, German, Italian, Spanish, Swedish, and Yiddish—while the following sections reversed the process by translating the other languages into English. The Yiddish section by itself made language history, in that modified Hebrew characters were for the first time transliterated into roman type. Within the privacy of the *Britannica* family, however, it was felt that the Funk and Wagnall dictionary was many years out of date, or at least greatly inferior to Merriam-Webster. When this was brought home to Benton, he entered on protracted negotiations aimed at acquiring the G. and C. Merriam Company.

Preble, meanwhile, conceived of a small family encyclopedia for

---

[1] The *Britannica Book of the Year* became a vehicle for Benton's writing, as will be seen, and in addition for such world figures as the prime minister of Great Britain, and former heads of state including America's Lyndon Johnson, West Germany's Ludwig Erhard and Japan's Shigeru Yoshida.

the Latin American market, which came to birth eventually as the sixteen-volume *Enciclopedia Barsa*,[2] published in Spanish. This in turn led to the publication for Brazil of a Portuguese *Enciclopedia Barsa*, whose projected appearance Benton announced in Brazil early in 1960 when he was on a Latin American tour with Governor Adlai Stevenson. The Spanish and Portuguese encyclopedias were reference works of about five or six million words, roughly comparable in size to the *Britannica Junior*, though more advanced in content.

Major efforts were also made by Benton and Preble to invigorate the business and editorial aspects of the British subsidiary of the *Britannica*. John Armitage, editor of the *Fortnightly* and former education editor of the London *Times*, became the London editor of the *Britannica*. As such, he worked closely with a committee of scholar-advisers from Oxford University, Cambridge University, and the University of London to oversee articles written for the *Britannica* by authorities in Great Britain, the Commonwealth, and the whole of Europe. There has been no chauvinism in the choice of people thought to be best qualified to write articles for the *Britannica;* non-American experts in special fields of knowledge account for up to one-half of the material in the encyclopedia.

One distinctively personal contribution which Benton made to the renovation of the British subsidiary had its origin at the 1948 Geneva Conference on Freedom of Information at which he and Hector McNeil were the chairmen of the American and British delegations, respectively. The two men were in close daily contact for more than a month, and the deep impression the Englishman made on the American had an offer as one of its by-products. Benton told McNeil that if the Labour government were ever voted out of power, there would be a place for him in the Britannica organization, provided he wanted it. When the Labour government was later defeated in a general election, the old offer was renewed and accepted. McNeil was made chairman of the board of directors of the British subsidiary, and then its managing director. He held both posts until his untimely death in 1955.

McNeil was the instigator of friendships that developed between Benton and leaders of the British Labour party, such as Hugh

---

[2]The name Barsa derives from the names of the principals in the Latin American company created to market the sets, Barrett and de Sa.

Gaitskell and Harold Wilson. As socialists, these men knew that many American businessmen were ready to believe that British Labourites were a band of airy-fairy theorists with no capacity to deal with events on the move in the hard world of reality. On this account, Gaitskell and Wilson were reportedly all the more fascinated to discover an American millionaire like Benton who did not think in stereotypes but chose a Labourite socialist like McNeil for a key place in his very capitalistic business organization simply because of the man's competence. Nor did Benton himself ever regret the choice. On the contrary, he often expressed the conviction that if McNeil's life had not been cut short, many business woes which later beset the British end of Britannica operations would have been avoided.

In the meantime, Benton brought other British leaders into an intimate relationship with the *Britannica* in both the United States and England. One of these was Geoffrey Crowther (later Sir Geoffrey and now Lord Crowther). Largely responsible as an editor and businessman for the stunning success of the *Economist*, Crowther became a *Britannica* director and vice-chairman of the board of editors. Another was Stanley Morison, who also joined *Britannica*'s board of editors and rendered invaluable services not only to it but to many other interests of the Britannica company. In his politics, Morison was an ardent republican who several times refused knighthood because, as he privately explained, he "could not on principle make the kowtow to the Royal Sovereign." Yet leaders in Great Britain's world of publishing, letters, and scholarship readily made "the kowtow" to him, and they affectionately called him "the gray eminence of Fleet Street." He was a member of the British Academy, one of the six men among its membership of 185 who was not a university professor. He was a member of the editorial board of the London *Times*, a former editor of the *Times*'s celebrated *Literary Supplement*, the author of a two-volume history of the *Times*, the world's leading calligrapher and typographer, the designer of Times New Roman, the world's most widely used typeface. It was said on Fleet Street that Morison's recommendations generally were decisive in the choice of editors of the London *Times;* reportedly, it was through Morison that Sir William Haley, after a career as head of the *Manchester Guardian* and then of the BBC, became the editor of the *Times*. It was Morison who also recommended to Benton that Haley be made the editor of the *Encyclopaedia Britannica,* and this was eventually done under circumstances to be related later.

In addition to Britannica matters, Muzak also claimed Benton's attention. If his post–Benton and Bowles business career is viewed as a single whole, Muzak stands out as the only venture he originally went into solely to make money; the $50,000 yearly salary he drew from the enterprise, plus an expense account, were important factors in the economics of his design for living. Back in 1948, soon after he left the State Department, he could have sold Muzak to the Columbia Broadcasting System for $2 million, half in cash and half in stock; if he had done this, the $1 million in CBS stock would have increased ten to fifteen times in value in the next few years. But he declined the CBS offer, hoping that Muzak could be used as a vehicle for converting his pre–State Department idea of subscription radio into subscription television. The hope, however, was shelved after he was appointed to the Senate in late 1949 and his attention was fully absorbed in Senate work.

In retrospect, Benton felt that while he was still in the Senate, Muzak should have applied for the five television licenses which the FCC was then willing to give to one company. This could have been done at a cost of something like thirty cents for each application— though the value of such a television station in a major market later ran between $10 and $20 million. Benton always looked upon his failure to make Muzak an obvious path into television as an inexplicable major business blunder. When he once got around to asking his lawyer, A. M. Gilbert, why *he* had not taken the initiative in urging Muzak to apply for the television licenses, Gilbert answered truthfully enough, "I never thought of it." Nor did Harry Houghton, the president of Muzak. Nor did Benton while he was in the Senate.

The missed opportunity was particularly galling when Benton later learned of an episode which occurred while he was concentrating on his Senate work. Leaders in commercial television had held a meeting to discuss the future organization of the industry. Toward the end of the get-together, Paul Porter, the former FCC chairman who represented Paramount, said to the others: "It's all very well for us to talk here about our plans, but we shall have to wait to see what Bill Benton intends to do." Porter later claimed that there was nothing hyperbolic in his note of caution. He meant it as a sober warning that Benton might shake up the television industry by mounting a drive for subscription television, just as he had previously frightened the radio industry with his short-lived, and self-aborted, plan for subscription radio.

The drive, however, never materialized. After leaving the Senate, Benton was no longer interested in trying to make Muzak a point of entry into the field of subscription television. Partly by accident, partly by inadvertence, partly by his absorption in politics and in the educational opportunities he saw in the *Encyclopaedia Britannica* and Britannica Films, he had missed the vital factor of timing where television was concerned.

His program for installing Muzak in airplanes and airport terminals, in banks and factories and insurance companies and buses and elevators, made rapid and orderly headway. But by 1958 his boredom with the whole enterprise inclined him toward the idea of selling Muzak. Several events which coincided at this time set the stage for the actual sale.

Robert Preble was due to retire as president of the Britannica company. Benton felt that Harry Houghton, the president of Muzak, could succeed Preble as president of the Britannica until a younger man was found for the job. The proposed shuffle, however, would leave vacant the presidency of Muzak, and the question arose of who was to fill it. In the middle of the conjectures on this score, a representative of the Marine Midland Bank called on Benton with a pointed question. When did he mean to pay off loans aggregating between $500,000 and $600,000 which he owed the bank? The first of the loans dated from the fall of 1947, when Benton borrowed $81,000 to buy the Britannica art collection. Subsequently, he had borrowed more money from the bank as his expenses continued to exceed his income while all his assets were tied up in the Britannica company, Britannica Films, and Muzak. Only part of the total amount he owed the bank had been spent on specifically personal needs. Benton regularly gave to charitable causes 30 percent of his income—the maximum allowable income tax deduction for philanthropy—even during this period when he had to get bank loans in order to do so.

"I haven't any intention of paying off the loan at all," Benton blithely told the representative of the bank. "As a matter of fact, I intend to continue to borrow because I need money in excess of my income. You're in the business of loaning money and I'm in the business of borrowing it." The shaken bank representative replied, "Well, the bank examiner has been in and has asked what your intentions are. You should have some idea about how you intend to pay off your loan." Benton did have an idea. Muzak was an easily marketable asset. By selling it, he could pay off the loan to the Marine Midland Bank, dispose of the question about who should run Muzak, refinance himself, gain time, and again have on hand the means to cover the continuing deficit between his regular income and his political, philanthropic, and other expenses.

At this juncture, John D. Wrather of Texas approached Benton with a cash purchase offer for Muzak, and the deal was closed. The selling price of $4,350,000 netted Benton more than $4 million on his original investment, though he gave 20 percent of the profit to his business associates in Muzak. His mother, had she been alive, would have been pleased by her son's action in getting rid of the company whose slogan was "Music that is not to be listened to." In Elma Benton's view, Muzak wasn't music at all, and she refused to let her son install a Muzak outlet in her apartment. Wrather, for his part, reportedly said later on: "Bill Benton is supposed to be a smart man, but I stole Muzak from him." True or not, Wrather managed the transaction skillfully. To meet his down payments to Benton, he drew $1 million in cash out of Muzak. Then he used Muzak profits to meet the six successive payments as they fell due. Still later, he made Muzak a worldwide enterprise by using the same promotion ideas and phrases Benton had originally popularized in the United States. Its sales and profits quadrupled and quintupled. Within less than ten years, it was earning some $2 million yearly before taxes. Benton, however, never once regretted the sale. He found his other business interests more challenging—and financially rewarding.

Early in Houghton's tenure as president of the Britannica company, work was begun on the editorial development of an encyclopedia for high school students. The venture was inspired by the huge success of the *World Book Encyclopedia*. If the *Encyclopaedia Britannica* was the Cadillac of the trade, *World Book* was the Chevrolet. It sold at around half the *Britannica*'s price and was outselling it two or three sets to one. The Britannica product that was meant to compete with *World Book* in its own mass market was

variously known as "Project X" or as "Benton's Encyclopaedia"
—the latter on the theory that a man's name is often the best name
for a product. While preliminary developmental work on the venture was still underway—$300,000 had already been spent on it—
Britannica officials learned that *Compton's Pictured Encyclopedia*
could be bought.

Frank E. Compton, the creator of the set that bore his name, had
died in 1950. But for thirty years before his death, there had been
an intense rivalry in Chicago between his encyclopedia and the
World Book published by Mr. Quarrie. Both encyclopedias were
aimed at the high school market. Both companies hired schoolteachers as summer salesmen. Both sets were of excellent quality.
Some school librarians preferred one, and some preferred the other.
But in the competition between the two, *Compton's* had the edge at
the time of Frank Compton's death. It was more lavishly illustrated.
It contained a "fact index" in every volume, and this widely publicized feature served to separate the short entries from the main
articles. *World Book*, by contrast, carried short entries and main
articles together in the same alphabetical order. With Compton's
death in 1950, however, there was a change in the competitive position of the two encyclopedias. Mr. Quarrie offered to sell his *World
Book* enterprise to Marshall Field III, and Benton, indirectly, had
helped persuade Field to buy it. *World Book* was then incorporated
into Field Enterprises; under inspired management, its sales soared
to a point where they would outstrip *Compton's* by a ten-to-one
margin. In the encyclopedia field a great sales volume clearly was
to be found with a high school encyclopedia rather than a scholarly
adult set.

Compton's widow had sold his company to her husband's nine
principal associates. The nine in turn had agreed among themselves
that no one would sell his stock to an outsider unless all nine did so
together. Perhaps because they were getting old, or perhaps because
they were reeling under the fierce competition of the *World Book*,
the nine owners were receptive to the idea of selling *Compton's* to
the Britannica company. A deal was closed. *Compton's* was purchased for $9 million in cash, and Britannica junked its own plans
to bring out a family encyclopedia specially edited for use by high
school students. The material in the fifteen volumes of *Compton's*
filled a knowledge gap midway between the level of reference material in the fifteen-volume *Britannica Junior Encyclopaedia* for ele-

mentary school children, and the twenty-four-volume *Encyclopaedia Britannica.*

Meanwhile, Benton had benefited greatly from a decision he made in 1953 to install Maurice B. Mitchell, a former vice-president of Muzak, as the president of Britannica Films. Mitchell combined talents rarely found in one person. An exceptionally articulate man and a brilliant speaker, he was deeply committed to the advancement of education, fertile in devising plans for new business growth, and a skilled leader who knew how to pick able associates. Under his direction, and with the help of his associates, the film company consolidated its position as world leader in visual aids to education, particularly in classroom talking pictures. Its camera crews, stimulated by specialists in the company and its advisory board, roamed the world to make teaching films that were tied directly to the curriculum. Indeed, the film library they built up could not now be duplicated for less than $40–$50 million. The films themselves were not merely an enrichment of instruction by books and teachers, nor were they a replacement of the latter. They were designed to fit into an educational system as a whole, often meeting problems of instruction that could not be handled in any other way.

As an incidental by-product, the films served as a potent source of advertising for the Britannica name they bore. The point here was brought home to Benton after he bought the Compton Company, at a dinner with the nine former owners. In the course of the table talk he was asked how he could have been so shrewd as to start Britannica Films, which "advertised" *Encyclopaedia Britannica* to tens of millions of schoolchildren every week. Benton tried to assure his guests that nothing resembling what they implied had been in his mind. Long before he had even dreamed of acquiring the *Britannica* he had wanted to enter the field of classroom talking pictures because he believed it to be an important educational venture that would in the long run turn out to be a good business investment. The former owners of *Compton's,* however, remained convinced that Britannica Films had been launched as a promotion device to popularize the name "Encyclopaedia Britannica." They were wrong in their assignment of motives but were right in emphasizing that Encyclopaedia Britannica Films did in fact focus the eyes of tens of millions of schoolchildren every week on the name of the *Encyclopaedia Britannica.*

Benton felt that the film company should be on the alert for educational ventures that went beyond talking pictures. This attitude enlarged Mitchell's opportunity to make the film company all the more venturesome, and in this he had Benton's full support. "Mitch," Benton once wrote him, "you are not making enough mistakes lately." It was another way of saying that he was being too cautious by Benton's lights, though even "cautious boldness" meant sinking many millions of dollars in projects with no certainty of a payoff.

One of these projects was TEMAC, a word coined by combining initial syllables of "teaching machines." TEMAC, a system of "programmed learning," enables the student to instruct himself and proceed at his own pace. In any given subject, many hundreds of questions are laid out in careful sequence, so as to take the student forward in small steps, question by question. The correct answer appears opposite each question at the right of the page, but covered by a flap which the student must slide downward as he goes. If his answer is incorrect he pauses to study or review, but if he answers correctly, he proceeds to the next question, and so on in a process that takes him through a full course of instruction. In addition to TEMAC, the film company also acquired the new Wirtz-Botel system for teaching elementary mathematics, which was to be adopted for California schools and widely used elsewhere.

To provide a corporate house for these and other ventures initiated by the film company, a new company, the Britannica Press, was to be created. There was to be a further change in corporate structure when the name of Encyclopaedia Britannica Films was changed to Encyclopaedia Britannica Educational Corporation, and in it was concentrated most of the Britannica company's interest in the school and library field—films, books, TEMAC, Wirtz-Botel, and the like. Some 170 salesmen would sell Britannica publications as well as Educational Corporation products to schools and libraries. Many additional lines of growth will be touched on in due course, and especially those involving the rapid international growth of Britannica ventures. But to keep Benton's personal life in focus, it must here be stressed that he was never "just a businessman" consumed by business. He lived a public life as well, and he continued to devote much of himself to it all the while that he was presiding over developments in his steadily expanding business empire.

26

Public Service Generalist

Despite the impressive earnings of his companies, Benton never served as a director of a company that was not his own—and only two companies listed on the New York Stock Exchange ever asked him to serve as a director. One, a major Hollywood studio, wanted him to merge Britannica Films with the studio and thus become its largest stockholder and chairman of the board. The proposal was turned down. It seems fair to suggest that Benton was never sought as a director for any other public corporations for the same reason that some of the ablest men of his generation—for example, Beardsley Ruml and Raymond Rubicam—were never sought as directors. They, like Benton, were men with original ideas, addicted to asking root-of-the-matter questions that management generally chose to overlook or to gloss over. In a word, they were "trouble makers," and publicly owned corporations are wary of men of that stamp.

American public life gained what Benton was not asked to give— or would have refused to give—to what he termed "other people's companies." Specifically, as of 1968, he served on twenty-six boards and twenty-eight committees devoted to various public interests. It is doubtful whether there were many other Americans of his day who equaled the simple arithmetic of these involvements, and probably few others regulated their approach to public service by the two rules Benton imposed on himself. First, he would give his name to a board or committee only if he was prepared to share the responsibility for the work to be done. This meant not only attending meetings but long hours of studying questions to be decided at them. The second rule was a corollary to the first. By sharing responsibility for the work to be done, he felt it was his duty to contribute financially to its support. In practice, this meant that Benton in his post-Senate years not only devoted about one-third of his time to public service organizations, but, as indicated earlier, contributed to them the full 30 percent of his rapidly rising personal income that the law allowed.

He was, however, no "fat cat." His effect on the organizations of which he was a member was once described and judged by Professor John Kenneth Galbraith, who had been chairman of the "domestic panel" of the Democratic Advisory Council, created during the Eisenhower administration to rally intellectual opposition. Benton was chairman of the panel's subcommittee on education. "Time after time, meeting after meeting," said Galbraith, "there was one man who had done his homework thoroughly—Benton. At the end of every meeting there was one man who had peppered the session with endless, audacious, innovative, practical ideas—Benton." Then, addressing the criticism of Benton usually sounded by his detractors, Galbraith added, "So what if he does flap his wings now and then? He's got a hell of a lot to flap his wings about."

A variant of this view was expressed by Representative Carl Albert, chairman of the platform committee at the 1964 Democratic National Convention. One man and one woman from each state make up this committee, and Benton had represented Connecticut on platform committees at the Democratic National Conventions of 1952, 1956, and 1964, as he was also to do in 1968. But in 1960 he could not serve because he alone in the Connecticut delegation supported Adlai Stevenson. Except for Senator Dodd, a Johnson supporter, all the rest were solidly behind John Kennedy. One of the Kennedy delegates was Congressman Chester Bowles, who represented his state on the platform committee and served as its chairman.

At the 1964 convention, Benton was the most experienced hand at platform writing—which he once described as "the art of the qualified sentence"—a literary form requiring skills not generally found among delegates chosen to draft the party platform. When the 1964 work was finished, Carl Albert in a note to Benton said: "Your many ideas and proposals were notable for the sound judgment in which they were grounded. Your leadership was accepted as a matter of course. No member of the platform committee had a greater impact on the final document than you."

But this was just a sideline.

For twenty years Benton was an active trustee of the University of Chicago, of Carleton College, and for ten years of Hampton Institute. When his son Charles became a trustee of Chicago and Hampton, Benton became a "life" or honorary trustee. He made the same transition at Carleton when he was granted an honorary degree. He is still an active trustee of the Universities of Connecticut and Bridgeport, and of Brandeis University. He is keenly interested in the University of Connecticut and has been directly involved in the university's swift growth in recent years—hinged to a $62 million building program. In the specific case of Brandeis University, Benton is one of a handful of trustees who are not Jewish. His interest in the institution had little to do with a "liberal" commitment to the betterment of "interfaith relations." He felt that Brandeis as an institution of higher learning under the leadership of its first president, Abram Sachar, and his successor, Morris Abrams, radiated the same exciting spirit of adventure that was present at the University of Chicago under its first president, William Rainey Harper, and again later under President Robert Maynard Hutchins. He wanted to help Sachar, and Abrams, fulfill the promise of the institution as a community of scholars and students pursuing excellence in education.

> Abram Sachar [Benton once said] reminds me of George Edgar Vincent's description of William Rainey Harper as a "steam engine in pants." Some time during my first year as a member of the board, I saw a report about Brandeis's money-raising activities, and discovered that this new university in the previous year had matched or exceeded the money raised by the University of Chicago, traditionally known as one of the "big three" in the money-raising business [Yale, Harvard, and Chicago]. So I turned to Dr. Sachar at a board meeting and I said, "Dr. Sachar, with its capacity to raise money, if Brandeis has academic leadership, within twenty-five years it should be the world's greatest university; all it takes is money and leadership." Sachar snapped back, "It won't take us that long!" My guess is that he may be proven right.

In addition to university trusteeships, the wide range of Benton's interests is mirrored in the many other public bodies with which he is connected. He is currently a trustee of the American Assembly (connected with Columbia University), American Shakespeare Festival Theatre (at Stratford, Connecticut), Aspen Institute,

Committee for Economic Development, Committee for a National Trade Policy, the Cradle Society, Eisenhower Exchange Fellowships, Fair Campaign Practices Committee, Institute of International Education, Kennedy Library Corporation, National Committee for the Support of the Public Schools, and the Eleanor Roosevelt Memorial Foundation. He is a member of the Cleveland Conference,[1] the Advisory Committee on the Arts for the National Culture Center (the Kennedy Center in Washington), the Adlai E. Stevenson Memorial Fund, and many others—including the fourteen-member Committee for the Preservation of the White House.

Though a full account of Benton's work for these various organizations falls outside the scope of this narrative, several matters are worth a passing comment. The first concerns the founding of the American Assembly. Averell Harriman and his brother had offered their family home, Arden House, to Columbia University when General Dwight D. Eisenhower was the president of the university. Eisenhower invited Benton to lunch to seek advice on whether or not the gift should be accepted. Benton urged him to accept Arden House and to use it as the home of a Columbia-sponsored group modeled after the CED. The advice was taken, and the American Assembly was born. Benton, however, blundered in one respect. "I failed to insist," he later said, "that General Eisenhower in accepting the gift should also ask Harriman and his brother to put up at least $1 million and preferably $2 million in an endowment to finance the American Assembly. The lack of such an endowment has since been a source of embarrassment to the trustees."

The second matter concerns the now dormant Committee for a United Europe. The late General William Donovan was initially its leading spirit. He was succeeded by Paul Hoffman, who later induced Benton to help formulate the committee's policies for promoting the economic and political integration of Europe. Hoffman, as the first administrator of the Marshall Plan, had consistently

---

[1] The Cleveland Conference is the "Skull and Bones" senior society in the world of education. Its seventy members are, in the main, the leading professional educators in the country. Benton is one of the three or four present members who are not professional educators. The name goes back to World War I when a group of leading educators met to discuss ways to improve the Cleveland public school system. They decided that such meetings could be annually productive. The meetings are today two days in length, with no speeches and no publicity. Benton has found them more instructive and interesting than any other meetings he has attended anywhere in the United States. He has never missed one in the years he has been a member.

urged European leaders to extend beyond the life of the Marshall Plan the "all-European" approach they had shown in allocating Marshall Plan aid for their respective nations. Hoffman saw the need for basic studies that could contribute to that objective; the American Committee for a United Europe agreed to finance such studies, and Benton twice traveled to Europe with Hoffman to commission and pay for the studies and to encourage interested European groups. In this CED type of approach, they were guided by specific recommendations made principally by Jean Monnet, and by Robert Schumann and Paul-Henri Spaak. The studies helped to lay out the economic grounds for what later became the Common Market—though ten years after the birth of the Common Market, Benton had his own way of assigning credit for its actual birth and growth. "When I saw Jean Monnet in the mid-1960s," said he, "I told him I wanted to put up a statue to him on every village green in Europe, a statue which would show Monnet sitting on a big bronze horse."

The third matter concerns Benton's membership on the board of trustees of the Eisenhower Exchange Fellowships. When the program was being formed as a sixty-second "birthday present" to President Eisenhower, Thomas McCabe, who had been intimately associated with Benton in the early work of the CED, asked Benton to join the board. "Will there be any other Democrats serving as trustees?" Benton asked. "Yes," said McCabe, "Averell Harriman and Eleanor Roosevelt." This was good enough, and Benton accepted. But when the board of trustees met with President Eisenhower in the White House, Benton discovered that there had been an amendment to McCabe's reassuring word. The "two other Democrats" were not Averell Harriman and Eleanor Roosevelt, but James Byrnes and Oveta Hobby, both of whom had bolted the Democrats to campaign for Eisenhower in 1952—the campaign which led to Benton's own defeat for reelection to the Senate. Benton, who might have seen in this an alliance between a victim and his executioner, depersonalized the circumstances in which he found himself. As the only partisan Democrat among the sixty-odd trustees, he plunged into his work, not merely because he felt that the idea of the exchange fellowships was sound, but because of his personal devotion to Eisenhower and McCabe formed in earlier years.

Benton continued an active partisan political life—though at first, he was restrained by taboos in certain Connecticut quarters.

Although he was called on to introduce Senator John F. Kennedy at the "showcase" dinner of Connecticut Democrats in Hartford early in 1954, he did not participate that fall in the campaign for the state's Democratic ticket. The one brief political appearance he made was in response to a request by Joseph Lyford who was seeking election as congressman-at-large from Connecticut. Lyford had been Benton's campaign manager in 1950, and when he asked Benton to appear for a five-minute spot on one of his television programs, Benton did so. He would gladly have offered open support to Lyford and the rest of the party ticket. Indeed, in view of his recent prominence as a senator—and the scarcity of partisan "Yankee" leaders among Connecticut Democrats—one might have thought this active involvement in the campaign would have been welcomed. But the state party leadership felt Benton should stand aside lest he "bring the McCarthy issue into the state campaign."

Elsewhere, however, the outlook was different. At the request of the Democratic National Committee, Benton campaigned for 1954 Democratic candidates in several states. His stock among Democrats was particularly high in Joseph McCarthy's own state of Wisconsin, precisely because Benton had led the Senate fight against him. Two years previously, for that very reason, he had been invited to give the keynote speech at the state convention of Wisconsin Democrats. For the same reason in 1954 he was the featured speaker at a Democratic fund-raising dinner in Milwaukee for the gubernatorial candidate, Gaylord Nelson. This was one of the most successful fund-raising dinners in the history of Wisconsin's Democratic party, and much of the success was publicly ascribed to Benton's drawing power as a front-line veteran of the anti-McCarthy wars. Elsewhere the warm political welcomes Benton got reassured him that he had not battled Joseph McCarthy in vain. Still, he did not campaign in Connecticut until 1958, and then only in connection with his own abortive bid for the Democratic nomination to the United States Senate.

Meanwhile, there was a change in Benton's relationship with Adlai Stevenson. He had known Stevenson casually since the late 1930s. In the 1940s, following the death of Frank Knox, Stevenson, acting on behalf of the employees of the *Chicago Daily News*, had asked for Benton's help in getting Mrs. Knox to sell the newspaper to the employees. Then again, in the early months of 1952, Benton had served as a middleman between President Truman and Stevenson in connection with the possibility of Stevenson's nomination as the Democratic presidential candidate in that year. Subsequently, the two men had electioneered together in Connecticut. Yet again, Stevenson and his son John Fell had stayed for more than two weeks at a Benton villa on the Riviera in 1953. But the friendship formed by these encounters was not really firmly established until November 1953 when two of Stevenson's sons at Harvard were invited to join the Bentons in Southport for Thanksgiving dinner. A week before Thanksgiving, Stevenson called Benton to say that the boys could not be in Southport; they had to join their mother who was to go to Boston to be with them. "But," said Stevenson, "may I come? I don't have any place to go for Thanksgiving dinner." Benton urged him to come, and so he did, for a full four-day weekend. There were other guests, including a considerable number of students, some from foreign countries. As part of their entertainment on Thanksgiving Eve, they were shown a dozen or more Britannica films. Stevenson, on his own initiative, contributed to the entertainment. After each film, he expanded on the subject shown by giving an extemporaneous lecture. "Adlai," Benton asked him when the evening was over, "where did you learn so much about so many different things?" Stevenson replied in his characteristically self-deprecating way; "I have spent my life collecting useless information."

Stevenson, in fact, had an insatiable curiosity and a ravenous appetite "to know." His tour de force over the Thanksgiving weekend made Benton realize this, and as a result he asked Stevenson to become a director of the Britannica company and of Britannica Films. The invitation was accepted, and Benton later gave Stevenson about 5 percent of the film company's stock, besides making him the chairman of its board of consultants.[2] Stevenson's name had a value in itself, but his being on the board had nothing in common with a star's endorsement of a product, such as hair oil, for a fee. The sale of the company's products would not have been affected one way or another by his mere presence. Stevenson worked hard to help develop the film company's educational program, to advance

---

[2]This business relationship was modified in January 1961 when Stevenson accepted President-elect Kennedy's appointment to head the United States delegation to the United Nations. Since Stevenson had to leave the Britannica Film Company, he also had to give up his stock in it, saying with a half-comic sigh, "Alas, there goes my fortune!" He remained a director of Encyclopaedia Britannica, Inc., and also of the film company until his death.

the affairs of the *Britannica* as well, and to work with Benton on other matters.

One of these, the National Defense Education Act, grew in part out of Benton's first trip to the Soviet Union in 1955. The Soviet propaganda machine and the skill with which it functioned had interested Benton since his tour in the State Department. He continued to hope that some day he would be able to study at close range the media and management of Soviet propaganda. A year and a half after the death of Joseph Stalin, the official travel agency of the Soviet Union offered foreigners a $35-a-day "de luxe" visit to Russia; and this offer may have crystallized Benton's interest in making the study he had long had in mind. He scheduled a trip to the Soviet Union for the fall of 1955 to gather material for a *Britannica Book of the Year* article on Soviet propaganda. The party was to consist of his wife Helen and an interpreter, Robert Tucker (now head of the Russian Institute at Princeton University). But the party was enlarged by one when Helen, on the eve of the scheduled departure, broke her leg. Hampered by a cast, she could move around only in a wheelchair. It was then agreed that young John Benton, age thirteen, should come along so as to be on hand in order to push his mother's wheelchair. John would miss the opening part of his fall school term, but it was reasoned that this would be offset by educational benefits to be derived from the trip. John thus became the first American child to be admitted as a "de luxe" tourist to the Soviet Union after Stalin's death.

Leningrad, the first stop, was where the Bentons spent their first full day in Russia. It was here that Benton was accidentally diverted to a study of Soviet education—though he did not abandon his intended study of the Soviet propaganda machine. The shift occurred when he visited Leningrad's world famous library at eleven o'clock in the morning. The librarian who greeted and guided him remarked that no other American had entered the place since 1938, except for a Ford Foundation fellow who had been there early in 1955. In the library's great science reading room, Benton noticed that all its desks—perhaps four hundred—were occupied. He also noticed that none of the readers looked up as his own party and the librarian bustled in. The air of the place was one of intense concentration. "Who are these people?" Benton asked the librarian. "Are they university students?" The answer was no. They were factory workers who, after completing their night shift, came to the library to study for courses for which they could receive university credit. Benton's eyes and ears popped.

From that moment, Benton began to seek information about all aspects of Soviet education, about its content, scope, quality, incentives, facilities, teacher training, and rewards. He asked questions wherever he went, of pedagogues, scientists, heads of schools and colleges, commissars, the head of Tass, the foreign editor of *Pravda*, the editor of *Izvestia*, radio and television functionaries, textbook publishers. Every encounter during a day of interviewing was the subject of a memorandum which Benton dictated at night on his portable dictaphone. When all the discs were eventually transcribed in his New York office, they came to 75,000 words of straight reporting.

Benton in all this maintained a certain critical distance from his subject matter. He saw many defects in the system of Soviet education, at least when judged by American standards. But at a time when many Americans still thought of Russians as being a mass of peasants lost in the darkness of illiteracy, Benton's leg work and questions brought him abreast of a truth known only to few of his own countrymen. It was that the Soviet Union was placing a major part of its national resources into the education of its people, that the people themselves placed their faith in education, and that the quality of the education offered in mathematics, science, and technology was of a very high order and was singularly free of Marxist dogma. Benton came away from the experience convinced that the United States, whether aware of the fact or not, was being challenged by the Soviet Union to a cold war battle that could be won or lost in their respective classrooms. Indeed, he was to invent the phrase, "the cold war of the classrooms."

He had an inside reporter in the Soviet classroom in the person of his young son John. When the Bentons had moved from Leningrad to Moscow, young John at first had little to do but "kick around" the hotel. In his father's view, such idleness was scarcely educational. Partly to correct this and partly because of his new interest in Soviet education, Benton decided to put his son into a school, but not the kind attended by the children of American diplomats or other resident Americans. He got permission from the Russian authorities to send the youth to an institution bearing the formidable name "Moscow School Number One"—which taught all classes in English except for Russian literature. The United States embassy officials to whom Benton talked had never heard of such a school—a revealing commentary on the lack of contact between the embassy and the facts of Russian life around it.[3]

The late Marguerite Higgins was then in Moscow for the *New York Herald Tribune* and living in the same hotel as the Bentons. When she heard that John was attending a Russian school, she saw a chance to get an insider's view of terra incognita. She cornered the youth in the National Hotel, loosened his tongue with Coca-Colas, and got the story of his educational experiences. Her account was subsequently carried on front pages around the world by the *Herald Tribune* syndicate, and American photographers from other capitals flew to Moscow to take pictures of John. He was briefly an international celebrity. Enough so, that when the Bentons returned to the United States, reporters at the airport were looking for the youth, not his father. There was also a request from *Life* asking John to write an article about his experiences in a Russian school to accompany special photographs, and he became *Life*'s youngest contributor up to that time. Shortly after the article appeared, former President Harry Truman wryly observed to former Senator William Benton, "You are now known as the father of John, just as I want to be known as the father of Margaret."

Benton's own thesis about Soviet education—along with what he had discovered about Soviet propaganda—was detailed in a 30,000-word article he wrote for the 1956 *Britannica Book of the Year*. This article he titled "The Voice of the Kremlin." Then he sent his 75,000 words of memorandums to Allen Dulles, head of the Central Intelligence Agency, who reproduced them for distribution in the agency. In what was meant as a compliment, Dulles told Benton that his data constituted one of the more important studies of the Soviet Union that had lately come to his notice. Naturally, Benton was pleased, but he had no compliments to offer in return. "It only goes to show," he told Dulles, "that you are sending the wrong kind of people to Russia. You are sending a lot of flatfeet who must think they are playing at cloak-and-dagger games. What you

---

[3]Benton later discovered that there were scores of such schools conducted in many different languages where Russian boys were being trained to serve their country abroad as diplomats, scientists—or spies.

need are people who can gather and assess obvious and readily accessible information which points to where Russian society is trending, and the implications in such trends."

Later, Benton also gave a full set of his memorandums to John Gunther, who was about to leave for the Soviet Union to do research for his projected book, *Inside Russia Today*. At the same time, Benton did what he could to publicize his own findings about Soviet education and their meaning. In addition to the article for the *Britannica* yearbook, this meant magazine articles, appearances before congressional committees, speeches before target audiences; in a speech before the Association of College Presidents, for example, he drew on his newly gathered data about Russian education to propose—before any other public figure—and spell out the case for a vast program of federal scholarships at the college level in the United States. He made a stir with the things he had to report and urge. But a more traumatic event was needed to win for Benton the wide audience his subject merited, particularly in the election year of 1956. Indeed, the presidential contest that was shaping up absorbed most of Benton's own attention, for he was anxious to help Adlai Stevenson win renomination as the Democratic candidate.

Stevenson's friends were of two minds about whether he should seek the nomination. Some may have felt that President Eisenhower was certain of reelection merely by declaring his availability. Stevenson, therefore, would be well advised to sit out the 1956 race in the hope of being the Democratic candidate in 1960, when he would face a less formidable rival. Benton, for one, opposed this line of reasoning. He argued that no one could say for certain what would actually happen in the future. Perhaps Eisenhower would be too ill to run for reelection in 1956. Perhaps Stevenson himself would not be alive in 1960. Some chances, like those surrounding a presidential nomination, were not postponable. They had to be seized as they presented themselves or abandoned forever. This proved to be Stevenson's own view, and this time he was no reluctant candidate waiting to be drafted.

Benton later admitted that he had grossly misjudged the extent to which Eisenhower in the White House had gained stature with an electorate devoted to "Ikonology." What concerned him immediately was the fact that Stevenson faced strong opposition within the Democratic party. Former President Truman in particular had a marked antagonism toward Stevenson, which had grown out of the conduct of the 1952 campaign. Benton felt that he should draw on his own warm relationship with Truman in an effort to soften the latter's hostility to Stevenson.

As it happened, in May 1956 Truman was to sail for England aboard the liner *United States* to receive an honorary degree from Cambridge University. It is not entirely clear whether the former president threw out a "suggestion" that Benton accompany him on the trip, or directly "asked" him to come along, or just how Benton got himself invited as a traveling companion. In any case, the two made the ocean crossing together and spent their time talking past, present, and future politics—but Benton's interventions had no influence whatever in softening Truman's hard-set opposition to Stevenson. Nor could he shake Truman's obiter dicta that Stevenson could have been elected president in 1952 if he had not fired Frank McKinney as chairman of the Democratic National Committee and with that act disrupted the "organization" McKinney had built for victory.

Benton was a Connecticut delegate to the 1956 convention in Chicago, and was Connecticut's representative on the platform committee. Despite Truman's opposition and Kefauver's showing in some of the primaries, there was no stopping Stevenson in the convention. The major interest of the Connecticut delegation centered on the vice-presidential nomination. It was at this time that Abraham Ribicoff and John Bailey emerged in the full view of the national party as the first two "big time" supporters of John F. Kennedy for a post of national party leadership. Here was the near-fulfillment of Brien McMahon's 1952 theory that the steppingstone for a Catholic aspiring to be nominated for the presidency lay by way of the vice-presidential nomination. Here, too, was the beginning of the fulfillment of Benton's 1954 theory when he introduced Kennedy to the Jefferson-Jackson Day dinner in Hartford as a man qualified to gather around himself the "bloc" of New England votes. As for Benton, he did not at the 1956 convention tie himself to Kennedy's future. His interest and identity was that of a Stevenson supporter straight down the line. Later in the fall, under the direction of the Democratic National Committee, he campaigned for Stevenson all over the country. Yet Stevenson's cause in 1956 was even more hopeless than in 1952, even without the Suez war which erupted near election day. He was defeated by a landslide.

After the election, Stevenson and other Democratic leaders outside the Congress addressed themselves to an old political problem. Who would speak for the party when it did not control the White

House? Tens of millions of Americans who had voted for Stevenson were in no way represented by Democrats in the Congress. To insist, therefore, that the Democratic leadership in the Congress should speak for the party when the White House was in Republican hands, would seal the voicelessness of the unrepresented millions. It would be to place the interests of Democrats in the urban and industrial North—where presidential elections are won or lost—at the mercy of the Democratic congressional leadership that was largely southern in character, and rural in its approach to many vital matters.

In the circumstances, Stevenson and other party leaders like Governor Lawrence of Pennsylvania, took a closer look at the Democratic National Committee. In theory, the committee was the "official" body of men and women duly chosen by the party to manage its affairs between elections. In practice, however, the committee never was a formulator of policy on the leading political questions of the day. It wasn't even interested in such questions. It was primarily an organ that quarreled over patronage, raised and distributed funds, pumped out propaganda, registered voters, procured speakers, and stimulated the state party organizations for presidential nominating conventions and campaigns. If there was to be an intellectual voice of the national party when the White House was in Republican hands, the voice needed to be created as a policy-formulating organ.

After much discussion and analysis, a Democratic Advisory Council to the National Committee was created, comprised of major party leaders from around the country. The Advisory Council in turn formed two panels of "experts." The one on foreign policy was under the chairmanship of former Secretary of State Dean Acheson; the other, on domestic policy, as noted earlier, was under the chairmanship of Professor John Kenneth Galbraith. Benton became a member of both panels.

When John Gunther returned to the United States from the Soviet Union after completing his research for *Inside Russia Today*, he called Benton to say that the 75,000 words of material he had received from Benton made the latter "the best journalist who ever went to Russia."[4] This was a heady tribute from a leading professional in the business. Benton, though delighted, protested that he was no journalist, nor had he tried to be one. He had simply

---

[4]In the book Gunther's acknowledgments thanked "above all William Benton" for his "memoranda of unique interest and value."

talked to many people in Russia whom the journalists had overlooked. "That's exactly the point," Gunther answered. "That's
what made you the best journalist." He went on to urge Benton to
convert his material into a book. "I protested that it was too late
in the day to do that," Benton subsequently recalled. "Gunther
said it wasn't, and further, that he would write the preface to such
a book. I took him only half seriously, but afterward, the idea
increasingly appealed to me, particularly when the preface arrived
by messenger, hot off Gunther's typewriter. I was interested in
bidding for the 1958 Democratic Senate nomination from Connecticut, and felt that the book would help offset the lingering McCar-
thyite charge that I was 'soft on communism.' "

There was the making of a book not only in the original 75,000
words of the memorandums, but in the 30,000-word *Britannica*
yearbook article, supplemented by many other articles and
speeches. The aggregate amounted to around 200,000 words. It was
agreed that John Howe and Edward Barrett would recast and edit
all of this. Howe and Barrett went to Florida for a week of joint
work, at the end of which they produced an 80,000-word book ready
for publication after further polishing by Benton. It was titled
This Is the Challenge, and the publication date was set for the
early spring of 1958.

In October 1957 the Soviet Union's success in launching *Sputnik*,
the first artificial earth satellite, gave a melodramatic aura to the
title *This Is the Challenge*. Americans up to that moment were
ready to credit other nations with some aptitudes superior to their
own. But it was inconceivable that any nation, much less the Russians, could outstrip them in science and applied technology. When
Sputnik shattered this illusion, the shock spun many Americans
around to confront the challenge Benton had described. It led to
a critical examination of America's educational system and a new
interest in the nature of Soviet education, particularly in science,
the status of its teachers, its educational resources and content, and
the pressures on Russian students to excel if they expected to improve their lot.

Readers of Benton's article in the 1956 *Britannica Book of the
Year* had been alerted to these matters. But in the nation at large,
very little was known about the educational system of Russia. Benton's writings and speeches thus became the first major public
resource to fill the great gap in American public knowledge about a
subject that was suddenly at the forefront of the public mind. It

was so viewed by the *New York Times* book editors who included Benton's volume in their list of the 250 best books published in 1958.

Meanwhile, the short interval between the launching of *Sputnik* and the appearance of Benton's account of the Soviet educational system earned him an unwarranted reputation as a "Soviet expert." There followed a tide of invitations to write more articles, give more speeches, and appear before more congressional committees. Benton was bemused to find himself viewed as an expert on anything. In his private thoughts, he felt that his tendency to spread himself across many fronts of activity made him thin and superficial on any one front—except on the subject of travel, where he had come to claim expert knowledge. Still, few other people in the nation knew as much as he did about Soviet education, and the few that knew more lacked Benton's personal power and public forum. Benton used both, aided by his friends and Britannica associates, Adlai Stevenson and Anna Rosenberg. The threesome were foremost among Americans not then in the government who led the drive which culminated in the passage by Congress of the National Defense Education Act of 1958.

Benton regretted the need to justify federal support for the training of scientists and technicians as an aspect of military defense. He felt such support was warranted as a good in itself. But he accepted the fruits of the National Defense Education Act and went on to tackle the larger needs of American education when the Galbraith panel of the Advisory Council to the Democratic National Committee made him the chairman of its subcommittee on education. Its other members were Beardsley Ruml; Walter Heller, later chairman of the Council of Economic Advisers under President Kennedy; Philip Coombs, then director of the Ford Foundation's Research Department and later assistant secretary of state for cultural affairs; and Professor Seymour Harris, chairman of the Economics Department at Harvard. Benton, as chairman, did most of the editing of the drafts of policy to emerge from this group. But he credited the others with having provided the intellectual content of a statement that soon had the approval of the Democratic Advisory Council. The statement set forth a program for federal aid to all aspects and levels of education—school construction, teacher supply and training, teaching materials, and merit scholarships. It left its mark on the measures President Kennedy advocated for education, measures which were to be enacted in great part during his and the Johnson administrations.

27

Benton versus Bowles

Suddenly in 1958 Benton found himself in the painful position of contending with Chester Bowles for Connecticut's Democratic nomination to the United States Senate. The two men had been intimate friends for more than thirty years. Each owed much to the other, and this clash was not to their personal liking nor to that of their mutual friends, some of whom were forced to take sides between them.

No version of how the clash came about is complete, nor does one square with another. Benton saw the matter through one knothole, Bowles through another, and John Bailey through still another; and the same can be said of Abraham Ribicoff and Thomas Dodd, who were among the principal actors in the drama. To complicate matters further, it is hard to know whether the different versions retrieved from memory some years after the clash correspond to what the different actors actually thought and did in the hour of decision. Things standing so, it would be abuse of language to say that the version to be presented here is the whole truth and nothing but the truth. The most that can be claimed for it is an attempt to sift available evidence and to construct a coherent account of what seems to be the more plausible version of how the clash came about.

In the summer of 1957, Benton had talked extensively with Democratic leaders in Connecticut about the senatorial nomination that had to be made in 1958. He had told Bowles he would do this while Bowles was away for the summer so that he could assess the lay of the land. He did not know at that time that Bowles was interested in the nomination, or if so, how intense his interest was. Benton recalled that after the election of 1950 he had flown to Bermuda to visit Bowles to ask whether he was interested in running for the Senate in 1952. Bowles said he did not. The two then discussed a future for Bowles in foreign policy, which was to come to pass with the latter's appointment as ambassador to India. Even if Bowles had changed his mind about serving in the Senate, the conversations Benton had with Connecticut leaders in the summer of 1957 convinced him that while neither he nor Bowles was a front runner for the nomination, Bowles had little if any chance but that Benton might have a reasonable chance. The front runners were Dick Lee, the able mayor of New Haven, and former Representative Thomas Dodd, once the national youth administrator in Connecticut, who after V-J Day had been on the United States legal staff at the Nuremberg trials. Dodd had given up his House seat to run for the Senate in 1956 and was swamped in the Eisenhower landslide. Now his friends said he was "entitled to another chance."

Lee seemed to have the edge in the support of the party leaders and also to stand high with liberal voters because of his eye-catching work in redeveloping New Haven. Dodd, however, remained a strong contender, though he was opposed by a number of influential Democrats and fellow Irish Catholics. Indeed, the near equality of strength between Lee and Dodd raised the possibility of a deadlock at the state nominating convention. If that proved the case, the nomination might go to a compromise candidate. It was by no means likely that this would actually happen; but if it did, Benton hinged his own prospects to the possibility of being the compromise choice. Whether or not Chester Bowles was interested in the nomination, he remained an alternative possible choice of the convention in case neither Lee nor Dodd could prevail. Bowles had many more devoted followers in the state than Benton and could summon support from the personal political organization he had built, first as Connecticut's OPA administrator and then as governor. In these roles, however, he also had aroused hostilities which Benton was spared. One of the party leaders who were Bowles's antagonists was Francis Smith of Waterbury, a former state Democratic chairman and the brother of a high-ranking Connecticut judge. The Smiths, a rich Irish Catholic family, held a position of prestige in Waterbury not unlike that of the Kennedys in Boston.

Benton thus had neither Bowles's personal following nor his opposition by party leaders. He had friends in every contending camp, and he seemed to be the second choice of most foreseeable rival factions. His prospects, it should be emphasized again, were premised on a deadlock between Lee and Dodd in which he might emerge as a compromise candidate. He did not envision a direct clash with Bowles.

Benton did not have a chance to discuss all this in a face-to-face meeting with Bowles, nor can it be said that Bowles would have accepted Benton's conclusions even if they had been presented to him directly. In any case, Dodd made a sudden move in September. He called Benton to say that he was formally announcing his candidacy for the Senate nomination the next day, and he urged Benton to announce his own candidacy at the same time. Benton was Dodd's second choice and if Dodd couldn't make it, he preferred Benton to Lee or Bowles. With this alert from Dodd, Benton tried to reach Bowles in Maine by telephone, but Bowles was yachting off the coast and there was no way of reaching him. The next day, therefore, Benton issued an informal public statement saying that anyone who had ever served in the Senate could not but be interested in the possibility of returning to it. He added words of praise for Bowles, Dodd, and Lee as possible nominees.

When Benton finally established contact with Bowles, the latter did not indicate that he was disturbed by Benton's intended candidacy. Nor did he indicate that he was after the nomination himself and pursuing it according to his own strategic plan.

In the fall and early winter months, Benton's own calculations continued to be based on the assumption that Lee would be a candidate for the nomination. But then, on 13 February 1958, Lee surprisingly announced that his "obligations to the program of redevelopment and renewal . . . in New Haven must keep [him] from being a candidate for the Senate" that year. Many business and civic leaders in New Haven had doubtlessly urged him to stay on as mayor in order to complete the work he had begun. But his withdrawal from the Senate race proceeded from other considerations as well. For one thing, Bowles reportedly had spoken to him several times in late 1957 urging him not to be a candidate for the Senate nomination on the ground that it was Bowles's own opportunity and he was prepared for it. Lee was a friend of Bowles and looked up to him as a national and international figure. For another thing, at a Connecticut testimonial dinner for Adlai Stevenson in 1957, Dodd had reportedly told Lee that he did not intend to be a candidate for the Senate in 1958, but he later claimed that Lee had misunderstood him. Further, in pushing his own candidacy, Dodd had threatened a challenge primary after the convention—an option open to anyone who received at least 20 percent of the delegate vote at the convention. Lee was not willing to go into a slugfest with Dodd in a primary contest unless he had the full backing of Governor Abraham Ribicoff and the state Democratic chairman, John Bailey. Lee was not sure that he could get such backing.

In any case, at the time of Lee's withdrawal, Bowles was on his yacht in the West Indies. Perhaps he was in no position to telephone Benton of his own intentions. Benton learned of them in a newspaper announcement that Bowles was coming into the Senate race. Thus what Benton had never anticipated—direct rivalry with Bowles— now loomed instead of a possible clash between Lee and Dodd, with Benton the residual legatee.

Bowles may have assumed that his announcement would be followed by Benton's withdrawal. But whether or not Benton himself would have been willing to withdraw, he was no longer a wholly free agent. In the previous six months of effort to muster delegate strength, virtually all of Benton's support came from Irish leaders like Edward B. Bergin, the mayor of Waterbury, and Alphonsus Donahue, the Democratic leader in Stamford, who were disaffected with Dodd. As experienced politicians, they may have foreseen a possibility which Benton overlooked—that Lee would withdraw from the Senate race and that Bowles would come in. In any case, they had pledged Benton their support—and agreed to serve as co-chairmen of his campaign—on condition that he promise, which he did, not to withdraw from the contest no matter what happened. His withdrawal would have left them out on a limb—in the awkward position of having to choose between Dodd and Bowles. Benton had no chance to inform Bowles of this pledge before the latter announced his candidacy.

Where Bowles was concerned, an element of passion that touched his candidacy for the Senate nomination was traceable to the way he envisioned himself as a possible Democratic presidential candidate in 1960. All four of the main contenders for the 1960 Democratic nomination, Senate Majority Leader Lyndon Johnson and Senators John F. Kennedy, Stuart Symington, and Hubert Humphrey, faced barriers of one sort or another. Leaving Stevenson out of account, the Democratic presidential nomination still seemed to be "up for grabs" in the early spring of 1958. The lure of that prize may have been decisive in inducing Bowles to seek the intermediate prize of the Senate. He reasoned that if he could win the Senate nomination, then with the strong Democratic tide that had begun to run in the nation, he had a good chance to win the Senate seat. If he won the Senate seat, then with his fine record as an executive in the Roosevelt and Truman administrations, as a former governor and former ambassador to India, he felt he would be in a strong position to seek the presidential nomination. The ambition was honorable, and Bowles's talents were outstanding—even if his long-range plans in connection with the presidency seemed fanciful to John Bailey and to other Democratic leaders in Connecticut.

In any case, Benton was urged in the name of such long-range plans to withdraw from the Senate race and to throw his support to Bowles, who seemed convinced that he could win the Senate nomination if Benton agreed to help. Benton was equally convinced that Bowles's larger aspirations for the 1960 presidential nomination were unrealistic. The fact that Bowles came from tiny Connecticut would surely bar him from the presidential nomination, and if so, his approach to the Senate nomination as a step toward the larger objective was pointless. But there was more to the matter. Benton was reminded that he owed his original prominence in Connecticut politics to Bowles's difficult but courageous act in agreeing with Senator McMahon to appoint him a senator in 1949. Was it now Benton's turn to pay off an I.O.U. by withdrawing and throwing his support to Bowles? Benton acknowledged that debt—and the one dating back to 1935, when Bowles's stand made it possible for Benton to leave their advertising agency. He further acknowledged the debt he owed to Bowles as the presumably key man who had recommended him as assistant secretary of state. On the other hand, Benton, having failed to anticipate Bowles's move, had committed himself firmly to Bergin, Donahue, and others. Moreover, Bowles owed a number of debts to Benton. Not the least of these was the appointment as United States ambassador to India, which enabled Bowles to become an authoritative voice on United States foreign policy. The reply from the Bowles camp was that the real reason for Benton's standing pat was none of these. The real reason was Benton's deluded belief that since he was the second choice of virtually all of Bowles's delegates, and the second choice of most of Dodd's, he could win the Senate nomination for himself if there was more than one ballot.

All three, Benton, Bowles, and Dodd, campaigned across the state to influence delegates. They appeared on radio and television. They engaged each other in debates. They spent scores of thousands of dollars on travel, promotion, dinners for delegates. But campaign as they did, one fact finally stood out clearly from the increasingly

tangled, emotion-charged situation. It is that neither Benton nor
Bowles was a match for Governor Abraham Ribicoff in political
maneuver or political muscle. Ribicoff, who had been elected governor of Connecticut by a narrow margin in 1954, was standing for
reelection in 1958. His approach to the identity of his senatorial
running mate on the ticket was naturally influenced by how that
person could affect his chances for reelection and by whether that
candidate might become a potential rival to himself. In his own
calculation of consequences, he may have felt that neither Bowles
nor Benton could bring to the ticket any strong elements of support which Ribicoff did not already have from his four-year record
as governor. And each man was a potential rival. With Lee out of
the race, the only alternative source of supplementary support lay
in securing the Senate nomination for Dodd and with it a block of
Irish Catholic votes for the ticket. It was also in Ribicoff's interest
to have the decision of the convention so decisive as to discourage
any Senate hopeful with 20 percent of the convention vote from
appealing over the head of the convention and forcing the party
into a postconvention challenge primary. He could assume that
neither Bowles nor Benton would do so, although Dodd threatened
just that. An open battle between a labor-liberal candidate like
Benton or Bowles with some organization support and a popular
rank-and-file figure like Dodd could not only mangle the prospects
of winning the Senate seat but, more importantly, could risk the
loss of the governorship.

It was a view shared by John Bailey, who would have preferred
Benton or Bowles to Dodd, a maverick who could turn on him. Yet
he counted on the fact that Dodd was a vote-getter and was especially popular in Hartford, where 40 percent of the state's Democrats reside. Above all, Bailey wanted the state party to emerge
intact from the nominating contest.

To observers at the convention scene, it seemed clear that Ribicoff
was in firm control of the convention. (In this matter, he had the
backing of Francis Smith, Bowles's enemy. Smith later told Benton
in Southport, "I would have liked to support you but I knew I could
defeat Bowles with Dodd, and I didn't know whether I could defeat
him with you.") Ribicoff, however, did not publicly declare himself
in Dodd's favor. The choice of the Senate candidate, said he, should
be decided by a "free and open convention." That is what Stevenson
had done at the 1956 Democratic National Convention when he

denied himself the traditional right of a presidential nominee to pick his vice-presidential running mate and left the choice up to the convention. Ribicoff—with Bailey concurring—further declared that they would "pass" their own votes at first, but would then vote for the candidate who had more than 50 percent on the first ballot, with the hope that a massive vote switch would follow, to give the top man more than 80 percent of the total.

Benton vigorously protested that this was an "abdication of leadership." By seeming to leave the decision up to the convention instead of following tradition and indicating plainly whom he wanted as a senatorial runningmate, Benton claimed that Ribicoff would later be in a position to say to the respective supporters of Benton and Bowles: "I really wanted your man; I knew he would make the best Senator; but what could I do? I had to follow the wishes of the convention." On the other hand, said Benton, if Ribicoff really meant to leave the decision up to the convention, he should let the delegates reach a consensus "in the time-honored way," on a sequence of votes taken after the first ballot. This would signal to all other delegates who depended on the patronage of the governor that the convention really was open.

Ribicoff, a skilled tactician, had carefully assessed the pattern of votes before there were any roll calls. He concluded that Bowles would outstrip Benton on the first ballot but would still fall short of Dodd's strength by about 100 delegates. He made no forays against the Bowles camp but let its members "roll along" on the theory that this would be better for party harmony afterward. But because Benton was the weaker figure in pledged delegate strength—with about 160–70 delegates on the eve of the convention—both the Ribicoff and Bowles people made the Benton camp the object of a political blitz. Benton's delegates were caught in the middle, between pressures from Ribicoff and Bowles. On the night before the voting, 60 or 70 of Benton's delegates were captured for Dodd or Bowles, leaving Benton with only about 100 when the balloting began.

On the first and sole ballot, Benton and Bowles combined got fewer votes than Dodd. "You may not have the quantity," said a veteran Connecticut political reporter to Benton, "but you sure have the quality." That was one small consolation after a tormented, tormenting, and time-consuming experience that ended in a shambles. There was another small consolation. Because Benton and Bowles combined got fewer votes than Dodd on the first ballot, it was hard to claim that they had killed each other off. Benton continued to believe that if he had withdrawn, 90 percent of his delegates would have gone to Dodd, but that if Bowles had not come into the race he might have been able to win Lee and other Bowles men, plus Smith and others opposed to Bowles. Thus, he reasoned, he might have had a chance. To this day, their mutual friends have found it difficult to understand the complex story of how the two men came into open rivalry on the convention floor. Benton and Bowles never tried to explain themselves to each other, and neither might have fully persuaded the other, but they did manage to reweave the frayed strands of their long friendship.

Ribicoff went on to carry the state by a historic 246,000, while Dodd won the Senate seat easily. Bowles had settled for the Democratic nomination in Connecticut's second congressional district—comprised of four thinly populated eastern counties—and was elected to the House of Representatives. John Bailey, hoping to assuage hurt feelings on all sides, had offered Benton the Democratic nomination as congressman-at-large from Connecticut. When Benton declined, Bailey proposed that he run as congressman from the Fairfield district, a traditionally Republican stronghold. This too was refused. Benton had less chance to carry Fairfield than to win as congressman-at-large. Had he followed Bailey's advice, he would have been carried into the House of Representatives in the 1958 Democratic sweep of Connecticut, and reelected in the Kennedy wave of 1960. From there he might have laid the ground for a strong bid for the 1962 Senate nomination. But he told Bailey that he was too old to start the tough grind up the long ladder of seniority in the House of Representatives. Besides, he had far too many other things to do to which he attached far greater importance than a junior seat in the House.

As the 1960 Democratic National Convention drew closer, Benton was urged to join the Ribicoff-Bailey commitment to Kennedy. It would have made sense for him to do so, given his continued hope of returning to his great and unrequited love—a seat in the United States Senate. Benton, however, would not fit in with the tactical plans of Ribicoff and Bailey, though the two men could be of vital importance to his continuing senatorial aspirations. He persisted in the hope that Adlai Stevenson would declare himself a candidate for the Democratic presidential nomination, and he meant to help him get it. Though Stevenson in 1960 was unwilling to give a positive sign of aggressive interest in being nominated for a third time, Benton still refused to fall in line with the move toward Kennedy among Connecticut Democrats. With Stevenson's knowledge and approval, he gave his temporary backing to their frequent companion, Senator Hubert Humphrey, who was now a formally announced candidate against Kennedy.

Benton, in his post-Senate days, remained convinced that Humphrey was a man of exceptional gifts. On grounds of personal affection alone, he remained in close touch with the man. He visited him at his home in Waverly, dined and stayed overnight with him in Washington, went to Minnesota at his request to campaign for Eugene McCarthy. He was ready to help Humphrey wherever and whenever possible. The need for a special kind of help arose on the eve of the 1960 preferential primaries in Wisconsin, where Humphrey and Kennedy were contending for delegate support. When Benton learned that Humphrey didn't have enough money to take his wife, Muriel, with him on his Wisconsin campaign, he sent him a check for $5,000. Subsequently, Humphrey was asked on a Washington television show about who was putting up the money for his Wisconsin campaign, and he answered simply, "Bill Benton." The reply hit the front pages of the Connecticut papers. It later led to an honest error that slipped past Theodore White and crept into his notable book, *The Making of the President—1960*. In White's version, John Bailey got in touch with Benton and threatened to ride him out of the Democratic party in Connecticut unless he stopped contributing to Humphrey's campaign. Benton's version was different in every respect. "It was wholly out of character for John Bailey to say anything like the words Teddy White ascribed to him," Benton related. "John Bailey did get in touch with me, but what he said was this: 'Since you gave $5,000 to Hubert's campaign, I want you to even the accounts by giving $5,000 to Jack Kennedy's campaign.' I told John that if Jack was nominated for the presidency, I would give him $10,000, which I later did."

When Humphrey's bid for the Democratic nomination foundered in the West Virginia primaries, Benton still held back from jumping on the Kennedy bandwagon. He continued to hope that Stevenson would declare himself a candidate for the nomination. "I still thought," said he, "that Adlai would make the best president of all available men in the Democratic party." At a later date, Benton surmised that "Adlai may have figured he would settle for secretary of state and I doubt it occurred to him that any Democratic president would do other than appoint him to the post. His desire for the secretaryship now seems obvious to me in everything he did from '52 to '60. To prepare himself, he took a trip around the world in '53. Then he made his trip through Africa—he invited me to join him on it and I made a very great mistake because I didn't. Then in the spring of '60 there was the two-month trip he and I made through South America. Why was he doing all this foreign traveling? I think he was trying to position himself beyond challenge for the post of secretary of state in any future Democratic administration."

On the eve of the 1960 Democratic Convention in Los Angeles, Benton went after the presidential nomination for Stevenson harder than Stevenson himself had ever done. Others joined Benton in that effort. They included Eleanor Roosevelt, Herbert Lehman, Tom Finletter, Senator Mike Monroney, who was the "campaign manager" of the effort, and James Doyle, the former Democratic state chairman of Wisconsin. Monroney needed help, and it was Benton who advanced much of the money that enabled Doyle to go first to Washington and then to Los Angeles where he organized the emotion-charged demonstrations for Stevenson inside and outside the convention hall. But it was all to no avail. Benton, for example, was the only delegate from Connecticut for Stevenson. He supported him to the bitter end ; Senator Tom Dodd was the only Connecticut delegate for Lyndon Johnson; the other forty delegates from Connecticut were for Kennedy, and as their numbers were duplicated in other state delegations, John F. Kennedy was acclaimed the 1960 presidential candidate. "Eleanor Roosevelt, Herbert Lehman, Mike Monroney, Hubert Humphrey and I," said Benton afterward, "were more faithful to Adlai than he was to himself."

It was later reported—and Benton still believes—that Stevenson at the convention had virtually been offered the post of secretary of state on condition that he make the speech placing Kennedy's name in nomination as the party standard-bearer for the presidency. It was also later reported that he had been offered the vice-presidential nomination on the same condition. Why would Stevenson reject such offers? Benton, who has joined in the speculation about this question, understood the answer to go like this: Stevenson had assured Stuart Symington and other candidates in the 1960 nominating race that he would not personally seek the nomination, nor would he venture a "laying on of hands" on anybody. He promised strict neutrality. Thus he didn't feel he could nominate Kennedy without breaking faith with Symington and others.

Two postscripts need to be added here. Presented in reverse chronological order, one concerns Stevenson's appointment in January 1961 as the United States representative to the United Nations. The other concerns the Benton-Stevenson trip throughout Latin America in the early months of 1960.

Right after the 1960 election, a very highly placed figure in the federal government approached Benton to ask if he would accept the United Nations appointment if it should be offered. The answer was a flat no. It was a rough, tough, brutally unpleasant assignment. Subsequently, in January 1961, Benton visited Stevenson at his home in Libertyville, Illinois. President Kennedy had announced that he would appoint Dean Rusk as secretary of state, and that Stevenson had been offered the post of United States representative to the United Nations. Stevenson had not yet decided whether to accept, and Benton was at Libertyville to talk over the decision that had to be made soon. "In what I had to say to him," Benton recalled, "I was naturally influenced by my own unwillingness to accept the same appointment. But in addition I told Adlai that if he took the assignment, it would almost certainly disqualify him for a future appointment as secretary of state. On the other hand, if he did not go to the UN, he would remain a powerful figure waiting on the sidelines to be called as Rusk's successor."

The advice to Stevenson did not imply any criticism of Rusk's talents. Benton had come to know Rusk in the State Department in the immediate postwar years and thought highly of him. Rather the advice, proceeded from a piece of vital statistics: that secretaries of state tend to have a high political mortality rate, particularly if they come to their post without either political muscle or independent standing in the power structure of the Congress, or with virtually no prior intimate working relations with a new president. Cordell Hull, who served as secretary of state longer than any other man in American history, owed his power of survival to the strong political base he had built in the Congress when he was one of its members; besides, he had maintained fairly close contact with Franklin D. Roosevelt in the latter's pre-presidential years. None of this was true in Rusk's case. He had no personal political power base, nor had he been close to the Congress prior to his appointment as secretary of state. He was unknown to President-elect Kennedy. It seemed reasonable to assume, therefore, that he could be a casualty of the slings and arrows which cut down many secretaries of state.

Benton's reasoning did not take into account the care and skill with which Rusk must have studied the assorted ambushes in which secretaries of state were cut down, in order to learn to make as small a target as possible. The future would show that despite frequent predictions that he was "through," he had remarkable survival powers in his highly vulnerable post. This Benton could not be expected to foresee when he advised Stevenson not to accept the United Nations assignment but to keep himself available as Rusk's successor. Stevenson was no better at foreseeing Rusk's durability. Yet he finally decided to accept the United Nations assignment. Why? On the night before he made his decision, he had dined with George Ball, an older and closer friend than Benton. Ball urged him to take the appointment, saying that the chance to be secretary of state had passed Stevenson by, perhaps forever. The United Nations appointment was probably the best offer he would ever get. It was the one way Stevenson could stay in public life. If he turned down the United Nations offer, he would be out of public life and would condemn himself, by his own standards, to years of frustration. Benton had minimized this essential point, and he later came to see that Ball had been right. Stevenson, out of public life in a Democratic administration, would be doomed to frustration.

The second postscript, told out of chronological order, concerns the Benton-Stevenson trip throughout Latin America in early 1960. The trip itself entailed a visit to twelve countries—Mexico, Guatemala, Costa Rica, Panama, Colombia, Ecuador, Peru, Chile, Argentina, Uruguay, Brazil, and Venezuela. Benton and Stevenson talked to eleven of the twelve presidents in these countries, and with the prime minister of Peru, whose president was in Europe. They talked with cabinet ministers, leaders of the opposition, labor leaders, students, educators, and school administrators. Benton, as always, dictated a report at the end of the day about everything he had seen or heard and mailed the discs to his New York office for transcription. The total wordage came to around 160,000. This would be no small achievement for a man who sat still and did nothing but write day after day for two months. Yet the discipline that was

required to record anything at all during such a trip can be inferred
from the preface Benton wrote for the book he published in 1961
under the title *The Voice of Latin America,* based on his dictated
reports. An extract reads:

I would not recommend to the tourist seeking a good time the
regimens to which Governor Stevenson and I were subjected.
Always our schedule of 16-hour days was unusual. Our Latin
American hosts and the U.S. embassies vied with each other in
homicidal hospitality. Often this meant ceremony and protocol; the 2½- or 3-hour luncheon with its emphasis on speeches
rather than informal give and take with a few key people; the
late dinner and reception with toasts and speeches and brandy
still being served at 1 A.M., six hours before plane time. When
we wanted to visit the rector of a University and a few of his
professors, often we arrived to find a couple of hundred professors with students and a schedule of speeches. All of this
was complimentary and much of it was instructive, but it was
not the best way to relax—nor was it always the best way to
learn the facts of political life.

The first day of our journey—in Mexico City—was not
untypical. The city is 7,500 feet high and my doctor had
warned me we should allow a full day to adjust ourselves to the
altitude. Our tourist plane from Chicago arrived at night an
hour or more late. Dinnerless, we got to the hotel about 10:30
to find the Overseas Press Club waiting for us in their new
clubrooms. We met with them until about 1 o'clock, gulping
scrambled eggs and Coca-Cola.

The next morning, we were up at 7. At 9:30 our able and
hard-working ambassador, Robert C. Hill of New Hampshire,
had the entire staff of the embassy to greet us in the embassy's
gardens—about five or six hundred people. We gave little
speeches. Then we had our "briefing" by Ambassador Hill and
his embassy officials—until sometime around noon when we
called on Foreign Minister Manuel Tello. This visit was followed by his three-hour formal luncheon of welcome, and this
in turn by a visit to the Palacio de Bellas Artes with the famous
Mexican Artist Rufino Tamayo, to see his murals. Back at the
hotel at 5:05 for a call at 6 on Pres. Adolfo Lopez Mateos.
From the president's mansion we were rushed to the U.S.

Embassy at 7:30 to stand in line to shake hands with 750 people. We were still on our feet after 10:00—and with no supper—but with a well-pleased ambassador and staff.

The Voice of Latin America, which first appeared in condensed form as an article in the 1961 *Britannica Book of the Year*, was published in full-length book form later that same year. The fiasco at the Bay of Pigs had already occurred, and there were many bleak overtones to that event. One of them was the way in which the White House had apparently kept Stevenson in the dark about the planned American involvement in the invasion of Cuba by exiles from the Castro regime. Thus, in his innocence about the facts of the matter, Stevenson's reflex reaction at the United Nations was to deny flatly that the United States had any part in the abortive invasion. But then came the belated disclosure in Washington that the United States had been deeply implicated in the Bay of Pigs invasion. It was a cruel blow, undeserved by a man whose standing in Latin American eyes, as Benton saw the matter during the 1960 Latin American trip, was described by Benton as follows (in *The Voice of Latin America*):

> Throughout the trip, Governor Stevenson was infinitely patient. The entire two-month-long journey was a great personal triumph for him. He seems known to almost every Latin American. He was besieged everywhere by admiring crowds seeking his autographs, bows, handshakes and smiles. Though we traveled strictly as private citizens, his appearance became a triumph also for the United States; he symbolizes, in his learning, his wisdom and wit, his urbanity, oratory and his humane qualities, the characteristics the Latin Americans most value in intellectual and political leaders.

The belated disclosure that Stevenson was personally innocent of any involvement in the Bay of Pigs affair enhanced his moral authority and personal prestige in the eyes of some of the United Nations delegates. But it also disturbed many to discover that a former presidential nominee, whose 1960 appearance in Latin America had been a "triumph for the United States," had been kept outside the inner circle of policy makers in the Kennedy administration.

There were further passages in Benton's preface to *The Voice of*

Latin America which had a bearing on the future course of events. In one, for example, he drew a picture of social and political instability in Latin America growing out of the sharp contrasts between poverty and wealth, and progress and backwardness, dwelling side by side. Thus:

> We saw modern buildings, rising at a feverish rate in Mexico City, in São Paulo, Brasilia and elsewhere—buildings that for brilliant architecture and imaginative use of local materials have no counterpart in the United States. In Lima, Rio de Janeiro and most of the big cities we also saw festering slums in the very shadows of tall luxurious apartment houses—slums where as much as 20% of the city's population exists in unbelievable squalor. We dined in presidential palaces adorned by tapestries, serenaded by bands and surrounded by magnificently gold-encrusted trappings from the 19th century. And we ate hamburgers with university students in the Tunjuelito of Bogotá. . . . We saw thousands of sleek, expensive automobiles in oil-rich Caracas and barefoot Indians pulling wooden plows in the fields of Peru—where the per capita income is only $100 per year.

To Benton, three great Latin American problems seemed of paramount importance. They were the lack of economic development, the threat of communism, and the paucity of education. In treating each of these in his report, he had a question to pose. Could the United States and the free world—through a better understanding of Latin American conditions and trends—develop policies better designed to advance the freedom, the progress, and the security of all? The current world struggle, said he, plus the immense variety of Latin America and its rapidity of change, were forcing upon Latin America and North America alike the need for a better understanding of their common goals. He welcomed any signs that pointed to a start in the planning of measures oriented toward such goals. Active cooperation was a far wiser course than letting things happen, as had been generally true in the past.

But it was on a somber note—amplified throughout the report—that Benton completed his preface:

> It would be false to say that I felt encouraged at the end of the trip. Yes, we had met gifted and indeed heroic men along

the way. The social projects they had begun were visible on all sides. Nevertheless, when I said my good-bye it was with a foreboding fear that the start of better things to come might be despoiled in the not far distant future. Whether or not this happens will depend in large part on the quality of hemispheric leadership—and not least in this balance will be the skill and leadership of the United States. This fact should be kept in mind by the reader as he peruses this report. Our presidents for decades to come will need the support and informed judgments of concerned citizens.

The Voice of Latin America was widely praised when it was published in 1961, and by no one more than leading members of the new Kennedy administration. Arthur Schlesinger, Jr., said it was the best book about Latin America he had ever read, and Benton replied that this was a commentary on the paucity of scholarship in the United States about Latin America. But though the text anticipated virtually all the major Latin American problems that were to plague the Kennedy and Johnson administrations, the necessary answers to those problems were slow in forthcoming. So slow, that as late as 1965, with only moderate revisions, the material in *The Voice of Latin America* remained sufficiently current to warrant reissuing the book in paperback.

28

The Best Ambassadorship

In December 1960 after President-elect Kennedy had appointed Chester Bowles as undersecretary of state and Dean Rusk as secretary of state, Bowles telephoned Benton to ask if he would be willing to go to Rome as the United States ambassador. "Rusk and I would like to recommend you to the president when we see him tomorrow," Bowles observed, "but if you are sure that you don't want the post, we'd rather not make the recommendation." He explained that there had been trouble with other proposed appointments. He didn't like to recommend people, only to have them refuse an embassy when it was offered to them directly by the president-elect.

Throughout his career, Benton had been approached many times with implied offers of an ambassadorial appointment and had declined every time. "An ambassador," he used to say, "spends 90 percent of his time doing things he doesn't want to do for the privilege of the other 10 percent." Benton, now sixty, immediately declined the prospect of the mission to Rome. He wondered nonetheless whether Kennedy himself knew of the telephone call. The point was cleared up for him by Clare Booth Luce, who had been the ambassador to Rome during the early Eisenhower years.

One of the ground rules for the Benton friendship with both Henry and Clare Luce was the right of mutual criticism without fear that the friendship would collapse. A month after President Kennedy's inauguration, Clare Luce suddenly hurled a barbed question at Benton. Why had he turned down the appointment to Rome? Benton answered that he had never really been offered the ambassadorial post. Then he went on to tell the story of Bowles's telephone call. Mrs. Luce dismissed the answer. The call, said she, had been a direct offer; it would not have been made unless Kennedy knew about it beforehand. Benton should have had enough sense to realize that. He insisted that he didn't know that. Anyway, it made no difference since he didn't want the post. But he was curious. How did she know that he had been approached about his interest in the Rome embassy? She explained that the source was her husband. Henry Luce on a recent visit with Kennedy had asked him, among other things, why Benton had been "left out" of the new administration. Kennedy replied that it was not by decision of his own. "I offered him the embassy in Rome," said Kennedy, "but he turned it down."

There had been a long history to Henry Luce's relationship with Kennedy, and Benton gained an insight into some of it when the Luces were guests of the Bentons on a yachting cruise during the second summer of Kennedy's administration. "For several days in succession on board the yacht," Benton recalled, "Harry spent all his time on deck, busily writing some sort of manuscript. I finally asked him what he was up to. He told me that he was revising the preface to the book *While England Slept*, which Kennedy had published in his early twenties soon after graduating from Harvard. I then asked Harry why he had written the original preface. His answer was a three-letter word: 'Joe'—meaning Joseph P. Kennedy. I began to understand why President Kennedy never denied the great part his father played in careful long-range preparations bearing on his career and success."

In 1960, Luce in his magazines had opposed the election of Kennedy as president. But his opposition was largely pro forma. The reality was that the Luce publications had regularly shown Kennedy in a highly favorable light in the widespread coverage they gave him, starting with his bid for the Democratic nomination and then for the presidency. This fact eventually led to a question which President Kennedy put to Benton at one of their encounters in the White House. The president knew of Benton's intimacy with Henry and Clare Luce, and he asked Benton out of the blue: "Do you think there's any possibility that Luce could ever be converted into a Democrat?" "Well," said Benton, "his magazines gave you wonderful treatment in your presidential campaign." When the president agreed, Benton suggested that Luce may have accounted for Kennedy's winning margin of one-tenth of 1 percent. "If he'd really gone after you," Benton said, "it's my belief you wouldn't be president." Kennedy promptly replied, "That's right. I agree on that.

That's why I asked you the question." To which Benton said: "The answer to your question is an unequivocal 'No.' "

As the 1962 election year drew near, Benton continued to hope that somehow he might secure the Democratic nomination for the Senate. The same circumstances and forces which secured his appointment in 1949 again seemed to be operating in his favor. Connecticut was represented in the Senate by Thomas Dodd, an Irishman, and furthermore it had as governor a man who was born in Ireland, John Dempsey. This worked against the possible nomination of Mayor Richard Lee of New Haven, a Catholic of Irish ancestry. This worked in Benton's favor. Furthermore, Senator Dodd, like Senator McMahon before him, might prefer a businessman rather than a lawyer, and a man who could finance his own campaign. He had encouraged, not discouraged, Benton's hopes for the 1962 nomination. Even Governor Ribicoff, who was now Kennedy's secretary of health, education, and welfare, had told Benton that he did not expect to come back to the state. He had suggested, perhaps in jest: "John Bailey is going to run you for the Senate!" But this seemingly favorable chance was suddenly eclipsed by a decision reached by Abraham Ribicoff in the spring of 1962.

Ribicoff was thought to entertain the honorable ambition of a seat on the Supreme Court. It was rumored that Kennedy had offered him the attorney generalship but that he had preferred the health, education, and welfare post as less of a potential handicap to an aspirant to the Supreme Court. A Court vacancy seemed imminent because it was clear that Justice Felix Frankfurter, aging and in poor health, must soon resign. Frankfurter, however, conscious of the need to resign, let President Kennedy know in person and in writing that he would not step down from the Court if his place would go to Ribicoff. The justice arranged a meeting with Benton to tell him so, and Benton brought Adlai Stevenson along. Frankfurter's grounds for this opposition to his likely successor are obscure, but apparently the president felt compelled to fall in with the justice's position. When Ribicoff learned that an appointment to the Supreme Court was apparently out of the question in the foreseeable future, he decided that he would rather serve in the Senate than in the cabinet. He thus secured President Kennedy's pledge of support if he left the cabinet to seek the Democratic 1962 senatorial nomination from Connecticut; his decision in the matter was conveyed to Benton by John Bailey in March 1962. It put an end to Benton's own hopes of being the senatorial candidate.

Later, in reviewing his political errors, Benton felt he had made a mistake in his brusque telephone refusal of the proposed ambassadorial appointment to Rome. "I should have told Chet Bowles that I wanted to talk to President Kennedy about it," he said. "Then at an arranged meeting, I should have said: 'Mr. President, Harry Truman told me I had the best voting record in the U.S. Senate. You need me in the Senate much more than you need me in Rome. Can I go to Rome now on condition that you will support me for the Senate nomination in 1962? Abe Ribicoff tells me that he is not coming back to the state. Tom Dodd will tell you that I have his unequivocal support. Won't you discuss the matter with Tom and John Bailey and Abe? It will help build me up for the Senate if I served a couple years in Rome. I could learn some Italian and develop myself with the Italian voters in Connecticut, the biggest bloc of voters in the state. Prescott Bush will be a formidable candidate and I can use that kind of buildup.' This would have been the language that the president would have understood. If I had spoken this way, and secured the hope of President Kennedy's support, I should have gone to Rome." Another man might have seen the possibilities at the time, but Benton, with his peculiar insensitivity to some of the nuances of politics, did not.

As an afterthought, Benton admitted: "Unfortunately, I am not as good at politics as I am in business. I did not foresee the potential developments and the risks of the future. I did not think about the fact that Abe Ribicoff might change his mind, that other things might happen. In 1960, I just knew I had a lot of things to do in the next two years which I preferred to Rome. I thought I'd be willing to take on London, where my role as publisher of the *Encyclopaedia Britannica* would be a big advantage to me. I asked for it again in 1960, as I had when I was asked about Paris in 1948, and learned it had been promised to David Bruce."

Aside from the proposed appointment to Rome, there were other indirect approaches to Benton about a place in the Kennedy administration. Two of these grew out of his book *The Voice of Latin America*. One entailed the post of assistant secretary of state for Latin America, and the other the Buenos Aires embassy, which as presented to Benton would have made him the senior United States ambassador in all of Latin America. But he deflected these approaches. He had too much to do. Then, early in 1963, President

Kennedy, through an intermediary, offered to make Benton the American ambassador to UNESCO, the first United States member of UNESCO's executive board to hold ambassadorial rank. This was something that struck a spark of interest. Benton made some independent inquiries about the nature of his duties, and by arrangement called at the White House on 9 March 1963 to give his answer to the president.

In the presidential office, Kennedy delayed coming to the point of the meeting by asking Benton straight off: "Tell me about all these new techniques in the field of education that you're experimenting with in the Britannica, about these new ways to teach mathematics and these new teaching machines. I'd like to hear about those."

"Where did you hear about them?" Benton asked.

"Hubert Humphrey has been telling me."

Benton explained the nature of the new developments. Then he interrupted himself with a characteristic Bentonism. Seemingly, it came straight off the top of his head, though there was, in fact, much brooding behind it. "Mr. President," said he, "if I can perfect the Britannica Schools in Chicago where we're now trying to train high school dropouts with all these new techniques, I'm going to give Hubert Humphrey the state of Minnesota as a franchise." And he added: "I'm tired of Hubert having to scrounge around the country without any money. I didn't like his not having any money to take his wife along to Wisconsin when he was campaigning against you—so that I had to send him $5,000. I'd like to try to make him a millionaire—like the Kennedys!" The president responded with enthusiastic laughter.

When they turned to the business at hand, Kennedy said that he knew of Benton's role as assistant secretary of state in getting UNESCO launched at the London Conference in the fall of 1945. He knew how he had pushed the UNESCO legislation through the Congress, and had subsequently been chairman of the United States delegations to the first two general conferences of the organization. "You are," said he, "the American founding father and patriarch of UNESCO, and your background will prove a great asset if you accept the ambassadorial post."

Benton, who knew how much UNESCO had changed since its founding days, countered by saying: "My going back to UNESCO as a founding father, Mr. President, is just like Thomas Jefferson coming back to Washington and trying to understand the Pentagon." Still, he did not turn down the offered appointment. "I'm going to tell you something that will surprise you," Benton continued. "The UNESCO ambassadorship—that nobody ever hears about or talks about—you don't have a big queue outside your office asking for it as for the post in London—it's the best ambassadorship you've got to offer. It's absolutely the number one top ambassadorship in the entire world for anyone who would like to be an ambassador."

Kennedy exclaimed, "What!—Why?"

First, said Benton, the ambassadorship would only require two months of his time in 1963, and three months in 1964. He would not have to entertain congressmen or businessmen or go to elaborate protocol dinners—or worry about de Gaulle. Second, all the meetings of the UNESCO executive board were held in Paris in April and May, and September and October, the most beautiful months of the year. It was like the AFL-CIO going to Miami in February for its meetings. In the third place, education, science, and culture were interesting, changing, and challenging. "Yes," said Benton in an enthusiastic summary, "this is the premier ambassadorship that you've got to bestow on anybody with other things to do! But nobody knows it except me!"

"By God, Bill," Kennedy said earnestly after he recovered from what appeared to be genuine surprise, "it's wonderful to have a guy in here who's not complaining."

Benton had a few ideas to press on the president. He said he wanted the president to become known as the world leader in the field of education, and he wanted to work to that end as Kennedy's ambassador to UNESCO. With the president's own intellectual interests, the leadership role was suited for him—and for the United States. The president, taken with the idea, cut in to suggest that Benton talk the matter over with McGeorge Bundy, the special assistant for national security affairs. Benton went on to say that he also wanted to talk to the president's brother, Robert, who had just written a major article for the *Saturday Evening Post* on information and cultural exchanges and United States propaganda. The previous summer, Robert Kennedy had been in Aspen, where he had as his guests a group of foreign students, many of them with socialist or communist leanings. As he had done at his various stops on a trip around the world, he spent all day at Aspen listening to the students' complaints about the United States. The *Saturday Eve-*

ning Post article reflected his grasp of the whole subject of information and cultural exchanges, and showed a better understanding
of the matter than any other cabinet officer had. "I hardly know
your brother," he said to the president, "but I want you to tell him
that I'll be around to see him because I want his help in connection
with the UNESCO assignment. I wouldn't take the assignment unless I thought I could help make UNESCO a more important factor
in world affairs. Your brother will understand this."

"I'll tell this to Bobby," the president replied. "There's not a
week that he's not annoying me about these foreign students. He's
talking to me about them all the time."

In that interview with President Kennedy, Benton found that
there was one thing about UNESCO which the president knew in
painful and intimate detail: a book UNESCO had published on race
relations in the Soviet Union. The text was a whitewashing piece
of propaganda that could as well have been written in the Kremlin.
In alluding to it, the president said rather helplessly, "Bill, I suppose there is nothing you can do about this Russian propaganda
through UNESCO." Benton felt that Kennedy showed a greater
generosity of attitude than he would himself have shown in the
president's place. "You bet your life there's something to do about
it," Benton said emphatically. "I'm going to do my best to see that
it doesn't happen again and that we set up a system in UNESCO so
that it is unlikely to happen again."

Right after the meeting with President Kennedy, Benton called
on McGeorge Bundy to restate the argument for positioning the
president of the United States as a world leader in education.
Bundy, like the president, was taken with the idea. It was Benton's
subsequent view that had Kennedy lived and been reelected, the goal
would have been pursued seriously. As it was, it was left to Kennedy's successor, Lyndon B. Johnson, the former schoolteacher, to
come by his own route to the same idea.

Before leaving for Paris as ambassador to UNESCO, Benton
spent some time in the State Department preparing for the assignment. Here, among other things, he heard many complaints about
René Maheu, the French intellectual who was UNESCO's director
general. The department had strongly but vainly opposed Maheu's
election to that post and continued to register its objections to him.
The result was a protracted feud. Benton had known Maheu since
the earliest days of UNESCO's history and had a high regard for

his intellectual capacity, although he also understood the grounds for the department's objections. But on balance he felt that the department's continued opposition was self-defeating. He so told Secretary of State Dean Rusk when he accepted the ambassadorship to UNESCO. He said he would go to Paris not to feud with Maheu, but in part to help end the feud. That meant that he would try to cooperate with the director general to promote the work of UNESCO in ways that would serve the enlightened self-interests of the organization and those of the United States as well.

Subsequently in Paris, Benton learned that Maheu, for his part, was disturbed by his relations with the United States and its State Department. One of the reasons grew out of his visit to Washington some months previously. As the head of a world organization that was part of the United Nations structure, he had wanted to pay his respects to President Kennedy. The State Department, however, had apparently been unwilling or unable to make the necessary arrangements even on a ceremonial basis. Maheu was emotionally upset by what he took to be a deliberate slap at UNESCO. The depth of his feeling was evident when with great passion he said to Benton, "I'm never going back to Washington again." It was Benton's turn to be distressed. He knew that Maheu by skillful tactics had come to wield great influence among the underdeveloped countries who looked to UNESCO for leadership in education, in science, and in modernizing their respective cultures. To snub UNESCO by snubbing Maheu made no diplomatic sense when seen from the standpoint of its effect on the underdeveloped countries. "You come back to Washington," Benton told UNESCO's director general, "and I'll see that you have a chance to meet President Kennedy and tell him about UNESCO's work, and what the United States can do to promote it." The promised meeting would materialize at the end of October 1963, three weeks before the president was assassinated.

In resuming work with UNESCO, Benton was straightaway faced by an old reality he protested after UNESCO's first general conference in 1946. United States Foreign Service and Civil Service personnel were nominated for UNESCO assignments either when they were toward the end of their careers or were marking time before a place could be found for them somewhere else. In 1946 Benton had urged the need to assign top professional United States personnel to UNESCO headquarters on a long-term basis. Now, in 1963, he tackled the old problem from a new angle. Why was it that the ablest of United States personnel *themselves* did not want to serve for any length of time at UNESCO—or at any other United Nations agency? One reason was that under United States Civil Service and Foreign Service regulations seniority and pension rights stopped accruing to any man loaned to a United Nations organization after three years. United States personnel, in a sense, "turned themselves over" by scurrying back from the international organizations to a United States agency in order to protect their place on promotion lists and future retirement benefits. By contrast, the French could pick out their brightest young men, assign them to an international agency, and keep them there for years while they steadily rose in its hierarchy. Their seniority and pension rights continued to accrue to them within their own government as if they had been working for it all along—as of course they were. Precisely in this way, many French civil servants like René Maheu had worked their way up from the ranks to become key officials in international agencies—a prospect that was closed to United States officers unless they were willing to sacrifice seniority and retirement benefits.

It was Benton's conviction that United States regulations should be brought abreast of these facts of international life. If they were not, the key posts of deputies and operating officers in the United Nations agencies would go by default to the personnel of countries other than the United States. Benton thus began a siege operation with the object of bringing about necessary changes in United States Civil Service and Foreign Service regulations. He would carry the argument directly to President Kennedy, who had previously been unaware of the issue. It was to be Benton's opinion that if Kennedy had lived, he would have strongly supported a change in the regulations. The whole issue, however, still remains unresolved at the time of this writing.

Benton was more successful in handling several other problems he faced when he began his UNESCO duties. One was the Soviet Union's effort, as in the case of the notorious pamphlet on race relations within Russia, to use UNESCO as a vehicle for Soviet propaganda. He repeatedly protested all efforts to debase the UNESCO imprimatur on the publications it issued. His hard stand led to the formulation of new rules for UNESCO publications, and the use of UNESCO as a propaganda forum was largely eliminated. Every time the Russians engaged in a propaganda outburst in the executive board, Benton automatically countered with a firm reminder that the proper place for political polemics was the United Nations in New York, and not UNESCO; such polemics interfered with UNESCO's dedication to science, culture, and education and were out of order. These repeated reminders slowly sank in; other members of UNESCO's executive board became tired of the Soviet diatribes, and the Soviet representatives themselves finally concluded that their tactics did not pay off. A concurrent general easing in United States–Soviet tensions led the Russians to replace their representative at UNESCO who had been foremost in bombast and bluster. The polemics virtually stopped. In Benton's last executive board session in the fall of 1968, Vietnam, long a favorite subject for Russian polemics, was not even mentioned. Benton reciprocated by avoiding the subject of the Soviet occupation of Czechoslovakia. In the forum of UNESCO, the United States and the Soviet Union discovered that they often had a basis for mutual cooperation. The executive board debates could often be long, dull, fruitless, and debilitating. But they were no longer an exercise in tirades as in the late 1950s and early 1960s. Even debates about the textbooks in the Arab territory under Israeli control were restrained in tone.

Above everything else, there had been a profound shift in UNESCO's governing ideas and work from its founding days. Immediately after V-E Day and V-J Day, many people were confident —if somewhat naively in a hurry to prove it—that *understanding* was an answer to mankind's ills. They believed that if misunderstandings in the world could be overcome, tensions would be relaxed and relations among people could be improved. UNESCO was a major focus of such hopes. Its primary and overriding aim was to help prevent World War III. It was to employ education, science, and culture as a means toward maintaining peace among the great nations. Many then hoped, quite literally, that UNESCO would contribute significantly to building the structure of peace through "intellectual togetherness." It would promote free inquiry and free communications. It would destroy the insularity that breeds suspicion, contempt, and conflict.

Further, an immediate objective of UNESCO in the wake of World War II was the repair of war-devastated schools, universities, libraries, and cultural monuments. Benton himself, at the London Conference of UNESCO in November 1945, gave $75,000 worth of *Encyclopaedia Britannica* sets to European libraries. The libraries had been unable during the war to buy encyclopedias; besides, the gift fitted in with the vision of an overall need to create a background for free inquiry and free communication. Significantly, however, Benton at this time made no gifts of *Britannica* sets to the underdeveloped or emerging countries. It was in the more developed countries that wars traditionally began, and they were at the center of UNESCO's long-range as well as immediate postwar objectives. By the time Benton returned to UNESCO in 1963, however, the objectives and programs of the organization had made an almost 180-degree shift away from the great military powers to the needs of the less-developed countries. There had also been a shift from an attempt to preserve world peace by mutual understanding to a program whose main object was to help underdeveloped countries in the fields of education and science.

Benton had a natural interest in this new point of emphasis. Moreover, he agreed that some scientific and cultural projects could be better pursued cooperatively under UNESCO auspices than by a single nation. But because of UNESCO's limited financial resources —its total regular budget in the mid-1960s was about 20 or 25 percent of the budget of the University of Chicago—he consistently urged UNESCO to adopt an order of priorities for its work. He warned that without an order of priorities, UNESCO, in its well-meant attempt to attack the problem of illiteracy, could lunge blindly into bottomless quicksands. He felt that UNESCO would be better advised to use its slim financial resources to conduct experiments in selected areas designed to test the effectiveness of new teaching techniques and their associated new media in the battle to overcome mass illiteracy. Several such experiments were begun and Benton followed them closely. René Maheu didn't know very much about them and seemed at first to have no great zest for them. But as a man highly sensitive to political nuance—and muscle—he showed a marked change of attitude after he discovered that President Kennedy was himself keenly interested in the experiments with the new teaching techniques.

The discovery took place at the meeting between the president and Maheu which Benton had arranged. Held at the end of October 1963 in the White House, it was meant to be little more than a brief ten-minute ceremonial visit, but Kennedy extended it to four times its scheduled length. Benton who was present, immediately afterward dictated a memorandum for the State Department summarizing what had transpired. His account reads in part:

The President started right in after Maheu. He said, "Tell me about what you want the United States to do for UNESCO? I want a strong UNESCO. How can we help?" Maheu answered, "I want your intellectual understanding and support and comprehension of UNESCO, your perception and insight into UNESCO and its problems." He intrigued the President by not saying, "I want more money," or "a bigger budget," or "more American scientists." So now the President said, "Tell me about these new types of educational techniques UNESCO is using. They are one of the reasons why I sent Senator Benton to UNESCO as ambassador."

I broke in to say at this point: "Mr. President, you know there's a conflict of interest here because the *Encyclopaedia Britannica* is interested in all these techniques and I don't want Mr. Maheu to think you sent me to UNESCO to promote the *Encyclopaedia Britannica*'s teaching machines." He looked at me coolly and said, "I sent you there because you had a conflict of interest. It is an important extra factor that qualified you for the job." It seemed to be his way of implying that I was old enough and rich enough to be trusted not to try to corrupt UNESCO or to try to get UNESCO to sell our teaching machines to Nigeria.

At any rate, after Maheu under further close questioning by the President described the three experiments underway in teaching techniques, I diverted the conversation to a point that bore on my own immediate interest in getting U.S. government employment rules changed so that abler U.S. personnel would be sent and kept at international agencies like UNESCO. I said to Maheu, "I want you to tell the President about your relations with the French Foreign Office and about how you've been on leave of absence for 17 years and how this permitted you to go up through the UNESCO hierarchy and become Director General. I want you to tell him that if you went back to the French Foreign Office tomorrow, it would be with full seniority and all its accrued benefits." The President asked, 'Is that true?' Maheu answered yes and gave him the details after which I said, 'Mr. President, I welcome the opportunity to have Mr. Maheu serve as my illustration of why our own system has got to be changed.' "

Maheu left the meeting inspired and grateful, persuaded that Kennedy meant business when he spoke about strengthening UNESCO. Even after the president's assassination, Maheu often recalled the meeting before various audiences, including his executive board, and Benton repeatedly alluded to the president's question, "What about these new techniques in the field of education?"

Benton last saw President Kennedy for fifteen minutes on 18 November 1963. He had been reluctant to break in on the president so soon after the lengthy meeting with Maheu. But a matter concerning the White House approach to certain UNESCO appointments, including the United States National Commission for UNESCO, could not wait. Benton felt that the State Department was being "excessively timid" about the matter and decided to take his own views to the President. Kennedy immediately agreed with those views, and Benton then returned to a theme he had advanced in March when he accepted the ambassadorship to UNESCO. He said again that he wanted to help make President Kennedy the world's leader in the field of education. Thus when the National Commission for UNESCO met in Washington, he wanted to bring the members to the Rose Garden at the White House for a photograph with the president, and with prints for each commission member. It would be a small gesture, but the members of the commission carried weight with the national organizations they represented and would use their influence to make these organizations responsive to the president's lead in the field of education. Kennedy, who understood this kind of language by instinct, quickly assented to the proposal. "Bring the commission members around," said he. "I want to see them." Four days later, Kennedy was dead. It was President Johnson who received the full commission in the fall of 1966.

For Benton, as for countless other people, the pattern of many understandings and promises of better things to come was broken by the assassination of President Kennedy. All these, as they affected the operations of the presidency and of the United States government generally, had to be rewoven strand by strand. Benton had never been a Kennedy intimate; the difference of almost two decades between their ages was one among the barriers that had stood in the way. Yet he had long admired Kennedy, even when convinced that in 1960 Stevenson was the Democrat best qualified to be president; and this admiration was strengthened on the few occasions when he saw at close range how Kennedy worked. After the assassination, when the Kennedy Library project was being organized at Harvard, Benton was invited to be a member of the board of trustees. In addition to a quick acceptance of the invitation, he arranged for the Britannica company to publish a book, *A Tribute to John F. Kennedy.* All the profits from the sale of the book were turned over to the library; at the time of this writing, they have exceeded $125,000.

In May 1964, Benton went to the Soviet Union for a stay of ten days. Since his first visit to Russia in 1955, he had returned to the country four times under different circumstances. One evolved from the "Dartmouth Conference," organized by Norman Cousins, the editor of the *Saturday Review,* which brought together a group of Soviet intellectuals to start a "dialogue" with a counterpart American group, one of whose members was Benton. The Russians reciprocated by inviting the Americans to meet with them in Yalta for a continuation of the discussion, and again Benton was part of the American contingent.

Another visit to the Soviet Union grew out of Benton's summertime practice of renting a yacht for a cruise with his family and friends to distant places. In 1960, as in several previous summers, the yacht was the *Flying Clipper,* the finest sailing yacht of its kind in the world. Owned by a Swedish publisher and shipping magnate, it is 205 feet long, with a crew of thirty-five, representing a mixture of professional sailors and holidaying Swedish Eagle Scouts. The *Flying Clipper,* with the Bentons and their friends aboard, cruised the North Sea in the summer of 1960, and one of the stops was Leningrad. It was a memorable stop for Benton, partly because of the armed Russian soldiers who guarded the yacht—a supreme symbol of capitalism—every moment the vessel was in port and who insisted on inspecting the passports of all members of the Benton party every time they went ashore or returned to the yacht. But it was also memorable mainly because of a visit to the Leningrad Library by Stanley Morison, who was along on the yachting trip. Morison, a celebrated medievalist as well as a scholar in calligraphy, wanted to see a rare manuscript with the signature of the Venerable

Bede. Benton secured the necessary permission for him, and Morison, with some awe, reported that the last signature on the last withdrawal slip for the manuscript was dated in 1935, and the signature on it was that of Stanley Morison. In the period between 1935 and the anchoring of the *Flying Clipper* in Leningrad in 1960, apparently not a single scholar with an interest in the important figure of the Venerable Bede had shown up in the Leningrad Library to look at one of his rarest manuscripts.

During that same visit to Leningrad, Benton answered a question which his own conduct had aroused in the minds of some of the Russians. Amid a feverish tour of Leningrad bookstores, where he cross-examined managers and noted customers' purchases, one of several Intourist guides he wore out on the trip asked him a question. Perplexed by this obvious capitalist who had come to Russia on his eminently capitalist yacht only to spend his time covering nearly every bookstore in town, she asked, "Tell me, please, Senator Benton, are you a member of the ruling imperialist clique in America?" Benton snapped, "You're damn right I am." The guide appeared relieved to have her stereotype restored.

After the 1960 visit, Benton and his wife were invited to Russia in 1962 as the first guests of the Institute of Soviet-American Relations, formerly known as the Society for Soviet-American Friendship. All expenses for the thirty-day tour were paid by the institute, and the red carpet was out at every stop from Moscow through Tashkent and Samarkand all the way to Novosibirsk, the latter Russia's "scientific city" and a rare privilege for Benton to visit.[1] Benton was puzzled by the invitation and assumed that it was related to his having written *This Is the Challenge*. The Soviet minister of higher education, Viacheslav Yelutin, whom he had met in 1955 and cited in the book, said of it, "I cannot speak of any other area you covered, but in the field of education, you were reliable and accurate." He also speculated that the invitation might be due in part to *The Voice of Latin America*. A Soviet journalist told him it had been "translated into Russian and read by high officials in Moscow." Benton retorted that he wished he could get it read in Washington. Yet another reason for the invitation was advanced by Eleanor Roosevelt. She assumed that the Russian leaders "understood the importance of the *Encyclopaedia Britannica* as an

---

[1]Benton described it in a 1962 *Saturday Evening Post* article advancing his earlier theme of "the cold war of the classrooms."

educational medium," and the importance of Benton in shaping its form and substance. Llewellyn Thompson, the United States ambassador to Moscow, added his own speculation. He assumed that the Russians were intent on seducing Benton into heading an American-Soviet friendship society. To this, Benton snorted that Thompson had been in the Soviet Union too long. In any case, Benton was given lavish attention—huge hotel suites, cars and chauffeurs, guides—and his only expense was a small bill he had to pay everywhere for his son John, whose presence evidently had not been approved by the Russian bureaucracy.

Through these visits, Benton enlarged his knowledge of the Soviet Union, and widened his circle of contacts with Russia's principal politicians, administrators, educators, scientists, encyclopedists, and managers of mass communication. Each visit, moreover, was followed by his efforts through articles and speeches to communicate to an American audience the realities of what he had learned while in the Soviet Union.

The trip to Russia in May 1964 grew out of a luncheon conversation with the Senate Foreign Relations Committee chairman, J. William Fulbright, and a later one with Fulbright and Ambassador-at-Large W. Averell Harriman just before Benton left for the springtime Paris meeting of UNESCO's executive board. The three men agreed that there were signs of change in Soviet society and an apparent easing in the friction-laden way the Russians approached their relations with the United States. But there were some questions to be asked. Did the so-called detente have any depth, or was it but a surface illusion? Which aspects of the detente were only tactical maneuvers? Which aspects represented an authentic desire of Soviet leaders, perhaps responsive to pressures from Soviet society itself, to remove some of the still explosive causes for conflict between Russia and the United States?

Fulbright was aware of Benton's impending departure for Paris and suggested that when UNESCO's agenda permitted, Benton should take a short leave and go to Moscow, in the hope of gaining insights into the unresolved questions of concern to American foreign policy makers. Benton liked the suggestion. So did Harriman, who joined Fulbright in urging Benton to make the trip to Moscow. As was his habit on all his trips, he dictated extensive memorandums on what he saw and heard. Also, as always, his memorandums contained material that was richer than the pages he later felt at liberty to put into public print. The 1964 trip bore fruit in one long article published in the 1965 *Britannica Book of the Year*. Reprints of the article were widely distributed, and the response justified an amplification of the text for another book, *The Teachers and the Taught in the U.S.S.R.*

While in Russia, Benton talked with some thirty leading Soviet officials, capped by an unexpected interview with Nikita Khrushchev. Some of his talks involved the political problems of prime interest to Fulbright and Harriman—Germany, disarmament, nonintervention in the affairs of other countries, and international trade. But the theme running through many of his conversations was of greatest interest to himself—Soviet education. As developed by Benton, his new book made a logical sequel to the earlier *This Is the Challenge*. *The Teachers and the Taught*, nearly a decade later, reported the Soviet Union's continuing progress in applying television and other new forms of teaching techniques to the education of its population.

Though he had gone to Moscow with the intention of inquiring primarily into political issues, the educational focus Benton gave to *The Teachers and the Taught* was justified, paradoxically, on political grounds. For one thing, Soviet progress in mass education seemed to be affecting the course of Soviet politics.[2] For another, five months after Benton's visit to the Soviet Union in May 1964, but before *The Teachers and the Taught* appeared in book form, Nikita Khrushchev was removed as the head of the Soviet Union. This placed a question mark after some of the political topics which Benton had discussed earlier with Soviet leaders. It did not, however, affect the picture that emerged from his discussion of educational progress.

On his trip to Russia, Benton had taken along many copies of the volume *A Tribute to John F. Kennedy*, which he gave to various Soviet officials. He later described their response as being "emotional and passionate;" since "Kennedy's personality had penetrated not merely throughout western Europe, but throughout the entire world, including the people and officials of the Soviet Union." Indeed, said Benton, he was "taken by surprise by the deeply felt and warmhearted response of the Soviet officials" to the Kennedy book. "It wasn't," said he, "that Kennedy had been young, or hand-

---

[2]Averell Harriman was quick to recognize this, and he circulated Benton's reports as "required reading" in the State Department.

some, or gay and witty, though these surely were elements in the response. It was more because his fame had been growing as a great world leader in the field of ideas—in the field of education. He was a symbol of hope for the world of a better life ahead."

Benton had not dared hope to see Khrushchev, and was delighted when he was told that he was to have an interview with the Soviet leader. At the same time, he regretted that he had already exhausted his supply of copies of *A Tribute to John F. Kennedy* and had none to give to the Russian leader who had sorely tested Kennedy beginning with their first meeting in Vienna on through to the Cuban missile crisis. In May 1964, of course, Benton could have no intimation that Khrushchev would be forced out of the Kremlin in October. In writing later of his meeting with Khrushchev, Benton said the Soviet leader's face "was deeply lined and impassive, and he looked very tired. His eyes seemed a bit glazed. I did not know whether I had his attention. Suddenly his face lit up and he began to talk and I couldn't tell what he was leading up to." But then Khrushchev found his range and commented on a variety of political topics. Benton summarized what he had to say in *The Teachers and the Taught*.

The meeting ended with an unusual twist. As Khrushchev was talking, someone handed him a note of reminder that Benton had to catch a plane back to Paris. "I do not know how long he would have continued to talk if this interruption had not occurred," Benton later said. "Khrushchev had shown no inclination to stop after an hour and a half. He appeared momentarily disconcerted. I assume he had rarely been told that an interview was terminated, and it must have been just as rare for anyone to walk out on him. I should not have left. I made a mistake. His office could easily have telephoned the airport and told the plane to wait for me. I should have had enough sense to ask him to do this."

Mistake or not, it led to a scene resembling a chase sequence in a spy film. Khrushchev's powerful limousine was waiting to take Benton to the airport, and when it got underway, the driver raced it at eighty miles an hour down the center of the highway. Marked by a broad white line, the center throughway is reserved for the cars of very important Soviet officials. At the airport, there was no pause for check-in. The car careened through the airport gate and raced to the end of the runway where the plane was waiting to take off. The car screeched to a halt in front of the jet, and in seconds Benton was in the plane, making a dramatic exit from Moscow.

In this same period, Benton was shocked and saddened by the deaths of two old friends—Beardsley Ruml and Galen Van Meter.[3] On the brighter side, there was the marriage of Paul Hoffman to Anna Rosenberg, with Benton signing the wedding register as the witness to their union. But then, suddenly, in July 1965, there was another break-off in the circle of Benton's closest friends. Adlai Stevenson died.

For the preceding week Benton had been with Stevenson almost continuously in Europe. They had met on a Wednesday in Geneva to attend some meetings arranged by the State Department, and they dined together that night. Then on Thursday Benton spoke at a closed meeting of European representatives about the work at UNESCO, and on Friday Stevenson spoke at an open session about the worldwide problems of urbanization resulting from the rush of people to the city. It was to be his last public speech, and one of the last photographs of Stevenson was taken in Geneva, showing him and Benton at a luncheon meeting with *Britannica* colleagues. Saturday the two men met in London and drove out to Chequers to have lunch with Prime Minister Harold Wilson and to spend the afternoon discussing foreign policy. They drove back to London that evening, where Stevenson stayed with Ambassador David Bruce and Benton at Claridge's. Over cocktails, Stevenson asked Benton and Bruce to play tennis the next morning. The invitation was greeted with laughter; Benton and Bruce were too tired.

At eleven o'clock Sunday morning, Stevenson and Benton drove out to have lunch with Stevenson's aunt, the former Mary Borden, then Lady Spiers, the wife of General Sir Edward Spiers. From there they went on to Oxford for the afternoon and for dinner with Lord Franks, who as Oliver Franks had been the British ambassador in Washington. He was now the master of Worcester College, of which Stevenson was a fellow.

During these drives from London over the English countryside, Stevenson and Benton, sitting alone in the back seat of the car, talked steadily about their future plans, especially Stevenson's. It

---

[3]Ruml occupied an office next to Benton in his last years and had become his closest personal associate except for Van Meter, his golf companion at Southport.

was later said that Stevenson meant to resign his United Nations post in protest against President Johnson's actions in sending United States troops into Santo Domingo, and in protest also against the emergent shape of American policy in Vietnam. Benton, for his part, heard nothing of the sort from Stevenson in the course of their last days together. It is true Stevenson had long been critical of the influence of McGeorge Bundy in shaping America's national security policies and had once asked Benton with some asperity, "When has Bundy ever been right?" But he said nothing to Benton indicating an intent to break with President Johnson either because of Santo Domingo or Vietnam. He did, however, reveal that he thought he wanted to resign the United Nations post at the end of the coming session of the General Assembly. Benton himself didn't know how seriously to take this; it could have been another of Stevenson's exercises in speculating out loud about his uncertainties. Moreover, it was Benton's view that Stevenson would not wish to resign if President Johnson really wanted to keep him, and surely could not do so until he had a successor. Stevenson was inclined to agree on the latter point, and after more talk, suggested a number of likely successors. His first choice was Senator Eugene McCarthy; his second was Senator John Sherman Cooper; his third was Chester Bowles.

Much of the talk between the two men was centered on the question of what Stevenson would do if in fact he did resign. Even while Stevenson was at the United Nations, Benton kept him on the Britannica payroll at $25,000 a year; this accumulated to his account, and it amounted to around $125,000 when he died. The arrangement stemmed from Benton's desire to maintain Stevenson's interest in the Britannica companies, though he could do little work for them while at the United Nations. Stevenson, for his part, was weighing a different proposal if he retired from the United Nations and he talked to Benton about it. It had been proposed that he become counsel to the law firm of Paul, Weiss, Rifkind, Wharton, and Garrison with which he had been previously associated. "Why," said Stevenson to Benton, "Judge Rifkind tells me I would only have to give the firm 80 percent of my time."

Benton, unimpressed, shot back: "Adlai, that is the most preposterous suggestion ever made to you. You shouldn't have been spending 80 percent of your time for any law firm when you were forty, and today, when you are a major world figure, you shouldn't spend even 40 percent of your time for any law firm. You're too old to fuss with clients and their minor problems. I'll give you $100,000 a year and a $100,000 a year expense account if you will work for Britannica."

"Well," said Stevenson, "what would I do?"

"You would be the greatest 'working ornament' Britannica ever had," Benton answered. "You could contribute greatly to our developing educational programs, and help expand our film company into a broad-based educational company. You could inspire our young executives and salesmen. You could help us expand into a worldwide publishing and educational force. You could help push us all over the world. Your association with the company could arouse the interest of all countries in the new educational technologies—teaching machines, the new mathematics, the use of films and audio-visual materials. And you'd still have time to play your key role as a world figure—because I wouldn't dare hope to take even 40 percent of your time." Stevenson reflected on this barrage and agreed to come to Southport the following weekend to play tennis—and to discuss in greater detail the opportunities and the terms of the offer.

In London a week after their Geneva meeting, Benton gave a luncheon at Claridge's for Stevenson and Robert Hutchins, along with the three principal officers of the London Britannica office and their wives. The luncheon broke up at three thirty, and Stevenson asked if he could have the key to Benton's suite at the hotel, since he had to hold some meetings that afternoon and preferred to hold them in the suite instead of the residence of Ambassador Bruce. Benton gave him the key and said goodbye. Then, his own bags already packed, he left for the London airport to catch a six o'clock plane to New York.

Stevenson himself went over to the BBC studios to make a television tape recording for its "panorama" program. He was met by Mrs. Marietta Tree, who worked with him at the United Nations. Later, with Mrs. Tree, he went back to Claridge's to return Benton's key, saying to her: "I don't need the suite. I shall save Bill Benton an extra day's charge." He was always careful about money, including other people's. But then, several blocks from the hotel, while walking with Mrs. Tree, he dropped to the sidewalk opposite Hyde Park. The time was 5:25 P.M. Marietta Tree knelt beside him to breathe into his mouth in a desperate hope that she could revive him: the London newspapers called it the "kiss of life."

An ambulance swerved up, and Stevenson was rushed off to a hospital. He was dead.

Benton knew nothing about Stevenson's death until, in mid-Atlantic, he was given a radio message from Ambassador Bruce conveying the news and advising Benton to return to London immediately from New York. The plane landed at nine thirty in the evening. There were arrangements for a quick turnabout, an interview by the AP, a tape recording for NBC, and a telephone call for Benton from Vice-President Hubert Humphrey. The vice-president was to head the official United States delegation leaving Washington for London at eleven o'clock that evening aboard the presidential plane to escort Stevenson's remains back to the United States. Humphrey wanted Benton to come to Washington and make the London flight as a member of the official delegation. Benton demurred. He couldn't get to Washington in time. It was best for him to go back to London on his own at once and there join the party from Washington. He was airborne for London forty-five minutes after his arrival in New York and was waiting at the London airport with the British foreign secretary when the presidential plane landed.

Stevenson had many good friends who were men, some going back to his boyhood days, but it seemed to Benton that Stevenson had scarcely any intimate friends who were men. Benton considered himself as close to Stevenson in the last years of his life as any man was allowed to be. They shared numerous interests and dined and traveled together often. Still, Stevenson never spoke to Benton about the latter's work in UNESCO, though it was a United Nations agency. Nor did he ever once discuss with Benton the fact that Benton had picked up the financial tab on a number of Stevenson's undertakings. It also struck Benton as being psychologically interesting that Stevenson reserved his gift of intimate friendship for women who were highly cultivated, very intelligent, often brilliant, and often very rich. They included Mrs. Marshall Field III, Mrs. Eugene Meyer, Mrs. Mary Lasker, Mrs. Alicia Patterson Guggenheim, Mrs. Philip Graham, Mrs. Marietta Tree, Mrs. Edison Dick, Lady Jackson (Barbara Ward), Mrs. John Gunther, Lauren Bacall. All possessed exceptional human traits. All were deeply devoted to him, as he was to them. "The most important four-letter word in dealing with unique women of this kind," Benton once said, "is a word that is seldom mentioned as a four-letter word. It's T-I-M-E. Adlai brought to these women the gift of wit and gaiety, and insights into world affairs. They were his joy in life. But above all, he gave them time."

Still, knowing this aspect of Stevenson's life, Benton was not quite prepared for what Mrs. Marshall Field had to say as the two stood on the steps of the American embassy in London when the casket bearing Stevenson's remains was carried out to a waiting hearse. Mrs. Field knew that, as a young couple in Chicago, Adlai Stevenson and Alicia Patterson had been engaged to be married. The engagement was broken off, but in all the years that followed, they remained deeply devoted to each other. "How fortunate Alicia Patterson was," Mrs. Field said to Benton as the casket moved past them. "She died before Adlai."

In the ceremonies at the United States embassy in London, then back across the Atlantic for the ceremonies in the Washington National Cathedral, Benton did what was expected of him as a member of the United States official delegation. But he did his mourning as a member of the Stevenson "family," which included the governor's three sons, their wives, and his sister and her husband. He found time on Friday morning to write a memorandum delivered by messenger to President Johnson, containing the suggestions Stevenson had ventured about his possible successor at the United Nations. On Saturday he said a final farewell to a cherished friend when Stevenson's casket was placed aboard a plane in Washington for the flight to Springfield, Illinois, and then to the family burial place in Bloomington. Benton accompanied Mrs. John Gunther back to New York. He later learned that even before Stevenson's body had been returned to Washington from London—and hence before Benton's note reached President Johnson—Johnson had moved quickly to persuade Justice Arthur Goldberg to leave the Supreme Court in order to be Stevenson's replacement at the United Nations—and to appoint his close friend and personal legal counsel, Abe Fortas, to the Goldberg vacancy.

29

Fortune / Future

In the first ten years after Henry Luce launched *Fortune* magazine, Benton often invoked the right of their friendship to denounce the magazine. He repeatedly told Luce that *Fortune* was a "disgrace" to his company—that he was merely putting out a magazine for the benefit of the wives of businessmen. He urged Luce to change the name of the magazine from *Fortune* to *Future*—because it would "make sure that the editors would have to know what the hell fortune is all about." He felt that the name *Fortune* permitted the editors to put into the magazine any kind of "junk" about business that crossed their minds. But under the name *Future* they would have to be alert. They would "have to think about the things that the men who make great fortunes are thinking about—since the future is the heart of fortune." He also wanted Luce to have his reporters "write stories not only about the triumphs but about the soft underbellies of the big corporations—soft underbellies full of opportunities for men who think about the future." This line of criticism reached its height in 1940–41, when Benton was trying to organize the American Policy Commission at the University of Chicago. Luce finally got annoyed with Benton's harping and, between acts at an opera, snapped at him: "Bill, I'm tired of listening to you. You can have the magazine if you think you can do better with it. You take it."

Benton didn't take it, nor did he subscribe to *Fortune*. He denied even reading it in his later years.[1] But he brought to his own enterprises the future-minded outlook he had urged on Luce in the course of his polemics about changing the name of his magazine. In

---

[1]Nonetheless, he noted (accurately) in 1968 that the *Britannica*'s $200 million sales volume would put it 360th among *Fortune*'s top five hundred businesses—if it were publicly owned.

doing so, he massively proved his point that "vast fortunes are made by men who think about the future"—though he had long since ceased to be concerned with his personal wealth. He did not stop to count his net worth or even to estimate it. "A truly rich man," Benton once observed, "is someone who doesn't know within $50 or $100 million what he is really worth." In fact, if he sold his companies or "went public" by listing them on the stock exchange, it is conceivable that they would be valued as high as $400–$500 million. Yet he refused even to consider selling or going public.

Benton never "felt rich." He once stated that despite the salable value of his enterprises, he would not put his and his wife's personal wealth "at more than a couple of million dollars, mostly hers." As for the companies, though he and his family owned them outright with no outside stockholders, he thought of them as "educational trusteeships" and of himself as a "custodian" with an obligation to develop them for the sake of education itself. Did his professions about the matter have the hollow ring of a Rotarian's talk about "service"? His critics answered yes. His files contradict the critics, and his overt acts square with the files.

Part of the Benton "business story" has been told through the time when Harry Houghton served as president of the parent Britannica company. What remains to be told here is the story extending beyond 1962 when Houghton retired.

The natural choice to succeed him was Maurice ("Mitch") Mitchell who had distinguished himself as president of the Britannica Films company. Mitchell's immediate need on becoming president was to deal with the consequences of the company's rapid growth at home and, particularly, overseas. Cash advances to support its swift international expansion had burdened the company heavily. Installment buying, inevitable in encyclopedia sales, is a firmly established aspect of the American economy. Britannica could thus borrow from American banks on accounts receivable. But in many countries overseas, installment buying was unheard of, or at least new and strange; it was difficult for the company to borrow local funds to finance installment accounts, and it had to draw on its American resources. In addition, in expanding the overseas sales force, division heads in the field often had been lax in the kind of salesmen they engaged or in the sales practices they condoned in areas like Canada, Great Britain, and Australia. In many such countries, there were no well-established techniques for checking credit or making collections. Many mistakes had been made in developing export markets; accumulated losses ran into millions.

The remedy called for firm and precise administrative action. This was slow in coming. The sales executives were earning too much; Mitchell could not easily break their mesmeric grip. At the same time, there was a further and in a sense more important matter that needed attention. Because of the company's rapid growth, its key elements got out of touch with each other; they had to be drawn together and reformed into teams of people who were not only eager for success in their own special areas of activity but also willing to cooperate with their colleagues. This applied not only to the separate enterprises but to the editorial and sales enclaves within a single enterprise. Traditional enmities had to be stopped. Benton realized that Mitchell came to the presidency of the Britannica company without the "book man's" traditional knowledge—meaning the knowledge of the highly priced field sales executives. He thus spent many hours with his chief lieutenant, to help strengthen his grasp of the difficult and often frustrating world which the "book men" knew almost by rote. All this went hand-in-hand with a collaborative effort between the two men as they pressed ahead with necessary reforms and company reorganization. As progress was made, the way was cleared for further collaborative effort in guiding the company's growth in new directions.

Benton made a point of avoiding responsibility for day-to-day operations. But it was also his policy and his practice to maintain a drumfire of memorandums—thousands of words on an average day—addressed to his associates in Chicago and elsewhere. Suggestions, questions, criticisms, compliments, comments relayed from friends around the world, engulfed the associates. He constantly prodded them to develop new products, to improve the quality of old ones, to adopt sales and promotion techniques with greater impact. Working for Benton was no rest cure. But it could be an exciting opportunity for productivity by men of imagination and strong nerves. More than 90 percent of the company's new business was developed within the company through the growth of old products and the development of new ones; a scant 10 percent of the new business was represented by the acquisition of other enterprises.

One of these new products was a new and greatly improved *International World Atlas*—prepared and published in line with

Benton's expectation that the company's most significant growth would come from abroad. In line with that same view, he threw his weight behind a plan for a French-language *Encyclopaedia Universalis* designed for sale to the French-speaking peoples of France, North Africa, and Canada.

Strangely, the French nation, in which modern encyclopedias originated, had no encyclopedia in a modern sense. The famous *Larousse* is but a dictionary by *Britannica* standards. Yet while Benton saw the opportunity to enter a field that had gone by default in the French-speaking world, he was intimidated by the prospect of entering it alone. In the first place, to publish an encyclopedia in France for French-speaking people required the approval of the French government. Second, Benton doubted whether that approval would be given to an American-owned company in view of France's strident nationalism. Thus in casting about for a French partner who might secure the necessary approval, Benton made his initial approaches to Larousse and Hachette, respectively, the two entrenched French publishers, whose competitive and financial power Benton respected. But because of the monopoly business deals common in France, neither of the two firms would join a collaborative venture with Britannica unless the other did. After years of negotiations, the two French firms made a final offer. It called for a three-cornered partnership, with Larousse, Hachette, and Britannica each having a one-third interest in the proposed new venture. It was, in Benton's view, a triangular arrangement which would have completely disfranchised Britannica. He turned it down. In search for what he still felt was a needed French partner, he settled on the newly formed Club Français du Livre. A relationship with the book club had been established by Britannica's editorial executive vice-president, Howard Goodkind. A fifty-fifty deal was arranged in which each partner was to put up around $500,000. After more than a year of effort, the French government gave its approval. It was the first such agreement Britannica ever made, in which it was not the sole owner.

The *Encyclopaedia Universalis* is to be a thirty-million-word set in twenty volumes, approaching the size of the *Britannica* itself. To reduce the financial burden on the publishers, a sales technique was adopted which had been followed by the *Britannica* in the first 130 years of its existence. As in the case of a magazine, the subscriber to the set pledges himself to buy the volumes in advance as they appear serially. Thus with the profits from volume 1, volume 2 is produced; profits from volume 2 make possible the publication of volume 3, and so on. Subscriptions to volume 1 of the new set greatly exceeded original expectations, and the venture now clearly is a solid success.

Meanwhile, progress was made on another front with an international angle. An "international module" was created which would contain basic material appropriate for an encyclopedia published in any area or language of the world. To this basic material—50 to 80 percent of the ultimate set—would be added special regional material to bring total wordage to ten or fifteen million. The international module enables Britannica to enter new foreign language markets with a specially edited encyclopedia without starting over each time from the beginning. Despite some skepticism, Benton backed the program. The first cycle of the experiment has been completed by a staff of forty people, at a cost of some $1.8 million. Now special editorial material is being added for the maiden sales effort in Japan to be followed, if it meets expectations, in other languages and other regions. Benton has encouraged still other experimental ventures or acquisitions which could contribute to the company's growth overseas. One of these, developed in Vienna, is known as the Anglo-tutor. It consists of a home language laboratory with text, tapes and records for the teaching of English in Italian, German, French, and Spanish. Current work is underway to do the same for the teaching of English in Japanese. In another direction, Benton's eye on the international market accounts for the translation into Arabic of *Compton's Illustrated Science Dictionary*.

While this kind of attention helped boost the company's international sales volume past $50 million by 1969, Benton did not overlook prospects in the domestic field—especially since a salient trend in education points to the start of education for children at a much younger age than has hitherto been the case. "By the year 2000," says he, "it is hoped that the Ph.D. degree—or its counterpart as of today—will be awarded to youngsters of eighteen or nineteen." With this kind of acceleration of the learning process in prospect, Benton prompted the Britannica company to start work on developing of a "pre-school encyclopedia" for children between four and eight who are not yet ready for *Britannica Junior*, or indeed, cannot as yet read.

The prosperous *Yearbook* business, meanwhile, became the core

of a burgeoning mail-order operation. An early venture into mer-
chandise unrelated to books and education had an unhappy result
which angered and embarrassed Benton. In its full implications he
saw that it compromised the *Britannica* name and was a disruptive
departure from the company's educational mission. This waywardness was stopped, and the mail-order operation was recast so that
it settled into an increasingly profitable traffic in books, sets of
books, annuals, and the like. George Collins, the vice-president
heading the mail-order division, was constantly in quest of new
mail-order products, and Benton examined each one selected, and
produced lengthy comments on how to improve their quality. The
results paid off handsomely. The *Britannica Book of the Year* is
the second largest selling book in the United States, year after
year; *Great Ideas Today* is one of the largest selling books annually; *Compton's Yearbook* has annually been earning a million
dollars before taxes; the yearbook division as a whole exceeds by far
the annual earnings of the Book-of-the-Month Club. Still, Benton
was not content with the kind of coverage of knowledge the year-
books provided. He reasoned that if people would pay $8.95 for a
yearbook about what happened last year, many would pay $8.95
for a yearbook about what was going to happen next year, or in
the decade ahead. Information about the future was more important
to them and to their children than the data about what happened
last year. In this conviction, he pelted his associates with memorandums spelling out what he had in mind, overcoming their objections, and prodding them to launch a yearbook dealing with the
future. The result, published for the first time in October 1968, was
The Britannica Yearbook of Science and the Future; its editorial
advisory board is headed by Dr. George Beadle, a Nobel Prize
winner in biology and former president of the University of Chicago.

The reception accorded the new yearbook led company executives
to forecast a 1969 profit before taxes of three-quarters of a million
dollars on the one volume alone. Seizing on this augury, Benton
drove home his favorite theme about new products to be developed
within the company by asking his associates a pointed question.
What would it cost to acquire a company with a new product that
would earn $750,000 before taxes in its second year? He gave them
the answer: ten or twenty times what it cost to develop the *Yearbook
of Science and the Future* within the *Britannica* itself.

Benton is similarly optimistic about another and major new product, developed by Britannica and sold by the Educational Corporation as well as the Britannica company. This is a twenty-volume set called *Annals of America*, a collection of the basic documents embracing all significant aspects of American thought and experience from the discovery of America to the present. The project, conceived and directed by Mortimer Adler, comprises 2,202 selections grouped chronologically. A "conspectus," somewhat like Adler's *Syntopicon* for the Great Books, fills two volumes with a topical index and provides an overview of the twenty-five "great issues" of continuing concern to the American people. The *Annals* is the first Britannica set to employ computerized typesetting, thus enabling the editors to direct the computer to retrieve all material relevant to a particular topic, properly organized and set in type. The first use of the retrieval arrangement resulted in a three-volume set, *The Negro in American History*, tracing the black man's experience on this continent from 1968 back to the fifteenth century. Other such "subsets" will follow as demand indicates, many of them "fascicles" as small as 32 pages, and proportionately inexpensive. While the entire *Annals* project was in preparation, Benton was, as usual, its sharpest critic, constantly asking questions about its quality. It had not occurred to him that anything he had written might be included in the set. He was pleasantly surprised when the editors sought his legal permission to include his 1944 essay for the CED, "The Economics of a Free Society," and extracts from his Senate bill of particulars against Joseph McCarthy. Benton gave permission quickly without turning to lawyers for advice.

There have been sharp and costly disappointments as well. Benton was never satisfied with the progress of the Britannica Schools. Their original aim had been to enable school dropouts to complete their secondary education and prepare for college by the use of programmed instruction. The concept of the schools was subsequently enlarged to provide correspondence courses through which employed people could continue their education and upgrade their skills. The whole operation is fully accredited by educational authorities, and the tested performance of the students has shown notable results. Benton, however, continued to be a severe critic of the schools and the correspondence courses. In his view, they have not realized their potential, while low enrollments have meant losses amounting to hundreds of thousands of dollars.

In addition, Benton has been disappointed by the slow progress made in winning acceptance for the Educational Corporation's TEMAC teaching machine program, and for the Wirtz-Botel "new math" program. Both are operating in the red. He also regretted the failure of a project—shut down in 1968—which entailed teaching by phonograph record, and the failure of his company to develop a remedial reading program for which he had agitated. He consoled himself with the hope that his company could learn from its mistakes and apply the lessons to new ventures. One of his recurring complaints, however, is denied by the heads of the two Britannica companies, and he himself sometimes admits that he may be mistaken in charging his major executives with failing to seek new creative and executive talent for the companies. Significant talent has been developed from inside, often from the ranks of salesmen—as were Arthur L. Sikking, executive vice-president in charge of Britannica sales, and Roger Graver, vice-president of the international sales division. Yet Benton aims a cannonade of questions, suggestions and criticisms at his executives, all with the object of stimulating them to ferret out talent wherever it can be found.

In 1964, there was a major addition to Benton's enterprises when Britannica—in what the president of McGraw-Hill called "the publishing acquisition of the century"—bought the G. and C. Merriam Company, publishers of the Merriam-Webster dictionaries. The Merriam Company, founded in 1831, had acquired the estate of Noah Webster in 1847 along with the final plates and unbound sheets for the second edition of Webster's great work. Copyright laws in the nineteenth century, however, were unclear, and the Webster family sold earlier and obsolete plates and dictionaries to other companies. The name "Webster" thus became generic, and some ten companies in all emerged as publishers of so-called Webster dictionaries. But precisely on this account, the name "Merriam" preceding "Webster" took on great importance. The G. and C. Merriam Company, with its "Merriam-Webster" dictionaries, became America's foremost dictionary publisher. When the Britannica company as the publisher of the *Encyclopaedia Britannica*—which first appeared in 1768—bought the Merriam Company, two of the oldest and most distinguished reference works in the English-speaking world were joined together. At the end of the protracted negotiations that finally led to the merger, Benton said: "Merriam like Britannica is the custodian of a great and cherished tradition. The union of these two companies and of their scholarly resources enhances the opportunities of both to contribute to the advancement of knowledge." From a business standpoint, as well, each company gained strength from the other. Britannica, as the publisher of many million individual volumes annually, used its book manufacturing knowledge to reduce Merriam-Webster production costs while maintaining or raising the quality of the dictionary's production. Conversely, with the acquisition of Merriam-Webster, Britannica was in a position to abandon the old Funk and Wagnall vehicle for its seven-language "world language" dictionary. The "Britannica" dictionary then became a special three-volume edition of *Webster's Third New International Dictionary* with much of the third volume devoted to the seven-language feature.

In the spring of 1966, Britannica again expanded when it bought the publishing company of Frederick A. Praeger, Inc. Benton admitted that in this transaction he was as much interested in "acquiring" Fred Praeger personally as his company. Praeger had been in the field of publishing in his native Vienna but fled a week before Hitler marched in. He arrived in America, penniless at age twenty-three. When the United States entered World War II, he was mustered into the army as a private and eventually became a first lieutenant in Intelligence. After V-J Day, he became civilian head of the publications branch of the information control division of the United States Military Government in Hesse, Germany. In 1950, at the age of thirty-five, he started his publishing firm with $4,000 of borrowed capital. Bit by bit, he made it a leading American publisher, specializing in books on international relations, foreign area studies, the Communist world, and military affairs—"Books that matter" was his slogan. Praeger's publication of Milovan Djilas's *The New Class* became a world classic and won him the Carey-Thomas Award for creative publishing. The firm also became a leading publisher of books about art, architecture, design, and archaeology, and it gained special distinction for its inexpensive World of Art series, published in both cloth and paperback editions.

Benton saw in the international nature of Praeger's book list and resources a companion piece to Britannica's global publishing and distribution programs. He was also attracted by Praeger's innovations in other fields, including the Special Studies series, dealing with specialized areas of international economics and development and United States economic and government affairs. These are important works but their market is limited to a few specialists. Praeger printed them by offset from typed manuscript—and sold them at premium prices. The firm is also active as the official or contract publisher for leading foundations and institutes, including the Council on Foreign Relations and the Hoover Institution. Frederick Praeger, in turn, saw in Britannica's research and editorial facilities, its domestic and international distribution machinery, and its resources, a means to intensify and enlarge his own publishing programs. At the age of fifty, Praeger sold his company to Britannica for $3.2 million in cash. Since then, about as much more has been invested in the Praeger company's development.

But in October 1968, Frederick Praeger—still the independent soul—decided to leave the Britannica complex and the firm he had founded to seek new challenges in his native Austria. (He was succeeded by his long-time associate and financial vice-president, George Aldor.) Nevertheless, the Britannica-Praeger merger led to further proliferation. The Praeger company acquired Phaidon, Ltd., of England, one of the world's leading art publishers. Under Britannica management, Phaidon's lavishly illustrated books of old and new masters are being adapted to paperback, and the firm is thriving. The company has also acquired a healthy minority interest in the distinguished British publisher, Weidenfeld and Nicolson, Ltd., which works closely with the Praeger company and Britannica. The signs point to the emergence of a unique, multinational combination of interrelated publishing activities in which the combination as a whole will have more strength than the sum of its parts.

In addition to the foregoing European acquisitions, Britannica acquired a highly respected Canadian publisher in 1968—the Centre de Psychologie et de Pédagogie, of Montreal, founded in 1955 as a cooperative publishing venture by teacher-authors. By 1968 its sales exceeded $4 million and it was the largest publisher of French-language textbooks in Canada.

In his approach to his business ventures, Benton never showed the serenity which Mark Twain ascribed to a Christian with four aces. He never lacked confidence in his ability to build successful businesses. Yet he wanted his postwar ventures to be profitable primarily in order to provide the means for steadily improving and expanding the educational opportunity they represented. And profitable they were. When Benton took over the *Britannica* with $100,000 in working capital, its sales volume was $3 million; the current sales volume exceeds $200 million. Yet while Benton has found a measure of pride in this record, few things ever embarrassed him more than did an article in *Fortune* magazine in the spring of 1968 which listed him among America's sixty-six wealthiest men. The author of the article estimated Benton's personal wealth as between $150 and $200 million, a figure based on the author's guess about the combined value of Encyclopaedia Britannica, Inc., and the Encyclopaedia Britannica Educational Corporation. In case of a sale, as has already been implied, the value of the two enterprises might amount to two or three times what *Fortune* estimated it to be. Benton, however, rejects outright all thought of a sale.

Neither company has been a source of common stock dividends that could swell the Bentons' personal assets. Neither has ever declared any such dividends. Benton's return from the Educational Corporation over twenty-five years was exactly $80 a year, representing $20 paid him at each director's meeting, held four times a year, for a total of $2,000. His salary—smaller than that of many of his associates—and his expenses are paid by the parent company, but they are modest by today's corporate standards.

In Benton's view, he has been something akin to the English aristocracy who were "land poor." They had land but no money. In his case, he has been "company poor." He has had very valuable enterprises, but no personal treasure chest full of money that would warrant placing him among the people listed in the *Fortune* article. With the publication of the article, he felt that any recipient of a contribution he made to a worthy cause might expect a gift one hundred times larger. He was more concerned about the way the article would affect his children's attitude. So he fired off a memorandum to his sons, Charles and John, and to his daughters, Helen and Louise, saying:

> Your mother and I do not follow the practices of some of the very rich. We have been pleased to buy Reginald Marsh pictures for as little as $100 or even $25—and have never attempted to buy Matisses or Picassos. We have no chauffeur. We have no full-time servants except Ivy and the two gardeners.

The *Fortune* story is very embarrassing to me because it cannot be denied that I could sell the companies and would immediately become one of the very rich. But your mother and I haven't the faintest idea of selling the companies. I think all of you understand this. But how can we prove this, or prove that we may not change our minds?

You children have never thought of yourselves as among the very rich. You're quite right. You're rich by middle class standards. You're not rich by the standards of the rich. Please don't change your attitude because of this unfortunate and ·unhappy and unwarranted and illegitimate publicity!

His children understood all this, as well as the fact that their parents' stock was destined for the Benton Foundation. But someone in very high authority—President Lyndon B. Johnson—had a moment of fun in the White House at Benton's expense as a "rich man." The occasion was after Mr. Johnson's announcement that he would neither seek nor accept the 1968 presidential nomination from the Democratic party. The way was now open for Vice-President Hubert Humphrey to seek it. President Johnson, meaning to adhere to a "nonpolitical" position, had given instructions that no one of his administration should side with any of the rival contenders for the party's presidential nomination. The instructions, strictly construed, applied to Benton as well; in his UNESCO role he, like any other ambassador, was part of the administration. Benton, however, did not stop to consider this kind of construction. Hubert Humphrey was his old and cherished friend, whose exceptional talents had won Benton's admiration since they served together in the Senate. By a reflex motion of his heart and head, he publicly gave his name as well as his time, thoughts, and money to the Humphrey cause. He became one of some twenty-five founders of the United Democrats for Humphrey; then he helped launch Citizens for Humphrey, and bent every effort to the organizational drive to win the presidential nomination for his friend. Secretary of State Dean Rusk, protocol-minded, told Benton that what he was doing didn't square with President Johnson's orders. Benton said he would take it up with the president, and did.

"Mr. President," said Benton earnestly, "your secretary of state has told me that I'm out of order as one of your ambassadors in being on Humphrey's organizing committee. He says that you have instructed all your ambassadors not to take sides on the presidential candidates, and that includes me. Yet here I was a few days ago, sitting at the head table with George Meany and Governor Sanford and Senators Harris and Mondale while we launched Hubert for the presidency."

After a Texas-sized roar of laughter, the president said: "Why Bill, I don't think of you as an ambassador. I just think of you as a multimillionaire. . . . You're like an old fire horse who hears the fire alarm go off. I couldn't expect you to do anything but what you are trying to do for your friend Hubert."

"Well," said Benton, "I'm glad to have that cleared up, and I shall tell your secretary of state."

Benton's UNESCO responsibilities required that he be in Paris leading the United States delegation while the presidential campaign was at its height. But he notified President Johnson that he would return home in mid-October for the last two weeks of the campaign. Because he had been away, and also because he felt so strongly that Humphrey *deserved* to be president, he had been slow to comprehend the scope of the incredible difficulties which dogged his friend's campaign. He had been working diligently for Humphrey at long distance, but when he returned to America he redoubled his efforts to raise money and support in Connecticut and Illinois, and in countless behind-the-scenes endeavors.

When it was over and Humphrey had lost his valiant fight by a surprisingly slim margin, he knew exactly what to do. He immediately urged the vice-president to join the Britannica family, to bring his talents to a role like that which the late Adlai Stevenson had filled. Humphrey agreed to the proposal after satisfying himself that the new responsibilities would not conflict with a commitment he had already made to the University of Minnesota and Macalester College. It was arranged that he would devote a quarter to a third of his time to Britannica and Educational Corporation interests. A Washington office was created for his use. He promptly began to familiarize himself in detail with the full range of Britannica products and to map out activities that would advance the company in the world of education which he had served so long as legislator and vice-president. Like Governor Stevenson before him, Humphrey presided over the Educational Corporation's board of consultants as well as serving on its board of directors and that of the Encyclopaedia Britannica Company.

But to resume with dollars-and-cents matters. Repeatedly, Benton has flatly refused even to consider turning his companies into public corporations with stocks listed on the stock exchange. He argued that only by retaining full personal control over them, with no outside stockholders, would he be free to make the kind of decisions that could best serve the educational purposes of his various enterprises. More directly, he observed that if the Britannica were publicly owned, he would not have been at liberty to do some risky and seemingly foolish things—which paid off. For example, he would not have acquired ERPI and launched Britannica Films, when experts would not touch it. He would not have defied the judgment of an experienced "book man" like Robert C. Preble, who advised against the heavy investments involved in the seemingly wild scheme to publish the Great Books of the Western World. Nor would he go public when doing so might threaten Benton's felt obligation to manage his enterprises in ways which would adhere to the educational standards of the University of Chicago itself—and he was constantly mindful that it was through the university connection that he had been in a position to acquire the enterprises in the first place.

He felt strongly enough on this point to include in his will a section addressed to his sons admonishing them in the language of Deuteronomy never to let the Britannica company "go public." He felt personally bereaved whenever he saw important educational vehicles, owned by other men, being taken over by corporations which in his view were interested only in earning profits for stockholders. That was his quick reaction, for example, when he heard that Norman Cousins had sold the *Saturday Review* to the McCall Corporation. Benton saw in Cousins a brilliant, courageous editor who had turned the *Saturday Review* into a vital instrument for public education about the great issues of contemporary life. Besides, he was a topflight businessman. He had built a struggling magazine into an enterprise with a circulation exceeding that of the *New Yorker*. These talents appealed so strongly to Benton that he repeatedly tried to lure Cousins into key posts in his own companies.[2]

Cousins, for his part, had a twofold motive in selling the *Saturday Review*. He was then deeply involved in a national campaign to win

---

[2]Cousins did serve for a time on the boards of directors of the two Britannica companies and the Benton Foundation.

public support for what later became the nuclear test-ban treaty, and he needed money to help finance that public effort—as well as other public causes of interest to him. At the same time, he was nagged by the prospect that in the event of his death, the inheritance tax on his estate might cut so deeply as to jeopardize and weaken the magazine. The sale of the magazine to McCall was rooted in such considerations. Benton, however, was not at first fully aware of why Cousins acted as he did. He assumed that his friend may have merely wanted to join the ranks of the rich. So instead of congratulating Cousins for having become a "millionaire," he wrote him a sorrowful note, expressing the fear that Cousins would no longer be free to keep the *Saturday Review* a major voice in public affairs. "There are around 40,000 millionaires in America," Benton observed in his note. "But there is only one *Saturday Review*. Why did you sell it?" He was partially consoled when Cousins explained the motives behind the sale.

How was the *Encyclopaedia Britannica* to be improved? When it was founded in 1768 by a "Society of Gentlemen" in Edinburgh, its first editor, William Smellie, age twenty-eight, set forth the aim of the *Britannica* in a preface to the first edition: "To diffuse the knowledge of Science, is the professed design of the following work." Smellie was later to become the official printer of the University of Edinburgh and a distinguished naturalist. Yet the first edition, which appeared on the eve of the industrial revolution—and of the American Revolution—was largely a rewrite of available scientific material, clipped and pasted together by a skillful editor. Its three thousand subscribers could read a long article, for example, on midwifery, made famous—or notorious—because Andrew Bell, the engraver and partner in the *Britannica* enterprise was tossed into jail for his graphic and explicit engravings illustrating the article. Yet even as a scissors and paste-pot project, the early *Britannica* had to keep pace with rapidly changing events, and insofar as was possible, to foretell them. As Benton himself observed, in a summary of the early years:

> In 1769 when *Britannica* was one year old, James Watt learned how to make an effective steam engine. From this came factories, railroads, steam-driven ships. And out of these came factory towns, world trade, and a new economic system. Adam Smith published *The Wealth of Nations* in 1776. At almost the

same time Richard Arkwright patented the roller spinning frame. In 1770 when *Britannica* was two, James Hargreaves patented the spinning jenny. In the thirty-two years between *Britannica*'s founding and the end of the eighteenth century, the industrial and scientific revolutions changed the world forever. The first vaccine was developed by Jenner, the first electric-current battery was made by Volta, the planet Uranus was discovered by Herschel, and Cavendish established that water is a compound of hydrogen and oxygen (which he then called "dephlogisticated air"). Such investions and discoveries multiplied commerce enormously with new demands for machinery, for power, for trade—and for education! And these in turn stimulated the division of labor, the rise of specialization and specialists, and the proliferation and fragmentation of knowledge. Thus the last third of the eighteenth century brought forth more changes than the first two-thirds. The last third of the twentieth century promises to do the same—to bring even more change than the first two-thirds, which ushered in the electronic and atomic age.

As new editions came out after 1768, *Britannica* continued to reflect the rapidity of change. The three volumes with three million words, produced in 1768–71, grew to eighteen volumes by the third edition of 1787–97. "So it has grown," Will Durant noted, "from edition to edition, through two hundred years. . . . how many of us have foraged in that harvest ten times a day, and pilfered from that treasury?" As the editions multiplied, the so-called middle classes of Western Europe were being given the means to become as well informed as the aristocracy and the clergy. "That, after all," adds Will Durant in *The Age of Voltaire*, "was the basic revolution." *Britannica* was from its beginning, as now, a measure for those who could read of mankind's increasing knowledge and achievement.

Each succeeding edition advanced the frontier of knowledge a little further. Each looked ahead of where things currently stood, and asked some leading questions about where they might trend. In the eighth edition, for example, completed on the eve of the American Civil War, the *Britannica* dealt for the first time with mental illness, the victims of which were still treated with occasional bleedings or the lash. "In concluding this brief historical retrospect," the article read in part, "we cannot refrain from expressing our surprise that the study of mental diseases has been deemed of so little interest or importance hitherto, as to form no part of the curriculum of medical education in this country." Sigmund Freud was then four years old. Two generations later, for the fourteenth edition published in 1929, Freud wrote a famous article that is still part of the *Britannica*'s entry on psychoanalysis—and in doing so, joined the extraordinary list of contributors to the *Britannica*, which includes men like Edward Everett (the first American contributor), Sir Walter Scott, James Mill, Malthus, Ricardo, DeQuincey, Macaulay, Bunsen, Matthew Arnold, T. S. Huxley, Sir Julian Huxley, Shaw, Marie Curie, Masaryk, Elihu Root, Einstein, Stephen Leacock, Trotsky, James Harvey Robinson, and hundred of others.

Knowledge, however, does more than increase. It changes its shape and character. New specialties split off from old ones; new forms of expertise develop; whole new sciences may be born. The encyclopedia that would report on the state of knowledge must reflect these changes in its own changing patterns of editorial organization. At the same time that knowledge proliferates and fragments it also becomes more subtly interrelated. Yet no encyclopedia can cover all the knowledge that there is to be recorded. The editor must decide, in association with specialist advisers, what can go into a set of books, and what must be eliminated. Today, midwifery might rate a column, whereas in the first edition of the *Britannica* it rated eighty. The expansion of knowledge is so great that if an edition did not rigorously delete, the size of a set would grow to one hundred and then to two hundred volumes. Where, for example, is the space to come from to take care of a new major article on space exploration? Here is a hard decision for an editor. It is also his responsibility to decide how best to keep his set genuinely up to date in each area of knowledge, preserving what may be old but still important, or displacing the old with new material when the old has in fact been rendered obsolete. All these considerations entered into the *Britannica*'s policy of continuous revision of its volumes—as against the old policy of bringing out a new edition once in a blue moon.

To guide the whole editorial process, Benton had created a board of editors, chaired by Robert Hutchins, back in 1943. He conceived of the board as a kind of clearinghouse for ideas, untrammeled by precedent—a potential new addition to the world network of universities, linking and coordinating them with one another and with the general intelligence of the world. Yet in the early and middle 1950s, the board of editors and Benton discovered that the process of continuously revising the *Britannica* was not doing all it should. It was not really keeping up with the proliferation of knowledge and was, moreover, certain to fall further behind each year. In 1957, therefore, Hutchins and the board of editors, prodded by President Robert Preble, approved a massive ten-year program of heavy, substantive, and costly revision and updating.

Measurable progress was slow in the first five years. While major changes that could be made right away were attended to, plans were laid and a staff assembled to get at a major reorganization of big articles and groups of articles. Progress became much more rapid by 1962, and finally, in the 1968 printing, the main job was completed. By then, *Britannica* editors had read and evaluated critically every word in the set. In ten years, they had changed 33 million of its 36 million words. In the last five years of the decade 5,800 entirely new articles, by 1,489 contributors, went into the set. The basis was thus laid for a sounder program of future annual revisions.

But even while this work was underway, Benton and Hutchins were not satisfied that the *Britannica* was all that it should be. The year 1968 loomed large in their thoughts as the two-hundredth anniversary of the *Encyclopaedia Britannica*'s first publication. It would also mark the twenty-fifth anniversary of Benton's becoming its publisher—and twenty-five years, besides being one-eighth of the total life of the set, was the longest period of time any one man had served as the *Britannica*'s publisher. On a foundation of the past, he and Hutchins wanted to give full rein to a function which both men felt the *Britannica* should fulfill as it faced the future. Benton gnawed away at the problem in his incessant memorandums:

> Bob Hutchins keeps insisting that he wants a "twentieth-century encyclopedia." We feel that the *Britannica* has become by far the greatest reference set ever published in any country, or language, or by any publisher. But is a reference set enough? Hutchins wants the set to be an educational set as well as a reference set. How could a young man "read for the law" in *Britannica*? If he was interested in philosophy, how

could he educate himself in philosophy? There isn't any guide to all the articles on the law, or to all the articles on philosophy. (I remember about twenty years ago when the Oxford faculty was revising all the articles on philosophy, and there were four hundred of these.) Couldn't the *Britannica* offer a young man more than a guide to Roman law, or Soviet law? If he wanted to refer to the *Britannica* for help, with its tradition and its connection with the world's great universities, over and above its admitted role as the world's leading reference set— what vital educational function could the *Britannica* perform for a reader seeking more about a broad subject than partial references to it spread through a whole set at different places?

In 1960, Benton and Hutchins made an agreement. Benton would underwrite a project which would bring together eminent scholars from all over the world to consider the revised and expanded aims of the *Britannica* as it entered its third century. The group would be under Hutchins's direction at his Santa Barbara Center for the Study of Democratic Institutions. It would consider how the editorial content of the *Britannica* could be made more intelligible and educational, and thus become a truer repository and conveyer of coherent human thought.

What came to be known as the "Santa Barbara project" had a stormy career, part of which ran concurrently with a storm over another matter. In the late 1950s, Benton, with Hutchins's encouragement, had installed Harry Ashmore as the new editor of the *Encyclopaedia Britannia*. Ashmore, a southerner by origin, was a noted journalist who had gained national celebrity for his moral and physical bravery during the school desegregation crisis in Little Rock, Arkansas. As the editor of the *Arkansas Gazette*, he had risked himself greatly in speaking out against the tactics of Governor Orval Faubus and the mob which was bent on preventing the desegregation of Central High School. His courage under fierce pressure won the admiration of both Benton and Hutchins, and Ashmore's extensive experience as a journalist and editor seemed to qualify him as an "educable" editor for the *Britannica*. At the very outset, however, a sharp disagreement developed over where he was to do his work. It was Benton's understanding that Ashmore had agreed to establish himself permanently in Chicago, where the editorial operation was centered. It was Ashmore's understanding that he could divide his time between Chicago and Santa Barbara, where Hutchins was located. Hutchins, for his part, tended to side with Ashmore, saying that his nearby presence would provide "an opportunity to educate the editor of the *Britannica*."

As the months went by, Ashmore spent more time in Santa Barbara and less in Chicago—where he came to be called "the phantom editor." Benton called him many more pointed things, but none of Benton's heated insistence moved Ashmore to Chicago. It was a costly dispute, but Ashmore in the end resigned as editor and established himself permanently in Santa Barbara. However, he maintained a connection with the *Encyclopaedia Britannica* by taking over responsibility for coordinating the preparation of the *Britannica Perspectives*—that eventually formed the heart of the "Santa Barbara project."

These articles were a series of twelve book-length essays. Each addressed an area of human knowledge, and more broadly and prospectively than the particular coverage of the *Britannica*.[3]

The authors chosen were generally acknowledged to be leading authorities in their fields. Each of the authors met in lengthy seminars and meetings with associates in his own field of special interest. Then they met with each other, not only in the United States but in Europe. Every effort was made to secure cross-fertilization among the various disciplines. It was one of the major editorial concepts of the twentieth century, but it was also expensive. The editorial cost alone was $1 million, with at least another million going into printing and other costs.

The twelve book-length essays were published in three volumes by Britannica in time for the bicentenary celebration of 1968, as a bonus to accompany new sets of the *Encyclopaedia* itself. They were also published in individual volumes by Praeger. The focus of the essays is on what lies ahead for man. "*Britannica*," Benton was fond of saying as he quoted Lord Crowther, "tells you what you need to

---

[3]Their titles: "Nature: Man and the Cosmos"; "Human Nature: Man and His Environment"; "The Technological Order: The Conquest of Nature and Its Consequences"; "The Legal Order: The Law—Its Ways and Byways"; "Mathematics and Logic: Retrospect and Prospects"; "The Social Order: The Promethean Dream: Society in Search of Itself"; "The Economic Order: The World after Keynes"; "The Political Order: Democracy in a Revolutionary Era"; "Education: The Learning Society"; "Linguistics: The Labyrinth of Language"; "The Fine Arts: Modern Situations in the Arts"; "Religion: The Search for Final Meaning."

know. *Perspectives* tells you what you ought to be thinking about."
Judged from a commercial standpoint as a publishing venture, despite a good critical reception for the set and lavish praise for some
of the essays, *Perspectives* could only lose money. Benton, however,
characteristically pointed to the educational merit of the venture.
It was, said he, the kind of thing a privately held firm could offer,
free of stockholder pressures for profit for profit's sake. Moreover,
it was his hope that the most significant value of the essays would
prove to be the influence they would have on the newly launched,
long-range, $25 million program to improve the *Britannica* further.

Another substantial publishing venture built around the *Britannica* bicentennial was the only one in Benton's career that did not
grow out of a major editorial investment that he approved from
the beginning and ultimately underwrote. It was a photo-offset reproduction of the first edition of 1768–71, faithfully done on carefully chosen paper closely resembling the original and bound in
simulated leather complete with imperfections in the "hides." Benton belatedly approved the idea, and then only reluctantly. It had
the odor of vanity publishing. But the public relations people
wanted to have it and the sales department thought it might be helpful as an "add-on" inducement to *Britannica* sales. So he agreed—
at a cost of about half a million dollars.

It is still questionable whether the first edition replica has in fact
helped boost *Britannica* sales. But the great stir its publication
caused among book reviewers, and the demand for it, warranted
selling the three-volume set to the regular book trade—at $79.50—
through the Praeger company. Meanwhile, Benton sent a worried
memorandum to his *Britannica* associates in Chicago. Would there
not be a danger, he asked, that one hundred years from now, the
replica—by then a century old—could be fraudulently palmed off
as a genuine three-hundred-year-old first edition? He was assured
that no expert could be deceived.

Being future-minded, Benton gave much thought to possible
changes in the technological form the *Britannica* might take, and he
was not always pleased with the visions he conjured up. He confessed that he had been made unhappy by a "computerized glimpse"
he got of "a *Britannica* coming to subscribers by pushbutton." It
did violence to his own bias as "an unscientifically inclined book
lover and publisher." But he rallied his spirits by adding sardon-
ically: "The logic behind forecasts of what the computer *will* do

because it *can* do it persuades me that one day the principal market for sets of the *Encyclopaedia Britannica* as we now know it may be for collectors of fine leather bindings !"

Never mechanically inclined, Benton took a perverse pride in being the only resident of the Waldorf Towers who had to send for a bellboy to tune his color television set. Yet he also knew that the new technology was revolutionizing publishing and education, and he continued to insist that the Britannica company itself should be alive to the opportunities for seizing the initiative in launching new educational ventures. Moreover, despite his naiveté in the world of mechanical gadgets, he did not hesitate to put the company's prestige and money behind publishing applications of the new technology—when he was persuaded that he was receiving sound advice from more technologically sophisticated associates. Persuasion was not easy, for he really had no conception of how a computer works. But he saw that the computer had its uses in publishing, as in the decision to set type for the *Annals of America* by computer, and to offer, produce, and market subsets retrieved by computer from the main body of the twenty-volume set.

Another triumph of persuasion occurred in connection with Britannica's latest pioneering venture, called the Britannica Library of American Civilization. What it represents is a library of 20,000 volumes. But instead of being printed, bound, and housed in a half-mile of shelves, it can be contained in a space much smaller than a breadbox—all made possible through the new technique of ultra-microfiche. *Fiche* is the French word for "index card," and through photographic reduction of 60 or more diameters, a volume of 400 or more pages can be reproduced cheaply on an almost indestructible acetate fiche. Inexpensive "readers"—magnifying and rear-projection devices about the size of a small portable television set—which can be manipulated easily to the desired page at the user's own pace bring the micro-miniaturized pages back to life size. The entire library, with necessary appurtenances like multiple indexes, includes scores of volumes so rare as to be quite beyond the resources of most libraries. Yet all this will sell for just over $15,000, a price expected to make it a major boon to new or underfinanced libraries anywhere in the world.

Benton, however, remained restless. When he read a *New York Times* story telling of the impact new federal appropriations for education were having on educational media, he sent the item to the

Britannica president, Maurice Mitchell, with a memorandum:

> The story again makes me wonder whether we are adequately
> staffed. I wrote to you the other day about our potential need
> of people who have had experience in our fields outside of the
> *Britannica* itself. But as I read the story, I think perhaps we
> need expanded horizons not so much in the traditional fields of
> textbook publishing, as in the new developments in education
> which are implicit throughout the story.
>
> Note that the *Times* states, "The most striking recent devel-
> opment in education is in the audio-visual field. . . ." Television
> plays the key role here. . . . I know there is nothing new for
> you in any of this. Nothing really new for me either. But it
> reminds me again of how rapidly our field is opening up. . . .
> Shouldn't we have a top executive in Britannica expending his
> full time on behalf of the *Britannica*, the Press and the Film
> Company—constantly studying and exploring new technolog-
> ical opportunities, and am I right that Bob Hutchins has made
> this same point? I think it would be a good thing if you took
> this *Times* story and my memorandum as an excuse to review
> the matter. I think it is overwhelmingly probable that in areas
> outside the field of books, others are going to seize the lead
> away from us, even if we are well equipped to take the lead, but
> I feel we should know what is going on so that we can take the
> leadership when we think the opportunity is unusual. I well
> remember how the textbook industry sat around on its hands
> and let us go into classroom motion pictures.

The ensuing search for a "top executive" who could spend time
on exploring new ideas in the field of education—outside of book
publishing—ran the course of a circle, leading to another Benton—
Benton's older son, Charles. Charles, after graduating from Yale,
joined Britannica Films, then taught school for a year, as part of
his preparation for a serious career in education. He rejoined
Britannica Films as a salesman, covering the state of Illinois, and
became a prize-winning salesman. He was promoted in measured
stages to the presidency of Britannica Films. In the realignment of
the companies at the end of 1966 he was made the president of the
newly formed Encyclopaedia Britannica Educational Corporation.

Benton's attitude toward his children has always been that of an attentive father, but he has no dynastic feelings. He has made it clear that the children would have no place in his companies by the mere fact of inheritance. If they wanted a place it would have to be earned by a record of performance. He would help guide and support them in their preparatory efforts, but he would not be a crutch for them to lean on. This was his repeated message to Charles, and to his younger son, John. After graduating from Yale, John was sent to King's College at Cambridge in order to round out his formal education with a master of arts degree. He then went to work as an "intern" in the International Institute for Educational Planning based in Paris and connected with UNESCO. The object was to expose him to the thoughts and experience of educational planners whose main concern is with the educational systems for the developing countries. John followed this up with a year of working for French Educational Television, and intervals of selling the *Britannica* at Lyons, Geneva, Rome, and San Diego, California. It is not an easy life, being a *Britannica* salesman, but it is the heart of the book company. If John Benton is ever brought into the managerial end of the enterprise, his fluency in French could well lead him into Britannica's overseas operations. At the time of this writing, John, now twenty-six, has not set a final course, and the senior Benton is not pushing him.

Of the two Benton daughters, Helen was married to John Nicholas Boley right after he graduated from Princeton at the age of twenty-two. He then went to the Yale Law School, and upon his graduation, the young couple settled in Chicago, where Boley was engaged by the city's largest law firm, Mayer, Friedlich, Spiess, Tierney, Brown & Platt. The other daughter, Louise, after graduating from Finch College, went to work for the Encyclopaedia Britannica Educational Corporation, where she is in charge of all the corporation's displays and exhibits at educational conventions. These convention exhibits—twenty or thirty each year—are major sales efforts, and Louise, an energetic, humorous extrovert, demonstrates films for potential buyers, manages the hospitality suite where educators are entertained, and mothers the salesmen who man the exhibits. She enjoys her job and does it with aplomb and skill. Despite repeated efforts, neither her father nor the company executives can persuade her to relinquish it for a "better" one.

Benton's anti-dynastic feelings were put to a test in early 1967 and were not found wanting in force or form. At that time, when

Charles Benton was thirty-six years old—the same age at which his father left Benton and Bowles—he resigned from the presidency of the Encyclopaedia Britannica Educational Corporation. His intention was to devote full time to a study of the educational uses of the new media, and to explore business possibilities which he could own and run free of supervision by his father and Maurice Mitchell.

To this end, Charles first created a nonprofit enterprise wholly independent of his father and the Britannica companies. Called the Fund for Media Research, the enterprise was launched with a research contract supported by the United States Office of Education and calling for a study of television in the school systems of the sixteen largest cities. His next move involved Films, Inc., a subsidiary of the Encyclopaedia Britannica Educational Corporation. Films, Inc., distributes 16-millimeter versions of "entertainment" motion pictures produced by major Hollywood studios like MGM, Fox, and Paramount; its traditional clients have been schools, and also clubs, service groups, church associations, and the like. The elder Benton strongly denied that there was any substantial educational potential in these entertainment films, but Charles saw the matter differently. He argued that the better entertainment films currently being produced dealt with the realities of human existence in ways which made them ideal take-off points for serious discussions and were so being used increasingly by schools and churches.

After much discussion between the father and son, Charles exchanged a large block of his stock in the Encyclopedia Britannica Educational Corporation in return for the sole ownership of Films, Inc. He also resigned from the boards of both Encyclopaedia Britannica, Inc., and the Britannica Educational Corporation. It was understood that he would turn over to the William Benton Foundation much of his remaining stock in the Educational Corporation and would also bequeath to the foundation his common stock in the Encyclopaedia Britannica company. While all these matters were being tidied up, Charles zestfully swung into action with his own company, Films, Inc. Within six months, and backed by a million dollars in working capital which he provided, he added a highly regarded line of German geographic films to his enterprise and launched a major venture in Canada.

After Charles cut his ties with the complex of Britannica enterprises, the presidency of the Educational Corporation was assumed by Dr. Warren Everote, a veteran executive who had previously held high positions in the Britannica companies. Today, the Educational Corporation offers an extraordinary range of instructional materials for a school curriculum. At one end, for example, there are imaginative teaching materials in reading and the most extensive programs available in the earth sciences, biology, and general science. At the other end, the technical skill and camera artistry which distinguished Britannica films from their earliest years have been put to use in pioneering new ways for teaching the humanities. Dr. Everote, himself a chemist, explained the new focus on the humanities in terms that had a special appeal to the unscientifically inclined Benton. "Our company," said Everote, "has used the technological device of films to do something in response to the concerns of leading educators who fear that the human qualities of man will be submerged by technology." The subjects chosen for the films dealing with the humanities are drawn from historic events, court cases, and significant current events—all vivified on film and accompanied not only by a filmed commentary made by teachers of exceptional ability but also by study guides. Leading educators have praised the aggregate product as being the most impressive effort of the educational motion-picture industry. And in addition to teaching motion pictures themselves, are film strips; eight-millimeter loops in fool-proof cartridges that a student or a group can project over and over to learn a single concept; transparencies for overhead projectors; recordings; programmed instruction— virtually the whole gamut of the new technology for the classroom.

Since all the stock which Benton and his wife own in the Britannica company—amounting to three-fourths of the common stock— will be left to the Benton Foundation, and since only the common stock has voting rights, the trustees of the foundation will control Britannica.[4] Moreover, because the Bentons also plan to leave to the foundation their 53 percent control of the Britannica Educational Corporation, the trustees will also decide, among other things, who will be the board members of the two companies, how the Britannica company and the Educational Corporation will be managed, and who their managers will be.

Benton had two main objects in mind when he created the foun-

---

[4]Benton anticipates that the stock owned by all his children will ultimately be owned by the foundation, and he is trying to work out that arrangement during his lifetime.

dation bearing his name. First and foremost, he wanted to protect beyond his own lifetime the integrity of the Britannica companies as educational instruments. By vesting their future control in public-minded trustees of the foundation, he could insure the companies against the prospect that after his death the companies might come under the control of bankers and businessmen who thought first and foremost of profits with minimum regard to educational aims. The second object in creating the foundation was to make it the receiver of dividends from the Britannica companies that could be used in support of philanthropic endeavors its future trustees felt were worthwhile.

In the latter matter, Benton insisted that the trustees must have an unquestioned right to make their own decisions. Yet he also expressed the hope that the foundation would lead an effort to raise the quality of the mass communications media. It was a hope that flowed naturally from the course of his adult life. For in several of his careers he had substantially influenced and been influenced by the mass media. As a young man in the advertising business, for example, he and Chester Bowles had made great impact on the development of radio. Subsequently, at the University of Chicago, he had helped give radio new stature as a medium for serious information and education. In the State Department, in domestic politics, at UNESCO, and in his Britannica enterprises, the communications media were of central importance to all that he said and did.

Furthermore, he often recalled the rebuffs he got from the great foundations when he asked them to support the University of Chicago's pioneer ventures in educational radio and in educational talking motion pictures. He noted that, until the advent of the Ford Foundation, the principal foundations had largely ignored the educational potentialities in the broadcasting media. He hoped that this would not be true of his own foundation. Questions remain to be settled regarding the relationship between the foundation and the Britannica companies. But gifts from Encyclopaedia Britannica, Inc., and from Benton have provided it with enough funds to start the development of a modest program along the lines of Benton's interest in the mass media.

In his various memorandums addressed to the trustees of the foundation, titled "Guidance Notes in Case of My Death," he requested the trustees to give first preference among projects on which they agree to those projects of interest to the faculties of the University of Chicago. At the same time, without insisting that the trustees govern themselves by the letter of his opinion, the suggestions he made to them appear best in a "guidance note" he wrote to the trustees in 1955 which still stands as a statement of his central conviction. After commending the University of Chicago and the field of communications as prime objects which he hoped the trustees would bear in mind, Benton said:

> I suggest to the trustees of the foundation . . . that they undertake no projects that the older established foundations would undertake on an adequate scale. In the foundation field as in no other with which I have had experience, there is the need for what businessmen like to call "risk money." I hope that the trustees of the Benton Foundation, in line with the spirit and attitude I have myself been unable to repress during much of my life—will continue to favor those things which seem risky, unorthodox, hazardous, and even unlikely to succeed—but which, with success, offer more than ordinary promise and in some cases very exceptional promise.

In case there was any doubt about what he meant, Benton re-emphasized his thoughts by adding:

> No foundation was ever prepared to put up money to implement the Report of the Commission on the Freedom of the Press. This has been most unfortunate. The idea will remain a good one and should be financed. The failure of any foundation thus far to put up the money, after almost a decade, illustrates not only the timidity of the foundations but their lack of understanding of the high significance of the media of communications.

He subsequently added to this point of emphasis a long list of possible directions the foundation might explore. Some, of course, may be vetoed because they involve a common interest with one company or the other, and no foundation may advance the interests of a business enterprise. But the ideas are far-ranging. For example, Benton felt that the foundation might work to stimulate educational innovations in school systems; help foster the growth of educational television; conduct research on the possible uses of new communications technology in helping schools and colleges meet the challenge of quantity and quality posed by the rapid increase in

student population; experiment with new means of combating illiteracy, especially in the world's underdeveloped areas; support an
objective evaluation of the structure and functioning of the Federal
Communications Commission, with recommendations to remedy its
weaknesses; study the relationships of Congress to broadcasting, as
well as the impact of the new media on political campaigns. Further,
Benton felt that the foundation might take an educational television
station and run it as a model. It could cooperate on a large scale
with Great Britain's efforts to develop a University of the Air, now
called the Open University. It could subsidize publications like the
Columbia Journalism Review, subsidize professorships and seminars
in the field of communications, and so on. A full list of Benton's suggestions about what the foundation could conceivably do, would
read like a collection of X-rays showing needs, missed opportunities,
and potentialities in the wide world of communications.

30

The Benton Medal

"Mr. Chairman—distinguished prevaricators—oppressed colleagues—my incredulous children—and other embarrassed guests—"

Bill Benton, who was beginning a speech on the evening of 1 February 1968, had come a long way to reach the dais where he stood in the Gothic-styled Hutchinson Commons at the University of Chicago. On the reel of time played backwards, it was twenty-five years to the day since he became the publisher of the *Encyclopaedia Britannica*. It was almost thirty-two full years since his resignation from Benton and Bowles and his chat in New York with Robert Maynard Hutchins. It was four months short of forty years since he married Helen Hemingway, and again four months short of forty-seven years since he graduated from Yale and went to work for the National Cash Register Company. It was also two months short of April Fools' Day, his birthday, when he would be sixty-eight years old.

His mother, Elma Hixson Benton, had been dead for a quarter of a century. In her lifetime, she was determined that he would not repeat what she called "the pattern of failure" among the male members of her family. For by her exacting standards, none of them had amounted to very much. Not her husband, Charles Benton, the professor of romance languages who never published enough to be noted. Not her father, Daniel Webster Hixson, the Union soldier and state senator, who never learned the monetary difference between addition and subtraction. Not her deceased father-in-law, the Congregationalist missionary, Reverend William Benton. Not even her grandfather, John Orr, who was merely a rich farmer. Because her standards were so demanding of achievement, she had trained

589

on her son, Bill, a barrage of criticism, unrelieved by a spoken word of praise to the day of her death—though it was her word of praise that he craved.

Still, the music of the spheres played a coda in an ironic key where this mother-son relationship was concerned. In Benton's life after Benton and Bowles, his interests, like his mother's, centered largely in the sphere of education, and here he made an impact beyond any that might have occurred to Elma in her wildest dreams for her son. More than that, he owed his effectiveness not only to the traits which showed up in the remarkable women in his family line, but even to those which showed up in the men who had formed "the pattern of failure." The elements which made for "failure" in their case needed a stiffening agent to convert "failure" into "success," and that element Benton had. It was the element of combination in which a Puritan's passion to improve himself and his environment was blended with a Cavalier's zest, courage and will to risk and to decide, and to imprint himself on his environment.

The combination made Benton no saint, and no "easy man." It made him a man born to have no rest himself, nor to allow much rest to other people. It made him respectful of truth, and disrespectful of dogma. It enabled him to discover obvious things to which wise men were blind, and to reach for them in rational ways—which seemed outlandish to prudent and discreet people. It made him hardheaded, and an enthusiast even for seemingly lost causes. It made him a man who found his vision of the ideal less in his successes and more in what he reckoned to be his failures. There was also another aspect to the man. In the full tilt of battle for serious objectives, there were times when his effect on the people who worked with or for him was like a jackhammer pressed against the nerve of a tooth. He was contrite only after the goal in view was attained, and he asked to be forgiven—just as he forgave some associates who abused his trust.

Benton was not unaware of the negative aspects of his drive, or of their effect on other people. When he saw an early draft of this biography and felt he was being portrayed in too favorable a light, he proceeded in the fashion of a Puritan diarist to write me a twelve-page, single-spaced letter detailing all the vices of which he felt he was guilty. Moreover, he sent along the names of people who he knew had very harsh things to say about him, and I was urged to seek them out and listen to their estimates of what he was like.

Mavericks like Benton usually incur enmity on a grand scale, yet the net of the things said of him by his critics was relatively small in scope. In points of detail, however, what was said was ardently said. His critics, for example, say that he "devours" the men who work for him, and that with his incessant memorandums and explosions he "keeps everything in turmoil." Benton did not protest the latter accusation. Rather, he quoted with relish one associate who paraphrased a line on Fred Friendly and heart attacks: "Bill, you'll never get an ulcer, but you sure are a carrier!"

His critics say he "blames other people for his mistakes." Yet Benton has always had a high tolerance of mistakes, his own and those of subordinates, as in the case where he "found fault" with Maurice Mitchell for "not making enough mistakes."

His critics say he "claims a monopoly of credit for the work of other men." This was one charge which angered Benton—because he considered it to be false. He claims credit for his ceaseless search for talented and daring executives, whose work often does redound to his benefit. He also observes that he sets the pace for the work of his associates. He is, for example, at the dictaphone when other men in comparable positions of wealth are relaxing at the beach. He is poring over company reports or some new or projected editorial product when other men are reading a novel. When others are at the theater, he is watching new educational films in his home, amassing critical notes which he immediately translates into more dictation. The same merciless regimen—only rarely interrupted—prevails when he takes a summer "day off" at Southport or a winter month at Phoenix. These times differ from the norm only in one respect. Since he is free of the telephone (which he dislikes), he can spend even longer hours at work.

His critics say that Benton "has an insatiable craving for recognition." This, to Benton, is a preposterous charge. He points to the long years when he actively and anonymously sought recognition for his clients or causes, from Benton and Bowles to the University of Chicago, the State Department, CED, UNESCO, and Britannica enterprises. The critics grant the anonymity of his efforts in the early days, but when they insist that their charge is true for the later years, Benton has a compelling answer. It is that he treats himself like any other client; that to a great degree, he as publisher and chairman personifies the *Britannica;* that when he is on the center of the stage, the *Britannica* is figuratively at his side. Since only he can transfer his publicity value to his companies, he would be foolish if he failed to do just that.

His critics say he "always talks and never listens"—although some will concede that they have been startled when he later recalled the precise details of a conversation he seemingly had "tuned out."

One critic quoted Thomas Jefferson to describe the abrasive effect Benton often has on associates: "It is unfortunate for our peace that unmerited abuse wounds, while unmerited praise has not the power to heal." Benton freely admits that he can be abrasive and even intemperate but, in his view, this happens under circumstances that warrant his being abrasive. He is, after all, a very articulate man, and when he wants to correct what he feels is the waywardness of an associate, he does so in terms that are vivid and pungent and have a telling effect. He almost never does this in a face-to-face confrontation, but rather by the device of a dictated memorandum. In this way, he can tone down his blast the next morning before it is actually delivered, and he almost always does so. But even in a toned-down version, the effect is often staggering—partly because he is always direct, and never resorts to irony to press his line of attack.

Some of Benton's critics say he is unable to use any form of humor or wit. In this, they misread the man. He has a special kind of humor which he uses sparingly, but with impressive effect when he does so. In 1966, for example, the Center for the Study of Democratic Institutions assembled a glittering audience to honor Paul Hoffman on his seventy-fifth birthday. The speaker's table was studded with men of note. Near the middle of the program Averell Harriman lauded Hoffman in a superb speech that was witty, deft, and affectionate. To many in the audience this was the evening's high point. Then Benton rose with a sly grin and, rasping over his near-chronic laryngitis, proceeded to "give the lowdown on Hoffman . . . in terms of the seven deadly sins."

He accused Hoffman of pride, "shamelessly embarrassing his friends by showing them up, nonchalantly doing things they cannot equal." Was Hoffman covetous? "He is positively greedy! Whenever he sees a challenging job to be done he grabs it, does it and seeks out another. He is not only greedy; he is insatiable." And so it went, through lust (for new honors for his friends), envy (of Eisen-

hower as president-maker to Hoffman, so Hoffman stole the president-maker role). And gluttony (for punishment), anger (he called
Joe McCarthy a liar), and on down the list. When he finished his
voice was gone and his audience, still choked with laughter, found
its. He sat down to an ovation.

On balance, Benton sees himself in a clear perspective. He readily
grants the validity of some of the complaints his critics lodge
against him. He is stung by others and is angered by still others.
Yet he can don a stoic's mask in an instant, and no one but he
knows what really rolls off his skin and what hurts deeply beneath
surface appearances.

Several more things remain to be said in this general connection.
First, Benton's files reveal that the most frequent cause of his criticism of a business associate has been his feeling that the associate
was not fulfilling his own potential to the maximum degree. Among
these were associates who admitted that they resented Benton's acts
and words all the more because later events proved him right. There
were also those who admitted that while they freely denounced him
on one count, they were proud of him on other counts—for example, his repeated reminders that the only reason Britannica needs
to make a profit is to enable the company to improve the quality of
its products. Benton, for his part, will forgo the affection of his colleagues in exchange for their respect, and he has their respect in an
overwhelming degree. Finally, Benton's files reveal many cases
where his most severe critics turned to him for help when they were
in need, and the aid was almost always forthcoming, in ample measure and without fanfare. Not only the critics but assorted strangers they referred to Benton have benefited from his help—whether
in the form of a job, a chance for a new start, financial assistance,
the underwriting of a worthy cause. Yet the one constraint which
Benton imposed on my use of the material in his files was his insistence that I respect the privacy of the help he has rendered and not
disclose the names of persons or the circumstances under which
they were aided.

While Benton's associates in public service causes were unstinting
in their praise for his work, the society around Benton was slow to
see that once he had left Benton and Bowles there was a sharp
change in the direction his life took. No matter what he did or how
well he did it, he was rarely credited with any deeply felt personal
commitment to the task in hand. He was seen as the "huckster," the

"Madison Avenue idea man" engaged to "advertise" the University of Chicago or the CED or the State Department, or who used "slick tricks" to win a seat in the Senate. When he supported dozens of worthy causes, he was seen not as a man who had a fund of ideas to contribute to them but rather as a "fat cat" to be stroked only for the purr of money he might emit. Over a long stretch of years the society around Benton was as slow to assign him a place of value as his mother was reluctant to speak a word of approval about anything he did. Because he moved in so many different societies he had no readily identifiable "image." A writer, he was not known as one. To politicians he was no politician. To businessmen he was not a businessman.

Nevertheless, in the passing years, different organizations and institutions came to see what the passing days had hidden about Benton's various contributions in different fields of endeavor. He was an early "hero" to the Jewish community in the United States, and Benton in return described that community as being "the most penetrating and generous in its approach to politics and to education." Indeed, every major Jewish organization in the United States has honored him with its highest award. There was the Man of the Year Award from the Hebrew Immigrant Aid Society; a silver plaque from B'nai B'rith; the Keys to Freedom Award created in honor of his career by Hadassah; the Human Relations Award from the American Jewish Committee; and a trusteeship of Brandeis University, followed by an honorary degree from it. In other directions, the CED which Benton helped found accorded him special recognition on the occasion of its twenty-fifth anniversary dinner. The State Department gave him its Distinguished Honor Award—number 46 in the State Department records—and second only to an award for physical bravery, usually bestowed posthumously. Then again, in 1968 alone, in addition to an honorary degree from Brandeis, Benton was awarded honorary degrees from Dartmouth and Notre Dame.

Then, again, in the *Britannica*'s native city, the University of Edinburgh also honored Benton on his twenty-fifth anniversary as publisher and the bicentennial of the *Encyclopaedia*. With pomp and circumstance the city and the university inaugurated an unprecedented series of Britannica Lectures. And in October 1968 unique tribute was paid both the publisher and his work at a white-tie banquet in London's historic Guildhall. Preceding the dinner, Prime Minister Harold Wilson gave a reception for Benton at 10 Downing Street, where Benton presented his old friend with a gold bicentenary medallion. At the banquet itself the prime minister toasted Benton for his leadership of "the present and most distinguished period of the *Britannica*'s history. For over twenty-five years now," Mr. Wilson continued, "William Benton has been publisher/proprietor—a continuous period of leadership unequaled in the *Britannica*'s long history. Bill Benton can look back on these years as a quarter-of-a-century of progress in which *Britannica*'s business has increased thirty-fold. In this period the University of Chicago, reluctantly persuaded by Bill Benton to accept the *Britannica* as a gift, has received more than $30 million in royalties—a reasonable return on a gift! I am delighted to see my old friend Bill Benton here with us this evening and we pass on our congratulations to him for his part in the most recent chapter of the *Britannica*'s history."

The prime minister then went on to pay a surprising tribute to Benton. Pointing out that six years earlier he had "spent some time in Chicago seeing the work of the *Britannica*'s educational films . . . division," he also pointed to a result. "It was what I saw there, together with the studies I had made of the use of radio and television for higher education in the Soviet Union, that led me to make my proposal for a University of the Air which one of my fellow guests tonight, Miss Jennie Lee, has now brought to the very verge of fruition as the Open University.[1] I believe this is one of the most exciting developments of our time. I believe that when it is established we will be leaving the United States far behind and I believe that its potential impact on the educational requirements of developing countries goes far beyond the imagination of any of us here tonight to conceive."

Benton had a surprise of his own to reveal in his response to Wilson's toast. "I am pleased," he said, "to announce tonight for the first time publicly that by reason of our respect for this responsibility Mrs. Benton and I plan to bequeath our stock ownership of the Britannica Corporation to the William Benton Foundation. As Dr. Hutchins told you we have indeed regarded ourselves for

---

[1]Lord Crowther, vice-chairman of the *Britannica*'s board of editors, was named chancellor of the Open University.

twenty-five years as the trustees of the *Britannica*. With our deaths the responsibility will pass to the trustees of the foundation. Two of the trustees are here with us tonight: Dr. Hutchins, chairman of *Britannica*'s board of editors, and Charles Benton, our son, who came especially from Chicago to be present tonight to hear this announcement."

Earlier, Benton's own chief of state, President Lyndon B. Johnson, had paid his own special kind of tribute to Benton. In December 1967 the Smithsonian Institution in Washington had arranged a two-hundredth anniversary *Britannica* exhibit. With President Johnson in attendance, Benton used the occasion to announce the presentation of a fifty-three-volume elementary reference library to 665 grade schools, and a fifty-seven-volume secondary reference library to 335 junior and senior high schools. The choice of the schools was made by the United States Office of Education, and the gift itself was made in the name of President Johnson in recognition of his exceptional efforts to expand educational opportunities for all peoples. Before the ceremonies began, Benton joked with the president: "Can't you teach me to be as good in politics as I am in business?" And in the course of his preliminary remarks before making the presentation of the gift, Benton publicly observed to Johnson: "I have lasted longer as publisher of the *Encyclopaedia Britannica*—twenty-five years—than you are likely to last as president." Johnson, entering into the spirit of things, began his speech of acceptance of the gift by remarking:

> Senator Benton did say to me coming up here that he wished that I would give him what information I had on politics. I don't know how a man could be very learned in that field and have such a poor poll unless there is something wrong with politics or polls. But I may need to know something about business. . . . I agreed with Senator Benton that I would tell him what little I knew about politics if he would tell me all he knew about business.
>
> The first thing he did was get up here and make a prediction. I thought he was bragging for a moment about how long he had been connected with the *Encyclopaedia Britannica* until I found out he was predicting what a short time I would be president. Let's just leave it this way: He is better at explaining things than he is at prophesying.

Then, in a serious turn of mood, President Johnson paid his respects to Benton's "very generous and farsighted act" in placing reference libraries in "poor schools attended by our poor children." More pointedly, he turned to Benton to bestow an accolade on him, saying: "What makes me prouder than ever, Senator, is that for many years you have been in the forefront of a movement in this country to get the federal government deeply concerned about giving every boy and girl all the education that he or she can take."

"It's coming too late," Benton was heard to murmur in a comment on the recognition he was receiving. But then he added, "Still, I'm alive." So he was—and is, with an animal energy and a ferment of ideas that makes much younger men seem old by comparison when placed alongside him.

Above all, he was alive to the fact that while he had graduated from Yale, it was Robert Hutchins and the University of Chicago that had educated him—and opened the door to great new outlets for his life force. The university, for its part, was alive to the fact that Benton had served its interests with distinction and openhanded generosity. Leaving out of account his contributions in other forms, the *Encyclopaedia Britannica,* which he had tried to acquire for the university or have it acquire, had returned under his management since 1 February 1943 more than $33 million in royalties and other payments to the university. The Rockefeller family and foundation, taken as a group, had contributed far more —perhaps three or four times the $35 million in personal gifts which John D. Rockefeller, Sr., made to the university. But if university income from endowments at 4 percent per annum is capitalized, and if the rapidly rising rate of royalties the *Britannica* pays the university—now annually in excess of $2 million—is capitalized, then Benton's current "gift" from *Britannica* sources represents an endowment of $50 million.

The University of Chicago has a policy which prohibits the award of honorary degrees to any except scholars for scholarly attainment. Yet in recognition of Benton's contributions to it, the university used the occasion of his twenty-fifth anniversary as publisher of the *Britannica* to create a new award, the highest it has ever given to anyone. It had never before issued a medal, named after an individual, which the university itself paid for and designed. Nor have Harvard, Yale, or Columbia ever done anything of the sort. The University of Chicago now did so by creating the William Benton Medal for Distinguished Service. A committee comprised of university trustees and faculty members was to be formed to award the medal to future recipients. But the medal clearly stamped "No. 1" was hung around Benton's neck at the banquet in his honor on 1 February 1968 in Hutchinson Commons. Benton regards it as the supreme honor of his life.

In the months immediately preceding the event, there had been changes in the circle of Benton's closest associates and friends. Henry Luce, with whom he had enjoyed a very special relationship, was dead. John Howe, who had selflessly served Benton for thirty years, was dead; his place was taken by Bruce L. Felknor, a writer of distinction who had directed the Fair Campaign Practices Committee. Maurice Mitchell had resigned the presidency of the Britannica company to become the chancellor of the University of Denver; his place in the company was filled by the thirty-nine-year-old Charles E. Swanson, who had done an outstanding job managing the Canadian operations of the Britannica and had become Mitchell's executive vice-president. Charles Benton, who had left the Educational Corporation, had been succeeded by Warren Everote. The post of editor-in-chief for the *Britannica* itself, which had been occupied on a provisional basis by Warren Preece after Harry Ashmore resigned, was now filled by Sir William Haley.

Benton first met Haley in 1945 when the latter was the governor of the BBC. Then for nine years he was the editor of the London *Times*. Haley, in Benton's view, was "the most distinguished editor in the Western world." His place in British life was so secure that Benton felt it would be presumptuous even to try to lure him from London to Chicago. However, after the *Times* was sold to Lord Thompson, Stanley Morison, who had recommended Haley as editor of the *Times* years before, now—shortly before his own death—urged Benton to invite Haley to assume the post of editor-in-chief of the *Britannica*. This was done, and Haley accepted. To prove to the British tax authorities that he was not merely temporarily absent from Great Britain but meant to reestablish himself in Chicago, he had to go as far as selling all his furniture—since a storage in London would be taken as presumptive evidence of an intention to return to the city. But Haley, after little more than a year as editor-in-chief, found himself in opposition to certain fundamental policies of the Board of Editors, and elected to resign. He returned to his native Island of Jersey, outside the United Kingdom. Editorial responsibility then reverted to Warren Preece, who retained the title of general editor he had assumed upon Haley's appointment. Preece, and the Board of Editors, had become warm friends and admirers of Sir William, and the parting caused keen regret on all sides, specifically including Benton.

The dinner in Benton's honor on 1 February turned out to be more than a celebration of Benton's association with the *Britannica* and the university. It was a celebration of his life, and the people invited to the dinner were those who had touched his life or had been touched by it. Some of the people invited could not attend, but they sent warm messages:

From President Johnson: "Your testimonial honors a man whose achievements could almost fill the index of the book he has published for a quarter of a century. . . . He has set a standard of patriotism and service which few can equal—and none can surpass." *From former President Eisenhower:* "I have admired Bill Benton's vision and understanding as well as his extraordinary capacity for energetic action." *From former President Truman:* "I would . . . like to add a personal salute to you for your many contributions in your important public service assignments." *From Prime Minister Harold Wilson:* "I know of old the contributions he has made to the cause of education nationally and internationally."

From Ambassador Chester Bowles: ". . . There has never been anyone else like him and I doubt there ever will be." *From Senator J. William Fulbright:* ". . . There is no man in America for whom I have a greater respect and admiration. . . ." *From Senator Eugene J. McCarthy:* "My congratulations for his leadership as publisher and for his many contributions to education. . . ." *From Speaker of the House John W. McCormack:* "He is one of the most dedicated men I have ever met, a gentleman in every respect and an outstanding American." *From Senate Majority Leader Mike Mansfield:* ". . . Bill has become a tradition in our generation—a tribute in itself to a great man, a great scholar, teacher, public servant, a great American." *From Governor Nelson Rockefeller:* ". . . a highly appropriate public recognition of Senator Benton's outstanding contributions to education."

From Secretary of State Dean Rusk: "We shall . . . be with you in spirit as you honor this distinguished statesman who has so devotedly given his time and talents to the cause of freedom and higher education in the finest American tradition." *From General Robert E. Wood:* "The success of the *Encyclopaedia Britannica* is a testimonial to his ability, fortitude, and know-how, and an achievement which does him proud." *From Senator John Sparkman:* "I look upon him as one of the most public-spirited citizens of this country." *From UNESCO Director General René Maheu:* "Senator Benton may be truly described as one of the founders of UNESCO. . . . One of the significant features of our time has been the achievement of a real fabric of international cooperation in education, science, and culture. Senator Benton has been one of the leaders of this historic development. In this he has demonstrated eminent qualities of vision and energy, but above all, of generosity. . . ."

There were other messages from the presidents of the colleges and universities on whose boards of trustees he had served: From John W. Nason, president of Carleton College; from Abraham Sachar, president of Brandeis University; from Jerome H. Holland, president of Hampton Institute; from James H. Halsey, chancellor of the University of Bridgeport; from Homer D. Babbidge, Jr., president of the University of Connecticut. Still other messages were there from Harry Scherman, chairman of the Book-of-the-Month Club; DeWitt Wallace, cochairman of the *Reader's Digest;* James E. Webb, head of NASA; Philip Coombs, director of the International Institute of Educational Planning; Arthur Goldberg, ambassador to the United Nations; and many more.

As one glanced around Hutchinson Commons at the 470 guests, and as one took in the identity of these people, they presented many reference points for different aspects of Benton's life. All had stories of their own to tell. There was John M. Bailey, chairman of the Democratic National Committee, and Governor John Dempsey of Connecticut, who could tell of Benton's life in the politics of the state. There was Senator Mike Monroney, officially representing the Senate, who could tell of Benton's hand-to-hand combat with Senator Joseph McCarthy. There was Loy Henderson, a leading figure in the career Foreign Service, now retired, who could tell of Benton's fight to organize the United States information program and to strengthen the Foreign Service itself. There was Illinois Secretary of State Adlai Stevenson III, who could tell of Benton's relationship with his father. There was Mortimer Adler, who could tell of Benton's steadfast support of "Benton's Folly," which resulted in the majestic publication of the Great Books of the Western World. There was Theodore Yntema, formerly financial vice-president of the Ford Motor Company and the first director of the Research Committee of the CED; he could tell of Benton's determination to maintain the intellectual independence of the economists on the staff. Every table buzzed with anecdotes about Benton—gay, tender, outlandish, bemused, respectful—enough of them to fill several volumes if only they could be collected. A special aura seemed to envelop a center table directly before the raised dais but removed from it by several feet. Here, surrounded by her children, sat Helen Hemingway Benton, more beautiful than ever, confining her show of pride to a gentle, soft smile.

Some of the speakers of the evening, sitting on the dais with Benton, were already legends in their own right. But they had been chosen to speak about aspects of Benton's life because each in his own way embodied and wrote large the same aspect, beginning with a touch that would have seemed contrived had it not happened naturally. The master of ceremonies was Fairfax Cone, chairman of the University of Chicago board of trustees and a man who, like Benton, had found his way to the university after a dazzling, successful career in the advertising business. Cone had also worked under Albert Lasker at Lord and Thomas and was one of the three partners in the firm of Foote, Cone, and Belding, to which Lasker turned over Lord and Thomas in the 1940s.

The first speaker of the evening was Vice-President Hubert Humphrey, who had come from Washington for the occasion with his wife, Muriel, as a complete surprise to Benton. The vice-president could have touched on his close association with Benton in the Senate, and he could have added something about the way in which Benton wanted to "make him a millionaire—just like the Kennedys." But his touch was more deft. As if in an allusion to the way Benton himself had long been America's "No. 1 No. 2 man," Mr. Humphrey observed that he was himself the first speaker of the evening; then he added: "Let me tell you how good it is to be first. The office of Vice-President is seldom understood by the people and sometimes less by the occupant. It is the only office that has humility built into it." Then turning "to my dear friend Bill Benton," he observed on the level of family intimacy: "You deserve everything they are going to say about you—good and bad." Humphrey added:

> I sent him a telegram—and I'm a rather frugal man—in fact I just decided to ask for a refund from Western Union since I seem to have gotten here ahead of the telegram.
>
> Here is what I said, Bill. "Excellence in scholarship—greatness in a human being—what a happy combination. This is the inspiring story of William Benton. Few men in public or private life have been more consistently devoted to truth in learning. Few have been as imaginative in blending the finest traditions of the university with the genius of private enterprise, thereby making available knowledge to our own and other peoples."
>
> That's what I wrote when I sat at my desk. But I'm never very good when I sit at my desk. . . . When I see this man tonight, I see the zest of life that he so exemplifies—constant effervescence, yet with a great constructive purpose. His stimulating mind . . . provocative, creative, courageous. What a wonderful thing it is to be able to come and be with him. . . . I've come here because you've given me the priceless gift of your friendship. We will ever be indebted to you, Bill.

Senator Paul Douglas spoke, and embodied the worlds of the university and of the government which Benton had also bridged. Douglas recalled that when he was a University of Chicago professor of economics, Vice-President Benton had been told "by many well-heeled Chicagoans" that the best way to improve the university's public relations was by firing Douglas. "I half expected this to happen," Douglas continued. "Instead, I was surprised one evening when I heard him befriend me over the radio. It proved to be the first of many kindnesses which he was to extend to me and my wife." Douglas had more to add in a reference to Benton's career in the State Department: "Bill shocked the staid members of the Foreign Service by insisting that diplomacy was something more than tea and cocktails." He then detailed the way in which Benton as assistant secretary of state had added a dimension to American foreign relations "which they have never entirely lost." But Douglas offered his own estimate of Benton's "greatest contribution to American political life." It was that he "started the whole train of events which ultimately led to the censuring of Senator Joseph Mc-

Carthy. . . . Bill's part in starting the decline of what came to be known as McCarthyism needs to be rescued from the obscurity of history. . . . Nothing has become you better, Bill. The money you've made, the honors you have received, are little, compared with the fact that you initiated the process that led to McCarthy's censure."

Paul Hoffman spoke of Benton the businessman, but confessed it was "hard to segregate from his many fields of action those that are strictly business." He led into his subject by noting that "Bill Benton's contribution [to the Committee on Economic Development] cannot be exaggerated." He said Benton thought of his "Economics of a Free Society" document "as CED's Declaration of Independence, which indeed it is." "Speaking personally," he continued, "I would designate it as more the Genesis in CED's Bible, and Bill was its Moses." Then Hoffman touched the high points in Benton's outsized career in business, saying that he was the "supreme example of the concept of 'how to succeed in making money without really trying.' " He observed that Benton's interest in *Britannica* profits was keyed to improving the set and the company. Hoffman concluded: "Bill could, of course, be wallowing in wealth if EB were made a public company and he sold even half his stock. However, not only has he no intention of having EB go public—I urge you not to suggest any such action to him. I did once, just once, and I got a lecture on the fact that EB was a trust to be administered not for private profit but in the public interest. I don't want to hear that lecture again."

Then there was Robert Maynard Hutchins. On the paneled wall behind the dais featuring portraits of University of Chicago presidents, one could see the portrait of Hutchins painted when he was still spoken of as "the boy president." He was no longer a boy. He was a year short of being seventy—but still looking magnificent, still full of yeasty ferment and ironic wit. More than any other man, this was his evening as much as it was Benton's, for it was he who had been the marriage broker between Benton and the university. He recalled how it was in the beginning with an allusion to Benton:

A Yale education, vintage 1921, and a brief, though sensational, stint in the advertising business form, at first glance, an odd preparation for a vice-presidency at the University of Chicago. But closer scrutiny shows that these experiences were providential.

The Yale class to which the Senator and I belonged, voting

in the middle of the senior year, reported they were overwhelmingly Episcopalian and 75 percent Republican. They chose as their favorite novel *A Tale of Two Cities*, closely followed by *Lorna Doone*. Their favorite magazine was the *Saturday Evening Post*, their favorite newspaper the *New York Tribune*, and their favorite poem *Crossing the Bar*, perhaps because of some confusion about the meaning of the words. They added that Yale's greatest need was a successful athletic policy.

Thank God for the generation gap.

As for the advertising business, Senator Benton's biography in the *Encyclopaedia Britannica* summarizes his career by saying, "Many of the techniques now traditional in that business originated with him. Some of them have had such an effect on American culture that he has more than once apologized for thinking of them." [2]

After a youth misspent in ways like these, Bill Benton was driven by his genius and a sense of guilt to return to the work of his father and of that remarkable woman, his mother, who, after his father's premature death, distinguished herself as a teacher and educational administrator. Yale she could forgive as the place, after all, where the Bentons had been going since the dawn of history. But she could not forgive the advertising business.

Hutchins went on to recapitulate Benton's career at the University of Chicago and in the public world beyond it. But he placed his heaviest emphasis on Benton and the *Britannica:*

General Robert E. Wood of Sears, Roebuck offered the *Britannica* to the University. The offer would not have been made except for Bill Benton. It would not have been accepted except for him. The company would not have been operated as an educational institution except for him.

And the fact that he and he alone has been able to determine the policies of the company has enabled it to do what no publicly owned corporation and no university could attempt, to take the risks inherent in offering people what they ought to have in the face of unanimous assurances that they did not want it and would not take it. . . . To take these risks, to exercise this independent judgment, successfully over a quarter of

---

[2] It was Hutchins himself who wrote the biographical entry.

a century requires a very unusual man. It requires, in fact, a genius. Bill Benton has raised to new heights the ancient name of *Britannica* and added new glories to it. The trouble is he is unique. For the sake of the university, and *Britannica*, and the future of education, we must hope he will live a thousand years.

The university's president, Dr. George W. Beadle, a Nobel Prize winner in biology, spoke of how Benton's impact on the university "still persists in the folklore and legend of the place, to be recalled at such relaxed times as Saturday luncheons at the round table of the Quadrangle Club." And Dr. Beadle countinued: "One of the folktales—and it does not sound apocryphal from my association with Bill—is the remark of a faculty member who had been subjected to Bill's searching interrogations. He is reputed to have said, 'He's on you like a swarm of fire ants.' There also is the remark of the famous [Swedish-born physiologist] Ajax Carlson, who subjected Bill to long, piercing scrutiny at the round table and finally announced with great disappointment: "If I could only figure out what makes you go, I'd bottle it and make a fortune." Then, after stressing Benton's devotion to the university and contributions to it "as friend, patron, and champion," Dr. Beadle, on behalf of the university presented him with the William Benton Medal.

To all this, Benton replied:

It must have occurred to you, as it did to me, during these extravagant speeches, that if this fellow Benton is such a sterling character, why can't he stop dictating all those memoranda? They drive people nuts. . . .

My friends, I have sat here patiently, in unaccustomed silence for what seemed like hours, listening to men wiser and better than I can ever hope to be—for in truth Bob Hutchins, Paul Hoffman, Paul Douglas, and Hubert Humphrey are giants who have inspired and profoundly influenced my life. I acknowledge these men my masters—but their pitfall tonight is simply that they do not know the real Bill Benton as well as I do. . . .

I now intend to set you straight. I'm going to tell you about the *real* Bill Benton:

He was born of extremely good and virtuous parents—and for the rest of his life remained a square—a total, complete, unchangeable square. . . .

Mr. Benton is, at bottom, an extremely *shy* fellow. I doubt if some of you believe *that*—I sometimes find it hard to believe myself. But after the closest possible examination of his habits I return to the conviction that he is a shy man—who conceals his shyness with a display of fervent purpose and alarming salesmanship.

Mr. Benton is also a man with a serious case of educationophilia. [He is] a maniac about trying to help get other people educated—not himself, mind you. For himself there has never been enough time to be both Saint Paul *and* Mortimer Adler.

Bad luck has made his life a series of triumphs. He was persuaded by Chet Bowles to go into business with him and the Great Depression struck. . . .

[At the University of Chicago, he] persuaded Bob Hutchins to bring the president of Czechoslovakia to the university faculty, and World War II promptly broke out.

Benton went to the State Department and the Russians blockaded Berlin, the British withdrew from Greece, and the Communists took over China.

He became a Democratic politician, and Paul Hoffman negotiated the Eisenhower landslide.

He . . . supported Adlai Stevenson or Hubert Humphrey for president in 1960, and you know what happened to them.

Not long after that, the University of Chicago, impressed with his track record, made him a life trustee—to get him out of the ranks of those who make the decisions.

His strength of character is best reflected in the fact that as a young man he turned down an invitation to become a professional gambler. Yet all his life he has been addicted to the needle—of the dictating machine. . . .

He has only been able to hold onto his suffering associates because his wife, Helen, goes around after him binding up their wounds.

It has been suggested here tonight that he has a magic hand for making money, that only a genius would have purchased the then ailing and depressed *Encyclopaedia Britannica*. As Bob Hutchins has informed you, rarely has such a legend been founded on such an infirm foundation. The reason that Bill Benton financed the *Encyclopaedia* was simple: he was trying to help out, and he could not say no to a couple of friends. . . .

That's the real story of Bill Benton, a tactless, not too likable fellow, who all his life has worked much harder than necessary trying to make ends meet.

My friends, when a man has heard what I have heard to-night, he has heard the obituary he hopes his wife and children will hear—and he should be ready for the grave. But I have, I trust, a surprise in store for so orderly a fate. . . .

It has been my high privilege to serve this great university for thirty-two years. . . . It is my determination to serve it as best I can for yet thirty-two more, or at least until that career, the facts of which have been so stretched tonight, can be stretched no further down the years. In thirty-two years I shall only be one hundred. When he retired at seventy, Coach Stagg fixed his eyes on Bob Hutchins and said, "Young man, I'll be coaching football when I'm one hundred." And so he was. . . .

I give thanks to the university and to the preceding speakers for the great honor done me tonight. Henceforward I shall try to deserve it.

An illuminated parchment scroll accompanying the medal reads: *William Benton, visionary public servant, perceptive student of foreign affairs, staunch supporter of education, discriminating publisher, astute businessman, co-founder of UNESCO and of the Committee for Economic Development, creator of the "Voice of America," whose talents he has shared freely with his fellow men.*

Index

609